THE JOHANNINE EPISTLES

RUDOLF SCHNACKENBURG

THE
JOHANNINE
EPISTLES

INTRODUCTION AND COMMENTARY

Translated by
Reginald and Ilse Fuller

CROSSROAD
New York

1992
The Crossroad Publishing Company
370 Lexington Avenue, New York, NY 10017

Originally published under the title *Die Johannesbriefe*
Herders Theologischer Kommentar zum Neuen Testament 13/3
©Verlag Herder KG Freiburg im Breisgau 1975

English translation © 1992 by The Crossroad Publishing Company
Based on the 7th edition of the German original (1984)

Printed in the United States of America

Library of Congress Cataloging-in-Publication Data

Schnackenburg, Rudolf, 1914–
  [Johannesbriefe. English]
  The Johannine epistles : introduction and commentary / Rudolf
Schnackenburg : translated by Reginald and Ilse Fuller.
       p.   cm.
  Translated from the 7th ed. of Die Johannesbriefe.
  Includes bibliographical references and index.
  ISBN 0-8245-1176-X (set)
  1. Bible. N.T. Epistles of John—Commentaries.   I. Bible. N.T.
Epistles of John. English. New Revised Standard.   1992
II. Title.
BS2805.3.S3613   1992
227'.94077—dc20   92-5
                                                          CIP

CONTENTS

Contents

Contents

Contents

Contents

PREFACE

The present volume is a translation of the 7th edition of the German original. Since the appearance of the 6th edition in 1979 much further literature has appeared, including works on the Gospel of John. All of this has contributed many new insights into the Johannine problem. Reference should also be made to the supplementary volume to the German commentary on the Gospel of John: *Das Johannesevangelium IV: Ergänzende Auslegungen und Exkurse* (Freiburg im Breisgau, 1984). As far as the Johannine Epistles are concerned, the most important event that has occurred is the appearance of Raymond E. Brown, *The Epistles of John* (Anchor Bible 30; Garden City, NY, 1982). This commentary takes note of and appropriates all the more recent literature. It runs to 812 pages. In view of Brown's bibliography (pp. 131–46) and the further bibliographical references to the individual sections, I have refrained from adding any further bibliography of my own. Brown's interpretations are usually close to mine, though he sometimes takes a line of his own. It has not been possible for me to enter into a detailed discussion of his views. His commentary represents a definite advance and is a high point of contemporary scholarship.

To those English-speaking readers who are prepared to immerse themselves in the questions raised by the Johannine Epistles for exegesis, theology, and the history of religions, and in the interpretation of specific passages, this English translation of my commentary will, I venture to hope, be of service.

RUDOLF SCHNACKENBURG

ABBREVIATIONS

ANCIENT WRITINGS

Adv. Haer.	Ignatius, *Adversus Haereses*
Barn.	*Letter of Barnabas*
CHerm	*Corpus Hermeticum*
Const. Apost.	*Apostolic Constitutions*
Did.	*Didache*
H.E.	Eusebius, *Historia Ecclesiastica*
Herm. Man.	*Hermas, Mandates*
Herm. Sim.	*Hermas, Similitudes*
Herm. Vis.	*Hermas, Visions*
Ignatius	
Eph.	Letter to the Ephesians
Magn.	Letter to the Magnesians
Philad.	Letter to the Philadelphians
Rom.	Letter to the Romans
Smyrn.	Letter to the Smyrnaeans
Trall.	Letter to the Trallians
Mart. Pol.	*Martyrdom of Polycarp*

Qumran Literature	
CD	*Damascus Rule*
1QH	*Thanksgiving Hymns*
1QM	*War Scroll*
1QS	*Community Rule*
1QpHab	*Habakkuk Pesher*

MODERN WORKS

AnBib	Analecta Biblica
AntChrist	F. J. Dölger, *Antike und Christentum*
ATAbh	Alttestamentliche Abhandlungen
ATANT	Abhandlungen zur Theologie des Alten und Neuen Testaments
BA	*Biblical Archaeologist*
BAGD	W. Bauer, W. F. Arndt, F. W. Gingrich, and F. W. Danker, *A Greek-English Lexicon of the NT*
BBB	Bonner biblische Beiträge
BDF	F. Blass, A. Debrunner, and R. W. Funk, *A Greek Grammar of the NT*

Abbreviations

Bib	*Biblica*
BS	*Biblische Studien*
BFCT	Beiträge zur Geschichte der biblischen Exegese
BJRL	*Bulletin of the John Rylands Library*
BWANT	Beiträge zur Wissenschaft vom Alten und Neuen Testament
BZ	*Biblische Zeitschrift*
BZNW	Beihefte zur *ZNW*
CIL	*Corpus inscriptionum latinarum*
ConNT	*Coniectanea Neotestamentica*
CQR	*Church Quarterly Review*
CSEL	Corpus scriptorum ecclesiasticorum latinorum
Cult. bib.	*Cultura bíblica*
DBSup	*Dictionnaire de la Bible, Supplément*
DivThom	*Divus Thomas*
Enchir. bib.	*Enchiridion Biblicum*
ETL	*Ephemerides theologicae lovanienses*
EvT	*Evangelische Theologie*
Exp	*Expositor*
ExpT	*Expository Times*
FRLANT	Forschungen zur Religion und Literatur des Alten und Neuen Testaments
GCS	Griechische christliche Schriftsteller
GGA	*Göttinger Gelehrte Anzeigen*
HNT	Handbuch zum Neuen Testament
HTKNT	Herders theologischer Kommentar zum Neuen Testament
HTR	*Harvard Theological Review*
ICC	International Critical Commentary
Int	*Interpretation*
JBL	*Journal of Biblical Literature*
JR	*Journal of Religion*
JTS	*Journal of Theological Studies*
LTK	*Lexikon für Theologie und Kirche*
LumVie	*Lumière et Vie*
MandLit	*Mandean Liturgy*
MTZ	*Münchener theologische Zeitschrift*
NKZ	*Neue kirchliche Zeitschrift*
NovT	*Novum Testamentum*
NRSV	New Revised Standard Version
NRT	*La nouvelle revue théologique*
NTAbh	Neutestamentliche Abhandlungen
NTD	Das Neue Testament Deutsch
PG	J. Migne, *Patrologia graeca*
PL	J. Migne, *Patrologia latina*
PWSup	Supplement to Pauly-Wissowa
RAC	*Reallexikon für Antike und Christentum*
RB	*Revue biblique*

Abbreviations

REB	Revised English Bible
RechScR	*Recherches de science religieuse*
RegNT	Regensburger Neues Testament
RevQum	*Revue de Qumran*
RevThom	*Revue thomiste*
RGG	*Die Religion in Geschichte und Gegenwart*
RHPR	*Rebue d'histoire et de philosophie religieuses*
RHR	*Revue de l'histoire des religions*
RTP	*Revue de théologie et de philosophie*
RVV	Religionsgeschichtliche Versuche und Vorarbeiten
SANT	Studien zum Alten und Neuen Testament
SB	*Sitzungsberichte der Deutschen Akademie der Wissenschaften zu Berlin*
StT	*Studia Theologica*
StudEv	*Studia Evangelica*
SvExA	*Svensk exegetisk Årsbok*
ThGl	*Theologie und Glaube*
TLZ	*Theologische Literaturzeitung*
TQ	*Theologische Quartalschrift*
TRu	*Theologische Rundschau*
TU	Texte und Untersuchungen
UBSGNT	United Bible Societies *Greek New Testament*
VD	*Verbum Domini*
WUNT	Wissenschaftliche Untersuchungen zum Neuen Testament
ZNW	*Zeitschrift für die neutestamentliche Wissenschaft*
ZTK	*Zeitschrift für Theologie und Kirche*
ZWT	*Zeitschrift für wissenschaftliche Theologie*

THE FIRST EPISTLE
OF JOHN

INTRODUCTION

1. External Form and Genre

1. 1 John, which was eventually accepted among the Catholic Epistles (see p. 5), is not to be classed formally as a letter of the Hellenistic type, for it has no name of the sender, addressees, or opening greetings, nor is there a farewell greeting at the end! At the same time it is not a product of literary art either, couched as it were in the form of a letter "in which an unknown author is dealing with an unknown public."[2] As far as its subject matter is concerned, the author evidently is familiar with the religious and ethical conditions of his readers, at least in general terms (2:18-27; 4:1-6; 5:21). He expects to be recognized as one peculiarly qualified for the proclamation of the Christian message (1:1-4; 4:14). His purpose in writing is to strengthen true faith and mutual love, and the joyful certainty of fellowship with God (1:3) and of eternal life (5:13), which that brings. This general Christian goal of salvation is endangered by certain heretics and enemies of the faith. The polemic against these antagonists is by no means confined to the two sections 2:18-27; 4:1-6, but in fact pervades the entire document.[3] It does not deal systematically with a particular theme like Hebrews, *Barnabas,* or the middle part of *1 Clement.* This means we can in no way call it a "tract."

It is more difficult to explain the absence of a conventional epistolary beginning and end. There was a tendency at the time, as we can see in the apocryphal

---

1. See O. Roller, *Das Formular der paulinischen Briefe* (BWANT 4.6; Stuttgart, 1933) 55ff. See also F. O. Francis, "The Form and Function of the Opening and Closing paragraphs of James and 1 John," *ZNW* 61 (1970) 110-26; on 1 John, see pp. 121ff. ("secondary" epistolary character, at the beginning thematic thesis, at the end resumption of the theme, related to prayer and eschatology).

2. A. Jülicher and E. Fascher, *Einleitung in das Neue Testament* (7th ed.; Tübingen, 1931) 188ff. The thesis of the literary "epistle" as distinct from the letter was especially advocated by A. Deissmann, *Light from the Ancient East* (New York, 1927) 217ff.; however, he regards 1 John as a "religious diatribe." For a contrary view, see Bonsirven, 10; Vrede, 146; P. Feine and J. Behm, *Einleitung in das Neue Testament* (9th ed.; Heidelberg, 1950) 259.

3. See the formulas *ean eipōmen* (1:6, 8, 10); *ho legōn* (2:4, 6, 9); *mēdeis planatō hymas* (3:7); *ean tis eipē* (4:20); see further the antitheses in 3:8, 10, 14f.; 4:8; 5:6b, 10b, 12b, 19.

literature, to enhance the authority of a document by attributing it pseudony-
mously to some authoritative figure of the past. In view of this, the absence of
the sender's name is all the more striking, especially in a letter (cf. the *Letter
of Aristeas,* the *Epistle to the Laodiceans,* and the *Epistola Apostolorum*). It
cannot be explained from a deliberate intent to mystify in order to suggest John
the Apostle. After all, he is not mentioned in GJohn (Gospel of John) either.[4]
Unlike other writers such as the author of 2 Peter, the author of 1 John is not
concerned to portray himself as one of the recognized apostles. He remains
completely anonymous,[5] though he does claim authority as a preacher (cf. 1:1-4;
Excursus 1). This raises the question of whether the absence of an opening
address is due to a different epistolary convention. Hebrews does not have one
either, though it does have an epistolary conclusion. The suggestion that the
address was changeable is untenable, because it is contrary to the epistolary conventions of antiquity.[6] There is much to be said in itself for Roller's opinion that
the epistolary form current in Asia Minor was different from the usual Hellenistic convention; this would account for the beginning of both Hebrews and
1 John.[7] Yet it can hardly be proved that letters in the ancient Near East were
delivered orally or by a messenger and that this led to a different epistolary form
still current there in Hellenistic times. Perhaps the author simply wanted to
introduce himself in the prooemium as a person of authority whom everybody
knew. Perhaps he deliberately wanted to give his writing a kerygmatic character,
different from ordinary letters. But in the final analysis the whole question
remains an enigma. It has been suggested that 1 John was a circular letter (see
p. 5 below). On the question of an ecclesiastical redaction that obscured its
original form, see pp. 15ff. below.

2. Since 1 John contains extensive parenetic sections (2:15-17; 3:11-24; 4:7-
12; 4:19-5:3), it could also be classified as a parenesis directed to a wider reader-
ship by a loosely connected series of injunctions (cf. James) or a meditation
revolving around a common theme (cf. *2 Clement* on repentance). Yet 1 John
is neither a homily[8] nor a tract. Although the frequent apostrophes[9] may conform to the conventions of preaching, the letter aims at being more than an
edifying discourse. It is a proclamation (1:1-3) and defense of the faith (4:4-6;
5:4-12) in an age that was all too familiar with conflict and conscious of its
eschatological significance (2:18; 4:1). The calm tone, sometimes solemn and
elevated (1:1-3; 3:1-3; 5:18-20), gives a glimpse of a serious and eager champion
of the true faith. This is due less to the unctiousness of the preacher than to

---

4. See F. Torm, *Hermeneutik des Neuen Testaments* (Göttingen, 1930) 143f.; 151ff.; idem, *Die
Psychologie der Pseudonymität im Hinblick auf die Literatur des Urchristentums* (Gütersloh, 1932).

5. See K. Aland, "The Problem of Anonymity and Pseudonymity in Christian Literature of the
First Two Centuries," *JTS* n.s. 12 (1961) 39-49, esp. 41.

6. Roller, *Formular,* 296ff.

7. Ibid., 213ff.; on Hebrews and 1 John, see esp. p. 237, followed by Feine-Behm, *Einleitung,* 259.

8. W. Soltau regards the main part, 3:1-5:5, as a homily, the beginning of which was removed
and replaced by 1:1-2:11 ("Der Verwandtschaft zwischen Ev Joh und dem 1 Joh," *StudKrit* 89 [1916]
232); similarly E. Lohmeyer, "Über Aufbau und Gliederung von 1 Joh," *ZNW* 27 (1928) 256ff., as
a homiletical writing; see further Dodd, xxi.

9. 2:1, 7, 12-14, 18, 28; 3:2, 7, 18, 21; 4:1, 4, 7, 11; 5:21.

Introduction

the grace and conviction of someone with a revelation to proclaim (see the frequent occurrence of "we know" and "you know," 2:20, 21; 3:2, 5, 14, 15; 5:13, 15, 18–20). The profundity of such Christian preaching (which of course always issues in parenesis) becomes evident when compared to similar exhortations in Jewish literature, as, for example, the *Testaments of the Twelve Patriarchs,* which have a stronger ethical orientation.[10] Nor can 1 John be regarded as a "substitute for an edifying discourse delivered directly to a particular congregation" (Büchsel).

3. 1 John is neither a letter to a single congregation like 2 John nor is it a circular letter like Colossians (see Col. 4:16) or 1 Peter. If it were that, an address would be almost indispensable.[11] It is equally unlikely that the author was addressing the Christian world in general; rather, he has a concrete situation in view.[12] He presupposes a pagan environment (5:21) in which gnostic trends were rife, where the true believers were battling with a false Christology (2:22–23; 4:2–3, 15; 5:1, 5–6). 1 John was apparently designed for a group of congregations in a limited area who found themselves in the same situation.[13] This brings Asia Minor to mind (on this see further, p. 40). If this epistle was intended to accompany GJohn,[14] this would have been clearly indicated. The epistle looks like an independent document, composed spontaneously for the sheer joy of proclaiming the Christian message (1:4), with a concern about the stability of faith (2:27) and a confidence in the reality of salvation (5:13). Dionysius of Alexandria called it "the catholic epistle,"[15] meaning that it was designed for general reading. This is certainly true so long as we remember that it was not addressed to all the Christians in the world but has a purview extending beyond that of a local congregation.

4. W. Nauck has proposed a new idea, which is both positive and constructive, to explain the character and tendency of 1 John.[16] Picking up the suggestions of earlier scholars that this epistle combines two different genres of discourse — namely, a series of antitheses plus a parenesis (see pp. 13–15) — he suggests that the document was developed in two successive stages, each responding to the contemporary situation of the recipients. Nauck considers it highly probable that the author had previously intervened in the affairs of the

---

10. J. C. O'Neill is of the opinion that the basis of the document was a heterodox Jewish admonitory writing, which was taken over by a Christian author and modified in a Christian direction (*The Puzzle of 1 John* [London, 1966]). The Jewish source, he thinks, was close to the Qumran texts and the *Testaments of the Twelve Patriarchs.* O'Neill discovers twelve admonitions in his source, but his hypothesis has not met with assent.

11. On the circular letter hypothesis, see Roller, *Formular,* 200ff.

12. Contra A. Harnack in *SB* (Berlin, 1923) 103; Lohmeyer, *ZNW* 27 (1928) 256; Jülicher-Fascher, *Einleitung,* 226; Windisch, 136.

13. So T. Zahn, *Introduction to the New Testament* (Edinburgh, 1909) 3:368; Büchsel, *Johannesbriefe,* 1; Vrede, 147; Bonsirven, 15; Chaine, 123; Feine-Behm, *Einleitung,* 259, et al.

14. See Belser, 1, 7; Vrede, 146–47; J. Sickenberger, *Einleitung,* 163–64. M. Meinertz also regards 1 John 2:14–15 as a direct allusion to GJohn (*Einleitung in das Neue Testament* [5th ed.; Paderborn, 1950] 275); however, see ad loc.

15. In Eusebius, *H.E.* 7.25.7, 10.

16. W. Nauck, *Die Tradition und der Charakter des ersten Johannesbriefes* (Tübingen, 1957). (The page numbers in parentheses refer to this.)

5

community or communities when the situation was still more critical: the false teachers had been doing their damage unchecked and had not been recognized as dangerous (p. 125). To accomplish his purpose the author utilized a polemical *Vorlage,* which he read before the assembled congregation, couched in sharp language. This style of rebuke was derived from the pronouncement of divine law. It had evidently done the trick (p. 126). The reason for returning to the polemical form in the present letter and commenting on it must be that the crisis had not been completely resolved. Many members of the community were apparently not yet entirely clear about the issue. If Nauck is right, 1 John is not a letter in the proper sense of the word, but an official missive to a group of readers who need strengthening now that they have survived the danger of apostasy (pp. 126–27).

This is an attractive suggestion. It focuses more strongly than usual upon the *Sitz im Leben* of the community and forces us to recognize that there are two layers in the document. Unlike earlier proposals along the same line, Nauck attributes both stages to the same author. Whether there are compelling reasons for questioning the integrity of 1 John on grounds of style and genre is something we shall have to consider later (see pp. 11–14 below). Nauck observes that the author of 1 John "distinguishes between sinners and righteous by calling his hearers' attention to the salvation they have appropriated through their baptism, which has brought them from darkness to light. He refers to the moment when they entered their Christian status and the promise they received that they would walk in the light" (p. 65). This observation is something worth holding on to. Even without his particular theory about the literary origins of the epistle, Nauck's observation brings out the character of 1 John more clearly. Despite its being conditioned by a concrete situation, the letter has an authority that gives it a lasting and universal significance. In short, it is a "catholic epistle," transcending its origin in time and space.

2. Style and Composition

Here we shall explore the author's style and the manner in which he expresses himself, but only insofar as these matters are important for the exegesis. We shall also take note of the structure of the document and the way in which its thought is developed.

Stylistic Devices

Compared with the Synoptic Gospels and the lively, impassioned and sometimes turbulent style of Paul, or with the artistry and literary expertise of Hebrews,[17] the Johannine writings show peculiarities which suggest that they should all be considered together (GJohn, 2 and 3 John as well as 1 John).

---

17. Cf. the judgment of E. Norden, *Die antike Kunstprosa* (2nd ed.; Leipzig/Berlin, 1909) 499–500.

Introduction

1. **Antithetical parallelism.** Here the same thought is expressed, first in positive terms and then in negative, or vice versa. See 1:5–10; also 2:4, 7, 10–11; 4:7–8; etc. The second phrase adds nothing to the development of the thought, at most a certain crescendo. This stylistic device gives emphasis to the statement, though to modern ears the effect is somewhat strange. A Greek or Roman, for all their love of antithesis, would not write like this.[18] R. Bultmann regards this style as characteristic of the *Vorlage* as he imagines it to have been;[19] however, it is generally typical of the Johannine literature. See, for instance, John 3:18a–b, 20–21, 36a–b; 5:22–23, 43–47; 6:53–54; 10:4–5; 12:44–49; 14:23–24; 15:6–7, 19a–b; etc.

2. **Pure antithesis.** This is not simply a reversal of the original saying. Rather, it uses opposite pairs of terms, for example, 3:7–10; 4:4–6; 5:18–19; 3 John 11. Although this is a common rhetorical device, which exploits the orator's personality to the full, in the Johannine writings it is based on their characteristic theological dualism. Here again we find the strongest contacts with GJohn; see John 3:3–5, 11–13, 19–21, 31–32; 5:24–29; 5:21–23; 8:41–47; 9:39; 10:25–26; 15:18–25; 16:20–22; 17:14–15; 18:36, 37. See also pp. 35–38.

3. **Repetition**

   a) As a concise recapitulation of the previous word or thought. Cf. 2:5c with 6a; 2:7b with c; 2:13 with 14; 2:24a with b (chiasm); 2:27c with 28; 3:4a with b; etc. The same phenomenon occurs frequently in GJohn; cf. 1:12 with 11; 3:33 with 32; 5:36 with 37; 6:38 with 39; 8:15 with 16, 55a with b; etc. It is surprising to find similar instances in the Mandean writings.[20]

   b) *Inclusio* — a Semitic device, that is, the framing of one or more verses in a thought unit with the same words: 1:2 ("was revealed"); 2:3–5; 2:18 ("last hour"); 2:19 ("from us"); 2:27 ("abides" "you abide"); 3:9 ("born of God"); 4:7–8 ("love of God–God is love"); 5:10 ("Son of God"); 5:16 ("what in not mortal"–"not mortal").[21] This acts as a drag on the movement of thought, making it circular and for our taste somewhat boring and old-fashioned, though in those days it had appropriate solemnity.

   c) Anaphora, that is, a series of sentences beginning with the same words: 1:6, 8, 10 ("if we say"); 2:4, 6, 9 ("whoever says"); 2:12, 13a, 13b *graphō* ("I write"); 2:14a, b, c *egrapsa* ("I write"); 5:18, 19, 20 ("we know"). This device occurs frequently in classical rhetoric, but with this author it creates an impression of calm solemnity or even of ponderousness, especially in conjunction with his other peculiarities. In GJohn the same word or phrase is often repeated at the end; see 8:14, 21–22, 24; 6:39–40; 10:28–29; 10:15, 17, 18; 16:16, 17, 19; 17:21-22.

4. **Variation,** that is, changes in expression, the use of synonymous phrases expressing the same idea. In combination they sometimes result in pleonasm.

---

18. On this difference between Semitic and Hellenistic parallelism, see E. Norden, *Agnostos Theos* (Leipzig/Berlin, 1913) 260f., 355ff. The repetition of the same words in Hellenistic parallelism is alleged to be un-Hellenistic.

19. R. Bultmann, "Analyse des 1 Joh.," in *Festgabe für A. Jülicher* (Tübingen, 1927) 141.

20. A typical example is the *Canonical Book of Mandaeans* 92: "Hearken not to the talk of all peoples and generations; let not their stumblings cause you to stumble, stumble not because of their stumblings! Be not interrogated at their tribunals, at their tribunals be not interrogated! Certainly have you held to established truth, Ye have held to the certainty about which I instructed you."

21. Similar examples occur in John 1:1–2, 29–34; 3:3–7; 5:31f.; 8:47.

These peculiarities of style often serve as valuable pointers for exegesis. Here are some examples:

1:1 "what we have seen"–"what we have looked at"
1:6 "to have fellowship"–2:3 "we know him"–2:5f. "to be (abide) in him"–2:9 "to be in the light"
1:8; 2:4 "the truth . . . in us"–1:10; 2:14c "the word . . . in us"
1:9c–9d "forgive . . . sins"–"cleanse . . . from all unrighteousness"
2:29–3:1: 3:9–10; 5:1–2 "to be born of God"–"to be children of God"
3:6bα–β "to have seen him"–"to know him"
4:6a–b, 7c–d "to be from God" (or "born of God")–"to know him"

These stylistic devices show that the Johannine writings are not devoid of artistry.

5. Association, that is, the attachment of one particular word or thought to another. This procedure sometimes provides a clue to otherwise surprising developments of thought. It also provides the key to the weak associations in Johannine thought which to us seems to some extent strange and illogical. Here are a few "association terms," selected from a vast amount of material, which in turn call forth new statements: 1:1→2 "life"; 2:8→9 "light"; 2:14→15 "the evil one" in association with "the world" (cf. 4:4b; 5:19); 2:17→18 "for ever" in association with "last hour"; 2:21→22 "lie"–"liar"; 3:8a→c "the devil" in association with "the Son of God"; 3:22→23 "the commandments"–"the commandment"; 4:12→13, cf. 3:24a→b the idea of God's abiding in the believer in association with the conferral of the Spirit; 4:15→16 "confess" in association with "believer"; 5:2→3 "the commandments of God"; 5:4→5 "faith"–"believe"; 5:6→7 "to testify"; 5:9→10 "the Son of God." On the section 5:13–21, which appears to be controlled by the law of association, see the commentary. From this it would appear that the author allows himself to be carried along as it were by the flow of association, though he holds the rudder firmly in a definite direction.[22]

Peculiarities of Style

Büchsel and Chaine are of the opinion that these peculiarities of style show that the author was a Semite by birth. What is certain is that his style is far removed from that usual in Greek or Hellenistic literature. Nor is it related in any way to that of Philo or Josephus. Some of these stylistic characteristics may have been admissible, just as in classical literature. That would be true, for instance, of antithesis, anaphora, and variation. But there they are used quite differently. This is especially true of antithesis and parallelism.[23] Even if there are no errors of grammar in the Greek by Koine standards,[24] there are still a

22. E. D. Freed, "Variations in the Language and Thought of John," *ZNW* 55 (1964) 167–97.
23. See p. 7, though for a contrary view see Deissmann, *Light*, 127ff.; it is the style of Hellenistic writing.
24. Also *hina* after a demonstrative pronoun (3:11–23; 5:3; 4:17, 21; BDF §394) or with a consecutive sense (1:9; 2:27; 3:1; BDF §390.5 is quite possible in Koine as is *ean* with the indicative (5:15) et al. (see ad loc.).

number of features to be observed which support the thesis of the more recent commentators that compared with the rich and differentiated use of prepositions in classical Greek the author of 1 John seems in this respect to be deficient and somewhat simplistic. His use of particles is sparing. He prefers asyndeton and *kai*, which, like the Hebrew *wĕ*, can express a variety of conjunctions. He dislikes complicated constructions. The personal pronouns *hēmeis* and *hymeis* are often placed next to the verb. Participles are used as substantives, often with the addition of *pas* (cf. Hebrew *kol*). Combinations of verb and noun or adjective from the same root are frequent; see 1:5; 2:25; 3:7; 4:10; 5:4, 10, 15, 16. Added to this there are many special phrases with good parallels in rabbinic usage. A list of these is given in A. Schlatter, *Sprache und Heimat des vierten Evangelisten* (BFCT 4,4; Gütersloh, 1902) 144–51. Some good examples for the Semitic foundation are "do the truth" (1:6); "believe in the name" (3:23); "pleasing in his sight" (NRSV "pleases him"; 3:22); "shut up his bowels" (NRSV "refuses help"; 3:17); "love . . . among us" (4:17).[25] Other peculiarities, such as the frequently occurring phrase "by this we know that" or *hina* ("that") should be ascribed to his personal style. We may suppose an author of Jewish birth, with Aramaic as his mother tongue, who has acquired flawless Koine Greek but has otherwise retained a Semitic feel for language.

It is more difficult to decide whether we have here the style of an old man.[26] That is very much a matter of personal judgment or taste. Paul would most likely have expressed himself differently in his later years. It is noticeable that the author tends to spread himself more and is inclined to recapitulate. The reason for this may be rhetorical, and due to a need for emphasis. One thing, however, can be observed. This is his frequent use of "little children" as a mode of address, the only example in the New Testament apart from a variant reading in Gal. 4:19 (John 13:33; 1 John 2:1, 12, 28; 3:7, 18; 4:4; 5:21) or "children" (2:14a, 18; cf. John 21:5). Although this may be simply an expression of intimacy or tenderness, it would be especially appropriate for an older man with preeminence and authority. We are at once reminded of the "elder" in 2 John 1 and 3 John 1. The regular address in sermons or letters was in any case "brothers," following Jewish usage.

Rhythm

For the rhythm of speech, parallelism and figures of three are determinative. See, e.g., 1:6, 8, 10; 2:4, 6, 9; 2:13–14a, 14b; 5:18–20. This gives rise to sentences consisting of two or three parts, as can be clearly seen, for instance, in 2:12–14. Two groups of three are combined in a similar-sounding initial phrase, such as "I write" (*graphō* or *egrapsa*). An analogous device may be observed in the

---

25. On Semitisms, see J. H. Moulton and W. F. Howard, *A Grammar of New Testament Greek* (Edinburgh, 1927) vol. 2, appendix, 411–85, esp. the examples on pp. 424, 429, 434, 437, 460ff.; see further J. Bonsirven, "Les aramaïsmes de S. Jean l'Évangeliste?" *Bib* 30 (1949) 405–31, esp. 425ff.; J. Héring, "Y a-t-il des Aramaïsmes dans la Première Épître Johannique?" *RHPR* 36 (1956) 113–21 (affirmatively, but with examples that for the most part are not convincing.

26. See G. Hoffmann, *Das Joh-Ev als Alterswerk* (Gütersloh, 1933).

Prologue of GJohn, where we have a mellifluent sequence of groups of twos and threes.[27] Such rhythmical patterns serve to break up a lengthy composition. In the case of 1 John there is the prooemium to be considered. This is governed by a pattern of duality in v. 1:

1:1a "was from the beginning"
   b "what we have heard, what we have seen with our eyes"
   c "we have looked at and touched with our hands"
   d "concerning the word of life"

Verse 2 is successfully enlivened in the middle part by a threefold pattern in the verbs:

1:2a "this life was revealed"
   b "and we have seen and testify . . . and declare"
   c "to you the eternal life"
   d "that was with the Father and was revealed to us."

After the main statement (a), calm and impressive as it is, there follows the vibrant central phrase (b), returning to the main statement which once again, with its two parts, places the accent on "with the Father" and "to us" (c). Again, v. 3 clearly has a ponderous two-part structure.

1:3a "what we have seen and heard
     we declare to you
   b that you also may have fellowship with us
   c and . . . our fellowship is with the Father"

Many detailed observations which cannot be pursued here would confirm our impression that the author's style is by no means devoid of artistry.

On the other hand, Lohmeyer's thesis is untenable.[28] He is of the opinion that 1 John is constructed in groups of seven. Unfortunately to make his point Lohmeyer has to keep on forcing the text in quite an arbitrary way. In his overall analysis the groupings are very uneven: Prologue (1:1–4) and Epilogue (5:13–21) seem to be just as important as the long section 2:18–3:24. Should there really be such a marked caesura after 2:6 ("first revelatory word," 1:5–2:6; "second revelatory word," 2:7–17)? The division is also very haphazard. In the prooemium the parenthesis in v. 2 is divided into two parts (before *hētis* comes a new division). The effect is to disturb the unity which forms an *inclusio.* These examples must suffice. Lohmeyer's suggestions have met with very little approval.

The Progression of Thought

a) These peculiarities of style are not without influence on the progression of thought. In particular the law of antithesis is at work. Typical of this are the transitions, like that from 1:6 to 1:7; from 1:8 to 1:9; from 2:1a to 2:1b; from 2:4

---

27. R. Bultmann allows only the parallelism to stand but for the most part brackets out the threefold structure (not in v. 1) on grounds of source criticism (*The Gospel of John* [Oxford, 1971] 13ff.).

28. E. Lohmeyer, *ZNW* 27 (1928) 225–63.

to 2:5; from 2:10 to 2:11; from 2:15a to 2:15b; etc. Longer sections may be constructed on the basis of association; see the commentary at 5:13–21. But usually when this happens the general line of thought is continued, as in 4:7–5:2 on the nature of love.

b) Characteristic for the movement of thought on a larger scale is the way the author circles around relatively few though crucial basic ideas. A case in point is his treatment of true faith in Christ and love that shows itself in practice in love of one's fellow Christians. Yet the suggestion that these two complexes alternate in a certain rhythm cannot be proved. In the first main section, 1:5–2:17, they are interwoven with one another, and in the middle of the thematic treatment of love, 4:7–21, the author returns to the topic of faith (4:14–16a).

Smaller units of thought with associated ideas, such as the assurance of fellowship with God through participation in the Spirit (3:24b; 4:13), the certainty that those who are begotten of God will be heard (3:21–22; 5:14–15), their freedom from sin (3:6, 9; 5:18), the certainty of victory for those who belong to God (2:14; 4:4; 5:4–5) show how the author or the Christian community possesses a firm stock of imagery. The author increases his emphasis on it by mentioning it wherever a suitable opportunity arises.

c) One characteristic development of thought may provide a valuable pointer to the seams between larger and smaller blocks of meaning. The author of 1 John likes to use a turn of phrase at the end of one section that will introduce the theme of the next, thus creating a transition, though at the same time blurring the lines of demarcation between the sections. This is noticeable where additions of this kind are unexpected, either from the point of view of logic or of style. For example: 1:7, where the phrase "and the blood" through "sins" introduces the theme of sin in 1:8–10, while in 2:29 the phrase "has been born of him" paves the way for the theme of being children of God in 3:1–3. In 3:10 "those who do not love their brothers" is appended so as to lead to the parenesis on fraternal love in 3:11–18. In 3:22 the entire sentence beginning with the *hoti*-clause, in itself dispensable, leads to "commandment of God." The end of 3:24, "by the Spirit" is perhaps the preamble for the theme of distinguishing the spirits in 4:1–3; 5:3–4. These are typical transitional verses introducing the theme of faith once more. For other examples, see the commentary.

3. The Structure and Unity of 1 John

Structure

On the question of the articulation of John there are two quite different views. One view regarded it as a highly artistic construct; the other compares the document with "the waves of the sea" (Hauck). T. Häring puts forward a very ingenious scheme, following other scholars, including A. E. Brooke.[29] According

---

29. T. Häring, "Gedankengang und Grundgedanke des 1 Joh" (1892); see further his commentary (1927).

11

to this view we have three successive series with ethical and eschatological theses alternating with one another. At the same time each section is amply subdivided. The resulting profile goes something like this:

Prologue: 1:1–4
A. 1. Ethical thesis: 1:5–2:17—Walking in the Light as the true sign of fellowship with God.
   2. Christological thesis: 2:18–27—Faith in Jesus as the Christ serving as the basis for fellowship with God.
B. 1. Ethical thesis: 2:28–3:24—Righteousness of life as a sign of being begotten of God.
   2. Christological thesis: 4:1–6—The Spirit proceeding from God confesses that Jesus Christ has come in the flesh.
C. The two theses combined:
   1. 4:7–21—Love as the basis of faith.
   2. 5:1–12—Faith as the basis of love.
Conclusion: 5:13–21.

In this scheme the divisions are not entirely justified by the text or development of thought, although the alternation between the ethical and the christological theses, of the theme of love and of faith as well as the combination of the two (3:23), may have been determined to some extent by the author's literary style. Above all, the strong caesura that occurs in 3:24 is completely ignored; 3:23–24 clearly forms a conclusion. This throws doubt on the whole analysis. M. Bogaert finds the key to the structure in a chiastic form, following the pattern A B C B' A'. This pattern, which is presumed to be a Semitic one, has been found by several scholars in GJohn, but it leads to arbitrary conclusions and cannot be convincingly verified from the texts.[30]

Those who find only a loose articulation in the document dismiss such analyses as purely subjective.[31] They either run into the danger of overemphasizing the formal and aesthetic aspects, or they are at the mercy of dogmatic considerations.[32] Such a warning is well taken. The author of 1 John has no intention of producing a systematic treatment like that of Romans or Galatians. At the very outset (1:1–4) he announces his intention of proclaiming the saving message of fellowship with God through Jesus Christ. But in so doing, he is carried along by his polemic against the heretics and his desire to strengthen the Christian community. So he sets out to teach and exhort them and keeps it up

---

30. M. Bogaert, "Structure et message de la Première Épître de s. Jean," *Bible et Vie Chrétienne* 83 (1968) 33–45. See also E. Malatesta, *The Epistles of St. John: Structured Greek Text* (Fano, 1966).

31. On the history of these attempts, see R. Schwertschlager, *Der 1 Joh in seinem Grundgedanken und Aufbau* (Diss., Gregorian; Coburg, 1935) 9–16. His own proposal may be equally untenable: I. Jesus' proclamation and his atoning blood (1:5–2:27); II. Jesus, the examplary Son of God (2:28–4:6); III. Jesus the revelation of God's love (4:7–5:17). E. Nagl attempts to find a rhythmic structure with a threefold pattern: first thesis: God is light (1:5–2:28); second thesis: God is righteous (2:29–4:6); third thesis: God is light (4:7–5:19) ("Die Gliederung des 1 Joh," *BZ* 16 [1924] 77–92). All such attempts are reminiscent of modern sermon outlines.

32. Büchsel, *Johannesbriefe,* 9.

Introduction

all the way through. This is how he develops his major sections, with one idea leading to another. The beginnings and conclusions constitute recognizable units of thought. Consequently, there should be some consensus among interpreters as to where the main caesuras lie. Distinct caesuras are found in 2:18 and 4:1, where in each case they are occasioned by a deliberate focus on the antichrists or false prophets.[33] In the major divisions that result, the progress of thought is not determined by a logical or carefully thought out scheme but is the result of the author's idiosyncrasies and particular associations of ideas (see p. 8). But he does not merely sail along without any particular plan. The interpreter must feel his way into the author's train of thought to discover its content and order, and then provide a convincing explanation of the author's intention. The subdivisions proposed in this commentary should not be understood as claiming to represent a deliberate plan on the part of the author. An appropriate summary is offered at the beginning of each major section with a brief justification in every case.

Unitary Character

We get quite a different view of 1 John's literary character if we apply source criticism and try to recover a *Vorlage* available to the author which he worked over in his own way, giving it the shape we know today. Such a procedure was attempted by Rudolf Bultmann, using the criterion of style.[34] Bultmann was following an earlier attempt along the same lines by Ernst von Dobschütz.[35] Bultmann detected two different styles, one didactic in character with thesis and antithesis, derived from the *Vorlage,* the other a homiletic and parenetic treatment developed by the author himself. At the conclusion of his essay Bultmann offers a reconstruction of the pattern as far as this is possible now that it is embedded in 1 John. With the deletion of a phrase or two here and there it consists of the following verses: 1:5-10; 2:4-5, 9-11, 29; 3:4, 6-10, 14-15 (24); 4:7 (8), 12, 16; 5:1, 4; 4:5, 6 (?); 2:23; 5:10, 12; (2 John 9). It is clear from this rough selection that Bultmann found it difficult to be sure himself. In any case the *Vorlage* has been absorbed for the most part into the parenesis.

A. Jülicher's sarcastic remark that attempts of this kind on the basis of style criticism tend to cancel each other out,[36] is certainly an exaggeration. Yet serious

---

33. For this reason the articulation proposed by Chaine is inadequate: I. Fellowship with God (1:5-2:28); II. Sonship to God (2:29-5:13). To place the section 2:28-4:6 under the theme "Sonship to God" (so A. Wikenhauser, *New Testament Introduction* [New York, 1958] 521; cf. F.-M. Braun in the *Jerusalem Bible,* and A. Feuillet in A. Robert and A. Feuillet, *Introduction à la Bible, II, Nouveau Testament* [Tournai, 1959] 688) does not commend itself. Although this theme comes out most clearly in 2:29-3:10 (cf. on 2:28-3:3 below, pp. 151-61), it is echoed later on (4:7; 5:1f.; 4:18); on the other hand, the parenetic section 3:11-24 and the dispute with the false prophets in 4:1-6 are not explicitly noted in this scheme.
34. Bultmann, "Analyse," 138-58.
35. E. von Dobschütz, "Johanneische Studien I," *ZNW* 8 (1907) 1-8.
36. A. Jülicher in Jülicher-Fascher, *Einleitung,* 225. For a critique of Bultmann, see F. Büchsel, "Zu den Johannesbriefen," *ZNW* 28 (1929) 235-41; further, although basically agreeing with Bultmann, H. Braun, "Literar-Analyse und theologische Schichtung im 1 Joh," *ZTK* 48 (1951)

doubts arise with regard to Bultmann's procedure and his results:

1. Whether there is some possible connection between the pattern Bultmann proposes for 1 John and the Revelation Discourses in the Gospel merits careful examination. The peculiarities of style are purely formal in nature and do not by themselves allow any conclusion about a source consisting of Revelation Discourses.

2. The change in style in the text of 1 John is in itself well observed and susceptible of a positive explanation, in part from the dual purpose of the document. For it is both a didactic and a polemical work directed against the heretics (e.g., 1:6–10), and at the same time a homiletical and parenetic work addressed to the community (e.g., 2:1–2).

3. The distinction between the *Vorlage* and the homiletical development is often hard to draw. Much would be gained, for instance, if 2:29b and 3:4a, which are anything but straightforward in their context, could be explained by attributing them to the source. According to Bultmann, they were combined so as to form a double verse ("Analyse," 147). Yet to extract them (2:29b) and combine them, thus passing over the important passage 3:1–3, raises problems. In 3:6–9 Bultmann again recognizes a fragment of the *Vorlage,* "though amply glossed for homiletical reading" ("Analyse," 147). The same applies to the difficult context of 3:19–20 (pp. 150–51) and of 3:24 (p. 151).

4. The removal of theological tensions, especially the one involving "Christ and sin" on the basis of this source analysis is questionable.[37] It can be explained just as easily if we assume a single origin (see Excursus 12).

5. Above all, this *Vorlage* would have to be a very peculiar creation consisting of an exhausting series of antitheses and stereotyped conditional sentences with participles used as nouns. Hardly anything like this is to be found in the literature of late Judaism or in gnostic texts.[38] As far as its contents go, the *Vorlage* would not provide us with Wisdom sayings, ethical directives, or even Revelation Discourses.

Bultmann's proposal, accepted by H. Windisch in his commentary, has been carried further by H. Preisker,[39] In his opinion the redactor has reintroduced the eschatology of the early church, which was unknown to Bultmann's *Vorlage.* In 3:13–14 (which Preisker, unlike Bultmann, ascribes to the redactor), he sees hints of an eschatological situation. In 3:19–21, he finds a fragment of a primitive eschatological sermon. He interprets 5:18b–20a as an eschatological Wisdom Discourse, introduced by a threefold *oidamen.* More importantly,

---

262–92; E. Käsemann, "Ketzer und Zeuge: Zum joh. Verfasserproblem," *ZTK* 48 (1951) 306–8, text and footnote.

37. "The concept of sin in the *Vorlage* and that of the author are different" ("Analyse," 148). On this, see H. Braun, *ZTK* 48 (1951) 276f.; Käsemann, *ZTK* 48 (1951) 262–92. Braun distinguishes still further themes and seeks to establish a *Vorlage* that is not pre-Christian but authentically Christian, edited by the author from a different point of view ("early catholic").

38. H. Becker (*Die Reden des Johannesevangeliums und der Stil der gnostischen Offenbarungsrede* [FRLANT n.s. 50; Göttingen, 1956] 24) refers to a Hermetic *kephalaia*-collection that has survived in Stobaeus (Frag. 11: Nock-Festugiere 3:54–57). But these are are only brief summaries. For a critique, see E. Haenchen, "Neuere Literatur zu den Johannesbriefen," *TRu* 26 (1960) 25f.

39. Preisker, Appendix to Windisch, 168–71.

Preisker exploits 2:18–25 and 4:1–12 for his hypothesis. Finally he suggests that the author of our present 1 John used two different *Vorlagen,* one in the shape of a Revelation Discourse à la Bultmann, the other an eschatological text. But that would mean tearing apart the thought world of 1 John, a document that is to be understood as a unity. Preisker's theory is hypercritical. From a methodological point of view we should resort to such hypotheses only when a unitary explanation of the work proves impossible.

Mainly for reasons of genre W. Nauck also seeks to distinguish between a *Vorlage* and a redaction, though ascribing both to the same author (see pp. 5–6 above). The following sections are in his view typical for the form and structure of the series of lapidary and apodictic sentences: 2:29–3:10; 1:6–10; 2:4–11.[40] From the perspective of genre Nauck would associate them with the proclamation of the reign of God in the Old Testament and its continuation in the dualistic teaching of Qumran (see the ritual of covenant renewal in 1QS 1:1–3:12).[41] The formal style originating in Jewish tradition and motifs emanating from Qumran (light and darkness, ethical behavior, confession of sin, etc.) were taken up in the early church's baptismal catechesis and traced further into the patristic age.[42] However justified Nauck's emphasis on baptismal parenesis may be, however remarkable the parallels he deduces from the Qumran texts, he does not really prove the unbroken continuity of the genre, as indeed Ernst Haenchen has shown.[43] Moreover, Nauck's suggestion that the author of 1 John picked up the original series of antitheses a second time and worked them into another document is open to serious doubt. Nauck's arrangement of the antitheses in rhythmical verse form is not worked out convincingly either.[44] The main objection, however, is that it is difficult to understand how they could ever have stood on their own. It seems best therefore to stick with the position that the document is a unity. The change of style from categorical assertion to homiletical parenesis may be credited to the author's own tendency. He needed to refute the heretics and confirm the believers in their Christian status and their ethical aspirations.

On Ernst Lohmeyer's structure analysis, see p. 10 above.

The Question of Redactional Additions

Turning from the question of 1 John's origin in a literary *Vorlage,* redacted into the curious document we have before us, we are faced with quite a different problem, which Bultmann has discussed in a recent essay.[45] Did the document, constructed as it was from an earlier source and then redacted, undergo a further redaction which gave it the final shape in which we have it today? Since John 21:24 leaves us with little doubt that there was such activity in the

---

40. W. Nauck, *Tradition und Charakter,* 1–26.

41. Ibid., 29–41.

42. Ibid., 41–66.

43. Haenchen, *TRu* 26 (1960) 22ff.

44. Ibid., 10f.

45. R. Bultmann, "Die kirchliche Redaktion des 1 Joh," *In memoriam Ernst Lohmeyer* (Stuttgart, 1951) 189–201.

Johannine school, this question has considerable weight. Bultmann resorts to this hypothesis to explain two considerations: (1) the destruction of its original character as a letter resulting from the addition of 5:14-21; (2) theological tensions arising from minor interpolations.

Bultmann can make a good case for assigning 5:14-21 to a later redaction. The original letter ended at 5:13 (cf. John 20:31). Verse 14 does not appear to follow logically after the previous verses. The topic raised in the last eight verses is partly new, partly different in kind from what was involved in the body of the letter. Thus the efficacy of prayer is qualified by "according to his will" (v. 14). The distinction between two classes of sinners (vv. 16-17) betrays a pedagogical and churchly concern. Verses 18-20 are evidently intended to sum up some of the main themes of the document. The conclusion forms a warning against idolatry which looks like a cliché (v. 21). Moreover, some of the style, Bultmann alleges, is un-Johannine, especially "has given us understanding"(v. 20), the absolute *ho alēthinos* ("him who is true," v. 20), "keep yourselves" (v. 21). The tensions Bultmann discovers between the final paragraph and the rest of the document are capable of resolution. Nauck has shown, *contra* Bultmann, that the situation of the Christians in the world and the attitude toward sin, a theme continued in the final verse (see the commentary ad loc.), is no different from what we find in the document as a whole and must be judged accordingly.[46] The riddle posed by the epistle's literary form and the peculiarity of 5:14-21 would of course be more readily explained on Bultmann's analysis. But there is still the problem of the final greeting, which remains unexplained. Was it missing altogether? Or was it intentionally dropped in order to add on this section? If so, why was it not removed to the end of the letter?

We become even more skeptical when faced by the interpolations Bultmann assigns to the redaction because of alleged tensions in style and theology. Three of them have to do with eschatology: (1) In 2:28 "when he is revealed" and "(before him) at his coming"; Bultmann takes the directive and warning to refer to God. We are to have confidence in God and he will not put us to shame. (2) In 3:2 "when he is revealed"; (3) in 4:17 he cuts out "the day of judgment" and supposes that the original text read differently: "so that we have confidence in this world because, as he (is in the love of the Father) so we, too, are in his love." Such a radical change arouses our suspicions. Next Bultmann assumes that the theme of atonement represents an interpolation: (a) in 1:7 "and the blood of Jesus," etc,; (b) the whole of verse 2:2; (c) 4.10b. Yet these theological motifs, suspect as they are to Bultmann, are certainly a part of Johannine theology, unless the Gospel itself was "laundered" in a similar manner.[47]

We should also point out that Bultmann himself has further complicated the origin of 1 John by this new hypothesis of his. He must, for example, assume that 2:1-3 has been worked over twice: there are the author's redactional additions to his *Vorlage* and then the additions of the ecclesiastical redactor (viz., 2:2).[48] These attempts to disentangle the document's origin inspire little

---

46. Nauck, *Tradition und Charakter,* 136-46.
47. See pp. 36-37 below; see further the commentary ad loc.
48. Bultmann, "Redaktion," 201.

confidence as Bultmann engages in them, employing the methods of style and content criticism upon a text that is quite readable, if not perfectly smooth.

4. Historical Presuppositions:
The Heresy Combated

If we are to understand 1 John we must try to form a picture of its contemporary background. In particular we must discover the motives of the opponents with which the epistle is in combat.

I. The epistle gives the impression of a community in an advanced state of development. The author keeps harking back to the message they had heard "from the beginning" (2:7, 24; 3:11; cf. 2 John 5). This suggests that they had been familiar with the Christian faith for a long time. The apostasy and departure of the antichrists (2:19), the intense activity of the false prophets (4:1), and the believing community's fight for survival (4:4–6) take up a whole page in church history. The author speaks as the representative of a circle of qualified witnesses who testify to the great event of salvation (1:1–3), to a generation that is no longer in direct contact with the foundation event. They depend for their faith exclusively on "hearing" (3:11).

The gnostic movement is in the ascendant. The imagery and terms of this movement have won out against the Pauline tradition and are creating a powerful impression. The parousia is still expected (2:28), though there is less excitement about it. It does not seem to cause any problems. All this presupposes a degree of development such as was reached only at the end of the first century C.E. Since there are hardly any concrete pointers, we must content ourselves with these general observations. Only the conflict with the opponents carried on all through the letter needs to be specially highlighted.

II. It is hardly possible to provide an exhaustive account of the heresy that is being opposed.[49] The meager hints and the formulas used in the letter are all we have to go on.

1. Although the problem of the heresy has often been discussed and is still a matter of debate, there is general agreement on the following points:

a) The author is fighting on a single front. Even though there may be different groups among the many antichrists (2:18) or false prophets,[50] they are united in their denial of the church's christological confession (2:22; 4:2-3). "Antichrists" and "false prophets" are only different terms arising from particular perspectives,[51] depending on whether it is eschatological (last hour, antichrist) or pneumatic (distinguishing of spirits). The repetition and separate treatment

---

49. See A. Škrinjar, "Errores in epistola 1 Jo impugnati," *VD* 41 (1963) 60–72; K. Weiss, "Orthodoxie und Heterodoxie im 1. Johannesbrief," *ZNW* 58 (1967) 247–55; F. Stagg, "Orthodoxy and Orthopraxy in the Johannine Epistles," *Review and Expositor* 67 (1970) 423–32.

50. So Brooke, who for that reason mistakenly argues that the letter is "directed against various forms of teaching" (pp. xxxix ff.). M. Goguel supposes three different groups (*The Birth of Christianity* [London, 1953] 407ff.).

51. See also the earliest citation of 4:2 in Polycarp 7.1: *pas gar, hos an mē homologē . . . antichristos estin.*

are due to the author's loose literary style. In fact there are other places as well where he makes reference to the christological differences (4:15; 5:15–16).

b) The heretics represent both christological error and a false ethic (1:5–2:11; to be inferred also from 3:4–24; 4:20–5:3). The doctrinal heresy and the ethical indifference spring from the same source and form a unified un-Christian stance.

c) The religious and ethical deviation under attack shows a gnostic tendency. This needs no further proof, given all the terminology employed and the ideological perspective.

d) The opponents are to be sought predominantly in a Gentile Christian milieu. This is evident from the method of argument, which makes no use of scriptural proof, from the preference for Son of God as a title for Jesus, and from other factors as well. A. Wurm has suggested that the opponents were Jewish and that the epistle defends the messiahship of Jesus against attacks from that quarter, but this theory has been generally rejected. An important counterargument is that such a denial of the messiahship of Jesus could never have arisen in a Christian community (cf. 2:19).

2. The issue today mainly involves the question of the type of gnosis which threatened the community. Was it a form of docetism? Or was it some other type of gnosticism unknown to us? Büchsel has introduced a new factor into the discussion. He maintains that it was not so much a heresy as "Christian prophecy gone wild," a "pneumatic Christianity" belonging to the "gnostic-pneumatic movement," which can be traced back to the conflicts of Paul at Corinth (pp. 4–5).

What are we to say to this? In the first place, the combination of pneumatic disturbances in the life of the community (1 Corinthians 12–14) with a dangerous view of the antichrist expressing themselves in doctrinal formulas (hence the creedal formulas which 1 John holds up against them) is highly dubious. Gnostic ideas developed into fanaticism by denying the simple way of salvation by faith. The message of the gnostics must therefore have been delivered in a pseudo-prophetic and charismatic mode. But the source of such fanaticism is generally different. Charismatic movements are characterized by undisciplined and falsely interpreted spiritual manifestations of a practical kind. With gnosticism, on the other hand, we find a perverted intellectual attitude—in fact, one might call it a false religious *Weltanschauung,* or a charismatic enthusiasm threatening the common life of the Christian community and its discipline, of which there is not a trace in 1 John. The letter is actually combating false doctrine and its practical consequences. We may therefore continue to call them "heretical teachers."

3. The christological heresy.

A. To understand the basic christological tenets of the heretics in 1 John we must first look at the confessional formulas that are brought to bear against them. These formulas are as follows:

a) 2:22; 5:1 "Jesus is the Christ"

b) 4:15; 5:5 "Jesus is the Son of God"; cf. the same title in 2:23; 3:23; 5:13 as well as 5:11–12, 20

c) 4:2 "Jesus Christ . . . come in the flesh"; cf. 2 John 7 "Jesus Christ . . . (coming) in the flesh"

d) 5:6 "This is the one that came by water and blood, Jesus Christ," etc.

These creedal formulas do not by themselves give a clear picture of the heresy under attack. They only provide evidence of certain tensions. There does seem to be an emphasis on the idea of messiahship (a). On the other hand, it looks as though there was a need to ward off a docetic misunderstanding either of the incarnation itself or of the crucifixion (b). The title Christ would have an entirely different meaning in each case. In the first case it would mean the one who brings salvation ([a] though also [d]); in the second instance it means a heavenly, preexistent spiritual being ([c] and [d]; cf. Cerinthus and his idea of a *Christus spiritalis*). Between these two poles, however, we find a frequent use of the title Son of God ([b] and elsewhere), coupled with each of the other three statements. It is practically interchangeable with the title Christ (cf. 2:22a with 2:22b and 23). Along with the formula (in 4:2) that speaks of Christ's coming or having come and the statement that he "came" in 5:20 (*hēkei*) we may compare "sending the Son of God" in 4:9, 10, 14 and his "appearing" in 3:8. Finally, the formula (in 5:6) that speaks of his coming stands in close relationship with the christological formula 5:5. Does the title refer to messiaship or to the preexistence of a divine being? Clearly, these formulas are not sufficient to settle the question.

B. To complete this picture we must add the positive statements of christological faith. Even if these are not directed emphatically against the heretics, they do, taken as a whole, create a picture of the faith in its light and shade which ought to protect the church against these dangerous influences. The most important examples of this, allowing for certain schematization, are as follows:

a) The emphasis on preexistence in the phrase "what was from the beginning" (1:1); "him who is from the beginning" (2:13a, 14b)

b) The presentation of the great salvation event in terms of incarnation (1:2, "was revealed"; 3:8a; cf. 4:9)

c) The emphasis on the atoning death of Jesus through the shedding of his blood for us (or for our sins) (1:7, "blood"; 2:2; 4:10, "atoning sacrifice"; 4:14, "the Savior of the world"; 3:8b, "to destroy the works of the devil"; 3:16, "for us"; 2:12, "forgiveness of sins": on account of his name)

d) The confession of the unique sonship and divinity of Jesus (4:9, "only"; 2:22, 23, 24; 4:14; 5:12; 2 John 9, "the Son," used absolutely;[52] 5:20, "the true God and eternal life"; 1:1 "the word of life")

All of these points are equally important to the author. Yet it is imperative to combine (d) and (a) internally. Because the Son of God (*logos*) is preexistent, "from the beginning," he is therefore a divine being and Son of God in a completely exclusive and unique sense (cf. John 1:1).

C. The author nowhere confronts the heretics with Johannine Christology in all its completeness. If the antiheretical statements under (A) appear to be

---

52. This means, of course, that the other *ho-huios-tou-theou* statements are to be interpreted accordingly.

referring to one or another of the points under (B), it must be understood that the heretics were denying all the crucial affirmations about Jesus Christ. In each case the author calls attention to one point or another. Christology is intricately linked to soteriology. The eternal, preexistent Son of God has appeared in order to impart the life of God (see 4:9; 5:11). For this purpose it is necessary for him to liberate us by his atoning death in which he shed his blood for our sins. This leads to the following points:

a) The incarnation formula: 4:2; cf. 1:2; 3:8
b) The identity formulas: Jesus is (truly) the Christ, or the Son of God: 2:22; 5:1;—4:15, 5:15
c) The soteriological statements: 5:6; cf. the references under (B, c).

All three groups, which in some places are closely connected (cf. 5:5–6) form a totality:
a) The incarnation of the preexistent One is the presupposition of real redemption. Only so does the Son of God truly come to us. Only so does the life of God actually appear among us and become a tangible reality. Only so does the Logos assume the flesh in which he will accomplish the bloody work of atonement.
b) No statement which denies the historic personality of Jesus or his pre-existence and divinity or his death for our salvation can do it justice.
c) The denial of the fact that the blood of Jesus takes away sins destroys the whole picture of faith in him, since this saving purpose, indissolubly bound up with his coming (3:8; 4:9, 14), is also given with the incarnation. From this it follows that the heretics reject any figure of salvation in the Christian sense. They specifically deny that Jesus had this significance. It is not at all clear what positive traits they ascribed to him as a historical person. Did they view him as the bearer of the Spirit? Did he become that at his baptism (5:6)? Or did they regard him as a prototype of the true gnostic, without emphasizing his moral qualities (cf. 2:6, 29; 3:3, 7)?

It cannot be proved that they entertained the idea of a *Christus spiritalis* temporarily associated with Jesus. The title Christ still retains its meaning, bringer of salvation (cf. "the Savior").[53] But at the same time it involved the preexistence and divine nature of the Son of God. This tendency can be observed already in the Gospel, where the title "Son" is often added to "Christ."[54] In the epistle, where there is no longer any concern with the problem of the "Jews," this combination is carried through without qualification (2:22; cf. v. 23).

4. Accordingly, the heresy that is being combated[55] can hardly be identified

---

53. So also in John 1:41; 4:29; 7:26, 27, 31, 41f.; 9:22; 12:34; but broadened in a universal sense as "Savior of the world" (4:42).

54. 11:27; 20:31; cf. also 1:34, 49.

55. Principal sources: Irenaeus, *Adv. Haer.* 1.21 (=Hippolytus, *Ref.* 7.33; cf. 10.21); 3.11.7; Epiphanius, *Pan.* 51.2, 3f.; 12.3; Jerome, *Vir. ill.* 9.—On the debate about his teaching, see H. Gladder, "Cerinth und unsere Evangelien," *BZ* 14 (1917) 317–32; C. Schmidt, "Gespräche Jesu mit seinen Jüngern nach seiner Auferstehung," *TU* 43 (1919) 403–52, 726–31; G. Bardy, "Cérinthe," *RB* 30 (1921) 344–73; Lagrange, *S. Jean,* lxxii f.

with the familiar christological views of Cerinthus,[56] although it shows certain contacts with them.

a) There is no trace in 1 John of the idea of two deities, a supreme power (*principalitas, quae est super universa,* or *deus super omnia*), as differentiated from an inferior, distinct power (*virtus quaedam valde separata et distans*).[57]

b) Connected with this doctrine of God in Cerinthus there is also a separation of the man Jesus, born of Joseph and Mary, from the spiritual Christ who descended upon him at his baptism. For in another passage Irenaeus tells us that Cerinthus, like the earlier Nicolaitans, held this Jesus to be the inferior divine power, the creator of the world (*fabricator*), allowing only the Christ to be of higher origin.[58] In view of this it would be wrong to interpret 1 John prematurely in a Cerinthian sense.

c) The denial of the incarnation, a point on which Cerinthus and the false teachers of 1 John are agreed, occurs in Cerinthus's case because he thinks the virginal conception in particular is incredible.[59] The Johannine heretics, however, reject the incarnation for general reasons of Christology and soteriology.

d) Again, the gnostics seem to deny redemption in the blood of Jesus more on grounds of principle—that is, because they reject the whole Christian doctrine of salvation, including sin and atonement. They do not share the specific christological perspective of Cerinthus. His idea of the spirit-Christ (*Christus spiritalis*) is associated with the idea of impassibility.

e) Finally, so far as the external evidence is concerned,[60] it tells us only that the Gospel was directed against Cerinthus. Consequently it must be accepted with caution.[61]

5. More careful attention than in the first edition needs to be paid to the docetists whom Ignatius of Antioch was combating. Although they cannot be placed on a par with the false teachers of 1 John and their Christology, there are nevertheless striking points of similarity in the polemical language used by the martyr-bishop and the author of 1 John. There are obvious affinities between the positions they are combating:

---

56. So R. Knopf, *Nachapostolisches Zeitalter,* 328ff.; Zahn, *Introduction* 3:365f.; Bardy, *RB* 30 (1921) 344–73; Lagrange, *S. Jean,* lxxii f.' Vrede; Chaine; Feine-Behm, *Einleitung,* 260; Wikenhauser, *Introduction,* 525; Feuillet, *Introduction,* 700f.; et al. Contra: see C. Clemen, "Beiträge zum geschichtlichen Verständnis der Johannesbriefe," *ZNW* 6 (1905) 271f.; Büchsel, *Johannesbriefe,* 65f.; H. Braun, "Literar-Analyse," 290. Cautiously W. Michaelis, *Einleitung in das Neue Testament* (3rd ed.; Bern, 1961) 298.

57. Irenaeus, *Adv. Haer.* 1.21.

58. *Adv. Haer.* 3.11.7: "alium quidem fabricatoris filium, alterum vero de superioribus Christum . . . descendentem in Iesum filium fabricatoris." The exact genealogy of the "Christ" is not made clear; the "*monogenes*" constitutes the beginning, and his Son is the Logos (ibid.).

59. Irenaeus, *Adv. Haer.* 1.21: "Iesum autem aubiecit non ex virgine natum (impossibile enim hoc ei visum est), fuisee autem Ioseph et Mariae filium, similiter ut reliqui omnes homines."

60. Irenaeus, *Adv. Haer.* 3.11.7; Epiphanius, *Pan.* 51.2.3f.; 12.3; Jerome, *Vir. ill.* 9.

61. The testimony of Epiphanius is particularly controverted; see Bardy, *RB* 30 (1921) 362ff. Cerinthus's opposition to John soon became embroidered with legend (cf. the story of their meeting at the baths, Irenaeus, *Adv. Haer.* 3.3.4). GJohn is supposedly directed against more than one front (Jerome: "adversus Cerinthum aliosque haereticos"); Irenaeus already mentions the Nicolaitans as well (3.11.7, following Rev. 2:6, 15?).

a) The heretics mentioned in Ignatius's letter to the Smyrnaeans refused to take Jesus' humanity or historicity seriously, his involvement in the "flesh." Ignatius accuses them of refusing to confess Jesus as *sarkophoros* (*Smyrn.* 5.2), insisting that his death on the cross (1.2) and his resurrection (3.1; cf. 3) occurred "in flesh." His birth, his passion, and his resurrection were real historical events which took place in historical time and so were real and trustworthy acts of salvation (*Magn.* 11). That is why Ignatius, like the Apostles' Creed, repeatedly insists that they are objects of confession (*Trall.* 9; *Smyrn.* 1).

b) The reason for this emphasis on the "fleshly" nature of Jesus' divine and human person, often characterized as "flesh and spirit," is its soteriological implication. Only by this means could we be truly redeemed: "for our sakes Jesus was nailed to the cross and of [this] fruit we are — that is, of his most blessed passion" (*Smyrn.* 1.2). "For he suffered all these things for our sake, that we might be saved" (1.2). This explains Ignatius's emphasis on the blood of Jesus: Whoever does not believe in the blood of Christ is warned of judgment (*Smyrn.* 6.1). By his blood we are firmly grounded in love (1.1). He can even call faith the flesh of Christ, and love his blood (*Trall.* 8.1). This gives the flesh of Jesus Christ and his blood a meaning similar to what they have in 1 John (4:2; cf. 1:7; 5:6).

c) The fruit of salvation effected by the bloody death of Christ upon the cross is applied concretely in the Eucharist, for which Ignatius uses similar terminology to that of GJohn, "flesh" and "blood" of Jesus Christ (cf. John 6:53–56) (*Philad.* 4; cf. *Rom.* 7.3; *Smyrn.* 12.2). The saving acts of the redeemer manifested in the flesh, his blood spilt in love, become effective in the recipients — an idea which, it should be noted, influences the sacramental background of John 19:34–35 and 1 John 5:7–8 (see ad loc.). Ignatius's heretics abstain from the Eucharist and prayer because they do not believe that the Eucharist is the flesh of the savior Jesus Christ, the flesh in which "he suffered for our sins" (*Smyrn.* 7.1).

d) The same people care nothing about *agapē* or about the widows and orphans, the afflicted, the prisoners, the hungry and the thirsty (*Smyrn.* 6.2; cf. *Trall.* 8.2). Here we find the same connection between christological heresy and moral indifference, the same neglect of fraternal love, as in 1 John. When these observations are taken together, some relationship between the two groups of heretics is undeniable.[62]

At the same time there are of course certain differences which cannot be overlooked. Ignatius's heretics are apparently genuine docetists, who reduce the existence and activity of Jesus Christ to a mere semblance. He counters this (*Smyrn.* 2; 4.2) again and again with the word "truly" (*alēthōs*). Jesus Christ is truly of the lineage of David according to the flesh, born of a virgin and baptized by John, was truly nailed to the cross, truly suffered and rose by his own

---

62. See P. T. Camelot, *Ignace d'Antioche: Lettres* (Sources chrétiennes; 2nd ed.; Paris, 1951) 27: "C'est le milieu que révèlent les épîtres de saint Jean, adressées, elles aussi, à des Églises d'Asie . . . ." See further Tillmann, *Joh-Ev,* 71; Dibelius, *RGG*² 3:317; Jülicher-Fascher, *Einleitung*, 227f. W. Lütgert goes too far when he says that Jesus is a spirit-being (*Amt und Geist im Kampf* [BFCT 15,4–5; Gütersloh, 1911]).

Introduction

power (*Smyrn.* 1-2; similarly *Trall.* 9; *Magn.* 11). This emphasis is missing from 1 John. There is no explicitly docetic Christology discernible in that document. For the rest, docetism appears in various guises,[63] but all of them are associated with a gnosticizing stance, a devaluation of the historic, unique act of salvation in Jesus Christ, in his flesh and blood. Furthermore, the heretical teachers as characterized in the letter to the Magnesians (9-10) have strong affinities with Judaism. They cling to Jewish opinions and customs such as the sabbath. There is no trace of anything like this in the letters of John.[64]

In the light of all this we must insist that the heresy which occasioned 1 and 2 John cannot be parallel with any other manifestation of heresy known from that era. Yet it has affinities with more than one such movement. They all play down the historic person of Jesus Christ as the unique and true savior. They all deny the way of salvation through his flesh and blood. In their precise christological interpretation of the figure of Jesus, these dangerous heretics, dissolving as they did the substance of the Christian faith, evidently went off in different directions. This can be seen by comparing the views of Cerinthus with those of the docetists in the letters of Ignatius, whose precise teaching, however, remains obscure. The Christology of the antichrists in the Johannine epistles also can no longer be described with certainty or precision. But it is one example of that pseudo-Christian tendency which manifested itself in gnosticism and was such a threat to the church.

6. Since the christological "lie" is the principal topic of interest, there is little to discuss about the other tenets of the heretical teachers. There is, however, one aspect of their teaching that we are informed about — their ethical and practical orientation. This is connected with their erroneous Christology.

a) These gnostics believed that they did not need to be saved by the blood of Jesus. See 1:7; 5:6; also 2:2; 3:8c-d; 4:10, 14.

b) The deeper reason for this is that they considered themselves superior to sin and refused to admit that they had any personal sins. See 1:8-10; cf. 3:6, 8; 5:18.

c) They did not consider themselves in any way to be under the law. See 2:3-4; 5:2-3; cf. 3:22, 24.

d) In particular they neglected the commandment of fraternal love. See 2:9-11; 3:10, 14-15; 4:8, 20; 5:2; cf. 3:23; 4:7, 11-12.

This attitude, strictly speaking, cannot be called libertinism. The typical formula "all things are lawful for me" (1 Cor. 6:12; 10:23) is missing. At all events, there is not a sign of the later perversion of deliberately committing sin in order to test one's own spiritual power.[65] It is a type of moral indifference, though it contains the seeds of libertinism and amorality. Any connection with the Nicolaitans of the Apocalypse, who had no scruples about taking part in

63. Cf. A. Grillmeier, *LTK* 3:470f.
64. On the Ignatian letters, see also J. Rohde, "Heresie und Schisma im ersten Clemensbrief und in den Ignatius-Briefen," *NovT* 10 (1968) 217-33.
65. See Irenaeus, *Adv. Haer.* 1.1.12; 20.2; 28.9; Clement of Alexandria, *Stromateis* 3.4.34.3f.; Epiphanius, *Pan.* 25.1ff.; 26.1ff. On this, see W. Bousset, *Hauptprobleme der Gnosis* (FRLANT 10; Göttingen, 1907) 74f.; Jonas, *Gnosis und spätantiker Geist,* FRLANT n.F. 33 (2nd ed.; Göttingen, 1954) 235ff.; H. J. Schoeps, *Aus frühchristlicher Zeit* (Tübingen, 1950) 255ff. (Gnostic nihilism).

pagan sacrifices (Rev. 2:14), cannot be proved. In particular, the gnostics of 1 John are never accused of indecent behavior or excess. Warnings like those in 2:15-17 could have been given for purely pastoral reasons. The letter contains no suggestion that the heretics were antinomians. On the contrary, "lawlessness" in 3:4 is really an afterthought, something no one would want to incur, while the commandment of God in 3:23 is addressed to the church, though since it is the "word of God" it is obviously intended as a serious incentive for the heretics as well (2:5). By contrast, the docetists with whom Ignatius of Antioch is arguing display an attitude of indifference vis-à-vis the love commandment similar to that of the antichrists in 1 John (see above under 5,d).

7. To be sure, there are connections with the contemporary opponents combated in GJohn, both in matters of Christology (1:14; 20:31) and in questions of morality (13:34-35; 14:15, 21; 15:10, 12, 17). Yet GJohn is taking issue primarily with those Jews who reject Jesus and only implicitly with the contemporary opponents of the author and his fellow believers. The evangelist is fighting on more than one front: the rejection of an exaggerated estimate of the Baptist plays no part in 1 John—see, e.g., 5:6.[66]

8. As for the way in which the Gnostics carry on their controversy over matters of faith, they must have developed a troublesome propaganda campaign. They had had some success, at least outwardly (cf. 4:5). Their personal claims and their low regard for their fellow believers fit the picture of arrogant pneumatics, a picture even more familiar in the later history of the gnostic movement, that of the Gnostics proper. The champion of orthodox Christianity conducts his defense above all in reliance on the strength that comes from God (4:4), the illumination of the Holy Spirit (2:27), and the power of truth (4:6). In this way he seeks to strengthen his readers and assure them of final victory (2:14; 5:4) and the certainty of their salvation (3:14; 5:13).

5. The Place of the Epistles
in the History of Religions

There is a widespread consensus today that a history-of-religions perspective is indispensable in Johannine studies. But given the exposure of the Johannine writings to so many religious influences from the surrounding world, it is still a matter of lively debate where exactly these writings fit in. It is impossible to pursue this problem here. All we can do is to draw attention to the views of other scholars in order to orient the reader,[67] and briefly indicate the position adopted

---

66. For GJohn, G. Richter assumes that all the antidocetic passages go back to a redactional layer that is close in affinity to 1 John ("Die Fleischwerdung des Logos im Johannesevangelium," *NovT* 13 [1971] 81-126; 14 [1972] 257-76). For the docetism, he refers to an unpublished dissertation by P. Weigandt ("Der Doketismus im Urchristentum und in der theologischen Entwicklung des zweiten Jahrhunderts" [Heidelberg, 1961]). This seems to confirm the connection with the docetists of the Ignatian letters.

67. L. Schmid, "Joh-Ev und Religionsgeschichte" (Diss., Tübingen, 1933); W. F. Howard, *The Fourth Gospel in Recent Criticism and Interpretation* (4th ed.; London, 1955); P.-H. Menoud, *L'Évangile de Jean d'après les recherches récentes* (2nd ed.; Neuchâtel/Paris, 1947) 30-50; idem,

Introduction

in the present commentary. In view of the results to which scholarship has led us in recent decades, it would be one-sided to interpret the Johannine writings exclusively from the standpoint of either Judaism or Hellenism.[68] This either-or has proved fruitful in discussion, but it has been misleading in the long run. The problem goes much deeper and is more complicated. Judaism was not entirely immune from external influences (cf. Hellenistic Judaism, the Essenes,[69] gnosticism[70]) and again the unmistakable influences that spread from Judaism and Christianity to (Eastern) Hellenism. Often it is difficult to decide which stratum should be given priority for any particular image or concept.[71] In particular,

---

"Les études Johanniques de Bultmann à Barrett," in *L'Évangile de Jean: Études et problèmes* (Rech. bib. 3; Louvain, 1958) 11–40, esp. 26–30; J. Behm, "Der gegenwärtige Stand der Erforschung des Joh-Ev," *TLZ* 73 (1948) 21–30; F.-M. Braun, "Où en est l'étude du 4° Évangile?" *ETL* 32 (1956) 516–31; E. Haenchen, *TRu* 26 (1960) 20–29.

68. C. H. Dodd indicates his openness to all sides in his valuable work *The Interpretation of the Fourth Gospel* (Cambridge, 1953). He allows a certain preference for the Hermetic literature (alongside of Hellenistic and rabbinic Judaism, gnosticism, and Mandeism), calling it "the higher religion of Hellenism." He does not as yet take note of the Qumran literature. See further C. K. Barrett, *The Gospel According to St. John* (London, 1955) 22–33 (the background of the Fourth Gospel is illuminated chiefly from Hellenistic Judaism; as yet he offers no judgment on the Qumran writings). Thoughtful and careful in their judgments are the studies of F.-M. Braun et al., "Hermétisme et Johannisme," *RevThom* 55 (1955) 22–42, 259–99; "L'arrière-fond judaïque du quatrième évangile et la communauté de l'Alliance," *RB* 62 (1955) 5–44; "L'arrière-fond du quatrième évangile," in *L'Évangile de Jean,* 179–96; "L'Évangile de Jean et les grandes traditions d'Israël," *RevThom* 59 (1959) 421–50; 60 (1960) 165–84, 325–63. Since the language and thought world of 1 John are related to GJohn, I may refer to my commentary on GJohn. For 1 John, more recent scholars underscore its relation to Judaism, particularly J. C. O'Neill in his special hypothesis (see above). But the Hellenistic-gnostic elements should not be overlooked. The controversy with the docetic heretics is enough to suggest that.

69. On Essenism, see W. Bauer in *PWSup* 4 (1924) 386–430; W. Bousset and H. Gressmann, *Die Religion des Judentums im späthellenistischer Zeitalter* (Lietzmann 21; 3rd ed.; Tübingen, 1926) 456–65; L. Marchal in *DBSup* 2:1109–22; F.-M. Braun, "Essénisme et Hermétisme," *RevThom* 54 (1954) 523–58; S. Wagner, *Die Essener in der wissenschaftlichen Diskussion vom Ausgang des 18. bis zum Beginn des 20. Jahrhunderts* (Berlin, 1960). The conviction that the Essenes, the Damascus, and the Qumran communities are related groups, and that the obvious differences in the accounts and the original documents are due to different stages of development, different branches, and local peculiarities has largely prevailed. See J. T. Milik, *Ten Years of Discovery in the Wilderness of Judaea* (London, 1957) 44–60. See also M. Burrows, *More Light on the Dead Sea Scrolls* (New York, 1958) 263–74; F. M. Cross, Jr., *The Ancient Library of Qumran and Modern Biblical Studies* (Garden City, NY, 1961) 49–70; K. Schubert, *Die Gemeinde vom toten Meer* (Munich/Basel, 1958) passim ("Essene").—On the relation between the Johannine writings and the Qumran texts, see the subsection "The Qumran Texts."

70. Whether it is possible to speak of "Jewish gnosticism" is admittedly a debatable question; H. J. Schoeps is strongly opposed (*Urgemeinde, Judenchristentum, Gnosis* (Tübingen, 1956]). See, however, L. Goppelt, *TLZ* 82 (1957) 429ff.; K. Schubert, *LTK* 4:1024ff. On Jewish mysticism, see H. Odeberg, *3 Enoch or the Hebrew Book of Enoch* (Cambridge, 1928); G. Scholem, *Die jüdische Mystik in ihren Hauptströmungen* (Zurich, 1957); idem, *Jewish Gnosticism, Merkabah Mysticism and Talmudic Tradition* (New York, 1960).

71. The *Odes of Solomon* are a typical syncretistic work, basically gnostic. See, however, J. Daniélou, *DBSup* 6:677–84; F.-M. Braun, *Jean le Théologien,* 224–51; S. Schulz, *RGG*³ 5:1339–42. On the question of dependence, a knowledge of GJohn and 1 John (cf. *OdesSol.* 3:3–4 with 1 John 4:19 and 4:8) on the part of the author of the *Odes* is undeniable; see Lagrange, *S. Jean,* xxxviii; Stauffer, *NT Theology,* 326 n. 829; F.-M. Braun, *Jean le Théologien,* 242–45; for a different view see Barrett, *John,* 55.

recent scholarship has raised the question as of whether gnosticism was a wide-spread current of thought which drew all varieties of culture into its sphere. Where and when it arose — not a few scholars believe that gnosticism had a strong Jewish component — need not be discussed here.[72] In one way or another the heretics of 1 John (see p. 17) fit into this general picture, like the Jewish gnostics in Colossians and the Pastorals. Many scholars rely in large measure on the gnostic texts for the interpretation of GJohn. We need to ask whether this is justified and, if so, to what extent.[73] We should be very cautious here, particularly in view of the Mandean problem.[74] The bulk of the relevant literature is considerable, and the question of the date and interrelationship of its various features is particularly urgent. Moreover, there is a dearth of preliminary studies on the subject. On the other hand, it is important for the exegesis that we should familiarize ourselves with the atmosphere and thought world of gnosticism, its outlook and its terminology. True, all these are features embedded in writings of a much later date which had been worked over for several centuries. But this is why the present commentary pays some attention to the Mandean writings as evidence of a non-Christian gnostic sect. After all, it may offer traces of much earlier gnostic beliefs. On the whole the Qumran texts have been the main focus of attention, and in fact they deserve special consideration. With the publication of the principal texts the parallels in language and theology can be judged with greater precision than was possible in the first edition. Of course, even here we must be careful not to overrate them or confine ourselves exclusively to these particular texts (see further below under "The Qumran Texts").

Relation to Judaism

1. Aside from the Qumran Texts

Some scholars have tried to find a strong influence of Judaism on both GJohn and the epistles. Such influences will always be significant, though in two different ways:

a) Language
Many terms and phrases can be understood only in the mouth of a Jew

72. See from the abundant literature H. Jonas, *Gnosis und spätantiker Geist;* G. Quispel, *Gnosis als Weltreligion* (Zurich, 1951); E. Peterson, "Gnosi," *Enc. Catt. Ital.* 6 (1951) 846–82; E. Haenchen, "Gab es eine vorchristliche Gnosis?" *ZTK* 49 (1952) 316–49; W. Frei, *Geschichte und Idee der Gnosis* (partial printing) (Zurich, 1958); R. McL. Wilson, *The Gnostic Problem* (London, 1958); R. M. Grant, *Gnosticism and Early Christianity* (New York, 1959); S. Schulz, "Die Bedeutung neuer Gnosisfunde für die neutestamentliche Wissenschaft," *TRu* 26 (1960) 209–66, 301–34.

73. See the commentaries of W. Bauer and R. Bultmann; see further E. Schweizer, *Ego eimi* (FRLANT n.s. 38; Göttingen, 1939); Becker, *Die Reden des Johannesevangeliums;* S. Schulz, *Komposition und Herkunft der Johanneischen Reden* (Stuttgart, 1960) (only to a limited extent). — In contrast, British scholarship shows great reserve on this matter; see R. Schnackenburg, *BZ* n.s. 2 (1958) 148ff.

74. On the present state of the question, see W. Baumgartner, *TZ* 6 (1959) 401–10; R. Macuch, *TLZ* 82 (1957) 401–8; F.-M. Braun, *Le Mandéisme et la secte essénienne de Qumran* (Orient et Bibl. Lov. 1; Louvain, 1957); S. Schulz, *TRu* 26 (1960) 301–29; K. Rudolph, *Die Mandäer, 1 Prolegomena: Das Mandäerproblem* (FRLANT n.s. 56; Göttingen, 1960) (standard work); idem., *Die Mandäer, II, Der Kult* (Göttingen, 1961); C. Colpe, *RGG*³ 4:709–12; J. Schmid, *LTK* 6:1343–47.

familiar with the Old Testament and in touch with rabbinic thought (see p. 9). The material assembled by Adolf Schlatter in his books *Sprache und Heimat des vierten Evangelisten* (1902) and *Der Evangelist Johannes* (1930) as well as the work of P. Billerbeck (*Kommentar* [1922–28]) should not be ignored even today.

b) Theology

Many ideas in the epistle can come only from a Jewish background. They show that this Christian theologian has his roots in Judaism. He did not merely acquire his ideas after his conversion to Christianity, but must have been familiar with them from his youth. This is particularly true of the whole complex of ideas relating to sin and atonement. Sin is the transgression of God's commandments. Some sins are mortal, others are not (5:16–17). Some commandments are light, others are difficult (5:3). People need divine forgiveness (1:9) and atonement through the shedding of blood (1:7). Closely connected with all of this is the idea of judgment (2:28; 4:17), which in turn leads to other eschatological and apocalyptic concepts, such as "the last hour," meaning the final time of evil (2:18) and the appearance of figures and powers at enmity with God. Of course, there has been a Christian development, as seen in the concept of the antichrists (2:18) and the false prophets (4:1) (see Excursus 7). In several matters the author of 1 John seems to be indebted primarily to the early Christian kerygma and the church's catechesis, but the acceptance and continuation of these ideas from Judaism is taken for granted. There is no attempt to hide their Jewish origin, thus suggesting an author who had been at home in a Jewish milieu from the cradle. Here are a few examples of this sort of thing. First, there is the devil or the evil one (2:13, 14; 5:18, 19) and his activity (see also 3:8; 4:4). This is not the pagan notion of demonology, nor does it imply a dualistic view of the world. The devil is the one who leads people astray. Then there is the attitude to petitionary prayer (3:22; 5:14–15) and intercession (5:16) and the idea of the Paraclete. All of this is dressed up in a Christian garb. Christ is the supreme counterpart of Satan, the one great righteous One, who is the advocate with the Father. To attribute such concepts to syncretistic influences would be inconceivable and farfetched. In addition, there are minor traits derived from Semitic thought, such as the heart as the seat of interior life (3:20–21) and the testimony of three witnesses (5:7–8).

On the other hand, allusions to Old Testament narratives are very rare. The only examples are references to the account of paradise (3:8) and the story of Cain and Abel (3:12). Perhaps the author's reticence in this regard is due to consideration for his readers, though it probably represents his preference for the core of Christian doctrine, that is, the proclamation of Christ.

Finally, not a few of his ideas are curiously ambiguous. They cannot be understood apart from their Jewish background, yet at the same time they are apparently influenced by syncretism, at least so far as the terminology is concerned. This includes such important doctrines as being children of God, eternal life (2:25), the vision of God (3:2), walking in the light (1:7), and the Redeemer (Savior, 4:14).

2. The Qumran Texts

The significance of the Qumran texts for the Johannine writings has been sufficiently evaluated in recent years,[75] though without producing any consensus about their actual relation to this literature. There are numerous affinities of language and theology. But it is not clear whether this is simply due to a common milieu, the world of late Judaism, or whether the Fourth Evangelist and the author of 1 John had closer contacts with the Qumran community. Was he associated with heterodox Judaism, including other phenomena such as apocalypticism and the Baptist movement?[76] Or do the connections between Qumran and Johannine writings come through the Christian communities in general rather than through the author personally? Did these connections come through Palestine, Syria, or Asia Minor (especially after 70 C.E.), when the Johannine community perhaps welcomed Essenes from Qumran into their ranks? It is premature to discuss these questions at this point. We will therefore content ourselves with marshaling a few points of contact which will be treated more closely in the commentary.

a) Some parallels of language have helped to clarify the issue. There is the phrase "doing the truth" (1:7) and the concept of truth in general. More particularly there is the range of vocabulary associated with the idea of sin, for which the Qumran texts exhibit a wealth of terminology. The meaning of "lawlessness" (3:4) and of error (4:6) is well illustrated by these texts. But it would also seem that "idols," mentioned in the last verse of the letter (5:21), does not really mean "idols" in the literal sense of the word but is used metaphorically to denote the abominations of sin (see ad loc.).

b) Other concepts for which there is plenty of evidence at Qumran are better placed in a wider framework because of their considerable theological importance. The prime examples are those dualistic sayings so typical of Johannine thought which now have their closest parallels in Qumran, such as light and darkness, truth and falsehood, God and the devil (Beliar), love and hate, etc. One can hardly attribute this dualism to gnostic influences (see Excursus 6). This kind of dualism, which holds fast to the supremacy of God and to faith in creation, can be studied in the Qumran texts.[77] The primary focus of this dualism is ethical despite its elevation to a cosmic dimension, both at Qumran and in the Johannine literature. Both of them speak of the realm of light and

---

75. See L. Mowry, "The Dead Sea Scrolls and the Background for the Gospel of St. John," *BA* 17 (1954) 78-94; F.-M. Braun, "L'arrière-fond," *RB* 62 (1955) 5-44; R. E. Brown, "The Qumran Scrolls and the Johannine Gospel and Epistles," *CBQ* 17 (1955) 403-19, 559-74; W. F. Albright, "Recent Discoveries in Palestine and the Gospel of St. John," in *The Background of the New Testament and its Eschatology* (Festschrift C. H. Dodd; Cambridge, 1956) 153-71; G. Baumbach, *Qumran und das Joh-Ev* (partial printing; Berlin, 1957); Cross, *Ancient Library,* 153-62; J. Smit Sibinga, "1 Joh tegen de achtergrond van de teksten van Qumran," *Vox Theolog.* 29 (1958-59) 11-14 —The alleged parallels are questioned by H. M. Teeple, "Qumran and the Origin of the Fourth Gospel," *NovT* 4 (1960) 6-25 (but not very convincingly).

76. See Schulz, *Komposition,* 182-87.

77. See F. Nötscher, *Zur theologischen Terminologie der Qumran-Texte* (BBB 10; Bonn, 1956) 79-133; H. W. Huppenbauer, *Der Mensch zwischen zwei Welten* (Zurich, 1959).

the realm of darkness. The point, however, is *walking* in light and darkness (1:6–7; 2:9–11). This doctrine of the Two Ways represents a biblical perspective further developed at Qumran.[78] Despite this common approach, a "relative dualism, at once ethical and cosmic," as Huppenbauer calls it, we should not overlook the substantial differences between Qumran and John. These differences cover both their doctrine and their ethics. The Qumraners talk about walking in the law of Moses and pursue a radical form of Torah piety. In the Johannine Epistles faith in Jesus Christ and obedience to his commandments, "which are not grievous," are what matters. Whatever is born of God overcomes the world (5:3–4). At Qumran there is love for all the children of light, but hatred for all the children of darkness. In the epistles there is only love as the hallmark of those who are born of God.

c) Another point of contact between Qumran and the Johannine community is their situation in the world. One has the feeling of being in the middle of a conflict between the powers of good and evil, a conflict involving not only human beings but also superhuman spirits. These spirits, however, are creatures that are subject to God. As Christians have to defend themselves against the false prophets and distinguish between the spirits, so the Qumraners speak of two kinds of spirits at work in the world. These spirits are in conflict with each other, striving to enslave the human race (1QS 3:13–4:26). In 1 John 2:13; 5:19 the power of evil or Beliar is overwhelming; the temptation to apostasy, great. But there are differences too. The Qumran community, sure as it is of the help of God and his angels, believes that the mortal conflict with the children of darkness still lies in the future. The Christian community, on the other hand, knows that the battle is already won because it is united with Christ (see 2:13; 4:4; 5:4, 20).

d) It is doubtful whether Qumran throws any light on the doctrine of sin in 1 John to the degree suggested by Nauck.[79] This is especially true of the problem of "the Christian and sin" (see Excursus 12). After all, the Christian doctrine of atonement through the blood of Christ provided an entirely new and quite different basis for this. But certain common motifs, such as the confession of sin (1:9), the duty of keeping oneself free from sin (see 3:9–10; 5:18), and mortal sin as the result of serious backsliding and apostasy, are unmistakable.

e) There are other sayings and turns of speech in 1 John where it remains doubtful whether the Qumran texts offer an adequate basis. This is particularly true of the important concept of "knowing (God)." True, the Johannine idea of knowing God has clear affinities with the Old Testament usage as further developed at Qumran[80] (cf. John 17:3 with 1QS 2:3; CD 3:20; 1QH 12:11; etc.). But in 1 John the idea of knowing God (see Excursus 3) has a special nuance directed against the gnosticizing heretics with their belief in a false way of

---

78. See F. Nötscher, *Gotteswege und Menschwege in der Bibel und in Qumran* (Bonn, 1958); W. Wibbling, *Die Tugend- und Lasterkataloge im NT und ihre Traditionsgeschichte unter besonderer Berücksichtigung der Qumran-Texte* (BZNW 25; Berlin, 1959) 61–64.

79. Nauck, *Tradition und Charakter*, 98–122.

80. See G. J. Botterweck, *"Gott erkennen" im Sprachgebrauch des AT* (BBB 2; Bonn, 1951); Nötscher, *Zur theologischen Terminologie*, 15–79; R. Schnackenburg, *LTK* 3:996ff.

salvation merely through gnosis and the vision of God. There are many things in John that can be explained from Qumran, but not everything.

Syncretism and Gnosticism

1. Relations with Hellenism

To begin with we have to correct the suggestion that the author of the Johannine Epistles betrays a close affinity with the thought and language of late Judaism. We must insist that he has a perfect command of everyday Greek and can use it to express himself simply yet not awkwardly. If he was Semitic by birth, he has become fully accepted as a citizen of the Greek world. In this connection the two shorter epistles use phrases and turns of speech that are common in the epistolary style of Hellenistic Greek (see the Introduction to 2 and 3 John).

When we look, however, for signs of familiarity with Greek philosophy or literature, the results are completely negative. Even as mediated through Philo of Alexandria, classical Greek thinking, the real spirit of the occident, is foreign to the author of the Johannine Epistles. He does not seem to be influenced by the popular philosophies of Stoicism and Cynicism. The world of Greco-Roman culture was familiar to him only to the extent that it had penetrated the eastern empire.

2. Relations with Near Eastern Syncretism

There are a number of important ideas in 1 John that are inexplicable without some contact with syncretism as it was gaining popularity at the time in various spheres of intellectual and religious life. This is particularly true of the mystery religions and even to some extent of Hermetic mysticism (*Tract.* I and XIII) and of magic (the Magic Papyri). Here we should mention particularly the idea of being born of God, which though it was a common term for baptism can hardly have been conceived without some outside influence (see Excursus 8). Further, such titles as Son of God and Savior (*sōtēr*) were not used unintentionally by the author of 1 John. With this we may compare Paul's use of *kyrios,* although for Paul this title had transcendent and absolute connotations. Terms like "truth," "light," "word of life" have a fullness and an individuality in the Johannine writings such as can hardly have been based exclusively on an Old Testament and Jewish background. Yet the question arises whether these and other key concepts in John, such as "to know" and "world," might not have some special gnostic resonance.

3. Relation to Gnostic Trends

a) In view of the heresy being combated in 1 and 2 John, there can be no doubt that the author was in contact with gnostic thought. He does not entirely reject this trend, for he claims that those who believe in Christ have seen, known, and recognized God (1 John 2:3; 3:6; 4:7; 3 John 11) and stand in fellowship with God (1:3, 6; 2:5-6; etc.). Only the gnostic way of salvation, divorced from the figure of the Savior, the Son of God made man, does he radically reject. Despite this repudiation of the heresy, however, it was an illuminating and fruitful encounter for him. So the question arises as to what the author may have learned and gained from gnostic thought.[81]

b) True, the characteristic Johannine dualism seems to find satisfactory explanation in late Judaism as the texts from Qumran now show (see above, "The Qumran Texts," section b). On closer inspection, the Johannine and gnostic dualisms are poles apart. The author of 1 John knows nothing of the metaphysical contrast between the divine and material worlds or of two basic principles hostile to each other. The divine Logos itself has become "flesh" (John 1:14) or, to put it another way, Jesus Christ has come "in the flesh" (1 John 4:2; 2 John 7). The polarity between the world of God, full of light and life, and this world, full of darkness and condemned to death, works itself out particularly in human nature. It becomes a religious and ethical separation inasmuch as human beings are recognized as children of God by their faith and love on the one hand or as children of the devil through their unbelief and hatred of their fellows (1 John 3:9-10; 4:4-10) on the other. Such a relative dualism, oriented toward the ethical behavior of human beings, finds a precedent in many writings of late Judaism, such as the Enoch literature, the book of *Jubilees,* and the *Testaments of the Twelve Patriarchs.* But it emerges in a sharper form in the Qumran texts. There are certainly further points of contact with gnostic dualism, not only in terminology but also in cosmology and anthropology. "But it should be noted that gnosis as we know it (all the evidence is after Christ) betrays a different feeling for the world from that of the Dead Sea Scrolls."[82]

c) Many favorite Johannine terms, for example, the pair "light and life," as well as "truth," "to know," and "to see," echo the thought of gnosticism and are based on the language used by the heretics. Though the Johannine author has integrated them thoroughly into his Christian theology, their form, application, and content have affinities with the language of gnosticism. The idea of the world in its characteristic Johannine sense (1 John 3:13; 4:4-5; 5:19) has a sense similar to the dualism with which it is so closely connected. Yet with all the apparent similarity, there is a fundamental difference in principle (see above).

d) Still greater caution must be exercised in regard to the Johannine letters and the gnostic redeemer myth. Many scholars see here a central motif and a dominant theme of gnosis, particularly in its pre-Christian form.[83] But it is also

81. See bibliography in the Appendix to *John I* (pp. 579ff.); see also E. Käsemann, *The Testament of Jesus* (London, 1968); L. Schottroff, *Der Glaubende und die feindliche Welt* (Neukirchen, 1970) esp. 228-96. Schottroff believes that she can find in 1 John an even more precise form of gnostic thought than in GJohn. For a contrary view, see K. Weiss, "Die 'Gnosis' im hintergrund und im Spiegel der Johannesbriefe," in *Gnosis und Neues Testament,* ed. K.-W. Tröger (Gütersloh, 1973) 341-56; the ideas are related at several points to gnosis. But the conclusion that the opponents were gnostics goes beyond the evidence (W. Schmithals, "Die gnostischen Elemente im Neuen Testament als hermeneutisches Problem," in *Gnosis und Neues Testament,* 359-81, esp. 374-80).

82. Huppenbauer, *Mensch,* 117ff.

83. R. Reitzenstein, *Das iranische Erlösungmysterium* (Bonn, 1921) 22ff., 33, 70ff., 84ff.; H. Schlier, *Religionsgeschichtliche Untersuchungen zu den Ignatiusbriefen* (Giessen, 1929) 5-81; Jonas, *Gnosis,* 122ff.; W. Staerk, *Die Erlösererwartung in den östlichen Religionen (Soter II)* (Stuttgart/Berlin, 1938) 67ff., 150ff., 422ff.; Bultmann, *John,* 61ff.; idem, *Theology of the New Testament*

being shown that scholarship has not yet come to terms with the difficult problems posed by the Iranian, Manichean, and Mandean texts.[84] There are no echoes in 1 John of the descent of the Son of man from heaven and of his return thither (see John 3:13, 31; 6:62). No one has succeeded in proving the gnostic origin of the characteristic expression in 1 John, "was revealed" (*ephanerōthē*), although such an origin has often been taken for granted.[85] It looks as though there was no myth of a redeemed redeemer in the heresy 1 John was combating. Rather, it was the gnostic understanding of salvation, without the redeemer figure, that was central. This meant that the gnostics were compelled to take issue with the *Christian* teaching about Jesus as the Christ. That is how the christological heresy may have taken shape.

Relation to the Early Christian Kerygma and to Genuinely Johannine Theology

We have already pointed out more than once that the author was indebted to the general tradition and catechesis of the Christian church, more than might appear at first sight, given the peculiarities of the Johannine diction. The parallels drawn from the history of religions should not be allowed to obscure the genuinely Christian elements. The core of the early church's christological kerygma is clearly vIsible in the Johannine Epistles despite their peculiarly Johannine form.

1. Contacts with the General Christian Kerygma

The following points should be especially emphasized:

a) Jesus' teaching about the fatherhood of God and the understanding of God as the Father of Jesus Christ is taken up by the author and appropriated in depth. This can be clearly seen not only in the fine passage in 1 John 3:1 but also in the way the theme of love is developed in 4:7–12, 14; 5:1–2. Fellowship with God means fellowship with the Father and with the Son (1 John 1:3; 2:22–25; 2 John 9). Moreover, Jesus Christ is the Son of the Father both in his preexistence (1 John 1:2) and after his return to heaven (2:1). The love of God is characterized as the love of the Father (2:15). The duty of walking in the right way emanates in the last analysis from the Father (2 John 4).

b) As regards the christological kerygma, no corners are cut. The author has

---

(New York, 1951, 1955) 1:174f., 2:6, etc.—The course of this whole scholarly orientation is described with critical illumination by C. Colpe, *Die religionsgeschichtliche Schule: Darstellung und Kritik ihres Bildes vom gnostischen Erlösermythus* (FRLANT n.s. 60; Göttingen, 1961).

84. Colpe, *Die religionsgeschichtliche Schule,* 171–93. After trenchantly criticizing the categories used hitherto, particularly the term "redeemed redeemer," with its manifold meanings, and the confusion of the archetypal Man (*Urmensch*) with the redeemer, Colpe proposes new and more appropriate categories. The previous model, combining Iranian and later gnostic texts, of a myth of a primitive redeemer wandering through space and time, reappearing all over the place, and leaving fossils behind, Colpe repudiates as "absolutely erroneous" (p. 191).

85. H. Schulte, *Der Begriff der Offenbarung im Neuen Testament* (Munich, 1949) 68ff. See further the commentary at 1:2.

a special interest in the incarnation because of the gnostic heresy. But he is equally concerned with the atoning death of Christ on the cross (1 John 2:2; 4:10; 3:16; 5:6) and with the parousia (2:28). All of these topics are constituent parts of his proclamation. His eschatological statements (2:18, 28; 3:2–3) are particularly remarkable, given the emphasis elsewhere on the present reality of salvation. The concern for salvation history is in no way played down in favor of a timeless mysticism.

c) The experience of the Spirit has left its marks on the community (1 John 3:24; 4:4, 6, 13). This does not mean that they have had ecstatic experiences of the Hellenistic type. It means an experience of faith grounded in the sacrament of baptism (cf. 2:20, 27; 3:9; 5:18).

d) Generally speaking, to know God means to believe in him (1 John 3:23; 4:16; 5:1, 4–5, 10–12). The emphasis is always on faith as the means of salvation. Faith takes many forms but it always has a confessional quality. It always means accepting Christ by decision of the will. That is something that never changes.

e) Most important of all is the ethical requirement of love for God and love of one's fellow believers. The two are intimately connected. Here is the very heart of the Johannine exhortation, the most precious heritage from the early church and from Jesus himself. This substitution of love of the fellow believer for love of the neighbor should not be misunderstood. It is not a misconstruing or altering of the command (cf. 1 John 3:17; 4:20, 21; 3 John 5). The rest of the parenesis (cf. 2:15–17; 5:21) reflects the general preaching of the church.

2. Authentic Johannine Elements

In this overall comparison with the social milieu and churchly matrix of the Johannine community the personal contribution of this early Christian theologian to the final shape of his work should not be underestimated. Not only did he accept suggestions from many different quarters, but he was himself a creative thinker.

a) One of his finest achievements is the way he combines so many different images and melds them into something truly Christian. We need only recall how he develops the idea of the believers as the children of God. They are begotten of God and derive their life from him. They become like him. The author is masterly in the way he presents the idea of fellowship with God and with the one Savior, Jesus Christ. He has successfully appropriated dualistic notions and christianized them. In developing the truly Christian elements, God as truth and love, he remains faithful to the early Christian kerygma, yet gives it an entirely new look. In Christology he puts the accents in somewhat different places. That is because of his struggle against gnosticism. Yet every time he is on target. He even draws on new terms such as "Logos," though at the same time avoiding any danger of being misunderstood.

b) He introduces some new features into Christian theology. We need only mention what is called, though not quite correctly or felicitously, Johannine mysticism. The formulas he uses for the immanence of God are unique, and despite possible parallels they can only be understood as his own creation. Many problems of the spiritual life, such as Christ and sin, love and fear, mysticism and ethics, have been grasped in a personal way and with a particular acuity. This of course is not meant to diminish the reputation of Paul.

We can only hint at such matters here so as not to overlook the strongest factor in Johannine theology, the genial, God-illumined, religious personality of the author.[86]

6. The Relation between 1 John and the Gospel of John

The question of the relationship between GJohn and 1 John was much discussed in the past, but today it has lost its interest. Yet it is still important if we are to evaluate the author and the way his work came into being. We may confine ourselves to a report on the current state of scholarship.

Language and Style

The two writings were compared very carefully by H. J. Holtzmann,[87] A. E. Brooke,[88] and more recently by C. H. Dodd,[89] W. F. Howard,[90] W. G. Wilson,[91] and A. P. Salom.[92] Like A. E. Brooke, most of the other scholars were convinced that the two writings are closely related. Yet Dodd, like Brooke before him, called attention to certain differences which convinced him that they were the work of two different authors. Here are the most important reasons for thinking so: 39 words in the epistle are absent from the Gospel. More importantly, 6 characteristic groups of words found in the Gospel do not appear in the epistle. Some of them have connections with the Old Testament: "scripture"(12 times in GJohn), "to write" (10 times), "law" (14 times). Among the christological terms we have "glory" (18 times) and "to glorify" (21 times). Then there are the characteristic terms of Johannine theology, for example, "to ascend" (5 times), "to descend" (11 times), "above" and "from above" (4 times). "to lift up, exalt" (5 times); the frequently used verb "to judge" (19 times and the noun "judgment" (11 times) to which in the epistle the only parallel is the phrase "the day of judgment" (4:17, which occurs only once). Howard reexamined

---

86. See P.-H. Menoud, "L'originalité de la pensée joh." *RTP* 28 (1940) 233–61.

87. Above all in *Jahrbuch für protestantische Theologie* (1882) 125ff.

88. Commentary, i–xii (in controversy with Holtzmann).

89. C. H. Dodd, "The First Epistle of John and the Fourth Gospel," *BJRL* 21 (1937) 129–56; commentary, Intro., xlvii–lvi. The differences between GJohn and 1 John are also emphasized by D. W. Riddle, "The later books of the New Testament: A Point of View and a Prospect," *JR* 13 (1933) 63–67.

90. W. F. Howard, "The Common Authorship of the Johannine Gospel and Epistles," *JTS* 48 (1947) 12–25.

91. W. G. Wilson, "An Examination of the Linguistic Evidence Adduced against the Unity of Authorship of the First Epistle of John and the Fourth Gospel," *JTS* 49 (1948) 147–56.

92. A. P. Salom, "Some Aspects of the Grammatical Style of 1 John," *JBL* 74 (1955) 96–102.— G. D. Kilpatrick makes two specific observations (on *alēthēs–alēthinos* and *apostellein–pempein*) in favor of the same style in GJohn and the Johannine Epistles ("Two Johannine Idioms in the Johannine Epistles," *JTS* n.s. 12 [1961] 272f.). (On the text criticism of 1 John 5:20, see, however, ad loc.).

these statistics and reduced their significance by observing (a) the way these terms are distributed in GJohn; and (b) the various meanings they represent in the framework of GJohn and the epistle. The previous work on the linguistic phenomena had been somewhat mechanical. Howard makes several valid observations on the subject which should not be forgotten when we consider the divergencies between the two documents: (a) GJohn has undergone a more extended process of composition, while the epistle was addressed to a specific situation; (b) the subject matter of GJohn is much richer than that of the epistle; (c) GJohn used both written and oral sources; (d) GJohn is far more exposed to Jewish influences through its use of Aramaic sources, whereas the epistle is written in colloquial Greek — the part played by a secretary must have been greater in the case of GJohn. Even though we may disagree in detail with Howard, we must take into consideration the different perspective of the two writings as well as the way in which they have been edited. Unfortunately, our knowledge about that is not very clear. GJohn remains, despite all its theological tendencies, a narrative of the career, death, and exaltation of the incarnate Son of God. The epistle is primarily a religious and ethical exhortation which takes familiarity with the history of the Christ-event for granted. Moreover, we must recognize that our modern ideas of authorship do not correspond to the way in which GJohn was edited.

Independently of Howard, W. G. Wilson, like A. P. Salom, succeeded in proving by a statstical analysis of the entire New Testament that the differences in language between GJohn and 1 John are minimal. The percentages of frequency for certain words, particles, prepositions, and peculiarities of speech, are less satisfactory for the Pauline homologoumena than for the Johannine writings. This is how the matter is to be assessed: Contrary to those differences which the critics have pointed out, the agreements in both writings regarding vocabulary, phraseology, and style are so marked that there is nothing to rule out the possibility of a common author so far as these considerations are concerned. But if many passages in GJohn are taken as redactional additions with close affinities to 1 John, it must be assumed that these were by different authors. Although these assumptions fail to convince in many respects, the arguments in favor of different authors for GJohn and 1 John have become stronger. I would therefore now like to assert more emphatically this point of view. Yet there are critics who maintain that both works were written by the same author.[93]

Theological Perspectives

The theological atmosphere of GJohn and 1 John is, when compared with the rest of the New Testament, so similar and shares so many basic motifs, that we can speak of a distinctive Johannine theology. Yet this still leaves room for different answers to the question of the identity of the author(s). Were they master and pupil, original writer and later redactor, or something else of that kind?

---

93. So W. G. Kümmel, *Introduction,* 445; J. Schmid, *Einleitung,* 623.

It has often been claimed that the three Johannine Epistles were the work of John the Presbyter who lived in Asia Minor, who is to be distinguished from John the Apostle, the son of Zebedee.[94] A comparison of GJohn and 1 John convinced Dodd that the Presbyter was a disciple of the evangelist and was a student of the evangelist's work—contrary to the opinion of many other scholars.[95] But for Dodd the important question is not so much the authorship as the fact that the Presbyter adheres more closely than the evangelist himself to the primitive apostolic kerygma and to the original church catechesis still current at the time. Is there such a divergence between GJohn and the epistles?

Dodd bases his hypothesis in the main on three considerations: (1) eschatology; (2) the atoning significance of Christ's death; (3)the doctrine of the Holy Spirit.[96] The question is whether GJohn is on these points further removed from the conventional theology of the church than 1 John. Following W. F. Howard we need to insist on the following points:

1. Even in GJohn there is a strong eschatological element. As Son of God and Son of man, Jesus is entrusted with the functions of an eschatological judge and given power to raise from the dead (John 5:20–29; 6:39, 40, 44, 54). The title Son of man appears in eight different chapters. The last day is seriously envisioned (6:39, 40, 44, 54; 11:24; 12:48). "The two conceptions of eschatology, partly realized already, partly as still a future event, are both present in the mind of the Evangelist" (p. 23). Though many critics dispute Howard's claim, this can only be done by arbitrarily eliminating the texts in question. As regards the parousia, things are not so simple. There is much debate about 14:3, while 21:22 is relegated to the Johannine appendix. It must be conceded that there is a stronger emphasis on future eschatology in 1 John. But it is not as great as to require a different author from that of GJohn. The concrete situation of the time provides sufficient explanation for the stronger eschatological expectation. For it was the acute danger of heresy that triggered the conviction that it was the "last hour," that the antichrist had come, and that the parousia and last judgment were at hand (2:18–25).

M.-E. Boismard has recently tried to establish a development of eschatology in GJohn.[97] He thinks he can detect this in certain doublets or parallel groupings in GJohn. One group represents a *"relecture"* (rereading) of the other. Against Bultmann's hypothesis of an ecclesiastical redactor who tried to bring Johannine eschatology belatedly into conformity with conventional early Christianity and its expectation of the end, Boismard thinks these passages represent a traditional eschatology (and Christology). They belong to the most primitive stratum in GJohn. A later redactor believed that the eschatological events had already been realized during the actual life of the church on earth.

---

94. See pp. 40–41 below.

95. Dodd, Intro., lvi.

96. Ibid., lii–liv. The first two points also play a part in Bultmann's theory of an ecclesiastical redaction; see above, pp. 15–17; see also Goguel, *The Birth of Christianity,* 367f., n. 1; H. Braun, "Literar-Analyse," 287.

97. M.-E. Boismard, "L'évolution du thème eschatologique dans les traditions johanniques," *RB* 68 (1961) 507–24.

He did not reject the traditional eschatology, but adjusted it to the contemporary life of the church under the promises of Christ (p. 523). Boismard attributes the eschatology of the epistles to a later stratum without deciding whether they go back to an author different from the evangelist. Perhaps the author of the epistles was a disciple of the author of GJohn. Alternatively both groups of material stem from the same author but were modified in later redaction (p. 524). This hypothesis raises several other difficulties. The realized eschatology in GJohn appears to belong to the central stratum and is in closest agreement with Johannine theology proper. It can hardly be ascribed to anyone other than the author of GJohn. By contrast, 1 John hardly looks like an approximation to traditional future eschatology. These questions, however, need further discussion.

2. Even if the atoning effect of Christ's death does not find such explicit expression in GJohn as it does in 1 John 2:2; 4:10 with the use of the word *hilasmos,* there is nevertheless the powerful witness of the Baptist to the Lamb of God in John 1:29, 36, and in the phrase about the "taking away" of sin (John 1:29; 1 John 3:5). Then there is the phrase "Savior of the world," which occurs both in GJohn (John 4:42), and in the epistle (1 John 4:14). The basic soteriological meaning of God's love for the world, a world in need of salvation, is the same in both writings (cf. John 3:16 and 1 John 4:9–10). Above all we should note the preposition *hyper,* so significant in early Christian theology, expressing the idea of Christ's vicarious sacrifice for sin, or at least hints of it (John 6:51; 10:11, 15; 11:50–52; 15:13; 17:19; 18:14; 1 John 3:16).[98]

3. C. H. Dodd fails to understand fully the doctrine of the Holy Spirit in 1 John (see Excursus 9). This is because for no reason he denies the Spirit's cooperation in the believers' birth from God and rejects the interpretation of "the divine seed" (3:9 REB) as a reference to the Holy Spirit. Dodd takes it to mean "word of God." This causes an artificial hiatus between the high Johannine doctrine of the Spirit in GJohn (3:5–8; 4:21–24) and that of the epistle. The acute tension Dodd finds with the Paraclete sayings in GJohn is explained from the fact that "charisma" in 1 John 2:20, 27, does not refer to the Holy Spirit, despite its performance of a similar role to that of the Paraclete in John 16:13. This results in an impoverished concept of the Spirit. It limits the epistle's teaching about the Spirit to those passages which speak of the Spirit's testimony to God (3:24; 4:13; cf. 4:1–6; 5:6–8). Further, he relegates it to "the realm of primitive or popular faith."[99] However, an organic interpretation of 1 John is possible only if we recognize the intimate connection between "spirit" and "life," between the work of the Spirit and the birth of the believers from God, and between the Spirit on the one hand and revelation and teaching on the other. If the emphasis is somewhat different, this is because of the conflict with heresy in the epistle, and the claim of the heretics to be the true pneumatics.

---

98. See M. Meinertz, *Theologie des NT* (Bonn, 1950) 2:288f.; K. H. Schelkle, *Die Passion Jesu* (Heidelberg, 1949) 131ff., 143ff.; A. Wikenhauser, *Johannes* (2nd ed.), 236f.; K. Romaniuk, *NovT* 5 (1962) 61–75.

99. Dodd, Intro., liv.

For the rest, we need only point out certain characteristic ideas and expressions which will enable the reader to see the close theological relation between GJohn and the epistle:

a) The statements about the nature of God (John 4:24; 1 John 1:5; 4:8, 16). The phrases in 1 John are felicitous in a way that complements what we find in GJohn (cf. 3:20–21; 7:17; 8:29; 14:31; 15:10 etc.; also 3:16; 14:21, 23; 16:27; 17:26).

b) The description of the realm opposed to God as one of darkness and death, its characterization by hatred, falsehood, murder, unbelief, and in general the dualistic perspective so characteristic of the Johannine writings.

c) The christological statements and titles, culminating in the pregnant image of the logos and the use of God as a predicate for Jesus (cf. John 1:1 and 1 John 1:1; also John 1:1c; 20:29 and 1 John 5:20).

d) The strong emphasis on the incarnation in John 1:14 and in 1 John 1:2; 4:2.

e) The description of salvation as achieved through faith and knowledge and generally through unconditional adherence to the Son of God made man.

f) The special quality of its "God-mysticism," and especially the typical Johannine formulas of immanence (see Excursus 4).

g) The description of the state of salvation as "having life" or, in a closely related phrase, as being "children of God" (see Excursus 8). The emphasis in both writings is on salvation as a present possession.

h) The demand for obedience to the commandments of God or of Christ or, alternatively, to the commandment of love, with insistence on its practical and effective aspect.

All of these points, which have often been noted, compel us to recognize the close affinity between the epistle and GJohn. The remaining differences in emphasis must be explained with Howard by the change in subject matter, the different genre of the two writings, the redactional method, and particularly the external circumstances (the combating of the heretical teaching in 1 John). These differences do not rule out the identity of authorship. Yet it is understandable that other scholars, even Roman Catholics,[100] presume a different author because of the undeniable theological differences and nuances in the longest of the letters. Nevertheless, the author must have stood in close contact with the evangelist, whether he was one of his pupils or a member of the circles which gathered around him, In this way he preserved the tradition of the evangelist.[101]

---

100. See Barrett, *John,* 110 (the same school of thought and tradition; cf. the hypothesis on p. 113); E. Haenchen, *TRu* 26 (1962) 8, 43 (different authors); F.-M. Braun, *Jean le théologien,* 33–41 (perhaps a disciple or disciple-secretary); Boismard, "L'évolution," 36 n. 3.

101. On the theological differences between GJohn and 1 John, see also E. Schweizer, "Der Kirchenbegriff im Evangelium und den Briefen des Johannes," in *Neotestamentica* (Zurich/Stuttgart, 1963) 254–71, esp. 266ff.; G. Klein, "'Das wahre Licht scheint schon,'" *ZTK* 68 (1978) 261–326.

The External Relation
between the Gospel of John and 1 John—Priority

The comparison of the two writings yields one positive result. It is impossible to regard the epistle merely as a companion piece to GJohn. It is a completely independent literary product. It neither presupposes the existence of the written Gospel, nor does it leave the reader to expect such a work dealing with the earthly life of the Son of God to follow.

This means that the question of the priority of the two writings is unanswerable. The argument that if the GJohn was completed earlier the epistle would be superfluous (Büchsel) does not hold up, for the struggle against the heretics, the main reason for the epistle, necessitated such specific instructions and warnings that the evangelist might well have felt it necessary to put pen to paper once more. We know very little of the internal conditions in the communities of Asia Minor. So we cannot judge whether the parenesis simply flowed along with the polemic or whether it was independent of it, and for the author an urgent and heartfelt concern. Most scholars today agree about the priority of the Gospel. Menoud's suggestion that the letter was composed between the dissemination of the gospel tradition in oral form and its completion in writing, has much to commend it.[102]

7. Readers, Authorship, and Date of Composition

The Readers

Given the literary genre of the document (see pp. 3–6), we reached the conclusion that 1 John was addressed to several communities in a limited area. Where exactly was that area located? This question would be answered if we could be certain who the author was (see the next section). The tradition going back to Irenaeus holds that the author was John the Apostle, the son of Zebedee, and points to Asia Minor as the place of origin. Irenaeus, who came from the East and had sat at the feet of Polycarp, the bishop of Smyrna (d. 156 C.E.), tells us that after Paul had founded the church in Ephesus, John had succeeded him and labored there until the reign of Trajan.[103] Irenaeus bases this information on the witness of "all the elders."[104] Although Eusebius accepts the famous quotation from Papias to the effect that there were two Johns, the apostle and the presbyter, he has no doubt that the tradition was referring to John the son of Zebedee.[105]

---

102. Menoud, *Jean,* 71–72.

103. *Adv. Haer.* 3.3.4; Eusebius, *H.E.* 3.23.4.

104. *Adv. Haer.* 2.23.3; Eusebius, *H.E.* 3.23.3.

105. The John of the testimonies of Irenaeus and Clement is for him identical with the apostle and evangelist, with the disciple "whom Jesus loved" (*H.E.* 3.23.1); the hypothesis of John the Presbyter is presented by Eusebius—evidently in dependence on the views of Dionysius of Alexandria (*H.E.* 2.29.6)—in favor of his judgment about the author of Revelation (*H.E.* 2.39.6).

With this external tradition the small amount gleaned from the internal evidence of GJohn is in agreement. The main area in which early gnosticism flourished appears to have been Asia Minor (see Colossians; Ephesians; 1 Tim. 4:1–5; 6:20; 2 Tim. 2:16, 23; 4:4). It is true that gnostic ideas appeared early on in Greece (1 Cor. 6:12; 8:1–3; 10:23) and especially in Syria. The personal testimony in 1 John offers some support to the external tradition, but no more than that.

More recently it has been suggested that GJohn and 1 John originated in Syria. This idea is based on the linguistic idiom which can be traced in Johannine Greek, as well as the alleged Syrian character of the gnosticism that is being combated. The former point has not been satisfactorily established, however. The linguistic idiom is more likely to be Palestinian if a Semitic background is accepted.[106] All it means is that the author was born in Palestine. There is not enough evidence to counter the strong witness of the ancient tradition going right back to the elders to make us relocate the Johannine writings in Syria rather than Asia Minor.[107]

F.-M. Braun considers Palestine a possible alternative and Asia Minor as the place where GJohn was edited in the form we now have it.[108] This is a carefully nuanced thesis that is gaining in credibility all the time, and having regard for the preliterary development of GJohn, it is well founded. Since 1 John did not undergo such a long process of development, it becomes obvious that Asia Minor must have been the place of its composition. The ascription *ad Parthos* appearing in later writers such as Augustine, Cassiodorus, etc. is curious.[109] Since this also appears as the heading of 2 John in two eleventh-century manuscripts,[110] the suggestion has been made that the "elect (lady)" is to be identified with Babylon (1 Pet. 5:13), which at that time was part of the Parthian empire. It is then supposed that this address was transferred from 2 John to 1 John. This is an ingenious hypothesis, but much too complicated. All we can be certain of is that the address originated in some mistake that we can no longer trace. It has no historical value.

The Author

The problem of authorship is, especially for those scholars who attribute GJohn and 1 John to the same writer (see pp. 34–39), part of the Johannine problem as a whole. The tradition of the early church since the time of Irenaeus

---

106. See Schlatter, *Sprache;* G. Kittel, *Die Probleme des palästinischen Spätjudentums und das Urchristentum* (Stuttgart, 1926) 45–51; idem, *ZNW* 35 (1936) 282–85.

107. See Feine-Behm, *Einleitung,* 109; Meinertz, *Einleitung,* 228; Michaelis, *Einleitung,* 124f.; Wikenhauser, *Introduction.*

108. F.-M. Braun, *Jean le Théologien,* 308–19, 396f.

109. Bede, *Introductio in epistolas catholicas* (*PL* 93:9f.) says that many ecclesiastical writers, among them Athanasius, offered evidence of this address.

110. Zahn (*Forschungen* 3:92ff.) supposes that the title *Ad virgines* in 2 John attested by Clement of Alexandria (*Adumbrationes*) goes back to a confusion of *parthous* and *parthenos;* here the first reading is allegedly the original (vice versa Ambroggi, 206–7). Otherwise, see A. Bludau, *TG* 11 (1919) 232ff.

(d. 202 c.e.) and Clement of Alexandria (d. ca. 211 c.e.) ascribes both GJohn and 1 John unequivocally to John the Apostle, the son of Zebedee. Irenaeus is quite explicit about 1 John (*Adv. Haer.* 3.16.5, 8). Clement, who frequently cites the letter, also wrote a commentary on it, though it is only extant in fragments of a Latin translation by Cassiodorus[111] Next we have the valuable testimony of Dionysius of Alexandria. He gives us his own critical observations about the authorship of the book of Revelation, which led him to place GJohn and the "Catholic Epistle" side by side, treating them both as the work of the apostle John and ascribing Revelation to another John[112] For the Latin church in North Africa, Tertullian (d. after 220 c.e.) is an early witness[113]

The question of whether the apostle John is the author of GJohn is discussed in detail in the introduction to our commentary on the Gospel. Only a broader discussion of the Johannine problem will enable us to give a definite answer to the question whether the son of Zebedee can be considered the author of 1 John. In the meantime here are a few specific arguments against his authorship:

a) If the apostle John had been the author, he would have had to lift the veil of anonymity when dealing with the heretics. However, such arguments from silence are generally questionable, and in this case it is uncertain whether the identity of the writer was not obvious to the recipients of the day from 1:1–4![114]

b) The objections that the author of 1 John, unlike the evangelist, never refers to the Old Testament or offers anything concrete about the life of Jesus can be refuted simply by pointing out the character and literary genre of the document (see pp. 3–6).

c) On the positive side it would be more plausible to envision an anonymous writer who was a member of the Johannine circle (cf. John 21:24 — note particularly the *oidamen*). The writer considers himself in fact to belong to a circle of preachers (1:1–4). When he appears in person as an authoritative witness, he can do so as a member of a circle with apostolic authority from the first generation behind it (see Excursus 1.5). Consequently, those scholars who maintain in the last analysis that John the Apostle, the son of Zebedee, was the author of GJohn, have no difficulty in postulating a pupil of his or someone else associated with him as the author of 1 John (see p. 38).

Date

Since there is such a close relationship between GJohn and 1 John, their respective dates cannot be so far apart. The redaction of GJohn in its present form, according to the almost unanimous opinion, is to be placed around the turn of the first century of the Christian era. Even if we do not accept the idea of an immediate connection between the epistle and the redaction of the Gospel

---

111. *Adumbrationes* (GCS 3:209–14). The tradition that he thought John was the author of 1 John derives from *Strom.* 2.6.45.

112. In Eusebius, *H.E.* 7.25.6ff.; cf. the position of Eusebius himself, 3.24.17 and 25.2–3.

113. Tertullian, *Adv. Prax.* 15; *Scorp.* 12.

114. On E. Käsemann's hypothesis, see the Introduction to 2 and 3 John below.

(for the idea that it was an accompanying letter, see p. 39), this date may be accepted for the epistle. The early form of the gnostic heresy fits into that date perfectly.

A further clue for the *terminus ad quem* is to be found in the citations of 1 John in other literature. Polycarp certainly presupposes 1 John 4:2-3; 2 John 7 (Pol. 7.1). Justin Martyr (*Dial.* 123.9) is probably alluding to 1 John 3:1. It is uncertain whether the reference to the Paraclete in *2 Clem.* 6.9 is connected with 1 John 2:1. Whether the *Odes of Solomon* refer to 1 John (*OdesSol.* 3:3; cf. 1 John 4:10, 19) is open to question. There are certain affinities of thought with Ignatius and Clement of Rome, [115] but these are insufficient to justify the conclusion that the two authors were actually using 1 John. On the other hand, Eusebius (*H.E.* 3.39.17) tells us that Papias, writing about 130 c.e. quoted 1 John.

8. Textual Tradition—The Johannine Comma

The Textual Evidence

The most important Greek witnesses for the text of the Johannine Epistles are ℵ, A, B, and C. Of these A and C represent the Alexandrian text as they do in the Acts of the Apostles and in Paul. In addition there are two later uncials, P (tenth century) and Ψ (Athos, Gr. Lavra 172; eighth/ninth century); in P, 1 John 3:20-5:1 is missing. Further, the minuscules 6, 33, 81, 104, 323, 326, 1175, and 1739 are witnesses to the Hesychian text. Especially valuable is the last-named codex 1739 (Athos, Lavra 184), a parchment manuscript of the tenth century with important scholia in the margin (see esp. on 4:3).[116] The so-called Koine text is represented by K L S (S=Gregory 049) and the majority of minuscules.

It is much to be regretted that Codex Bezae (D), which at one time contained the Catholic Epistles between the Gospels and Acts, now has a lengthy lacuna of sixty-seven pages. Apart from a Latin fragment of 3 John 11-15 and the subscription *Epistulae Iohanis III explicit,* this principal witness to the Western text deserts us completely, and this loss cannot be compensated for by any existing version.[117]

The witnesses for the Old Latin are scarce and incomplete: h (palimpsest of Fleury; fifth century; contains 1 John 1:8-3:20); q or r (Freisingen Fragments; seventh century; contains 1 John 3:8-5:21).[118] In addition to this there are quotations from Cyprian, Pseudo-Cyprian (*De rebaptismo*) and those in Pseudo-

---

115. See Chaine, 97f. The use of *teleioun* in combination with *agapē* offers no adequate basis.
116. See E. von der Golz, "Eine textkritische Arbeit des 10. bezw. 6. Jahrhunderts," *TU* 17,4 (1899); K. Lake and S. New, *Six Collations of NT Manuscripts* (Cambridge, MA, 1932) 191-219, esp. 165-67; H. W. Kim, "Codices 1582, 1739 and Origen," *JBL* 69 (1950) 167-75.
117. See M.-J. Lagrange, *Critique textuelle II: La critique rationelle* (Paris, 1935) 529-32.
118. Merk still frequently adduces codex p (Perpinianus; thirteenth century), which, however, according to Lagrange (*Critique textuelle,* 546f.) offers only the Vulgate text.

Introduction

Augustine (*Speculum* [m])[119] The entire material will be clarified only by reference to the Beuron edition of the Old Latin text, which unfortunately has not yet reached the Johannine Epistles. Meanwhile the work of W. Thiele gives us some insight![120] We know that the oldest Latin texts were translated by Cyprian and Pseudo-Cyprian[121]— a very important consideration for the history of the Johannine Comma (see below).

In the Old Syrian version the Johannine Epistles are missing, as are the Catholic Epistles altogether. The Peshitta contains only 1 John along with James and 1 Peter. The Philoxeniana alone contains all the Catholic Epistles.

Among the other versions only the Coptic (sah and boh) is important.

The Textual Criticism of the Johannine Epistles

The idea of producing a new Textus Receptus, which became fashionable after the successful achievements of textual criticism in the last century, down to the work of Gregory (1908) seems to suggest a preference for the so-called neutral text, that is, mainly B and ℵ. This idea seems to have gradually faded out in modern research. The return to some of the readings of the Koine text, which J. Schmid notes in the latest editions of the New Testament,[122] is reflected as far as 1 John is concerned in the following passages: 𝔨 adds the article to *antichristos* in 2:18, 𝔥 omits it; in 2:20 *pantes* stands in B ℵ P pc as against *panta* in A C 𝔨 pl. (for further information see ad loc.); in 5:18 B A* have *auton*, ℵ 𝔨 *heauton*. At these places recent editions prefer in part the Koine reading. But as these examples show, there are usually no clear lines of demarcation between the Alexandrian and Antiochene forms of the text. Many secondary versions of the Koine text are still discarded in favor of the Alexandrian, and with good reason.

But we are inclined to ask whether the Vulgate readings may sometimes represent a good form of the text. Adolf von Harnack worked through the most important passages (2:17, 20; 3:10; 4:3; 5:17, 18) and recognized the value of the Old Latin and Vulgate as a witness to the text![123] He rejects only three additions to 5:20 plus the Johannine Comma (see below).[124] Regarding the additions to 2:17, he is cautious![125] The comparison of all the Vulgate variants which he cites

---

119. On Cyprian, see H. Freiherr von Soden, "Das lateinische NT in Afrika zur Zeit Cyprians," *TU* 33 (1909) esp. 224–31, 572–76; on the whole subject, see Lagrange, *Critique textuelle,* 540–51. Tertullian has himself translated his quotations from the Greek, according to Lagrange (p. 540–42).

120. W. Thiele, ("Untersuchungen zu den altlateinischen Texten der drei Johannesbriefe" (Diss., Tübingen, 1956) (see *TLZ* 82 [1957] 71f.). In print and available, *Wortschatzuntersuchungen zu den altlateinischen Texten der Johannesbriefe* (Freiburg im Breisgau, 1958); further, an essay on the Johannine Comma (see below).

121. Thiele, *Wortschatzuntersuchungen,* 41.

122. J. Schmid, *MTZ* 1,II,4 (1950) 72–81, esp. 79.

123. Harnack, *SB* (Berlin, 1915) 534–73, reprinted in "Studien zur Geschichte des NT und der alten Kirche," in *Zur neutestamentlichen Textkritik* (Berlin/Leipzig, 1931) 105–32.

124. Harnack, *SB* (1915) Appendix, 571f. (in reprint, 149ff.).

125. Ibid., 561–63 (in reprint, 138ff.).

at other places,[126] leads him to conclude that they do not represent an independent recension but that the Latin text must be regarded simply as a very ancient witness to the Greek text.[127] Yet Harnack's preference for the Vulgate readings has met with little assent.[128]

Given the state of uncertainty over the early history of the text, each case has to be decided on its own merits, and reasons given in every instance.

The Johannine Comma

The Johannine Comma is a clause added to 1 John 5:7 in several Old Latin manuscripts. It was printed in the Sixtine-Clementine edition of the Vulgate and has achieved a certain notoriety. However, scholarship has been able almost completely to solve this problem, and nowadays nobody defends its authenticity. It was added for dogmatic reasons and it does not even fit the context. On this matter we have, according to T. Ayuso, a veritable consensus. It will suffice to outline the history of the debate to summarize the results. The Sixtine-Clementine text of 1 John 5:7–8 reads as follows:

> [7]quoniam tres sunt, qui testimonium dant [in caelo: Pater, Verbum, et Spiritus Sanctus, et hi tres unum sunt. [8]Et tres sunt, qui testimonium dant in terra]: Spiritus et aqua, et sanguis, et hi tres unum sunt.

The controversy began in the sixteenth century when Erasmus omitted from his Greek text the passage from "in caelo" through "in terra" from the first two editions of his Greek New Testament (1516 and 1519). Only in the third edition (1522) did he reluctantly include them, following Codex Montfortianus.[129] The Complutensian Polyglot, which appeared earlier, had already included it. The controversy did not come to a head until the nineteenth and twentieth centuries. Despite the decree of the Congregation of the Holy Inquisition on January 1, 1897, which required the acceptance of the comma as authentic,[130] it was impossible to put the clock back.[131] Even Catholic scholars played a significant part in clarifying the textual history of the comma.[132] A more recent official pronouncement of the Holy Office on June 6, 1927[133] allowed Catholic scripture scholars to regard the comma as a later addition.

---

126. Harnack, *Beiträge zur Einleitung in das NT 7* (Leipzig, 1916) 56ff.

127. Ibid., 65.

128. See J. E. Belser, "Zur Textkritik der Schriften des Johannes," *TQ* 98 (1916) 148–84; Lagrange, *Critique textuelle,* 564–68.

129. See A. Bludau, "Das C. J. (1 Joh 5,7) im 16. Jh.," *BZ* 1 (1903) 280–302, 378–407.

130. See in the *Enchiridion biblicum* #135.

131. See the letter of Cardinal Vaughan (*RB* [1898] 149) and further references in Chaine, 136.

132. Above all, we should mention K. Künstle, *Das C. J. auf seine Herkunft untersucht* (Freiburg, 1905); numerous essays by Bishop A. Bludau (listed in *DBSup* 2:72f.); J. Lebreton, *Histoire du dogme de la Trinité* 1 (2nd ed.; Paris, 1927); M. del Alamo, "Los tres testificantes de la 1. Ep. de Juán," *Cult. bib.* 4 (1947) 11–14; T. Ayuso Marazuela, "Nuevo estudio sobre el 'C.J.,'" *Bib* 28 (1947) 83–112, 216–35; 29 (1948) 52–76. On the Protestant side, E. Riggenbach wrote a very challenging contribution to the discussion (*Das Comma Johanneum* [BFCT 31,4; Gütersloh, 1928]).

133. *Enchir. bib.*[2] #136.

Following the latest works on the subject it is possible to summarize the results of the discussion:[134]

a) The entire Greek textual tradition knows nothing of the Johannine Comma. It is not found in any of the uncials or quoted by any of the Greek fathers: "In view of the great Trinitarian controversy this is a compelling argument against its authenticity" (Wikenhauser). Of the Greek manuscripts, only four minuscules have the comma. And these assuredly only because of the Latin textual tradition: (1) Codex Regius (Gregory 88; twelfth century), where it is a later marginal gloss, according to Tischendorf, from the hand of a seventeenth-century librarian; (2) Codex Ravianus or Berolinensis (sixteenth century), which is a copy of the Complutensian imprint; (3) Codex Vaticanus Ottobonianus Gr. 298 (Gregory 629; fourteenth-fifteenth century or later), a bilingual manuscript in which the Greek has been conformed to the Latin; (4) Codex Montfortianus (Gregory 61; sixteenth century), which is also dependent on the Vulgate.[135] From this we gather that the Johannine Comma hardly became part of the Greek text,[136] but is really a problem in the textual history of the Latin version.

b) The most ancient manuscripts of the Vulgate (fu, am, harl) do not have the comma either. Only from the ninth century on does it find its way increasingly into the manuscripts of the Vulgate.[137]

c) As regards the Old Latin, the comma is found in a palimpsest at Lyons, viz., the Freising Fragments (q or r), both of Spanish origin; codex p (thirteenth century); and in a few quotations by ecclesiastical writers like Pseudo-Augustine, *Speculum* 2 (CSEL 12:314; eighth century), Cassiodorus, *Complexiones* (*PL* 70:1373, cols. 540 and 570), Ithacus Clarus, *Libri tres contra Varimadum* 1.5 (*PL* 62:359; ca. 389 C.E.), and *Liber apologeticus* 1.4 of Priscillian (d. 385 C.E.) or, according to others, of the Spanish bishop Instantius, a pupil of Priscillian (CSEL 18:6a, 380). The last of these is the most ancient witness.

d) The Johannine Comma was completely unknown in the East. How far it spread in North Africa is still open to question. Until recently it was assumed that the texts of Tertullian and Cyprian offer no proof of the existence of the comma in their versions of the Bible. It only appears as an allegorical interpretation of 1 John 5:8 in reference to the Trinity.[138] Not until the most recent

---

134. Riggenbach, Ayuso (see n. 132); see further A. Lemonnyer, *DBSup* 2:67–73; Chaine, 126–37; Ambroggi, 210–13; Meinertz, *Einleitung*, 278–81. Further opinions in Ayuso, *Bib* 28 (1947) 85ff. Ayuso's conclusions, taken over in the first edition, have been in part corrected (on the Spanish origin of the comma) by W. Thiele, "Beobachtungen zum Comma Johanneum (1 Joh 5,7f.)," *ZNW* 50 (1959) 61–73.

135. See Riggenbach, *Comma,* 11–14; Lemonnyer, *DBSup* 2:68; Ayuso, *Bib* 28 (1947) 94–96.

136. Thiele ("Beobachtungen," 72f.) it is true does not exclude this possibility, but we naturally ask how this addition could then have disappeared so opportunely from the Greek textual tradition (before the trinitarian controversies!) without leaving a trace.

137. See the lists given in P. Martin, *Introduction à la critique textuelle du NT* 5 (Paris, 1886) 148–52 (reprinted in Chaine, 127). Ayuso provides a critical apparatus for the Vulgate readings (*Bib* 28 [1947] 107–12),

138. See A. Bludau, "Das C. J. bei Tertullian und Cyprian," *TQ* 101 (1920) 1–21; Ayuso, *Bib* 29 (1948) 52ff. On Augustine, who does not himself quote the comma, though he does offer that allegorical interpretation, see A. Bludau, "Der heilige Augustinus und 1. Joh 5, 7f.," *TG* 11 (1919)

researches of W. Thiele, who examined the Johannine Comma in connection with other interpolations in the Latin Bible, could we entertain the possibility that Cyprian may have had the Johannine Comma in the text of his Bible![139] In that case the famous interpolation must have originated in North Africa, introduced, like many other additions, as early as the second century.

e) The Johannine Comma was particularly welcome in Spain, where Priscillian uses it as a basis for his doctrine of the Trinity. From different variants in the Spanish manuscripts we may conclude that this heretic already found the comma in the text he used, but in his familiar way altered it to suit his purpose![140] The original form of the comma in the Old Latin was, we are told by Ayuso, perfectly orthodox. It found its way into certain manuscripts of the Vulgate, beginning with $vg^{s\text{-}clem}$, sometimes in Priscillian's heterodox form![141]

There are still some unresolved problems regarding the Johannine Comma and its early history, but it is certainly a relatively early interpolation into the Latin Bible. It went on to play a role in Priscillianism and in the history of the Vulgate. It does not have the kind of dogmatic significance that has been attributed to it.

9. 1 John in the History of the Canon

1. Origen[142] and Eusebius[143] include 1 John among the homologoumena. It is a fact that this letter took its place alongside the other New Testament writings and was never seriously questioned in the ancient church. In the second century the Apostolic Fathers and the Apologists proved by citing the letter that they had a high regard for it (see p. 43). Other ecclesiastical writers of the second and third centuries, such as Irenaeus,[144] Tertullian,[145] Cyprian,[146] and Clement of Alexandria,[147] agree.

For the history of the canon the following evidence is important:

a) The Muratorian Canon (second half of the second century) cites 1 John

---

379–86; N. Fickermann, "St. Augustinus gegen das C.J.?," *BZ* 22 (1934) 350–58; Thiele, "Beobachtungen," 71f.

139. Thiele, "Beobachtungen," 68ff. As his principal argument he adduces the fact that additions to the Old Latin text are characteristic and that in the course of its history attempts were made to eliminate them. The subsequent insertion of such a long and widespread addition as the Johannine Comma would be a singular exception to the rule (p. 69). Büchsel already pleaded for a North African and second-century origin for the comma.

140. Ayuso in particular proved this (*Bib* 29 [1948] 56ff.).

141. Ibid., 64–71; see his conclusions, pp. 72–74.

142. *In Ioa.* 5.3 in Eusebius, *H.E.* 6.25.10; see also in *Lib. Iesu nave* 7.1.

143. Eusebius, *H.E.* 3.24.17; 25.2.

144. Irenaeus, *Adv. Haer.* 3.17.5, 8.

145. Tertullian, *Adv. Prax.* 15; *Adv. Marc.* 5.16; *Scorp.* 12 and often; cf. Rönsch, *Das NT Tertullians* (Leipzig, 1871) 545–55.

146. See the index in Hartel 3, 371f.

147. He not only cites it frequently (see the index in O. Stählin, GCS 4:25f), but has also commented on it (*Fragmente in Adumbrationes,* trans. Cassiodorus, GCS 3:209–14).

1:1 in lines 29–34, and in line 69 includes two other Johannine epistles as part of the canon.[148]

b) On Origen, see above. It is surprising that Origen describes 1 John with the words *panu oligōn stichōn* (in Eusebius, *H.E.* 6.25.10).

c) The canon in Codex Claromontanus,[149] Cyril of Jerusalem,[150] Canon 59 of the Council of Laodicea (ca. 360 C.E.),[151] Athanasius in his 39th Festal Letter,[152] etc., already speak of the three Johannine Epistles as canonical.

The letter therefore maintained a firm position in the Greek as well as the Latin church and was accepted as part of the canon from early times.

2. We do not know whether 1 John was rejected by the Alogi as they rejected GJohn and Acts.[153] In any case this sect, which arose during the struggle with Montanism in the second half of the second century, could not appeal to any prior tradition for their rejection of it. It is missing from Marcion's canon,[154] but that does not prove anything, given the drastic procedures of that particular heretic.[155] Among the various versions, the Old Syrian probably did not contain 1 John. The alleged allusions to certain passages in the letter in Aphraates and Ephraem Syrus are very doubtful.[156] The so-called Syrian catalogue published by Mrs. Lewis, which is considered older than the Peshitta, does not mention any of the Johannine Epistles. But this does not imply a rejection of these epistles. 1 John was accepted into the Peshitta not later than the beginning of the fifth century. It seems that the Catholic Epistles were late to be translated into Syriac. All the other ancient versions contain the epistle.

---

148. T. Zahn, *Geschichte des neutestamentlichen Kanons* (Erlangen/Leipzig, 1888, 1890) 2:6, 8; probably in line 69 there is also a reference to the two shorter epistles of John; see the Introduction to 2 and 3 John (pp. xf.).

149. According to Zahn, it was produced ca. 300 in Alexandria or vicinity (*Geschichte des neutestamentlichen Kanons* 2:157ff.).

150. Cyril of Jerusalem, *Cat.* 4.36 (ca. 350) in Zahn, *Geschichte des neutestamentlichen Kanons* 2:179).

151. Zahn, *Geschichte des Neutestamentlichen Kanons* 2:202.

152. Ibid., 211.

153. On the Alogi, see Irenaeus, *Adv. Haer.* 3.11.12, and esp. Epiphanius, *Pan.* 51; E. Schwarz, *Über den Tod der Söhne Zebedaei* (1904) 29ff.; T. Zahn, *Geschichte des neutestamentlichen Kanons* 1:220ff.; A. Bludau, "Die ersten Gegner der Johannesschriften," *BS* 22:1-2 (Freiburg, 1925). Epiphanius's remark that John pubished his Gospel, epistles, and Revelation "for the Church" (51.35.2) does not permit us to infer that the Alogi also rejected the epistle. See Jülicher-Fascher, *Einleitung,* 485; otherwise Bludau, 129ff.; Meinertz, *Einleitung,* 275 n. 3.

154. Harnack, *Marcion, das Evangelium vom fremden Gott* (2nd ed.; Leipzig, 1924), 35ff., esp. 69ff.; Marcion's "critical procedure [is] unique for its tendentious and arbitrary character" (p. 69).

155. According to R. Devreese (*Essai sur Theodore de Mopsueste* [Studi e Testi 141; Vatican City, 1948] 42), Theodore did not reject James, 1 Peter, and 1 John, as has hitherto been generally assumed, but simply failed to quote them (Ishodad of Merw, Introduction to his commentary on James).

156. See W. Bauer, *Der Apostolos der Syrer von der Mitte des 4. Jahrhunderts bis zur Spaltung der syrischen Kirche* (Giessen, 1903) 40ff.; Lagrange, *Critique textuelle,* 128f.; Chaine is more optimistic (p. 192).

157. Lagrange, *Critique textuelle,* 129.

EXEGESIS

THE PROOEMIUM (1 JOHN 1:1-4)

1:1 We declare to you what was from the beginning, what we have heard, what we have seen with our eyes, what we have looked at and touched with our hands, concerning the word of life — ²this life was revealed, and we have seen it, and testified to it, and declare to you the eternal life that was with the Father and was revealed to us — ³we declare to you what we have seen and heard so that you also may have fellowship with us; and truly our fellowship is with the Father and with his Son Jesus Christ. ⁴We are writing these things so that our joy may be complete.

* * *

The author begins this letter without the prescript which was customary in letters at that time[1] but in a manner similar to the Gospel of John, with a foreword (prooemium) couched in a lofty style. It is a résumé of important basic themes developed in the letter. What the author announces ("we declare," vv. 2, 3) in his capacity as a representative of those who have seen and heard is the manifestation of the eternal divine ("what was from the beginning") "word of life." The manifestation occurs in a perceptible, tangible personality at a particular point in time and history. This certainty of faith is beyond all doubt because it is based on a once-for-all, exclusive experience of this event of salvation. Those who proclaim it seek to share ("to you") it with the recipients of the letter by means of their witness of that same experience. In this way the witnesses will enable the recipient to attain with them the fellowship of faith. This will bring them to a living fellowship with him who appeared as the divine word of life, that is, with Jesus Christ. And through him they will attain finally to fellowship with God, the Father of Jesus Christ. For themselves the proclaimers expect to gain from writing this letter the joy of preaching the gospel.

---

1. On this, see Introduction, p. 3.

Three considerations come together here, as expressed in the tenses of the verbs. First, a retrospect to the once-for-all, unique event of salvation through which the eternal and divine appeared on earth (aorist). Second, the witnesses' certainty of their supreme experience of faith. They have been able to see with their eyes and touch with their hands. Here the verbs are mainly in the perfect tense. The time frame of the experiences reaches into the present. Finally, there is the perspective upon the present generation, to whom they wish to proclaim the faith and whom they wish to bring to the fellowship of faith with God (present tense), to make it possible for them to participate in a living fellowship with God. To express these three considerations, each important in its own way, in equally forceful terms and in a unified manner, was not an easy task for the writer. He begins with the powerful subject of his proclamation and assures his readers that he and his fellow witnesses became certain of these divine archetypal realities through their experiences. But this is interrupted by a brief description of the great salvation event, and finally the writer returns to his role as a witness, in order to impart fellowship with God to his readers in the preaching of faith.

It is not surprising that this battery of thoughts which the author tries to bring to light in the fundamental opening sentence makes the structure of this sentence unclear. The skeleton of it is clearly discernible:

"We declare to you
what was from the beginning,
what we have heard . . .
that you may fellowship with us."

Hearing and proclamation are coordinated. The "we" are mediators of what was heard, to the "you," who should accept it exactly in the same way as the "we" have accepted it themselves. But it is a matter of passing it along not merely as a message but rather as the experience and mediation of a higher reality. That is why the author makes a fresh start after "we have heard" ("what . . .") and shows in breadth and urgency how they have grasped the word of life with all their senses — until he gets entangled in the second "we have heard" (this time after "we have seen"). But also in this self-contained piece between the two occurrences of "we have heard" he hesitates and interrupts his train of thought once more. The addition of "concerning the word of life," inserted to clarify "what was from the beginning," produces the key word for a parenthesis, which again, with an *inclusio* ("was revealed" at the beginning and the end) expresses, attests, and announces the great event of salvation clearly. Although this makes the whole passage so intricate, the author handles it with great skill, gathering all the loose ends together and producing the accentuation he intends.

Finally, the author is also guided by his sense of rhythm,[2] which has influenced the more detailed formation of v. 1. For after the phrase "we have seen with our eyes," which contributes to the understanding of the matter, he adds the line that is parallel in rhythm and rounds off the thought ("what we have

---

2. On this, see Introduction, p. 9f.

looked and touched"). Further, v. 2, which with its change in rhythm is unusually lively and impressive, as well as v. 3, which again takes up the same line as v. 1, discloses an author who is in command of his style and writes with a natural self-assurance.

In order to understand this prooemium we must compare it closely with the Prologue of GJohn. Right at the beginning, the avoidance of the name Jesus Christ, the same starting point ("the beginning"), the central place of the term *logos,* and the importance of the statements about "life" lead to the same level of meaning. But more important is the common core idea that the *logos,* which bears within itself the fullness of divine life, "becomes flesh" at a particular moment in history (John 1:14) or "appears" (1 John 1:2) and discloses himself in his nature to the eyes of faith ("we have seen," John 1:14; 1 John 1:2). Verse 2 of the epistle's prooemium sounds like a résumé of the Gospel Prologue.

With this undeniable intellectual and literary relationship the special features of the introduction of 1 John must not be overlooked. Apart from a few formal divergencies,[3] there is also to be noted a certain change of emphasis. The Prologue appears like an all-embracing hymn to the Logos and as the overture to the narrative of the Johannine Gospel. It prepares for the puzzling rejection of the bringer of light and life on the part of the world (vv. 10–11). The epistle, however, is no longer concerned with the historic confrontation between the Word made flesh and the unbelieving world. It starts from the point where the Prologue speaks of those who recognized the divine revealer and bearer of life and accepted him in faith (John 1:13–14). The author of 1 John is concerned not with the fact as such that there was a circle of believers to whom his divine glory was revealed. This is not where the author places his emphasis, but rather on the certainty and reliability of their faith experience, which they can then proclaim later as the revelation that impacts "life." Thus he is more concerned to focus on his own time and his Christian readers. One senses at the very outset that their faith and their salvation are threatened. Yet Prologue and prooemium coincide exactly as to the content of their faith experience. In John 1 it involves receiving from the fullness of the Son of God (v. 16); in 1 John it is fellowship with God made possible by the acceptance in faith of the divine bearer of life — in both cases a real obtaining of salvation through the mediator of salvation, Jesus Christ. One may say that the opening of the letter presumes the Gospel Prologue or the Logos hymn embedded in it. It takes up the theme of the Prologue and exploits it for the purposes of relevant proclamation.

3.

John 1		1 John 1	
ἐν ἀρχῇ	v. 1	ἀπ' ἀρχῆς	v. 1
ἐν αὐτῷ ζωὴ ἦν	v. 4	τοῦ λόγου τῆς ζωῆς	v. 1
ἦν πρὸς τὸν θεόν	vv. 1, 2	ἦν πρὸς τὸν πατέρα	v. 2
ὁ λόγος σὰρξ ἐγένετο	v. 14	ἡ ζωὴ ἐφανερώθη	v. 2
ἐθεασάμεθα τὴν δόξαν αὐτοῦ	v. 14	ὃ ἐθεασάμεθα	v. 1
		or: ἑωράκαμεν . . . τὴν ζωὴν τὴν αἰώνιον	v. 2

Prooemium

EXCURSUS I

The Meaning and Significance of "Witness" in 1 John 1:1-4

It is a difficult question, sometimes taken too lightly, as to who is speaking in 1 John 1:1-4. Nor is it clear what the witness is that they desire to give to the readers of 1 John. Does it involve a claim to direct historic encounter with Jesus Christ? Or is it only an expression of faith elevated to ultimate certainty and equally available to subsequent generations of believers? It is important to decide this issue[4] not only for the question of the authorship of 1 John but also for the meaning of the message of salvation that is proclaimed to the recipients of the letter.

1. As far as the language goes, the plural "we" may be an authorial plural, common in epistolary style and equivalent to a singular (cf. v. 4).[5] However, the author generally speaks of himself in 1 John in the singular.[6] This makes it more probable that he is referring to a wider circle of witnesses. But this would mean that in v. 4 he incorrectly retains the plural—understandably enough though, given the flow of diction. In any case in pinpointing either himself in person or a larger group of witnesses he distinguishes between the "we" of the original messengers and the "you" who receive the message. This is different from those places where the "we" covers all believers in Christ.[7] In view of this, Harnack's thesis that the "we" in 1:1-4 is a *pluralis autoritatis* is completely ruled out.[8] True, the author speaks with authority, but this does not mean "that he also claims for his own person an authority as though the community itself were speaking" (Harnack, "Das 'Wir,'" 104). What sense would there be in speaking in the name of the "community of believers," since the addressees are themselves a "community of believers"? The difference between the "we" and the "you" lies deeper, in what "witness" really means. But Harnack does not allow for this.[9] This special sense of "we" referring to the idea of witness appears again in 4:14 (though hardly in 4:6).

---

4. Apart from all the Catholics, many Protestant exegetes still maintain that the author was a historical witness. A contrary view is taken chiefly by the scholars to be discussed below: A. von Harnack, E. Norden, H. Windisch, R. Bultmann, C. H. Dodd; further M. Dibelius, *RGG*[2] 3:348; A. Omodeo, *La mistica Giovannea* (Bari, 1930) 181; H. Brown, *Literar-Analyse,* 286; Käsemann, "Ketzer und Zeuge," 305; Haenchen, *TRu* 26 (1960) 14.

5. So Ambroggi, 225. For the rest, see the commentaries on 3 John 9. R. Bultmann holds fast to the view that the "we" denotes the first Christian preachers (*The Johannine Epistles* [Hermeneia; Philadelphia, 1973] 9ff.). They were "eschatological" contemporaries of Jesus. Since they are distinguished from "you," they are bearers of the tradition.

6. 2:1a, 7, 8, 12-14, 21, 26; 5:13.

7. 2:1b, 2, 3, 5, 18b, etc.—To be distinguished from the impersonal *ean eipōmen* (1:6, 8, 10) (= *ho legōn,* 2:4, 6, 9).

8. A. von Harnack, "Das 'Wir' in den Johanneischen Schriften," *SB* (Berlin, 1923) 96-113. He has been followed by H. H. Wendt, *Die Johannesbriefe und das joh. Christentum* (Halle, 1925) 33; H. Seesemann, *Der Begriff* κοινωνία *im NT* (BZNW 14; Giessen, 1933) 93 n. 1.

9. Harnack, "Das 'Wir,'" 105: "In no way does he express an eye witnessship in space and time."—*Per contra,* see M. Barth, *Der Augenzeuge* (Zurich, 1946), but his methodology is open to question.

2. In effect, the controversy boils down to this: Do the speakers here claim to be witnesses who have actually seen and heard the historical occurrences, to have been close companions of Jesus Christ during his days on earth?[10] Or are the massive phrases in v. 1 susceptible of some other interpretation?

The strictly realistic interpretation, which emphasizes the historical connection of the speakers here with Christ, stands in contradiction to the author's concern, which is not with the historical as such but with the divine veiled in earthly vesture ("what was from the beginning"). Despite all the manifestations in "signs" (John 2:11; 11:40), despite the self-revelation in words and works (John 14:10; cf. 10:38), this can be apprehended only by the believers. There is in John no preeminently historical interest in eyewitnesses (*autoptai,* Luke 1:2) or in the personal companions of Jesus (Acts 1:21). Rather it is a religious concern. True, given the temporal and spatial conditioning of the incarnation, this may imply a historic connection with the divine bearer of life. But this is a point that has first to be examined.

The interpretation of the statements in v. 1 as referring to the risen One[11] is based no less on a misunderstanding. Such an interpretation not only narrows the perspective unduly and disregards the clear reference to the incarnation in v. 2, but misses the basic difference between the resurrection narratives and what is said in the prooemium of the epistle. In particular, the references to "touching" and "seeing the hands and feet" in Luke 24:39 (cf. John 20:25, 27) are intended to affirm the bodily reality of the risen One and to overcome the suspicion that the appearances were merely hallucinations. In 1 John 1:1 the verbs that speak of physical apprehension serve to dispel all doubt about the reality and tangibility of the eternal and divine in bodily vesture![12] The aim therefore is not to reach certainty about the external form of the appearances but to lay hold of the unattainable, nonsensible reality of the divine. It finds this reality manifested and incarnated in a person. The purpose of Luke 24 is to remove all doubt about the presence of a particular form and figure. In 1 John 1:1 it is emphatically asserted that a reality which certainly existed (the phrase "what was from the beginning" is put first) appeared in a particular form. The physical seeing and touching of the body of the risen One in the Lucan account has the purpose of arousing faith (in the resurrection) on the part of the disciples. The Johannine statements, however, *include* the affirmation of faith in a christological sense (cf. John 1:14 with 1:12).

3. Are these phrases intended to reproduce merely a peculiarly "massive" impression of the faith experience as something that is open to all believers? For

---

10. The author may have been associating himself with a witness already dead.

11. Bisping, Belser, Loisy, Vrede; see also Bonsirven, 82f.; Ambroggi, 223; Barth, *Augenzeuge,* 104f.; H. J. Vogels, *TRu* 39 (1940) 17.

12. The verbs of sensuous apprehension are uttered as "a bold stroke." In a similar sense already H. Conzelmann, "Was von Anfang war," in *Neutestamentliche Studien für R. Bultmann* (Berlin, 1954) 194–201. See also J. Beutler, *Martyria: Traditionsgeschichtliche Untersuchungen zum Zeugnisthema bei Johannes* (Frankfurt am Main, 1972) 218f., 283f.; J. L. Houlden, commentary, 47f. In the same sense as in my commentary, see M. de Jonge, *De brieven van Johannes* (Nijkerk, 1968) 34–36.

the terms used we may compare Acts 17:27a and *Corpus Hermeticum* 5.2[13] The object of such knowledge, described as it is in these texts in the language of sensible experience, is the invisible infinite God. Its source is to be found in Stoicism.[14] But the interpretation that is available for Acts 17:27a is inapplicable 1 John 1. In the former case we have a human quest for the divine vision to apprehend God in tangible form. In 1 John 1 we have a divine offer of the eternal and divine in real and tangible form, that is, in the incarnate Son of God. The popular philosophy of Stoicism with its everyday imagery barely conceals the pantheism and monism of its thought. Such language is poles apart from the doctrine of the incarnation, with its strongly personal conception of God.

The witnesses in 1 John 1:1–4 are seeking to convey to their addressees a special experience that was unique to themselves. There is not a single word to suggest that the recipients could share the same unique experience (cf. by contrast "not far from each one of us" in Acts 17:27). The special role of *hēmeis* ("we") as witnesses is further highlighted by the peculiarly Johannine use of the verb "to testify,"[15] particularly in combination with the verb "to see" (v. 2). In John 1:34 (cf. 32); 3:11, 32; 19:35; 1 John 1:2; 4:14) the term "witness" is combined with the verb for seeing. But this seeing does not necessarily involve physical perception. In 3:32 "to see" is used with metaphorically with "to hear" to express the immediacy of heavenly experiences of the Son of man. But in earthly connections and in historical contexts (1:34; 19:35) it is impossible to exclude the physical element in the experience of the witnesses since otherwise their experiences would be invalidated. Consequently, in doubtful cases, where the faith of the witnesses and the immediacy of their experiences are in the forefront, and where nevertheless this experience cannot be detached from its historical context, physical sight cannot be ruled out altogether. Such is the case here, as in 1 John 4:14.[16] That which is actually "seen" and "testified" is an object of faith (v. 2, "life"). But it is something that can only have been experienced in the historical, physical form ("was revealed"). Hence the sequence of the three verbs in v. 2 offers a firm basis for concluding that the speakers of 1:1–4

---

13. CHerm 5.2: ἄφθονος γὰρ ὁ κύριος φαίνεται διὰ παντὸς τοῦ κοσμοῦ, νόησιν ἰδεῖν καὶ λαβέσθαι αὐταῖς ταῖς χερσὶ δύνασει καὶ τὴν εἰκόνα τοῦ θεοῦ θεάσασθαι. See Norden, *Agnostos Theos,* 17; W. Scott, *Hermetica* (Oxford, 1924–26) 1:158f. (with rearrangement of the text); 2:161 applies the "image of God" to the visible universe. For a different opinion, see Nock-Festugière (1:61), who take the second sentence as a question and understand the image of God to mean the human intellect (see also Ferguson in Scott, *Hermetica* 4:369); this gives rise to a different meaning: just as one cannot see the human mind, so neither can one see God *directly,* but only through the order of the universe.

14. See Norden, *Agnostos Theos,* 14ff. Scott (*Hermetica* 2:156) reckons further with Egyptian influence.

15. H. Strathmann, *TDNT* 4:497ff.; I. de la Potterie, "La notion de témoignage dans saint Jean," *Sacra Pagina* 2 (Paris/Gembloux, 1959) 193–208 (with further bibliography). See also the commentary at 5:7ff.

16. N. Brox admittedly supposes that here, as in 4:14, "the real point, the element of witnessing has faded" (*Zeuge und Märtyrer* [Munich, 1961] 85). But at least the seeing (John 1:14) of the incarnate Logos is presupposed as the foundation for the testimony of faith.

must be regarded as people who have had a historical experience of the great event of salvation.[17]

4. Other exegetes understand these particular statements as "the peculiar way every fresh generation experiences anew the situation of Jesus' contemporaries,"[18] as "solidarity of the subsequent generations with the original generation," or again as "a later mystical experience."[19] According to these interpretations, however they may be further nuanced, the "we" could only be regarded as people who have heard, seen, and touched.

Windisch reminds us of the principle enunciated in *Pes.* 10.5b (Danby, p. 151): "In every generation a man must so regard himself as if he came forth himself out of Egypt." That is why it says in 5c (Danby, p. 167): "He brought *us* out from bondage to freedom." But according to Christian faith the salvation event is fundamentally tied to Christ, not to the first generation of Christians, and the role of Christ is unrepeatable. Dodd (pp. 13–14) points to the "feeling of solidarity which was so intensive in ancient communities" and also to the "I" of the Psalms, as well as Amos 2:10 ("I brought you up out of the land of Egypt and led you forty years in the wilderness") and Josh. 24:7 ("your eyes saw what I did in Egypt and you lived in the wilderness a long time"). But this involves an identification with earlier generations which was usual at all times with people who shared a common nationality or a common mentality or destiny. It is found even to this day, though no longer as frequently or as strongly. This is shown by many other examples which may also be quoted, such as Tacitus, *Agric.* 45 ("Mox nostrae duxere Helvidium in carcere manus"); Matt. 23:35; Gal. 1:23; Augustine, *Ep.* 88.8. In Luke 1:1; Heb. 1:2 there is an identification with contemporaries analogous to the way we use "our" era; it is not confined to our own personal life span. In Polycarp 9.1 we have an imprecise combination of the present personal experience with earlier events.

We should pay special attention to Irenaeus, *Adv. Haer.* 5.1.1, since this deals with an experience of Christ on the part of later generations. The passage reads: "Neque rursus nos aliter discere poteramus nisi magistrum nostrum videntes et per auditum vocem eius percipientes." The difference between this and the pro-oemium of 1 John is readily visible when attention is paid to the meaning and purpose of this turn of speech. These later Christians do not want to represent themselves as witnesses for the quondam Christ-event over against others, but "uti imitatores quidem operum, factores autem sermonum eius facti communionem habeamus cum ipso." This experience, which is rooted in a lively religious imagination — Christ stands before them as teacher — can be enjoyed by Christians at any time.

---

17. O. Cullmann also deduces that "seeing" in John 1:14 etc., although involving physical sight implies an interpretive perception ("Εἶδεν καὶ ἐπίστευσεν," in *Aux sources de la tradition chrétienne, Mélanges offerts à M. Goguel* [Neuchâtel/Paris, 1950] 52–61).

18. Bultmann, *John*, 70f. n. 13 (on John 1:14).

19. Windisch, ad loc. — in this a further ground for suspicion is the way in which Windisch makes the gnostic mystical experience similar to Jewish and early Christian views of communion with the deity. In *OdesSol.* 7:4 the redeemer identifies himself with the redeemed in order that the latter may apprehend him; in John 1:1f. by contrast the witnesses stand *over against* the redeemer, full of wonder at being able to apprehend the divine in human form.

None of the supposed parallels adduced from Jewish, pagan, or Christian sources refers to such an urgent situation as the one in which the Christian faith finds itself over against the unique and great event of salvation, the appearance of the Logos of life upon this earth. This is an event which remains firmly and inextricably bound to its historic basis, which can never under any circumstances relinquish its innermost substance to a liturgical celebration (Passover) or simply serve to enrich the religious imagination (Irenaeus, *Adv. Haer.* 5.1.1). Those supposed analogies do not offer any real parallel to the typically Johannine idea of "witness," which presupposes an immediate experience and an urge to indoctrinate.

5. There can hardly be any doubt that the author must be included in a circle of witnesses, called and qualified, who experienced the direct historic presence of the incarnate Son of God. But there is still one difficulty left: it is hardly likely that there was still a sizable group of witnesses alive as late as this who had seen and heard. Even though the majority might be dead, the expression would indicate (note the present tense) that there were still a number of survivors around. This may be one of the reasons why there is cause to doubt the traditional view that it is John the son of Zebedee who is speaking. For—again according to tradition—he was an exception, still surviving in the postapostolic age.

Thus, while acknowledging the special use of "we" as opposed to "you," we have to look for a different explanation. The author, who is not himself a direct witness of the salvation event, is expressing a prophetic self-consciousness in which he appropriates to himself the experience of a witness who actually saw and heard. This may be a "prophetic plural," adopted by those who "think of themselves somehow as successors of the original apostles." They belong to a collegium "in which autopsy is as it were deposited."[20] E. Haenchen takes a similar view: "In the opening words the author is speaking in the style of a prophetic revelation, and thereby lending a proper weight to his concern."[21] Now it is hard to prove—except perhaps in the case of the Apocalypse—that a "prophetic collective" lies behind the Johannine writings, a more closely knit community of apostolic itinerant missionaries from whose circle the individual Johannine writings originate.[22] But one might modify this thesis by suggesting that there were still disciples of the original apostles alive, who, because of their close relationship with them, considered themselves entitled to represent those witnesses who had heard and seen, and to pass on their message. 1 John does not otherwise betray a "prophetic self-consciousness." Rather, the author has a powerful feeling for the strength of the tradition. He is a bearer of that tradition (see 2:7, 13f.; 24:2, 11), one who participated in the mission of the original apostles (see John 4:38; 13:20; 17:18; 20:21). He could count himself as a member of the circle of John bar Zebedee, as a disciple and representative of the "apostolic witnesses," who by their ties to the Son of God who appeared on earth "in the flesh" can give a unique and exclusive testimony of faith.

---

20. A. Kragerud, *Der Lieblingsjünger im Johannesevangelium* (Oslo, 1959) 102f.
21. Haenchen, *TRu* 26 (1960) 14.
22. See R. Schnackenburg, *BZ* n.s. 4 (1960) 305f.

6. What purpose do these emphatic assurances have for the document as a whole? If the speakers, as we saw, do not represent themselves as witnesses who have heard and seen out of a purely historic interest, why then do they make such a point of sensible apprehension? Is it only to give their own faith convictions a lasting expression? An attentive reading will show that already in this foreword the author focuses on the heresy that he is combating throughout the letter. We must avoid isolating the christological errors but must recognize in them the "first lie." They deny altogether the figure of Jesus Christ, the Savior, or, to put it differently, the meaning of Jesus Christ for redemption and salvation. That is the common denominator for all the different statements about Jesus Christ (see Introduction, pp. 18–20) and also the connection between the "christological" and the "moral" error. The opponents combated by the author proclaim a way to salvation in which the fulfillment of the commandments and brotherly love (2:3–14; 3:1b, 6; 4:7f.), the cleansing of sin by the blood of Christ (1:7; 5:6; cf. 2:2; 3:5, 16; 4:10, 14) and finally Jesus Christ himself as mediator of salvation are irrelevant. In the incarnation the profound otherness of the Christian way of salvation as contrasted with the "gnostic" way, as 1 John combats it, is most clear and obvious to the author. Gnosticism is poles apart from the historic event and will have no truck with a historic mediator. The Gnostics believe they can achieve salvation by an immediate knowledge and vision of God. The true believers in Christ, however, see quite a different pathway to salvation before them, and it is the only way. They cannot directly achieve the life of God or have communion with God, but only in and with the Son of God who came in the flesh in human history (5:11–12; cf. John 6:57). It is he therefore who is himself "the Way" and that in an absolute sense (John 14:6). In contrast to one trying to lay hold of God immediately as the Gnostic preaches, Christian faith proclaims the eternal and divine made flesh in a unique and final human form. Both the reality of the "flesh" and the divinity of the "Logos" hidden within it belong absolutely together. It is this unity that is the true object of faith and the great experience of salvation which has to be proclaimed. Upon the immediate witnesses of this fact falls the task, insofar as they comprehend its meaning in faith, to witness to it and to proclaim it at all times (1 John 1:1–4).

Both the historicity and in particular the form of the incarnation are characteristic of the great salvation event which God effected for the deliverance of humankind in Christ Jesus. This was recognized by the author of 1 John in his controversy with the gnostic heresy. Its historicity is emphasized in the course of the letter by such phrases as "sending" (4:9, 10, 14) or "having come" (4:2; 5:6, 20a). For the incarnation he uses the formula "come in the flesh" (4:2). His favorite term is the brief "was revealed" (1:2; 3:5, 8; 4:9). But the opening sentences of his letter are intended to put clearly before the readers at the outset what is meant by the historic self-revelation of God in Christ for faith, in opposition to the heresy of the false Gnosis.

* * *

1:1 The phrase "was from the beginning" at the very outset must be regarded as intentionally general (neuter), and mysteriously brief in its formulation. Its purpose is to suggest the depths that lead into the abysses of God.[23] The phrase "from the beginning," frequently used in 1 John,[24] refers for the most part to the doctrine proclaimed at the beginning (2:7, 24; 3:11) and is intended to move the readers to remain faithful to that doctrine as against the teachers of heresy who appeared only later. But there is a more profound, substantial reason for this early Christian principle of tradition. The message proclaimed "from the beginning" also includes the personal bearer of an archetypal Being ("him who is from the beginning," 2:13–14). And the recipients of the letter must remain faithful not only to the doctrine (2:24) but also to the Revealer himself (2:27; 3:6). The very first word of the letter prepares the ground for this important demand. It refers not to the beginning of the proclamation[25] but to the personal bearer of the archetypal Being. This is proved by the "was'" and by the use of the phrase "concerning the word of life." The neuter gender often appears in Johannine usage for the masculine.[26] The phrase "concerning the word of life," which disturbs the balance of the sentence, can be explained as due to the urgent need for qualification.[27] As far as the content goes, both phrases may be making the same point, the one at the beginning and the other at the end of v. 1. The preexistent Logos, and subsequently the incarnate One, incorporates in himself the fullness of the divine life, an idea that is no more clarified here than it is in GJohn. Only in the phrase "what was from the beginning" and in the term "the word" itself is there any emphasis on the eternal divine Being. Without dwelling on its meaning, the author at once directs our attention to the fact of its being made accessible in the incarnate Logos of life to the experience of faith.

It is an open question whether "beginning" refers to the beginning of creation (Brooke, Chaine) or to a primal timelessness and supratemporal state (Belser, Camerlynck, Bonsirven, etc.). Since "from the beginning" is not a verbal allusion to "in the beginning" in John 1:1–2 (cf. Gen. 1:1), and since the prooemium, unlike the Prologue to the Gospel, does not mention the activity of the Logos in creation, this expression may be intended only to express his preexistence and divinity. The Logos is the theme of the proclamation not in respect of his activity (*contra* Chaine), but in repsect of his primal divine Being (his "life"), disclosed to the believers through the incarnation (v. 2) in order to bring them into fellowship with God (v. 3).

The eternal-divine has now been heard by the present speakers. They saw him with their eyes and touched him with their hands. Precisely this "tangibility" of

---

23. See Häring: "The neuter gender, 'that,' 'what' serves in the higher, viz., religious language with its indefinite quality, to draw attention to the fact that this is something that cannot be expressed fully in human language." See also Bultmann, *Theology* 2:29ff.

24. 2:7 (bis), 13, 14, 24 (bis); 3:8, 11; cf. 2 John 5:6.

25. So H. H. Wendt, *ZNW* 21 (1922) 38–42, and *Johannesbriefe*, 31ff.; Goguel, *The Birth of Christianity*, 366.

26. Cf. John 3:6 with 5; 4:22 with 23; 6:37a with b; 6:39 with 40; 17:2 *pan ho* with *autois;* 17:10 with 9; 1 John 5:4 with 5.—BDF §138.1.

27. It would be possible to see in *ho ēn* a prefixed absolute nominative (Bonsirven), as is not rare in John (John 7:38; 17:2; cf. 15:2;—1 John 2:24, 27; BDF §466.1; J. H. Moulton-N. Turner, *A Grammar of New Testament Greek* [Edinburgh, 1963] 314, 316); but *apangellein peri tinos* is, as a comparison with v. 2 shows, the secondary construction, compared with the accusative.

that which is otherwise beyond human reach, this historic experience of One who transcends all time (as is shown by the repetition and crescendo of the verbs) is all-important. Thus it is possible to gain possession of the eternal-divine life in human form and consequently to participate in that life. The choice of verbs is deliberate and the order is intentional. The appearance of the Logos is the self-revelation of God. The correct response to that revelation is, initially, to "hear" it. Strictly speaking, this does not mean that the witnesses had actually "heard" the words of the incarnate Logos. Rather, they themselves heard the Logos as the "word" of God addressed to humankind. But his message must also be taken into consideration, since this message is primarily the personal testimony of One who was sent from God, the only Son of God (cf. all the "I am" predicates in GJohn). So that there can be no doubt that the great revelation of God's salvation took place in a personal form, the author adds: "That which we have seen with our eyes." As the perfect tense shows,[28] the speaker is concerned with the permanent effect of this hearing and seeing. It generates lasting knowledge and firm faith (cf. John 6:69; 1 John 4:16). Even more concretely we are led to the same point by the little ho-clause. In style and rhythm it forms a parallelism to the first two clauses: "what we have heard, what we have seen with our eyes, what we have looked at and touched with our hands."

Each time the second phrase is expanded beyond the verb. The two verbs in this second line belong together because of their aorist form. It is important to notice this stylistic method for several reasons. First, it may not be that the aorists in the second line express a different nuance of meaning compared with the perfects of the first line. Rather, they are used merely for the sake of variety.[29] Similarly, the author's sense of rhythm explains the curious insertion of "we have looked at" after "we have seen." It is hard to suppose, given the context and the author's linguistic usage, that the second verb of seeing is intended to add any further meaning of its own.[30] To spiritualize the "seeing" so realistically described in v. 1 ("with our eyes") and make it a "perceiving" in faith (faith is also part of "seeing") would in this context only be disturbing, and a step backwards. The crescendo of thought, strongly reinforced by the rhythm and word order, does not come out until the phrase "touched with our hands." In this way the manifestation of the eternal-divine in human, tangible form is considerably enhanced—and nothing more (see Excursus 1). Thus the sequence of the verbs forms a "marvelous crescendo" (Chaine), even further heightened by the ralentando in "we have seen."

---

28. On the meaning of the imperfect in general, see BDF §§318.4; 342. Regarding *akouein* and *horan* the difference between *heōraka* and *ēkousa* in John 3:32; Acts 22:15 is to be observed where the seeing is determinative; John 5:37; in 1 John 1:1, 3, on the other hand, the hearing (*akēkoa*) is equally essential.

29. See Radermacher on the use of tenses in Koine: "Sometimes the tenses are used at random without any perceptible difference of meaning" (*Neutestamentliche Grammatik* [Lietzmann I; 2nd ed.; Tübingen, 1925] 150); specifically on the perfect and aorist, p. 154; further Moulton-Turner, 68–71.

30. On the linguistic usage, cf. 1 John 4:12 with 20; John 1:38; 4:35; 6:5 (physical sight); 11:45 (cf. with 2:23 *theōrein*).—BAG 698, s.v. 1; Bultmann, *John,* 69 n. 2; M. Barth, *Augenzeuge,* 94f.; O. Cullmann, "Εἶδεν καὶ ἐπίστευσεν," 55.

Although not syntactically correct, the author inserts "concerning the word of life." Maybe he avoids the accusative because of the danger of misunderstanding.[31] In any case, he could certainly express the personal character of the object better — and that is the primary focus. Then another point: this makes it possible grammatically to reproduce the object of "declare" meaning "to report about somebody or something."[32] With "the word of life" we get a pregnant term with which the readers may be presumed to be familiar. In the light of all this there can be no doubt that the object is the same Logos as in John 1 (see ad loc.). A new feature is the addition of "the word of life," a point which, as we shall see in due course, is of utmost importance to the author. This is because he is concerned with the meaning of Logos for humanity, at least for the believers (for "us" and "you"). He sees this importance in the conferral of everlasting, divine life (cf. 2:25; 5:11-13) — another aspect of "fellowship" with God (1:3, 6). The (incarnate) Logos is able to mediate "life" because he possesses the fullness of life in himself (John 1:4; cf. 5:21, 26; 6:57), and because he, the Son of God, was sent into the world for the purpose of bringing this "life" to the world (1 John 3:9; cf. John 3:16; 6:40, 50-51; 10:10; 11:25-26). The addition is therefore a genitive of quality or apposition. The Logos possesses "life" within himself and is "life" in his whole nature. Such combinations of the genitive with "of life" are not unusual in the Johannine writings,[33] and point as a whole to the great gift of salvation conferred by the divine life. On the other hand, in the Mandean literature[34] "word of life" is only one term among many which in these texts, rich as they are in imagery and verbose in the extreme, in no way have the pregnancy and weight of the Johannine terms.

1:2   The mention of "Logos of life" leads the author to speak parenthetically of the appearance of the divine life in the world of humanity; overshadowed as it is by death. There he personifies "life" — as it may already have been in the genitive of apposition. Paul (Col. 3:4) and Ignatius of Antioch (*Ephesians* 7.2) also call Christ "our life." More importantly, however, the Johannine Christ himself says "I am . . . the life" (11:25; 14:6). This clearly refers to the Son of

---

31. Cf. *ho logos hon ēkousate*, 2:7; the accusative would have been misunderstood as "word of life" (Phil. 2:16); there is a similar objective genitive after *logos* in Matt. 13:19; Acts 13:26; 14:3; 15:7; 20:32; 1 Cor. 1:18; 2 Cor. 5:19; Col. 1:5; 1 Tim. 4:6. When *peri* is used, this meaning is excluded (*contra* Windisch).

32. *Contra* Lohmeyer, *ZNW* 27 (1928) 227.— In the New Testament see Luke 7:18; 13:1; John 16:25; Acts 28:21; 1 Thess. 1:9 and in Epictetus, *Diss.* 3.4.1; 18.1; Xenophon, *Anabasis* 1.7.2. See BAG 78, s.v. *apangellein* 1. According to J. Schniewind, *TDNT* 1:64ff., it has the same meaning as *anangellein* in 1 John 1:22, "in a highly specialized use" (66).

33. The strongest echo is *to phōs tēs zōēs* (John 8:12), but cf. also *ho artos tēs zōēs* (6:35a, 48); *rhēmata zōēs aiōniou* (6:68). There are many similar phrases in Revelation (:7b, 10c; 3:5; 11:11; 17:8b, etc.; 21:6c, etc.; 22:14, 19).

34. *MandLit* 33, as a designation for Jōkabar; *Ginza* 88.19; 289.11, as a name for Jawar-Zīwā. See also *MandLit* 90: "Praised be the First Life and praised be the word of the First Light." This emissary is also called the "Primal One," *MandLit* 134: "Praises be to the One who is first of all, and to the Son of the First Great Life, whom Life has created, equipped and sent into the ages"; but the same expression also occurs in the plural (*MandLit* 137). Neither the absolute uniqueness of the Johannine Logos nor his incarnation has any parallel in the Mandean writings.

God as the bearer and mediator of "life." This is confirmed for the reader by the unexpected appearance of "that was with the Father." The life was "made manifest"; this concise statement expresses the great event of salvation which took place at a precise point in history (aorist) in the world of humanity. As the verb "to be revealed" tells us,[35] it was a revelation indeed, a unique and final disclosure of the hidden being of God. God's epiphany in the person of Christ becomes the special theme of John 14:8-9. The Son is the supreme revelation of the Father to humankind and at the same time the way to the Father. The aorist *ephanerōthē* (as in 3:5, 8) refers to the incarnation. But in 1 John 2:28 it looks beyond that to the second manifestation (again *phanerousthai*) of the Son of God in the future, the parousia. The author of 1 John defends the incarnation against the false prophets of his own day (4:2). He has a profound theological grasp of its significance. Through the incarnation—and only through it—the eternal-divine ("what was from the beginning"), the invisible, becomes visible, tangible, revealed, and capable of being imparted in such a way that those who were hitherto condemned to darkness and to the world of death can have fellowship in the divine Being and partake of eternal life.[36] In this way Johannine theology shifts the emphasis from the event of Golgotha, which was so central to Paul (Rom. 3:24-25; 1 Cor. 1:23; 2:2; 2 Cor. 5:14, 19, 21; Gal. 3:13; Col. 1:20; 2:14-15) to the incarnation of the Son of God (John 1:14; 3:16; 1 John 4:9). This is true even though the death of Jesus on the cross is still important as the assurance of divine love and of God's atoning purpose (1 John 2:2; 3:16; 4:10). Already in the sending of the Son into the world (1 John 4:9, 14), in the coming of the light into the darkness (John 12:46-47), salvation is assured, even though the "coming by blood" (1 John 5:6) remains integral to the saving act. While Paul gives a stronger christological accent to the incarnation (Phil. 2:6-7)—that is, to its soteriological significance in ending the reign of terror of the demonic powers (Gal. 4:4)—in Johannine thought it acquires a soteriological character from the very outset. It is the descent of life eternal into the world of humankind alienated from God, the invasion of the absolute, indestructible power of life into this transitory cosmos, destined as it was to perdition (1 John 2:17).

---

35. *Phaneroun* in the Johannine writings has the predominant meaning of revelation in *acts;* see John 2:11; 3:21; 7:4; 9:3; 1 John 2:19, 28; 3:2ab, 10; 4:9. There is no revelation merely in word, even in John 1:31; 17:6. It is mainly oriented to the disclosure of the divine essence, and thus of his *agapē* (1 John 4:9), of the *doxa* (of Jesus as the one sent by God, John 2:11) of the *onoma tou patros* (17:6). That is how what was previously hidden is brought to light (cf. John 3:21; 1 John 3:10, which, however, does not need to have been previously completely unknown (cf. 1 John 3:2a with b; *contra* B. Weiss). The term, a favorite one in John (twenty occurrences) and in the New Testament generally (fifty-one occurrences), is very rare in profane Greek; see H. Schulte, *Der Begriff der Offenbarung im NT* (Munich, 1949) 67. It appears in the Johannine writings along with several synonyms (H. H. Huber, *Der Begriff der Offenbarung im Joh-Ev* [Göttingen, 1934] 72ff.), yet *apokalyptein* never occurs. Schulte supposes that *phaneroun* was common in gnostic circles (*Begriff,* 68ff.). For its use in Ignatius of Antioch, see H. Schlier, *Religionsgeschichtliche Untersuchungen zu dem Ignatiusbriefen* (Giessen, 1929) 34ff.; otherwise H. W. Bartsch (*Gnostisches Gut und Gemeindetradition bei Ignatius von Antioch* [Gütersloh, 1940]), who attributes *phaneroun* to the "church's vocabulary."
36. On incarnation, see P. S. Minear, "The Idea of Incarnation in First John," *Int* 24 (1970) 291-302.

Those speakers here assure us that they have seen this divine life embodied in a personal bearer. In a single verb, *heōrakamen* (which goes particularly well with *ephanerōthē*), the author summarizes all the verbs that speak of sensible apprehension in the middle of v. 1. The speakers bear witness to this fact (see Excursus 1) accordingly and proclaim it to the recipients of the letter. Once again the author refers to that all-important subject, this time in its complete form, *"eternal* life"[37] — which addition, however, adds nothing new. But by placing the attribute after the noun and repeating the article, the author emphasizes the uniqueness of this personified divine life and differentiates it from all other "life" on earth, which is threatened by death, limited in power, and therefore no real "life" at all.[38] The divine life is in its very essence eternal and indestructible, and for that very reason is what humanity longs for so deeply, threatened as it is by death and destruction. Steering back to their role as witnesses (from the beginning of v. 3 to v. 1) the speakers once more emphasize the amazing fact that the divine life which was with the Father has appeared precisely to themselves. The absolute use of the name of Father for God (John 1:1 "with God") provides yet another strong connecting link with the Gospel of John. The emphatic "we" betrays the same experience of bliss (*seelige Ergriffenheit*) that is expressed in John 1:14c, 16.

1:3 After the parenthesis in v. 2 the author explicitly refers back to v. 1 (*ho . . .*). For the third time he assures the audience that "we have seen" — this time placed before "we have heard," because seeing (as in v. 2) corresponds to the "manifesting" of life. The phrase "we have heard," with which the author picks up the original thread at the beginning of v. 1, provides at the same time a transition to the proclamation. The recipients also[39] are given this message of salvation. They too can have fellowship (in faith) with the circle of immediate witnesses of the great event of salvation. Through their close-knit fellowship with this group — that is, by sharing the same faith — they too may have fellowship with the Father and the Son, a principle of communication (*Kommunikationsprinzip*) that is apparent already in John 17:20–21. For this is the real purpose of the proclamation — or rather of the faith created by it — to "have" the Son and through him to "have" the Father (1 John 2:23; 5:11–12). Thus, v. 3b, which stands on its own grammatically,[40] goes closely with v. 3a. The pleonastic

---

37. Cf. the alternation of *zōē* and *zōē aiōnios* in John 3:36; 5:24; 6:53f. On the whole question, see J. B. Frey, "Le concept de 'Vie' dans l'Évangile de S. Jean," *Bib* 1 (1920) 37–58, 211–39, esp. 50ff.; H. Pribnow, *Die johanneische Anschauung vom "Leben"* (Greifswald, 1934) 27ff.; R. Bultmann, *TDNT* 2:870f.; J. Dupont, *Essais sur la Christologie de S. Jean* (Bruges, 1951) 163–65; F. Mussner, *ZŌH: Die Anschauung vom 'Leben' in 4. Ev. unter Berücksichtigung der Johannesbriefe* (Munich, 1952) 48, 177f.

38. See also the constantly recurring slogan in the Mandean writings: "Life is victorious," a reflection of the desire for a life of such indestructible power.

39. *Kai* before *hymin* is missing from ℵ Vg sy[h] sa bo, but is certainly original. These manuscripts have probably omitted it like *apangellomen hymin* in v. 2 or because it reduplicates *kai hymeis*.

40. Differently Vg: "societas nostra sit cum Patre," etc. But in that case an *ē* would be indispensable in parallelism with *echēte*.

phrase (*kai=de*) is certainly possible.[41] It has the meaning here of leading the fellowship with the proclaimers, which is promised to the recipients, to fellowship with God.[42] On the other hand, it has the further purpose of making it clear that the proclaimers themselves ("*our* fellowship") possess with perfect certainty this fellowship with the Father and the Son. The "fellowship" of the readers and proclaimers in v. 3a is therefore in the first instance—on the basis of the proclamation—a fellowship of shared faith (cf. 2 John 10–11). Since faith imparts life (John 3:16, 36, etc.), it at once becomes a real and supernatural fellowship because of this possession of "life." The proclaimers draw those who hear with faith into the sphere of the divine life, into that divine fellowship which they themselves enjoy already. The Father is mentioned first (cf. 2:22b) because he is the ultimate goal of the unity desired and the primary place is appropriate to his dignity. The addition of "with his Son Jesus Christ," which is coordinated with the earlier phrase, means in the context that fellowship with the Father can only be attained through the Son (cf. John 14:6–11; 1 John 2:23; 5:11–12). The solemn designation "Jesus Christ" (an apologetic point, directed against the false teachers? cf. 4:15; 5:4–5), like the solemn accentuation of v. 3b, along with the proclamation of salvation in v. 2, forms one of the climaxes of the prooemium. Fellowship with God—or alternatively possession of the divine life (5:13)—is the good news of the whole document (see Excursus 2). Above all, as this comparison with 5:13 shows, the prooemium does not seek to initiate fellowship with God or to reestablish it. All it wants to do is to make the readers conscious of it ("that you may know"). The proclamation is something that goes on all the time ("we declare"—present). It produces and confirms ever anew the faith of the Christians and their state of salvation. At the same time, v. 3b introduces the theme of God which is to be developed in the first paragraph (1:5-10). Just as the Prologue of John highlights the christological message of the Fourth Gospel, so does the prooemium of 1 John strike a basic chord which echoes again and again throughout the document and places the whole under a dominant theme: fellowship with God and association in faith with Jesus Christ, the true Son of God, who was manifested in history and confessed in the community of right faith.

1:4 By writing this letter[43] the author hopes to achieve the fulfillment of his own joy and that of his fellow witnesses.[44] Joy was something the Johannine

---

41. *De,* omitted from a number of manuscripts, is undoubtedly original. It usually stands in the fourth position, after *kai,* and is also abundantly attested outside the New Testament; see BDF §447.9. E. Mayser, *Grammatik der griechischen Papyri aus der Ptolemäerzeit* (Berlin/Leipzig, 1906–34) 2/3:131f.; Deissmann, *Light,* 151 n. 3. For the meaning, cf. John 8:16.

42. *Koinōnia* occurs in the Johannine writings only at 1 John 1:3, 6, 7.—The substantival form of the Johannine concept of fellowship is usually expressed with *einai en, menein en,* etc.; see Seesemann, *Der Begriff* κοινωνία, 92–99.

43. *Tauta graphomen* undoubtedly refers to the whole letter that follows, since when the author looks back he says *tauta egrapsa* (2:26; 5:13).

44. *Hēmeis* is to be preferred on grounds of text criticism to *hymin* (A^corr pl. Vg sy sa bo arm), since the latter reading smoothes out the former and reinterprets it as a reference to the joy of the recipients (see next note). *Hēmeis* is in an emphatic position (see BDF §277), but need not mean

Prooemium

Jesus repeatedly promised his disciples in the farewell discourses (John 15:11; 16:20, 22, 24; 17:13). By the addition of "my" he had designated them as a gift of God which he himself—through his communion with the Father (cf. 14:28)—possessed, and which was his alone to give. This joy, through the experience of close union in life and love with the glorified Christ (15:11; 17:13), is meant to be "fulfilled" (*plērousthai*), as distinguished from *teleiousthai,* represents not so much a climax as the realization of a possibility.[45] Since the writers of 1 John 1:4 are conscious of their close fellowship with Christ (v. 3), they already possess the joy that Jesus promises (John 16:22) and none can take away. To be "fulfilled" and never to lose that joy (perfect tense) is another "special joy" for the proclaimers as they enlarge and strengthen the circle of those who are brought into fellowship with God (cf. "to you . . . you also," v. 3). It is the joy of the sower who sees that the fields are white unto the harvest (John 4:36). In itself it might seem strange that the author speaks of his own joy and not that of the letter's recipients.[46] But the joy of salvation that the addressees experience is part and parcel of their union with God. For himself the author wants to emphasize that proclamation is a matter of giving and receiving. He never states explicitly that the joy of the proclaimers is "fulfilled" in the readers' joy over their salvation (Häring: "A meaningful testimony to mutual love").

EXCURSUS 2

Fellowship with God

The idea of fellowship with God is found in one form or another in every religion. Longing for nearness to God together with awe and reverence for him is one of the basic emotions of religion. It is the way they are combined and the ideas developed in the process that give each religion its particular character. This is equally true of Hellenistic syncretism, itself the product of an age of exceptional religious vitality. Here we must recognize what is peculiar to Christianity and especially to Johannine Christology.

1. As a basis for comparison it is important to recognize that 1 John can express its favorite ideas in various ways. Alongside of "to have fellowship with God," which sounds general enough and is only found in 1:3 and 6, one of the

anything more than "as far as we are concerned"; see 2:20; 3:14; 4:14, 19. There is no Aramaism here, since the personal pronoun would in that case come first.

45. See E. Gulin, *Die Freude im NT, II, Das Joh-Ev* (Helsinki, 1936) 67–71. He says it means the eschatological appearance of the object of joy; however, the meaning "to become full" is certainly not to be excluded (cf. on 2 John 12).

46. The corresponding deviations of the manuscripts are therefore to be regarded as secondary alterations: *hymōn* instead of *hēmōn* is offered by ACP 81 323 1739 2298 pm K Vg[cl] sy[pal] h bo arm. Vg adds: (ut) gaudeatis et (gaudium . . .). Bultmann interprets *hymōn* with reference to the joy of both writers and recipients included (*Theology* 2:82 n. 1). The UBS both times adopts the personal pronoun in the first person plural. Against this a plea is made by J. H. Dobson for *hymōn* instead of *hēmōn* ("Emphatic Personal Pronouns in the New Testament," *Bible Translator* 22 (1971) 58–60.

commonest phrases is "to be in God" (2:5; 5:20) or "to abide" (2:6, 24; 3:24; 4:13, 15, 16). This combination with the typical word "abide" is usually expanded (except in 2:6, 24) into a twofold or reciprocal formula ("we in God and God in us") or vice versa. Since fellowship with the Father and the Son is placed on the same level (1:3; 2:24), we must also include those passages which speak of "abiding in the Son" (2:27, 28; 3:6). We also find the reverse phrase, "God abides in us," independently of the reciprocal formula (4:12). In view of this it may not be methodologically wrong to include within our purview those sayings which speak of "abiding" in other entities closely connected with God, such as "truth" (1:8; 2:4); "his word" (1:10; 2:14; cf. 2:24; 5:10); "his anointing" (2:27); "his seed" (3:9); "eternal life" (3:15); "love" (4:12; cf. 2:5; 3:17). But each of these formulas of immanence requires separate investigation (see Excursus 4). Another expression for fellowship with God found only in John is "to have God (or the Son)" (1 John 2:23; 5:12; 2 John 9). Finally, "to know God" comes to the same thing. It occurs in the perfect tense in 2:3 (cf. 2:5); 2:13, 14 (cf. 1:3) with the same meaning. Though "to know God" is used in its own particular sense (cf. 3:1, 6; 4:6, 7, 8; see Excursus 3), nevertheless the complete knowledge of God stands in the closest relationship to that communion with him which is so much desired (see also John 17:3). All this shows the central significance of this idea, which has a strong connection to other leading concepts, especially that of a "child of God" (3:1–3). For our overall view we may already deduce from this survey the following characteristics:[47]

a) The Christians' fellowship with God is an intimate mutual relationship (cf. the reciprocal formulas). It is not solely a relationship of protection on God's side or of participation on the human side.

b) It may be represented as a mutual interpenetration and has more than a merely moral quality. The terms used for the "abiding" of the divine Being and life in the human are much too real for that.

c) The personality of God and of the human are never compromised: "God" is often represented as "the Father" or "the Son" or both at once (1:3).

d The way to fellowship with the Father is exclusively through the Son (2:23; cf. 5:12, 20). This is a basic christological principle.

e) Fellowship with God is never a momentary thing. It is an experience that is not limited in time, as in mysticism or ecstasy, but is in its very nature a permanent possession ("to abide"; "to have God"), a gift of salvation, and is related to "eternal life."

f) There are important conditions ("if . . .") and criteria ("by this we know") for fellowship with God.

Let us now take a brief look at related forms of expression and imagery on the periphery of early Christianity.

2. Jewish piety was more inclined to emphasize the majesty and

---

47. On this, see L. S. Thornton, *The Common Life in the Body of Christ* (2nd ed.; London, 1944) 156ff.; P. C. Bori, KOINΩNIA: *L'idea della comunione nell'ecclesiologia recente e nel Nuovo Testamento* (Brescia, 1972); J. M. McDermott, "The Biblical Doctrine of κοινωνια," *BZ* n.s. 19 (1975) 64–77.

Prooemium

transcendence of God,[48] even where his nearness is experienced. It therefore hardly offers any point of contact. In the history of Judaism the idea of the covenant is central, that is, the fellowship of the entire people of Israel with God. "I will be their God, and they shall be my people" (Lev. 26:11–12). Even after the covenant is impaired by Israel's unfaithfulness and apostasy—that is, even after God's judgment and punishment of his people—the great promise of the messianic age is renewed (Jer. 7:23; 11:4; 30:22; Ezek. 11:20; 36:28; 37:27; Zech. 8:8). This nearness to God is more than a merely moral relationship. Because of the Temple, it is represented as God's indwelling in the midst of his people (Ezek. 37:27; cf. 40–45; Zech. 2:10–13). Notable is the expression "God with us" (Isa. 7:14; 8:8; cf. Rev. 2:3). The Messiah, as the earthly representative of the heavenly God and King, the vice-regent of his kingdom, will be called "God with us" (Isa. 7:14). But this "with us" (Isa. 8:8) is not the same as "in us" in the full Johannine sense. In contrast to the Jewish concept, our author thinks in individualistic terms.[49] Later Judaism was much too concerned with the fulfillment of the works of the law and with notions of expiation and judgment to be attracted by a mystically oriented piety. Even if fringe groups[50] inclined toward a mystical cult as a means of achieving the union of the soul with God, they remained a closed circle, which does not change the overall picture, and they had no far-reaching influence beyond their own borders. If occasionally pious thinkers like Philo are concerned with the divine image in humanity and with ascent to union with God, they are influenced chiefly by Greek philosophy and Hellenistic mysticism.[51]

---

48. See W. Eichrodt, *Theology of the Old Testament* (Philadelphia, 1961, 1967) 2:30ff. Bousset-Gressmann, *Religion,* 358ff., esp. 373ff. The following authors, however, rightly place more emphasis on the kindly, fatherly traits of God: Moore, *Judaism in the First Centuries of the Christian Era* (Cambridge, 1927–30) 1:357ff.; 2:201ff. V. Hamp, *Der Begriff 'Wort' in der aramäischen Bibelübersetzung* (Munich, 1938) 73–79; E. Sjöberg, *Gott und die Sünde im palästinischen Judentum* (Stuttgart, 1938) 184ff.; 261ff.—For a balanced view, see J. Bonsirven, *Le judaïsme palestinien au temps de Jésus-Christ* (Paris, 1934, 1935) 1:196ff.

49. Although religious individualism became more widespread in the postexilic period, this did not lead to a mystical piety. The distance between humanity and God remains considerable, although one could approach the "Father in heaven" full of confidence (see Moore, *Judaism* 2:202ff. with a somewhat different accent, the rationalism of later Jewish theology). See Bonsirven, *Judaïsme* 1:220f.

50. For the Essenes, P. Volz assumes a mystery cult leading to the union of the soul with the deity (*Die Eschatologie der jüdischen Gemeinde im neutestamentlichen Zeitalter* [Tübingen, 1934] 131); similarly H. Preisker, *Neutestamentliche Zeitgeschichte* (Berlin, 1937) 255. Against this view, L. Marchel ("Esséniens," *DBSup* 2:1115) supposes that they were people who cared more for asceticism and were moralists rather than speculative thinkers. For their meals, see also Bousset-Gressmann, *Religion,* 460 (no thought of the mysteries).—The problem of Jewish mysticism has been little investigated for this period. However, since we now have the Qumran texts as evidence for an Essene group, and since these texts offer no evidence to confirm that type of piety (see further in the text above), that idea—already questioned in earlier times (see Bousset-Gressmann, *Religion,* 458ff.)—must be abandoned. On the beginnings of Jewish mysticism and its views (throne mysticism), see G. G. Scholem, *Die jüdische Mystik in ihren Hauptströmungen* (Zurich, 1957) 43–86; idem, *Jewish Gnosticism, Merkabah Mysticism and Talmudic Tradition* (New York, 1960) 9–35.

51. On Philo, see Bousset-Gressmann, *Religion,* 452f.; W. Völker, *Fortschritt und Vollendung bei Philo von Alexandrien* (Leipzig, 1938) 288ff., esp. 314.

Instructive is the stance of the devout at Qumran, where it mainly appears in the "hymns of praise" (*Hodayoth*). The devotees are filled with gratitude and joy for the knowledge they have received from God, the revelation of the divine "secrets," and their "lifting up" into fellowship with the "children of heaven." But all this is understood in quite a different way from mysticism and gnosis. The "elect" are always conscious of the great gulf between themselves and God. They are always mindful that they are "creatures of earth," "worms," and "sinners" (1QH 1:21ff.; 3:24f.; 4:29f.; 6:34; 10:3ff.; etc.). They praise God for having granted them to be "raised up to everlasting height" and for having "cleansed a perverse spirit of great sin that it may stand with the host of the Holy Ones and that it may enter into the community with the congregation of the Sons of Heaven" (3:19–22 [Vermes, p. 158]; cf. 11:13–14; 18:29; fragment 2, line 20). All this is nothing more than an association with the heavenly hosts and the hope of complete union with them. Their actual relationship with God depends on their faithful fulfillment of the law and on God's fidelity to his elect. "Those who please Thee shall stand before Thee forever; those who walk in the way of Thy heart shall be established for evermore" (4:21–22 [Vermes, p. 162]). This is reminiscent of 1 John 2:17, but there are no signs of any deeper fellowship with God or of actual union with him. Qumran piety remains for the most part what it was in the Old Testament.[52]

3. Again, the utterances of religiously attuned philosophy, especially Stoicism, have quite a different meaning from 1 John's conception of fellowship with God. This is true even if at first sight they sound familiar to Christian ears. There is a terminological echo in the New Testament itself, in Paul's speech on the Areopagus, for example (Acts 17:28). Both the first part ("in him we live") and the second, an explicit quotation from Cleanthes' hymn to Zeus and from Aratus's *Phaenomena* 5, breathe the spirit of contemporary popular Stoicism. It speaks of God as the Father of humankind and Father of the gods. It also speaks of humanity's kinship (*syngeneia*) with God and draws ethical consequences from the fact. An instructive example of this is the lecture of Epictetus. He asks what it means to call God the Father of mankind.[53] First he quotes an old Stoic precept: We have in the first place been brought into being by God, and he is the Father of humankind and of the gods. Epictetus goes on to develop what is common between humanity and God, viz., reason and will. Finally, he regrets how few are conscious of this dignity or make use of their minds in a manner that befits their relationship with God. Such teaching about the divine cosmic Reason (Logos), which is deeply grounded in the Stoic system and which speaks of Reason as a seed implanted in humankind, retreats into the background in popular presentations.[54] But it does reveal the great gulf between this kind of philosophy, which is at bottom pantheistic, and the

---

52. F. Nötscher, *Zur theologischen Terminologie der Qumran-Texte* (Bonn, 1956) 38–63; M. Burrows, *The Dead Sea Scrolls* (New York, 1955) 209ff.; idem, *More Light on the Dead Sea Scrolls* (New York, 1958) 293ff.; K. Schubert, *Die Gemeinde vom Toten Meer* (Munich/Basel, 1958) 62–69; S. Holm-Nielsen, *Hodayot: Psalms from Qumran* (Aarhus, 1960) 274–91; M. Mansoor, *The Thanksgiving Hymns* (Leiden, 1961) 65–74.

53. *Diss.*, 1.3.

54. Ibid., 1.9.4f.

Christian view of God. Correspondingly, when the Stoics speak of "fellowship with God" they mean nothing more than a purely natural affinity and relationship with the deity. In fact, by Christian standards it is something less than that, since they have no idea of the personality of God.[55] There is at this point no bridge between Stoicism and the Johannine concept of fellowship with God, which is intimate and personal and is based on the sharing of a common life. Philo of Alexandria is influenced by Stoicism, though he obviously derives his notions from other sources as well, such as mysticism and ecstasy.

4. We may further ask what is the relationship between the Johannine concept of fellowship with God and the piety of Greek "enthusiasm." Both in etymology and in content *enthousiasmos* is derived from *en theō*.[56] The religion of Dionysus, according to modern scholarship, is very ancient and drew the Greek soul under its spell from early times. With its ecstatic element it creates an entirely different religious atmosphere from the religion of the Olympic deities. It is a crazy world in which "sacred frenzy" reigns.[57] To this mystery piety, with its strong focus on experience, its wallowing in the inebriation of divine inspiration, there can be no greater contrast than the piety of the Johannine writings, with its emphasis on faith, its lucidity of mind, and its ethical sobriety—and, on the other hand, its fervent love. Though the author of 1 John has a high view of fellowship with God, a fellowship that is consummated only in the eschatological vision of God (3:2), he nowhere describes or even hints at any mystical experiences such as those of vision or ecstasy. He explicitly rejects any idea of a physical vision of God on earth (4:12; cf. v. 20). Nor does he describe in further detail the effects of *pneuma,* God-given though it be (3:24; 4:13). If the "anointing" of 2:20 and 27 is to be identified with the Spirit (see the commentary ad loc.) we find that it too stands preeminently in the service of the illumination and confirming of faith. Fellowship with God is attained through faith rather than through ecstasy. It is a continual experience of salvation, not a passing experience of sacred frenzy.

5. Ecstasy of a different kind is to be found in Gnosis, with its union in God, whether it be described as vision, deification, rebirth, or in other ways. But it lacks the theatrical element of the mysteries. Its way is not that of the *drōmenon,* the rite that was enacted in the mysteries, but knowledge of God, which liberates humanity from the material world, from the *timoria tēs hylēs,* and ascends into the higher world of light, to the heavenly spheres. These

---

55. Ibid., 2.19.26f. For the rest it is sufficient to refer to the relevant literature, including E. Rohde, *Psyche* 2:310ff.; A. Bonhöffer, *Epiktet und das NT* (Giessen, 1911) 51f., 358f.; M. Pohlenz, *Die Stoa* I (Göttingen, 1948) 338 etc. (with further bibliography); M. P. Nilsson, *Geschichte der griechischen Religion* (Munich, 1941–50) 2:379f.

56. See Rohde, *Psyche* 2:89ff.; R. Reitzenstein, *Die hellenistische Mysterienreligionen* (Leipzig, 1927) 333ff.; G. Schrenk, "Geist und Enthusiasmus," *Wort und Geist* (Festschrift K. Heim; Berlin, 1934) 75–97 (differentiates strongly between life in the Spirit and enthusiasm—they are mutually exclusive alternatives [p. 87]); F. Pfister, *Pisciculi* (Festschrift F. J. Dölger; Münster, 1939) 178–91 (*contra* Rohde); A. Oepke, *TDNT* 2:449ff.; M.-J. Lagrange, *Critique historique, I, Les Mystères: L'Orphisme* (Paris, 1937) 82ff.; H. Hanse, *'Gott haben' in der Antike und im frühen Christentum* (Berlin, 1939) 35ff.; M. P. Nilsson, *Geschichte der griechischen Religion* 2:379f.

57. See the picture offered by Rohde, *Psyche* 2:11ff.; W. F. Otto, *Dionysos: Mythos und Kultus* (Frankfurt am Main, 1933) 87ff.; Lagrange, *L'Orphisme,* 51ff.

concepts, more spiritualized than the sensuous and frenetic phenomena of the cult of Dionysus, are undoubtedly closer to the Johannine terminology and world of thought (see Excursus 3 on Gnosis). Yet there is a considerable gulf between their respective terms. The so-called *Mithras Liturgy* describes union with God as a kind of ascent of the soul. It conceives the ensuing *unio mystica* in the world above in ecstatic terms as a permanent indwelling of God in humankind. The mystic gives utterance to the prayer "Abide with me in my soul" (14, 24–25). This is — maybe with the exception of the idea of becoming the child of God (6, 2, 12) — perhaps the strongest point of contact with 1 John. But both in language (the reciprocal formulas of 1 John) and even more in idea, the differences are striking. Primarily, the believing Christians do not need to "step out of themselves" (*ek-stasis*) through illumination or vision, or to ascend from this earth to some higher world. Christians can find in this world (see 1 John 4:17c), by faith in the Son of God alone (3:23; 5:12, 13), their fellowship with God.

Let us now turn to the *13th Hermetic Tract* "Concerning Rebirth." Here the indoctrinated mystic, coached by Hermes, experiences rebirth. The mystic becomes detached from the impression of the senses. As the vision reaches its climax, in the consummate moment of deification, the mystic cries: "I am in heaven, on earth, in water, in the air . . . everywhere" (11). "Father, I see the All and myself in Mind" (13).[58] This is a mysticism of deification, with overtones of pantheism. Such mysticism, involving union with the deity, finds its strongest expression in the affirmations of identity which occur in a number of magical incantations. "I know you, Hermes, and you know me. I am you, and you I."[59] The Johannine statements are clearly poles apart from this sort of thing. They never obscure the boundary between humanity and God. The believer who is raised into the divine sphere (1 John 3:14), who is "born of God" (2:29), will never achieve identity with God. Rather, such a person will have real communion with God and will attain to participation in the divine life and love and all its blessings. That person becomes "a child of God" (3:1) and acquires a divine nature ("of God"); 3:10; 4:4, 6; 5:19), which must work itself out and express itself in concrete behavior.

The *Odes of Solomon* provide an example of this ecstatic and mystical piety in the syncretistic guise of Christian gnosticism.[60] To describe the intimate fellowship with God which the soul attains in its ascent to "the light of truth"

---

58. W. Scott attempts a conjecture (*Hermetica* 1:246): πάτερ, τὸ πᾶν ὁρῶ ἐμαυτὸν ὄντα, ἐν τῷ νοῖ ὁρῶ. Even if this construction of the text is too bold, it may nevertheless be a correct interpretation. In the all-embracing vision of the divine totality, the mystic enters into his/her true self (and probably for that reason is taken out of self, *kai emauton*). The visionary is divinized and becomes part of the All. Cf. 30.2: ἄλλος ἔσται ὁ γεννώμενος, θεοῦ θεὸς παῖς, τὸ πᾶν, ἐν παντί. Scott refers further in his exposition (2:391) to 11.20.

59. Magic prayer 2.7 in Reitzenstein, *Poimandres* (Leipzig, 1904) 20f.; see further pp. 242–44. See also *CHerm* 5.11; σὺ γὰρ εἶ ὃ [ἐ]ὰν ὦ, ὃ ἂν ποιῶ, σὺ εἶ, ὃ ἂν λέγω, σὺ γὰρ πάντα εἶ; on this see Nock-Festugière, n. 33 (pp. 68f.).

60. On the *Odes of Solomon* (second century C.E.), see R. Abramowski, "Der Christus der Salomooden," *ZNW* 35 (1936) 44–69; J. Daniélou, *DBSup* 6:677–84; F.-M. Braun, *Jean le Théologien*, 224–51; S. Schulz, *RGG*³ 5:1339–42; J. Schmid, *LTK* 7:1094f.

(38:1, a frequently occurring notion; cf. 4:9; 21:5) the *Odes* use a whole plethora of symbols. They speak, for instance, of conjugal love,[61] of being clothed in the form of the Redeemer,[62] of the divine indwelling,[63] of drinking milk from the breasts,[64] etc. What all this means is that redemption is accomplished through gnosis (cf. 8:8ff.;11:4; etc.) while the figure of the Redeemer ("Son," "Christ," or "Lord") is understood in terms of the gnostic redeemer myth.[65] But all this is cloaked in a symbolic language that is mystical, enthusiastic, and veiled in secrecy. These curious lyrics are permeated with gratitude for the gnosis which God has given and which leads to union with him. They are exuberant with the bliss of knowledge (see 11:7–8) and ecstatic jubilation (21:6ff.). To the author of 1 John, with his ethical and practical outlook, such symbols or imageries and the warmth of emotion they depict are utterly alien. Our author is not a mystic, if by mysticism we mean extraordinary experiences of union with God. Fellowship with the deity, in his view, is open to all who have faith in Christ. On the other hand, so intimate is their mutual union with him, and through him with God, that we might call it an "existential mysticism" (*Seinsmystik*).

6. Wherever we look, on closer inspection, the author of 1 John never loses his unique view of fellowship with God. Through Christ, the Son of God, the believers enter personally into fellowship with the deity in the reality of their being. It is a living fellowship in which they also acquire the hope of a consummated union still to come (cf. 2:25; 3:2–3). In no way can this final union with God be hastened, neither by ecstasy, nor by visions, nor by sacred inebriation or frenetic behavior, nor through elevated gnosis. The way to it is open to all through faith, provided they accept the divine testimony (5:9–10), viz., the message of human witnesses and proclaimers (1:2–3, 5). It is not reserved for a privileged elite, for prophets, mystics, or charismatics. It promises the same for all and demands the same from all. As far as his language is concerned, the author has gnosis primarily in mind, not without reason, for he was confronted by heretical gnostic teachers. But with his high estimate of the importance of ethics ("keep the commandments") he preserves the best of his Jewish heritage except that he improves on it in the light of Jesus' teaching (the love commandment, the absence of any idea of merit or achievement). What Jesus promises is not one whit inferior to the magic melodies of other movements so long as they do not deceive but call to action. It even surpasses them all since it can point to the great event of salvation which has already occurred, the epiphany of God in Christ.

---

61. *Odes Sol.* 3:3ff.; 7:1f.; 8:13, 22; 28:6; 38:11; 42:8f.
62. *Odes Sol.* 7:4; 17:4; 33:12; cf. also the putting on of the body of light in *Odes Sol.* 11:10f.; 21:3.
63. *Odes Sol.* 32:1; 33:8; cf. 10:2.
64. *Odes Sol.* 4:10; 8:16; 14:2; 19:1ff. 35:5.
65. See esp. *Odes Sol.* 3; 7; 10; 17; 29; 31; 42; on this, see Abramowski, *ZNW* 35 (1936) 44–69.

PART ONE

Fellowship with God Means Walking in the Light: Its Realization in the World (1 John 1:5-2:17)

Part One, 1:5-2:17, clearly forms a unit. It develops the theme of fellowship with God (1:6), already touched on in the prooemium (1:3). It lays bare the conditions for the realization of this fellowship (1:6, 8; 2:3, 9), draws out its implications for walking in the light (1:7; 2:9-11), and emphasizes the hurdles that face it from the "world," where the powers opposed to God are at work (2:12-17). This complex of ideas is not discussed systematically, but all through there is an unremitting conflict with the moral heresy of gnosticism (cf. the reference to the opponents' opinions with the words "if we say," 1:6, 8, 10; "whoever says," 2:4, 6, 9). The unity of theme is given not only in the metaphor of walking in the light, which appears at the beginning (1:5-7) and reaches its climax in 2:9-11, but also in other equivalents for fellowship with God. These are phrases picked up from the heretical teachers: "to know God" (2:3, 4); "to be in him" (2:5b) or "to abide in him" (2:6), which the author continues to use when addressing the community (2:13-14). The challenge to resist the evil one (2:13, 14) and the warning against the powers that are invading the world (2:15-17) also serve to strengthen fellowship with God. A new theme is broached in 2:18ff. In this section the author is concerned with the antichrists and their slogans. These are incompatible with the church's message and involve errors in Christology.

Scholars have different views about the subdivisions of this first main part. Neither style criticism with its hypothesis of an original written source (von Dobschütz, Bultmann) nor rhythmical patterns (Lohmeyer) offer suitable clues, since this whole part really defies clear and convincing analysis. To divide it up under the rubrics of "the message" (1:5-2:6) and "the commandment" (2:7-17), as F. Hauck does, breaks down, because his kerygmatic section is mainly concerned with ethics (from 1:7 on), and indeed with parenesis (2:1, 6), while the commandment section (2:9-11) contains kerygmatic statements just as much as the first section does. The whole passage would seem to be a loosely connected series of ideas put together at random. An initial series of small units developing like one cell from another continues from 1:5 through 2:2. At the end of the antithesis light—darkness, which dominates vv. 5-7, the word "sin" occurs! This word strikes the keynote for the following verses, 8-10, The fact of sin ("we . . . have sinned," v. 10) must be admitted, despite the divine imperative that we should walk in the light. But Christians are expected to triumph increasingly over the power of sin (2:1a), This idea serves as a bridge leading to the next thought, namely, that Jesus Christ is the atoning sacrifice and our advocate with the Father (2:1-2). But here the chain of thought breaks off. The transition from Jesus to "his" commandments is artificial and made more difficult by the uncertain meaning of the word advocate.[2] The previously dominant theme of sin is dropped at 2:2. With 2:3 the author makes a fresh start, slanting the main theme, that of fellowship with God, in a different direction. The central point now becomes "keeping the commandments" (vv. 3, 4) or "his word" (v. 5). This theme, basically covered in 2:3-6 and in vv. 5b-6, focused on Jesus and his way of life, becomes more specific in 2:7-11 with its reference to the one commandment, to love the brothers and sisters. First, this is described as a commandment that is both old and new (vv. 7-8). Then comes a new unit of thought, held together in vv. 7-8 by the key word "light." This is now openly and clearly defined as mutual love (vv. 9-11). At the same time these verses point back to the metaphor of walking in the light, which we met right at the beginning of Part One. Thus the whole section is rounded off. Nor is there any key word or thought to form a bridge between 2:12 and 13. A new paragraph begins at v. 13. The last third of Part One (2:13-17) contains admonitions to the members of the community: (1) advice and encouragement (vv. 12-13); (2) a word of warning not to love this world (vv. 15-17). This last section offers, as it were, an application of the previous train of thought to the needs of the readers.

As a result we are left with the following divisions—not that the author deliberately intended them, but they can be inferred from the text. The message: God is light and in him there is no darkness (1:5).

I. Fellowship with God, and sin (1:6-2:2).
    1. Fellowship with God means walking in light (vv. 6-7).
    2. The fact of sin is undeniable; sin must be confessed (vv. 8-10).
    3. Jesus Christ takes care of the removal of our sins (2:1-2).
II. Knowing God and keeping his commandments (2:3-11).
    1. Knowledge of God requires us to keep his commandments and to walk in the way of Jesus Christ (vv. 3-6).
    2. In particular the commandment is both old and new (vv. 7-8).
    3. Only the one who fulfills this command, that is, mutual love, is in the light (vv. 9-11).
III. Application to the readers (2:12-17).
    1. Words of encouragement: the readers have fellowship with God and are strong in the combat with the evil one (vv. 12-14).
    2. Admonition: the readers must not love the world and what is in it (vv. 15-17).

The result of this analysis is particularly valuable for the second paragraph:

---

1. Bultmann overlooks this point in his analysis ("Analyse," 140), when he brackets v. 7c and omits it from his hypothetical *Vorlage*.

2. For that reason 2:1-6 can hardly be included in the very general theme of "the significance of Jesus" (*contra* Büchsel).

1. It turns out that the phrase "by this we know" (2:3) continues the thesis of 1:6ff. with renewed determination. In confirmation of this, the opponents' arguments are introduced into the first paragraph three times with the words "if we say" (vv. 6:8, 10), and in the new section three times over with the words "whoever says" (2:4, 6, 9). The author likes to vary his wording in a way that makes no real difference to the meaning. This is shown by the different words he uses for fellowship with God.

2. This makes clear the antecedent of the word "him" (*auton*) (2:3ff.)—not Jesus Christ (2:1f.) but God himself. In this paragraph Jesus Christ is introduced with the Greek word *ekeinos* (NRSV "he," literally, "that one," 2:6; cf. 3:3, 5, 7, 16; 4:17).[3]

3. This shows that there is no major division before 2:7 (cf. Nestle). The theme of keeping the commandments is merely alluded to. The juxtaposition of plural and singular is typically Johannine; cf. John 15:10 with 12; 14:23 ("my word") with 15:21 (the same in 14:31 according to the reading in BLX al. lat.); 1 John 3:22 with 23; 2 John (4, 5) 6a with 6b. The transition is created by the idea of Jesus as the model for Christian behavior (v. 6). But he enunciates the old commandment, which on his lips, however, is the new commandment of love (v. 7; cf. John 13:34f.—to be amplified with "from him" as in 1:5).

THE MESSAGE: GOD IS LIGHT
AND IN HIM THERE IS NO DARKNESS (1 JOHN 1:5)

[5]This is the message we have heard from him and proclaimed to you, that God is light and in him there is no darkness at all.

* * *

1:5 To indicate the content of the proclamation (v. 3a) the author refers to a message about God.[4] This is because his major theme is fellowship with the Father (v. 3b). He links up with his earlier statement "we . . . have heard and we declare" (v. 3a), though with a slight change in the Greek (*anangellomen* instead of *apangellomen*).[5] In so doing he mentions that he and his fellow preachers have received this message from Jesus Christ ("from him"),[6] whose

---

3. That the *ekeinos* ought to be an *autos* according to the logic of the sentence as Bultmann thinks ("Analyse," 144), would be appropriate only if related to a more distant noun, in this case to Jesus Christ. The attribution of vv. 2:5c–6 to the parenetic redaction of the author in distinction from vv. 2:4–5b, which allegedly belonged to the *Vorlage,* demonstrates the fragile nature of this hypothesis. Bultmann himself shifts his ground as to whether *ho legōn en autō menein* should be regarded as a fragment of the *Vorlage.* See the stylistic echo in 2:4 and 9, which Bultmann assigns to the *Vorlage.*

4. *Angelia* occurs elsewhere only in 3:11, followed by a *hina*-clause=a command; usually to be understood as good news (Prov. 12:25; 25:25); without an adjective but in contrast to *kaka* (Isa. 28:9).—The transition *kai estin autē* with a reference to what follows is a linguistic peculiarity of the author; cf. 3:11, 23; 4:21; 5:3, 4, 11, 14.

5. Stylistic variation or nonessential change, since *anangellein* perhaps emphasizes more strongly the idea of "repeating what has been heard"; see P. Joüon, *RechScR* 28 (1938) 234f.; BAGD 51, s.v. 2. This word, a favorite one in Koine, often has a solemn resonance=“to proclaim"; cf. Schniewind, *TDNT* 1:61f., 64.

6. Classical, and occurring overwhelmingly in the New Testament, *akouein para,* though in the

revelatory activity during his earthly life is mentioned several times in the letter, though we can only infer that it is the basis of the proclamation (cf. 2:7f.; 3:11; 4:21; 5:11). It is not explicitly stated. Jesus alone was able to proclaim this message from God. It is hidden from human eyes (4:12; cf. John 1:18; 6:46). It is not elaborated here but presumed (cf. John 1:18; 3:32). As the Revealer, the Johannine Jesus is fond of claiming to be the "light" or "light of the world" (8:12; 9:5; 12:35f., 46; as well as 1:4, 5, 9). The author of John uses the term "light" to speak of the reality of God — not, however, in the sense of revelation, but in the sense of his heavenly fullness of being and moral holiness. The image of light is an almost inexhaustible treasure trove for the religious imagination of all time. In Johannine thought it is used in many different ways.[7]

The statement that "God is light" represents the core and keynote all through Part One. He is the revelation and the message, a point that does not have to be proved. The author imparts an inner attraction and warmth to the theme of fellowship with God. There is hardly any other idea that so fired up the religious yearnings of antiquity, especially in Hellenism, as that of life and light. To draw near to the heavenly world of light through gnosis and ecstasy was the blessed promise of all mysticism.[8] Much of magic was associated with light and was used to attain this goal.[9] For the Mandeans in particular, God was the "high king of light," the "pure radiance and supreme luminary which passes not away." He is the "Lord of all worlds of light" and so on. He is surrounded by angels in glory,[10] and to participate in this glorious world of light is humanity's greatest hope, sung by tongues that never tire. "The righteous who have heard

---

Koine *apo* is also possible; see Acts 9:13; BDF §173.1 and 210.3. See also A. T. Robertson, *A Grammar of the Greek New Testament in the Light of Historical Research* (New York, 1919) 613, 615.

7. See G. P. Wetter, *Phos* (1915); F. J. Dölger, *Sol salutis* (1920); O. Schäfer, *StudKrit* 105 (1933) 467–76; F. Auer, *ThGl* 28 (1936) 397–407; E. R. Goodenough, *By Light, Light* (1935); W. Bauer, *Das Johannesevangelium* (Lietzmann 6; Tübingen, 1933) 13f.; Bultmann, *John,* 43ff.; idem, "Zur Geschichte der Lichtsymbolik im Altertum," *Philol.* 97 (1948) 1–36; E. Percy, *Untersuchungen über den Ursprung der joh. Theologie* (Lund, 1939) 23–79; *Eranos-Jahrbuch* (1934). For late Judaism, see H. Odeberg, *The Fourth Gospel* (Amsterdam, 1929; repr. 1968) 139–49; S. Aalen, *Die Begriffe 'Licht' und 'Finsternis' im AT, im Spätjudentum und im Rabbinismus* (Oslo, 1951) (abundant material); Nötscher, *Zur theologischen Terminologie der Qumran-Texte,* 92–148. For GJohn, see also J. C. Bott, "De notione lucis in scriptis S. Joannis Ap.," *VD* 19 (1939) 81–91, 117–22; Wikenhauser, *Johannes,* 77–79; P. Feine and K. Aland, *Theologie des NT* (Berlin, 1949–51) 346–48; Dupont, *Essais,* 61–105; Mussner, ZΩH, 164–71; B. Bussmann, *Der Begriff des Lichtes beim hl. Johannes* (Münster, 1957).

8. See *CHerm* 1.32: εἰς ζωὴν καὶ φῶς χωρῶ as the aim of the tractate; before this §§6, 9, 12, 17, 21, 28; the so-called Λόγος τέλειος of Pseudo-Asclepius (P. Mimaut): ἐγνωρίσαμέν σε, ὧ ζωὴ ἀληθὲς τῆς ἀνθρωπίνης ζωῆς, ἐγνωρίσαμέν (σε), ὧ φῶς μέγιστον ἀπάσης γνώσεως; *Odes Sol.* 10:6: "And the traces of light were set upon their heart, and they walked according to my life and were saved"; cf. 6:17; 7:14; 11:11; 12:7; 29:7f.; the upper world of light (light of lights in *Pistis Sophia;* the *photismos* in the mystery religions. In addition to the literature in the previous note, see further Reitzenstein, *Hellenistische Mysterienreligionen,* 264f.; 292; W. Bousset, *Kyrios Christos* (Eng. trans. Nashville, 1971) 232ff.

9. See the magic prayer in which the magician stared into the world of light (Reitzenstein, *Poimandres,* 25ff.).

10. *Ginza* 5.17 etc. (see index s.v. *Lichtkönig, Lichtwelt*); *MandLit* 65.1f. "The place where all of life, splendor, light, and glory are"; *Ginza* 11.4ff.; 31.25ff.; 32.18ff. etc. (see index, s.v. *Engel des Lichtes, des Glanzes*).

the message and accepted it in faith ascend victorious and enjoy the vision of the abode of light."[11] Contrary to all ecstatic mysticism, the New Testament never loses sight of the distance between God and humanity. God dwells "in unapproachable light" (1 Tim. 6:16). The New Testament does not deny this general yearning for God, which was common in antiquity, but looks for its fulfillment only at the end, or only after death (cf. 3:2; also Matt. 5:8; 1 Cor. 13:12). Consequently, any reader, on hearing that God is light, would be touched as it were by a magic sound inviting him or her to enjoy that same light. But the author has a different intention. For he has no mystical proclivities. Verse 5 is formulated with an eye to vv. 6f., where walking in the light is presented as a moral obligation. Equally v. 5 is one of the great wisdom sayings, like John 4:24 (God is Spirit) and 1 John 4:16 (God is love). This view of God does not have a merely moral aspect, but rather the reverse. Rather his moral being derives from the depths of his nature. It is this theological profundity that renders the morality of the heretics untenable. In this Christian exposition of the divine being it must be insisted, contrary to all nature religion, that the light (whether sun or moon) is never elevated to divine status. Rather the reverse is true. The nature of God is made clear by the quality of light (see v. 7, "He is in the light"). This is very different from pagan mysticism. The heavenly glory does not permeate humanity in a magic sort of way. Humanity does not dwell ecstatically in heavenly light (note the moral emphasis in the phrase "walking in the light," vv. 6 and 7). This is poles apart from what we find in gnosticism. The antithesis between light and darkness is not one between two primeval principles (see below).

When the author wrote v. 5 he already had in mind the pernicious morality of the heretics which he is going to attack in the ensuing verses. This is clear from the negative statement "and in him there is no darkness at all." That is just the point. The opponents are walking in darkness (v. 6). Within the framework of the metaphysical assertion about the nature of God in v. 5, the author wants to emphasize only the unblemished holiness of the deity (cf. James 1:17), the fullness of his divine being.[12] He says nothing of another realm existing separately from him, the realm of evil.[13] The dualistic language in 1 John has primarily an ethical focus (see also 2:8-11). The gnostic dualism is transcended by the shift to a moral concern (see 3:8ff.) and by an emphasis on the superiority of God and the way in which he strengthens the Christians in their moral conflict.

---

11. *Ginza* 20.27f.; cf. 42.23ff.; 51.20ff. etc.—See G. Kittel, *Die Herrlichkeit Gottes* (BZNW 16; Giessen, 1934) 115-24; Jonas, *Gnosis und spätantiker Geist*, 103; Percy, *Untersuchungen*, 23ff.

12. For the way it is expressed, see the Mandean texts: ". . . he is the Light in whom there is no darkness, the Living One in whom there is no death, the Good One in whom there is no wickedness . . ." (*Ginza* 6.26-7.2). As a contrast to this: "(Go) to the world of darkness without a ray of light, to the world of persecution and of death without light forever" (*Ginza* 33.5ff.).—In the rabbis too we meet the expression "God is all light," but without the dualistic contrast, see Aalen, *'Licht' und 'Finsternis'*, 317f.

13. *Contra* Windisch, ad loc., according to whom darkness ought to "be a realm of its own, distinct from God"; cf. 2:8-11.

Fellowship with God

This ethical dualism in the use of the metaphor of light and darkness is found also in late Judaism. It is the main point in the *Testaments of the Twelve Patriarchs,* which have been known for a long time. Scholars may argue today about the Jewish or Christian provenance of this work.[14] But there can be no doubt that it provides evidence for later Jewish tradition. In *T. Levi* 19:1 we read: "Choose for yourselves light or darkness, the Law of the Lord or the works of Beliar."[15] This kind of thinking is now confirmed by the Qumran texts. These include a work called *The War of the Sons of Light and the Sons of Darkness* (1QM). The same idea also appears in the *Community Rule* (1QS). Here we have the same dualistic contrast applied to the realm of religious ethics. Whoever enters into the covenant of God must love "all the sons of light" and hate "all the sons of darkness" (1:9f.). Henceforth they must walk in "the way of light" (cf. 3:3, 20). In the instruction on the two spirits (3:13–4:26) the way of light is described in a catalogue of virtues (4:2–6) and is contrasted with the way of darkness described in a catalogue of vices (4:9, 11). This antithesis between light and darkness is paralleled by that between truth and falsehood. This may well be the closest approach to the dualism of the Johannine writings.[16]

In other religious texts of Judaism one misses the strong dualistic tension. They use the idea of light in quite a different manner. The Old Testament and the apocalyptic literature employ it mainly in eschatological contexts to describe the blessedness, peace, and perfection of the new age, the time of salvation.[17] For Philo, the light of knowledge stands in the foreground,[18] though occasionally he compares virtue with divine light.[19] Rabbinic theology speaks of the Torah, the Temple, and other important institutions as "the light of the world."[20]

---

14. For Christian origin, see esp. M. de Jonge, *The Testaments of the Twelve Patriarchs* (Assen, 1953); for the opposite view, see M. Philonenko, "Les interpolations chrétiennes des Testaments des Douze Patriarches et les manuscrits de Qumran," *RHPR* 38 (1958) 308–43; 39 (1959) 14–38; for a reply, see M. de Jonge, "Christian Influence in the Testaments of the Twelve Patriarchs," *NovT* 4 (1960) 182–235. See also B. Otzen, "Die neugefundenen hebräischen Sektenschriften und die Testamente der zwölf Patriarchen," *StT* 7 (1954) 124–57; F.-M. Braun, "Les Testaments des XII Patriarches et le problème de leur origine," *RB* 67 (1960) 516–49 (for Jewish origin).

15. See *T. Levi* 14:3ff.; *T. Gad* 5:7; *T. Benj.* 5:3; also *1 Enoch* 58:6; 92:4; *4 Enoch* (Greek) 30:15; on this, see P. Billerbeck, *Kommentar zum NT aus Talmud und Midrasch* (Munich, 1922–28) 2:427f.; Odeberg, *Fourth Gospel,* 140ff.; R. Eppel, *Le Piétisme juif dans les Testaments des Douze Patriarches* (Paris, 1930) 77–89; Aalen, *'Licht' und 'Finsternis',* 178–83.

16. See Otzen, *StT* 7 (1954) 124–57; Nötscher, *Zur theologischen Terminologie,* 92–99; H. W. Huppenbauer, *Der Mensch zwischen zwei Welten* (Zurich, 1959) 16–29; S. Wibbing, *Die Tugend- und Lasterkatalog im Neuen Testament und ihre Traditionsgeschichte unter besonderer Berücksichtigung der Qumrantexte* (Berlin, 1959) 61–68.

17. See Isa. 2:5; 9:1; 60:1–3, 19f.; Zech. 14:7; etc.; *1 Enoch* 58:3ff.; 96:3; 108:12; *Pss. Sol.* 3:16; Billerbeck *Kommentar* 2:428; Volz, *Eschatologie,* 364ff.; Aalen, *'Licht' und 'Finsternis',* 195–202.

18. See *Somn.* 1.72: τοῦθ' (= φῶς θεοῦ) ὅταν μὲν ἐπιλάμψῃ διανοίᾳ, τὰ δεύτερα λόγων δεύται φέγγη, πολὺ δὲ μᾶλλον οἱ αἰσθητοὶ τόποι πάντες ἐπισκιάζονται; Heres 264; *Migr.* 39; *Somn.* 2.74; *Fuga* 136; in addition *Somn.* 1.75, where there is a formal parallel to Ps. 27:1: πρῶτον μὲν ὁ Θεὸς φῶς ἐστι.

19. See *Leg. all.* 1.18; *Conf.* 61.

20. On the law, see already Ps. 119:105; Prov. 6:23; for the rest, see Billerbeck, *Kommentar* 1:237; Aalen, *'Licht' und 'Finsternis',* 273–80; Nötscher, *Zur theologischen Terminologie,* 108f.

Even if 1 John shows similarities to these writings in its dualistic way of thinking and its ethical emphasis, there are nevertheless certain differences. In 1 John there is no demonology such as we find in the *Testaments of the Twelve Patriarchs,* the only exception being the evil one and Beliar as the counterpart of God and Christ. Also missing in the *Testaments* is the realistic doctrine of salvation we find in the Johannine writings. In 1 John there is no separation of the sons of light and no condemnation of the sons of darkness. People are warned of but not consigned to damnation. Instead, the focus is on God, the epitome and source of light. Was this particular dualism gnostic in character, a gnosticism in contact with certain types of Judaism? That is a question that can hardly be answered at this distance in time. In 1 John 1:5ff. the strong moral accent in its doctrine of divine being is the main point in the author's attack on the gnostic heretics and their perverse notions about the divine light and the way to reach it.[21]

FIRST SECTION

FELLOWSHIP WITH GOD AND SIN (1 JOHN 1:6–2:2)

[6]If we say that we have fellowship with him while we are walking in darkness, we lie and do not do what is true; [7]but if we walk in the light as he himself is in the light, we have fellowship with one another, and the blood of Jesus his Son cleanses us from all sin. [8]If we say that we have no sin, we deceive ourselves, and the truth is not in us. [9]If we confess our sins, he who is faithful and just will forgive us our sins and cleanse us from all unrighteousness. [10]If we say that we have not sinned, we make him a liar, and his word is not in us.

2:1 My little children, I am writing these things to you so that you may not sin. But if anyone does sin, we have an advocate with the Father, Jesus Christ the righteous; [2]and he is the atoning sacrifice for our sins, and not for ours only but also for the sins of the whole world. * * *

1. Fellowship with God Means Walking in the Light
(1 John 1:6–7)

The fellowship with God that the heretical teachers claim ("we have") must be demonstrated to be illusory in character. This is achieved by the metaphor of light. They walk in darkness,[22] with which God has no contact whatever since he is pure light. The author has in mind their moral attitude and their

---

21. On 1:5, see the commentary on John 1:5 (1:246–49); see further E. R. Achtemeier, "Jesus Christ, the Light of the World," *Int* 17 (1963) 439–49; O. Böcher, *Der johanneische Dualismus* (Gütersloh, 1965); R. T. Stamm, "Creation and Revelation in the Gospel of John," in *Search the Scriptures* (Leiden, 1969); J. Chmiel, *Lumière et charité d'après la 1. épître de S. Jean* (Rome, 1971) 30–95; G. Stemberger, *La symbolique du bien et du mal selon s. Jean* (Paris, 1970) 40–49. For further discussion of Johannine and gnostic dualism, see Introduction.

22. *Skotos* occurs only here and in John 3:19; elsewhere it is always *skotia*. Comparison with 1 John 2:9, 11 shows that there is no difference of meaning.

consequent behavior, which is antagonistic to God, a point that comes out more clearly in the following verses (1:8, 10; 2:4, 9). Their practical behavior, their "walking,"[23] proves that what they claim is false.[24] The metaphor of darkness, a common one both within the Bible and outside of it,[25] speaks for itself. Darkness is the place where evil deeds are done, deeds that shun the light of day (cf. John 3:20f.). The same idea occurs in Paul, though there the contrast between light and darkness is more closely connected with salvation history (Rom. 13:12f.; 1 Thess. 5:4–8).

In v. 6 we have the first quotation of a slogan used by the heretical teachers whom the author is combating all through the epistle. Their slogans are often recognizable from the way they are introduced. The first person plural ("*we* say") as distinct from the verbs in v. 5 has an impersonal force, as does the substantive participle in the phrase "if anyone says" (Greek *ho legōn*, literally, "he who says") in 2:4, 6, 9 and "those who say" in 4:20. This does not mean that the people who use these slogans are still members of the community.[26] In this they are different from the opponents in 2:18ff. On the other hand, the introductory formula "if we say" is homiletic in style, warning the members of the community against the false notions held by the heretics. The author identifies himself by using the first person plural, warning them against sin and the ways of sin, while at the same time seeking to encourage them (v. 7). As W. Nauck has correctly observed, this seems to be based on the pattern of the Two Ways.[27] It echoes the baptismal catechesis (*reditus ad baptismum*).

The claim to possess fellowship with God is erroneous only on the lips of the heretical teachers (cf., on the other hand, 1:3), but it becomes so solely because of the way they behave. "To lie" means leading others astray in a wicked and malicious way. That is why Jesus calls the devil a liar (John 8:44). The false teachers, who are likewise called liars (John 2:4, 22a; 4:20), are not merely wrong in their behavior; they are actually antichrists (2:22b; cf. 2:18) and false prophets (4:1).

The religious and moral symptoms of this "lie" which are not conducive to salvation are emphasized by the further observation: "and do not do what is true" — "do," not "say." The phrase is linguistically related to the Hebrew *'āśâ 'ĕmet* ("do the truth")[28] and occurs also in John 3:21. It expresses the idea of

23. *Peripatein* in the sense of practical moral action (following the Hebrew *hālak;* in the New Testament, see BAGD 649, s.v. 2 ["decidedly Pauline"]) has in GJohn and 1 John retained its metaphorical significance (cf. John 8:12; 12:35b; 1 John 2:11), but in 2 John 4, 6 (bis) and 3 John 3, 4 comes close to the Pauline nonmetaphorical usage.

24. The *kai* in the *hoti*-clause has an adversative sense: "and yet" (BDF §442.1).

25. See Isa. 29:15; Job 24:13–17; 38:12f.; Ps. 10:8ff.; Sir. 23:18f.; *Pss. Sol.* 4:5; 8:8f.; *T. Naph.* 2:10, *oude en skoti ontes dynasthe poiein erga phōtos.* On this, see Aalen, *'Licht' und 'Finsternis',* 71f.; 233f.; 321ff.—The idea is also found in Hellenistic and gnostic texts; see Bauer, *Johannes,* 61 (on 3:20f.).

26. *Contra* Windisch, ad loc.; and J. Herkenrath, "Sünde zum Tode (1 Joh 5,16)," in *Aus Theologie und Philosophie* (Festschrift F. Tillmann; Düsseldorf, 1950) 119–38, esp. 121.

27. Nauck, *Tradition und Charakter,* 59–61.

28. Cf. Aramaic *'ābar qûštā'* in Tg. Hos. 4:1 (Lagarde, *Proph. chald.* 436, 3f.); the LXX not only translates it in this way in Gen. 32:11; 47:29; Neh. 9:33, where the subject as *God's* "doing righteousness, mercy, and truth," but also uses the same expression on its own initiative in Isa. 26:10; Tob 4:6; 13:6, where the reference is to *human* activity. See further *T. Rub.* 6:9; *T. Benj.* 10:3; 1QS

moral, not only intellectual, error (cf. "all who do evil," John 3:20). The ethical aspect is primary here and shows that we are right in our interpretation of "light" in v. 5. Indeed, light and truth are closely related, not only when they point to the saving revelation of God[29] but also when they highlight the moral holiness that proceeds from God and his ways.[30] Here the author might just as well have said "do what is right" (cf. 1 John 3:10). But falsehood and darkness, like truth and light, are common antitheses.[31]

1:7 Though the author repudiates the heretical claim to fellowship with God in v. 6, he will now show that walking in the light actually achieves this goal. Both metaphor and thought are reminiscent of the primitive Christian baptismal catechism (cf. Acts 26:18; Eph. 5:8-13; 1 Pet. 2:9, 12). In John 8:12; 12:35f. the same metaphor is used for Christian discipleship, which leads to salvation. But the presupposition for this is a moral life, "walking in the light"; on this see further 1 John 2:9ff. We are not told this time that God is light, but rather that God is in the light. There is a linguistic reason for this. Previously the author had been speaking about human beings. Now he shows that he is less concerned with the metaphor of light (which here breaks down) than with the actual point he is making. Only the pure, moral, holy being of God is really in the light.

A surprising consequence is drawn from this: "we have fellowship with one another." One would expect the author to say "we have fellowship with him," which is what several later manuscripts actually have.[32] Unlike the heretics, who boast of their personal experience and possession of God, the author is entirely rooted in the Christian fellowship and knows that the only way to God is in community, the community that preserves the message of Christ (cf. 1:3; 2:19). That is why those who walk in the light have an intimate and tangible assurance of their fellowship with God. They have their place in the true community of Christ.[33]

1:5; 5:3; 8:2; cf. 1QH 6:9; further 1QpHab 7:11f. "service of the truth." On the concept of *alētheia* in the Old Testament, see Bultmann, *ZNW* 27 (1928) 113-63, esp. 115f.; idem, *TDNT* 1:240; Büchsel, *Johannes und der hellenistische Synkretismus* (BFCT 2, 16; Gütersloh, 1928) 85; M. Zerwick, "Veritatem facere," *VD* 18 (1938) 338-42, 373-77. On the Qumran texts, see F. Nötscher, "'Wahrheit' als theologischer Terminus in den Qumran-Texten," *Vorderasiatische Studien* (Festschrift V. Christian; Vienna, 1956) 83-92; I. de la Potterie, "L'arrière-fond du thème johannique de vérité," *StudEv* (TU 73; Berlin, 1959) 277-94, esp. 282ff.; O. Betz, *Offenbarung und Schriftforschung in der Qumransekte* (Tübingen, 1960) 53-61.

29. See John 1:4f., 9; 8:12; 11:9f.; 12:35f.; also Rev. 21:23f.; 22:5. Bultmann, *TDNT* 1:240. Cf. *T. Levi* 4:3: φῶς γνώσεως ἐν τῷ Ιακὼβ καὶ ὡς ἥλιος ἔσῃ παντὶ σπέρματι Ισραήλ.

30. Cf. John 3:20f.; 1 John 2:8f.; also in Rev. 21:27, cf. 23-26, it becomes clear that the light of God's glory is at the same time a brightly shining moral holiness and therefore can only be contemplated with pure eyes (cf. Matt. 5:8). A close connection between *phōs* and *alētheia* in a religious-ethical sense will be found also in *T. Ash.* 5:3: πᾶσα ἀλήθεια ὑπὸ τοῦ φωτός ἐστιν (καθὼς τὰ πάντα ὑπὸ τοῦ θεοῦ). See also *CHerm* 13.9: τῇ δὲ ἀληθείᾳ καὶ τὸ ἀγαθὸν ἐπεγένετο, ἅμα ζωῇ καὶ φωτί, καὶ οὔκετι ἐπῆλθεν οὐδεμία τοῦ σκότους τιμωρία. True, Hermetic gnosis has a different conception of evil; it is not "sin" in the ethical sense, but ἀγνοία, ἀπάτη, τιμωρία τῆς ὕλης or τοῦ σκότους.

31. See Isa. 26:10; Tob. 1:3, 4:5 with 6; 14:7; *Pss. Sol.* 3:6; 14:1 with 2; 4 Ezra 7:114.

32. A* (probably); Clement; Tertullian; *Didache* (*tou theou*) p z sy[pal].—The change of *met' autou* into *met' allēlōn*, which most of the manuscripts offer, cannot in that case be explained (*contra* Bultmann, "Analyse," 139, 1; Büchsel).

33. *Met' allēlōn* cannot refer to our relationship with God (*contra* Häring), since elsewhere it

If we look back to the heretical teachers and their false slogans, we shall see how the author develops his argument from the end of v. 7 on. The author has a healthy Christian feeling of self-worth, and because of this he dares to write about the sinlessness of those who are born of God (3:9; 5:18f.) and of the love for brothers and sisters that pervades the community (3:14). But the claim of the heretical teachers that they have no sin (1:8) is one that the Christians cannot make for themselves without qualification. They dare not apply it to their own moral behavior or their own personal character. That would be typical of the heretics. Nobody can make this claim except the One who is sinless, Jesus Christ (2:1, 29; 3:7; cf. John 8:46). But in refuting the novel slogans of the heretics the author is in danger of contradicting what he has just said. On the one hand, he insists that fellowship with God means walking in the light, in a pure moral life according to the rule of the supreme and all-holy God. On the other hand, no Christian can claim to be without sin. The solution to the dilemma lies, for the author, in the fact that the Christian is not immune from sin, but that the blood of Jesus Christ cleanses from all sin.[34] The problem of "the Christian and sin" comes up again and again (2:1; 3:4–10; 5:16–18). This is not only because the author runs a risk in his attempt to refute the moral heresy but also because of his genuine pastoral concern (see Excursus 12).

The author therefore does not retract the requirement he made at the beginning of v. 7 when he said that Christians—unlike the heretics—should walk in the light. However, he does not base it on their absolute sinlessness, but indirectly admits that sin may occur even in the life of Christians (cf. 5:17). But the blood of Jesus cleanses them from sin. It is God himself, not only Jesus his Son, who does so, who draws them into the fullness of his light and enables them to walk in that light. There is nothing else that can cleanse from sin like the blood of Jesus.[35] (Note that the verb is in the active voice; cf. 2:2; 4:10; 5:6b—and for the basic thought, cf. Heb. 9:22). It performs this redeeming function again and again (note the present tense). By saying this and by adding "from all sin" the author makes it clear that he is not speaking of preconversion sin nor about sin's "active power" (Brooke).

Already at this point we can see how the moral heresy is closely connected with Christology (cf. 3:23). Because the heretics think they are sinless and regard sin as meaningless in their higher, pneumatic existence, they have no need whatever of Jesus or of redemption by his blood (5:6).

2. The Fact of Sin Is Undeniable: Sin Must Be Confessed (1 John 1:8–10)

1:8 Picking up the key word "sin" (v. 7), the author now introduces a new slogan of the heretics: "if we say." This sounds like a defense against a charge

always denotes a reciprocal relationship between human beings; see John 5:44; 6:43, 52; 13:14, 22, 35; 16:19.

34. Bultmann regards the last part of the verse as an interpolation ("Redaktion," 199f.); on this, see the Introduction, p. 16.

35. There is no sign of any polemic against some other way of catharsis, e.g., through gnosis and the mortification of the senses.

brought against them by the church. But it only shows even more blatantly that they are walking in darkness and are separated from God. Quite seriously, they claim they have no sin and in fact consider themselves sinless.[36] There is nothing in 1 John about sexual immorality or other gross sins, which were so rife in the later history of gnosticism[37] (2:16 is a general admonition addressed to the Christian community). Again and again the author upbraids the false prophets for their failure to love brothers and sisters. They hardly deny their *ability* to sin (cf. Brooke) as distinct from saying "we *have not* sinned" (v. 10). There is a deeper reason for their presumptuous claim, the gnostic conviction that pneumatics cannot be defiled by the material world and its impurities.[38] The author does not give us his own opinion of the matter because he is sticking to the slogans of the heretics as they were circulating at the time (vv. 8 and 10). He sees in them a dangerous poison that could destroy the Christian teaching about the need of redemption through the blood of Jesus (v. 7) and the Christian practice of confessing one's sins (v. 9). Such could be the effect on those who hear the gnostic slogans.

His condemnation of the erroneous view is constructed in terms parallel to v. 6. Instead of "we lie," he now says "we deceive ourselves," for "we do not do what is true," "the truth is not in us." Each time there is a crescendo. The active voice with a reflexive gives a stronger image ("we deceive ourselves") stressing the note of personal responsibility. It is a fatal error full of baleful consequences and due to one's own fault. Again, the claim to possess the truth is more pointed than it was in v. 6. Truth is understood as a divine reality[39] which does not dwell in that type of person. The same point is made in a different way in v. 10: "his word is not in us." Truth, like the word of God, is in objective reality given by God (cf. Chaine). It works in humankind as an "interior principle . . . shaping our inner life" (Brooke). The author hurls his accusations especially at those who claim immunity from sin. Such people have no divine spark in them at all.

In Greek thought truth is something entirely different. It means conforming with reality or accepting a logical fact. But neither does the Old Testament idea of God's truth in the sense of constancy or fidelity come anywhere near close to the Johannine usage.[40]

---

36. On *hamartian echein,* see John 9:41; 15:22, 24; 19:11. This phrase, which is peculiar to the Johannine writings, always conveys the idea of being actually tainted with sin, not merely being accused of it.—Phrases with *echein* are typically Johannine; cf. *agapēn echein* (John 5:42; 13:35; 15:13); *eirēnēn echein* (16:33); *charan echein* (17:13; etc.). For rabbinic parallels (*bĕyādô*), see Schlatter, *Sprache,* 101f.

37. See what Irenaeus says about the Valentinians in *Adv. Haer.* 1.1.12: τὰ ἀπειρημένα πάντα ἀδεῶς οἱ τελειόταται πράττουσιν αὐτῶν; and about the Carpocratians in 1.20.3, and the Cainites in 1.28.9 (et hoc esse scientiam perfectam, sine tremore in tales abire operationes, quas ne nominare quidem fas est).

38. See Irenaeus, *Adv. Haer.* 1.1.11 (Valentinians): διὰ τὸ φύσει πνευματικοὺς εἶναι πάντῃ τε καὶ πάντως σωθήσεσθαι δογματίζουσιν, etc.

39. On this concept of *alētheia,* see Bultmann, *TDNT* 1:245ff.; idem, *John,* 74 n. 2, etc.; idem, *Theology* 2:18f.; Wikenhauser, *Johannes* (2nd ed.), Excursus, pp. 181f. On truth, see my Excursus in *John* (New York, 1980) 2:225–37.

40. Attempts in this direction are unconvincing; see F. Büchsel, *Der Begriff der Wahrheit in dem Evangelium und den Briefen des Johannes* (Gütersloh, 1911); idem, *Johannes und der hellenistische Synkretismus,* 83–97; Percy, *Untersuchungen,* 80–124.

Its proximity to the language of gnosticism is unmistakable. Compare, for example, *Odes Sol.* 24:10ff.: "And the Lord destroyed the thoughts, / of all those who had not the truth in them. . . . So they were rejected, / because the truth was not with them." Or in Mandeism, *Ginza* 57.21f.: "We hear your praise, and into our heart Kušta entered and lay down"; ibid. 60.3–8: "Everyone who hears him speaking, whose eyes are filled with light . . . his heart is filled with truth." Yet a simple derivation from gnostic dualism is hardly likely. The Qumran texts show the direction in which it was possible for the Old Testament concept of truth to develop. Here truth is a central and all-embracing term denoting all the blessings of faith and salvation enjoyed by the "sons of truth" (1QS 4:5f.) or "the men of truth" (1QpHab 7:10). It is worth noting how the holy Spirit is associated with truth (1QS 4:21; cf. CD 2:12f.). Truth designates what belongs to God in contrast to the falsehoods of humanity (1QH 1:27); the "sons of his good pleasure" God instructs in "the counsel of his truth," "to be one with the children of (his) truth" (1QH 11:9ff.). But even here the distinctive Johannine note of truth in the sense of the divine being who reveals and communicates himself is not yet reached. It is something that can be understood only in the light of Johannine Christology and message of salvation. The Son of God made man embodies the fullness of divine grace and truth in himself (John 1:14) and with his coming brought it to humanity (John 1:17). As the truth and the life he has become the way to the Father for all who believe (John 14:6). This line of thought is developed further in GJohn (see 8:32, 36; 17:17; 18:27), and it lies behind similar sayings in the epistle. Clearly, then, the gnostic concept of truth, in spite of its formal similarities, is still a long way from the Johannine, while the affinity of the latter with Old Testament and Jewish thought is greater than it seems at first sight (cf. the twin terms in John 1:14, 17; and also 4:23f.).

1:9 In opposition to the perverse views of the heretics on the subject of sin, the author goes on to deal positively with the theme of "the Christian and sin" in the light of fellowship with God. He outlines his case with a few broad strokes. Verse 9 provides the basic answer of orthodox Christianity to that problem, showing how fellowship with God requires a life without sin. At the same time it faces up to the reality of sin in the Christian life. God himself clears away the obstacle of sin so long as people confess their misdeeds in penitence. Thus he restores them once more to unclouded fellowship with himself. The great chasm between gnosticism and Christianity is shown up in this reply. We find in gnosticism a self-assertive desire to find God, in Christianity a humble waiting to be brought back to fellowship with him.

The author does not ask his readers to confess their sinfulness in general terms but to confess each specific sin ("past sins").[41] Personal confession of sin, which was also a part of the Baptist's preaching by the Jordan (Mark 1:5 = Matt. 3:6), is an inheritance from the practice of Judaism.

---

41. *Homologein* is always associated with outward expression, not just with an inner attitude. In John 12:42, by contrast, it is associated with inner believing; in 1:20 it is opposed to *arneisthai,* and in 9:22 also it connotes open expression. For the confession of sin this passage is unique in the Johannine writings; otherwise it is always used in connection with Christian believing (1 John 2:23; 4:2, 3, 15; 2 John 7). For the confession of sin *exomologein* is generally used; see BAGD 277, s.v. 2a, and 568, s.v. *homologein* 3b. On James 5:10, see further below. Cf. O. Michel, *TDNT* 5:199ff., esp. 204f.; 215; 218f.

It was especially on the Day of Atonement that this practice was observed.[42] In rabbinic discussion the duty of confession is given a theological basis.[43] When a sin offering is presented, the one offering it has to specify his or her transgressions (Lev. 5:5). Otherwise such confession was not generally required.[44] Since it is God who has been offended and angered by sin, it is to him that these confessions of guilt are addressed (Ps. 51:6; cf. Gen. 20:6; 39:9; Lev. 5:19; 2 Sam. 12:13), although in certain circumstances it was the priest who heard the confession (Lev. 6:5f.) or to others (Josh. 7:19; *Sanh.* 6:2). In the Qumran community there was probably an annual festival of covenant renewal which included the admission of new members. The ceremonial for this occasion is preserved in 1QS 1:16–2:18 (or 3:12). Like Israel's Day of Atonement, this rite included a confession of sin in general terms. The Levites recite "the iniquities of the children of Israel, all their guilty rebellions and sin during the dominion of Satan" (1:23). At the same time the new members make a specific confession of their sin and guilt (1:24–2:1). Even so, the whole community may have taken part in this confession of sin, as suggested by CD 20:28ff.).

There is no indication in the text that 1 John 1:9 goes beyond this. We can, however, be assured that this passage represents one of the earliest pieces of evidence for the church's practice of confession.[45] The emphasis on the part played by God himself in giving absolution ("he who is faithful and just will forgive us our sins") makes it unlikely that the community itself or their leaders are standing in the background hearing the confessions and pronouncing absolution. To claim that this is similar to John 20:23 (Chaine, Ambroggi) is going too far in view of the difference between the two passages on the key point, viz., the subject of the verb. It is, however, possible that there was already a liturgical custom of confessing one's sins before the assembled congregation (cf. *Did.* 14.1) or before a smaller group of church members. But it is impossible to prove

---

42. Lev. 16:21; cf. 5:5; Isa. 7:19; Ps. 32:5; Prov. 28:13; Dan. 9:20.—Confession of sins was also practiced in Hellenistic paganism; see the material from inscriptions in F. X. Steinleitner, "Die Beichte im Zusammenhang mit der sakralen Rechtspflege in der Antike" (Diss., Munich, 1913); Reitzenstein, *Hellenistische Mysterienreligion,* 137ff.; Michel, *TDNT* 5:201, 26–45.

43. Cf. the impressive utterance of R. Simon and R. Jehoshuah ben Levi in the name of R. Shim'on ben Halaphta, that we should confess "like a robber, who is brought before a court for judgment. So long as he resists, he is beaten, but if he makes a confession, he receives his sentence. God, on the other hand, does not treat us like this; rather, as long as people refuse to confess their sins, they receive their sentence. But as soon as they do confess, they are acquitted" (*Pesiq.* 159a; see Billerbeck, *Kommentar* 1:170).

44. Cf. the wording of the confessions in Billerbeck, *Kommentar* 1:113f.; further the confession at the annual covenant feast at Qumran: 1QS 1:24–2:1; cf. CD 20:28–30. According to a *baraita* on *p. Yoma* 8, 9, the rabbis were not unanimous on whether it was proper for people to confess their sins to individuals. R. Jehuda ben Bathyra (ca. 110) required them to do so; R. Akiba (d. ca. 135) did not (Billerbeck, *Kommentar* 1:113). In the case of a delinquent whose greatest sin was known to the judicial authorities, it was sufficient to say: "Let my death be an atonement for all my transgressions." But only so could that person hope to attain to eternal life (*Sanh.* 6.2c; cf. 2a; Krauss, 187f.). See further Bonsirven, *Judaïsme* 2:99ff.

45. R. Seeberg, "Die Sünden und die Sündenvergebung," in *Das Erbe Martin Luthers* (Festschrift L. Ihmels; Leipzig, 1928) 22. This view is rightly opposed by B. Poschmann (*Paenitentia secunda* [Bonn, 1940] 68, 1), who however himself thinks (wrongly) of an inner confession of sins before God (p. 68). Bede, Theophylact, and Oecumenius also thought only of private confession to God.

this, not even from James 5:16,[46] or from 1 John 5:16.[47] The context in each case is quite different and presupposes a concrete situation quite unlike that in 1 John 1:9.

The absolution conferred by God on those who sincerely confess their sins is described in terms familiar from the world of the Old Testament. God himself is "faithful and just." That is his nature as described in Exod. 34:6f., where we read that it is his will to forgive sins.[48] These divine attributes enumerated in the farewell discourse of Moses in Deut. 32:4 and elsewhere appear closely related.[49] God's faithfulness, generally rendered as his "truth," is his fidelity to his promise to grant forgiveness to penitent sinners.[50] We are already reminded of this in Mic. 7:18-20. Such faithfulness is synonymous with righteousness. It is a holy attitude akin to mercy (see above, Exod. 34:6) and grace (Pss. 33:5; 119:64).[51] The Old Testament uses many different metaphors for deliverance from sins.[52] Those chosen here are canceling a debt[53] and cleansing or washing away of impurity.[54] The last of these metaphors is enhanced only by the phrase "from all unrighteousness." This is parallel to the end of v. 7, and at the same time contrasts our unholiness (which is the same thing as sin) with God's holiness and mercy (cf. Exod. 34:7; Ps. 51:4 etc.). The same point that was made in v. 7 about the blood of Christ is repeated here with reference to God himself. The author identifies the saving act of God with the work of Jesus as his mediator. The blood of Jesus or the person of Jesus himself is the sole and supreme way to salvation. God's atoning will triumphs ever anew in the blood of the One Man. Forgiveness of sins is not a bit of magic any more than it is in the Old Testament. Nor is it just a juridical transaction, as the metaphor of cleansing reminds us. It must be accepted as an act of God, of a God who is

46. Chaine: "without doubt an allusion to the same liturgical custom as Jas 5:16"; see also Ambroggi. Yet at this point in James the association with prayer for others and the healing of the sick creates a situation so concrete that it would be hazardous to draw a parallel between it and a generally worded text like 1 John 1:9. Much the same holds good for the confession of sin before the celebration of the Eucharist in *Did.* 14.1.

47. Poschmann thinks it probable that the sinner himself was concerned to have others pray for him and would naturally have confessed his sins (*Paenitentia,* 68). But the text makes it more probable that the initiative for intercession comes from fellow Christians who have not sinned (*ean tis idē* . . .). For more on this, see ad loc.

48. ἀληθινὸς καὶ δικαιοσύνην διατηρῶν καὶ ποιῶν ἔλεος εἰς χιλιάδας, ἀφαιρῶν ἀνομίας καὶ ἀδικίας καὶ ἁμαρτίας.

49. Pss. (LXX) 18:8f.; 32:4f.; 84:12; 88:15; 95:13; 118:160.

50. See Isa. 1:18; Jer. 31:34; 33:8; 50:20; Ezek. 18:21ff.; 33:11, 14ff.

51. Hence *dikaios* as used here does not mean without sin (Büchsel) as in 2:1, 29 and 3:7, since it is concerned with what is done to others. See also C. H. Dodd, *The Bible and the Greeks* (London, 1935) 45ff., 65.

52. *Hina* here is not final but consecutive; see BDF §391.5; Radermacher, *Grammatik,* 193; F. M. Abel, *Grammaire du Grec biblique* (Paris, 1927) 303; the Johannine passages are collected in Brooke, ad loc.

53. *Aphienai;* cf. Matt. 6:12; 18:27, 32—Exod. 32:32; Lev. 4:20; 19:22; Num. 14:19 etc. In Esth. 2:18 it means remission of taxes. In any case "remission" is a juridical concept; see Bultmann, *TDNT* 1:510.

54. Isa. 1:16; Jer. 40:8; Pss. 19:14; 51:4; Prov. 20:9; Sir. 38:10; etc. Rabbinic parallels are given in Schlatter, *Sprache* 126.

true to himself and his promises, a God who is the gracious author of salvation.[55] There is a slight hint here of the mystery of the *felix culpa*, though in a profound doxological sense. Sin, which destroys our fellowship with God, is constantly removed by him. In this way the fellowship between God and humanity is preserved and strengthened.

1:10 Once again the author turns against the heretics and their claim to sinlessness. That claim is so perverse and immoral as to compromise the holiness and truthfulness of God. In taking up their slogan for the third time ("if we say") the author recapitulates his second reference to it in different terms (v. 8).[56] Their denial of personal sinfulness is a crime against God. For God had spoken of the general sinfulness of humanity in the Old Testament revelation.[57] This is hinted at by the substitution of "his word" for "the truth" in v. 8. To deny human sinfulness is to make God a liar (cf. 5:10) and to place him on a par with the devil, the "liar and the father of lies" (John 8:44).

The "word of God" as it was given shape in revelation is presented here as a substantial reality. This seems to be an earlier stage in the personification (hardly a direct hypostatizing) of the word of God in late judaism.[58] The next point of contact for this metaphor is found in many of the sayings of Jesus in GJohn. The word of God is not only the expression of his thoughts; it is the bearer of and witness to the divine Spirit.[59] This has nothing to do with the idea of the Logos as representing the preexistent Son of God (cf. 1:1). The Johannine writings never claim that this personal Logos (always used absolutely, without the possessive pronoun "his"=God's) dwells within human beings (Philo's concept of the Logos is different). This is why the phrase "is not in us" occurs so frequently (see Excursus 4). The word of God has never come to dwell in those who oppose him, or to fill them with his Spirit. In their attempt to attain to God they fail to make room for his word and are unable to retain it in themselves.[60]

With this response the author peremptorily and conclusively denies to the gnostics any fellowship with God. They openly defy the will of God and shut themselves off from his salvation and life-giving powers.

---

55. Eichrodt says that the Old Testament had already developed a high concept of the forgiveness of sins (*Theology* 2:454: "So they experienced his remission of punishment as a free act of the divine Lord, in which each time the mystery of his approach to men in a desire for fellowship with them made itself known in forgiveness of sins."

56. The antithetical parallelism between vv. 8 and 9 does not require a distinction between the singular *hamartian* (v. 8) and plural *hamartias* (v. 9). The perfect *ouch hēmartēkamen* (v. 10) expresses the condition of sinlessness, of freedom from personal sin, and makes the same point as the phrase in v. 8 (*contra* Brooke).

57. Cf. Gen. 8:21; 1 Kgs. 8:46; Pss. 14:3; 53:2; Job 4:17; 15:14–16; Prov. 20:9. Late Judaism had a strong and sincere sense of sin; see Bousset-Gressmann, *Religion*, 390f.; Bonsirven, *Judaïsme* 2:89f.

58. See Billerbeck, *Kommentar* 2:305; Moore, *Judaism* 1:414ff.; O. Grether, *Name und Wort Gottes im Alten Testament* (Giessen, 1934) 150ff.; L. Dürr, *Die Wertung des Wortes Gottes im Alten Testament und im antiken Orient* (Leipzig, 1938) 122ff.; Hamp, *Der Begriff 'Wort,'* 108–67.

59. John 3:34; 6:63, 68; 8:31, 47, 51f.; 12:47f.; 15:3, 7.—On this, see Mussner, ΖΩΗ, 99–101.

60. See John 8:37; 5:38. In contrast to this, the disciples have "received" Jesus' word which the Father "gave" him (John 17:8, 14; cf. 14:23f.).

3. Jesus Christ Takes Care of the Removal
of Our Sins (1 John 2:1-2)

There is no need to take 1:5-10 (with additions by the author himself) as a Christian commentary on a *Vorlage* consisting of 2:1-2 (Bultmann), or 2:1-7 (Windisch). True, there is a striking change of vocabulary in 2:1-2. However, it is open to quite a different explanation. The author's argument with the heretics and his closely reasoned altercations have come to an end for the time being in 1:10. Now he turns directly to his readers, embarking upon a brief parenesis for internal consumption and providing it immediately with an authentic Christian motivation (Christ as the advocate). The author is afraid his readers might regard sin as a normal part of the Christian life (cf. 2:1a). Of course, he knows perfectly well that Christians do fall into sin (2:1b). So he reminds them that they have a powerful advocate before the throne of God to whom they can turn (cf. "on account of his name," 2:12). Because of that God will be even more ready to pardon them. This further eases the tension with 1:9, which seemed to have said all that was necessary about the forgiveness of sin by a faithful and gracious God. The role of Jesus Christ in the removal of sins is then developed further (2:2).

2:1 From now on the author frequently addresses his readers as "little children" (2:12, 28; 3:7, 18; 4:4; 5:21). This does not imply a major break in the development of the thought. But it does allow a moment's breathing space, like the phrase "I am writing these things," which does not refer only to the last verses. With loving persistence[61] the author turns to his Christian readers in order to help them understand correctly what he had said about the heretical teachers in 1:5-10.[62] The point in vv. 6f. still holds good: there is no room for sin in the Christian life. If in spite of this people continue to sin,[63] they have One, a mighty helper, who will secure the remission of their sins, Jesus Christ himself. The previous paragraph had focused on God (except for the end of v. 7), whereas 2:1-2 is a short compendium of early Christian teaching about Jesus Christ, the author of salvation who takes away our sins.

The present advocacy of Jesus Christ before throne of God for the faithful when they fall into sin on earth is described by the use of the title Paraclete. This word is unique in the New Testament to the Johannine writings and shows how close the epistle is to GJohn.[64] Of course, in the farewell discourses the title is

---

61. *Teknia,* diminutive of *tekna,* also the way Jesus addresses his disciples (John 13:33) need not imply any particular tenderness (cf. *probatia* John 21:16f.) compared with *probata* (10:1ff.). It implies that they have been well instructed; cf. the way rabbis addressed their disciples (Billerbeck, *Kommentar* 1:198). On the other hand, *teknon* in the Hermetic dialogues presupposes the correlative *pater,* and thus remains tied to the dialogue (5.2; 13.21).

62. *Tauta graphō* prevents our relating it to the letter as a whole (Brooke, Büchsel) in view of the specific object: *hina mē hamartēte.*

63. For this limitation of a previously expressed general statement, cf. John 1:12; 3:32f.; 5:23a-b; 12:42 with 37, 39.

64. On the Paraclete, see the Excursus in R. E. Brown, *The Gospel According to John XIII-XXI* (Anchor Bible 29A; Garden City, NY, 1970) 1135-44 (with bibliography); G. Johnston, *The Spirit-*

applied to the Holy Spirit (14:16, 26; 15:26; 16:7). There its functions on earth as the Spirit of truth are distinct from those of Jesus Christ as the Paraclete in heaven.[65] But this only goes to show what broad meaning the term has. The role of the risen One before the throne of God is consistent with what Jesus did for his disciples while he was still on earth. At that time he had been their protector (John 17:12), and before his departure he asked the Father to preserve them from the evil one (17:15). Now, when they fall into the sins of infirmity, he prays for the believers before the throne of God. The same understanding of Jesus' intercession at the right hand of God is also found in Rom. 8:34 and Heb. 7:25.

The Mandeans also have a messenger (helper, or advocate), but he does not have a function such as this. In the main he is sent to the lost soul, to guide it upward to the realm of light.[66] The idea of the paraclete is derived from the Old Testament and late Judaism. In the wide range of views concerning advocates, witnesses, and mediators, both human and superhuman (angels, the Holy Spirit, and in rabbinic theology such derivatives as Torah, good works, etc,),[67] advocacy for sinners takes precedence over all the other functions and covers a variety of activities.[68] As regards the terminology, it is important to note that the term "paraclete" found its way as a loanword into the language of the rabbis. In early Christianity the idea of Jesus as mediator and advocate is more common than the title Paraclete.[69]

What "paraclete" means in 1 John 2:1 is clear from the context. Jesus is the advocate with the Father for Christians when they sin, for he is close by him ("with the Father").[70] It does not say that it is his task to defend them against

---

Paraclete in the Gospel of John (Cambridge, 1970) esp. pp. 75–79 and chap. 7 on the more recent studies.

65. See Windisch, "Die fünf Johanneischen Parakletsprüche," in *Festgabe für A. Jülicher* (Tübingen, 1927) 110–37, esp. 114; W. Michaelis, "Zur Herkunft des Johanneischen Paraklet-Titels," in *ConNT* 11 (Lund, 1947) 147–62, esp. 147f. and n. 3; G. Bornkamm, "Der Paraklet im Joh-Ev," *Festschrift für R. Bultmann* (Stuttgart, 1949) 12–35; C. K. Barrett, "The Holy Spirit in the Fourth Gospel," *JTS* n.s. 1 (1950) 1–15, esp. 7ff. J. Behm, *TDNT* 5:800–814; S. Schulz, *Untersuchungen zur Menschensohn-Christologie im Johannesevangelium* (Göttingen, 1957) 142–58; D. E. Holwerda, *The Holy Spirit and Eschatology in the Gospel of John* (Kampen, 1959) 26–38.

66. Cf. *MandLit* 191 ("helper"); 202; 225 ("messenger"); *Ginza* 328.25ff.; 346.15ff.; 389.29ff.; 456.19ff.; 477.19ff. ("Helper"); *Book of John*, 60.15ff.; 69.3ff. ("messenger, assistant"). Bultmann's attempt (*John*, 552f., etc.) to explain the Johannine Paraclete from this material has been shown to be impossible, esp. by W. Michaelis, "Zur Herkunft"; see also Menoud, *Jean*, 57–60.

67. See Nils Johansson, "Parakletoi" (Diss., Lund, 1940) and the abundant material developed there. Johansson expands the range of perspective, perhaps too broadly (cf. esp. "Guide," pp. 46ff.; 186ff.).

68. See Gen. 18:23ff.; 20:7; Exod. 32:11ff., 30ff.; 1 Sam 7:8f.; 12:19ff.; Jer. 18:19f.; Job 42:8, 10; 2 Macc. 7:32f.; 15:12, 14; Eichrodt, *Theology* 2/3:448ff.; P. Heinisch, *Theologie des AT* (Bonn, 1940) 202f.— For late Judaism, see esp. 4 Macc. 6:28; *2 Apoc. Bar.* 85:1ff.; John 10:3ff. *As. Mos.* 11:11ff.; 12:6f.; Eccl. 11:2; 4 Ezra 7:106ff.; *4 Enoch* (Greek) 64:5; etc.; see Volz, *Eschatologie,* index under "Fürbitte"; Johansson "Parakletoi," 65f.; 120 (on *3 Enoch*); Billerbeck, *Kommentar* 3:643 (on 1 Tim. 2:1); 769f. on James 5:16; Moore, *Judaism* 1:537ff.; 2:219.

69. See Johansson, "Parakletoi," 180ff. The attempt to understand "Son of man" chiefly from the idea of "Advocate" is to be rejected. Similarly, it is hardly convincing when Bornkamm ("Der Paraklet," 20ff.) and S. Schulz (*Untersuchungen*, 153f.) find one of the main roots of the Johannine Paraclete sayings in the Son of man tradition.

70. To be understood in a local sense as in 1:2; see BDF §239.1; Mayser, *Grammatik* 2.2:371, 11ff. (*contra* Findlay, 110 n. 1).

the accusations of Satan (cf. Rev. 12:10). The forensic meaning of "paraclete" is here overshadowed by Christ's high-priestly role.[71] This is made plain not only by the high-priestly prayer (John 17) but also by the cultic terminology that is used in the following verse. As he is about to leave his disciples, Christ assures them that he is "sanctifying himself" for them (John 17:19). So now he is called the atoning sacrifice for our sins. His death is a sin offering that fulfills this promise. The whole picture is strikingly reminiscent of Heb. 7:25ff. The high priest, who is "holy, blameless, undefiled, separated from sinners," has offered himself once and for all and now lives forever to be the advocate of those who "by him draw near to God." The contacts between Hebrews and the Johannine writings are rich and profound in other respects, too, and point to a common tradition in early Christianity.[72] In addition to the idea of God as faithful and merciful (1:9), we now have Jesus Christ as the priestly advocate and mediator. He relieves the faithful of all their anxiety about their salvation, now once more endangered by sin, and he assures them that in spite of their weakness they can draw near to the throne of grace (cf. Heb. 4:16; 10:19ff.).

Jesus Christ is also distinguished with the epithet "righteous." This is hardly in order to designate the permanency of his role as advocate (Windisch), but rather to stress its efficacy. God will not abandon the advocacy of those who "do righteousness," who conform to his will (cf. 3:7).[73] On the other hand, he will not hearken to sinners (John 9:31). It is still more probable that the author adds this to show how Jesus became our advocate before the throne of God. It is because he died "as the righteous for the unrighteous" (1 Pet. 3:18 — probably an echo of Isa. 53:11), or because he offered himself for sinners as a holy and blameless high priest (cf. Heb. 7:26f.). With this, following his usual style (see 1:5, 7), the author leads into the next verse.

2:2 The author now widens out his argument. Following up his reference to Jesus Christ[74] he continues to discuss his role in the removal of sins.[75] This consideration refers back to what Christ had done originally to remove the guilt of

---

71. See O. Moe, "Das Priestertum Christi im NT ausserhalb des Hebräerbriefes," *TLZ* 72 (1947) 335–38, esp. 338; see Spicq, "L'origine johannique de la conception du Christ-prêtre dans l'Épître aux Hébreux," in *Aux sources de la tradition chrétienne* (Festschrift M. Goguel; Neuchâtel/Paris, 1950) 258–69, esp. 263f.; J. Behm, *TDNT* 5:812 n. 91 (but thinks the forensic meaning is connected with it; O. Cullmann, *The Christology of the New Testament* (2nd ed.; Philadelphia, 1963) 106f.

72. See C. Spicq, *Hébreux* (Paris, 1952) 1:109–38, esp. 121–27. How far this is influenced by contact with Qumran need not be discussed here; on the latter point see C. Spicq, "LÉpître aux Hébreux, Apollos, Jean-Baptiste, les Hellénistes et Qumran," *RevQum* 1 (1958–59) 365–90.

73. See Bonsirven, *Judaïsme* 2:156f.—If this is already true for the "righteous man" in the Old Testament, it is even more true of Jesus; on the designation of Jesus as *ho dikaios* in the New Testament, see further Luke 23:47; Acts 3:14; 7:52; 22:14; 1 Pet. 3:18; 1 John 2:29; 3:7; also John 16:10.

74. In classical Greek *houtos* would be preferred; see BDF §277.3, 290.1. However, "the usage is an old one, though foreign to Attic" (§277.3). In the New Testament it is as frequent in Luke; thus 1:22; 2:50; 4:15; 7:12 (*v.l.*); 8:42 (*v.l.*); 8:52 (*v.l.*); 9:36; 11:14; cf. *autos de* or *gar* (Matt. 3:4; Mark 6:17; Luke 3:23; John 2:24; 4:44). The emphasis of *autos* is weak; cf. G. B. Winer-W. F. Moulton, *A Grammar of New Testament Greek* (Edinburgh, 1882) §22 (pp. 180f.).

75. Bultmann ("Redaktion," 200) regards v. 2 as an interpolation (on this, see the Introduction, p. 16).

sin, a removal that remains effective for all time (note the present tense, "is"). He is and remains the great atoning One. This does not mean that he goes on offering sacrifice in heaven—that would be outside the purview of the New Testament (cf. Rom. 6:10; Heb. 9:12, 28; 10:10, 12, 14; 1 Pet. 3:18). Rather, the idea is that his blood retains its redeeming and cleansing power (cf. 1:7; Heb. 9:14). The expression "atoning sacrifice" (Greek *hilasmos*), which occurs only here and in 4:10, is a verbal substantive with a strong active force.[76] It can be understood here either as a substitution of an abstract for a concrete or as a neologism for "sin offering."[77] The phrase "atonement for sins" clearly betrays its Old Testament roots (LXX *hilaskomai peri,* "to make atonement for") and, like forgiveness of sin in 1:9, shows whence the author got it. But he does not draw his ideas about sacrifice exclusively from the Old Testament. Like Hebrews, he also utilizes ideas further developed in the theology of later Judaism about the vicarious suffering and death of the righteous martyrs.[78] Take, for instance, the prayer of Eleazar before he was burned at the stake: "Be merciful to your people and let our punishment be a satisfaction on their behalf. Make my blood their purification (*katharsin*) and take my life as a ransom (*antipsychon*) for theirs" (4 Macc. 6:28f.). But above and beyond such martyrdom for the people,[79] the death of the Messiah acquires a universal import.[80] This is hardly comparable to the arrogance of the gnostics, who as pneumatics think they are superior to the suffering incurred as a punishment for sin.[81] Nor is it a question of the general need for atonement, but for the far-reaching scope of Christ's redeeming work. Without making a special point of it, the author speaks in a truly "catholic" manner. He knows he is proclaiming the definitive message of salvation (cf. 1:1–3). The positive kerygmatic formulation of the phrase and the way he rounds it off mark the conclusion of the theme with which he has been dealing, the theme of sin.

---

76. Like *hagiasmos, peirasmos, phōtismos,* etc.; see BDF §109.1; *hilasmos* = rabbinic *kappārâ;* see Schlatter, *Sprache,* 146. See further T. C. G. Thornton, "Propitiation or Expiation? Ἱλαστήριον and ἱλασμός in Romans and 1 John," *ExpT* 80 (1968) 53–55 ("expiation"); H. Clavier, "Notes sur un mot-clef du johannisme et de la sotériologie biblique: ἱλασμός," *NovT* 10 (1968) 287–304 (principal meaning: "reconciliation" according to John 12:32).

77. See BAGD 375, s.v. 2 (otherwise *thysia* and *holokautōma peri hamartias,* Heb. 10:5–8). Bauer rightly refers to Ezek. 44:27 (cf. the parallels 43:27; 44:11), further to Num. 5:8; 2 Macc. 3:33; on this, see Dodd, *The Bible and the Greeks,* 94f.; F. Büchsel, *TDNT* 3:317f.

78. See Moore, *Judaism* 1:546; Bonsirven, *Judaïsme* 2:98; H. W. Surkau, *Märtyrien in jüdischer und frühchristlicher Zeit* (FRLANT n.s. 36; Göttingen, 1938) 9–82; E. Lohse, *Märtyrer und Gottesknecht* (FRLANT n.s. 46; Göttingen, 1955) 64–110.

79. See Billerbeck's summary judgment on those rabbinic sayings which also give evidence of suffering on the part of the Davidic Messiah (*Kommentar* 2:292), but the idea of the Messiah suffering for the sins of the *world* is never found in rabbinic literature.

80. GJohn is very interested in the universal scope of Christ's redemptive work; see 1:29; 3:17; 4:42; 10:16; 11:52; 12:24, 32, 47; 17:18, 20.

81. See Irenaeus, *Adv. Haer.* 1.1.12: καὶ ἄλλα δὲ πολλὰ μυσαρὰ καὶ ἄθεα πράσσοντες . . . ἑαυτοὺς δὲ ὑπερυφοῦσι τελείους ἀποκαλοῦντες καὶ σπέρματα ἐκλογῆς.

SECOND SECTION
KNOWING GOD AND KEEPING HIS COMMANDMENTS
(1 JOHN 2:3-11)

[3]Now by this we may be sure that we know him, if we obey his commandments. [4]Whoever says, "I have come to know him," but does not obey his commandments, is a liar, and in such a person the truth does not exist; [5]but whoever obeys his word, truly in this person the love of God has reached perfection. By this we may be sure that we are in him; [6]whoever says, "I abide in him," ought to walk just as he walked.

[7]Beloved, I am writing you no new commandment, but an old commandment that you have had from the beginning; the old commandment is the word that you have heard. [8]Yet I am writing you a new commandment that is true in him and in you, because the darkness is passing away and the true light is already shining. [9]Whoever says, "I am in the light," while hating a brother or sister, is still in the darkness. [10]Whoever loves a brother or sister lives in the light, and in such a person there is no cause for stumbling. [11]But whoever hates another believer is in the darkness, walks in the darkness, and does not know the way to go, because the darkness has brought on blindness.

* * *

1. Knowledge of God Requires That
We Should Keep His Commandments
and Walk after the Example of Jesus (1 John 2:3-6)

There is a noticeable parallel in sentence structure between 2:3-5a and 1:5-7. After setting out his thesis in v. 3 (cf. 1:5) the author proceeds to refute the claims of the gnostics in v. 4, just as he had done in 1:6, branding them with similar epithets (2:4b; cf. 1:6b). Then their wrong behavior is contrasted with the right, and the latter is given the assurance of salvation (2:5; cf. 1:7). The whole short paragraph is a fresh application of the same basic theme, except that the negative idiom "not walking in the darkness" is now applied positively, "keeping the commandments." This all goes to show that fellowship with God and knowledge of him are one and the same thing, as is further corroborated at the end of v. 5c, "we are in him." This fresh illumination of the same theme points up one of the author's characteristic traits, though it also has a concrete reason of its own. This is the gnostic slogan "I know him." The Christian preacher picks up this slogan and interprets it in terms of the orthodox doctrine of salvation and its requirements.

The object of religious knowledge here can also be Jesus Christ (1:13a, 14b; cf. John 1:10; 14:7, 9; 16:3; 17:3), though the hymn in the previous paragraph does not actually refer to him.[82]

In 2:1-2 Jesus Christ is evaluated in terms of his role as advocate and redeemer for us. 1 John cannot be concerned with knowing who Jesus of Nazareth really was when he walked among us (cf. John 8:28; 10:38; 17:8, 23, 25 — a knowing that has a close

---

82. Calmes, Büchsel (see also Windisch, Dodd) *contra* most recent commentators.

affinity with believing). That much is clear. But neither does the knowledge of his divine nature and being as a way to fellowship with God (cf. 2:23; 5:11f.) stand in the foreground here. That would result in a shift of perspective compared with 2:1–2 and would lead to an abrupt ending (unlike 2:23f.). On the other hand, everything becomes intelligible when we interpret "to know him" as the knowledge of God and place it in parallelism with 1:6ff.

To know God is an idea full of rich associations evoking strong emotions in contemporary religious language. The author of 1 John has deliberately adopted it as part of his vocabulary, like fellowship with God. But since "to know God" has a different nuance according to one's individual religious perspective, an important question arises here. What did the author of 1 John take as his starting point, and in what sense did he adopt the idea of knowing God?

EXCURSUS 3

Heretical Gnosis and Christian Knowledge of God

1. The idea of knowledge of God in 1 John is derived neither from Greek culture nor entirely from a Jewish background. As far as the false teachers are concerned, the idea of knowledge of God ties in with that cultural current to which this slogan lent its name. In Hellenistic literature the term "knowledge of God" is extremely rare.[83] On Greco-Roman soil, knowledge is the result of careful observation, speculative thought, systematic reflection, and logical deduction. This is the way the Greek philosopher arrives at the source and ground of his being, that is, the first cause, the unmoved mover (Aristotle). Against this "the fact remains that we find ourselves in an entirely different world when we examine the material which has in common with Greek culture nothing but the use of the Greek alphabet."[84] By this is meant that treasure of religious testimonies mainly of oriental provenance which—despite all its differences—means saving knowledge, the proper way to redemption, as gnosticism understood it.[85]

The relationships are rather different with the Old Testament and late Judaism. In the Old Testament, knowledge of God is not primarily a rational process. Rather, it is a response to the divine revelation and election. It involves a reciprocal relationship and manifests itself in cult and worship and in

---

83. See Norden, *Agnostos Theos,* 87ff.; Bultmann, *TDNT* 1:120f.

84. Norden, *Agnostos Theos,* 95.

85. On this and on the difficult problem of the rise of gnosticism, see Jonas, *Gnosis* (amid all the varieties of gnostic manifestations, there was a unitary gnostic "feel for the world"); Bultmann, *TDNT* 1:692ff.; L. Cerfaux, *DBSup* 3:659–701 (against a pre-Christian origin of gnosticism and its influence on John); S. Pétrement, *Le dualisme chez Platon, les Gnostiques et les Manichéens* (Paris, 1947) 132–59; M. P. Nilsson, *Geschichte der griechischen Religion* 2:556–96; Quispel, *Gnosis als Weltreligion* (its main roots are in Judaism); R. McL. Wilson, *Gnostic Problem* (see esp. pp. 64–96), "Gnosticism and Christianity in NT Times"—perhaps the best treatment of this problem); Grant, *Gnosticism and Early Christianity;* S. Schulz, *TRu* 26 (1960) 209–66, 301–34.

obedience to God's commandments.[86] In Pharisaic and rabbinic Judaism knowledge of God is increasingly restricted to the confession of monotheism and to fidelity and obedience to the precepts of the Torah. Inasmuch as it regards the revelation of God in history as a means of access to a knowledge of him and requires its practical expression in the keeping of his commandments, the Johannine idea of the knowledge of God comes somewhat close to this. Yet there is a considerable difference, as is shown by a quotation from *Sipre Deuteronomy* 11:22.[87] "Would you know who spoke and the world came into being? Then learn Haggada [the art of scripture interpretation]. Thereby you will come to know God and cleave to his ways." The knowledge of God in rabbinic Judaism involves a strict adherence to the law and its interpretation (which is often allegorical). But this allows for so much maneuvering that scholars with a Greek education like Philo of Alexandria were able to discover the heights and depths of philosophy and mysticism in the Old Testament revelation.[88] But 1 John never follows this detour, nor does it indulge in allegorical exegesis. A closer approximation to John's idea of the knowledge of God can be found in the Qumran texts. There knowledge, insight, and similar terms play an important part.[89] But there the emphasis is on the knowledge that comes from God and is hidden from humanity, being imparted only by special revelation. That was the special privilege enjoyed by the scripture scholars at Qumran. It involves both the correct interpretation of the Torah and the uncovering of eschatological mysteries. "My eyes have gazed on that which is eternal, on wisdom concealed from men, on knowledge and wise design (hidden) from the sons of men; on a fountain of righteousness and on a storehouse of power, on a spring of glory . . ." (1QS 11:6f.). Such knowledge is made possible by the Holy Spirit, which God gives to his elect: "I have as one with understanding known thee, O my God, by the spirit which thou hast given to me, and I have faithfully hearkened to thy marvellous counsel. In the mystery of thy wisdom thou hast opened knowledge to me, and in thy mercies (thou hast unlocked for me) the fountain of thy mind" (1QH 12:11ff.). Of course this kind of knowledge can

---

86. See Botterwick, *'Gott erkennen' im Sprachgebrauch des Alten Testaments* (with older literature); W. Zimmerli, *Erkenntnis Gottes nach dem Buche Ezechiel* (Zurich, 1954); Nötscher, *Zur theologischen Terminologie,* 23–26.—M.-É. Boismard regards the eschatologicsl expressions of Ezekiel and Jeremiah about the "new heart" and the corresponding "knowledge of God" as comparable with the Johannine expressions (*RB* 56 [1949] 366–71, 388–91).

87. *Sipre Deuteronomy* 11:22 §49 (see Billerbeck, *Kommentar* 3:776); see further Moore, *Judaism* 2:289ff.

88. In Philo, the Hellenistic, gnostic, and Old Testament concepts merge with one another, and it is often hard to say which one is dominant. But Philo's starting point is the Old Testament, and his method is the allegorical interpretation of scripture. See H. Windisch, *Die Frömmigkeit Philos* (1909) 60ff.; Bultmann, *TDNT* 1:702; E. Bréhier, *Les idées philosophiques et religieuses de Philon d'Alexandrie* (2nd ed.; Paris, 1925) passim; E. Stein, *Die allegorische Exegese des Philo aus Alexandreia* (BZNW 51; Giessen, 1929); Völker, *Fortschritt und Vollendung,* esp. 189ff.; Pétrement, *Dualisme,* 216ff.

89. See W. D. Davies, "'Knowledge' in the Dead Sea Scrolls and Matthew 11:25–30," *HTR* 16 (1953) 113–39; Nötscher, *Zur theologischen Terminologie,* 38–79; Betz, *Offenbarung und Schriftforschung,* 6–15, 18f., 135–40. See also the following note.

hardly be termed gnostic even if it does bring illumination and redemption.[90] Nor does it lead to the kind of fellowship with God which 1 John has in mind. Since, however, this knowledge is mediated by a divine revelation, it does have some affinity with gnosticism. This is true despite the fact that its starting point is more likely to be found in apocalyptic. Once again, heterodox Judaism may have proved a gateway to gnostic thinking. On the other hand, there are features in the Qumran texts that do show some connection with the knowledge of God as it is found in 1 John. Both speak of God in personal terms. Both are aware of the distance between humanity and God. Both hold fast to revelation in history and to salvation history in particular. Above all, both are aware of the necessity of obedience. All of this is in both traditions an inalienable part of their Jewish heritage and quite different from anything in gnosticism. Thus, the Qumran texts do in fact serve to some extent as a bridge. But they are not a complete explanation of Johannine usage.

The author of 1 John takes over the phrase "knowledge of God" from the heretical teachers he is opposing. It is significant that he uses the term, alongside of "seeing God," for a direct vision of God (1 John 3:6; cf. John 14:7, 17; 3 John 11). He appropriates these slogans, using them to address the Christian community (3:6; 4:7f.; 5:20a). Yet he sees the way to such gnosis and its precise nature in a very different light. If it is true that the slogan "to know God" was used in the competition between the religions,[91] then the author of 1 John has joined the fray and beaten the same drum as the gnostics in the hope of winning recruits for Christianity. It is our task to throw light on the distinctively Christian element in the Johannine concept of the knowledge of God.

2. What did John's opponents mean by the knowledge of God? To answer that all we can do is to point out the general direction of their thought, for we have no precise information about their theology and spirituality. All we know is that for them the knowledge of God leads to fellowship with him (cf. 1:6; 2:5c). They are convinced that they are "in the light" (2:9). Their goal is their own divinization; "this is the glorious goal for all, to have acquired gnosis: to become divinized."[92] Or again, those who have acquired gnosis are good and holy; indeed, they are already divine.[93] It is possible that the gnostics of 1 John were not so precise about the way such knowledge of God was achieved, though they may have encouraged ecstatic visions of God (cf. 4:12, 20; 3:6b). The ascent to life and light is described in Poimandres without any reference to ecstasy. Poimandres only offers advice for this earthly life: "The person who is guided by *Nous* (Greek *ennous*) will acquire self-knowledge" (§21). In addition, the divine assistance is promised (§22). Progressive emancipation from the trammels of the bodily senses, something achieved at the dissolution of the material

---

90. See B. Reicke, "Traces of Gnosticism in the Dead Sea Scrolls?" *NTS* 1 (1954–55) 137–41; Schoeps, *Urgemeinde,* 30–46, 85 ("analogous" development in Judaism; in the Qumran texts no sign of Hellenistic-pagan gnosis); K. Schubert, *LTK* 4:1025 (the terms have a "gnostic character"); Cross, *Ancient Library,* 154f. (takes a similar line).

91. Norden, *Agnostos Theos,* 109.

92. *CHerm* 1.26a.

93. *CHerm* 10.9.

body, is also promised (§24). The *Hermetic Tractate 13,* on the other hand, allows for "rebirth in the Spirit already here on earth through ecstatic vision (§13). Both answers are therefore possible. It is not ecstasy that lies at the heart of gnosticism but deliverance from the world of darkness, of the material, and of death, and the return of the soul into the realm of light from which it had come and to which it yearns to return from this alien world. Whether this happens already now in ecstasy or must wait until after death is a secondary question. At the same time contempt for all material reality, which is characteristic of this type of spirituality, provides a strong impulse toward ecstasy. The way of salvation in gnosis, however, always involves a knowledge of the soul's origin and destiny, of its pneumatic nature and its "thrownness" into this lower, alien world. This is what really matters. With this knowledge as such, redemption and rebirth are initiated and basically achieved. The purer and more intensive this gnosis is, the more completely does the gnostic participate in the divine life and light. "Holy is God, who wills to be known and to be known by his own."[94] It is highly probable that the heretical teachers in 1 John shared this basic principle of all gnosis, even if the typically gnostic questions about the soul's origin, destiny, and nature[95] do not surface. 1 John gives no detailed account of their teachings, unlike the later Christian apologists. All he does is to oppose a few of their slogans.

3. The Christian gnosis espoused by the author of 1 John is completely purged of all non-Christian elements. As a result he "has produced one of the supreme intellectual achievements of all time."[96]

In particular the difference between his idea of the knowledge of God and the non-Christian gnosis of the heretics might be summarized as follows:

a) By knowing God he is looking not for human self-understanding but for a genuine experience of God, leading to fellowship with him.

b) Such knowledge of God is dependent on a revelation quite different from anything found in gnosticism. In the mystery religions the initiate is drawn into an experience that is at once sensual and suprasensual, for example, a mysterious vision of the upper and nether worlds.[97] In Hermetic mysticism the initiate is enlightened and instructed by his "father," the god Hermes (so Hermes, *Tractate 13*), or by Poimandres, the "mind of the supreme Power" (*nous tēs authentias,* §2). This occurs in a kind of spiritual slumber (§1) in which the initiate is instructed how to attain to this liberated gnosis. The Christian, on the other hand, believes in a revelation that happened at a particular moment in history and became the subject of public proclamation (1 John 1:3, 5). The Christian receives this revelation at the hands of messengers. It is not imparted in a secret

---

94. *CHerm* 1.31.

95. [Ἡ] γνῶσις, τίνες ἦμεν, τί γεγόναμεν· ποῦ ἦμεν [ἢ] ποῦ ἐνεβλήθημεν· ποῦ σπεύδομεν, πόθεν λυτρούμεθα· τί γέννησις τί ἀναγέννησις (Clement of Alexandria, *Exc. ex Theod.* 78.2). Cf. *Acts Thom.* 15. These formulas are also known to the Stoic philosophers, though they use them in a different way; see Epictetus 1.6.25; Seneca, *Ep.* 82.6; Marcus Aurelius, *In sem.* 8.52. See also Norden, *Agnostos Theos,* 102f.; Reitzenstein, *Hellenistische Mysterienreligionen,* 285ff.

96. Hanse, *'Gott haben' in der Antike,* 105; see also on the independence of Johannine "mysticism," Omodeo, *La mistica Giovannea,* 106ff.

97. See Apuleius, *Metamorphoses* 11.23.

rite of initiation nor through some exalted dream, but by listening faithfully to the divine message (1 John 2:7, 24; 3:11).

c) The revelation leading to the knowledge of God and to fellowship with him is mediated by his incarnate Son, Jesus Christ. He is the mediator of salvation, indispensable in the role he plays. The emissary from the upper world of light, or whatever he is called in the gnostic systems, is a very different kind of figure, a mythological being in whom the idea of the gnostic redemption is clothed. His mission is a timeless one and can be heard at any time by those who are receptive to it. It is the call of truth which comes to the soul from beyond this material world. Into this world the initiate is thrown, being recalled to the world of light and life.[98] The coming of the emissary is a permanent or constantly repeated fact[99] or, insofar as it envisions a historical figure as in Manicheism,[100] is prototypical in character. This is because the emissary is meant to portray nothing else but the fate and destiny of every soul. "The Coming One is however in the last analysis identical with those to whom he comes. Life in the last analysis is identical with life. The stranger comes to strangers in the world and in a remarkable way the nature and destiny of the emissary and those to whom he is sent are interchangeable."[101] A notable instance of this is the "Song of the Pearl," which comes in *Acts of Thomas* 108ff., also known as the "Hymn of Souls." Here the "son of the king," who is also the redeemer, may at the same time be the soul itself![102] Again, in the *Odes of Solomon* the true son of God appears alongside of the adopted son, that is, the redeemed human being. One term merges into the other![103] It is easy to understand how puzzling and confusing such trains of thought must have been for the Christian doctrine of redemption. They "dissolved" Jesus (*v.l.*, see NRSV margin, 1 John 4:3). They reduced the historically unique incarnate Redeemer, with his irreplaceable and unrepeatable bloody death as an atonement for sin and the salvation of the world, to a more or less mythological notion. The author of 1 John was clearly aware of this danger and fought against it might and main.

d) What are the consequences of this for practical behavior here on earth? That is a question which non-Christian gnosis hardly raised. They were too

---

98. See Jonas, *Gnosis* 1:120ff.; Pétrement, *Dualisme,* 164ff.

99. An example of the "coming of the emissary of light" and his "preaching" in the world will be found, for example, in *Ginza* 57–61, of the "leading" of his own up to heaven in *Odes Sol.* 22.

100. On this, see Jonas, *Gnosis* 1:303f.; Reitzenstein, *Iranische Erlösungsmysterien,* 17f., 34f., 55f.; Pétrement, *Dualisme,* 200ff., 299ff.; H.-C. Puech, *Le Manichéisme* (Paris, 1949) 1:78ff. The addition of the so-called hymn-cycles became important for the elucidation of Manichean gnosticism; see H. Boyce, *The Manichaean Hymn-Cycles* (Oxford, 1954). These hymns are discussed in Colpe, *Die religionsgeschichtliche Schule,* 69–100, with considerable clarification of the gnostic redeemer myth (pp. 171–208).

101. Jonas, *Gnosis* 1:126; cf. Reitzenstein, *Iranische Erlösungsmysterien,* 55f. R. Abramowski, "Der Christus der Salomooden," *ZNW* 35 (1936) 59: "Absolute identity in form between the fate of Christ and the fate of humanity both in humiliation and in exaltation."

102. Jonas, *Gnosis,* 1:320; Pétrement, *Dualisme,* 165f.; G. Bornkamm, *Mythos und Legende in den apokryphen Thomas-Akten* (FRLANT n.s. 31; Göttingen, 1933) 111ff.; A. Adam, *Die Psalmen des Thomas und Perlenlied als Zeugnisse vorchristlicher Gnosis* (BZNW 24; Berlin, 1959) 56f., 81f.

103. See Abramowski, *ZNW* 35 (1936) 52–62.

preoccupied with the soul and its salvation. But the question of moral behavior becomes for the Christians the overriding concern, when seen in the light of their Savior's ethical requirements. Whoever would know God and attain to fellowship with him must keep his commandments (2:3–5). God's emissary is not a prototype of the Christian's destiny, individual and cosmic, but a pattern for moral behavior in this world (2:6). More than this, the Son of God made man makes highly concrete demands on the Christian, for the Son is the source of redemption; and for that the Christian owes a debt of gratitude (2:1f.). Primarily this means the love of brother and sister (2:7ff.). Moral obedience is the indispensable condition for eternal salvation, which even though expected joyfully and with confidence (2:28; 4:17) continues to be no more than a matter of hope (3:3).[104]

* * *

2:3 The "now" (Greek *kai*, "and") does not merely join this verse to the previous verses. On the contrary, "by this" places all the emphasis upon the following[105] conditional clause, "if we . . . ." The author is concerned with a criterion for distinguishing between false and true gnostics. The litmus test is whether they keep God's commandments.[106] The frequent occurrences of the phrase "by this we may be sure"[107] show how the epistle's addressees were threatened by the self-confident, misleading slogans of the false teachers and how much depends on such distinguishing marks. This "being sure" has a diacritical sense quite different from when the same verb is used for "knowing God," as can also be seen from the tense of the verb in the same verse. There is always a criterion available. Hence the present tense expressing a *rule,* whereas when the author speaks about the knowledge of God as a permanent possession he uses the perfect tense.

The criterion already mentioned, "if we obey his commandments," is typically Johannine even in its wording.[108] Paul prefers a different word for "keeping"

---

104. On the knowledge of God in John, see further M.-É. Boismard, "La connaissance de Dieu dans l'Alliance Nouvelle d'après la première lettre de s. Jean," *RB* 56 (1949) 365–91; Suitbertus a S. Joanne a Cruce, *Bib* 39 (1958) 450–57; J. Alfaro, "Cognitio Dei et Christi in 1 Jo," *VD* 39 (1961) 82–91; A. M. Denis, *Le thèmes de connaissance dans le Document de Damas* (Louvain, 1967); J. E. Ménard, "La 'connaissance' dans l'Évangile de Vérité," *RechScR* 41 (1967) 1–28; B. E. Gärtner, "The Pauline and Johannine Idea of 'to know God' against the Hellenistic Background," *NTS* 14 (1968) 209–31 (principle: "like through like"); I. de la Potterie, "La connaissance de Dieu dans le dualisme eschatologique d'après 1 Jn 2, 12–14," in *Au service de la Parole de Dieu* (Mélanges A. M. Charue; Gembloux, 1969) 77–99, esp. 93–96 (eschatological knowledge of God according to Jer. 31:31–34, no relation to gnosticism).

105. Cf. John 13:35; 1 John 3:16, 24; 4:2; 5:9. Contrary to this, the demonstrative pronoun in 2:5b; 3:19; 4:6 (*ek toutou*) refers to what precedes.

106. See A. Humbert, *L'observance des commandements dans les écrits johanniques* (Studia Moralia; Rome, 1962).

107. See the passages cited in n. 105; see also M.-É. Boismard, *RB* 56 (1949) 371ff.

108. *Tērein* occurs with this meaning 12 times in GJohn, 6 times in 1 John, and 5 or 6 times in Revelation (according to whether it is taken in an ethical sense in 1:3; 3:3; 22:7, 9) meaning "to observe" or "to hold fast" (in memory).

the commandments (Greek *phylassein*),[109] following the Septuagint. But the other word for "keeping" the commandments (Greek *tērein*) is a good New Testament usage[110] and has some precedent in the Septuagint.[111] Even more important than this is the fact that moral obedience is a typical emphasis of Johannine Christianity. The Johannine Jesus requires it from his disciples as a proof of their love for him (John 14:15, 23). It is a precondition of his love for them (15:10). Keeping his commandments assures them of eternal life (8:51f.). In a similar vein the author of 1 John is never tired of demanding the same practical expression of love for God (5:2f.). It is the ground for the continuance of fellowship with God (3:24) and the precondition for having their prayers answered (3:22). Despite all the speculation and mystical profundity which impresses us so much in the Johannine writings, they are eminently practical and down to earth in their moral concern. This leads to a practical Christianity diametrically opposed to a mysticism divorced from action and to unworldly speculation. It is precisely by this ethic of obedience that the author maintains his links with the teaching of Jesus in the Synoptic Gospels,[112] and with the basic moral attitude of earliest Christianity.[113] In this matter he stands closer to Judaism than to pagan syncretism.[114] There were many different kinds of gnosticism at that time. Along with the mud of libertinism there flowed the clear waters of pure morality. Many of the gnostics must have struggled seriously and radically for emancipation from material realities.[115] But the gnostic ethic is no answer to the call of a personal God, no justification before the forum of the eternal judge. This is the reason why they could fall into the abyss where for the sake of freedom immorality became the order of the day. It was this perversion of moral sensitivity that roused the ire of their opponents, especially Irenaeus (see Excursus 3). The clarity and simplicity of the Christian ethic owe not a little to the Johannine writings.

2:4 The criterion we have pinpointed is now applied to the heretical teachers. Their gnostic slogan, "I have come to know him," is contrasted with their actual

---

109. *Tērein* in 1 Tim. 6:14; *phylassein* in Rom. 2:26; Gal. 6:13; 1 Tim. 5:21.

110. Matt. 19:17; 23:3; 28:20; Mark 7:9; Acts 15:5; James 2:10.

111. See Prov. 3:1, 21; Tobit 14:9; Sir. 29:1; (substantive *tērēsis*) Wis. 6:18; Sir. 35:23; *per contra*, the LXX translates Hebrew *šāmar* with *phylassein*, *not* with *tērein* (*contra* Chaine et al.).

112. Matt. 5:19; 7:21; 23:23; Mark 10:25, 28; Luke 10:37; etc.

113. Acts 2:37f.; 3:19; 17:30f.; Rom. 2:6ff.; 1 Cor. 8:1-3; Gal. 5:16; 1 Pet. 1:17; James 1:25; 2:14, 17, 18, etc.; Rev. 2:23; 20:12f.; 22:12.

114. See Billerbeck, *Kommentar* 3:776 ad loc. However, it is obviously accentuated differently in the rabbinic idea of "fulfilling the commandments" (*miṣwōt*) as compared with the action-oriented ethic of early Christianity. The Jew aspires to "fulfill the commandments" (*ṣālag miswōt;* see Billerbeck, *Kommentar* 4:11f.), while the disciple of Christ is meant to strive to realize concretely the one commandment of love.

115. See Bousset, *Hauptprobleme,* 321; Jonas, *Gnosis* 1:233ff.—The ascetic tendencies of Basilides, Valentinus, and Marcion, as well as that in Manicheism, are expressions of a different basic attitude from that in Christian self-restraint, for they devalue the material world on principle. Moreover, early Christianity is critical of asceticism precisely because of its misuse in gnosticism; see H. von Campenhausen, *Die Askese im Urchristentum* (Tübingen, 1949) 44ff.; R. Schnackenburg, *Die sittliche Botschaft des NT* (2nd ed.; Munich, 1962) 163-71.

behavior (note the conjunction "but"=Greek *kai* adversative). The condemnation is delivered in terms almost identical to 1:6 and 8. Instead of "we lie" we now have "is a liar," underscoring their distance from God and their antagonism toward him (see on 1:6). The second term, already familiar from 1:8, not only denies such a liar and tempter ("in such a *person*" — not "in it") the truth of his claim, but beyond that his possession of truth altogether. He lacks the divine nature which alone makes possible a genuine knowledge of God.[116] In this sense "the truth" is synonymous with the "Spirit of truth" (cf. 4:6; John 14:17). To enjoy genuine gnosis a person must be "of the truth" (cf. John 18:37; 1 John 2:21; 3:19).

2:5 In contrast to the gloomy picture of the false gnostics who claim to know God but do not keep his commandments, the author draws a cheerful picture of the genuine Christian who "obeys his [God's] word." The divine commandments are now defined and summarized as God's word.[117] Just because they are his word — that is, a revelation of his will — they involve an unconditional obligation. Behind this word imparted by God there is a profound theological idea. It is like being entrusted with a treasure that must be guarded as a sacred deposit (see John 5:38; 1 John 1:10). But it also involves obligations and must be translated into concrete behavior. It becomes a person's judge (cf. John 12:48).

For the Christian the attempt to obey the will of God made known to us in Christ is a sign that one bears the divine love in oneself. Only so (genitive of quality)[118] can the depth and fullness of the Johannine thought be comprehended. Love is what marks those who are born of God. But it must then be put to the test and proved in practical obedience to his commandments (cf. 4:7ff.). Conversely, keeping the commandments becomes the hallmark of this divine status. Divine love is not simply love toward God (objective genitive). That is clear from the context of v. 4: truth and love are kindred terms for what Christ in his divine being bears within himself. This is the point the author seeks to underscore. This divine nature has no other outward sign than moral fidelity. Here is the ethical and practical simplicity that makes the Christian idea of love so different from that of the gnostics. In the *Odes of Solomon* love is an enthusiastic yearning for God, the soul's encounter with the beloved in mystical

---

116. *Alētheia* is not identical with *gnōsis* (*contra* Windisch), but stands in a double relationship to it; either it is the content of revelation and therefore the object of knowledge (John 8:32; 2 John 1) or — so here — the presupposition of true knowledge, involving the imparting of a divine nature to human beings (John 8:43f.; 14:17; 2 John 2).

117. *Logos* is also a wider concept than *entolai*, insofar as it includes the word of revelation laid hold upon in faith; cf. John 8:51; 14:23; 15:20; 17:6; Rev. 3:8, 10.

118. That the objective genitive does not do complete justice to Johannine thought is the feeling of many modern interpreters as contrasted with older ones; however, see already Westcott, *Johannine Epistles,* ad loc.: "The fundamental idea of 'the love of God' in St John is 'the love which God has made known, and which shows his nature.' This love communicated to man is effective in him towards the brethren and towards God Himself."—The subjective genitive, regarded as possible by Büchsel, makes no sense in this context and indeed is ruled out by the formulation of the language. For more on the subject, see the commentary on 3:17; 4:12. M. Zerwick calls this genitive "*generaliter determinans*" (*Graecitas biblica* 25–28).

ecstasy.[119] The author of 1 John does not regard the fulfillment of the commandments as simply a first step toward a higher mystical life with God. On the contrary, when a person faithfully observes the word of God, the divine love is realized to the full.[120] Neither is this Johannine idea of perfection (Greek *teleiousthai*) an eschatological event (corresponding to the eschatological term *telos*),[121] nor does it derive from the Greek idea of perfection as a progressive development.[122] Rather, it denotes, as the term "perfect love" indicates (4:18), a condition of perfection in deed (hence the perfect tense in John 17:23; 1 John 4:12, 17, 18) or the fulfillment of works up to the point of their completion (cf. John 4:34; 5:36; 17:4; 19:28). But this perfection is not reached in stages through human endeavor. Truth and love by and large are granted as gifts when the believer is born of God, though they must be manifested in faith and in keeping the commandments. The perfection of God's love, which consists in the harmonious correlation between being and obligation, is also the fruit of cooperation between God and humanity. The passive form ("is perfected") shows how it is God who takes the initiative in this process. Only as one born of God and beloved by him is a human being able to reciprocate this love and keep God's commandments.

The words "by this we may be sure" hark back to the beginning of v. 3, forming an *inclusio*. Once again the point is hammered home that "keeping (and fulfilling) God's word" is the sole criterion for fellowship with him.

2:6 The last phrase is accompanied by a second gnostic slogan, although the author himself seems to have contributed something to the shaping of it, since "abiding in him" is a favorite Johannine phrase.[123] With the expression that follows he is concerned with the obligation[124] of walking after the pattern of Christ.[125] With this, the general requirement of keeping God's commandments

---

119. *Odes Sol.* 3:2–8; 7:1f.; 8:1, 13, 22; 16:2f.; 23:3; 40:4; 42:7–9. See Excursus 10, 4b.

120. Büchsel prefers to take *alēthōs* with the relative clause. The contrast, however, is not between a presumed activity of the divine will and an actual one, but between doing and not doing. The real point lies in the final clause. This corresponds to the prepositive use of *alēthōs* which is elsewhere attested in GJohn: 1:47; 4:42; 6:14; 7:26, 40; 8:31. It is postpositive only in 17:8, and there for the sake of euphony.

121. *Contra* Bultmann, *John,* 516 n. 3 ("eschatological sense") and Preisker, *Neutestamentliche Zeitgeschichte,* 169 ("Love, as it ought to be at the *telos*"). See further BAGD 811, s.v.; Westcott, ad loc.; P. J. Du Plessis, ΤΕΛΕΙΟΣ: *The Idea of Perfection in the New Testament* (Kampen, 1960?) 174ff.

122. The linguistic root probably lies in the Hebrew *gāmar;* cf. the rabbinic usage given in Schlatter, *Sprache,* 135, 150 (in the sense, however, of the Jewish idea of suffering). The same concept of perfection occurs frequently in the Dead Sea Scrolls; see 1QS 1:8; 2:2; 4:22; 8:9f., 20f.; 9:6, 8f.; 1QSa 1:17, 28; 1QM 14:7; 1QH 1:36; 4:30. The Dead Sea Scrolls *tmym* and *twm* for it. See R. Schnackenburg, *Geist und Leben* 32 (1959) 420–23; Du Plessis, ΤΕΛΕΙΟΣ, 104–15.

123. See Excursus 4.—*Menein en autō* could, because of the rapid switch of phrases, have the same meaning as *einai en autō;* cf. also 2:10 with 9; 3:24; 4:12, 13, 15; but it may have been the idea of ethical stability that gave the verb "abide" its particular nuance.

124. *Opheilein* occurs in this sense also in 3:16; 4:11; 3 John 8. To apply the term as a tool for style criticism and make it a Christian (parenetic) comment on the *Vorlage* (Bultmann, "Analyse," 143f.) is arbitrary. It occurs also in GJohn (13:17; in a somewhat different sense, 19:7).

125. The Pythagoreans also spoke of their master as *ekeinos ho anēr* (Iamblichus, *Vita Pythag.* 18.88; 35.255). See further p. 72 n. 3.

(which was just as much the duty of the pious Jew) acquires a distinctive Christian stamp. It is not just a general code of law, even if it be the venerable Decalogue, that is the Christian's code of conduct. Rather, it is the teaching of Christ himself, not only by word but also by the example of his life. It is not for nothing that this phrase is preceded by the word "abide." If fellowship with God is to be real and lasting, it requires constant fidelity to the great paradigm (note the words "just as," Greek *kathōs*)[126] that is, Christ himself. For Christ's life of obedience to God was crowned with his death on the cross (cf. John 14:31). In saying this the author may have already had in mind what follows, for he speaks in concrete terms of the love of brothers and sisters. It is just here that the example of Christ shines at its brightest (3:16; cf. John 13:14f.). Given his strong emphasis on practical behavior (3:18) the author can find no better way than to point to the person and teaching of Christ.

EXCURSUS 4

The Johannine Formulas of Immanence

Unlike the formulas that Paul uses to express his "Christ mysticism" ("in Christ," "Christ in us," etc.) the Johannine formulas have received little attention to date![127] Because of their association with the idea of "abiding in him," we will refer to them succinctly as "formulas of immanence," and this despite the fact that they require quite different explanations. The almost complete disappearance of the formula "in Christ" and the substitution of "abiding in him" (1 John 2:24, 27f.; 3:6; cf. John 6:56; 15:4-7), the typical formula of reciprocity (John 6:56; 15:4ff.; 14:20; 17:23 — Paul says either "in Christ" or "Christ in us"), the expansion of the formula to include the Father (1 John 2:24; 3:24; 4:13; 5:20; cf. John 17:21-23), the change in the meaning of *pneuma* in Johannine theology (in Paul it is the key to basic understanding) — all this shows how far apart Paul and John are in the way they think and express themselves. Paul can use "in Christ" and "in the Spirit" as alternatives. This is because for him the risen Christ is essentially a pneumatic being (Rom. 1:4; 2 Cor. 3:17). We look in vain for such an illuminating formula in the Johannine writings (Rev. 1:10 represents the traditional language of prophecy). Without pursuing these differences any further at this point, let us see if we can throw light on the Johannine formulas of immanence in all their distinctiveness.

---

126. Imitation, not discipleship in the sense of following the master's footsteps. The author does not use this metaphor. *Akolouthein* remains in the Johannine writings a literal following on the part of the disciples, or a following in faith (John 8:12; 10:4, 5, 27; 13:36f.).

127. See R. Borig, *Der wahre Weinstock: Untersuchungen zu Jo 15, 1-10* (Munich, 1967) 199-236.

The Johannine Epistles

I. GROUPING OF THE MATERIAL

1. Divine Attributes and Energies in Humanity

Connections with ideas familar elsewhere can be found chiefly in what the Johannine writings have to say about the divine attributes and energies within human beings. In 1 John such a claim is made for "truth" (Greek *alētheia,* 1:8; 2:4; cf. 2 John 2), for the divine Logos (1:10; 2:14; cf. 2:4), for the "anointing" (*chrisma,* 2:27), for the "seed" (Greek *sperma,* 3:9), for the "love of God" (3:17; 4:12; cf. 2:5). To have "life abiding in (oneself)" (3:15) means very much the same thing. In the Old Testament and in later Judaism the Spirit of God is conceived of in the main as a living and active power, both in the people of God as a whole and in the individual. It will become complete and perfect in the expected time of salvation.[128] Yet the ancient texts have more to say about the outpouring of the Spirit and less about its indwelling. In the thanksgiving psalms (*Hodayot*) of Qumran it is often said that God "gave" his (holy) Spirit to people (1QH 12:12; 13:19; 16:11; 17:17; frag. 3, line 14) or "shed" it upon them (1QH 7:7; 17:26; frag. 2, lines 9, 13). But the sole purpose of this is to enable them to have knowledge and to give them strength for pure and moral behavior. The closest parallel to the Johannine language is when Paul speaks of the Spirit's "dwelling" or "indwelling" (Rom. 8:9, 11; cf. 1 Cor. 3:16).[129] It is doubtful, however, whether the Johannine idea of "abiding" has any connection with the indwelling of the Spirit (cf. Matt. 12:38f.), as Hauck thinks. The idea is often found in literature outside of the Bible. According to Philo, the divine Logos or Spirit inhabits the soul in its search for God.[130] The *Testaments of the Twelve Patriarchs* comes closer in feeling to the Old Testament when it says that nothing evil dwells in the soul of the righteous, but only the fear of God.[131] The Mandean writings tell us how Kušta (Truth) "enters our heart" or how "our heart is filled with Kušta."[132] With all their differences in detail, these evidences all have in common an inward-looking mystical yearning, a contemplation of the holiness of the soul, which aspires to the radiance of the divine.

2. The Indwelling of God Himself in Humankind

It is not a big step from this to the idea of God himself dwelling in humankind. John is certainly familiar with this image, as is clear from John 14:23. This

---

128. First in an extraordinary manner in the prophets: Num. 11:25, 29; 1 Sam. 10:6f., 10; 19:23; Mic. 3:8; etc., for the age of salvation in all the righteous: Isa. 32:15; Ezek. 36:26f.; Joel 3:1ff. etc. See Eichrodt, *Theology* 2:57ff.; Heinisch, *Theologie,* 88f.; Moore, *Judaism* 1:421; Bousset-Gressmann, *Religion des Judentums,* 394ff.; Bonsirven, *Judaïsme* 1:210ff.; (with restrictions) Hamp, *Der Begriff 'Wort,'* 116–20.

129. See Billerbeck, *Kommentar* 3:239; Hauck, *TDNT* 5:576; Michel, *TDNT* 5:125 nn. 2, 3; G. Pecorara, "De verbo 'manere' apud Ioannem," *DivThom* 40 (1937) 170f.

130. Philo, *Post.* 122; *Gig.* 28; cf. *Spec. leg.* 4.49.

131. *T. Gad* 5:4; cf. *T. Sim.* 5:1.

132. *Ginza* 57.21f. 60.3–8; cf. 271.29f. In contrast to this void, darkness, rottenness in the soul of the wicked, see *Ginza* 276.7f., 33f.

passage has a word from the same root as "abide," the Greek word *monē,* which the NRSV translates "home" but which literally means "dwelling place." This offers a clue to what John means when he speaks of "abiding." The late Jewish and rabbinic idea of the *shekinah* living in Israel or in the faithful provides no close parallel to this intimate, individualistic type of mysticism![133] The *Testaments of the Twelve Patriarchs* speaks of God dwelling in humankind and of God's gracious condescension in so doing as his *katoikein* ("dwelling") in them![134] The idea is expressed even more strongly in Philo, who speaks of God entering the soul of the wise, "as if he were walking around in a city" (Greek *emperipatein*)![135] The author of the Johannine writing is conscious of being surrounded by this kind of religious atmosphere, though there is no trace of his borrowing any particular terminology.

3. Abiding in God and His Realm

The most forcible expression of this idea in 1 John occurs in a spatial metaphor: People dwell within an area or a realm. See especially the phrase "abides in death" (1 John 3:14). It is possible to reside in the realm of death, for the author tells his readers earlier that they had passed from the realm of death into life (Greek *metabainein;* cf. John 5:24), and to "live in the light" (2:10) — that is, to sojourn in the realm of light (cf. John 12:46). Similarly, in 2:5c and 5:20c it says "we are in him" and in 4:16 "God abides in him." Since the way to dwelling and abiding in God can only be achieved through Christ, the analogous sayings about "abiding in Christ" are closely connected with these ideas (2:24, 27, 28; 3:6). Perhaps "abide in love" (4:16) is also to be understood as abiding in the realm of God. However, the spatial metaphor is not pressed here, since it is immediately followed by the formula of reciprocity: "They abide in God and God in them." The metaphor is toned down in a similar way in the phase "in the teaching" (2 John 9)"; "in my word" (John 8:31); "in love" (John 15:9f.); cf. also "does not stand in the truth" (John 8:44). [136]

By using such language the author shows how he has turned the idea of indwelling around. That he can do so without further ado is typical of the Johannine phraseology. It warns us not to overpress his metaphorical language. Indeed, it has become almost a stereotypical formula, almost parallel to the variation between "in Christ" and "Christ in us," which we find in Paul. Moreover, it teaches us that the indwelling of divine attributes and life-giving powers in humankind, like its converse, the idea of our abiding in them, may only be a purely linguistic analogy to the identical mode of expression in reference to God.

4. This brings us to the peculiar sayings that we have called formulas of reciprocity (3:24; 4:13, 15, 16). In GJohn there are many different ways of speaking about our fellowship with Christ (cf. 14:20; 17:21, 23, 26). In formulations

---

133. On this, see Billerbeck, *Kommentar* 1:794; Moore, *Judaism* 1:434ff.
134. *T. Zeb.* 8:2; *T. Dan.* 5:1; *T. Jos.* 10:2f.; *T. Benj.* 6:4.
135. *Somn.* 2.248; cf. *Deter.* 4.
136. Cf. *emeina en tē alētheiạ tou Kyriou* (*T. Jos.* 1:3).

of this kind the real concern of the author comes out clearly. The way he varies his expressions prevents us from taking the metaphor too seriously and makes us concentrate on the reality of our union with Christ. They are all different ways of expressing our fellowship with God as this particular Christan author understands it (see Excursus 2). The formulas of reciprocity are no: meant to express our identity with God. There is no mystery language here. Yet they mean more than just being close to God, praying and singing psalms with fervor![137] As a result we cannot draw any real parallels from non-Christian literature.

II. THE MEANING OF THE IMMANENCE FORMULAS FOR JOHANNINE THEOLOGY

1. Immanence Formulas and "God-Mysticism"

The Johannine idea of fellowship with God is distinctive. It is certain of its faith and is accessible only through faith. It is a reality grounded in the sacrament, and the best way of describing it is by means of these immanence formulas, which, though obscure, are full of meaning. These formulas do not become really clear until light is thrown on them by the texts of GJohn. The evangelist speaks about Jesus in a very similar way. Jesus speaks of his profound ontological relationship with his Father. This makes the unity of the Christian with God an extension of the fellowship between the Father and the Son (14:20; cf. 10:17, 21, 23). Or, to put it another way, the fellowship of the Christians with one another when they are united with God is modeled on the union between the Father and the Son (17:11, 21, 22). The metaphysical uniqueness of the Father–Son relationship, however, remains intact. The Son "knows" the Father (8:55; 10:15; 17:25) in a more profound and intimate manner (cf. 1:18; 3:32). It is only through the Son and in him that the believers come to know and see the Father (14:7, 9). They do not have the same relationship or interaction with the Father (5:17, 19), or the same immediate understanding or certainty that their prayers are being heard (11:41f.) as the Son enjoys. They do not have the same certainty that God has loved them from all eternity (5:20ff.; 17:24) as the Son has. They have it only in an approximate way through their association with the Son (see 16:26f.). The Christian can never say like Christ: "The Father and I are one" (10:30; cf. 17:11). But through Christ the Christian is brought into a profound fellowship with God, as profound as is possible without the loss of one's personality. This is what the immanence formulas express so beautifully by combining two different ideas to describe our unity with God in order to make one and the same point. We are in God, and God is in us. In both cases we have between God and ourselves the person of Christ as the mediator of this union, the living bond between ourselves and God![138]

---

137. Cf. Deut. 31:8; Josh. 1:5; Pss. 16:8; 17:8; 23:4; 25:16; 36:8; 38:22; 46:8; 57:2; 63:9; 71:12; 91:1ff.; etc. The thought, both metaphor and expression, always implies God's protection and assistance (God with me, by my side); it never approaches mystical communion (God in me). On *Odes of Solomon,* see Excursus 2, 5.

138. See further the discussion in Mussner, ZΩH, 151ff. and the graphic presentation on p. 153.

2. Immanence Formulas and Johannine Ethics
(The Substitution of "abiding" for "being" in These Formulas

Johannine mysticism is distinctive because of its strong ethical orientation. Fellowship with God is an eschatological reality, but it must be given practical proof. This is what the immanence formulas express. They also render yet another service. Not in vain do they use the verb "to abide in" instead of "to be in," which would have been just as possible. Even the bare statistics (which ignore all the various nuances of the term) lead us to suppose that there must be some deeper reason for this. "Abide in" occurs in GJohn 41 times, in 1 John 22 times, in 2 John 3 times, compared with 52 times in the rest of the New Testament. The relatively short document before us includes almost a fifth of all the New Testament occurrences, and the Johannine writings as a whole contain a third. On closer inspection this use of "abide" in 1 John plays a double role. On the one hand, the author uses it in the indicative to encourage the believers in their struggle against antichrists (2:27a; 3:24b; 4:13; cf. John 14:17; 2 John 2) as well as in their moral conflict (3:9; 5:18). On the other hand, the majority of the occurrences are found where the author is exhorting them both directly and indirectly to persevere in the truth (2:24; 4:15; cf. 2 John 9), to abide in Christ (2:27c, 28), and to fulfill the commandments, especially the commandment of love (2:10, 17; 3:15, 17; 4:12, 16). For the author it is a matter of principle that the life-giving powers of God are permanent (the believer *has* eternal life, 5:12, 13). He, the author, is convinced of that. But in practice he is aware of the dangers that constantly beset the attitude of faith (2:27c), and of the constant allure of the world (2:16f.). The anointing, the illumination and instruction that come from the power of God's Spirit, abides in the believers (2:27a). Yet the author deems it necessary to warn them about the propaganda and wiles of the antichrists or false prophets (2:18ff.; 4:1ff.). He feels obliged to remind them of the outward marks of the heresy (2:22; 4:2f., 15; 5:5f.). The divine seed abides in those who are born of God, making it impossible for them to sin (3:9). Yet there is sin in the lives of Christians (2:1b; 5:17). They may even lapse completely into the realm of death (5:16b). Such problems arose out of the experiences of a long-established community. The shocking paradox of Christian existence in this world is that it is at once secure yet still insecure. It is this that has led to the frequent use of the verb "to abide." The indications always point back to the blessed state of salvation expressed in the immanence formulas. But they are accompanied by the imperative, which makes clear the preliminary character and the threatened state of our union with God in this world (see Excursus 12).

* * *

2. In Particular the Commandment is Both Old and New
(1 John 2:7–8)

God expects us to keep his commandments. There is one commandment in particular that is the acid test of our obedience to him: the command to love brothers and sisters (vv. 9–11). Here indeed is the very heart of Christian morality, the very place where the false gnostics (v. 9) come to grief. But before he gets to the point, the author inserts a section (vv. 7–8) to show that this commandment is both old and new. This makes sense only if the opponents were in his eyes "innovators" (cf. 2 John 9). To hold fast to the old, to what was preached from the beginning, is for the author the seal of truth. Any novelty that is not a part of the original teaching has departed from the one truth, which comes from God. Hence it is "a lie" (cf. 2:19, 21). The author can hardly be thinking of new commandments which the false teachers have invented themselves.[139] Rather, he has in mind their disregard of the chief commandment of the Christian moral code, the sign of true knowledge of God and of fellowship with him. But the moment he mentions the old commandment, the author remembers that Jesus himself had called it a new one, so in v. 8 he explains why this is so.

2:7 He begins by addressing his readers: "Beloved"—as he often does from now on.[140] The ensuing argument is closely connected with what has gone before. Commandment in the singular harks back to commandments in the plural in vv. 3 and 4. This is no more remarkable than the same change between 3:23 and 24 and between 2 John 5 and 6. The commandment is old in a relative sense. The readers have heard it like this from the very beginning, that is, from the moment they became Christians.[141] Ever since then they have lived under its imperative (note the perfect tense: "You have had").[142] while everything they have heard later that contradicts the original tradition is new,[143] and lacks the required authority. Who was it who taught the readers this decisive commandment? We are not told. It must have been those who originally preached the gospel to them, those who were called and authorized to proclaim it. But in the last analysis the word comes from Christ himself. It is a dominical saying.

2:8 Here we have a hidden reminder of Christ, not just an ingenious play on words.[144] It brings the author to the other side of the matter ("yet"=Greek *palin,*

139. Büchsel suggests participation in pagan cultic meals (cf. 5:21), similar to those which the prophet Jezebel and the Nicolaitans of Rev. 2:20 and 2:14f. allegedly encouraged and the orgies often associated with such meals. However, if that were the case, the letter would have been more polemical. Once again, the point of the attack is the lack of mutual love.

140. 1 John 3:2, 21; 4:1, 7, 11. In the Paulines and the other Catholic Epistles this form of address is by no means rare.

141. To connect *ap' archēs* with creation and the commands as a primeval command of human reason in general is misleading (Bisping; Rothe; W. Lütgert, *Die johanneische Christologie* [2nd ed.; Gütersloh, 1916] 215f., etc.).

142. The imperfect indicates duration, but here it also suggests incomplete action in verbs of command and petition; see BDF §328.

143. *Kainos*=unknown, something that has not been around before; *neos,* by contrast=new, fresh. See BAGD 394, s.v. 2, and 536, s.v. 1a; see further Büchsel, ad loc.

144. Windisch (ad loc.) offers a few parallels to the "ingenious word-play with 'old' and 'new.'" On 2:8, see also G. Klein, *ZTK* 68 (1971) 261–326; A. Vicent Cernuda, "Engañan la oscuridad y el mundo: la luz era y manifiesta lo verdadero," *EstBib* 27 (1968) 153–75, 215–32 (meaning: "Darkness deceives but the light already discloses the truth").

"again")![145] This old commandment is also a new one. It was none other than Jesus himself who called the commandments to love one another a new commandment which he gave to his disciples (John 13:34). To suggest that Christian love for the neighbor is universal in contrast to Jewish particularlism (Chaine) destroys the connection with John 13, and this idea is never so much as mentioned in 1 John 2. In John 13:34 Jesus enjoins upon his disciples the same love for one another as that with which he had loved them. They must be ready for active service as he was. They must give themselves to the uttermost (John 13:1) as he, their master, did when he washed their feet and gave his life for them (John 15:13; cf. 1 John 3:16). This self-effacing, dedicated love is the new element in the Christian commandment of love. Such love is the final revelation of the paradoxical love of God for this sinful world (cf. 4:9f.; John 3:16). It becomes visible and effective only through the eschatological mission of the Son of God and his demonstration of his love, even to death on the cross. The eschatological novelty of this love commandment is part and parcel of that love of his. Here lies the clue to that apparently insignificant relative clause (Greek relative ho, "that"). This clause refers back to the whole sentence and makes everything clear: the novelty of the command derives from Christ himself. It is "in him" and "in you," the Christians to whom the letter is addressed, that it is new. Only if the author was thinking of Christ when he wrote v. 7 could he suddenly speak of him ("in him") in v. 8 (cf. "from him" in v. 5). The new commandment is "true" (Greek alēthes),[146] not because it was not taught like this before,[147] but because it was not realized in this way. As far as Christ is concerned, this claim is completely true. But the Christians being addressed[148] might be put off by it. Yet 1 John does not share our modern squeamishness about hurting our "humility" by such self-confidence. The speakers here are so confident that they have passed from death to life because they love the brothers and sisters (3:14). The author encourages his younger readers to feel confident about their victory over the evil one (2:13c, 14c; cf. 5:4). This is not human arrogance, for they can never forget that all their strength comes from the One who dwells within them (4:4).

In making the claim that the novelty of the love commandment is realized in those who are truly Christian, the author elucidates and bases it in the clause beginning "that . . . ." This poses for our exegesis a difficult problem because of the metaphorical way in which it is expressed.

1) We can dismiss the suggestion that it defines the content of the commandment

---

145. On the meaning of *palin*, see BAGD 607, s.v. 4.

146. *Alēthes* does not express logical truth, but connotes the newness of the love command as manifested in Christ and in the recipients of the epistle. For this meaning of *alēthēs*, see Acts 12:9, and the use of *alēthōs* (= "really") with verbs (Acts 7:26; 12:11; 17:8; 1 John 2:5) and with the copula (John 1:47; 8:31; cf. Matt. 14:33; Mark 14:70 par.; John 4:42; 6:14; 7:40).—Through the addition of *en autō*, etc., it acquires a stronger relation to personal action. On the use of *alēthēs*, see C. Maurer, *Ignatius von Antioch und das Joh-Ev* (Zurich, 1949) 47.

147. *Contra* Chaine, who thinks that it was a new piece of information precisely for those coming over from paganism.

148. The reading *en hēmin* AP 323 1739 2298 al.h sy^hmg Jerome Hilary is too weakly attested compared with *hymin*.

(*hoti*-recitative).[149] for the clause has nothing to do with a commandment. The metaphor of light and darkness is used in a way similar to Rom. 13:12—the darkness (night) is passing.[150] The light (the day or the sun) is already appearing.

2) Nor does it refer to the rising of the true light of Christ as a result of the incarnation (1:9).[151] The incarnate Son of God says he will be in the world as its light for only a short while (12:35; cf. 9:5). For this brief interval he can rightly claim to be the light of the world.

3) When John 1:5 says that the light (i.e., the Logos) shines in the darkness, this is not a true parallel. Admittedly, the present tense of the word "shines" might suggest that this is still going on from the evangelist's standpoint. The revelation of Christ is being continued in the church's proclamation.[152] But in any case, John 1:5 looks backward, to the fact that the Logos was the light of all people. Only 1 John 2:8 looks toward the full coming of the light in the future. 1 John 2:8c explains further how the love command is realized in the Christian life. The true light radiates from Christians through the way they live. Thus the interpretation of "the true light" in 1 John 2:8 as a reference to Christ personally should be ruled out.

The picture language describes a situation that includes all faithful Christians ("in you"). Taken in connection with 1:5–7 and 2:9–11, this can mean only that the divine realm of light is expanding and the power of the good is advancing victoriously. Only in a remote way can Christ be included in this consideration: The time frame indicated by the word "already" begins with his first appearance in the incarnation, an appearance that has already taken place (1:2; 3:5, 8). But it also includes the second appearance, which is still to come in the parousia (2:28). Neither the beginning nor the end can be separated from one another. Since he came into the world, it has been possible for people to receive the light of life (John 8:12, here understood as the blessings of salvation) and to walk "in the light" in a religious and moral sense (1 John 1:7). But only at the parousia will the light of goodness acquire its full power. At the same time this connection with Christ is not accentuated here, but only the general situation in salvation history. The true light[153] of morality according to the standard of divine holiness, and with the power of light and love proceeding from God himself, is advancing, for through Christ the love command has been expounded and realized in a way hitherto unknown (hence the "new"). The light which is Christ scatters the darkness of sin and all the powers opposed to God which lurk behind it. All this takes on substance and reality in the true Christian life. The author believes that he has seen this happen in his own experience. It serves to guarantee that something new has taken place.

Only such a thoroughgoing religious and ethical interpretation of "light"

149. For older scholars, see in Bisping; more recently Windisch.

150. Vg. "transierunt" is not an exact translation.

151. Windisch, ad loc.; Stauffer *Theology*, 127; Bultmann, *Theology* 2:82.

152. So Bultmann, *John*, 47f.; Wikenhauser, ad loc.; but it is more accurate to take it as a statement of basic principle: the Logos as the bearer of light is suited and competent to be the light of a universe in bondage to death. See Mussner, ZΩH, 80f.; 165f.

153. *Alēthinon* means this light in contrast to other supposed inauthentic light—probably a polemic against the gnostic heresy, which also spoke of light. On the linguistic usage, see Maurer, *Ignatius*, 48.

Fellowship with God

explains what it means to live and walk in it. This thought controls what follows in the succeeding verses. There is a shift in the metaphor. In v. 8c the fulfillment of the new commandment is itself the light, a radiance of the divine nature. In vv. 9–11, on the other hand, it is presented as a walking in the light (cf. the similar shift from 1:5 to 7).

3. Only the Fulfillment of This Command—That Is, Mutual Love—Guarantees Being in the Light—That Is, Fellowship with God (1 John 2:9-11)

2:9 At last we are told what the commandment is—the love of brothers and sisters. The converse, hatred of brother or sister, incurs the sternest condemnation. Like the contrast between light and darkness, there are no halfway stages between love and hate. Once again, the heretical opponents are given their say ("whoever says," as in vv. 4 and 6). They are now condemned to utter darkness for hating their brothers and sisters. The opposite is also true: "walking in darkness" (1:6) is exposed through hatred. In form the verse is reminiscent of 2:4. The claim to be in the light is just another way of saying "we have come to know God" or "we are in him" (2:5b). The author refutes this claim by insisting that the reverse is true. These enthusiasts who fail to practice love are "in darkness." They are far from God.

Here for the first time the author broaches his favorite theme, the command to love brother and sister. It is a theme that recurs again and again (3:10ff., 23; 4:7, 11ff., 20f.; cf. 5:16). This is not just an old man constantly repeating himself, nor is it the pedantry of a moralist. No, the problem is so crucial that it surfaces from many different perspectives. Sometimes the author is refuting the gnostics. At other times he is delivering an in-house admonition. Here, in 2:9–11, he is indulging in polemics. Love of brother and sister is the essential prerequisite for fellowship with God. Just as GJohn knows no halfway house between faith and unbelief,[154] so both Johannine writings constantly draw a contrast between love and hatred.[155] This picture in black and white is not just a peculiarity of the author. We find the same thing in the Synoptic Jesus.[156] The use of "not loving" as an equivalent for "hating" is of Hebrew origin.[157] Following the example and directives of Jesus, 1 John lays down strict standards for the Christian love of brothers and sisters. This is shown by the concrete imperatives to share one's personal possessions with the brother or sister in need (3:17), and even to lay down one's life for them (3:16).

154. Cf. John 3:18, 36; 5:24, 38–47; 6:36–40; 8:24; 12:37–43, 44–50; 20:31.
155. John 3:19f.; 7:7; 12:25; 15:18f., 23–25; 1 John 3:13–15; 4:20.
156. Cf. esp. Matt. 5:43ff.; 6:24=Luke 16:13; Luke 14:26—On the idea of mutual love (=love of neighbor), see esp. Matt. 5:22–26; 7:2–5=Luke 6:41f.; 18:21ff.; 23:8; 25:34ff. See Excursus 5.
157. Cf. Deut. 21:15–17; 2 Sam. 19:7; Prov. 13:24; Mal. 1:2–3 (= Rom. 9:12); Michel, *TDNT* 4:135 nn. 2 and 3; on *misoun* in the New Testament, see also Rom. 7:15; Rev. 2:6; 17:16.—The sharp contrast between love and hate appears also in the Dead Sea Scrolls: 1QS 1:3f., 9f.; 4:1; 9:16, 21; 1QH 14:24; CD 2:15; 8:16ff.

2:10 The author wants his readers, unlike the heretics, to fulfill the commandment to love the brothers and sisters. He therefore formulates his central thought in a positive way, so that the members of the Christian community are admonished at the same time (cf. "abides"). The central motif here is "being in the light." But then comes a second motif: "in such a person there is no cause for stumbling." Does this mean there is nothing to make them stumble? That is how most recent commentators take it.[158] That would mean switching over to a completely different metaphor.[159] Of course, the author is perfectly capable of changing the metaphor like this. It might mean: there is nothing in such a person to cause offense in the brothers and sisters.[160] This would confirm our observation that the author intends at the same time to address the inner life of the community. It would, however, be best to translate the words "in such a person" as "in the light" (neuter instead of masculine). In the realm of the light there is no offense, no cause of stumbling, for those who walk in the light. This translation is supported by the way the same motif continues in a negative sense in v. 11. Here we have an indirect warning of the danger of stumbling. This point is similar to John 11:9: "Those who walk during the day do not stumble, because they see the light of this world." We have the same metaphor here, though it is applied differently. The present passage also contains the promise that whoever loves brother or sister will never stumble, but will enjoy perfect fellowship with God (cf. 3:2).[161]

2:11 With an adversative conjunction ("But") the author now turns the same thought into its converse, thus repeating what he had said at the end of v. 9. Such repetitions create an awkward impression, but they serve as a bridge to continue the argument. Moreover, we have here an impressive picture disclosing the ultimate consequences of hating brothers or sisters. It cuts one off from God and condemns a person to "living in the darkness." Living in the darkness means walking in it, too. It must of course be remembered that the image of walking in the darkness was used in 1:6 to explain *how* we are excluded from fellowship with God. Here in 2:11, however, it becomes the *consequence* of being cut off from fellowship with God. Accordingly, the picture painted here brings out the tragic and perilous situation for those who find themselves opposed to God. The image of walking in the darkness is also used by the Johannine Jesus in several other places (8:12; 11:9f.; 12:35). The style and character of the imagery in John 12:35 are close to what we have here. But Jesus only threatens

---

158. Brooke; Windisch; Hauck; Stählin, *Skandalon* (1930) 179–83; Ambroggi.

159. Bauer's divergent translation (BAGD 753, s.v. 3) "in him there is no stain" is not justified. Stählin, it is true, points to a development of meaning in the direction of a metaphorical sense, again differentiated (*Skandalon*), but it is not so colorless as Bauer's translation suggests.

160. So Büchsel, ad loc., and the first edition of this commentary.—The *en* should in that case be interpreted here exactly as it is when used with *skandalizein*; cf. Matt. 11:6=Luke 7:23; Matt. 13:57. Cf. also the rabbinic use given in Schlatter, *Sprache,* 147. That *en* denotes a "quite particular relationship of its own" (Stählin, *Skandalon,* 181) is true at most when used with *en Christō,* which according to Stählin has a double meaning: through Christ to disbelieve in Christ (pp. 115, 226). Originally it indicated the object against which a person stumbled.

161. On 2:9–11, see Chmiel, *Lumière et charité,* 96–131.

the possibility of darkness, whereas in 1 John 2:11 it has already come for those who hate the brothers and sisters.

All told the metaphor is rather different in GJohn. There Jesus himself is the light of the world (cf. already 1:9). He shines on all of humankind and thus becomes the source of light. In 1 John the light—this may be the original form of the metaphor[162]—means simply the holiness in which those who are bound to God live and have their being. The substantive difference is still more important: the light that Jesus gives is the *revelation* and the gift of being able to walk in the light of faith (cf. John 12:36). In 1 John walking in the light means religious and moral behavior (1:7) or its consequences (2:11). The imagery is relevant for unbelievers (John 12:35f.) and for those who are cut off from God by their hatred of brothers and sisters (1 John 2:11). This is where it warns them of the uncertainty and danger at the end of the way of darkness (catastrophe).

The phrase "does not know the way to go" is reminiscent of the gnostic promise to lead humanity to saving knowledge.[163] Taken in this sense, these words would be a direct denial of the gnostic claim. It is like an insult flung in their faces. But it is only a metaphor, and put in these negative terms it serves as a threat, perhaps a threat of condemantion (cf. "go to destruction," Rev. 17:8, 11).

The author now gives a deeper reason for this aimless wandering in the darkness, and the accompanying warning of a dreadful end: the darkness itself has blinded their eyes. The Greek verb for "to blind" (*typhloun*) is used in John 12:40 (quoting Isa. 6:9) for the blindness of unbelief. In 2 Cor. 4:4 it is said that "the God of this world has blinded the minds of the unbelievers." What blinds them is the power at enmity with God. But there is no direct reference to Satan in 1 John 2:11. The forceful phrase "has brought blindness" does not imply that light and darkness confront each other like two metaphysical principles or mythological powers. The frame of the metaphor, walking in darkness, remains unbroken. When we have been in the darkness for a long time (cf. v. 10), we can no longer see!164 A similar active role is played by the darkness in John 12:35. In GJohn, however, the blindness of the unbelievers is due to their moral failings (cf. 8:21, 24, 43ff.; 9:39, 41; 12:39f., 42ff.). In like manner 1 John 2:11 says that those who hate become increasingly trapped and entangled in evil. Eventually they cannot escape from the darkness. This is the obscure secret of obduracy, though they have only themselves to blame (cf. John 3:19). At this point the author goes on to a counterattack against the arrogance and conceit of the gnostics. Here we have the climax of his argument with those dangerous heretics and their contempt for Christian morality.

At the same time the author returns to the image he started with (1:6f.). In this way he has worked out for his community what fellowship with God requires. It means to be free from sin and to keep the commandments, especially the commandment of love. This moral requirement is inseparable from the

---

162. See R. Bultmann, "Zur Geschichte der Lichtsymbolik im Altertum," *Philol.* 97 (1948) 1–38; *John,* 52ff.; *Theology* 2:192f.

163. See Excursus 3. Many passages in GJohn also give the overall impression that the author is not unfamiliar with the language of gnosis; see below on 2:20.

164. The aorist *etyphlōsen* is to be taken in a complexive or constative sense (BDF §332), as the conclusive result of an action spread over a longer period of time.

religious promise. It is the foundation of the Christian religion and its promise of salvation. Here the counterfeit currency of the false teachers and their novelties become crystal clear![165]

EXCURSUS 5

The Love of Brothers and Sisters

A constantly recurring theme in 1 John is brotherly and sisterly love (2:9–11; 3:11–18, 23; 4:7, 11f., 20f.; 5:1f.). With this theme the author is pursuing a double goal. First, he seeks to refute the heretical teachers and their morally destructive opinions by furnishing sure criteria to make the difference clear (2:9–11; 4:20f.). Second, he seeks to instruct his fellow believers by showing them what it means to live the Christian life (3:18) and by cementing their fellowship with one another. These goals are closely connected and often coincide. But in order to clarify certain problems he has to keep them apart. How does the hatred of brother and sister show itself in the opponent? What do they and what do their adversaries, the true believers, mean when they speak of brothers and sisters? How then can the love of Christians and battle with the world coexist?

1. THE TITLE "BROTHER" AND "SISTER"

Only once (3:13) does the author address his readers as brothers and sisters, and there he has a special reason for doing so. It is because he wants to use the example of Cain and Abel. Generally he prefers to call them "children" (Greek *teknia* or *paidia*). This is because he wishes to assert his authority over them (cf. 2 John 1 and 3 John 1). Of course he knows that Christians in the earliest church generally addressed one another as "brothers and sisters." That is clear from 3:16f. and 5:16. It is typical of the Johannine writings that they never use

---

165. A related use of the metaphor of light–darkness is used in *Odes of Solomon*. But it is in the consequences drawn from the metaphor that the meanings diverge. Similarities do occur, however, e.g., *Odes Sol.* 15:2: "Because he [the Lord] is my sun, / and his rays have restored me; / and his light has dismissed all darkness from my face"; or 18:6: "Let not the light be conquered by the darkness, / nor let truth flee from falsehood"; or 21:3: "And I stripped off darkness / and put on light"—but the moral aspect is lacking. The way of salvation here consists in knowledge (gnosis), the reception of truth, ascent into the realm of light; it does not feature any moral requirements. For this gnostic dualism, see Percy, *Dualisme,* 23–79.—*Per contra,* the metaphor of light and darkness is used quite similarly to John in the Dead Sea Scrolls, and the idea of hardness of heart is expressed clearly; see 1QS 3:20f.: "All the children of righteousness are ruled by the Prince of Light and walk in the ways of light, but all the children of falsehood are ruled by the Angel of Darkness and walk in the ways of darkness"; 4:11: "The ways of the spirit of falsehood are these: greed, slackness in the search for righteousness, wickedness and lies, haughtiness and pride." Following this, eternal destruction is predicted for such people. See further 1QS 11:10; 1QM 1:6f., 16; 3:6, 9, etc. (sons of darkness); 13:5 ("their lot is darkness"); 13:11f. Belial is in darkness and sets his mind on evil. His lot is cast with the angels of destruction, and they all walk in the laws of darkness": 15:9f.—further material in F. Nötscher, *Gotteswege und Menschenwege,* 91–96.

the term "brothers and sisters" in a casual way, it never gets to be like a worn-down coin. These Johannine Christians know their brothers and sisters because they have all been born from the same Father (1 John 5:1f.). They share the same family traits (3:10), the same ties to Jesus and his teaching (1 John 2:7f.; cf. 2 John 5f.). True, Jesus had spoken about the love of friends (15:12ff.). But 1 John 3:16 understands his challenge to follow his example and make the supreme sacrifice as a call to mutual love. It is quite likely that when the risen Lord called the disciples his "brothers" (John 20:17) this led to even deeper understanding of what it meant to call one's fellow Christian a brother or a sister.

The early church adopted this title from Judaism, as can be clearly seen from Acts.[166] At first the Christians formed a special group within the larger Jewish community, like the Pharisees[167] or the Essenes,[168] the members of the Community of the New Covenant at Damascus,[169] and the closely related community of Qumran.[170] The sayings of Jesus in the Synoptic Gospels[171] leave no doubt that the disciples felt themselves to be bound to call each other "brother" after the example of their Lord. The Johannine usage is patterned after this general custom of early Christianity. But as we have already noted, it has acquired a deeper significance in the light of Johannine theology.

It should be further noted that this use of the title "brother" is also found in pagan religious communities. This can be seen both from inscriptions and from literary evidence.[172] This fact is important for 1 John in another way too. It may be assumed that at that time there were not many unattached religious individuals, especially in the Orient. There was always an urge to join some group or other. How then did things stand with the heretical teachers in 1 John? And what lies behind their hatred of the brothers and sisters which we so often hear about in 1 John (2:9; 3:15; 4:20; cf. 3:10, 12, 13)?

166. See Acts 2:29, 37; 3:17; 7:2; 13:15, 26, 38; 22:1; 23:1, 5, 6; 28:17 in addressing the Jews; in contrast to this, the Christians among themselves 1:15; 3:22; 6:3; 7:23; 9:30; etc. The title of "brother" in Judaism has mainly a religious as opposed to an ethnic sense; see H. von Soden, *TDNT* 1:145f.

167. Josephus, *Jewish War* 2.166.

168. Ibid., 2.122.

169. See CD 6:20; 7:1f.; 14:5; 20:18.

170. 1QS 6:10, 22; 1QSa 1:18; 1QM 13:1; 15:4, 7.

171. In Matt. 5:22, 23f.; 7:3ff. = Luke 6:41f.; 18:15 = Luke 17:3; 18:21, 35 the Jewish usage is simply taken over (cf. Matt. 5:47). Thus passages like Mark 3:33ff. par.; Matt. 23:8; 25:40; 28:10; John 20:17; Luke 22:32 are basic for a deepened Christian understanding of the designation "brother."

172. Cf. the technical use at the Serapeum at Memphis (Deissmann, *Bible Studies* [Edinburgh, 1909] 140), in the *Mithras Liturgy* (A. Dieterich, *Eine Mithrasliturgie* [Leipzig/Berlin, 1923] 149f.), in *Poimandres* (closing prayer; see Reitzenstein, 154), among the Mandeans (*Ginza* 20.12ff.), in the mystery religions (Vettius Valens 4.11), in a judaizing sect in the Crimea (B. Latyschew, *Inscr. Pont. Eux.* 11, 449ff.), in an Egyptian mystery congregation (evidence in Nilsson, *Geschichte der griechischen Religion* 2:584. For further information, see K. H. Schelkle, *RAC* 2:631-40.

2. THE OPPONENTS' HATRED OF BROTHERS AND SISTERS

As the letter shows, the heretical teachers came from within the Christian community (2:19). Externally the separation was complete, though they do not yet seem to have become a cohesive group. The author tells us there were "many false prophets" (4:1). But nowhere did they form a single closed sect (contrast the Nicolaitans in Rev. 2:6, 15). He regards all who do not belong to the true Christian community as part of the "world" (3:13; 4:4-6; 5:4). Whom then does the author have in mind when he accuses the heretics of "hating brothers and sisters"? It is most unlikely that he would pay any attention to the interior concerns of the opponents, or their behavior among themselves. Perhaps there were class distinctions among them as in the later Manichean community (cf. Augustine). But for that the expression "to hate" would be too harsh. Everything points to the fact that the opponents' hatred is directed toward the orthodox Christians, especially their leaders. Those to whom the author has close ties are having to suffer from the hatred of the world (cf. 3:13). However, this hostile front cannot be limited to the false teachers. But that they are making enemies of those who remain firm in their loyalty to the church is all too understandable. At the same time, however, the schismatics were trying to expand their numbers by wooing those members of the community who were beginning to waver (cf. 2:20f., 27; 4:1-3). Did they actually use the title of brother or sister? It cannot be proved that they did so. The epistle always takes the title brother or sister seriously and never speaks of false ones. Again, in 2:9-11 the polemic is presumably directed against those who were formerly brothers or sisters. They are now unfaithful and no longer members of the community but infected by gnosticism![173] Both in form and content the rebuttal ("whoever says," 2:4, 6) with its key word "commandment" (2:3-8) forms a single unit. It is so harsh ("is still in the darkness," v. 9) that the author can hardly be thinking of them still as Christians. Language just as polemical as this is used by Jesus in GJohn against unbelievers (cf. 3:19-21; 8:21-24, 40-44; 12:35, 46-48). There is another possibility: when the author accuses the heretics of hating the brothers and sisters he is using the term "brother" in a broader, less-focused sense, meaning no more than fellow human beings (cf. 3:15). On the other hand, the example of Cain and Abel (3:12) warns us not to evacuate the term of its original profound meaning. For the author it is more than just a conventional title. He is convinced that all should be brothers and sisters, following Jesus' word and example.

3. THE MUTUAL OR RECIPROCAL LOVE OF CHRISTIANS

When the author urges his readers to love one another (3:11, 23; 4:7, 11, 12; cf. 2 John 5), he is clearly thinking of life within the community. This is how Jesus formulated his new commandment—he was thinking of the inner circle

---

173. So Windisch, Excursus, p. 115.

of his disciples (John 13:34; 15:12, 17). The combination of parenesis and polemics often leads to an overlapping of the two expressions, love for brothers and sisters on the one hand, and reciprocal love on the other. In 3:11 the author is thinking of Jesus' charge to his disciples to love one another. Although the polemical aspect predominates, it is the love of brother and sister that he has in mind (v. 10). This is what distinguishes the children of God from the children of the devil. The point is driven home by the example of Cain and Abel (vv. 14–15). But the polemic gradually subsides, giving way to admonition for the common life of the community and the moral behavior of the individual Christian. At the same time the believers must not expect the world to love them (v. 13). However, they must always be prepared for the ultimate sacrifice, following the example of their Lord (vv. 16–18). We can understand why the author, having delivered the midrash on Cain and Abel, should go on to talk about the love of brothers and sisters. But he never tells us what he means by these terms. In v. 13 the author is thinking of the faithful members of the community as contrasted with the world. But in v.14 it would limit the author too much if in contrast to the heretics' hatred of the brothers and sisters he were now declaring—and with emphasis to boot (note the pronoun "we")—that the Christians loved one another. Brothers and sisters here include everybody, even outsiders, with whom the Christians are in contact. Of course, they have to fight the world (cf. 4:4; 5:4). They must close their ranks in self-defense (5:21; 2 John 10f.). But nowhere does the author preach hatred. As he develops the theme of mutual love (3:16–18) he seems to be concentrating more on the inner circle of the believers.

In chapter 4 we have a general discussion of the nature of love![174] Only where the author envisions its concrete application does he speak of reciprocal love. Even in the final verses he keeps within the bounds of community parenesis (cf. v. 19). One may wonder whether (v. 20) in casting an eye upon someone with a perverse attitude, he has in mind a false gnostic or a Christian who is falling by the wayside. The sharp tone of v. 20, reminding us as it does of 2:9, supports the former view. The antithesis between the "invisible God" and the "visible" brother or sister shows that this kind of love embraces the whole human race. Of course, this motivation is possible within the bounds of the community. But in 4:21 we get another motif: "brothers and sisters" now has a wider sense. The author is clearly referring to the double commandment of love, the love of God and neighbor. On the other hand, 5:1–2 continues a train of thought that confines it to the orthodox, to those who are born of God. Clearly, there is a curious oscillation here between a narrower and a wider understanding of Christian

174. On mutual love, see M. Bouttier, "La notion de frères chez s. Jean," *RHPR* 44 (1964) 179–90; N. Lazure, *Les valeurs morales de la théologie johannique* (Paris, 1965) 241–47; J. Coppens, "La doctrine biblique sur l'amour de Dieu et du prochain," *ETL* 40 (1964) 252–99; idem, 'Aγάπη and ἀγαπᾶν dans les lettres Johanniques," *ETL* 45 (1969) 125–27; A. Wei Yuey-shan, *L'amore fraterno, segno della comunione con Dio secondo la 1. Ep. di Giovanni* (Fribourg, 1969); Chmiel, *Lumière et charité*, 132–55. Further, the view has been advanced that mutual love in John implies the limitation of love to the inner circle of the believrs. See, e.g., E. Käsemann, *The Testament of Jesus* (London, 1968) 65: "the object of Christian love is not one's neighbour as such . . . the object of Christian love for John is only what belongs to the community under the word on what is elected to belong to it, that is the brotherhood of Jesus." But stronger differentiation must be made here.

love. This may be because the author wants to find an umbrella term for the Christians' activity of love. If they are true to the commandment of Jesus, Christians should never exclude anyone, brother or sister, from their love. But the particular area for this love is to be found in the Christian community, consisting of brothers and sisters in the faith. This is similar to the behavior of the earliest community at Jerusalem (Acts 2:44–47; 4:32–37). Paul likewise warns his readers (1 Thess. 4:9f.; 5:15; Gal. 6:10). Justin gives us explicit evidence on the matter: "We say also to the heathen: You are our brothers" (*Dial.* 96); see also Tertullian, *Apol.* 39![175] It is therefore incorrect to speak of a narrowing of love of neighbor to love of (Christian) brothers and sisters in John![176] This is seen even more clearly when the warnings given to the members of the Qumran community are compared with the Johannine teaching. The Qumraners are to love the "sons of light," that is, the fellow members of their own community. But they are to hate the "sons of darkness."[177]

THIRD SECTION

APPLICATION TO THE READERS:
ASSURANCE OF THEIR STATE OF SALVATION IN GOD
AND ADMONITION TO REJECT ALL LOVE OF THE WORLD
(1 JOHN 2:12–17)

[12]I am writing to you, little children,
because your sins are forgiven on account of his name.
[13]I am writing to you, fathers,
because you know him who is from the beginning.
I am writing to you, young people,
because you have conquered the evil one.
[14]I write to you, children,
because you know the Father,
I write to you, fathers,
because you know him who is from the beginning.
I write to you, young people,
because you are strong
and the word of God abides in you,
and you have overcome the evil one.
[15]Do not love the world or the things in the world. The love of the Father is not in those who love the world; [16]for all that is in the world—the desire of the flesh, the desire of the eyes, the pride in riches—comes not from the Father but from the

---

175. On the designation "brother" and on mutual love among Christians as the early church continued to develop, see Harnack, *Mission and Expansion,* 404–7.

176. See Bauer on John 13:34 and 15:13. A. Nygren, *Agape and Eros* (Philadelphia, 1953) 153ff. (he calls it "particularism"); E. Stauffer, *Die Botschaft Jesu damals und heute* (Bern, 1959) 47; H. Montefiore, *NovT* 5 (1962) 164ff.—For a contrary view, see J. Huby, *Mystiques paulinienne et johannique* (Paris, 1946) 183ff.; Bultmann, *Theology* 2:82.

177. See 1QS 1:3f., 9f.; 9:16, 21f.

world. [17]And the world and its desires are passing away, but those who do the will of God live forever.

* * *

With 2:12 a new section begins. The problem here is with the context rather than with the word-by-word exegesis. What is the meaning of the six apostrophes in vv. 12–14? They are clearly divided into two groups, as shown by the introductions "I am writing" and "I write." Each of the two groups also falls into three parts. Are they solemn assurances to the reader each carrying its own weight? Or are they meant to serve as an introduction to the commandment not to love the world in vv. 15–17? If the latter, the emphasis would lie on those verses, with the entire section focused on them.

Büchsel would place the commandment to love brother and sister (vv. 7–11) in contrast to the prohibition of love of the world (vv. 15–17). In Büchsel's view, vv. 12–14 do not stand on their own, but are to be connected with vv. 15–17. They contain a radical prohibition of love for the world. There are several objections to this interpretation: (1) From a linguistic point of view there is nothing in vv. 7–11 to correspond to the phrase "do not love" in v. 15. The sentences in vv. 9–11 condemn the opponents for hating the brothers and sisters (vv. 9, 11). They are living and walking in the darkness (v. 11). The opposite of love for the world is not the love of brothers and sisters but the love of God (cf. vv. 15b, 16). (2) Verses 12–14 hark back to the whole section 1:5ff., applying it directly to the lives of the readers. Verses 12–14 contain directives ("do not love") that are too important to be merely a transition ("you know," cf. 2:3ff.), going beyond the presumed framework of 2:7–17. (3) The sixfold repetition of the phrase "I am writing" or "I write" at the beginning of each sentence gives weight to the because-clauses that follow, and not to what comes before vv. 12–14. But suppose one follows Brooke and Büchsel and takes the phrase "do not love . . ." as the object of "I am writing" or "I write," and the because-clauses correspondingly in a causal sense, then one would expect a repetition of the phrase "do not love." This would then be the main point. At the very least this admonition should have been made earlier (perhaps before or after v. 12). It should not limp along after a sixfold introduction![178]

We shall have to take 2:12–17 as a separate section connecting up with 1:5–2:2 and 2:3–11. The author now turns directly to his readers, having refuted the errors of his opponents. He seeks to assure his readers of their salvation (vv. 12–14), and he urges them to reject all evil love of the world (vv. 15–17).

1. Words of Encouragement:
The Readers Have Fellowship with God and Are Strong
in the Combat with the Evil One (1 John 2:12–14)

2:12 The readers are addressed as "little children," varying the Greek word in v. 14 (*teknia* in v. 12; *paidia* in v. 14). As in 2:1, 28; 3:4, 18; 4:4; 5:21, the author is addressing his readers generally with a friendly word of paternal assurance and admonition.

---

178. There is no parallelism between *graphō hymin* in vv. 7, 8, and *graphō* (*egrapsa*) *hymin* in vv. 12–14. In vv. 7 and 8 the two words are unemphasized, whereas in vv. 12–14 we have a deliberate stylistic device.

Windisch connects the address "little children" and the corresponding "because" clauses with baptism. That would only make sense if there were a clearer reference to baptism as a salvific event in these verses. When the author speaks of forgiveness "on account of his name" this is hardly a reference to baptism in the name of Jesus (cf. 1 Cor. 1:13, 15; Matt. 28:19; Acts 8:16; 19:5 "into the name"; Acts 2:38 "upon the name"; 1 Cor. 6:11 "in the name"). The recipients of the letter have the right to bear the name of Christ. It is their privilege to call upon his name (cf. 2:1f.). That is why God has forgiven their sins.

According to the interpretation given above, the because-clauses are really causal as more recent commentators think. They tell the readers what the author wishes to reassure them about. Independently of the present commentary, B. Noack has taken this line more recently with additional supporting arguments.[179]

The harsh condemnation of those who transgress the commandments (2:4) and the dire threat against all who fail to practice the love of brothers and sisters (2:11) would naturally cause fear and anxiety in the Christian readers. Are they really "walking in the light"? Do they really have fellowship with God? To reassure them the author takes up (as he had already done in 2:1f.) the central Christian motif of their bond with Christ (2:12, "on account of his name"; 2:13a, 14b, "you know him who is from the beginning"; 2:13b, 14c, "you have conquered the evil one," i.e., the adversary of Christ). The thought clearly revolves around the theme of "fellowship with God, and sin." The false gnostics had failed both in attitude and in behavior in relation to the ethical demands of God. But the Christians are equally aware of their own inadequacies. There are, however, differences. True Christians follow the way of salvation humbly, as directed by Christ, and are victorious through his strength.

2:13 Following the words of assurance addressed to his readers generally, the author turns specifically to two age groups, fathers and young people. He is not giving instructions to different classes of people as Paul does in his household codes[180] to various members of the family (husbands, wives, and children), and social orders (slaves and masters). Nor does the Johannine author seek to highlight certain groups in the community like the Pastoral Epistles.[181] Rather, he tries to strengthen both young and old in the conflict over religion and morals. The order of the age groups is the same as in the Pastorals.[182] The designations "fathers" and "young people" are filled with too much meaning to be a purely "rhetorical figure" for Christians in general (Dodd).[183]

---

179. B. Noack, "On 1 John ii.12–14," *NTS* 6 (1959–60) 236–41.

180. Eph. 5:22–6:9; Col. 3:18–4:1; cf. 1 Pet. 2:18–3:7.

181. Men and women (1 Tim. 2:8–15; Titus 2:1–8); widows (1 Tim. 5:3–6); officeholders (1 Tim. 3:1–13; 5:9–16, 17–21; Titus 1:5–9); slaves (1 Tim. 6:1–2; Titus 2:9–10).

182. See 1 Tim. 5:1–2; Titus 2:1–8.

183. In his reference to mystic experience of "all grades and levels of existence simultaneously" in *CHerm* 11.20; 13.11, Dodd overlooks the completely different character of these passages. If 1 John wanted to attribute to all Christians the natural strength of youth and the maturity of old age in its experience of faith he would have had to make this clearer than he does with his brief apostrophes.

The author, having just been thinking of Jesus, assures the fathers that they "know him who is from the beginning." The readers can understand who the object is in the light of 1:1. It reminds them once again of the salvation spoken of in the prooemium. For them, too, the "life" has appeared. That is what it means to "know" him who is from the beginning (2:3f. makes a similar point). This is more than purely intellectual understanding; it also involves personal contact with him who is the mediator of salvation. Knowing Christ in this way—or, more correctly, having come to know him[184]—they are assured of fellowship with God (1:3, 6; 2:3, 5). They have this because their sins have been forgiven for Christ's sake (2:12). They enjoy a living relationship to God through Christ.

The author writes to the "young people" that they have conquered the adversary, the evil one, the counterpart of "him who is from the beginning." This designation for Satan appears to be derived from the language of the earliest Christian community.[185] It is the author of this epistle who has contributed a profound view of the contrast between Christ and Satan. This is expressed in terms of Johannine dualism. Christ is not merely the sinless One (2:1, 29; 3:7) over whom Satan has no power (cf. John 14:30). He is also the One who has destroyed Satan's power (3:8) and protects the believers from his onslaughts (cf. 5:20 with 19). Just as Christ reveals the truth of God and champions God's cause in the struggle for the hearts and minds of people in this world, so is the evil one the representative of all that is opposed to God (5:18f.). He is an active aggressor, who, however, can never harm those who are born of God (5:18c).[186] There are other texts that deal with the conflict between the two sides and with the victory of God, such as 4:4 and 5:5. But in these texts the primary focus is on the question of faith, whereas in 2:13f. it is the moral struggle that is paramount. In the final analysis, however, it is one and the same struggle (cf. 3:23; 5:3ff.; also Rev. 14:12). Just as the moral and christological heresy are closely connected (cf. 1:7), so too the evil one tries to tempt people to abandon their faith in Christ and to allure them into sin. He seeks to win them over to his side. It is a subtle point that it is precisely the young people, the very ones for whom

---

184. This perfect tense, denoting completion of the condition and expressing the fellowship achieved with Christ or God, is to be distinguished from the simple *ginōskein*, which is frequently related to *pisteuein;* see John 7:26; 8:28, 32; 10:38; 14:20; 16:3; 17:8, 23, 25; 1 John 3:1; 4:6, 7, 8; 5:20, and of course also with the perfect form(s) in John 6:69; 8:55; 14:7 (*v.l.*), 9; 17:7; 1 John 4:16; 2 John 1.

185. See Matt. 13:19; Eph. 6:16; perhaps also Matt. 6:13; 2 Thess. 3:3. See further *Barn.* 2.10; 21.3; *Mart. Pol.* 17:1; the Agrapha in *Ps.-Clem. Hom.* 3.55 (Klostermann, *Apocrypha* III [Kleine Texte 11²] #46, p. 10) *ho ponēros estin ho peirazōn; Ps.-Clem. Hom.* 19, 2. (Klostermann #49, p. 11) *mē dote prophasin tō ponērō;* see also the report about the martyrs of Lyons in Eusebius, *H.E.* 5.1.6; F. Dölger, *Die Sonne der Gerechtigkeit und der Schwarze* (Münster, 1918) 63f. Among the rabbis "the Evil One" is not a usual designation of Satan according to Billerbeck (*Kommentar* 1:422 and 665), though possible; similarly Büchsel, *Johannes und der hellenistische Synkretismus,* 104. Cf., however, the frequent occurrence of this designation among the Mandeans, as given in the index to *Ginza,* s.v.; *MandLit* 222; *Odes Sol.* 14:5: "Let me be preserved from evil" (*bīšā'*).

186. For the later development of the antithesis between Christ and the evil one, see Dölger, *Die Sonne der Gerechtigkeit,* 63f.

the moral struggle is most acute, who receive the encouragement and assurance that they are winning the victory over the evil one.

2:14 We have here a new trilogy of addresses to the reader, repeating much of what has been said in vv. 12–13. Most striking is the way it begins with the aorist "I wrote" (Greek *egrapsa;* NRSV "I write")

Three main explanations have been offered for this aorist: (1) It is a reference to an earlier letter. (2) It is a reference to earlier passages in the same letter. (3) It is an epistolary aorist, to be translated in English with the present tense (so NRSV). The first suggestion is unacceptable because there is no identifiable passage in 2 or 3 John to which it can refer.[187] To suppose an earlier letter, now lost (see Windisch), would be too easy a way out of the difficulty. Moreover, the sequence would be unusual. Again, if the author wishes to repeat what he had already said, we would expect him to quote it verbatim (cf. 1 Cor. 5:9 and 11). The second suggestion (cf. Brooke), though not impossible so far as the content goes (v. 14a=2:3?: v. 14b=v. 13a; v. 14c=v. 13b), does not explain why the author repeats what he has already said in this peculiar manner. The third possibility is to be preferred. Verses 12–14 are thoroughly in accord with epistolary style. Thus "I sent" in Acts 23:30; Phil. 2:28; Col. 4:8; Eph. 6:22; Philem. 12 refers to something happening at the time the letter was written and sent off. Also "I am writing" in 1 Cor. 5:11; Gal. 6:11; Philem. 19, 21 and, most importantly, in 1 John 2:21 is best explained this way.[188] A similar use is evidenced in profane letters, where "I write" refers almost certainly to the letter just being written.[189]

The aorist *egrapsa,* translated "I write," seems simply to be a variant of the present tense. The author has a predilection not only for varying his expressions but also for a certain rhetorical sound and rhythm (see Introduction, p. 8).

What the author says he is writing is almost identical in wording down to v. 14a (v. 14c is only a little bit longer) as in vv. 12–13. Presumably v. 14a is intended to make the same point, though from a higher perspective of fellowship with God, like v. 12.[190] The Christians who are being addressed are already enjoying the salvation they desire. They have received the forgiveness of sins (v. 12) and in effect they know the Father (v. 14a). They have attained this through the Son, the One "who is from the beginning" (cf. 1:1–3). Thus it is not an abrupt shift when v. 14b says that the "fathers" have known him who "is from the beginning." That is why they have fellowship with the Father. They are firmly anchored in fellowship with Christ.[191]

---

187. *Contra* H. H. Wendt, *ZNW* 21 (1922) 140ff.

188. BDF (§334) disputes this for *graphein* ("on the other hand always . . . *graphō*"), evidently following the cautious judgment of Mayser, *Grammatik* 2.1:143f. Radermacher also includes as an example of epistolary style 1 Pet. 5:12 (*egrapsa*), 2 John 12 (*ouk eboulēthēn*), 3 John 13 (*polla eichon grapsai soi*) and refers to "Paul" in general terms (*Grammatik,* 156). Calmes, Bultmann ("Analyse," 144 n. 1), Büchsel, Chaine, and Ambroggi adopt the same solution.

189. Deissmann points out two examples of *egrapsa* from private letters of the second century C.E. and from the second half of the same century, as well as examples of *epestele* and *ephas[k]e* in the oldest known Greek private letter from the beginning of the fourth century B.C.E. (*Light from the Ancient East*).

190. See M.-É. Boismard, *RB* 56 (1949) 377ff., esp. 380.

191. On 2:12–14, see further J. Bruns, "A Note on John 16:33 and 1 John 2:13–14," *JBL* 86 (1967) 451–53 (comparison with Heracles as victor over death; but that is too farfetched); I. de la Potterie,

In true Johannine style, the message for the young people is repeated three times, though in different words (v. 14c). In v. 13b they are assured that they have conquered the evil one. The middle phrase indicates the source of their power. It is that the word of God abides among them. That word is not a weapon for combat as in Eph. 6:17, but rather the power of God at work within them (cf. John 5:38; 6:63b; 8:31; 15:3; 17:14, 17). The aphorism stands in contrast to 1 John 1:10, where the heretics are said not to possess the word of God. The young warriors for Christ are told, though with a special nuance, that they have the same thing as their experienced fathers have. They are in living fellowshp with God. From that fellowship they derive the power to overcome the evil one. It would appear that the young people are in particular need of these assurances. Moreover, the indicative of the verb "abides" allows the imperative to be heard along with it (cf. the beginning and end of 2:27).

2. Admonition: The Readers Must Not Love the World and What Is in It (1 John 2:15–17)

The author is convinced that his readers have fellowship with God. He forcefully reassures them that they are in a state of grace. At the same time, however, he is aware of the temptations they are still exposed to from the world. Hence this brief admonition with its neat and rhythmical three-part structure![192] Note also the impressive contrasts[193] and the effective motivation (v. 17). We have here a minor model of early Christian parenesis. It deals with a theme that never loses its urgency and is always a lively topic, the theme of the Christian's relationship to the world. To avoid any misunderstanding we must define precisely what is meant by "world" in this connection.

At first sight one would be tempted to connect the "world" with the evil one (vv. 13b and 14c), the adversary of God who has been overcome by the young Christians (cf. the "ruler of this world" in John 12:31; 14:30; 16:11). Yet, as we discovered, vv. 12–14 stand on their own. Neither in the reasoning of v., 16 nor in the motivation to beware of the world in v. 17 is there any mention of the satanic ruler of "this" world. This means that

---

"La connaissance de Dieu," in *Au service de la Parole de Dieu,* 89 (he refers to Jer. 31:34: "they shall all know me, from the least of them to the greatest"). The reference is important, although there is hardly a direct connection with that passage here. De la Potterie also draws a connection with 1 John 4:20 ("you *all* know"). In point of fact the addresses "fathers" and "young men" may be merely an extension of the idea to cover all believers. This is how the verse is explained by Thüsing (pp. 70–74). The author knows that those whom he addresses as children are at the same time fathers who have joined *him* as witnesses. He is telling us that we have the strength of young men in our victorious struggle against the evil one. De la Potterie regards these verses in the light of their literary character as a solemn declaration of a kerygmatic type placed at the beginning of the section 2:12–28 (p. 88).—A different view is taken by Houlden (pp. 70f): "Fathers" probably means "presbyters"; "young men" probably "deacons" (this interpretation is improbable).

192. The whole parenesis falls into three parts (vv. 15-16-17), as does *ta en tō kosmō* (v. 16). Side by side with it a two-part structure consisting of antithesis (vv. 15a–16b; at the end of v. 16 *ouk-alla;* vv. 17a–17b) and coordination (v. 15a *ton kosmon-mēde ta en tō kosmō;* v. 17a *ho kosmos . . . kai hē epithymia autou*).

193. Verse 15b *agapa ton kosmon-agapē tou patros;* v. 16 *ek tou patros-ek tou kosmou;* v. 17 *ho kosmos-ho de poiōn to thelēma tou theou;* v. 17 *paragetai-menei.*

the concept of the world and the meaning of the admonition have to be gleaned from the immediate context.

2:15 This admonition against loving the world and the things that are in it is developed along the following lines: the love of this world is dangerous because it is filled with evil desires and is under their control. We are not told who was enmeshed by these evil desires. Only this much is clear: it is not the world as such, nor the world as God's creation that is evil. The trouble is that the world attracts evil desires like a magnet (see further Excursus 6).

The motivation the author urges upon his readers in v. 15b shows that the love of the world is incompatible with the life-style that befits the children of God. Since it is contrasted with the love of the world, the love of the Father should here be translated "love *toward* the Father" (objective genitive).[194] It does not mean the love of God for us.[195] The author wishes to say this because he had spoken earlier (v. 14a) of the knowledge of the Father. The Father's love for us (subjective genitive) does not fit the phrase "is not in them," which means the same as "you do not have the love of God in you" (John 5:42). The love referred to here is therefore something that belongs to humankind, and fills them inwardly. Yet this love toward God is not to be taken in a purely moral sense. It is not a virtue or an achievement. Rather, it is a mode of being, originating in God's love. It can only develop in those who are born of him (cf. on 2:5). In the final analysis, therefore, love toward the Father is only the flowering of the love granted by God to the believers. This opens up a profound contrast between the "world" and God, between "love of the world" and love of God. This contrast comes out even more clearly at the end of v. 16. But already behind the motivation in v. 15b there lies this same perspective of Christian dualism. This verse is not just a simple appeal to the readers, urging them to love God. Rather, it is a reminder of the love of God which they have already received.

2:16 This verse gives the reason (note the conjunction "for") for the warning against the world. There are three evil desires filling the world. They are summed up in v. 17 in the words "its desires." These desires are opposed to God by their very nature: "they do not come from the Father." They are not meant to be a catalog of vices; they simply describe the evil that is in the world ("all that is . . ."). All that is in the world is exemplified by these three items. The important point for the author is that the world is full of evil desires, not what these desires actually are. The desire of the flesh is particularly condemned. This reminds us of the "auxiliary troops" in Paul which support the power of sin, the flesh with its desires![196] The three items cited in the genitive case — flesh, eyes, life (so Greek; NRSV "riches") belong to what is earthly and transitory. There

---

194. Windisch and Büchsel leave the genitive hanging in the air.

195. So AC 33 642 808 z; a few minuscules (94 307 329 al.) try to do justice to both readings with *theou kai patros*. That is un-Johannine.

196. In John 1:13 also, only natural sexual desire is intended (*thelēma tēs sarkos*) in contrast to supernatural begetting from God (*contra* Büchsel), and John 3:6; 6:63 (*hē sarx ouk ōphelei ouden*) envisions the antithesis natural, transitory–supernatural, divine.

is no value judgment involved here. They become evil and objectionable only when they excite evil impulses in human beings (genitive of origin). Desire may flare up and knows only too well how to misuse them. What the ultimate roots of desire are we are not told, though the differences from the gnostic view of the matter ought to be clear![197]

We should not look for a strict scheme of thought behind these three items. They illustrate but do not schematize. There is a close parallel to this summary of evil desires in other literature, for example, Philo![198] One could also compare 'Abot 4:21: "Jealousy, lust, and ambition put a man out of the world (Danby, 455). The Christian author does not need to take over an earlier scheme, he simply coins his own formulation.

This association of evil desires with the flesh is foreign to Judaism. The *yēṣer hārā'* (which is not identical with actual desire) played an important role in rabbinic thought. But it is based on a psychosomatic and holistic view of human nature![199] This leads many scholars to think that the author is influenced here by Hellenistic philosophy, at least as far as his vocabulary is concerned.[200] The same terms can be found in Paul, though with a particular nuance derived from his distinctive use of the term flesh.[201] Now the Qumran texts have their own concept of "flesh," developed from the Old Testament yet still explicable in Jewish terms.[202] Many passages in the Dead Sea Scrolls reflect the same perspective as in GJohn: "flesh" means humanity in its creatureliness, mortality, and weakness. But over and above this, "flesh" is associated with sin. Even the elect still belong to the "company of ungodly flesh" (1QS 11:9) and must "stagger because of the sin of the flesh" (1QS 11:12). The creaturely weakness of the flesh finds its expression in the inclination to sin (see 1QH 13:13–16). Quite close to this is the thought of 1QH 10:22f.: "Thou hast not placed any support in gain, [nor does] my [heart delight in riches]. Thou hast given me no fleshly [*yṣr bśr*] refuge." In a similar way, the whole early Christian community turns it back on the flesh and its desires. The "desire of the flesh" in 1 John 2:16 encompasses

---

197. Cf. the similar ideas in *Ginza* 26.6–8; 44.6–8; Reitzenstein, *Iranisches Erlösungsmysterium* (Hymn II, 40; Reitzenstein, 25): "and observe the world . . . , which is wholly given to desire."

198. Especially *Decal.* 153 *epithymias ē chrēmatōn ē doxēs ē hēdonēs;* cf. *Decal.* 151; *Opif.* 79; *Prob.* 31.

199. See Moore, *Judaism* 1:479ff.; Billerbeck, *Kommentar* 4:1, 466–83; Bonsirven, *Judaïsme* 2:18ff.; Lietzmann, *An die Römer* Excursus on Rom. 7:14 (HNT 8; 4th ed., 75–77); Büchsel, *TDNT* 3:168f.

200. Epicurus in Plutarch, *Mor.* 1096C (*hai tēs sarkos epithymia*); Plutarch himself: *Mor.* 101B (*tais tēs sarkos hēdonais*) etc.; Diogenes Laertius 10.145. See Lietzmann, 75f (he compares especially the Philonic terminology and assumes Hellenistic influence for both); Chaine, ad loc.; E. Schweizer, *TDNT* 7:140f. See also N. Lazure, "La convoitise de la chair en I Jean, II, 16," *RB* 76 (1969) 161–205 (further meaning: all evil efforts of human beings, following biblical and Jewish tradition). I do not understand how Lazure can say, after my commentary and those of others, that they take up a position "in an exclusively Hellenistic sense" (p. 162).

201. For a formal comparison, see Gal. 5:16; Eph. 2:3; for the sense, see Rom. 1:24; 6:12; 13:14; Gal. 5:24. See also 1 Pet. 2:11; cf. 1:14; 2 Pet. 2:10, 18; cf. 1:4; Jude 8, 23 (without *epithymia*).

202. See K. G. Kuhn, "πειρασμός–ἁμαρτία–σάρξ im NT und die damit zusammenhängenden Vorstellungen," *ZTK* 49 (1952) 200–222; Nötscher, *Zur theologischen Terminologie,* 84f.; H. Huppenbauer, "בשר 'Fleisch' in den Texten von Qumran (Höhle I)," *TZ* 13 (1957) 298–300; R. E. Murphy, "Bśr in the Qumran Literature and Sarks in the Epistle to the Romans," *Sacra Pagina 2* (Paris/Gembloux, 1959) 68–76; R. Meyer, *TDNT* 7:110ff.

all evil motivations arising from the psychosomatic nature of humanity. The author has particularly in view the overwhelming sexual urges which drive human beings to excess, the consequences of which can be devastating. Contrasted with the more refined "desires of the eyes" are the coarser sexual perversions typical of paganism. These were especially dangerous for the young Christian community.[203] The damming up of this wild current of vice was the main object of early Christian parenesis[204] which the author appropriates for himself. Yet the desire of the flesh is not limited to the sexual realm but includes gluttony, drunkenness, and the like.

The desire of the eyes had from early times been associated with covetousness.[205] But apart from the envious and greedy eyeing of earthly treasures (Sir. 14:9 etc.) the eyes are used for lustful glances arising from unbridled desire (Job 31:1; Matt. 5:27-29; cf. 18:9; Mark 9:47). Hence the second desire, just like the first and the third, can be part of the Johannine characterization of the "world."[206] Since this is not a catalogue of vices in the technical sense, the author must be talking of the allurements of the world in stirring up sexual passions. He wants to impress upon his readers the power of temptation. It is the eyes that lead most directly and quickly from external observation to evil thoughts latent in the human heart (cf. Mark 7:21-23).

The climax comes in the third item, the pride of life (NRSV "riches"). Pride is a perverse attitude of mind making us forget our dependence on God and leading to self-glorification.[207] At the same time it prevents people from paying attention to their fellows. Here, as in 3:17,and in many other places,[208] "life" means income, property, or wealth (hence NRSV "riches"). The genitive, as with "*of* the flesh" and "*of* the eyes," denotes the origin or source of the desire.[209] The author also appears to be indebted here to the general moral teaching of early Christianity, which was strongly influenced by the teaching of Jesus about the dangers of wealth, especially according to the Lucan tradition.[210] Pride leads

---

203. Cf. Rom. 1:24ff., perhaps following late Jewish polemic; 1 Cor. 6:9; 1 Thess. 4:5; 1 Tim. 1:10; *Did.* 2.2; *Barn.* 19.4; Athenagoras 13.19 etc.

204. 1 Thess. 4:3ff.; 1 Cor. 5:1ff.; 6:12ff.; 10:8; 2 Cor. 12:21; Gal. 5:19; Eph. 5:3; Col. 3:5; 1 Tim. 1:10; Heb. 13:4; 2 Pet. 2:10; Jude 7f., 10; Rev. 21:8.

205. Chrysostom, *In Matt. hom.* 4.9; Thomas Aquinas, *Summa theologica* I, II q. 77, a. 5; Estius; Belser; Vrede; Ambroggi.—Another special meaning is lust of the eyes and prurient curiosity; so Augustine, *Confessions* 10.53 and *In Joa. tr.* 11.13, followed by many later writers (see Camerlynck, as well as Ambroggi).

206. So modern writers such as Loisy, Windisch, Büchsel, Bonsirven; see also Chaine.

207. Cf. Wis. 5:8; James 4:16; *1 Clem.* 13.1; 14.1; 16.2; 21.5; 35.5. *Herm. Man.* 6.2, 5; 8.5; *Did.* 5.1; Diog. 4.1.6. For profane writers see the lexicons.—*Alazoneia* always appears to refer to speaking boastfully or to external expressions of superiority, whereas *hyperēphania* or *typhos* (=darkness) designates interior pride.

208. In profane literature, papyri, LXX (Prov. 31:14; Cant. 8:7; 1 Esdr. 7:26) and New Testament (Mark 12:44; Luke 15:12, 30; 21:4), see BAGD 142, s.v. 3; R. C. Trench, *Synonyms of the New Testament* (New York, 1871) 87ff.

209. Cf. Wis. 5:8 *ploutos meta alazoneias;* not to be taken as an objective genitive as in Polybius 6.57.6 *hē peri tous bious alazoneia.* Büchsel takes *tou biou* as a qualitative genitive.

210. See Mark 10:23ff. par.; Luke 6:24; 11:41; 12:15, 16-21, 33; 14:12-14; 16:9, 19-31.

to self-satisfaction and cuts us off from God. It is the same thing as arrogance. But the translation "pride of life," is incorrect.[211] The way back to God is more difficult, the delusion greater than it is with the desire of the flesh or the eyes.

All these characteristic traits of the world are far removed from what God wants from us. Once again, the author calls God "Father," perhaps because he wants (as in v. 17) to highlight the eternal constancy of the divine reality in contrast to the creatureliness and mortality of the world. *"From the Father"* (Greek *ek* with genitive) does not denote origin, but as often in John, nature.[212] It does not mean that everything in the world comes *from* it; rather it means that evil behaviors are altogether worldly and as such are contrary to what God wills. In a similar way Jesus in GJohn reassures his disciples that the world hates them because they do not belong to the world.

2:17 As a strong incentive or admonition, the author speaks of the transitory nature of the world. He is not thinking in philosophical terms about the contingent character of reality. Nor does he have the theological doctrine of creation in mind, or the temporal limitations imposed on it by God. The fragility of the world becomes visible from the contrast between God and the world. God, and everything that pertains to him, is permanent; everything else transitory. There is no reason here to extend this reflection in the direction of salvation history.[213] Neither in "passing away"[214] nor in "forever" (which is purely formal in meaning)[215] is there any eschatological accent. The present tense in the phrase *"are* passing away" is not intended to be emphatic as though the world were already well on in process of dissolution (contrast the "now" in v. 18). Rather, it is used in contrast with "lives" (Greek *menei,* literally, "abides"), expressing the idea of stability. The time is not "grown short"(as in 1 Cor. 7:29–31) owing to the fast-approaching end. Johannine Christianity is more certain than Paul that the world is still going on and that Christians must hold their own in it (cf.

211. Accordingly the view of P. Joüon (*RechScR* 28 [1938] 479–81) that at the heart of this attitude there is a presumptuous confidence in riches does not quite fit the case, still less Chaine's interpretation that the author has in mind a perverse ambition on their part to raise themselves to a higher social and cultural level.

212. Especially significant in this connection is *ek tēs alētheias* John 18:37; 1 John 2:21; 3:19. *Einai ek theou* occurs frequently: 7:17; 8:47; 1 John 3:10; 4:1–3, 4, 6, 7; 5:19; 3 John 11. On *einai ek tou kosmou* see further John 8:23; 15:19; 17:14, 16; 18:36; 1 John 4:5. There is no doubt that *ek* originally denoted origin in a local sense, like *ek tōn anō* (John 8:23=*anōthen,* John 3:31), *ek tōn katō* (John 8:23=*ek tēs gēs,* John 3:31), and causal origin, like *ek tou diabolou* (John 8:44; 1 John 3:8, cf. 12); especially clear in the phrase *gennēthēnai ek* (John 1:13; 3:5, 6, 8; 1 John 2:29; 3:9; 4:7; 5:1, 4, 18). But sinse quality is defined principally by origin, *einai ek* later became a qualitative way of speech in which the element of origin faded. See Bultmann, *Theology* 2:23f.

213. See Windisch, Chaine, Dodd.

214. Cf. on 2:8.

215. The phrase *eis ton aiōna* is also found in inscriptions; see Dittenberger, *Or. inscr.,* 194, 35; 332, 33; 515, 56; *Syll.* ³814, 50; cf. E. Peterson, Εἷς θεός (1926) 168ff.—In the Johannine writings it connotes unlimited duration, which only God possesses; see John 4:14; 6:51, 58; 8:35, 51, 52; 10:28; 11:26; 12:34; 13:8; 14:16; 2 John 2.

John 17:15; 1 John 4:17).[216] Lust and desire, which make the world so attractive, are just as transitory as the world itself.[217]

A. Vicent Cernuda interprets this part of the verse thus: "The world and all its desires are deceptive, but those who do the will of God are firm in their resolve not to be deceived by the world."[218] *Paragein* can certainly mean "lead astray," but this meaning is very questionable for 2:8 and 17, because it has no object in the accusative. The context contains temporal phrases, and there is evidence for *paragein* and *paragesthai* in the sense of "to pass away" in the Septuagint (2 Esdr. 9:2; Ps. 143:4).

Those who "do the will of God" resist the world and its desires. This, like the phrases "do the will of God" and "obey the commandments of God" (2:3, 4, 5; 3:22, 24; 5:2, 3) is an Old Testament and Jewish expression, but it is more successful than these phrases in avoiding a nomistic misunderstanding. The thought of v. 17 has strong echoes in the apocryphal writings of late Judaism, especially *2 Apoc. Bar.* and *4 Ezra*.[219] It can be found also in Philo, though with a slightly different nuance.[220] It is here that we must look for the source of early Christian teaching, not, for example, in Mandeism. True, Mandeism also has a powerful ethic which is highly practical too. But despite the similarities, it is quite different from anything in Christianity, being gnostic and dualistic in its orientation.[221] In GJohn the phrase "to abide forever" is identical in meaning with "to have eternal (divine) life."[222] This Johannine idea of life is not particularly interested in future judgment or the world to come. This is what makes 1 John 2:17 so different from the apocalyptic drama that is found in texts like *2 Apoc. Bar.* and *4 Ezra* (see above) and gives it an accent of its own. It is not a catastrophic "passing away" of the world but the abiding paradox of both passing away and abiding that gives the expression its stamp. The substitution of "God" for "Father" in v. 16 must not tempt us to draw far-reaching theological conclusions.[223] What "forever" means is clear enough from common Jewish-

216. Cf. R. Löwe, op. cit., 124: "Here (in the Johannine writings and in Jas) the two eons disappear altogether and make more room for the horizontal perspective. Above is God with his good gifts, spirit, light, and eternal life, beneath the world in ignorance, night, and sin." But this assessment is exaggerated.

217. *Epithymia* without *autou* (A 33 323 1739 h sa arm) is the weaker reading (*contra* Büchsel).

218. Vicent Cernuda, *EstBib* 27 (1968) 153–75, 215–32.

219. See *2 Apoc. Bar.* 21:19; 31:5; 40:3; 48:50; 73:4f.; 74:2; 83:10ff.; 4 Ezra 4:11, 26; 6:20; 7:96, 112; further *4 Enoch* 65:6ff.; *Apoc. Abr.* 17; *T. Iss.* 4, 3, 6; *Sipre Deut.* §47, etc.; see Schlatter, *Der Evangelist Johannes* on John 8:34 (p. 213).

220. In Philo the idea becomes spiritual and ethical; "life" consists in goodness and virtue; wickedness and evil are "death" (*Fuga* 58); cf. *Deter.* 48, 49; *Congr.* 87; *Heres* 290; *Fuga* 55.

221. See *Ginza* 39.14f.: "do the will of your Lord so that you may ascent victorious to the realms of light"; further 42.23ff.; 219.7–36. For a parallel to v. 17, see *Ginza* 78.8f.: "the children of darkness perish, but the children of power and life endure"; further 16.25–27; 35.6–8; 62.10.—Without ethical application, *Odes Sol.* 5:12–14.

222. =*zēsei eis ton aiōna* (6:51, 58); similar phrases in 8:51f.; 10:28; 11:26.

223. Chaine is of the opinion that this is a recollection of God as Creator and that "to do his will" means to use material things in accordance with the divine plan. However, the contrasted term *kosmos* in 2:15 does not connote creation.

Christian usage.[224] With the word "forever" the paragraph comes to a linguistically satisfying conclusion. The Old Latin texts add "as also he himself [God] lives forever," or something like it.[225] But this cannot be original. The manuscript support for it is inadequate, although the addition is consistent with Johannine style (cf. 1:7; 3:3, 7; 4:17). The idea behind it is taken for granted in Johannine thought and requires no special emphasis.

EXCURSUS 6

The "World" in 1 John 2:15-17

The paragraph 1 John 2:15-17 presupposes an understanding of the "world" that occupies a special place of its own in the Johannine writings, marked as they are by a rich and varied use of language.[226] The "world" here is a dangerous reality, and people have to be warned against it. It is neither completely evil, nor is it neutral, let alone good. It never appears in this half light anywhere else in the Johannine writings. It is either God's creation (= "all things" [NRSV "the world"], John 1:10b; cf. 3:17, 24), or it is the world as alienated from God, the domain of Satan, the ruler of (this) world (John 12:31; 14:30; 16:11). A kind of intermediate position is taken in those passages which speak of the Son of God coming or being sent into the world.[227] There the world is regarded as the habitat and abode of humanity. As a result of sin and humanity's distance from God, the world becomes a realm of darkness, though illuminated by Jesus, who is "the light of the world" (John 3:19; 8:12; 9:5; 12:46). But since the people who

---

224. Cf. *thelēma tou theou* (John 9:31; Rom. 1:10; 12:2; 15:32; 1 Cor. 1:1; [so too in the exordium of other letters]; Eph. 6:6; 1 Thess. 4:3; Heb. 10:36; 13:21; 1 Pet. 2:15; 3:17).

225. sa: quemadmodum ille qui est in aeternum; cypr. (*testim.* III, 11 19): quomodo (et) ipse manet in aeternum; (*De mortal.* 24), Lucif., Zeno: quomodo (et) deus manet (manebit cypr., *Hab. virg.* 7) in aeternum; Augustine, *In I Joa. tr.* 2.10: sicut et ipse (ille) manet in aeternum; Augustine, *In I Joa. tr.* 2.14; Pel., Rur.: sicut et Deus manet in aeternum. On all of this, see A. von Harnack, *SB* (Berlin, 1915) 561f. Since the whole Greek textual tradition knows nothing of this addition, and since Jerome did not adopt it in the Vulgate, it can hardly be regarded as original.

226. This excursus is not intended to discuss the concept of "world" per se, but only to call attention to one aspect of it which hitherto has received little attention. On the Johannine concept of world, see R. Löwe, *Kosmos und Aion* (Gütersloh, 1935) esp. 124ff.; H. Sasse, *TDNT* 3:894f.; R. Bultmann, *Glauben und Verstehen* (collected essays; Tübingen, 1933) 135-39; idem, *John,* passim (see index s.v. *kosmos*); idem, *Theology* 1:15ff.; Percy, *Untersuchungen,* 125ff.; Wikenhauser, *Johannes,* 174-76; Meinertz, *Theologie* 2:286f. L. Schottroff assumes a unitary dualistic and gnostic concept of the world for GJohn and 1 John (*Der Glaubende und die feindliche Welt* [Neukirchen, 1970]). Against this, see O. Böcher, *Der johanneische Dualismus,* 76-127; N. H. Cassem, "A Grammatical and Contextual Inventory of the Use of κόσμος in the Johannine Corpus with Some Implications for a Johannine Cosmic Theology," *NTS* 19 (1972-73) 81-91. See further J. Becker, "Beobachtungen zum Dualismus im Johannesevangelium," *ZNW* 65 (1974) 1-87 (assumes an interior development of the Johannine communities). — On the dualism in Qumran, see also J. H. Charlesworth, "A Critical Comparison of the Dualism in 1QS iii, 14-iv, 26 and the 'Dualism' Contained in the Fourth Gospel," *NTS* 15 (1968-69) 389-419 (reprinted in *John and Qumran,* 76-106); P. von der Osten-Sacken, *Gott und Belial: Traditionsgeschichtliche Untersuchungen zum Dualismus in den Texten aus Qumran* (Göttingen, 1969).

227. John 1:9; 3:19; 6:14; 9:39; 10:36; 11:27; 12:46; 16:28; 17:18; 18:37; 1 John 4:9.

live in the world are in need of salvation, it becomes the world (*kosmos*) in a different sense, the object of God's mercy and love (John 3:16; 1 John 4:9).[228] In 1 John 2:15ff. the author issues a warning against the world as the abode of evil desires (v. 16). Unbelief and hatred directed against God's emissary and all who belong to him have hardened part of the human race,[229] making the "world" a designation of all that is hostile to God.[230] But it does not have that meaning in 2:15ff. At the same time the author is so familiar with the idea of the world as a realm opposed to God that the phrase crops up again in the parenesis at the end of v. 16. If "world" were used here in the same sense as in v. 15, the reasoning in v. 16 would result in a vicious circle. However, the desire to express positively what he had said negatively in the phrase "comes not from the Father" leads the author to add "but from the world."

The world that the reader should not love is not the human world but the material world and all that is in it ("all that is in the world"). The assessment of this "world" is a negative one. The author is thinking not of its character as God's creation but of its dangerous character since the fall.

The "world" is not inherently corrupt like the evil one.[231] Rather, it is filled with bad desires (v. 16). That is what makes it so dangerous and so full of temptation. It is not stated in so many words, or even hinted at, that the world is derived from an evil principle. Moreover, in 2:15f. the author can still think of the world as God's creation, although he does not actually say so here, which is understandable. There are similar warnings in the Mandean literature, but there they are based on gnostic, dualistic thought. The world for Mandeism is not merely a place of moral perfidy; it is rotten to the core, It is "darkness without light . . . foul smelling . . . a place of persecution and death without life forever . . . ."[232] In the *Book of the Dead* the soul is blessed which has left this world: "Thou hast left corruption behind, along with the foul smelling corpses among which thou wast sojourneying, the abode of the vile ones, the place which is nought but sin, the realm of darkness, hatred, jealousy, and enmity. . . ."[233] These denigrations of the world have an entirely different basis from the warnings of the Christian author, for as we read elsewhere, "this world was not created out of a desire for life . . . it was created because of the errors

---

228. Cf. also *ho sōtēr tou kosmou* (John 4:42; 1 John 4:14) and further statements like John 1:29; 3:17; 6:33, 51; 12:47.

229. John 1:10c; 7:7; 14:17; 15:18f.; 17:14, 25; 1 John 3:1, 13.

230. See especially the phrase *ek tou kosmou (toutou) einai* (John 8:23; 15:19; 17:14, 16; 18:36; 1 John 2:16; 4:5), which always expressed the strong contrast with God (*ek tou theou*); on this, see Bultmann, *John,* 161 n. 3; Percy, *Untersuchungen,* 128–31.

231. At other places where the typically Johannine concept "world" occurs, the same assertions are made as those about the evil one. All who believe in Christ overcome the world (5:4f.), just as they overcome evil (2:13b, 14c; cf. John 16:33). This world is under judgment (John 12:31), as is the ruler of this world. In 1 John 2:15 it is not possible to substitute "evil one" for *kosmos,* for that would be much too weak an assertion.

232. *Ginza* 14.22ff.; cf. 33.3ff.; 241.31f.; *Book of John* 55.1f.; *MandLit* 161f.

233. *Ginza* 511.8ff.=*MandLit* 159; *Ginza* 568.25ff.; 572.25ff.; *Book of John* 93.2f.; *MandLit* 12.6; 143.8f.; 161f.; 198; 227.

(of the planets), for the planets . . . lead the human race astray and into sin."[234] This cosmological dualism also lies at the root of Iranian and Manichean religion,[235] and is typical of gnosticism.[236] In 1 John 2:15ff. the "world" offers the evil desires only a place to live and play. It becomes evil because of what happens in it. Those who ally themselves with it find themselves ensnared in the evil passions that are in it. So the antithesis between God and the world is not metaphysical but moral. That is why the love of the world and the love of God cannot coexist (v. 15b). In effect, people must choose between one and the other. The "world" in 1 John 2:15ff. is nothing other than an abode of evil passions (see v. 16); it is liable to collapse along with everything that it shelters (v. 17a). Again, the pessimistic judgment about the world as the realm of the evil one in 1 John 5:19 goes beyond what was said in 2:15ff. This is rather one of those sayings about the "ruler of this world" (cf. the contrast with the "Son of God" in 5:20a). It is this purely moral contrast that colors the idea of the world in 2:15.

When we ask whence this concept of the world in 2:15 is derived, we are reminded of other sayings in the teaching of the early church. The closest parallel occurs in James 4:4. Here we find the same pointed contrast between God and the world, a contrast that is moral in nature. Friendship with the world means enmity toward God. But this is only one saying among many others which continue to occur through the Apostolic Fathers.[237] Paul had a major influence on these formulations.[238] His parenesis is slanted more in the direction of salvation history than is the case with 1 John. Paul regards "the world" or "this world" as existing under judgment (1 Cor. 6:2; 11:32). Its form is passing away (1 Cor. 7:31). Those who believe in Christ belong in their true nature to the age to come. They should therefore possess the goods of this world as though they had them not, using them with a certain detachment (ibid.). This urgent eschatological motivation is lacking in 1 John. But these are only differences of nuance. By and large early Christian teaching was formulated by the same attitude toward the "world" or "this age."

Once again, the early church seems to be indebted at this point to late Judaism. Quite a number of the parenetic sections in the *Testaments of the*

---

234. *Ginza* 247.9ff.; cf. 242.9–16. How the realm of darkness arose is not described (cf. *Ginza* 70ff.), though its dualistic origin is certain; see further *Book of John* 55.10ff.; *MandLit* 4.

235. See Reitzenstein, *Iranisches Erlösungsmysterium*, 25; Pétrement, *Dualisme*, 196–204.

236. Cf. *CHerm* 6.4: ὁ γὰρ κόσμος πλήρωμά ἐστι τῆς κακίας, ὁ δὲ θεὸς τοῦ ἀγαθοῦ. But there are also other Hermetic statements that contradict it (10.10: the world is not evil, but neither is it good; 9.4: the earth is the abode of evil, not the world; Asclep. 27: the world is an icon of God). On this ambiguity in the Hermetic literature, see W. Bousset in his review of J. Kroll, *GGA* (1914) 697–755; Pétrement, *Dualisme,* 179f. Jonas sees in this the protest "which the Greek spirit was compelled to register against the depravation of the concept of the cosmos" (*Gnosis* 1:153f.). Percy believes that he sees here stoic-astrological influence (*Untersuchungen,* 134f.).—Other gnostic texts will be found in *Odes Sol.* 20:3; *Exc. ex Theod.* 74; *Pistis Sophia* 32; 41; 96; 100. However, the contrast here changes more into that between "matter" and "spirit." See further Bousset, *Hauptprobleme,* 91ff.; Jonas, *Gnosis* 1:146ff.; Pétrement, *Dualisme,* 190ff.

237. Cf. James 1:27; 2 Pet. 1:4; 2:20; Ignatius, *Rom.* 7.1; Polycarp, *Phil.* 5.3; 9.2; *Barn.* 4.3; *Herm. Vis.* 1.1, 8; *2 Clem.* 5.6f.; 6.6.

238. 1 Cor. 5:10; 7:31; Gal. 6:14; Eph. 2:2; Rom. 12:2 (*ho aiōn houtos*).

Twelve Patriarchs,[239] the Damascus Document,[240] as well as the apocalyptic literature,[241] breathe a similar spirit. The person who is single-hearted ". . . shunning eyes (made) evil through the error of the world, lest he should see the perversion of any of the commandments of the Lord" (*T. Iss.* 4:6).[242] There are urgent warnings against everything that arouses passionate desire, such as wine, women, and wealth (*T. Jud.* 13ff.), against riches and gluttony (*T. Benj.* 6:2f.; *1 Enoch* 108:8f.), against the "three snares of Belial": lasciviousness, wealth, and desecration of the Temple (CD 4:15ff.). In the Qumran texts the warnings are even more pointed in view of the "dominion of the Angel of Darkness over the children of falsehood." For the Angel of Darkness may even lead the "children of righteousness" astray (see 1QS 3:21ff.). Symptomatic for the "spirit of false-hood" is a whole catalogue of vices (1QS 4:9ff.). Other passages speak of the "dominion of Satan." His rule, however, is of limited duration and lasts only until the destruction of the "children of darkness."[243] The "chosen ones of God" seek to withdraw into a life of purity, separating themselves from evil influences through purification, prayer, and a strict moral life. Above and beyond this they seek to "atone for the land" by a radical observance of the law and by whole-hearted attempts to please God (1QS 8:6, 10; 1QSa 1:3). Insofar as the Qumraners are thinking of the two antithetical realms of light and darkness, we might suspect here a cosmic dualism. But apart from the fact that they have no concept of the "world," there is no tendency to devaluate the material world in principle as in gnosticism. God is the creator and all things are under his control, even the "spirits of darkness." "From the God of knowledge comes all that is and shall be" (1QS 3:15). To him they look for eschatological renewal (1QS 4:25; 1QH 13:11f.). Light and darkness are envisioned as two different realms of power. But even this apparent dualism is still oriented toward salvation history and ethics. Thus it definitely remains within the limits of late Judaism.[244]

Following the normal teaching of the earliest Christian church, which was influenced at this point by late Judaism, the author takes up a distinctive concept of the "world" which does not exactly echo the harsh "Johannine" tone. It does, however, easily lead into the pregnant view of the "world" as the antithesis of the divine sphere. The typically Johannine concept of the "world" has a gnostic sound, but it is closer in reality to the earliest church's view of the "world," with its concern for morality and salvation history, than might appear at first sight.

---

239. *T. Iss.* 4; *T. Jud.* 13; *T. Benj.* 8.

240. CD 2:14–17; 4:13–18; 6:14–17.

241. *2 Apoc. Bar.* 73.4f.; 4 Ezra 4:26ff.; 14:20f.; *1 Enoch* 48:7; 108:8f.; cf. Volz. *Eschatologie,* 7, 68.

242. It should certainly be translated thus, following the better reading (Charles). Riessler takes a different view.

243. "Dominion of Satan": 1QS 1:18, 23; 2:19; 1QM 14:9; 4QMa 6; cf. 1QS 3:22f.; 4:19; 1QM 1:15; 14:10; 17:5; 18:1, 11.—On Belial, see H. W. Huppenbauer, "Belial in den Qumrantexten," *TZ* 15 (1959) 81–89.

244. Cf. Nötscher, *Zur theologischen Terminologie,* 82–86; Huppenbauer, *Der Mensch zwischen zwei Welten,* 95–115, esp. 108f.

PART TWO

The Contemporary Situation of the Christian Communities: Their Struggle to Defend Themselves against the "Antichrists," Their Expectation of Salvation and Their Religious and Moral Task (1 John 2:18–3:24)

With 2:18ff. we begin a new part. Up to this point the author has been speaking of the Christian community in a didactic and parenetic way without regard to the particular moment in time of salvation history. Now, however, he focuses his attention on the "last hour" (2:18) and what it requires. His reason for doing so is the emergence of heretical teachers who deny the central point of the christological message, the saving significance of Jesus Christ. These christological heretics are in fact identical with the moral heretics of Part One (see Introduction, p. 17). The reason for his concern is that it endangers the very heart of his saving message (1:1–3). Because their denial of Christ is so pernicious, he stigmatizes them as "antichrists." This is how the author interprets the present situation, enabling him to warn his churches and alert them to the need to hold fast to their confession of faith in Christ as it had been delivered to them. True, he does not think in terms of salvation history to the degree that Paul does. But the present conflict leads him to develop his thinking in that direction. He had already mentioned how the word of life had come and how important that was (1:2; cf. 3:8). But this demands the future appearance of Christ in the parousia (2:28). Only then will the salvation they have already received as children of God be complete (3:2, "now . . . not yet been revealed"). This major section, 3:4–24, filled with parenetic concern as it is, does not leave salvation history in the background. Rather, it is placed under the motif, "all who have this hope" (3:3). In any case it is not advisable to begin a new section with 3:4ff. The author was already steering toward this admonition in 2:29 ("everyone who does right"; cf. 3:7) and is only distracted by the theme of our being born of God, or of being children of God. With 3:3 ("purify themselves") he finally reaches the theme.

It is more difficult to decide where the section should end. Contra the attempts to include 4:1-6 in this section (Häring, Brooke) or, even worse, to continue it down to 5:13, there is clearly a break at 3:23f.: (1) Faith in Christ and mutual love, embracing personal sanctification and fulfillment of the commandments, are summed up in 3:23 (cf. 2:18-27 and 2:28-3:17 or 20). (2) The word about fellowship with God in 3:24a gives the impression of a final chord, resuming the main motif of Part One (cf. 2:5, 10; 1:6). On the other hand, 3:24b forms a transition. The possession of the Spirit as the mark of knowledge is a new idea, paving the way to the problem of "distinguishing the spirits" in 4:1ff. This raising of a new topic at the end of a section dealing with an unrelated theme is consistent with the author's style (see Introduction, p. 9f.).

The train of thought in this part of the letter is marked off in a way reminiscent of 1:5-2:17. Following the altercation with the heresy, in this instance a christological one, 2:18-27, and a positive presentation of the hope of salvation in 2:28-3:3 (this digression is here rather special) there follows a parenetic admonition in 3:4-24, similar to 2:12-17. In comparison with Part One the author develops the parenesis further here. It is easy to see why. Its main thrust is on the false moral stance of his opponents and the contrasting stance of Christian orthodoxy. Thematically, however, the author is no longer concerned in 3:4-24 with the moral heresy, but is combating it only in an indirect and latent fashion. The first part of the epistle sets the stage for the understanding of this latent polemic. The leading role played by the parenesis is obvious from the fact that the opponents are no longer given their say directly. Note the absence of "if we say" or "whoever says." The believers are simply warned to beware of their seducers (3:7). By and large this section is addressed to the orthodox Christians, to those who are "born of God" (cf. also 3:11, 13, 18, 21). It is concerned for the most part with in-house problems of Christian living (cf. 3:16f., 19f., 21f.).

Finally, it would be hard to imagine the author returning to the same theme again and again without any clear plan. But that would be exactly what would happen with the theme of "mutual love" if we were to alter the framework and extend it. This theme seems rather to belong to three different sections of the letter, each time focusing on one aspect of the subject (2:7-11; 3:11-18; 4:7-21). The opponents are mentioned again in 4:1ff., although that passage seems to be dealing with the same group of people. This time, however, they are referred to as "false prophets." This is because "Spirit" and "prophecy" go together like "Christ" and "antichrist." Also in Part Three the author is moving over to the "testing of the spirits" and to "distinguishing what is authentically Christian."

It will be seen that the author develops his thought in a peculiar way, paragraph by paragraph. Perhaps he wrote one paragraph at a time. In any case, the same complex of ideas, more or less, surfaces from different perspectives. He also tends to recapitulate his thought, though with variations in style. So it is not surprising to find familiar thoughts resurfacing in a manner similar to what preceded. Cf. 3:5 and 16 with 2:1f.; 3:6, 9 with 1:6; 3:11ff. with 2:7ff.; 3:19 with 2:4; 3:24 with 2:5.

Some scholars, like Vrede and Chaine, think that the main theme in 2:29-5:13 is the Christian status as children of God. This, however, is untenable, not only for the reasons given already but because this theme does not stand on its own. It occurs frequently as a motivating factor (2:29; 3:9; 4:7; 5:1, 4, 18). Except in 3:1-3 it never has any independent significance of its own. The author is fond of omitting any connecting link between one section and another, making it difficult to mark off one from the next. But as we have already indicated, there is good reason to highlight 2:18-3:24 as a special section on its own. For it is colored by the notion of salvation history and eschatology. This is clear from 2:18. However, neither salvation history nor eschatology provides an organizing principle (cf. Büchsel). The author is led to make a fresh start in view of the christological heresy, refuting it but then going on immediately in his usual manner with further admonitions to his churches.

We would therefore propose the following structure:

I. The "Last Hour." The heretical teachers as antichrists, their expulsion from the community of true believers (2:18-27).
1. It is the "last hour" and the heretical teachers are "antichrists" (2:18).
2. The community has expelled the antichrists who had arisen in their midst and has been confirmed in the truth by the Holy Spirit (2:19-21).
3. By denying the Christian faith, the heretical teachers identify themselves as antichrists, thus forfeiting their fellowship with the Father and the promise of eternal life (2:22-25).
4. The readers must hold fast to the true faith in Christ, illumined as they are by the Holy Spirit (2:26-27).

II. The Christian hope of salvation (2:28-3:3).
1. The parousia is a matter of hope and requires holiness (2:28-29).
2. Christians have the gift of becoming children of God and are promised even greater glory (3:1-3).

III. The religious and moral task at the present time (3:4-24).
1. The avoidance of sin (3:4-10).
   a) Union with Christ rules out sinful behavior (3:4-8).
   b) The children of God cannot sin (3:9-10).
2. The practice of mutual love (3:11-20).
   a) The message of mutual love, as the story of Cain and Abel shows, reveals the good and evil in humankind (3:11-12).
   b) The nature and effect of hatred: It is equivalent to murder and deprives its perpetrators of eternal life (3:13-15).
   c) The nature of mutual love: It is expressed by following the example of Christ in action (3:16-18).
   d) A special fruit of mutual love: It gives us peace of heart in the sight of God (3:19-20).
3. The admonition concluded (3:21-24).
   a) Those who keep the commandments will receive an answer to their prayers (3:21-22).
   b) God's commandment can be summed up as faith in Christ and mutual love (3:23).
   c) The fruit of such obedience is true fellowship with God (3:24).

FIRST SECTION

THE "LAST HOUR." THE HERETICAL TEACHERS AS ANTICHRISTS, THEIR EXPULSION FROM THE COMMUNITY OF TRUE BELIEVERS (1 JOHN 2:18-27)

[18]Children, it is the last hour! As you have heard that antichrist is coming, so now many antichrists have come. From this we know that it is the last hour. [19]They went out from us, but they did not belong to us; for if they had belonged to us, they would have remained with us. But by going out they made it plain that none of them belongs to us. [20]But you have been anointed by the Holy One, and all of you have knowledge. [21]I write to you, not because you do not know the truth, but because you know it, and you know that no lie comes from the truth. [22]Who is the liar but the one who denies that Jesus is the Christ? This is the antichrist, the one who denies the Father and the Son. [23]No one who denies the Son has the Father; everyone who confesses the Son has the Father also. [24]Let what you heard from the beginning abide in you. If what you heard from the beginning abides in you, then you will abide in the Son and in the Father. [25]And this is what he has promised to us, eternal life.

[26]I write these things to you concerning those who would deceive you. [27]As for you, the anointing that you received from him abides in you, and so you do not need anyone to teach you. But as his anointing teaches you about all things, and is true and not a lie, and just as it has taught you, abide in him [=Christ].

1. It Is the "Last Hour" and the Heretical Teachers Are "Antichrists" (1 John 2:18)

2:18   With a new, yet already familiar address (2:14) the author places a concise statement at the opening of this new section, similar to the "message" from God at the beginning of Part One (1:5). This time it is a statement that it is the last hour in salvation history. The absence of the article underscores the categorical importance of this sentence! "Hour" does not look back to a lengthy series of moments in time, but is identical in meaning with time itself.[2] It is the time of salvation history, so supremely pregnant with our future destiny in the struggle between the powers of good and evil. It is the decisive period before the End (Mark 14:5-7, 13 par.) or parousia (1 John 2:28). This epoch, so important for the way God reckons the hours, though not calculable in human measurement of time, is discernible by certain signs (Mark 13:4, 29), and may have various designations.[3] GJohn does not offer any parallel for this, though it does know

---

1. Moulton 2:430; cf. BDF §258.
2. BAGD 896, s.v. 3; for GJohn, cf. further phrases with *erchetai* (4:[21], 23; 5:25, 28; 16:2, 4, 25 [32]), which signify a time that is important in salvation history.
3. Cf. *en tais eschatais hēmerais* (Acts 2:17 [without article]; 2 Tim. 3:1; Jas. 5:3); *ep' eschatou tou chronou* (Jude 18; cf. 1 Pet. 1:20); *ep' eschatōn tōn hēmerōn* (2 Pet. 3:3).—Different expressions also occur in Jewish apocalyptic. In the Dead Sea Scrolls this time is called "the end of the days" (1QpHab 2:5; 9:6; 1QSa 1:1; etc.; cf. CD 4:4; 6:11, "last time," "time of wickedness" (1QpHab 5:7f.; 7:7, 12; 1QS 4:16; etc.—Phrases with *qēs* =end, time); see K. G. Kuhn, *ZTK* 47 (1950) 208f.; Nötscher, *Zur theologischen Terminologie,* 167-69.

the eschatological hour of the resurrection of the dead and the judgment.[4] The last hour does not mean the whole period since the coming of Christ or since his resurrection. But neither is it a phase or particular period within time as it draws to its close.[5] The author looks forward to the parousia (2:28) and regards the emergence of the antichrists as a sign of the last times (2:18d). But this does not imply a precise chronological scheme for his eschatology. With the warning signal "antichrists have come," all he means to say is that his own time has an eschatological importance. He wishes to alert his leaders in the face of impending danger. Although, like other early Christian theologians,[6] he takes for granted the imminence of the parousia, he makes no attempt to calculate its precise date. He has the same eschatological sense of time that all of the other New Testament authors have—particularly the author of Revelation (1:3; 3:11; 6:10; 22:7, 10, 12, 20).

In GJohn of course there is a palpable shift of emphasis. Here Jesus speaks of the hour "which is coming and now is," when the true worshipers shall worship the Father in spirit and truth (4:23), or when the dead will hear the voice of the Son of God (5:25). In other words, the eschatological time has come with the person of Jesus. The promises are being fulfilled and the gifts of the Spirit are already present. Eternal life, which the believer received from Jesus, the heavenly bearer of life (cf. 5:26; 6:57), appears to make any expectation of the future unnecessary. Yet the impression is created only by the heavy concentration on the person of Christ, the eschatological revealer and mediator. As has already been shown in the discussion about the Johannine concept of "life" (see Pribnow, Mussner), all this is invariably qualified by Semitic thought, which cannot imagine the consummation apart from the resurrection of the body. This means it is hardly possible to deny the authenticity of the constantly recurring refrain in 6:39, 40, 44, 54 ("and I would raise them up on the last day") or the "eschatological prospect" in 5:28f. or to assign it to an ecclesiastical redactor. Only the perspective has been shifted. The present eschatological hour of Jesus and the future resurrection of the dead and the last judgment are merged together. The author of 1 John, on the other hand, knows that in Christ the "life was revealed" (1:2) and that faith in Christ has conquered the world (5:4). But in the conflict with the heretical teachers and with the reality of sin in the Christian life he becomes aware of the danger that besets the eschatological situation of the Christians at the present time. This explains why he is more open to the provisional character of salvation, as the earliest Christians were, and why he reverts to ideas and terminology of the earliest church as these are found in its catechetical teaching.

The author's affinity with early Christian eschatology becomes immediately apparent when he says "As you have heard." He is appealing here to the

---

4. John 5:28f.; cf. also resurrection or judgment "on the last day" (6:39, 40, 44, 54; 12:48).

5. Cf. Westcott, ad loc., appealing to the absence of the article (on this, however, see above in the text). The second interpretation mentioned is supported by those explanations of the antichrist as the forerunner of the real antichrists still expected; see further in the text.

6. 1 Cor. 7:29ff.; 16:22; Rom. 13:11; Phil. 4:5; 1 Thess. 5:1ff.; 2 Thess. 2:2; Heb. 10:25, 37; Jas. 5:8; 2 Pet. 3:9; *1 Clem.* 23.2; *Did.* 10.6; *Barn.* 4.1ff.; 21.3, 6; Ignatius, *Eph.* 2.1; *Herm. Vis.* 3.9; Justin, *Dial.* 32.3f. A stronger support for the eschatological-apocalyptic world view will be found in Cyprian; see *De mortal.* 2.15.25; *Ad Demetr.* 3.4.23; *De unit. eccl.* 16; *Ad Fortun.* 1; *Ep.* 58.1.7; 61.4; 67.7.—A. von Harnack offers as his judgment: "Until beyond the beginning of the third cent. this belief continued in wide circles; but its high point was the time up to Marcus Aurelius" (*Mission und Ausbreitung,* 121).

tradition, to the official Christian teaching.[7] He regards the imminent expectation of the antichrist as part of that tradition. We shall never completely understand the origin or meaning of this term (see Excursus 7), but it clearly comes from the early church.

There was then a widely held conviction of the coming of the antichrist in the early church, and the author takes up this concept in order to describe heretical teachers with whom he is engaged in combat. This is obviously his own idea, as is shown by the use of the plural and by the fact that nowhere else in the New Testament is it connected with heresy (its use is confined to 1 and 2 John). The sequence of the two sayings about the antichrist (in the singular), and of the antichrists (in the plural) is probably due to the author. He is applying and interpreting the early Christian tradition. Note the omission of the article before "antichrist" in the best manuscripts,[8] which results in a clear parallelism.

Thus the suggestion is hardly tenable that the antichrists mentioned here are in the author's mind merely the precursors and representatives of the real antichrist, whose personal appearance still lies in the future.[9] True, no formal identification is made (though cf. 2 John 7). Yet the parallel structure shows that it is a consciously interpreted tradition. The future "is coming" is replaced by the perfect "have come" (2:18), and there is an emphatic contrast between the singular and the plural ("many") which follows. The "so" before the "now" does not emphasize any new event different from the one already mentioned. There is no "already" as in 4:3. Rather, it should be taken similarly to the Greek word *kai* in the comparative clause ("so in fact now").[10] If the designation of the heretical teachers as antichrists is meant to be taken only metaphorically, or as a simile, its meaning would be perfectly straightforward. Taken literally, however, it would be quite different from the early Christian concept of the antichrist. Another curious factor would be the complete silence regarding the person and activity of the real antichrist.

But this should not be regarded as a "tendentious interpretation," on the part of the author. It is not as though he wanted to deconstruct the traditional eschatology of Jewish apocalyptic and replace it by a new one, limited to the present — a tendency that critics have attributed to GJohn![11] The suggestion that

7. On this use of *akouein*, cf. 2:7b, 24; 3:11; 4:3; Eph. 4:21; 1 Tim. 4:16.

8. B ℵ* C Ψ 1739 5 623 Orig. Epiph. without article; A ℵ pl. with article. For that reason it is better omitted (*contra* Vogels, Merk).

9. Belser, Camerlynck, Vrede, Charue, Ambroggi, Michl. Cf. already Estius: (Antichristus) "nam omnino venturus est; sed *interim* iam Antichristi facti sunt." For a contrary view, see Bonsirven; Chaine; B. Rigaux, *Les Épîtres aux Thessaloniciens* (Paris, 1956) 278f.—contrary to his earlier view in *L'Antéchrist*, 386.

10. BDF §453.2; the *kai* can also stand in both parts of the comparison (as in Rom. 1:13; Matt. 18:33). For 1 John, cf. 2:27b.—The *kai* in 4:3, where the temporal aspect is primary (*nyn . . . ēdē*), does not mean "also" but "and."

11. H. J. Holtzmann, *Lehrbuch der neutestamentliche Theologie* (2nd ed.; Tübingen, 1911) 2:575–78; R. Bultmann, *Glauben und Verstehen*, 134ff., and more esp. 133 n. 1; idem, *John*, passim; he states his basic thesis, for example, on p. 433 (on John 12:31): "if in the evangelist's mind the myth has not lost its mythological content and become historicized, his language on the other hand serves to eliminate the traditional eschatology of primitive Christianity." See also M. Goguel, who, however, contends that there was a return to the primitive eschatology in 1 John ("Eschatologie et apocalyptique dans le christianisme primitif," *RHR* 106 [1932] 381–434, 490–524). Similarly W. Grundmann, *Aufnahme und Deutung der Botschaft Jesu im Urchristentum* (Weimar, 1941) 159f.—For a critique, see G. Stählin, "Zum Problem der johanneischen Eschatologie," *ZNW* 32 (1934) 225–59,

this passage leaves no place for any future expectation is ruled out by the powerful imagery of the "last hour," which, given the context of 2:28, can only mean the period preceding the parousia. Rather, the author is proposing a time scheme similar to what we find in the book of Revelation. It keeps well within the framework of early Christian eschatology. Compared with 2 Thess. 2:3ff. it is certainly remarkable that in 1 (and 2) John the "antichrist" is used as a collective term. But the description and characterization of this traditional eschatological phenomenon remain vague and uncertain, both in the New Testament and for a long time afterward![12]

EXCURSUS 7

The Expectation of the Antichrist: Its Earlier History

1. In his expectation of the antichrist, the author refers specifically to the early Christian preaching (see 2:7, 24; 3:11; 4:3). To corroborate this all we have is a single reference, albeit one that provides abundant evidence, namely, 2 Thess. 2:3ff. It is obvious that Paul is not giving his readers any revelation here that is essentially new. Rather, he is basing himself on teachings already familiar to his readers in order to calm down their exaggerated expectations of an immediate parousia. This passage enhances the supposition that the mysterious desolating sacrilege of Mark 13:14; Matt. 24:15, alluding to Dan. 8:12; 9:27; 11:13 (12:11) is a reference to the antichrist. Finally, the visions of the antichrist in the book of Revelation (13:1ff.; 19:19ff.) are undoubtedly connected with the expectation of the community, though the seer may have interpreted it in his own way![13] However, 2 Cor. 6:15 is not to be connected with the idea of the antichrist. The identification of the antichrist with Beliar—in late Judaism an equivalent of Satan[14]—belongs to a later period![15]

In 2 Thess. 2:3ff. the antichrist—as a technical term it was only coined by 1 John 2:18, 22; 4:3; 2 John 7 (cf. Polycarp 7.1)—is called "the lawless one," the "one destined to destruction" (v. 3). He is considered to be God's strongest enemy.

---

esp. 236ff.; B. Aebert, *Die Eschatologie des Joh-Ev* (Würzburg, 1936); W. F. Howard, *Christianity According to St. John* (London, 1943) 106–28; C. K. Barrett, "The Place of Eschatology in the Fourth Gospel," *ExpT* 59 (1947–48) 302–5; H. Blauert, "Die Bedeutung der Zeit in der johanneischen Theologie" (diss., Tübingen, 1953; Wikenhauser, *Johannes,* 257–80; O. Linton, "Johannesevangelist og eskatologien," *SvExA* 22–23 (1957–58) 98–110; A. Corell, *Consumatum est: Eschatology and Church in the Gospel of St. John* (London, 1958) 101–9.

12. See Westcott, 92f.; further, Excursus 7 (at the end).

13. See J. Ernst, *Die eschatologischen Gegenspieler in den Schriften des Neuen Testaments* (Regensburg, 1967) 168–77.

14. All through the *Testaments of the Twelve Patriarchs* (Beliar); see further 1QS 1:18, 24; 2:5, 19; 1QM 1:1, 5, 13; 4:2; 11:8; etc. (Belial); CD 4:13, 15; 5:18; 8:2; 12:2; *Jub.* 1:20; 15:13; *Asc. Isa.* 2:4; 3:11, 13; 5:15; *Sib.* 3:72. See further Bousset-Gressmann, *Religion des Judentums,* 334 n. 3; 514 n. 1; Baudissin in Hauck's *Realencyclopedie* 2:548f.; Windisch, *Der zweite Korintherbrief* (KEK; Göttingen, 1970) 215. W. Foerster, *TDNT* 1:607; B. Noack, *Satanas und Soteria* (Copenhagen, 1948) 58ff.; Rigaux, *Thessaloniciens,* 266–72.

15. *Asc. Isa.* 4:1ff.; see in the text under 4. *Contra* the interpretation of 2 Cor. 6:15 as a reference to the antichrist (cf. Lietzmann, ad loc.; Windisch, ad loc.; Foerster, *TDNT* 1:607; Noack, *Satanas.*

He "exalts himself and considers himself greater than any god" (Dan. 11:36) or anything that is called holy. He takes his seat in the temple of God and calls himself God (v. 4). At his parousia, Christ will slay this enemy of God "with the breath of his lips" (2 Thess. 2:8; cf. Isa. 11:4). This eschatological phenomenon is therefore conceived as a human being, an individual personality. Later he is described more explicitly as a tool of Satan, who can work miracles and lying signs by the power of his spirit in opposition to God (v. 9) and by satanic deceit lead people astray (v. 10). Inasmuch as his appearance was also called a "parousia" (v. 9), the similarities and differences are obvious. He is a counter-Christ, appearing immediately before the coming of Christ himself. He raises the banner of Satan just as Christ raises the banner of God![16]

The description of the beast from the abyss in Rev. 13:1ff. exhibits several similar traits. It derives its power from the dragon, Satan (vv. 2, 4). It blasphemes against God (vv. 5f.). It allows itself to be worshiped (v. 8). Finally, it is defeated by the Messiah (19:19ff.). But there are also significant differences. The beast oscillates between being a political power (the Roman Empire) and an individual personality. In view of the primary vision (Daniel 7) and of the connection of one of his heads with a particular ruler (Rev. 13:3), the beast in Rev. 13:1ff. seems to symbolize an institutional power. But already the beast from the earth (13:11ff.) appears as the lackey and precursor of the first beast, suggesting a single individual. Moreover, the exegesis of 17:9ff. (esp. v. 11) confirms this. The seer, in a typically apocalyptic manner, exploits the symbol in two directions. Compared with the situation in Paul, the contemporary background (the Roman Empire) and the Nero mythology are noticeably transformed. There are other differences too, namely, the bloody persecution of the Christians (Rev. 13:7) and the transference of deceptive signs to the second beast, the beast from the earth (13:13ff.).

The trait that comes so strongly to the fore in the verses that follow, that is, the lawless one who takes his seat in the Temple of God in Jerusalem,[17] forms a bridge leading back from 2 Thess. 2:4 to Mark 13:14; cf. Matt. 24:15. Accordingly the desolating sacrilege, apparently a reference to the altar of Zeus in the Daniel prophecy, set up by Antiochus Epiphanes in Jerusalem when he committed an act of sacrilege on entering the Holy of Holies (cf. 1 Macc. 1:54),[18] in Christian understanding, must be applied to the antichrist. The so-called Little Apocalypse invites its readers to a special understanding ("let the reader understand"), adding to the name (which is neuter) a masculine participle (Greek *hestēkota;* NRSV "set up").[19] In this Marcan text (Matthew refers explicitly to

16. On this passage, see further J. Schmid, "Der Antichrist und die hemmende Macht (2 Thess 2, 1–12)," *TQ* 129 (1949) 323–43, with further bibliography. See also C. H. Giblin, *The Threat to Faith: An Exegetical and Theological Re-examination of 2 Thess. 2* (Rome, 1967); W. Trilling, *Untersuchungen zum 2. Thessalonicherbrief* (Leipzig, 1972) 77–86 (observes a parallelism between 2 Thessalonians 2 and 1 John in relation to the reception and application of traditional views).

17. On this point, see M. Dibelius, *An die Thessalonicher I, II, an die Philipper* (HNT 11; Tübingen, 1937).

18. Cf. J. Goettsberger, *Das Buch Daniel* (Bonn, 1928) on Deut. 9:27; 11:31ff.; similarly F. Nötscher, *Daniel* (Würzburg, 1948) on the same passage; A. Allgeier, *Biblische Zeitgeschichte* (Freiburg, 1937) 276f.

19. Also among Catholic writers, where the temporal-historical interpretation prevailed for a long time, the following scholars opt for it now: J. Schmid, *Das Evangelium nach Markus* (3rd ed.;

the Danielic prophecy) there is a reference to the early Christian conviction that there was a mysterious personality arrogating to itself the prerogatives belonging to a holy place ("where it ought not to be"). Especially when the Synoptic Apocalypse is understood as a parousia discourse these mystifying expressions would be recognized as references to the mighty adversary of God, the antichrist, who precedes the parousia.[20]

2. The passage in Mark 13:14 raises the pressing question of the Jewish background to the early Christian doctrine of the antichrist. Was late Judaism, especially in its apocalyptic form, aware of anything like this? It is necessary to be cautious about this question, despite the positive view of Bousset-Gressmann.[21] All we can say for certain is that in Jewish apocalyptic there was an expectation that the last times would be terrible, marked by the rise of a mighty empire in opposition to God.[22] It is easy to understand how after the fall of Jerusalem this pagan world empire came be identified with Rome, given the predilection for identifying the mysterious symbols of apocalyptic with contemporary events. We should pay attention to those passages in which this cosmic power opposed to God is embodied in a single personality. It is possible that such opinions were shaped by particularly vicious persecutors of the true worshipers of God, like Antiochus Epiphanes. The figure of the last great tyrant would then be "removed from history and mysteriously elevated to the status of a supernatural power transcending history" (Volz). Such an adversary of God is depicted by Daniel in his night visions of the king, especially in 11:36ff., a passage that seems to have influenced the wording of 2 Thess. 2:5.[23] Thus both of the great Jewish apocalypses have left traces of this perspective. The Syriac *Apocalypse of Baruch* depicts the last pagan ruler under the image of a cedar tree. He is eventually bound in fetters, carried off to Mount Zion, and killed by the Messiah. The same eschatological figure seems to be intended in 4 Ezra 5:6, where we read: "And one shall reign whom those who dwell on earth do not expect." The context here describes the signs of the last dreadful days (cf. 5:1). There will be extraordinary events, both on earth and in heaven, reminiscent of Mark 13, though different in detail. Then there is *As. Mos.* 8:2: "one that ruleth with great power . . . shall crucify those who confess to their circumcision; and those who conceal it he shall torture and deliver them up to be bound and led into prison." Here we have the same figure of one who persecutes the people of God in the

Regensburg, 1954) 242f.; and Rigaux, *Thessaloniciens,* 268 n. 3, for an allusion to the antichrist. Jerome considered the possibility that it refers to the antichrist (*In Matt.* 24:15 [*PL* 26:177]).

20. The interpretation in Mark 13:14 of the "desolating sacrilege" as a reference to the antichrist has now been questioned more strongly; see especially R. Pesch, *Naherwartungen: Tradition und Redaktion in Mk 13* (Düsseldorf, 1968) 139–44 (interprets it historically as a reference to the destruction of Jerusalem. Within the whole discourse of Mark 13 and the context of v. 14, the interpretation of it as a reference to the antichrist is indeed questionable. See also E. Schweizer, *The Good News According to Mark* (Richmond, VA, 1967) 272.

21. *Religion des Judentums,* 225f.; for a contrary view, see Billerbeck, *Kommentar* 3:637f.; Volz, *Eschatologie,* 282; Foerster, *TDNT* 1:607; Bonsirven, *Judaïsme* 1:465.

22. Volz, *Eschatologie,* 280–82; Bousset-Gressmann, *Religion des Judentums,* 256; Bonsirven, *Judaïsme* 1:464 (Gog and Magog). The foundation of this is already laid in the Old Testament; see H. Gressmann, *Der Messias* (Göttingen, 1929) 125, 240, 252 (Assyria as Antichrist).

23. See Dibelius on 2 Thess. 2:4.

last times. Finally, there are some passage in the *Sibylline Oracles*,[24] which form part of the same series.

We find then in Judaism the idea of a political ruler opposed to God, one who is annihilated by the Messiah (cf. Psalm 2). This antichrist (or rather "antechrist") lacks certain traits that are found in the Christian figure, who is the seducer causing the great apostasy before the end of the world.[25] In Judaism this figure has no need to perform lying signs through the power of Satan, like the lawless one in 2 Thess. 2:9f. or the false messiahs and false prophets in Mark 13:22, or the second beast from the earth in Rev. 13:13f. It seems that there was independent reflection on this complex of questions.

3. Some have attributed the diabolical traits of the antichrist to a remote mythological source. In older times the antichrist was identified with Satan. The role he played in the creation myths reappears, *mutatis mutandis,* in eschatological expectation.[26] However, Satan, the old dragon, is clearly distinguished from the antichrist, particularly in the book of Revelation. This makes it more plausible to assume that the early church was indebted to the teaching of Jesus as it worked out the idea of the antichrist, particularly where the parousia was concerned. In the great parousia discourse of Mark 13 we find the major elements of the later idea of the antichrist, though not yet combined with this figure: external persecution (Mark 13:11) and his blasphemous enthronement in the holy place (v. 14). Whatever the ultimate sources of this apocalyptic imagery may be, for the Christian community, which held fast to the revelation discourse of its Lord, this is a secondary question. Once more, it must have thought that the advance signs of the parousia as disclosed in Mark 13 were not the only source of its beliefs. The possibility of a purely oral tradition of the teaching of Jesus on this subject has to be kept in mind. Early Christian prophets may also have made their own contribution, as Revelation suggests.

There is one characteristic of the antichrist that is missing from Mark 13 but appears later on. This is his close association with Satan. Such a view may have been triggered by Satan's hostility to Jesus, as portrayed in the temptation story in the Gospels as well as by certain sayings of Jesus about Satan's activity (Mark 4:15; Luke 13:16; 22:31), rather than by more remote mythological memories.

4. The early church may therefore have contributed to the development of the idea of the antichrist. The extent to which this happened can never be gauged with accuracy, given the paucity of evidence. Where we can lay hands on it — and we can do so relatively early (2 Thess. 2:3ff.) — the antichrist is already a clearly defined figure. Certain advance signs are concentrated in his activity. Further, Paul refers in 2 Thessalonians to a person or power acting as a constraint (2:6f.), an idea not found anywhere else in the eschatological expectation of the early church. In a similar vein the author of 1 John speaks of the approaching appearance of the antichrist as if it were an early Christian tradition and goes on to

---

24. 2:167f.; 3:63ff.; 5:33f., 214ff.; 8:140ff.

25. See Billerbeck, *Kommentar* 3:638; for a different assessment, see W. Staerk, *Soter I,* 71 (the figure of the prophetic antichrist is already present in Jewish apocalyptic).

26. Strongly contested by W. Bousset, *Der Antichrist* (Göttingen, 1895) 88ff.; Bousset-Gressmann, *Religion des Judentums,* 254 (the antichrist as simply the devil in human form); H. Preisker, *RGG*² 1:375f.; W. Staerk, *Soter I,* 71; E. Lohmeyer, *RAC* 1:145f.

recognize him collectively in the heretical teachers of his time and their Christology. This eschatological imagery is further expanded in Revelation, where the contemporary historical background has to be taken into consideration.

The climax in the development of the antichrist concept is reached only after New Testament times, above all in writings that betray a Jewish background with subsequent Christian redaction. A particularly vivid example of this is to be found in the *Apocalypse of Elijah* ("son of lawlessness," 3:5, 13, 18; cf. "king of injustice," 2:3).[27] The originally distinct figures of the antichrist and the false messiahs claiming to be the Christ gradually merge into a single figure. That is especially clear in *Apoc. Pet.* 2. In *Did.* 16.4 the antichrist is "the world deceiver as a son of God," and he works signs and wonders. Likewise *Barn.* 4.3 probably refers to him as "the last offense." In *Ascension of Isaiah,* which has undergone Christian redaction, the antichrist is equated with "Beliar the great prince, the king of this world," who appears in human form as an unjust king descending from the firmament. In *Ps.-Clem. Hom.* 2.17 there is a gnostic picture of the antichrist and the parousia-Christ as counterparts. That scourge of the heretics Irenaeus, in his polemic against the gnostic Marcus, brands him as the precursor of the antichrist,[28] while Hippolytus writes an entire book on the antichrist.[29] In this broad and colorful picture the one certainly acknowledged fact is that the antichrist, the great adversary, will appear before the parousia of Christ himself.

* * *

2. The Community Has Expelled the Antichrists
Who Had Arisen in Their Midst and Has Been Confirmed
in the Truth by the Holy Spirit (1 John 2:19–21)

2:19 The following verses, which deal with the relationship between the orthodox community and the antichrists, provide a deep insight into the self-consciousness of the orthodox Christians. They know that they are supported by the true knowledge which is theirs only through the Holy Spirit ("You have been anointed"). "You know" is repeated three times. They display a strong feeling of fellowship, closing their ranks against everything that is un-Christian. These verses are governed by this contrast between the recipients ("you," vv. 20–21), with whom the writer identifies himself ("we," v. 19), and those who are outwardly and inwardly ("they went out . . . they did not belong to us") heretical teachers who have been expelled from the community. The author is less concerned with polemics than he is with the positive side of the question. They have been given strength enabling them to put up resistance. Having indulged in a brief rebuttal of his opponents (vv. 19, 22f., 26), he at once goes on to impress

---

27. Date of appearance uncertain. In its present form it certainly comes from the third or the fourth century c.e., though it may well use earlier sources, perhaps a basic document of Jewish origin. See G. Steindorf, "Die Apokalypse des Elias," *TU* 17,3 (Leipzig, 1899); E. Schürer, *Geschichte des jüdischen Volkes im Zeitalter Jesu Christi,* ⁴III (Leipzig, 1909) 361–66; P. Riessler, *Altjüdisches Schrifttum ausserhalb der Bibel* (Augsburg, 1928) 1272; J. P. Frey, *DBSup* 1:456–58; J. Jeremias, *TDNT* 2:925ff.

28. Irenaeus, *Adv. Haer.* 1.8.17.

29. On this and further points, see E. Lohmeyer, op. cit., 455f.

upon his readers (vv. 20f., 22f., 26) the need to be aware of the truth of their faith (v. 21). He assures them what a treasure they have in the gift of salvation (v. 24) and the promise that has been made to them (v. 25). Their solidarity as a community (v. 19) and their inner supernatural enlightenment (vv. 20, 27) are something they must never forget, for these are the surest guarantee that they will win the final battle.

The false teachers have left the community at a particular point of time (note the aorist tense).[30] They did so of their own free will; there is no sign that the community took the initiative in expelling them.[31] The author regards the outcome as inevitable. It was a process of elimination, necessitated by the very nature of the community, because the antichrists and the orthodox Christians were incompatible with one another. The latter "come from the truth" (v. 21). With a play on words he employs the preposition *ek* ("of," "from"), denoting both origin and affiliation.[32]

In v. 19b the author probes deeper in his reasoning. To remain in the Christian community[33] one has to belong to it by genuine, natural affinity. He has the impression that true Christians are drawn so much into the heavenly world of light and are so decisively and finally translated from the realm of death into the realm of life (3:14) that they become incapable of sin. They have a divine power within themselves which gives them moral strength (3:9). The coming of Christ has brought about a great divide between faith and unbelief (John 3:19). It has exposed the children of God and the children of the devil (1 John 3:10). This divide continues to operate in the Christian community. Heresy and immorality are simply different manifestations of the same ungodly way revealed and "judged" through Christ as such, just as faith and keeping the commandments are the object of God's will (1 John 3:23). The Christian church underwent a painful experience around the turn of the first century. The battle cut right across its ranks. But it was mitigated by the fact that whatever does not belong to it cannot in the long run remain within it. Equally, it was reassuring for the leaders that the rifts that were occurring ("many," v. 18) involved only fringe members of the community, though there were considerable numbers of them.

The exposure of those who do not belong by nature to the true Christian community is clinched by the final clause in v. 19c, "they made it plain." It is all part of the divine plan.[34] Since the whole verse refers to the antichrists, these must

---

30. On the aorist *exēlthan,* see BDF §80–81.

31. Such an exclusion from the community, which Chaine discusses in view of Jewish and Pauline practice (1 Cor. 5:2, 5), lies beyond the purview of the author—a significant difference from Qumran, where offenses against the law and ethos of the "community of God" were punished by temporary or permanent excommunication; see 1QS 6:24–7:25; 8:20–9:2.

32. See above on 2:16.

33. *Memenēkeisan,* pluperfect without augment, frequent in Koine; BDF §66.1; Radermacher, *Grammatik,* 83f.; Abel, *Grammaire,* §16b, n. 1. The pluperfect (instead of the aorist, which in itself would be possible) "expresses the duration of the possible event until the time of the speaker" (Moulton-Thumb, 233).

34. Behind *all'* we must supply *ou memenēkasin meth' hēmōn.* On this elliptical form, which is especially used in connection with the fulfillment of scripture (for GJohn cf. 13:18; 15:25) but also for the divine purpose in general (John 1:8, 31; 9:3), see BDF §448.7.—That *hina* can be used as

be the subject of *"they* made it plain."[35] This pronoun "they" does not include all, but only the heretical teachers. The "all" is only added later as an afterthought.[36] The effect is to brand the heretical teachers without exception as alien to the community ("they did not belong to us"). The author obviously intends to draw a clear line of demarcation here.

2:20 The group separated from the Christian community and not belonging to them, the antichrists, are emphatically contrasted with the people the author is addressing[37] as "you." These have an "anointing," i.e., the chrism.[38] This is probably picture language for the Holy Spirit, similar to "seed" in 3:9.[39] The anointing imparts knowledge of the truth (v. 21) and "teaches them about all things" (v. 27b). In the hour of his departure Jesus had promised to send the Paraclete, "the Spirit of Truth" (John 14:17; 15:26; 16:13). The author reminds his firmly established Christians that they are in possession of that Spirit ("you have") and the teaching the Holy Spirit ("it has taught you," v. 27b). But he does not reflect on the way in which they originally received the Spirit. Even if he knows of a sacramental rite conveying the Spirit ("you have received," v. 27a), the only thing that is decisive here is its continuing power ("abides in you"). It is not likely that the author is using the expression "anointing" (*chrisma*) in antithesis to antichristos in order to characterize the orthodox Christians as "anointed ones" (*christoi*) in contrast to *antichristos,*[40] for *antichristos* is chosen in contrast to *Christos* (v. 22), that is, in view of Christ himself. It is more likely that the two images, *chrisma* (anointing) and *sperma* (seed) have gnostic associations.[41] If

an introduction to an independent sentence (Radermacher, *Grammatik,* 170) is difficult to maintain (*contra* Windisch).

35. If the clause is to be translated "that it may be made plain that they do not all belong to us" it would be necesary to have an impersonal *phanerōthę̄* (cf. 3:2a; Diog. 9.2a). The personal construction requires the subject to be the same in the independent clause ("be recognized as those who . . ."); cf. 2 Cor. 3:3; BAGD 853 s.v. 2,b. *Contra* Camerlynck, Vrede, Windisch, et al.

36. Büchsel regards this expression as a Hebraism, but Koine also knows the same postpositive emphatic *pantes;* see BDF §275.5; Mayser, *Grammatik,* II, 2:99f.

37. It is not directly the adversative *kai* (="and yet"; BDF §442.1); but *kai* (perhaps based on the Hebrew *wĕ*) can indicate many different kinds of transitions (BDF §442.1).

38. *Chrisma* means not "anointing" but "oil for anointing," as in Exod 29:7; 30:25; 40:15 LXX; in v. 27b an active function is ascribed to it. The language is obviously symbolic.

39. Against this, see Reitzenstein, *Hellenistische Mysterienreligionen,* 396f. and idem, *Vorgeschichte der Taufe,* 184 n. 1; he connects the term with baptism, in which the oil, like the baptismal water, symbolizes the *teaching.* But in that case it would be necessary to interpret 2:27b impersonally. In view of John 14:28b; 16:13 the personal sense is to be preferred. Dodd also opts for interpreting the metaphor as a reference to the teaching or word of God (p. 62f.). But on this point, see J. Michl, "Der Geist als Garant des rechten Glaubens," in N. Adler, ed., *Vom Wort des Lebens* (Festschrift M. Meinertz; Münster, 1951) 143f. and n. 15.—In a penetrating study I. de la Potterie (*Bib* 40 [1959] 30–47) arrives at an interpretation combining both meanings, though giving priority to the (Spirit-inspired) word: "the oil of unction, that is certainly the word of God, not that it is always preached in an exterior way in the community, but in that it is recited by faith in the hearts and remains active there thanks to the action of the Spirit" (p. 44). J. Chmiel (*Lumière et charité,* 209f.) follows the interpretation of de la Potterie. See also M. de Jonge, 110–14; Houlden, 79 (compares Ignatius, *Eph.* 17.1); W. Grundmann, *TDNT* 9:572 (=Spirit).

40. Brooke, Büchsel, Bonsirven, Chaine.

41. Cf. *alālǭ chrismati* (Hippolytus, *Ref.* 5.7.19); *chrismati leukǭ* (Origen, *Contra Celsum* 6.27);

that is the case, the author must be confronting the false claims of the gnostics with the certainty that the Christians really possess those inner powers of divine grace, which enable them to have true gnosis. That there was already a sacrament of chrism (which was later featured in gnostic sects[42]) cannot be proved for this early period, though the term may already have been in use as a metaphor. W. Nauck tries to prove that chrismation was already an element in *Christian* initiation and that the author is basing his remarks here and in 5:7f. on that.[43] Even if it can hardly be proved that the rite of reception consisted of chrism, water baptism, and Eucharist (in that order), which is doubtful for GJohn (cf. on 5:7f.), the material cited from the missionary documents of Hellenistic Judaism (possibly of Essene origin), and *Joseph and Aseneth*,[44] is valuable for its sacramental ideas and its symbolic language. As for this epistle, it is sufficient to assume that "anointing" is a metaphor for the giving of the Holy Spirit in baptism (cf. 2 Cor. 1:21), especially since it can hardly be separated from the other metaphor of "seed" (3:9). The author attached no particular importance to sacramental anointing; what mattered was that the believers had had the presence of the Holy Spirit ever since their baptism, the true "oil of anointing."

It is difficult to decide whether the "Holy One" refers to God or to Christ. The latter is more likely.[45] Although the "Holy One" (of Israel) is an Old Testament predicate for God,[46] and is still called that in Rev. 4:8; 6:10, it is used as a designation for Jesus as an established title in John 6:69 (cf. Mark 1:24; Luke 4:34). In Rev. 3:7 he receives the divine designation "the faithful and true"; cf. Acts 3:14. Added to this is the further point that "from him" in v. 27a can hardly refer to anyone except Jesus Christ (cf. "he" in v. 25). The attribution of the sending of the Paraclete to both the Father (John 14:16, 26) and the Son (15:26; 16:7) and, further, the alternation between "know the Father" (1 John 2:14a) and "know him who is from the beginning" (i.e., the Son) in v. 14b shows that it does not make much difference which Person is being referred to. Everything depends on being empowered "from above," from the divine realm (cf. 4:2, 4).

---

chrisma (pneumatikon) (*Pistis Sophia* 81; 112; 128; 130; II *Jeû* 43; *Gos. Truth* 36; *Gos. Phil.* 68; 95 [H.-M. Schenke, *TLZ* 84 (1959) 15 and 18f.]). Mussner recalls the late Jewish idea of the oil of life flowing from the tree of life (ZΩH, 113); but it should still be noted that the primary association of *chrisma* in 1 John 2:20 and 27 is the communication of knowledge.

42. In addition to the previous note, see also *Acts Thom.* 27.157; *Odes Sol.* 36:6 and esp. the Mandean sacrament of unction (*MandLit* 34ff., 115ff.). On this, see Bousset, *Hauptprobleme,* 297ff.; H. Leisegang, *Die Gnosis* (Leipzig, 1924) 346, 350ff., 389; Dodd, 61; K. Rudolph, *Die Mandäer: II, Der Kult* (FRLANT n.s. 57; Göttingen, 1961) 155–74.

43. Nauck, *Tradition und Charakter,* 94f., 147–82.

44. Greek text according to the (defective) edition of P. Battifol, *Studia Patristica* 1–2 (Paris, 1889–90). Battifol wrongly assumes that the work is a late Christian romance. It should be noted that the reference is to a real though symbolically interpreted function: chap. 8 (p. 49): *chrietai chrismata eulogēmenǭ aphtharsias;* chap. 15 (p. 61): *chrismati christhēsǭ eulogēmenǭ tēs aphtharsias;* chap. 16 (p. 64); *chrismati kechrisai aphtharsias.* The idea of *aphtharsia* (parallel to *athanasia*) shows Hellenistic influence.

45. In favor of connecting it with God are Büchsel; Nauck, *Tradition und Charakter,* 94; Undecided are Windisch; Bonsirven; Charue; Ambroggi. In favor of connecting it with Christ are Belser; Camerlynck; Westcott; Brooke; Vrede; Chaine; Michl; de la Potterie, *Bib* 40 (1959) 35f.

46. Usually the "Holy One of Israel," esp. in Isaiah (1:4; 17:7; etc.); Pss. 71:22; 78:41; "the holy One" absolutely Isa. 5:16; Hab. 3:3; Bar. 4:22; Tob. 12:15.

The Spirit imparts knowledge, the knowledge of revelation that the unbelieving world, separated as it is from God, cannot comprehend.[47] Just as Jesus has a special knowledge of God and of divine realities,[48] so Christians initiated into divine truth by the Holy Spirit are included among those who "know." This is intended as a barb against the false gnostics.[49]

There is a long-standing debate whether to read *pantes* or *panta* ("all people" or "all things"). This is not easily decided. The manuscript evidence is pretty evenly balanced.[50] In favor of *panta* is the fact that "you know" (*oidate*) would otherwise have no object. Further, there is the phrase "teaches you all things" (v. 26; cf. John 14:26; 16:13). Against *panta* is the difficulty that such unlimited knowledge is restricted to Jesus (cf. John 16:30), and this could have caused the change from *panta* to *pantes*. However, this argument does not seem to hold in the light of John 14:26; 16:13; 1 John 2:27b. On the contrary, *pantes* must be regarded as the more difficult reading and the change to *panta* therefore more easily explained. Another point in favor of *pantes* is the parallelism with *pantes* at the end of v. 19. Against the heretics who by and large are hostile to God, *pantes* in v. 20 asserts that the believers as a whole have true knowledge of salvation. The author seeks to strengthen them with these comforting assurances (cf. 2:12–14) and to make them aware of the truth. If *pantas* were read, this would carry the wrong tone. But the next verse actually shows that the emphasis lies on "you know" ("You do not know . . . you know"). Also in this connection—otherwise than in v. 27b—it would not be obvious what the rich (*panta*) content of their knowledge is supposed to be. Thus *pantes* is to be preferred. The Achilles' heel of this interpretation is still the missing object. If an elliptical form of speech is unacceptable ("and[51] you all know it, namely, that you have the anointing")— which, however, contradicts the whole meaning of "you know" in the next verse—then it must be taken in a strong emphatic sense: "you have all wisdom." Although this kind of expression cannot be vouched for elsewhere, it is possible to go along with it, since the author perhaps wanted to avoid saying: "you have knowledge" (cf. 1 Cor. 8:1, 10).[52]

---

47. In GJohn "knowing" is always contrasted with "not knowing" on the part of the unbelieving Jews (1:26; [4:22]; 7:28; 8:14, 19, 54f.; 9:29f.; 15:21), and even the disciples do not have true knowledge until the coming of the Paraclete (4:32; 13:7; 14:7; 16:18).

48. John 5:32; 7:29; 8:14, 55; 13:1, 3; 16:30; 18:4; 19:27; (21:17).

49. The proximity of *ginōskein* and *eidenai* is easily recognizable; cf. John 2:24f. with 16:30 and 21:17; 3:10 with 11; 7:27a with b; 8:55a; 13:7b; 14:7a; 21:17c. The parallel between John 8:21 (*ginōsesthe tēn alētheian*) and 1 John 2:29 (*oidate tēn alētheian*) is especially important.—That the Johannine use of *oida*, especially in the sayings of Jesus about himself (7:27f.; 8:14, 19, 54f.; 14:7), is connected with the gnostic way of speaking can hardly be doubted; see Bultmann, *John,* ad loc.; and Seesemann, *TDNT* 5:118.

50. *Pantes* B ℵ P 598 1838 1852 sa arm Jer; *panta* AC ﬞ pl. Vg sy[h] bo eth *Did.* For *panta,* see von Soden; Harnack, *SB* (Berlin, 1915) 564; Vogels; Windisch; Büchsel. For *pantes,* see Tischendorf; Westcott-Hort; Merk; Lagrange, *Critique textuelle,* 565; Brooke; Bonsirven; Chaine; Dodd; Ambroggi. UBSGNT adopts *pantes,* but only with the lowest grade of reading (D). On the meaning of *oida,* see I. de la Potterie, "Οἶδα et γινώσκω: Les deux modes de la connaissance dans le quatrième Ev.," *Bib* 40 (1959) 709–25.

51. *Kai* is lacking in B h sa (a reading preferred by Westcott). That is perhaps evidence for such an interpretation.

52. It is noticeable that with the strong use of *ginōskein* in the Johannine writings there is not a single occurrence of *gnōsis*—compared with twenty-eight occurrences in the rest of the New Testament.

2:21 The author is using the espistolary aorist.[53] He wishes to reassure his readers emphatically (cf. 2:12–14) that[54] they "know the truth." The awkwardness of the phraseology, first negative then positive, is consistent with the author's usual style.[55] It is applied here in order to underscore the fact that "you know the truth." Thus the whole passage serves to continue and underline the thought of v. 20: "all of you have knowledge." Windisch thinks the author wants to suggest to them that "he at least knows more of the truth than his readers do," thereby seeking to justify himself for writing to them. That is not in accordance with his manner (cf. 1:3f.; 2:7, 27; 5:13). Rather, his intention is to confirm them in the knowledge that they possess the blessings of salvation.[56] There is no emphasis here on "truth" as a comprehensive term for all that the Spirit of truth teaches (John 16:13). But it does acquire another nuance when he makes his second point, reassuring them "that no lie comes from the truth." Whatever they know themselves comes from the Spirit of truth, from the divine realm. So, on the other hand, what the heretical teachers defend does not come from that source. There are only the two antithetical possibilities: "from the truth," that is, from God, or "from the world," that is, from the realm opposed to God (cf. 4:4f.). This is just how these heretical teachers show that they embody the spirit of the antichrist (4:3). For this kind of existential thinking, in which truth is a divine reality, thing and person cannot be separated (cf. again 4:3ff.). At the same time, v. 21b asserts that these antichrists (like all those who champion a lie[57] and embody it in themselves) are not themselves "from the truth" (cf. John 18:37; 3:19). This clinches the statement that they "did not belong to us" (v. 19). Thus, v. 21 confronts the readers who possess the Spirit and know the divine truth most sharply with those heretical teachers who not only fly in the face of truth but are themselves ungodly in origin and nature.

3. By Denying the Christian Faith, the Heretical Teachers Identify Themselves as Antichrists, Thus Forfeiting Their Fellowship with the Father and the Promise of Eternal Life (1 John 2:22–25)

2:22 After drawing this sharp distinction between the orthodox believers and the antichrists, the author goes on to describe their heresy and to strengthen his

---

53. See above on 2:14. It is not possible to take *egrapsa* as a reference to an earlier letter, to 2 John in particular, nor is it necessary; cf. *egrapsa* in 2:14 (*contra* Wendt, *ZNW* 21 [1922] 140ff. and Hauck).

54. To take *hoti* in a causal sense as most scholars do (except Bonsirven) creates difficulties. True, it seems to suit the combination of negative and positive in the first part of the verse, but in view of the third *hoti* it is untenable. (Cf. the forced explanations in Brooke, Windisch, and Hauck.) This is the reason why others take the third *hoti* as a recitative, depending on the second *oidate* (Belser, Büchsel, Chaine, Dodd). But this coordination of an accusative of the object (*autēn*) with an apodictic assertion is harsh from a linguistic point of view, and it is difficult to attribute such an intention to the author. With the causal *hoti* (similarly as with *hina*) one would expect a *tauta*, since *graphein* in 1 John never stands without an object (1:4; 2:1, 7, 8, 26; 5:13).

55. Joined with *alla*, e.g., 2:7, 16; 4:17–18; 3 John 11; with *kai*, e.g., 1:6, 8; 2:4, 27b.

56. Cf. 3:14; 5:13 (*hina, eidēte*, etc.); 5:18–20 (*oidamen*, three times); cf. also passages like 2:12–14; 4:4; 5:4, which pursue the same goal.

57. *Pan pseudos* is to be taken in a general sense and does not refer to the "other," that is, the moral heresy (*contra* Wurm, 133ff.).

case for designating them that way. It is significant that he does not begin by describing the heresy and then drawing consequences from it. Instead, he begins by emphasizing the vital distinction between his readers and the heretics. For the moment, however, he prefers to lead his readers to understand inwardly why these "liars" cannot enjoy fellowship with God and why they block their own way to salvation.

Further to the expression "no lie" in v. 21, everyone[58] who openly rejects the church's creed[59] is designated a liar. Indeed, they are liars *par excellence,* as the emphatic mode of speech "who . . .?" indicates.[60] This is not a straightforward error, but a set battle originating from the dark powers opposed to God and directed against the fellowship with him which Jesus opened up to humankind (cf. v. 22b and 1:1-3). They declare their false opinions publicly, seeking to spread confusion among the faithful (4:1ff.) who have found the blessings of fellowship with God (1:3; cf. 4:1ff.). That is why they are branded as his enemies (cf. 1:10; 5:10) who pursue the cause of Satan (cf. John 8:44).

It is important to note that it was the christological confession of the church that was at stake. Only this will show what was wrong with the heresy. "Jesus is the Christ"[61]— that is the church's confession which the liars deny.[62] The issue is not what it was with Judaism (cf. John 1:47; 4:25f., 29; 7:26f., 41f.; 9:22; 12:34), namely, messiahship of Jesus — at any rate not in this letter.[63] It is the question of the One who brought redemption, nothing more and nothing less. In GJohn too the twofold confession, "Jesus is the Messiah, the Son of God" (20:31; cf. 11:27, also 1:49) is the culminating christological affirmation. But in the epistle the issue at stake is no longer the controversy with Judaism but the object of faith, acknowledged briefly in the formula "in the name of his Son Jesus Christ" (3:23) or "in the name of the Son of God" (5:13; cf. also v. 20). The decisive nature of the shift from the Jewish concept of Messiah to the general term "Christ" in this passage becomes a certainty when we note the substitution of "the Son" for "the Christ" in vv. 22b and 23. In no way does the thought develop in the direction of suggesting that the denial of Jesus' messiahship as understood by the author and his readers involves also the denial of his divine Sonship. The

---

58. *Ho arnoumenos* is to be understood in the same way as *ho legōn* (2:4, 6, 9) and has a generic sense; see BDF §413.1, 2.

59. *Arneisthai,* the opposite of *homologein,* presumes, like the latter, a vocal expression; see BAGD 107, s.v. 2. Both verbs have a solemn proclamatory (and liturgical?) sound; see O. Michel, *TDNT* 5:210.

60. Apart from here only in 5:5. Unlike *ho antichristos, ho pseustēs* is no known figure. The term has a pregnant sense as in 5:5.

61. The repetition of the negative after verbs of negative import is classical and survives in the New Testament (Luke 20:27; 22:34; etc.); see BDF §429.

62. J. C. O'Neill thinks that because the words *Iēsous . . . ho Christos* are directed against the denial of Jesus' messiahship, the opponents must have been Jews (*Puzzle,* 5f.). But this conclusion is not necessary when we recall that the false teachers came from a Christian community (see 2:19). See also Kümmel, *Introduction,* 441 n. 21; M. de Jonge, "The Use of the Word χριστός in the Johannine Epistles," in *Studies in John* (Festschrift J. N. Sevenster; Leiden, 1970) 66-74; W. Grundmann, *TDNT* 9:570-71.

63. *Contra* A. Wurm, *Die Irrlehre im 1 Joh.* (BS 8,1; Freiburg im Breisgau, 1903) 10ff.; Clemen, *ZNW* 6 (1905) 272ff.; Belser. In addition, Büchsel and Windisch (the latter undecided) think of Jesus' messianic claim (without identifying the heretics with Jewish circles). See further Introduction, p. 18f.

only thing that is happening is that the title "Son" is being substituted for "Messiah," without any resultant shift of meaning. Messiah and Son of God mean the same thing.[64] Jesus, the historical Jesus, is truly the Messiah. As the Son of God, he stands in intimate fellowship with the Father and leads the believers into that same fellowship. On the other hand, "Messiah" is not synonymous with "celestial spirit" in the later gnostic sense, since in this epistle his office as Redeemer is just as strongly emphasized (cf. 3:5, 8, 16; 4:10, 14, 15; 1:5, 6).

Verse 22 begins with a clear contrast to "the Messiah." It reads "Who is the liar but the one who denies that Jesus is the Christ?" Because of this linguistic contrast the predicate noun "antichrist" is placed before "the one who denies . . . ," which must be taken with the subject "this." For "the one who denies" picks up the same phrase from v. 22a and makes the previous "this" explicit. From this pointed contrast of "antichrist" with "Christ" we have the clue to the use of the collective singular to denote a plurality of persons in v. 19. To express the pernicious attitude of the antichrists, the author not only says, as we might expect, "who denies the Son," but puts "the Father" first. He is not only recapitulating his argument, but making a fresh point. Having inserted "the Father," he is obliged to put "Son" instead of "Christ," which makes the contrast clear. He already has v. 23 in mind, as a result of which we get the overloaded clause in v. 22b, which becomes completely clear only when we get to v. 23. Now at last the author can return to his usual calm way of speaking. Verse 22b brands the liar as antichrist, echoed in turn by "Christ," which comes like a thunder clap. Then the author takes a leap in his thought. First, it is the Father who is denied. This shows that the author has not lost all his enthusiasm in his old age.

2:23 The claim that to deny the Son is to deny the Father shows that the author in his usual way is making a point with both positive and negative implications. This time, however, he begins with the negative one. The point is quite fundamental and typically Johannine (cf. John 12:44f.; 14:6b, 9b, 10–11). After the appearance of the Son of God (1:2; 3:8) no fellowship with God is possible("No one has seen the Father"),[65] which does not lead to him by way of living fellowship with the Son. The Jews, in their monotheistic pride, are denied true knowledge of God by the Johannine Jesus (7:28; 8:19, 55; 15:21; 16:3). But their alienation from God is an existential one. It is not only a matter of accepting God's emissary and knowing and honoring him (Matt. 10:40, cf. 41 – John 13:20). It is the only way that leads to a true relationship with God and to the attainment of the goal of salvation (John 14:6f.). The reason for this centrality of Christ, repeated often enough, is that salvation comes through his unity with the Father (John 14:10f., cf. 20; 10:30; 17:11, 21). The hidden God in heaven can only be reached through this single, true Revealer (John 1:18; 12:35f.) and divine Bearer and Giver of life (John 5:26; 6:57; 10:10; 11:26). The author presumes that these are the beliefs of his readers. He is addressing people who believe and know (2:20). But he is

---

64. Cf. also 5:5 with 5:1, and further Introduction, p. 18ff.

65. *Echein theon* elsewhere only at 2 John 9; it denotes communion more powerfully than *egnōkenai* (2:3f.; cf. 5c; John 14:7b) and *heōrakenai* (John 14:7, 9) and is perhaps an early gnostic expression; cf. H. Hanse, *'Gott haben' in der Antike*, esp. 105, 119ff.

recalling to their consciousness this basic Christian conviction which the heretical teachers threaten to obscure. Thus the positive statement of the thesis in v. 23b, which in itself would be superfluous, is more than just a stylistic peculiarity. In making it, the writer is thinking of his orthodox readers and seeking to impress upon them how fortunate they are in what they confess. Thus he is providing a transition to the direct address and admonition in v. 24.

2:24 Once again, as in the previous section (2:19-21), the author draws the contrast between the false teachers and his readers as sharply as possible. That is why the sentence begins in Greek with "you," with no connecting participle (NRSV "Let what you . . .").[66] Previously he had sought to separate them from all daily contacts with the antichrists and have them distance themselves inwardly from them. Now he is concerned with purity of doctrine (hence "you heard"). As before (2:7), the basis and motivation of his admonition are that which they have "heard from the beginning." It is the message they heard when they first became Christians. That should fill their minds and remain with them. What matters is not the way they heard it in the beginning but that the teaching they then received is the traditional doctrine of the community. That doctrine is based on the eyewitness testimony of those who were Christ's closest associates (1:1-3).[67] The traditional doctrine is not random material passed on to them and venerable on that account. It is the revelatory word of Christ himself, the pledge of eternal life with God (John 8:51). The message they have heard is to abide in them (cf. John 5:38; 1 John 2:14c). Or, to put it another way, they must abide "in the word of Christ" (cf. John 8:31; 15:7). The word of Christ or of God is a reality that takes up its abode in them, which lives and works in them. They must cling to it and let it abide in them, like the "anointing" (2:20) or "God's seed" (3:9).[68]

The word of Christ is itself so much the divine life and pneumatic reality (cf. John 6:63) that it becomes the bond between Christ and the believers. To abide in his word means to be in him (cf. John 15:7). But when we are in the Son we are also in the Father through the Son and with the Son. This point leads the author back to his basic theme of fellowship with God. Around the turn of the century the Christian community had to fight for its faith and defend itself against heresies that threatened the substance of this faith. Given this situation, it is significant that the word of Christ should take on the specific character of right doctrine, to be recognized as such by the principle of tradition. This comes out still more clearly in 2 John 9. Like moral stability (2:7ff.), christological orthodoxy is the sole key to continuing fellowship with God.

---

66. It is not an anticipation of the subject before the relative pronoun (BDF §475.1), but, since *hymeis,* like *en hymin,* belongs to the main clause, a case without construction placed in anticipation (§466.1) BDF rightly refer additionally to the rhythm (modeled on Hebrew parallelism?) through which two ideas are contrasted, here the idea of beginning with continuation (§466). See Moulton 2:423f., 447 — *Oun* in the Textus Receptus is a pedantic and not appropriate correction, for without it the contrast is sharper.

67. This principle can be seen in the Pastorals. The apostle reminds Timothy of the "sound words" (or teachings) which he has had from him (2 Tim. 1:13), words which, however, are in the last analysis the words of Jesus Christ himself (1 Tim. 6:3); cf. 2 Tim. 4:3f.; Titus 1:9.

68. The specific reference of "that which was heard" to the love commandment (Wurm, *Irrlehre,* 135-37) is unconvincing.

2:25 The author then is thinking of the same theology of the word of Christ that is familar from GJohn. This verse confirms that fact by pointing to eternal life. In his controversy with heresy, the Johannine Christ is always basing his demand for faith on the fact that the believers, and they alone, possess the divine life.[69] For to believe means to receive his word and witness (3:31, 32f.; 12:48; 17:8), to hear it and hold it fast (8:43, 47, 51f.; 12:47; 14:23; 15:20; 17:6). The only objection put forward against this is that in 1 John 2:25 eternal life is a promise (Greek *epangelia*) for the future, whereas in GJohn it is a present possession. The grammatical form of the sentence is no objection[70] and shows that eternal life is the content of the promise. But when GJohn calls for an instant decision of faith, thus emphasizing the immediate acquisition of salvation, the divine life is a continuing gift of salvation and will be realized in its full glory only at the "resurrection of life" (5:29; cf. 6:33, 40, 44, 54). Some texts do in fact focus primarily on the future (4:14, 36; 5:39; 6:27; 12:25).[71] This perspective comes about because the author wants to give his readers a motive for adhering faithfully to the right doctrine, for abiding in fellowship with God. Their salvation is not yet complete (cf. 3:2). From this point of view eternal life is still no more than a promise. It is possible that we have here, as in John 12:25, the aftereffect of the Synoptic conception. At any rate the author knows that Jesus himself[72] gave the promise of eternal life.

The term "promise" (*epangelia*) is totally missing from GJohn and not very common in the Synoptics. It acquired a deeper meaning only in the early church,[73] after the community was deprived of the physical presence of its Lord and came to yearn increasingly for the parousia. The church knew with certainty that the great Old Testament prophecies of salvation were already fulfilled in principle in Christ (Galatians, Ephesians, et al.). But gradually it became clearer that there were remnants of unfulfilled or only partially fulfilled promises left over (Pastorals, Hebrews, Catholic Epistles). It is among the members of this community, oriented as they were toward the future, and bearing the testimony and seal of their hope within themselves, that the author of 1 John has his place. As against GJohn, there is here an unmistakable openness toward the future. This has to do with

---

69. John 3:16, 18, 36; 5:24; 6:35, 40, 47; 8:51; 11:25f.; cf. 1 John 5:13.

70. The harsh construction *hautē–zōēn aiōnion* is the result of the way the sentence is developed. *Hautē* agrees with *he epangelia,* the predicate noun (BDF §132.1). *Zōēn aiōnion* is inverse attraction (BDF §295), occasioned by *hēn,* etc. The demonstrative pronoun thus points to what follows; a reference back to v. 24b is ruled out because of *tēn zōēn,* etc. The reading *hymin* (B 69 Vg) instead of *hēmin* is probably occasioned by *en hymin* in v. 24.

71. Bultmann connects the future tense "not . . . to an eschatological future, but to the moment of decision when, confronted by the word: He who will believe, will live" (*TDNT* 2:870). But that can hardly be right. See Pribnow, *Die johanneische Anschauung vom Leben,* 104ff., 149ff.; Wikenhauser, *Johannes,* 178–81; Meinertz, *Theologie* 2:278–82, 306; Huby, *Mystiques,* 172f., 211ff.; above all, Mussner, ZΩH, 136f., 176ff.

72. *Autos* can only mean Christ (*contra* Büchsel). Christ too is the source of the promise, the One "who has been heard from the beginning," and is therefore to be trusted. That is what *autos* is meant to suggest.

73. 1 Tim. 4:8 (*epangelian . . . zōēs tēs nyn kai tēs mellousēs*); Titus 3:7; Heb. 4:1; 6:12; 8:6; 9:15; 10:23, 26; 12:26; James 1:12; 2 Pet. 3:4, 9. This development is especially clear in Hebrews "Christians are in the tension between what is already and what is not yet (Heb. 8:5). They are beginning to tire and therefore to doubt the consummation" (Friedrich, *TDNT* 2:585). In 2 Peter the situation has become more acute than it was in Hebrews (ibid., 585).

the situation in which the letter was written. The present eschatological situation stimulates the hope for eschatological confirmation (cf. on 2:18).

4. The Readers Must Hold Fast to the True Faith in Christ Illumined as They Are by the Holy Spirit (1 John 2:26-27)

2:26 Looking back on the whole section about the antichrists (2:18-25), the author closes with a final word. The *inclusio* (v. 26) is a feature of his style (2:1; 5:13). He now calls the opponents "deceivers," pointing out by the use of the present tense (conative present) that their influence is still dangerous despite the outward separation.[74]

2:27 In contrast, the author again makes a fresh start (as in vv. 20 and 24) with a pointed antithesis: "As for you."[75] The anointing, that is, the Holy Spirit, which his readers have received from Christ ("from him") is still theirs.[76] With his illumination and strength they can still stand firm against the deceivers. The purpose of this final encouragement is also to give them confidence in the future, and the author sees a guarantee for this in the continuing ("you received"-"abides") power of the Spirit of God which lives within them.[77] He then adds a typically Johannine expression: they do not need anyone to teach them.[78] He can hardly have the heretical teachers in mind here, for he never refers to their activity as "teaching." What they "say" is from the world (4:5). He must therefore be referring to the recognized teaching of the church (cf. 2 John 9f.), though without any particular emphasis.[79] Büchsel thinks he is trying to assure them that they are not subject to any teaching authority. But that is quite unthinkable for a writer who makes faith and fellowship dependent on the traditional proclamation (1:2, 3, 5; 2:7, 24; 3:11). The only point is that hand in hand with hearing and faithful reception of the Christian message from the beginning goes the interior indoctrination of the Holy Spirit. This is what gives them their (subjective) certainty.

In v. 27b, "abide [imperative] in him" cannot be the main clause,[80] coming as it does

---

74. *Planān* does not mean "to lead astray into sin" (Büchsel), but "to lead into error" (cf. on 1:8), to divert from the way of faith and salvation; cf. also *to pneuma tēs planēs* (4:6).

75. Again, a nominative without any construction, placed as an anacolouthon at the beginning, as in v. 24 (see commentary on that verse).

76. P 33 323 1739 2298 h Vg sy[h] offer the reading *menetō*, but this is probably an assimilation to v. 24a.

77. We are not to think of a sacramental-magical viewpoint, as though *chrisma* were "apotropaic substance" (Windisch), for no other reason than because this would mean attributing to *chrisma* the personal function of instruction.

78. Cf. John 2:25; 16:30; instead of the *hina*-clause, the infinitive would stand, as in classical Greek and as is the case in the rest of the New Testament: Matt. 3:14; 14:16; 1 Thess. 1:8; 4:9; 5:1; Heb. 5:12, but also in John 13:10.

79. See P. Couture, "The Teaching Function in the Church of 1 Jo 2, 20. 27" (diss., Gregorian University, 1966-67).

80. Against Westcott, Brooke (with hesitation), Windisch, Bonsirven, Chaine, Dodd; with Belser, Büchsel, Hauck.

149

after several clumsy subordinate clauses. To take it that way would be too complicated, while the clause beginning "and so" denotes the consequence, rather like 2:18.

The principal activity of the Holy Spirit, that of teaching (cf. John 14:26), coming as it does from God, carries with it the seal of truth ("is true") and is from inner necessity immune from all falsehood and deception ("is not a lie"). This final repetition in a negative form is presumably a deliberate barb directed against the pernicious "lie" (v. 21) of the heretical teachers. Verse 27b is expressed in a somewhat roundabout way, though it does serve to strengthen the confidence of the readers in the Spirit as the teacher of truth internally. Yet the author is unmistakably steering toward the final warning (v. 26c, cf. 24a).

The clause beginning "But as" could — if looked at out of context — contain an admonition to abide in this anointing or the teaching it brings (cf. v. 24).[81] But the following verse, which takes up the phrase "abide in him," tells against this. This is because the admonition can only refer to abiding in Christ. In this case "abide" (v. 27c) must be an imperative (as in NRSV).[82] In the light of this, the aorist "taught," following the present "to teach" (Greek present subjunctive) in the clause beginning "and so" seems to mean that the urge to abide in Christ was already conveyed by the Spirit when they began their Christian life. Now, however, he is particularly enlightening about the errors of the heretical teachers, thus protecting their association with Christ. By taking the final "him" to refer to Christ, the reference of this pronoun in the other two places in v. 27 to Christ is assured (cf. also the "he" [Greek *autos*] in v. 25). As a consequence there is an intimate relationship between the Spirit and Christ. It was from Christ that the Christians received their anointing, and it is his anointing that teaches them. The Spirit's main task, on the other hand, is to introduce the believers into the Christian community and to keep them there (cf. John 14:26; 16:14f.). True, it is usually God who gives the Spirit (3:24; 4:13), while in GJohn the term "Spirit of Christ" is never found. Yet this passage continues in a similar vein about the utterances of the Spirit as does John 16:7, where the sending of the Paraclete is ascribed to the Son. The admonition to abide in Christ is primarily oriented in the context to true faith in Christ. But since it was this faith that established living fellowship with Christ (John 3:16, 18, etc.), it is at the same time oriented to a fully ontological union with him (cf. v. 24).

---

81. Büchsel takes *en autǭ* in an impersonal sense, relating it to the *kathōs*-clause; but in that case one would expect *en toutǭ menete*. *Autos* can stand for *ekeinos* or *houtos,* used adjectivally (Moulton-Thumb, 145f.; BDF §288.2; Mayser, *Grammatik* II, 2:75ff.; but that is not the case here.

82. ℵ al. offer here the easier reading *meneite* (future as opposed to the aorist *edidaxen,* perhaps as a reminiscence of v. 24, just as the same manuscripts had earlier simplified *to autou chrisma* into *auto.*—The indicative is accepted by Westcott, Loisy, Brooke, Vrede, Chaine (though with doubt). But after the solemn assurance that the Spirit guarantees the truth, this would be an anticlimax; as a result, what we have here is an admonition.

SECOND SECTION

THE CHRISTIAN HOPE OF SALVATION
(1 JOHN 2:28-3:3)

[28]And now, little children, abide in him, so that when he is revealed we may have confidence and not be put to shame before him at his coming. [29]If you know that he is righteous, you may be sure that everyone who does right has been born of him. [3][1]See what love the Father has given us, that we should be called children of God; and that is what we are. The reason the world does not know us is that it did not know him. [2]Beloved, we are God's children now; what we will be has not yet been revealed. What we do know is this: when he is revealed, we will be like him, for we will see him as he is. [3]And all who have this hope in him purify themselves, just as he is pure.

In this new section, beginning with 2:28, the author is obviously guided by the key phrase "abide in Christ" (2:28; cf. 3:6) in the direction of parenesis (2:29; 3:3). But he is still holding back for the moment, focusing on the present reality of salvation. Christian preaching is not merely ethical admonition with a religious tinge, but proceeds from God's saving action toward humankind. That is the source of its obligations and motives for religious and ethical activity, exploiting the very tension between present salvation and its final realization. To put it concretely, the author is clearly looking back to baptism. It was there that the faithful were "born" as children of God (cf. 3:9), there that they received the pledge of full salvation (3:2). Early Christian moral teaching consists largely of baptismal catechesis, presenting the Christian under various images, such as "being born," "new creation," and "rebirth" (see Excursus 8). In these ways the abundant grace of their salvation, the "newness" of their lives, and the obligation to holiness are brought home to them. Typical of the baptismal catechesis is the inner connection between being and obligation, between the state of grace and moral behavior. Being demands obligation, though obligation is anchored in being. Seen in this light, the section 2:29-3:10 forms a unity. Doing what is right and refraining from sin become a mark of being born of God or being a child cf God. *Per contra,* others are separated from God and are children of the devil (cf. 2:29; 3:7f., 10). The deeper reason for this is that "Those who have been born of God do not sin" (3:9), and "no one who abides in him sins" (3:6). The sharp division between those who belong to God and those who belong to the devil is enhanced by the antithetical language. It is impossible to combine doing of sin with doing what is right.

In this section, 2:29-3:10, W. Nauck, like E. von Dobschütz before him, thinks he is able to distinguish a *Vorlage* (*Tradition und Charakter,* 15-19) whose literary form is related to the apodictic divine law, as found in the Old Testament (pp. 29-33) and in the rite of reception at Qumran (pp. 34-41). He thinks it goes back to the baptismal teaching, but was later reapplied in the defense against the heretical teachers (pp. 65f., 123). But it is hard to imagine that this series of antitheses (2:29 after the second "that" [Greek *hoti kai*]; 3:4, 6, 7b, 8aα, 9aα, 10bα) could ever have existed on their own. So although we have to accept the two tendencies pointed out by Nauck; the passage in its entirety must be regarded as an original unity.

In the whole section 2:29–3:10, vv. 1–3 of chapter 3 stand out. The author of 1 John seeks to introduce his readers to and congratulate them on their dignity, the gifts they have received, and the promises involved in their present state of salvation. Thus we get a brief digression, more kerygmatic in character. However, that does not belie the admonitory purpose of the section as a whole.

1. The Parousia Is a Matter of Hope
and Requires Holiness (1 John 2:28–29)

2:28 With "And now"[83] the author returns to his previous admonition (v. 27), "abide in Christ." He repeats it in view of the expected parousia. In this admonition he summarizes the need for loyalty to the faith in view of the heretical teachers (v. 27) and for moral purity ("does right," v. 29) in the face of the Lord who requires accountability. The author softens the imperative by addressing his readers tenderly as "little children" (cf. 2:1, 12). They must make an effort on their own. But the whole idea of abiding in Christ acquires a greater ontological profundity in the light of v. 24.

In view of the parousia the author rounds out the argument begun in 2:18. The last hour, the time when the powers opposed to God are active, ends with Christ's return. The author does not divulge the exact timing of this eschatological event any more than Jesus himself did (Mark 13:32). It is not necessarily expected in the immediate future (note NRSV "when," translating Greek *ean* = "if").[84] It is not entirely peculiar to this author that he speaks of Christ's being "revealed" (cf. Col. 3:4; also 2 Cor. 4:10f.). But it gives his proclamation a special flavor, for he has already spoken of another "revelation" of Christ, namely, in the incarnation (1:2; cf. 3:5, 8). The two events, bound together by the use of the same verb, may be regarded as a single, all-embracing manifestation or epiphany of God. In both events the divine becomes visible in our earthly, human world. Both are displays of God's majesty. Already at the first appearance the Son of God comes to destroy the works of the devil (3:8). One difference there certainly is this: The first coming was an epiphany only of God's love (4:9), of his redemptive purpose (3:5). It was an infusion of divine, life-giving power in the world of humanity (1:2; 4:9; 5:11f.). But in the parousia, Christ appears also as the Ruler and Judge. Thus the thought ends up in harmony with the faith of the early Christian church. Perhaps that is why the author adds the technical term parousia, which had become traditional in the community.[85] This is the only occurrence of it in the Johannine writings. There was no other term so suitable in a Hellenistic

---

83. A temporal contrast between *nyn* and *ean phanerōthē* (as in 3:2), leading up the the parousia, is ruled out by *menete; nyn* denotes consequence ("now therefore," "as things now stand"); cf. BAGD 546, s.v. 2; BDF §442.15 (Hebraism); especially J. Jeremias, *ZNW* 38 (1939) 119f.

84. See BAGD 211, s.v. 1, d, with biblical examples: Abel, *Grammaire* §68n (p. 296) with classical examples.

85. See Matt. 24:3, 27, 37, 39 (not yet in Mark); 1 Thess. 2:19; 3:13; 4:15; 5:23; 2 Thess. 2:1, 8; 1 Cor. 15:23; Jas. 5:7, 8; 2 Pet. 1:16; 3:4.—Bultmann regards *ean phanerōthē* and *en tē parousiā autou* as interpolations ("Redaktion," 196f.); see Introduction, p. 16.

environment, announcing the arrival of God as king.[86] This second revelation highlights the difference between the incarnation and the full royal and divine majesty of Jesus Christ displayed over the entire world.

Before the royal throne and judgment seat of Christ, Christians who have proved their loyalty to the community can come with "boldness," that is, with the assurance of a good concience.[87] The term "be ashamed" comes from the language of the law court. It does not refer to a psychological attitude, the embarrassment of those who are summoned before a judge (*aischynesthai* = middle voice), but rather objective conviction and condemnation (*aischynesthai* = passive voice).[88] The preposition *apo* can in this case be either synonymous with *hyper*, as often in Koine,[89] or perhaps be understood as a metaphor for the guilty stumbling backward or being rejected.[90]

This verse shows once more just how close the author stands, despite his own theology, to the common ideas of the early church and how harmoniously he has fitted both together. His announcement and explanation of the last hour vibrate with genuine theology, following the general line of early Christian teaching and interpretation. Once this is recognized, it is impossible to dismiss his clear view of the parousia as a survival of more primitive views which he had already in principle outgrown (cf. 3:14; 5:12) or as a veneer that a later circle may have imposed upon the pure Johannine theology.[91]

Many scholars would prefer to begin a new section at 2:29,[92] organizing it under the theme of "children of God." Actually, v. 28 might form a conclusion to the previous section

---

86. See Deissmann, *Light from the Ancient East*, 372ff.; Dibelius, Excursus on 1 Thess. 2:19 (HNT XI³, 14–16); BAG 635, s.v.; A. Oepke, *TDNT* 5:867f.

87. *Parrhēsia* originally meant "courage" or "frankness in speech" and soon moved from the realm of politics (the privilege of the free person) into the sphere of morality, being combined with the idea of friendship. It was first carried over into the relationship between humanity and God in Hellenistic Jewish literature (Josephus, *Antiquities* 2.52; 5.38; 9.226). According to Philo, even a slave enjoyed *parrhēsia* in relation to his master, so long as he had a clear conscience (*Heres* 6f.). In the same way a person cleansed from sin and striving to love God can *eleutherostomein* ("be free of speech") to his/her Lord, the Lord of the whole earth. This original meaning of *parrhēsia* comes out in the intercessory prayers in 1 John 3:21f.; 5:14, whereas in 2:28; 4:17 the idea of judgment brings out the element of confidence in a pure conscience. On the history of the term, see E. Peterson, in Festschrift R. Seeberg (Leipzig, 1929) 1:283–97, esp. 292; H. Schlier, *TDNT* 5:879ff. See also H. Jaeger, "Παρρησία et fiducia," in *Studia Patristica*, ed. K. Aland and F. L. Cross (Berlin, 1957) 221–39.

88. In Prov. 13:5 *aischynesthai* and *parrhēsian* (ouk) *echein* are also associated, *aischynesthai* in the passive (the wicked behave shamefully — the middle would make no sense). If the meaning "to be ashamed" is attested in several passages in the LXX (as in Sir. 4:26; 21:22; 22:25; 41:17ff.; Sus. 11 Theod.), as well as in the New Testament (Luke 16:3; 1 Pet. 4:16). In 1 John 2:28 being not ashamed is the consequence of belief in Christ. On this idea, cf. Jer. 12:13; Phil. 1:20; 2 Cor. 10:8; *1 Enoch* 62:10; 97:6 and *b. Ber.* 46a: "May his will be that the householder should not be put to shame in this world nor confounded in the world to come" (Goldschmidt, *Kleine Ausgabe* 1:200).

89. BDF §210.2; Robertson, *Grammar*, 636; cf. Mayser, *Grammatik*, II, 2:378f. on *apo* denoting origin.

90. Cf. the picture in *1 Enoch* 62:10; Matt. 7:23; 25:41; also BAG 25, s.v. 2.

91. Bultmann thinks that 2:28 may belong to the ecclesiastical redaction or else have a different meaning (*Theology* 2:88); for a contrary view, see H. Braun, "Literatur-Analyse," 287.

92. Bisping; Belser; Vrede; Bultmann, "Analyse," 146; Chaine; Dodd; Nauck, *Tradition und Charakter*.

with v. 29 clearing away the difficulty of the grammatical subject in v. 28. However, v. 29 does not give the impression of a fresh start, either in its form or in its content. The thought of "who . . . has been born of him" does not seem to be central. The introductory conditional sentence with the emphatic "righteous" stresses the grammatical subject, "every one who does right." Verse 29 is the continuation of v. 28, but at the same time develops the thought further in the final phrase. With 3:1 the author has unmistakably introduced a new thought, that of being children of God.

2:29 "Righteous," as the context suggests, and as is actually said, can only refer to Jesus Christ.[93] True, he had already once before (1:9) been designated as "just," but there in conjunction with "faithful." There it meant that his justice emanates from his faithful and gracious attitude in the forgiveness of sins. The sinless One (2:1; 3:5), who at the same time becomes the moral pattern for Christians (3:7; cf. 2:6; 3:6, 16; 4:17), can only be Christ. But in 2:29 "righteous" cannot be taken in any other sense. The *kai* ("and"; NRSV omits) before "everyone," although not universally attested,[94] is probably original. It compares the one "who does right"[95] with the righteous One, and does so in a way that is clearly defined a little later in 3:7b. On the other hand, the end of v. 29 is reminiscent of 3:10b. That leads us to expect a different conclusion to this verse. The present text forces us on purely grammatical grounds to connect "of him" with "righteous." The possibility of the translation "being born of Christ"[96] must be rejected out of hand in the light of the firmly established Johannine concept of "being born of God."[97] However, anyone who seeks to avoid this dilemma by appealing to a sentence in the *Vorlage*[98] is bound to agree that the author had in mind the thought of what follows and that this resulted in a contamination. The author begins his parenesis by saying: If you know that he (Christ) is righteous, then you acknowledge[99] that everyone who abides in him (cf. v. 28; 3:6) must do what is right. But the intervening thought asserts that those in fellowship in Christ are born of God, and that restricts this requirement. Conversely, it makes doing what is right a mark of being born of God.[100] It turns out to be impossible to

---

93. With Westcott and Brooke, *contra* Camerlynck, Loisy, Vrede, Büchsel, Chaine, Charue, et al. Windisch and Dodd leave it open.

94. It is missing from B ℵ al. sy^h sa bo arm, Aug. Ambr.

95. An Old Testament, Jewish phrase similar to *poiein tēn alētheian* 1:6 (see ad loc.), cf. Rev. 22:11; further *plērōsai pasan dikaiosynēn* (Matt. 3:15); *poiein dikaiosynēn* (Matt. 6:1; Rom. 10:5); *ergazesthai dikaiosynēn* (Acts 10:35; Heb. 11:33; Jas. 1:20).

96. Brooke takes this possibility seriously, referring to John 1:12 and to being "born of the Spirit" (John 3:5ff.); but in John 1:12 the Logos is not thought of as the principle of begetting while being born of the Spirit is contrasted with being born of the flesh and with the mere water baptism of John the Baptist, an idea more easily explicable.

97. John 1:13; 1 John 3:9; 4:7; 5:1, 4, 18. For the rest, see Excursus 8.

98. Windisch; Bultmann, "Analyse," 146, who, however, is bound to concede that the framework (*ean* . . . and *ginōskete hoti*) is the author's own formulation; W. Grundmann, *Aufnahme und Deutung*, 158 n. 1; H. Braun, "Literar-Analyse," 269.

99. *Ginōskete* is undoubtedly an indicative (Büchsel, Chaine). The introductory clause with *ean* requires a sequel consisting in the acknowledgment of a fact. Such acknowledgments are generally stated in the form of an assertion (2:3, 5; 3:16, 19, 24; 4:2, 6, 13; 5:2). In favor of an imperative (Vg, Bisping, Belser, Windisch, Hauck, Dodd) the parallel to *menete* would be the strongest argument.

100. The explanation "that everywhere, and absolutely everyone . . ." (Belser) ignores the *kai* before *pas*. So there is no attack here on the false teachers.

explain v. 29 without assuming that the author has opted for certain fixed formulations as he has done already in 3:4ff.

2. Christians Have the Gift of Becoming Children of God and Are Promised Even Greater Glory (1 John 3:1-3)

3:1 In an urgent tone ("See")[101] the author calls the attention of his readers to their present state of salvation. He had already told them that the surest defense against the heretics and their dangerous influence was the instruction they had received from the Holy Spirit (2:20f., 24, 27). Now in a similar vein he tells them that in their moral conflict they have as a bastion against the onslaughts of the devil (see vv. 7f.) not the human heart in its weakness but God and his blessings of salvation. The love of God the Father himself sustains the Christian over the abyss of worldliness and sin. In the alien world, cut off from God, they are still his children. The loving relationship between Father and children is conferred on them to the fullest extent. So great is the Father's love ("what love the Father has given us"; Greek *potapēn*, "how great").[102] "The Father" — it is the Johannine Jesus who speaks in this absolute way[103] — bridges the gap between the Creator and his creation, between the King of the universe and the citizens of earth. Such a closeness to God, which allows people to become his children ("that we should be called . . .")[104] is an unmerited gift ("has given"). Late Judaism also looked for such a relationship with God, but only as a pledge of his grace in the coming age of salvation. "And I shall be a father to them, and they will be sons to me. And they will all be called 'sons of the living God.' And every angel and every spirit will know and acknowledge that they are my sons and I am their father in uprightness and righteousness. And I shall love them" (*Jub.* 1:24f.). This quotation from the pre-Christian book of *Jubilees* is related to the Qumran writings. Its language is identical to that of 1 John. But in *Jubilees* it is a promise for the future, the longed-for goal of salvation history, whereas in 1 John it is already present as a joyous reality (perfect "has given").

Clearly the message about the loving Father echoes the simple words of Jesus when he spoke about the heavenly Father.[105] It is just as clear that there is a new

---

101. The phrase has a similar function to *ide*, which has already become a fixed formula (BAG 220) calling attention to something; cf. Mark 13:1; John 4:29; 7:52; Acts 13:41 (quoting Hab. 1:5); Rom. 11:22; Gal. 6:11. See Schlatter, *Sprache*, 148.

102. *Potapos* (older form *podapos*) properly = qualis; here also = quantus. Cf. Mark 13:1 and BAG 701, s.v.

103. *Ho patēr,* used absolutely in the Synoptists only at Matt. 11:27 = Luke 10:21; Matt. 24:36 = Mark 13:32; Paul usually says *theos (kai) patēr* or adds another word to the phrase. By contrast, *ho patēr* is used absolutely in GJohn 75 times, in 1 John 12 times, in 2 John twice.

104. On the construction with a *hina*-clause instead of an infinitive, see BDF §394; Radermacher, *Grammatik,* 190, 192.

105. Cf. Matthew 6; 23:9; Luke 3:36; 15:11ff. etc. Yet we are not to conclude without qualification from the designation Father, or from God's fatherly love, that our status as children of God is one of the blessings of salvation spoken of by Paul and John. In Matt. 5:9; Luke 20:36, being a child of God is an eschatological concept. Only on the basis of the experience of the Spirit does Paul speak of the believers' "sonship," which they experience in prayer (Rom. 8:16ff.; Gal. 4:5ff.). In John

element here in the Johannine writings, for they add that we are children of God (see Excursus 8). In GJohn the term "Son of God," as Jesus prefers to call himself, acquires an exalted dimension. In a similar way "the Father" has acquired a solemn resonance, The distinctive love of the *Father,* of which Jesus assured his disciples in the intimate circle of the upper room (16:27) is now extended to all who love the Son and prove it by keeping his commandments (14:21). This is attested in 1 John 3:1 for all who belong to the fellowship of true believers ("us").[106] The *distinctive* love of the Father, which made them his children and designated them as such, is still to be differentiated from the redemptive love of God to humanity in general in the bondage of death (John 3:16; 1 John 4:9, 14, 16). This perfect love, indicated by their designation as children, presupposes faith in the Son (John 1:12) and must of necessity be proved by their doing what is right (1 John 3:10).

This great gift of salvation is a cause for great joy. The Johannine terminology makes the difference clear between what it means for Christians to be the children of God as the result of grace, and Christ's own divine Sonship, which is ontological. Nowhere in the Johannine writings—in contrast to Paul[107] are Christians designated "sons of God." This is not because "child" implies a different relationship from "son."[108] Rather, it seems that John has coined a new usage. Paul himself apparently assumed that there was a difference between our sonship by grace and the ontological sonship of Christ, as he shows by the absolute phrase "the Son" (of God).

The actual term "child" does not express all that the author means by this relationship. In a brief independent clause (v. 10b) he adds: "and that is what we are."[109] This realistic sentiment surely stems from his sacramentalism (John 3; see Excursus 8) and presupposes the possession of the Spirit. The Spirit is the supernatural reality which elevates the relation of the child to God above a merely juridical or moral level.

Typically Johannine is the statement in v. 1b. The world does not recognize the Christians because it is cut off from God. Christians do not belong to the world and the world does not love them (cf. John 15:19; 1 John 3:13). Such a

---

the status of children becomes a fully present state of salvation. Cf. E. Lohmeyer, *Das Vaterunser* (2nd ed.; Göttingen, 1947) 30f.; Wikenhauser, *Johannes,* 75f.

106. B Ψ K* al. have *hymin,* which may have been caused by the forms with second person plural in 2:29 and *idete* in 3:1.

107. Rom. 8:14, 19; Gal. 3:26; 4:6, 7; In addition, see *huiothesia* (Rom. 8:15, 23; Gal. 4:5; Eph. 1:5). On this, see W. Twisselmann, "Die Gotteskindschaft der Christen nach dem NT" (diss., Tübingen, n.d. [1940]) 56–72.

108. *Teknon* means in the first place simply biological offspring; cf. Matt. 2:18; 27:25; Luke 16:25 (the rich man after his death); Acts 2:39; 13:33; Rom. 9:8. By contrast *teknia,* which the author of 1 John uses in addressing his readers, emphasizes their difference in age, though it can be merely an expression of tenderness. The linguistic difference is carried through in 1 John to its logical conclusion. In 2 John 1, 4, 13; 3 John 4 (cf. Rev. 2:23), the members of the church are called *teknia,* evidently because of the metaphor (*kyria!*). On the other hand, the expression *teknon theou* is missing from the two shorter Johannine epistles.—That *takna* and *huioi theou* mean the same thing is evident from a comparison with Rom. 8:15 and 16; 8:19 and 21.

109. *Kai esmen* is missing in א al. The two words cannot be a later gloss, for they are too well attested. They were probably left out because of the poor grammatical connection or because of carelessness.—One cannot make *esmen* dependent on *hina* (cf. Vg *simus*), since "the present indicative after *hina* is of course only a corruption" (BDF §369.6; Radermacher, *Grammatik,* 173 n. 4).

recognition is possible only between equals, between the Father and the Son (John 10:15; 17:25), between the Son and his own (John 10:14, 27; 1 John 1:13, 14). On the other hand, such recognition is possible between the world and the false prophets (cf. 1 John 4:5). The deeper reason[110] for this is the fact, frequently stated in GJohn and 1 John,[111] that the world itself does not know the Father of these children of God.[112]

3:2 Turning from the subject of their present salvation and its joy ("now") the author again addresses his readers as "beloved," as in 2:7, and directs their attention away from the present to the future. This will lead to an even greater crescendo, showing that salvation history is not just an external framework for his thought. It is the temporal aspect that he brings out here ("now"–"not yet"). The prospect of future consummation opened up by the parousia (2:28) reveals a reality that has hitherto been invisible ("revealed"). In GJohn resurrection on the last day (6:39, 40, 44, 54) was not just tacked on by a redactor to Jesus' sayings about eternal life. Similarly here, the author of 1 John has no intention of omitting any reference to the revelation of God's children in glory (cf. Rom. 8:19ff.). The resurrection is obviously presumed here, for otherwise the word "revealed" would be hardly intelligible. But either he has no interest in the resurrection of the body, or else he deliberately suppresses it. All he says is "what we shall be." Otherwise he is quite vague about it.[113] He thus avoids all the problems about the intermediate state which figured so largely in Jewish apocalyptic.[114] All he is concerned with is the glory of the children of God, which at present is hidden but which later will be revealed.

In v. 2b[115] he is at last able to say something definite about the future life of the children of God. He probably gleaned this knowledge from the traditional eschatology of the early church, as in 5:20 (cf. "you know," 3:5, 15; "we know," 5:15).

Whether the words "when he is revealed" refer to the parousia (as in 2:28) or resume "has not yet been revealed" from v. 2a, with the ellipse of "what we shall be" (meaning "when it appears what we shall be"), is not certain. The context appears to favor the second possibility.[116] (1) The "not yet" produced a sharp tension, which is resolved by the "when" (Greek *ean*)—again to be understood in a temporal sense as in 2:28. (2) From 3:1 on, the focus has been on the Father, God, and no change of person is likely. (3) The following pronouns in the third person (*autō, auton,* v. 2b; *ep' autō,* v. 3) would in that case naturally refer to Christ. He is also the likely object of the term "seeing" ("we shall see

---

110. *Dia touto* points to the following *hoti*-clause as in John 5:16, 18; 12:39.

111. John 7:28; 8:19, 55; 15:21; 16:3; 17:25; 1 John 3:6; 4:8.

112. The reading *hēmas* is to be preferred as in v. 1a to *hymas* (ℵ* P ℓ al.). Cf. the continuation in v. 2 in the first person plural.

113. On *ti* instead of *tines,* see BDF §299.2.

114. See Volz, *Eschatologie,* 256ff.

115. "With the *oidamen* one misses a *de* from a formal point of view" (Büchsel), but the asyndeton belongs to the style; the addition of *de* in ℓ al. sy^pal sa bo is an attempt to smooth out the text.

116. *Contra* Westcott, Häring, Windisch, Bonsirven, Dodd.—Bultmann would omit *ean phanerōthē* ("Redaktion," 197f).

him as he is") rather than God. In 3:3 Christ is introduced with *ekeinos* (literally, "that one"; NRSV "him").[117]

Following this the eschatological escalation and full realization of our new status as children of God will consist in our being like him. Although *homoios* can also mean "similar," rather than "equal," we should not read into those two words the same contrast as in English. But it would be better not to speak of "*equality* to God" here. Strictly speaking, likeness to God (cf. John 5:18, "making himself equal with God"; Phil. 2:7, "equality with God") is never promised to the believers in the New Testament. Yet it would seam that certain rabbinic phrases[118] for the eschatological restoration of life in paradise anticipate an even greater proximity to God, a closer assimilation of human nature to the divine, than was the case originally. "God has now made the promise come true, 'eritis sicut deus'" (Volz, *Eschatologie,* 395). However, the rabbis have no intention of placing human beings on the same level with God, even in the future Garden of Eden. These Jewish sayings are nowhere near that type of deification which pagan syncretism takes so seriously. There human beings actually become "God."[119] This presumes a pantheistic conception of the deity,[120] which has always been ruled out in the Old Testament and Judaism, as well as in Christian thought,

---

117. F. C. Synge offers a new proposal with a different punctuation, "Now are we sons of God, and he has not been manifest. What we shall be we know, because if he is made manifest we shall be like him, because we shall see him as he is" (*JTS* n.s. 3 [1952] 79). But this is to destroy the parallel *esmen–esometha,* to which *nyn–oupō* points, and makes *oupō ephanerōthē* superfluous. The second *hoti*-clause in 2b would then give the reason why we shall be like Christ at the parousia—a not very illuminating explanation (see the commentary). It is better to take the construction after the analogy of 3:14.

118. *Pesiq. R.* 11 (46b): "in this world the Israelites have held fast to God, for it is written: 'those of you who held fast the Lord your God are all alive today' (Deut. 4:4); but in time to come they will be like God for our God is a devouring fire, as it is written: Deut. 4:24: 'For the Lord your God is a devouring fire.'"—See Billerbeck, *Kommentar* 3:777; according to *Sipra Lev.* 26:12 (111b), the righteous, when they see God, who loves to walk in their midst, will be struck with fear at the sight of his countenance; but he says to them, "Why do you fear me? I am as one of you" (see Volz, *Eschatologie,* 395, and more material given there).

119. *Theousthai, apotheousthai,* etc. are terms repeated constantly in literary mysticism and gnosis; see *CHerm* 1.26; 13.1 (*theiotēs*); 13.7, 10 (Scott 1:256, 8 conj); 10.6; Asclepius, *Epil.;* Stobaeus, *Exc.* 24.4. The visionary is addressed directly as God (*CHerm* 13.2: *allos estai ho gennōmenos theou theos pais*), just like the initiate in the preaching of the Naassenes in Hippolytus, *Ref.* 5.8.22; Clement of Alexandria *Exc. ex Theod.* 76; among the Pythagoreans on a golden tablet: *olbie kai makariste, theos d'esē anti brotoio* (see Bousset, *Kyrios Christos* [Eng. trans.]) 430. Further evidence in Clement of Alexandria and Hippolytus is given by Scott, *Hermetica* 3:292f. The same meaning is attached to the usage in the mystery religions, where the mystic puts on the robe of the deity after initiation; for the Isis cult, see Apuleius, *Metam.* 11.24; for Mithraism, see Porphyry, *De abstinatione* 4.16; for Babylon, see F. J. Dölger, *Ichthys* (Rome, 1910) 1:115. "By initiation the mystic was born again to a superhuman life and became like the immortals" (F. Cumont, *Die orientalischen Religionen im römischen Heidentum* [3rd ed.; Leipzig/Berlin, 1931] 92).

120. See Reitzenstein, *Poimandres,* 234ff.; Bousset, *Kyrios Christos* (Eng. trans.) 166: "This *unio mystica* takes on a completely pantheistic, speculative color in the prophetic consecration of Hermes"; 431f.: "The characteristic thing is that here all boundaries between divine and human fade away in an utterly astonishing fashion."

with its Old Testament–Jewish roots. Despite its bold formulas about unity with God, Johannine theology nowhere teaches a mystical identity between God and humanity (see Excursuses 2 and 4). After the parousia we shall be close to God and we shall see him. But although the language is similar, it has a radically different meaning from the Hellenistic mysteries or gnosticism, with their idea of deification. We must not translate it "to be equal with God," as though to be children of God already included being similar to him. Otherwise there would be nothing more for us to attain (B. Weiss). "Being a child of God" is above all to experience the love of the Father; it is not the child's similarity to him. This state of being remains hidden in this world and will only become visible in the coming era when all that is hidden will be brought to light![121]

The basis of this likeness to God which will then be unveiled lies, according to the author, in our seeing him. Does the clause beginning with "for" give the reason for this experience? In other words, do we know we are like God because we see him? Is our seeing God the cause of our becoming like him? Scholars belonging to the history-of-religions school assume the latter and find in this passage the Hellenistic concept of deification through the vision of God![122] On purely linguistic grounds it does not seem that the *hoti*-clause should be taken as explaining why "we know," because in that case the author would have said "by this we know."[123] Moreover, we find the same construction in 3:14, where the second *hoti*-clause (translated "because") explains *why* "we know." Actually the idea of becoming like God through seeing him would be quite unusual in the Johannine writings. In the whole of the New Testament it occurs only in the much-discussed passage of 2 Cor. 3:18. But there it is prepared for by a midrash about the "glory" on the face of Moses. As in the construction in 1 John 3:14, nothing else is said in 3:2b except that we shall see him in the eschatological consummation. The deeper reason for arguing from seeing God to being like him is not mentioned. The more philosophical basis for this, namely, that like can only be known by like,[124] must be ruled out. But it can still be asked whether to see God as he is requires immediate proximity to him, or whether the consequence of this is an assimilation to God granted by grace![125] Or does seeing God presuppose a communication of the divine glory, on the ground that only one transformed into God can see him? (*2 Apoc. Bar.* 51:5, 8).[126] In the final analysis

---

121. See Volz, *Eschatologie,* 115f.; we would more likely expect here *apokalyphthē;* but John always has *phanerousthai* (except in the citation in 12:38).

122. Bousset, *Kyrios Christos* (Eng. trans.) 222. Reitzenstein, *Hellenistische Mysterienreligionen,* 357f.; Windisch ad loc.—*Contra* Büchsel, *Johannes und der hellenistische Synkretismus,* 82 n. 3; Twisselmann, "Gotteskindschaft," 91 n. 1; M.-J. Lagrange, *RB* 38 (1929) 68–81; 201–14.

123. 2:3, 5; 3:16; 4:2, 13; 5:2.

124. See Windisch, ad loc., and the texts he adduces there, together with *CHerm* 11.20 *to gar homoion tō homoiō noēton.*

125. Cf. Wis. 3:9; 5:5, 15f.; 6:19; 4 Macc. 9:8; *2 Apoc. Bar.* 51:8ff.; *4 Enoch* 22:8ff.

126. An account of the transformation made possible by the vision will be found in the text quoted by Windisch, *2 Clem.* 17.16. This text is inspired by Jewish ideas, as shown by the claim that the resurrected will be *like* angels; cf. Luke 20:36; Volz, *Eschatologie,* 396f. H. J. Schoeps, *Theologie und Geschichte des Judenchristentums* (Tübingin, 1949) 423f. 1 John speaks immediately of the redeemed being *like* God, though that idea, a late Jewish one, is much closer to what he means than the Hellenistic idea of deification.—On the other hand, *Odes Sol.* 7:18f. and 13:1f. are influenced by gnosticism. Here subject and object of vision are reciprocal. See also *MandLit* 86.

both amount to the same thing; proximity to God and transfiguration into glory belong together. In any case becoming like God seems to be the consequence of glory, the radiant light of divine glory. Already in late Judaism the Messiah and those who participate in eschatological salvation[127] were expected to share in this divine prerogative. But in GJohn this prerogative had become an ontological possession of the Son of God![128] Yet the Messiah permits those who believe in him to share in this divine sonship (John 17:22 — the final fulfillment is held in reserve until they enter into the heavenly world of light, John 17:24). In this context "seeing" and "glory of light" are interdependent ("to see my glory," John 17:24; cf. also John 1:14). This has a different meaning from the Hellenistic idea of deification as a result of vision. According to *1 Enoch* 38:4, the Lord of spirits beams his light upon the saints, the righteous, and the elect (cf. *2 Apoc. Bar.* 51:3, 5), while according to *1 Enoch* 62:16 the elect "shall wear the garments of glory. These garments . . . shall become the garments of life from the Lord of the Spirits." Thus we have here an event of grace. Glory is one of the blessings of salvation received by the righteous as a gift![129] It is not just that the seeing of God deifies them. Rather because they are being deified (if we may still use that expression), they see.

The idea of seeing God is found both in Judaism[130] and in Christianity![131] It is a component part of the eschatological hope. In the Johannine writings there is a polemic against any direct seeing of God on earth (John 1:18; 5:37; 6:46; 14:8f.; 1 John 4:12), but that is no objection against the whole notion. On earth, people see the Father in the Son (John 14:9; 12:45). The addition of "as he is" leaves this way of experiencing God on earth open to the believers. It promises the unveiled sight of God ("face to face," 1 Cor. 13:12) only at the eschatological consummation.

The crescendo and crown of salvation which the future brings hardly lie in the fact that our present status as God's children is to be dissolved and replaced by equality with God. Rather, that status will then unveil its hidden glory, which is our likeness to God. This will probably—though precise Johannine texts are lacking—be brought about by the granting of divine glory in all its fullness. As a consequence—just as in Pauline thought—the only sequel will be a revealing of the children of God (Rom. 8:19).

3:3 Likeness to God and seeing God together sum up the whole content of Christian hope. This is the only occasion in the Johannine writings when hope is mentioned—apart from the reference to Jewish hope in John 5:45. Hope is

---

127. See Volz, *Eschatologie*, 397.

128. John 1:14; 2:11; 12:41; 17:5, 22, 24.

129. Cf. on the other hand *CHerm* 11.20 *ean oun mē seauton exisasēs tō theō, ton theon noēsai ou dynasai.*

130. See Billerbeck, *Kommentar* 1:206-15 (on Matt 5:8); Volz, *Eschatologie*, 396; F. Nötscher, *'Das Angesicht Gottes schauen' nach biblischer und babylonischer Auffassung* (Würzburg, 1924) 170ff.; W. Michaelis, *TDNT* 5:339.

131. Matt. 5:8; 1 Cor. 13:12; 2 Cor. 5:7; Rev. 22:4. Cf. Michaelis, *TDNT* 5:364ff.

here directed toward God ("in him").[132] It is not merely a verbal promise (cf. Matt. 5:8; Rev. 22:4), but also a promise of his love, a love already granted, the reality of being children of God. This does not, however, lead to a complacent assurance of salvation. On the contrary, it incites the believers to moral action. The dynamic of the Pauline ethic, which develops its powerful incentive from the salvation already possessed: "Become what you are," permeates the Johannine theology too. In the shape of a categorical announcement the author states that those who have this hope[133] purify themselves.

"To purify" is in origin a cultic term, meaning to withdraw from the profane, to make something fit for worship.[134] But the cultic rule in the mystery religions that only those who have consecrated themselves can see God, cannot apply here. Consecration is not a precondition but an ethical requirement. That requirement arises from the certain expectation of seeing God.[135] In fact "to purify" had long since become an ethical concept.[136]

The ethical and parenetic character of this passage is underscored by the brief clause "as he is." This, like 2:6 (cf. v. 29), sets Christ before us as our supreme example. As he is righteous (2:29), so too is he pure, that is, from sin (3:5). The ethic of the Sermon on the Mount, requiring spotless purity in the children of the heavenly Father, mirrored in a pure and simple heart (cf. Matt. 5:8; 6:22f.), is further developed here for the Christian state of salvation, Christ as our model. There can be no idea here of self-righteousness or self-glorification, falsely understood. The statement is a logical deduction from the boundless gift of God's grace, and the future consummation, still hidden but awaiting completion from God.[137] Verse 3 is apparently not a polemic directed against the heretical teachers, any more than the whole section vv. 1–3. Rather it reminds the believers of the fullness of salvation and the blessed state awaiting them. The polemic will come up in the following sentences, which form an antithesis to what is said here.

---

132. *Epi* with the dative refers to the one from whom fulfillment is expected, not to its real basis ("on the basis of fellowship with him"—so evidently Büchsel). Cf. Rom. 15:12; 1 Tim. 4:10; 6:17 and with *pepoithenai* (Matt. 27:43; Mark 10:24 *v.l.*) Luke 11:22; 18:9; 2 Cor. 1:9; Heb. 2:13; cf. BDF §235.3 and 187.6; BAG 287γ.

133. *Elpida echein;* cf. Rom. 15:4; 2 Cor. 3:12; Eph. 2:12; in addition (*theos*) *dous elpida agathēn en chariti* (2 Thess. 2:16). Hope is therefore the gift of God's grace and the blessing of salvation.

134. Cf. Exod. 19:10; Num. 8:21; 19:12; etc.; 1 Chron. 15:12, 14; 2 Chron. 29:5, 15, 18, 34; etc.— John 11:55 (the opposite in 18:28); Acts 21:24, 26; 24:18.

135. *Contra* Brooke, Windisch.

136. Cf. Jas. 4:8; 1 Pet. 1:22. On the ethicizing of holiness, see R. Asting, *Die Heiligkeit im Urchristentum* (Göttingen, 1930) 34; Hauck, *TDNT* 1:123; Eichrodt, *Theology* 1:137, 271; 2:334ff.; on *agnos,* see Trench, *Synonyms,* 313ff.

137. Cf. Augustine, *In epist. Joa tr.* 4.7 (*PL* 35:2009): Quis nos castificat nisi Deus? Sed Deus te nolentem non castificat. Ergo quod adjungis voluntatem tuam Deo, castificas teipsum. Castificas te, non de te, sed de illo, qui venit ut inhabitet te.

EXCURSUS 8

Being Children of God and Being Born of God

I. THE INNER MEANING OF THE JOHANNINE TERMS

1. Being Children of God and Being Born of God

1 John often speaks of Christians being born of God (2:29; 3:9; 4:7; 5:1, 4, 18). The question is, Does this mean the same thing as being children of God? The answer to that question will determine whether "child of God" (3:1, 2, 10; 5:2) is merely a polite form of address, not to be taken seriously, or whether conversely, to be "born of God" has any important significance. In 3:9 and 10 the alternation between "born of God" and "child of God" occurs without any change of meaning. The same is true in 5:1 and 2. Thus "has been born of him" in 2:29 introduces the theme of being children of God, which is developed in 3:1. Especially important is the analogy of the human parent and offspring, which lies behind 5:1b. Like the metaphor of "God's seed" in 3:9, it shows that the author is serious about the comparison with natural begetting. But the phrase is not merely an analogy. The child of God is not his seed; rather, the seed of God abides in the child. The relationship is not merely one involving legal adoption or moral association (the love between father and child). It is an ontological one ("that is what we are," 3:1). But being a child of God is not a natural status; it belongs to the realm of the supernatural. This claim receives full endorsement if the plural reading in John 1:13 is adopted. Here the natural and supernatural are confronted with each other with all possible clarity (cf. 3:6).

There may also be a warning in 1 John against a naturalistic interpretation of being born of God. This warning occurs in the contrast between the children of God and the children of the devil. All the emphasis is placed on the moral behavior of those who are born of God (cf. 2:29; 3:9f.; 4:7; 5:1f.). True, the ontological basis for this is laid bare and is regarded as essential (3:9). But if that is all that is involved, to be a child of the devil would be an equally biological fact. But this is just what the author wishes to avoid. He never speaks of people being "born of the devil." Those who commit sin are revealed as children of the devil (3:8, 10; cf. John 8:41, 44). Nowhere does he speak of the devil's seed. There is no antithetical parallelism after 3:9, for v. 10 is deliberately formulated in different terms. However much the author is concerned with the antithesis between the children of God and the children of the devil, he avoids treating them on the same level. Being a child of God is more than a matter of moral behavior, while being a child of the devil is less than a biological relationship. To be a child of God means something more. It is a supernatural, ontological reality, lacking in those who are children of the devil, and it is manifested in their character and behavior (3:10).

2. Being Born of God and Baptism

In 1 John being born of God and being the child of God are equivalent. This is because it is not the process but the effect and the condition of being born of God that are being envisioned (note the perfect tense; on the only aorist, 5:18, see ad loc.). The epistle focuses on what it means to be a child of God and on its moral implications. It is not interested in the miracle of the event itself. GJohn is quite different. In the dialogue with Nicodemus this is just the question Nicodemus asks, "How can these things be?" (3:9; cf. v. 4). And the reply of Jesus leaves no doubt for a Christian audience that this takes place in baptism (3:5). The Holy Spirit is the decisive factor in this supernatural event (3:6). Therefore we must conclude that in 1 John baptism is tacitly presumed to be the place where we are born of God. However, the author's concern with practical morality obscures this fact. He is not speaking about the dogmatic necessity of baptism but about the new spirituality and moral attitude of the baptized. Faith in Christ (5:1) and love (4:7) or doing what is right (2:29) are not preconditions, still less means, but rather criteria for being born of God. This is clearly proved by 5:4 and 3:9-10. Therefore it is possible without any difficulty to recognize a uniform view behind all these sayings. In the process of being born of God in baptism, a person becomes a new creature, one "born of the Spirit" (John 3:6) or "born of God" (1 John). That person embodies the way of God as contrasted with the way of the devil (1 John 3:10) and the way of the "world" (1 John 4:4f.; 5:4, 19).

That is why it is misleading to suppose that the creative agent in rebirth in John is the word of God.[138] James 1:18 and 1 Peter 1:23 offer no direct parallel to 1 John 3:9. James 1:18 ("by the word of truth") may be connected with the idea of sowing the seed — that is, the word — of God (Mark 4:14ff. par.). 1 Peter 1:23 highlights the creative word of God borne by the Spirit as the decisive factor in the baptismal rite (the "living and enduring word of God"; cf. Eph. 5:26). The Johannine texts keep exclusively to the analogy of "being born" and view it as the creative act of God or the Spirit.[139] In John the theology of the word of God is not connected in any way with the idea of being born of God.

3. Being Children of God as the Presence of Salvation and Its Blessings

Since in Johannine theology being a child of God is derived from being born of God, it cannot be understood in a purely moral sense. It is a blessing of salvation granted by the grace of God. It not only is intended for the end-time (Matt. 5:9) but is already a present reality. The children of God in the Johannine sense, those who already believe in Christ, are born by baptism into a new life. They have been raised above the sphere of the flesh and have been accepted into the life of fellowship with God. They are able to triumph ("conquered," 1 John 4:4; 5:4) over Satan. As representatives of God they fight for him in the midst of a world still under the thrall of the evil one (5:18f.). The term "child of God" can be understood only against the background of Johannine eschatology, with its idiosyncratic emphasis on present realization. The clearest expression of it is to be found in passages that speak of life eternal as a present possession (John 3:16, 18, 36; 5:24; etc.; 1 John 3:14; 5:11-13).

---

138. Cf. on 3:9; and further Thornton, *The Common Life*, 200ff.
139. See Mussner, ZΩH, 111-23.

4. What It Means to Be Children of God

Here then is the clue to what it means to be children of God in the Johannine sense. The believer becomes a child of God (cf. John 1:12) through an act of divine begetting, being born from above. In this act of God the believer receives the divine Spirit as the principle of life (cf. "God's seed," 1 John 3:9). Thus the believer comes to belong to the heavenly, spiritual sphere, the realm of the divine. Behind this stands the axiom that origin determines nature: "What is born of the flesh is flesh, and what is born of the Spirit is spirit" (John 3:6). Since the natural or carnal human is imprisoned in the lower, earthly realm, birth through the Spirit must come "from above," from the heavenly realm of the divine (John 3:3, 7). To be children of God must be a gift, like having the Spirit of God ("has given," 1 John 3:1; cf. 3:24; 4:13). Although "being born of God is, for John, no more than a metaphor, it is connected with the idea of life. To be born of God therefore means to be equipped as a human being with a divine principle of life, the life of the Spirit, the impartation of the divine life of the Spirit (F. Mussner). The gracious gift of God is matched on the part of the human recipient by a humble, joyous gratitude for life (1 John 3:1).

By the same token, to be a child of God is not the final fulfillment of salvation. As the divine life awaits the final resurrection on the last day (John 5:29; 6:39, 40, 44, 54), so, although we are already children of God, it has not become clear what we will become eventually (1 John 3:2). Since it speaks of our being "like him," it may be inferred that "the glory" will be achieved in the heavenly world of God (cf. John 12:4; 17:24). At the same time this is different from Paul, for whom we are already children or sons of God, while at the same time we hope to become so later (cf. Rom. 8:15 with 23). In 1 John all the emphasis lies on our present status as God's children. It says nothing about its future aspect.

It is God's begetting that creates our status as his children. That status is achieved only when we are completely permeated with the divine nature. Essential to this is our moral attitude — above all, love. The two things, ontological ground and the personal attitude of the child of God, cannot be separated, according to the author of 1 John. This becomes intelligible only with the statement that those who are born of God cannot sin (3:9; cf. 5:18). Then again, love is declared to be the criterion of our being born of God (4:7). To be a child of God says something not only about what we are but also about how we are to behave. Note how easily the author moves from "being born of God" (3:9) to "being of God" (3:10; cf. 4:4 with 5:4). To be a child of God becomes an all-embracing characteristic of the Christian person in the indissoluble unity of that person's supernatural being. It is a comprehensive term for our gracious elevation and moral perfection, which together provide a model of what it means to be a Christian.

II. THE SOURCE OF THE JOHANNINE CONCEPTION

Where did the Johannine idea of being children of God come from? And where did the idea of being born of God come from? This is a highly complex problem.

The idea is so rich and profound that it must be derived from more than one source. Different areas in the environment of early Christianity must have contributed to it without any single main influence being discernible that would exclude all others.

1. Relation to the Old Testament and Judaism

The idea of being a child of God is not unfamiliar to Old Testament theology, though it was only later, viz., in the Hellenistic age, that it was transferred from the people of Israel as a whole to the pious individual.[140] The designation of Israel as son of God can be traced a long way back (Exod. 4:22f.—where there is a deliberate contrast between the firstborn son of Yahweh and the firstborn son of Pharaoh). Hosea 11:1ff. (cf. Isa. 43:1-7; 63:8f.; Mal. 1:2f.) makes a great point of the love between the Father and the son (cf. 1 John 3:1, "what [great] love"). But this is based on Israel's election and covenant (cf. Deut. 14:1f.; Isa. 1:2ff.; Mal. 1:2f.; *Jub.* 2:20; 19:29). Moreover, the passage referring to the creation and formation of a people by God as its Father are rooted in this key concept of Old Testament thought (cf. Deut. 32:6ff.; Isa. 43:6f.; 63:16f.; Mal. 2:10). That this people or the individual members thereof were formed by this Father like the potter with his clay and so became his own property to which he clings so lovingly is a key concept in the Old Testament. But the Old Testament never speaks of Israel's being begotten by God![141] Right up to the time of the individualizing of this concept[142] we have aftereffects of the covenant theology (cf. Wis. 12:19-27).

Closer to 1 John is another line of thought which emerges in later Judaism. This is the expectation that in the messianic age the elect or redeemed will become children of God. How this idea originated and developed can already be seen

---

140. The devout individual speaks of God as his/her Father; see Sir. 23:1, 4; 51:10; 3 Macc. 5:7; 6:8; 7:6. The Wisdom of Solomon speaks more frequently of individuals as "God's children" (2:13, 16, 18; 12:21; 14:5 etc.). On the use of "Father" as a name for God in rabbinic Judaism, see G. Dalman, *The Words of Jesus* (Edinburgh, 1909) 186f.; Bousset-Gressmann, *Religion des Judentums,* 377f.; Moore, *Judaism* 2:203ff.; Billerbeck, *Kommentar* 1:219f.; Bonsirven, *Judaïsme* 1:138f.; Sjöberg, *Gott und die Sünde,* passim; Twisselmann, "Gotteskindschaft," 26-35.

141. On the idea of a divine act of "begetting" in late Judaism—something that can hardly be proved, where the texts reflect it, though in quite a different sense—see Billerbeck, *Kommentar* 2:421ff.; 3:840ff.; 4:453ff.; K. H. Rengstorf, *TDNT* 1:666-68 (comparing a proselyte to a newborn child; Büchsel, ibid., (on Psalms 2:7; 109; and Prov. 8:22ff.); the matter is judged in a more positive light by Twisselmann ("Gotteskindschaft," 81; the term, he claims, is not found, though the idea is present); O. Michel and O. Betz believe they can prove still more positively the presence of the idea in (nonrabbinic) Judaism, especially on the basis of certain Qumran texts ("Von Gott gezeugt," in *Judentum, Urchristentum, Kirche* [Festschrift J. Jeremias; BZNW 26: Berlin, 1960] 3-23). However, the text 1QSa 2:11 (the Messiah is "begotten of God") is disputed and 1QH 9:35f. ("For Thou art a father to all [the sons] of Thy truth, and as a woman who tenderly loves her babe . . .") is hardly more than a metaphor and a comparison. As a result, the judgment remains seriously open to question: "the divine Sonship promised to the community of the end-time is interpreted by him [John] by the statement which in the sect applies only to the Messiah: The believers are begotten of God" (p. 22).

142. Volz does not regard the relationship of father to children as a purely individual one (*Eschatologie,* 395). For being children of God applies to all members of God's holy people, not just to the individual by himself or herself.

from Mal. 3:17f. Here the faithful servants of Yahweh become like sons, who remain permanently in their father's house and will be spared on the day of judgment (cf. Wis. 2:18; 5:5). Gradually, to be a child of God becomes a privilege granted by him, admitting one to the joys of salvation (cf. *Pss. Sol.* 17:27, 30; *Jub.* 1:24f.; *1 Enoch* 62:11; *As. Mos.* 10:3; and esp. Matt. 5:9, where this eschatological dignity becomes quite clear in the context of the beatitudes). This saying of Jesus does not restrict divine sonship to the people of Israel, as is often the case in the Jewish texts (cf. *Pirqe 'Abot* 3.14) in favor of a purely religious and ethical assessment. 1 John 3:1 seems to be aware of this development ("that we should be called children of God"), but it believes that Christians have already become so.

2. Relation to the Mystery Religions

Since the early Christian concept of being born of God is not found in Judaism, it has been suggested that it is the result of the "hellenization" of Christianity, particularly under the influence of the mystery religions. One thing cannot be doubted: the Alexandrian Jew Philo, although remaining basically faithful to his ancestral religion, was so keen to combine the wisdom of the Greco-Roman world with the Mosaic religion of the law, that he speaks without reserve and in the most varied connections of God's not having left himself without witness![143] When he is speaking allegorically, there may be nothing wrong with that. This was for him a picturesque description of God's creative activity. To be sure, Philo was indebted for much of his terminology to the pagan mystery religions as well as to philosophy. Is it not possible that early Christianity also imbibed something from that source? The early church could well have had contact with these secret cults, more by merely existing alongside of them than by entering into controversy with them.

Yet this view is open to question for the following reasons: (a) Whether these secret cults had any idea of new birth in an initiatory rite is open to doubt![144] True, the idea of renewal is found there and was described in metaphors of this kind![145] (b) On the other hand, despite the similarity in terminology, the Johannine

---

143. Cf. the text cited by Windisch in his excursus after 1 John 3:9. He cites *Spec. leg.* 1:317–18; *Conf.* 63.146 for the idea of being sons of God—the latter passage is especially significant for the relation God–Logos–human beings. That Philo was decisively influenced by (Platonic and) Stoic philosophy may be seen from a comparison with Epictetus, *Diss.* 1.9.6: *dia ti mē eipē [tis] auton kosmion; dia ti mē huion tou theou;* cf. (with a Platonic basis—Plato, *Tim.* 28c; 37c) 1.3.1f.; 9.7; 13.3; 19.9; 2.16.44; 3.24.15f. See further on Plato, Epictetus, and Philo, G. Schrenk, *TDNT* 5:954ff.

144. F. Büchsel endeavors to prove that the mysteries thought only in terms of adoption (*TDNT* 1:666ff.). He cites further literature. See also N. P. Nilsson, *Geschichte der griechischen Religion* 2:660: "It would appear that that idea is an interpretation of the rite, rather than its basis."

145. Cf. Hippolytus, *Ref.* 5.8.40f., on the Eleusinian mysteries: *hieron eteke potnia kouron Brimō Brimon* and the interpretation *hē genesis hē pneumatikē, hē epouranios hē anō. Ref.* 5.8.10: The Samothracians envisioned two men, the created Adam and that *tou anagennōmenou pneumatikou;* the so-called *Mithras Liturgy* (Dieterich, *Mithrasliturgie,* 12) speaks of *metagennasthai;* in the Isis rite of consecration, according to Apuleius, *Metam.* 11.21, the initiates become *quodammodo renatos;* for the Attis cult we have an inscription (*CIL* 6:510): *Taurobolio cribolioq(ue), in aeternum renatos.*— Cf. H. Usener, *Das Weihnachtsfest* (2nd ed.; Bonn, 1911) 151ff.; Dieterich *Mithrasliturgie,* 134ff.,

idea, so far as we can ascertain, is by no means identical![146] There is no direct parallel here to the Johannine idea of being born of God. Further, in John the term "rebirth" (Greek *palingenesia*) is missing. (c) The evidence covering the development of this concept of regeneration in the mystery cults comes from a later period, and it must be doubted whether they were already developed so strongly at the beginning of the second century. The influence of the Christian rite of baptism on the mystery religions cannot be ruled out![147]

We must therefore be careful in claiming that John took over the idea of being born of God from the mystery religions. At the same time there may have been a borrowing of terminology. Indeed it is noticeable that similar metaphorical language is found in other manifestations of Hellenistic syncretism. In Hermetic mysticism we find the notion of birth in the spirit,[148] in which people attained to a new, higher existence. The way to this is not some sort of initiatory rite, but an ecstatic vision releasing one from the bodily senses![149] The concept of rebirth is found also in gnostic texts![150] But despite the similarities in terminology, closer investigation shows that there are profound differences in content between the non-Christian or heretical texts and the Johannine. Since this is particularly obvious in the case of the gnostic texts, let us pay special attention to them.

3. Relation to the Gnostic Texts

With their pneumatic nature and knowledge, the gnostics, who had experienced a rebirth, regarded themselves as different from the rest of humanity. In this connection it seems worth noting that 1 John also speaks of Christians as people with a special nature. They are born of God. They come from him and are separated from those who are "of the world" (4:4f.). But the gnostic attitude behind the idea of rebirth is quite different. The gnostics are "pneumatics by nature."[151]

157ff.; Reitzenstein, *Hellenistische Mysterienreligionen,* 47ff.; 245ff.; Bauer, *Johannes,* Excursus, 51–53; Windisch, Excursus on 1 John 3:9.

146. For a critique, see J. Dey, "Παλιγγενεσία," *NTAbh* 17.5 (Münster, 1937); K. Prümm, *Der christliche Glaube und die altheidnische Welt* (Leipzig, 1935) 2:310ff.; idem, *Religionsgeschichtliches Handbuch für den Raum der altchristlichen Umwelt* (Freiburg, 1943) 213ff., esp. 327f.; Twisselmann, "Gotteskindschaft," 10–19; Huby, *Mystiques,* 163ff.; Wikenhauser, *Johannes,* 93f. (concedes that the terminology is related).

147. See M. Dibelius, *Die Isisweihe* (SA Heidelberg, 1917) 51f.; Dey, "Παλιγγενεσία," 73; Prümm, *Christlicher Glaube* 2:312; also C. Clemen, *Religionsgeschichtliche Erklärung des NT* (2nd ed.; Giessen, 1924) 32ff. on the age when the mysteries flourished.

148. *CHerm* 13.3: *kai eimi nyn ouch ho prin, all' egennēthēn en nō,* here the same as *palingenesia* (13.1, 7, etc.) and *genesis tēs theotētos* (13.7).—Many scholars assume that Johannine Christianity was influential on this; so M.-J. Lagrange, "L'Hermétisme," *RB* 35 (1926) 252–62; Twisselmann, "Gotteskindschaft," 20f. For a contrary view, see among others Huby, *Mystiques,* 167 n. 2.

149. Reitzenstein speaks of a "vintage mystery" (*Hellenistische Mysterienreligionen,* 43); Nilsson (*Geschichte* 2:586), following Nock, of a "mystery religion in words," and more frequently elsewhere of a "mystery of the book."

150. See Hippolytus, *Ref.* 5.8.23, in the so-called *Preaching of the Naassenes: anagennēthentes pneumatikoi, ou sarkikoi* (cf. also 8.18); Clement of Alexandria, *Exc. ex Theod.* 76.4 (*anagennōmetha*) and 80.1.

151. Irenaeus, *Adv. Haer.* 1.1.11: cf. 1.1.8; further Clement of Alexandria, *Strom.* 3.4.30: *huioi physei tou prōtou theou;* 4.165.3: *hyperkosmion physei; Exc. ex Theod.* 2.2: *to sperma to pneumatikon* (that is placed in the soul from the beginning). See also *Odes Sol.* 41:9f.: "For the Father of truth remembered

Their transformation is caused by gnosis, even though it may be clothed in sacramental rites.[152] In gnosis people discover the pneumatic core of their souls, which is unworldly and supraworldly. Thus souls are redeemed from the bonds of matter, from the alienation of the ungodly world, into which they had been cast and banished.[153] So too they can only remember their original pneumatic nature. *Per contra,* John contains no hint of this kind of predetermination of people to be either gnostics or nongnostics.[154] All people are primarily "flesh" and must be equipped anew by being born of God for a supernatural, pneumatic life which they had not known before. This can be attained only through faith in Christ, the bringer of life, and through the sacrament of baptism.[155]

So if Johannine theology was influenced to some extent by Hellenistic language, it made use of these already existing images in its own particular way in the interests of the Christian doctrine of baptism and endowment of the Spirit.

4. Relation to the Early Church and Jesus

In its substance and core the Johannine view is embedded in the early Christian proclamation as a whole (see above under 1). Should it not be indebted *genetically* to the kerygma of the community? Should not the primary source for the formulation of the idea be sought here? The earlier writings of the New Testament in particular include several texts that make a similar use of this image of begetting or birth to express the Christian experience of salvation. Thus 1 Peter 1:23 speaks of our "being born anew" (cf. 1:3). In 2:2 the readers are compared to "newborn infants" (*artigennēta brephē*). The same image is used in vv. 2f. for parenetic purposes. There are various other methaphors of the same type such as being begotten by the word of God or being begotten by God and being nourished with the milk of moral and religious instruction. The same salvation event always lies behind the differing language, namely, baptism.[156] To what extent James 1:18 comes from the same background remains an open question. But Titus 3:5 clearly alludes to it when it speaks of "washing" (NRSV marg.), and here it is designated by the term "regeneration," without exploiting the symbolism any further.

These various terms in the New Testament writings allow us to conclude that the early church adopted the analogy of begetting or birth for the saving event of baptism from quite early days, though without any hard and fast terminology. Preachers and writers were free to adopt their own similes for what it meant to become Christians through faith and the sacramental mysteries. In this broad, yet clearly focused field of imagery in the early Christian proclamation the author

---

me; / he who possessed me from the beginning. / For his riches begat me, / and the thought of his heart."

152. Cf. Clement of Alexandria, *Exc. ex Theod.* 78.2: Not only the bath (of baptism) redeems us, but also gnosis . . . ."

153. See Reitzenstein, *Hellenistische Mysterienreligionen,* 53ff.; Jonas, *Gnosis* 1:106ff., 202ff., 320ff.

154. Predestination in the Christian sense is something different; see Excursus 12 (at the end).

155. See Mussner, ZΩH, 123–26.

156. Cf. K. H. Schelkle, *Die Petrusbriefe. Der Judasbrief* (HTKNT 13.2; Freiburg im Breisgau, 1961) Excursus, pp. 28–31.

of 1 John has his own special place, with his own distinctive language about being born of God.

It is impossible to say with certainty where the early church derived its main incentive to use the analogies of begetting and birth for its sacrament of baptism. That originally the idea of the cleansing of sins was more conspicuously in the foreground can hardly be doubted (cf. 1 Cor. 6:11; Acts 2:38; 22:16; Heb. 10:22), particularly in view of the connection with John the Baptist. But the idea of Christian baptism involves the baptism of the Spirit (Mark 1:8 par.; Acts 1:5; 2:38; 11:16; 19:2ff.; etc.), and this must already have opened the door to further reflection. Moreover, the Johannine theology of baptism takes the action of the Holy Spirit as its focal point, basing this upon the words of Jesus to Nicodemus (John 3:3ff.). That these words are impossible in the mouth of the historical Jesus can only be seriously maintained by those who are skeptical of the entire Jesus tradition in the Fourth Gospel![157]

THIRD SECTION

THE RELIGIOUS AND MORAL TASK
OF THE PRESENT (1 JOHN 3:4-24)

The parenetic section which now begins is the longest of its type. It was heralded by "purify themselves" (3:3), and belongs essentially to Part Two. Alongside of the strengthening of faith (2:18–27) there is the moral admonition, culminating in the commandment of mutual love in 3:11ff. Side by side with the christological heresy, the moral poison in the attitude of the adversaries in the last hour is vigorously combated. True, there was a very direct challenge against moral indifference in Part One, under the rubric of fellowship with God (1:8ff.). Now the challenge is resumed with reference to Christ as the sinless Redeemer (3:5ff.), and the saving fact of our status as children of God (3:9f.). This time it is an even more powerful challenge. As the parenesis unfolds, we can recognize its connection with the previous section (3:5-8; cf. 2:28f.; 3:9–10; cf.3:1f.). The heretical teachers are not the object of such a strong attack as they were in the dogmatic section (2:22f.). But after v. 7a there can be no doubt that the focus here is on the real opponents and seducers and that the polemic is a very pointed one. Here we see the way Johannine thought develops in its distinctive mode. The sentences form a series of antitheses, following this pattern: first a negative admonition to avoid sin (vv. 4–10), then a positive admonition to practice mutual love (vv. 11–20). This pattern had already shaped the structure in 1:5-2:11.

1. The Avoidance of Sin (1 John 3:4-10)

[4]Everyone who commits sin is guilty of lawlessness: sin is lawlessness. [5]You know that he was revealed to take away sins, and in him there is no sin. [6]No one who abides

---

157. On being sons of God, see I. de la Potterie, "Naître de l'eau et naître de l'Esprit: Le texte baptismal de Jean 3,5," in I. de la Potterie and S. Lyonnet, *La vie selon l'Esprit* (Paris, 1965) 31–63; J. Gallot, *'Être né de Dieu': Jean 1, 13* (AnBib 37; Rome, 1979).

in him sins; no one who sins has either seen him or known him. ⁷Little children, let no one deceive you. Everyone who does what is right is righteous, just as he is righteous. ⁸Everyone who commits sin is a child of the devil; for the devil has been sinning from the beginning. The Son of God was revealed for this purpose, to destroy the works of the devil. ⁹Those who have been born of God do not sin, because God's seed abides in them; they cannot sin, because they have been born of God. ¹⁰The children of God and the children of the devil are revealed in this way; all who do not do what is right are not from God, nor are those who do not love their brothers and sisters.

This section, 3:4–10, is "one of the most thoughtful and most challenging" (Büchsel) in the entire epistle. It expounds the profound problem of the Christian and sin, refusing to compromise at all with the realities of sin. Not-being-allowed-to-sin is forced into not-being-able-to-sin (v. 9b). At the very outset it must be stated that the entire section is parenetic in character. It offers no theoretical discussion about the relation between the Christian state of salvation and the active powers of evil. The converse of this statement in positive terms, the concrete conclusion as it were, begins with the moral challenge or admonition that we should love one another (v. 11). Thus 3:11ff. also highlights the categorical statements in 3:4–10. Their purpose is to emphasize as much as possible the Christian renunciation of sin, which is characteristically theirs and which they are enabled to fulfill because they are born of God. This they can do both in theory and in practice. At the same time these verses are intended to distinguish between the children of God and the children of the devil, just as the true confession of Jesus in 2:22 separates the genuine Christian from the antichrist. But their purpose is not to teach the Christians that they are superior to sin or invulnerable to the power of evil. That is exactly the heretical teaching which their adversaries, with their false gnostic pride, are guilty of, the very thing which the author was combating in 1:8ff. There is no contradiction between 1:6 and 1:8, nor between 1:8ff. and 3:4ff. The only difference here is that the issue is pursued in a particular direction. The author is able to make a powerful appeal to the believers because they have been equipped with supernatural armor and have in Christ an exalted model.

a) Union with Christ Rules Out Sinful Behavior (3:4–8)

3:4 The polemic against sin begins with a twofold assertion, branding sin as "lawlessness." The drift here is not easy to grasp.

First: Who are the objects of the polemic? The heretical teachers or the believers who have not yet overcome sin? More likely the latter, since (1) the wording is different from 1:6ff.; 2:4ff.; and suggests that the author is quoting a slogan of the heretics; (2) the admonition to abide in Christ (v. 6) seems to be addressed to the believers like 2:27f.; and (3) v. 4 presents a general motif before going on to talk specifically of Christ (vv. 5–8) and of our being children of God (vv. 9–10). It would also be hard to understand what distinction the gnostics would find, given their indifference toward sin, between sin and lawlessness!¹⁵⁸

---

158. Wendt (*Johannesbriefe*, 60f.) assumes that the gnostics distinguished between *hamartia* =

If, however, this verse is directed against the believers, it assumes that they have a clear profile of what lawlessness means. If the sin in question is lawlessness, it must be abhorred. It is unlikely that the author is moving away "sharply from Antinomianism and radical Paulinism" (Windisch). Though he speaks continually of keeping the commandments (2:3, 4; 3:22, 24; 5:2), he never fights for a rehabilitation of the law. The crescendo from sin to lawlessness in 3:4 is all the more remarkable since the two terms are often used synonymously in the Bible.[159] We seem to be left with just two ways of explaining this. One springs from the ongoing development of the term "lawlessness" within Christianity. In the descriptions of the evil times preceding the parousia, the word "lawlessness" is used to brand the works of Satan in opposition to God. The antichrist is called the "lawless one" (2 Thess. 2:3, 8), while in Paul's opinion the "mystery of lawlessness" is already at work (2:7). According to the Freer ending of Mark, "this age of lawlessness" (NRSV marg.) is under the thrall of Satan. Again, in early postcanonical writings we find the same narrower eschatological idea of lawlessness.[160] We would therefore suggest that *anomia* should be translated as "evil" rather than "lawlessness." In the context of 1 John 3 this would make excellent sense. Perpetrators of sin declare that they are secret allies and colleagues of Satan. They submit to the power of Christ's adversary (vv. 7–8) and prove themselves to be genuine children of the devil (vv. 9–10). The eschatological perspective here closely follows the early Christian tradition — given what he has already said (2:18, 28). Alternatively, it is derived from the vocabulary of Hellenistic paganism, which forms the background of the readers. Given the vague idea of sin which prevailed in this intellectual milieu,[161] *anomia* suggests lawless, wicked behavior, which arouses more disgust than "sin." This view is strengthened to a degree by 5:17, where the author takes up the term *adikia,* a word that apparently gained currency in the life of the community and became synonymous with *hamartia* ("sin"; NRSV translates *adikia* by "wrongdoing"). The first suggestion is, however, to be preferred, and it has the support of other scholars too.[162] Above all, the Qumran texts support the theory that such a concept, enhanced in a dualistic and eschatological direction, was taken over by the early church from Judaism.[163] For

---

apostasy from the holy mysteries and *anomia* = transgression of the laws prescribed by the magistrate for human society.—There is no evidence to support this, and it is artificial. Also M. Goguel maintains that the passage is directed against heretics (*The Primitive Church* [New York, 1964]).

159. Cf. in LXX: Pss. 31:1 (= Rom. 4:7); 50:4; 58:4; 102:10; further Heb. 10:17; *1 Clem.* 8.3; 18.3, 5, 9; *Herm. Vis.* 2.2.2; *Sim.* 7.3; but also Epictetus, *Diss.* 2.16.44; 3.26.32; Philo, *Spec. leg.* 1.188. See also Dodd, *The Bible and the Greeks,* 79f.

160. *Did.* 16.4; *Barn.* 4.1; 14.5; 15.7; 18.2. According to the last passage, which occurs in the doctrine of the Two Ways (of light and darkness), the whole of the present aeon is a *kairos tēs anomias.* It would easily be possible for such a concept to have developed quite soon in the early church — perhaps under Jewish influence. Cf. also *2 Clem.* 20.2: *dyo autō hodoi prosetethēsan, nomou te kai anomias; Apoc. Pet.* 1.3.—Cf. Rigaux, *L'Antéchrist,* 257.

161. Cf. O. Hey, "ἁμαρτία," *Philol.* 83 (1927) 1–17, 137–63; G. Stählin and W. Grundmann, *TDNT* 1:296ff.

162. I. de la Potterie, " 'Le péché, c'est l'iniquité' (1 Joh III, 4)," *NRT* 78 (1956) 785–97 (with further supporting arguments); see also Nauck, *Tradition und Charakter,* 16 n. 1, who refers additionally to the fact that the LXX already translates *bly'l* with *anomia.*

163. See J. Becker, *Das Heil Gottes: Heils- und Sündenbegriffe in den Qumrantexten und im Neuen Testament* (Göttingen, 1964).

the latter had an abundant terminology for this purpose, denoting lawlessness, sinfulness, falsehood, rebellion against God, and similar behaviors. Of these, '*wl* and '*wlh* provide the closest equivalents. This much-used term (according to the Kuhn concordance) occurs about twenty-six times, denoting the reign of the evil one in the end-time, the spirits at work in it, and the human beings who have succumbed to its power (see 1QS 3:19, 21; 4:9, 17, 19; 5:2; etc.). But God "has ordained an end for falsehood, and at the time of visitation He will destroy it forever" (1QS 4:18f.). There is also a strong emphasis on the antithesis between falsehood and truth, the very core of the divine nature (see 1QS 3:19; 4:23; 6:15; 1QH 11:15f., 25f.). Noteworthy is the admonition: "O just men, put away iniquity" (1QH 1:36). The same idea lies behind 1 John 3:4. The crescendo in v. 4b, "sin is lawlessness," is not a definition, for there is no article with the predicate noun. It introduces not a general truth but a specific point, a well-known fact, in its way emphasized![164] The sin in question is one that the readers presumably knew about, one that they abhor as diabolical.

3:5 In contrast to this godless realm of sin and lawlessness, Christ leads us away from everything that hints of sin. The author reminds his readers next about the teaching familiar to them from a key phrase in the baptismal catechism:[165] Christ was revealed to take away sin (v. 5a). Then he goes on to present Christ as the model of perfect holiness. In Christ there is absolutely no sin (v. 5b). The present tense is significant. The author is no longer looking back on the earthly life of Christ as in v. 5a, but rather to his separation by nature from all sin ("sin" has no article: from everything that goes by the name of sin).[166] The sinlessness of Christ is here not the ground of our redemption, as in 2 Cor. 5:21 or 1 Pet. 3:18. Nor is it a general parenetic motif, as in 1 Pet. 2:21ff. Rather, it is a proof of the incompatibility between sin and the divine nature. The tacit consequence is this: Since therefore you are delivered from your sins by Christ (v. 5a), you should no longer have anything to do with sin (v. 5b). But at that point the author is reminded of the seducers (v. 7), so he shapes v. 6 to say that freedom from sin is the hallmark of those who are really in fellowship with Christ, and who have actually seen and know him![167]

Verse 5 also contains familiar and authentic Johannine insights. The incarnation is expressed in the same terms as in 1:2 and 3:8 by the phrase "was revealed." The purpose of Christ's coming is defined as "to take away sin." This turn of speech sounds like an echo of John 1:29, but there is no doubt that the latter passage alludes to Isa. 53:4, 11, 12 and that *airein* means "to take upon oneself, bear." Thus the context in 3:5 requires us to translate it "set aside, remove." Instead of the singular "*sin* of the world" (John 1:29 = the entire weight of sin), 1 John 3:5 has the plural "(our) sins,"[168] reminding the believers that they have been

---

164. BDF §273.1.

165. Cf. 1 Cor. 15:3; Heb. 1:3; 1 Pet. 3:18; Rev. 1:5.—Acts 22:16; Eph. 2:1ff.; Col. 2:13; Heb. 10:22.

166. Cf. the present *hilasmos estin* (2:2). It points to the permanent efficacy of Christ's redeeming work and his role as mediator.

167. See Stemberger, *La symbolique*, 198–205.

168. *Hēmōn* is missing from BAP 33 323 1739 al. h sy[h] sa bo arm Tert. Fulg., but is found in אC ᵏ Vg sy[p] pm. The shorter reading is the more probable one since there is no *hēmeis* in the context. This makes the emphasis on *hamartias* still stronger.

delivered from their sins. We already know from GJohn (8:46; cf. 14:31) that Christ is sinless ("in him there is no sin"). While v. 5a emphasizes the once-for-all character of redemption, v. 5b highlights the ontological difference.

3:6 Just as Christ is immune from sin, so it is with the Christian who is united with him. This is firmly asserted as a consequence of our fellowship with Christ — so convinced is the author of God's superiority over the power of the evil one (cf. 4:4; 5:3–5). But he also presumes — like Paul in Rom. 6:1–11 that Christians have renounced the power of sin and submitted to God in fellowship with Christ. This means that this verse is neither a purely soteriological statement, denoting the inability to sin, nor is it a piece of ethical parenesis, admonishing the believers to avoid all sin at all cost. "No one sins" is neither an *apodictic* statement ("cannot sin") nor is it a disguised imperative ("should not sin"). Rather, the categorical present tense is meant to suggest an observation and a rule. It is pointed indirectly against the gnostics with their disregard of the divine commandment. This comes out in the sequel. Those who sin lose their credibility as people who have "seen" Christ or "known" him, "To see" is a Johannine term for the experience of faith leading to fellowship![169] The perfect tense expresses the relevant connection. "Has known" is simply used for variation and is directed against their slogan with its claim to have "known" him (cf. 2:13a, 14b). The word *pas* ("all") emphasizes that this rule knows no exception. Those who claim fellowship with Christ on the ground of their gnosis, but feel no need to refrain from sin, fall under the judgment of this saying: Nobody who sins really has true union with Christ. Sin is an unmistakable sign of division. If we interpret this sentence to mean "we become sinless through our vision of Christ," we are turning the sentence on its head![170]

3:7 Here the author makes a fresh start by addressing his readers as "little children" as in 2:1, 12, 18, 28. He expresses his abhorrence of sin in even stronger terms. Once again he argues from our union with Christ, but this time pictures him in positive terms as an example for the righteous and godly who have turned their backs on sin completely. In doing so he links up with 2:29 and does so because of the pernicious views of his adversaries. He is warning his readers of the artful wiles employed by the heretical teachers. The danger is that our bond of faith with Christ and our living union with him will be loosened as a result (cf. 2:24, 27; 5:3f., 16, 20).

Only those who do what is right[171] can call themselves righteous, even as he, Christ, deserves without question to be called righteous, since he is completely free from sin (v. 5b; cf. 2:1). From this it would again appear that the heretical

---

169. Cf. John 6:36; 14:9; also in relation to God: 14:7, 9; 3 John 11. Physical sight (Windisch; cf. Büchsel) is ruled out because of the combination with *egnōken*. Moreover, it is altogether off the track to suggest that it is an experience any Christian can have.

170. *Contra* Windisch, who as a result reaches conclusions that are untenable (deliverance from sin is the consequence not of the atoning work of the Redeemer but of the "impression made by the sinlessness of his personality").

171. Action (*poiein*) is emphasized, as in 1:6 (*ou poioumen tēn alētheian*); cf. John 7:17; 13:17. It is not making a point about faith without works as in Jas. 1:25; 2:12ff.—Verse 7b is the opposite of *pas ho poiōn tē alētheian* in v. 4, just as vv. 7–8 in their entirety are a parallel development to vv. 4–6.

teachers claim to be righteous without feeling any obligation to prove that they are so by their deeds.[172]

3:8 In the antithesis the sinner is branded as belonging to the devil. In John 8:44 the devil is called a "murderer from the beginning" and the "father of lies." In this verse, as the context shows, it is stated in general terms that he has sinned from the beginning, A comparison with John 8:44 seems to show that by the word "beginning" the author has the story of paradise in mind. The beginning of creation is not what he is speaking about; there is no suggestion that the devil was God's antagonist in a dualistic sense. The counterpart here is Christ. The battle of Satan against the divine realm of holiness is staged within the framework of human history. At the beginning, and still today ("has been sinning"; present tense in Greek) he makes his foul stench of sin felt. We can hear the harsh judgment passed on the children of the devil. But not until v. 10, where we have the contrast "being born of God," is this motif completely developed.

Verse 8 is thus still staying with the theme of association with Christ, which excludes all sinful behavior, and in v. 8b the author pursues further the salvation-historical contrast between the devil and Christ (cf. 2:13, 14; 5:19f.). Whoever is one with Christ must know that he appeared on earth ("was revealed," as in v. 5 above) to destroy the works of the devil. The phrase "Son of God" may remind us of the temptation story (Matt. 4:3, 6; Luke 4:3, 9). But the author likes to use this title for Christ anyhow, and in speaking of "the works" he is hardly suggesting the temptation story, which was a battle of words. Rather, they are the sinful works of Satan![173] To destroy (Greek *lyein*)[174] the works of the devil means their radical annihilation, like "to take away" in v. 5. There it highlights the remorseless antithesis in nature and operation between the devil and the Son of God. Whoever takes the side of Christ must in consequence relinquish the devil and his works. Whoever sins and does the works of the devil is fighting against Christ. Despite the similarity to v. 5, the context shows that this verse looks beyond the redeeming death of Christ on the cross, beyond his victory in principle over the devil, toward the continuing battle against the works of the devil, a battle in which the believers are also involved. At the same time it forms an *inclusio* which rounds off the argument.

b) THE CHILDREN OF GOD CANNOT SIN (3:9-10)

3:9 From a new perspective, already adumbrated in v. 8, vv. 9-10 develop the impossibility for Christians to continue in sin. They have been born of God (cf. 2:29) and are therefore his children (3:1-2). Similarly, in v. 9 we are told categorically, as in v. 6, that everyone who is born of God does not sin, but then the author digs deeper. Christians have an ultimate ground of being. Their existence is supernatural, for God's seed abides in them. This metaphor of God's seed is

---

172. Yet this point is not necessarily contained in this, since to "commit sin" (v. 4) provides the occasion for the antithesis, "to do righteousness." Or the idea of Christ as the righteous One may have given rise to this motif.

173. See Noack *Satanas und Soteria,* 76f.

174. *Lyein* is a vivid metaphor suggested by tearing buildings down (John 2:19; Eph 2:19; often in profane literature). In its metaphorical sense it denotes complete abolition or destruction (so esp. of laws, Matt. 5:19; *to sabbaton,* John 5:18; 7:23; 10:35; and even *ton Iēsoun,* 1 John 4:3 *v.l.;* see ad loc.).

akin to "being born of God." But the analogy to human begetting is not strictly carried out as it is in 1 Pet. 1:23. This shows that the reality of salvation is more important in the author's mind than the analogy itself. Where it comes from is sufficiently indicated by the phrase "of God." The focus shifts to the abiding reality of the divine powers which manifest the nature of those who are born of God. "God's seed" can hardly mean anything other than the Holy Spirit (cf. 3:24; 4:13). This is similar to John 3:6, where the effect of being born from above or of water and the Spirit is designated as being "spirit." "Seed" is therefore a metaphor, similar to "anointing" in 2:20, 27. "Seed" is usually preferred for the word of God.[175] But in the present context it is used for the divine Spirit. The Christians' inability to sin is therefore regarded as a necessary consequence of this divine principle of light which they have had within themselves since they were baptized and were born of God. This is more than a mere moral inability to sin, as we find, for instance, in Stoicism.[176] It presupposes an ontological likeness, an idea already adumbrated in the Old Testament, with its promise of a new heart and a new spirit[177] forming part of the messianic hope.[178] The language of divine begetting and of the seed of God is, however, more reminiscent of gnostic terminology.[179] But it is only a linguistic echo; the ideas themselves are basically different (see Excursus 8).

The author is concerned to emphasize that to be a Christian means to be absolutely separated from the domain of sin. Lest this be misunderstood, he adds in v. 9b that those who are born of God have become unable to sin. We must be careful not to minimize the importance of this statement. At the same time, however, we must not forget what it presupposes. Alongside the supernatural act of divine begetting, the author takes for granted that the Christians abide in Christ (v. 6). This necessitates a fervent effort to cultivate faith and love, purity from sin, and holiness (cf. 2:6, 24, 28f.; 3:3, 7b, 16b). The divine principle of life in the human heart is not something magical. It never excuses us from moral endeavor, but calls and awakens us to it. Those who hate their brother or sister and "murder" them do not have the life of God abiding in them (3:15). The abiding of the seed of God in the human heart (v. 9a) requires for its growth the imperative, to live as God wills (4:16).

---

175. Matt. 13:3ff. par. 24ff.; (*spora*) 1 Pet. 1:23; cf. Jas. 1:18, 21. This interpretation is followed here and in 1 John 3:9 by Clement of Alexandria, Augustine, Bede, and many moderns including B. Weiss, Büchsel (in *Johannes und der hellenistische Synkretismus,* 59; otherwise ad loc.).

176. See Seneca, *Ep.* 72.6: sapiens recidere non potest, ne incidere quidem amplius; Plutarch, *De Stoic. repugn.* 2; Epictetus, *Diss.* 4.8.6. Similar assertions made by Philo (*Leg. all.* 3.68; *Fuga* 117) are influenced by Stoicism. Yet contrary assertions are also found; see Philo, *Fuga* 157f.; *Virt.* 177; Epictetus 4.12.19 also doubts immunity from error. See also S. Kubo, "I John 3:9: Absolute or Habitual?" *Andrews University Seminary Studies* 7 (1969) 47–56.

177. Jer. 24:7; 32:40; Ezek. 11:19; 36:26f.

178. *1 Enoch* 5:8f.; *Jub.* 5:12; *Pss. Sol.* 17:32; Volz, *Eschatologie,* 391; cf. now also 1QS 4:19–23; further 1QH 16:11ff. (on the ground that the Spirit has now been imparted).

179. Cf. the gnostic doctrine of the divine "seed" which dwells in the true gnostic and makes him/her a *physei pneumatikos* (Irenaeus, *Adv. Haer.* 1.1.11; Hippolytus, *Ref.* 5.8.112f.; Clement of Alexandria, *Exc. ex Theod.* 1, 2, 38, 40, 49, 53). This "spiritual seed" is the innermost kernel of the soul of the pneumatic person: ὕπνος δὲ Ἀδὰμ ἡ λήθη τῆς ψυχῆς ἡ συνεῖχε μὴ διαλυθῆναι τὸ σπέρμα τὸ πνευματικόν, ὅπερ ἐνέθηκεν τῇ ψυχῇ ὁ Σωτήρ (*Exc. ex Theod.* 2). See Reitzenstein, *Hellenistische Mysterienreligionen,* 245ff., 399; Dieterich, *Mithrasliturgie,* 121ff.; Dodd, *The Bible and the Greeks,* 75–77.

Mutual love is the response we owe unconditionally to God's love for us. Only so can God continue in fellowship with us (4:11f.). The divine begetting, which is the basis for our inability to sin (3:9), is not an isolated supernatural act of God. It has to be proved internally by a moral life as children of God. Only the act of God's grace and the shaping of our lives according to his will lead to what the author understands as our being the children of God in all its fullness. This is certainly an idealistic view, and it needs to be constantly corrected by seeing how Christians really behave in this world (cf. 2:1; 3:20; 5:17) — which may explain the forceful expression in v. 9. This author may appear at first sight to be contradicting himself, but there is a unity here in tension. For in John as in Paul sacrament and ethics are inextricably intertwined and conditioned by the state of salvation which Christians enjoy in this world. The language may be different, but the problem "Christians and sin" is pretty much the same for John as it was for Paul (see Excursus 12).

3:10 If to be born of God makes sin impossible, then sinning becomes a differentiating characteristic. If people do not practice righteousness,[180] it then becomes obvious ("revealed") that they are children of God![181] It is noticeable that the phrase "born of the devil" never occurs. Loyalty to the devil does not, like loyalty to God, rest on an event like the sacrament in which we are born of God. Rather, it grows out of what a person does and therefore has a purely moral character.[182] Also it is not unimportant that in v. 10b the author does not, as we might have expected after v. 9b, say "is not born of God." All he does say is that they "are not from God." This corresponds to "is from the devil" (NRSV "to be a child of the devil"). This is a weaker way of putting it, which lays more stress on the mode of origin. Again, we must not infer from v. 9a that to be a child of God is only moral in nature. This polemical verse is only intended to refer to the two contrasted groups in a highly suggestive way.

The division of people into righteous and ungodly is quite familiar. *Jubilees* 15:26ff. contrasts the uncircumcised children of perdition or sons of Beliar (v. 33) with the children of the covenant which God made with Abraham. In the *Apocalypse of Abraham* 13f. an unclean bird, Azazel (=godlessness), tempts Abraham, but the angel of God drives the bird away and says to him, "for you have selected here [the earth], (and) become enamored of the dwelling place of your blemish. Therefore the Eternal Ruler, the Mighty One, has given you a

---

180. Many Latins, including the Vg apart from codices DZ, viz., Tert., Cypr., Luc., Aug., Ps.-Aug. (*Speculum*), further the Greek codices Ψ, sy hmg sa Orig., read instead of this *ho mē ōn dikaios*. Almost all of the Greek manuscripts, and also the Old Latin manuscripts h and q, have the contrary reading. The former reading is especially favored by Harnack *SB* (Berlin, 1915) 465f. The argument, which is confined to internal evidence, is not convincing since the author of 1 John bases the status of being children of the devil on the *doing* of evil.

181. *En toutǭ* stands in the middle here in such a way as to point both backwards and forwards (cf. Windisch); the dependent phrase contains a double point: *tekna tou theou tekna* and *tou diabolou*, the first covered by v. 9, the second by v. 10b.

182. In John 8:41ff. being children of the devil is derived positively from the sinful desires of the defendants. This moral deviation is here contrasted with physical descent from Abraham, to which their partners in the dialogue appeal.

dwelling on earth. Through you the all-evil spirit (is) a liar, and through you (are) wrath and trials on the generations of men who live impiously" (13:8–9). According to the *Testament of Dan* (4:7) either God or Beliar can rule over people's souls, and according to 5:1 God or Beliar can inhabit them. The devil, who appears in late Judaism under various names as God's counterpart, though in strict subordination to him,[183] created a following among men and women, superior in numbers and political power over the elect, those faithful to God in this world, more often the devout Jews[184] Not a few of these writings stem from circles close to the Essenes and the Qumran sect. In the Dead Sea Scrolls the contrast between the children of God and the children of the devil is stronger than anywhere else. Despite this, the term "sons of God" is avoided for those who belong to God, and not a single instance of it has been found to date. At the same time their opposites, those who act against God, are marked only by their having succumbed to the realm of sin and evil, to Belial and his hosts but not for having been born of the devil. The Qumraners call themselves "the elect," "the sons of light," "the people of God." They clearly distinguish themselves from the sons of darkness, from those who belong to Belial[185] They express this by separating from them and shunning them. Their religious and ethical dualism is reminiscent of the way John contrasts the children of God and the children of the devil. The author of 1 John seems to have been not uninfluenced by these Jewish ideas. The example adduced from the Old Testament which soon follows (Cain, v. 12), also supports this possibility. Under the lodestar of divine begetting, the Johannine language acquired greater precision and force. The final phrase, "and those who do not love . . . ," states in concrete terms in what for the author the faithlessness of the children of the devil and the loyalty of the children of God consist. It is clearly a transition to the following section, which explicitly deals with the theme of mutual love.

2. The Practice of Mutual Love (1 John 3:11–20)

[11]For this is the message you have heard from the beginning, that we should love one another. [12]We must not be like Cain who was from the evil one and murdered his brother. And why did he murder him? Because his own deeds were evil and his brother's righteous. [13]Do not be astonished, brothers and sisters, that the world hates you. [14]We know that we have passed from death to life because we love one another. Whoever does not love abides in death. [15]All who hate a brother or sister are murderers, and you know that murderers do not have eternal life abiding in them. [16]We know love by this, that he laid down his life for us — and we ought to lay down our lives for one another. [17]How does God's love abide in anyone who has the world's goods and sees a brother or sister in need and yet refuses help?

---

183. See Bousset-Gressmann, *Religion des Judentums,* 332ff.; Volz, *Eschatologie,* 85f., 286f.; Bonsirven, *Judaïsme* 1:244ff.

184. See especially Wis. 2:23f.; *Jub.* 10:8ff.; 11:5; 19:28; *Apoc. Abr.* 13:7ff.; 14:5ff.; 21:2; 22:6; *Testament of the Twelve Patriarchs* passim, esp. *T. Rub.* 4:11; *T. Sim.* 5:3; *T. Levi* 19:1; *T. Iss.* 6:1; 7:7; *T. Naph.* 2:6; 3:1; *T. Ash.* 1:8; 3:2; *T. Jos.* 20:2; *T. Benj.* 3:3f.; 7:1; *1 Enoch* 8; 53ff.; 69.

185. See Excursus 6.

[18]Little children, let us love, not in word or speech, but in truth and action. [19]And by this we will know that we are from the truth and will reassure our hearts before him [20]whenever our hearts condemn us; for God is greater than our hearts, and he knows everything.

Already in Part One the commandment of mutual love (2:7–11) gave concrete shape to the general requirement that we should keep God's commandment (2:3–6). In a similar way the practice of righteousness (3:4–10) is now given specific application and is illustrated in connection with mutual love. The clearest and most awesome instance of sin, which lays bare what the world is like when alienated from God, is the hatred that leads to murder. At the same time, vv. 16–18 show how in practice the author thinks of moral behavior as a proof of our true nature (vv. 7–8, 9–10). The un-gnostic character of his message or the transmutation of gnostic ideas into Christian ones, is nowhere expressed so powerfully. The author lived in an age when the attractions of gnosticism were very strong, but he has robbed this temptress of all her sweet and dangerous venom. This section is a masterpiece, dealing with the meaning, character, and rewards of practical Christian love.

a) The Message of Mutual Love,
   as the Story of Cain and Abel Shows,
   Reveals the Good and Evil in Humankind (3:11–12)

3:11 This verse begins with the same phrase as 1:5, except for the conjunction *hoti* (NRSV "for"), which links up with the final word of v. 10 but introduces a main clause.[186] The author begins his theme (which was so important to him) with a certain emphatic solemnity. The word "message"[187] takes on the meaning of "commandment," because of the *hoti*–clause. The author regards the commandments as the essential message of Christ, just as conversely faith in the name of Christ appears as a commandment (3:23). As earlier, in 2:7, he adds the further point that the readers have heard this from the very beginning of their acquaintance with Christianity. To neglect this message would be a dangerous innovation. "To love one another"[188] is the same as "to love brother or sister (or several brothers or sisters)" (vv. 10b, 14, 16b, 17). This is not to restrict the universal love of neighbor to a cliquish mutual love, as might be inferred from vv. 13–15, where the world's hatred is directed against those whom they should regard as their own brothers and sisters ("all who hate brother or sister," v. 15). Thus their murder of others (in the context, the Christians) becomes fratricide, like Cain's murder of Abel (v. 12). Conversely, Christians will not cease to love when

---

186. *Hoti*=for, BDF §456.1; BAG 594, s.v. 3, b.

187. Since *angelia* also gives a good sense it is not necessary to adopt the reading *epangelia* (אCP Ψ 1739 al. sy[h] sa[codd] bo Did. Luc; the same manuscripts have in part the same reading in 1:5). In the New Testament *epangellia* never means commandment, which is probably the usual meaning in profane Greek; cf. Polybius 9.38.2 and Liddell-Scott, 602, s.f. 2, where evidence is given for a juristic use of the word.

188. For rabbinic parallels, see Schlatter, *Johannes*, 289, on John 13:34.

confronted with a hostile world![189] "John has in mind the *Christian* brothers and sisters. But this does not exclude others, it includes them" (Büchsel).

3:12 As a horrendous example—the only Old Testament allusion in 1 John— the author recalls Cain's murder of his brother. With the same formula, *ou kathōs* ("not like"), John 6:58 introduces another parallel from the Old Testament, the story of the manna. The author has embroidered the story in the light of its background. First he says that the murderer was "from the evil one." As elsewhere in 1 John (2:13, 14; 5:18, and perhaps 19 also) the adjective *ponēros* should be taken as a masculine and seems to point to 3:8, "of the devil." This makes Cain the representative of the devil's children![190] Cain's satanic origin and behavior are brought out—a second emphasis in John, and a special one—in his "murder" (*esphaxen*) of his brother. This crass expression[191] may be suggested by the brutal killing of Christians in the earliest persecutions under Domitian (cf. Revelation). Be that as it may, he thus recognizes the true face of the "world" (v. 13) and the hate-filled scowl on the face of the old enemy of God, the "evil one." This interpretation of Cain's deed as the work of the devil in a human act is in agreement with the judgment passed on Judas in GJohn (cf. 13:2, 27).

The author asks why Cain committed this wicked act. His answer is: "Because his own deeds were evil." This is the same reason GJohn gives for unbelief (3:19) and hatred (7:7) toward Jesus. The author goes on to add: "And his brother's (works) were righteous." He is not offering a psychological explanation for what Cain did (cf. Büchsel). Rather, he is reflecting on the objective basis for his act, the first murder. It was because of his moral defects—the third comment on the Old Testament story—that Cain resorted to this crime, which opened up a chasm between him and his righteous brother Abel![192] This brief Christian midrash[193] is a continuation of the remarks about the children of God and the children of the devil. It shows that sinfulness is not only the symptom ("revealed," v. 10) but also the root of their status as children of the devil.

---

189. See Justin, *Dial.* 96.2: *hois* (the Gentiles) *hēmeis hapasi legomen hoti Adelphoi hēmōn este;* Tertullian, *Apol.* 39.8: Fratres autem etiam vestri sumus iure naturae matris unius, etsi vos parum homines, quia mali fratres.

190. There is at least one late Jewish parallel to this, viz., *Apoc. Abr.* 24:5: "Cain, who had been led by the adversary to break the law."

191. Cf. Judg. 12:6; 1 Sam. 15:33; 1 Macc. 1:2; etc.; Rev. 6:4, 9; 18:24. The sacrificial term *sphattein* (cf. Gen. 22:10; Lev. 1:5, 11; etc.; Rev. 5:6, 9, 12; 13:8) does not occur here.

192. This predicate is applied to Abel in Matt. 23:35; Heb. 11:4 in common with late Jewish tradition (it does not yet appear in Gen. 4:3ff.—*contra* Chaine); see K. G. Kuhn, *TDNT* 1:6ff. The Mandean figure Hebel-Zīwā has quite different traits: *contra* Lohmeyer (*ZNW* 27 [1928] 242 n. 2) he is the envoy from heaven.

193. Jewish interpretation makes Cain among other things a model of unbelief (see *Tg. Ps.-Jon.* on Gen. 4:7), of the rebel against God (Philo, *Post.* 38f.; *Migr.* 74f.), of the egoist and a man of greed (Philo, *Deter.* 78; Josephus, *Antiquities* 1.60f.). Early Christian exegesis may well have drawn from this rich tradition of interpretation in accordance with its needs (see Heb. 11:4; Jude 11). The nearest parallel is *T. Benj.* 7:5, where Cain is a model of envy and fratricidal hatred.

b) The Nature and Effect of Hatred: It is Equivalent to Murder and Deprives Its Perpetrators of Eternal Life (3:13-15)

3:13 The paradigm of Cain and Abel influences the following verses, especially v. 15. But it is developed entirely from a Christian point of view and independently of the paradigm and the author expatiates on the nature of hatred and love.[194] As an aside, he glances at the old story in the Bible, treating Cain as a type of hatred. One can hardly say that in v. 13 the author is comparing the fate of his readers with Abel, for in v. 14 Christians attained to life, the opposite of what Abel did. Rather, the author seeks to show that hatred belongs to the very nature of the cosmos and leads to eternal death. Hatred, as it already reared its head in Cain and drove him to commit murder, is a characteristic of the world at enmity with God. Hence the readers, whom the author appropriately addresses as brothers and sisters (the only time in 1 John) should not be surprised when they incur hatred. *Kosmos* ("world") is used differently here from 2:15. It means the unbelieving human race at enmity with God, which first vented its rejection and persecution on God's emissary and then, as Jesus predicted in GJohn, did the same to his disciples (John 15:18f.; 17:14). The thought, though not developed any further here, clearly points back to GJohn.

3:14 Verse 14 develops the contrast between the world alienated from God and the Christian community ("we"). This is done not to provide the reason for the world's hatred, as in John 15:19; 17:14, but to show where this sort of hatred leads. This picture of the community, which has attained to the realm of divine life, serves to highlight what hatred leads to. As far as the Christians are concerned (the "we" is emphatic), they belong to the realm of God, whereas those who hate are still under the power of death. The clause beginning "because . . . " in v. 14a gives the reason (as in 3:2) for their knowledge. Otherwise it would suggest that one can attain to life through love, an idea not found in John. The path to the divine life leads through faith and being born of God in baptism (cf. John 1:12f.; 3:15f.; 5:24; etc.). Love is the sign that we know those who are born of God (1 John 3:10; 4:7). *Oidamen* ("we know") is stronger than *ginōskomen*. We live in the knowledge that we possess the divine life (cf. 5:13). The symbol of moving from one house or area into another[195] involves the sharpest possible distinction between death and life. The perfect "we have power" expresses the finality of this transition. The present actuality of the divorce between the world and the believers is expressed by the present tense "we love" and the plural "the brothers" (so Greek; NRSV "one another"). This points concretely to each individual believer (cf.

---

194. Lohmeyer's attempt (*ZNW* 27 [1928] 242ff.) to interpret the whole section 3:11-24 using this as a foil is not convincing.

195. Cf. Luke 10:7; John 13:1; *Mart. Pol.* 6.1; J. H. Moulton and G. Milligan, *The Vocabulary of the Greek New Testament,* rev. H. Moulton (London, 1978) 401, s.v. (citing *P. Tebt.* 2.316, 21; Dittenberger, *Or. inscr.* 458.7. Cf. BAGD 511, s.v.; J. Schneider, *TDNT* 1:520.

3 John 5). Elsewhere 1 John always uses the collective singular.[196] The curse of those who do not love consists in being imprisoned ("abides") in the realm of death. Whatever else they may claim (cf. v. 6b), they basically deceive themselves about their state of salvation. They are like unbelievers, and the wrath of God remains upon their disobedience (John 3:36). God has not accepted them into his realm of life and salvation![197]

3:15 A further consideration leads to the same conclusion. Those who hate are excluded from the life of God. They commit one of the most dreadful sins, for hatred is equivalent to murder. The expression "murderer" reminds every reader of Cain, who was mentioned a little earlier, the one who killed his brother (v. 12). There is no reference here to Satan (John 8:44; so Chaine), who, according to v. 12 apparently stood behind the deed of Cain. The author would hardly have wanted to say of those who hate God and their fellow human beings: "who hates his brother or sisters." With an eye on Cain the author now concludes that all who hate are guilty of murder—which reminds us of the judgment of Jesus in the Sermon on the Mount (Matt. 5:21f.)[198] The same idea is also found more than once in late Judaism—for example, in the fine word in *T. Gad* 4:6f.: "Just as love wants to bring the dead back to life and to recall those under sentence of death, so hate wants to kill the living and does not wish to preserve alive those who have committed the slightest sin. For among all men the spirit of hatred works by Satan through human frailty for the death of mankind; but the spirit of love works by the Law of God through forbearance for the salvation of mankind."[199] For the author of 1 John this idea is presupposed in the conclusion of v. 15. The ancient principle that the murderer forfeits his (physical) life (Gen. 9:6) is here applied to the spiritual, supernatural life.[200] The predicative sense of "abiding" should therefore not be pressed. In the author's opinion those who are guilty of hatred are totally devoid of eternal or divine life (note the absence of the article with the word "life"). They remain in the realm of death (v. 14b). But in focusing on those who lose the divine life as a result of their hatred, he can hardly be thinking of his readers, for that would not be compatible with v. 14. Rather, as "all" (*pas*), which elsewhere invariably refers to the heretical teachers, shows he must be thinking of the opponents.

---

196. The addition of *hēmōn* in a few manuscripts is of no consequence. On the other hand, the addition *ton adelphon* (+*autou*) (CP ᵏ pm. sy sa) in v. 14b emphasizes the specific nuance of the preceding plural. However, it is too weakly attested compared with BℵA 33 323 1739 al. h q Vg bo arm Did Luc. Aug., and it weakens the absolute claim of the assertion.

197. On this idea, see Mussner, ZΩH, 96–98.

198. The material connection consists in the fact that the intention begind the external deed is just as important. However, the point of Jesus' saying according to 5:20 (*perisseusē*), to say nothing of its content (anger, abuse) is somewhat different.

199. See further the rabbinic sayings in Billerbeck, *Kommentar* 1:365, 367.

200. The author evidently wanted to adduce a general proposition: "You know that murderers do not have eternal life abiding in them," but immediately he goes on to apply it to the supernatural, divine life. The same easy transition from natural to supernatural or eternal life occurs in John 11:25f.; cf. 5:24–29.

c) The Nature of Mutual Love: It Is Expressed
by Following the Example of Christ in Action (3:16–18)

3:16 After this horrifying glimpse into the abyss of hatred, the author proceeds to give us his positive assessment of the nature of love and how it operates. The standard for this is set by the example of the Son of God. Jesus' surrender of his life for us[201] provides the best illustration of the nature of genuine love (*tēn agapēn*).[202] Christ, who has not been mentioned for some time (vv. 7f.) is re-introduced with the pronoun *ekeinos* (NRSV "he"). His example shows that genuine love is expressed in deed as well as in an extraordinary measure. The degree to which life is surrendered acquires a special significance when contrasted with Cain. Those who hate deprive others of life. Those who love sacrifice their lives for others. The wording here points clearly to the sayings about the Good Shepherd (John 10:11b, 15b, 17, 18). This being so, *hyper hēmōn* (NRSV "for us") should be translated "in favor of us," "for our good" (cf. John 10:11b, 15b). But since the completion of Christ's deed of love the Christian community is aware that the surrender of life by the Son of God is a representative sacrifice for themselves and for the sins of the whole world (1 John 2:2; 4:10, 14; cf. John 6:51; 17:19 — sacrificial language). Alongside of the shepherd imagery, we have the saying about Christ's supreme service to his friends in John 15:13, which serves as a foil for 1 John 3:16a.

The style of the phrase "we ought" (Greek *opheilomen*) is curious.[203] But it makes the point that the love Jesus showed to his disciples in deed provides a pattern for mutual Christian love. This is a challenge which Jesus never explicitly uttered, but the author deduces it from Jesus' command that we should love one another "as I have loved you" (John 15:12; cf. 13:34).

3:17 The author places all his emphasis on the deed of love. For this reason he goes on to cite a second example which points up the possibility of such a deed of love in the concrete circumstances of his community. The laying down of one's life remains an exception. But the distribution of one's earthly goods to the needy brothers and sisters is often adduced as a compelling imperative for Christians. *Bios* ("life"; NRSV "goods") means here as in 2:16 (and Mark 12:44=Luke 21:4; Luke 15:12, 30) "livelihood," "possessions." "This world's" is presumably added to indicate its temporary nature, as in 2:16f.[204] The parable of the Good Samaritan (Luke 10:30–37), which also describes instant practical help, seeks primarily to draw attention to the object which demands our loving aid. It is every person in need whom we encounter, even if that person is a stranger

---

201. John regularly says *tēn psychēn theinai* (on the other hand Mark 10:45=Matt. 20:28 says *tēn psychēn dounai*), although the corresponding rabbinic word is *nāthan;* see Schlatter, *Sprache,* 103. As regards the image of the shepherd in John 10:11, 15, Bultmann asserts that the meaning "to stake one's life" is appropriate (*John,* 370 n. 5). In 1 John 3:16 a literal laying down of life is implied, as in John 10:17, 18; 13:37f.; 15:13. Cf. already F. Spitta, *ZNT* 10 (1909) 78.

202. Thus, not as in h Vg *caritatem Dei* but to denote its nature in an absolute sense.

203. See on 2:6 (further 4:11; 3 John 8); it also occurs in GJohn, viz., in the paradigm of the foot-washing, 13:14.

204. Rabbinic parallels will be found in Schlatter, *Sprache,* 149.

or an enemy of our people. In 1 John 3:17 we have a discussion of mutual love. This should not be regarded as a narrowing of the love commandment. All that is changed is the orientation.

As an incentive for the deed of love, the author plays on our emotions of sympathy and compassion (*splanchna*)[205] and regards it as a terrible crime when people refuse to help the needy. This epistle has very little interest in psychological processes per se, though it does not ignore them completely.[206] When the strings of compassion are regarded not in purely human terms but as divine impulses in the human being, the final question becomes more readily intelligible. Tacked on as an *anakolouthon* it denies in the form of a meditative question that the *agapē* of God dwells in those who refuse to help a brother or sister in need. The genitive "of God" is a genitive of quality.[207] It is the equivalent of the adjective *theios* ("divine"), otherwise unusual in the New Testament. The divine life-style of love expresses itself in human beings as a love for God and for brothers and sisters. In a heart that suppresses the emotions of charity, the essential characteristic of the divine nature cannot survive. "Those who practice love have the love of God immanent in their hearts as a living power and a principle of action" (Bonsirven).

The imperative requiring Christians to distribute to the needy from their own bounty persists in early Christianity following the stringent admonition of Jesus (Luke 6:38; 12:33; Mark 10:21; etc.), even after its heroic expression in the earliest community in Jerusalem (Acts 2:44f.; 4:32). This can be seen from James 2:15f. as well as in 1 John 3:17. In this way[208] almsgiving, which had been practiced in Judaism as the preeminent work of righteousness under the law (cf. Acts 3:2ff.), was internalized (Matt. 6:2ff.) and radicalized in the sense of unconditional discipleship to Jesus (Mark 10:21 par.). Almsgiving also played an important part in the life of the Mandeans.[209] *Ginza* 188.31ff. is very similar to 1 John 3:17 when it says "those who drive the poor and needy from their doorstep and refuse to give them alms" cannot ascend to the light. *Ginza* 284.5f. shows that this is not only meant as an external exercise. For alongside of "belief in the powerful, primary life" there is a demand for sympathy and compassion for the needy. According to the Mandean *Book of John* 101.24, almsgiving is more important than wife and child. At the same time, however, there was a high standard of

---

205. To be derived from Old Testament usage; cf. Gen. 43:30; Jer. 31:20; Prov. 12:10; Sir. 30:7; in the New Testament cf. Luke 1:78; Col. 3:12; Phil. 2:1; similar expressions Deut. 15:7; Jas. 2:15f.; *T. Zeb.* 7:2–4; 8:1–3. See P. Dhorme, "L'emploi metaphorique des noms de parties du corps en Hébreu et en Akkadien: Les entrailles," *RB* 31 (1922) 514–17.

206. See 3:19f.; 4:17f.

207. *Theios* occurs only in Acts 17:29; 2 Pet. 1:3, 4, evidently under Hellenistic influence.— It is instructive to compare *T. Gad* 5:2; *Hopōs ezōsēte to misos to diabolikon kai kollēthēte tē agapē tou theou*. Most exegetes opt for an objective genitive. Büchsel, however, takes it as a subjective genitive. But his argument that in the context as a whole there is nothing about the love of God fits his explanation. Bonsirven interprets it much as we have done in the text.

208. See Matt. 6:2ff.; Mark 12:41ff.; 14:5; Acts 10:2; 24:17; Billerbeck, *Kommentar* 4:551ff.

209. See the indexes in M. Lidzbarski.

care for the poor, as, for example, in the community of the new covenant in Damascus.[210]

3:18 Repeating his affectionate address, "Little children" (cf. 2:1), and with a forceful admonition (cf. 2:28), the author brings his argument to a conclusion. In doing so he sums up from his exposition what love really is (v. 16). It means selfless service to the uttermost for the brothers and sisters (ibid.). It is fulfilled in deed, particularly in the sharing of one's own goods (v. 17). Warning them of merely using specious words, the author is apparently hitting out at the gnostics, with their readiness of tongue (cf. 2:4, 6, 9) and failure to act in the spirit of love. The phrase "in truth"[211] strengthens "in . . . action" and corresponds to the double formula in v. 18a. There is a parallel to this forceful saying in James 1:25; 2:12, 15–17, and also *T. Gad* 6:1 "Love one another in deed and word and inward thoughts." The un-gnostic character of Johannine Christianity is brought out clearly in this verse as well as its mysticism—if that is the right word for his striving for fellowship with God.

d) A Fruit of Mutual Love:
   It Gives Us a Peace of Heart in the Sight of God (3:19–20)

3:19–20 Looking back ("by this")[212] to his description of mutual love, the author promises that those who practice it will be rewarded ("we will"—future tense).[213] It will be a token that they are "from the truth." Compared with the phrase "in truth" (v. 18), this turn of speech has a deeper meaning. As in John 18:37, it suggests an origin from the divine sphere (cf. John 8:47), our belonging to God. Therefore it is intended to assure those who practice love of air fellowship with God (cf. 3:14). If because of our weakness and inclination to sin our hearts condemn us, God, who knows everything, will reassure us. God is greater than our hearts, greater than our consciences when they condemn us.[214] He will also remember our deeds of love.

In this broad outline what follows seems clear enough. But in particular the long sentence is a *crux interpretum,* and many exegetes think it cannot be explained without assuming that there has been a corruption in the text.[215] However, we

---

210. See CD 14:14–16. See also H. Bolkestein, *Wohltätigkeit und Armenpflege im vorchristlichen Altertum* (Utrecht, 1939).

211. See H. Preisker in the appendix to Windisch's commentary, p. 166.

212. *En toutō* does not always point to what follows; it clearly points to what precedes in John 16:30; 1 John 2:5b; on 3:10, see ad loc.; see also *ek toutou*, 4:6.

213. The reading *ginōskomen* (ℵ al. Vg Aug.) is probably an assimilation to the usual formula (2:3, 5, 18; 3:24; 4:2, 13; 5:2). At the same time, the future may be an attempt to make it agree with *peisomen.* This logical future makes little difference to the meaning: "that puts us into the position to recognize it" (Belser).

214. The Stoic terms *syneidēsis, physis, kathēkon,* and others occur nowhere in John; he confines himself to Jewish-Christian modes of expression. For the conscience pronouncing a sentence of condemnation, see esp. *T. Gad* 5:3. The righteous and humble shrink from behaving unjustly, *ouch hyp' allou kataginōskomenos, all' hypo tēs idias kardias.*

must try to make sense of the best-attested text. The grammatical construction also poses a related problem.

Here we have to make a decision between two interpretations that have been carefully developed:

1. The first interpretation understands *peisomen* (NRSV "will reassure") to mean "persuade," "convince" and makes the *hoti*-clause dependent on that verb. But a difficulty at once arises. In the best manuscripts *hoti* occurs twice, once before *ean* and again before *meizōn*. Since the omission of the second *hoti* in some manuscripts[216] is obviously a later simplification, it is undoubtedly original. But in practice it has to be disregarded, a procedure followed by the Vulgate and most other versions (except sy).

2. The other interpretation takes *peisomen* to mean "quieten" and provides a good deal of supporting evidence in its favor.[217] It goes on to combine with this the phrase *hoti ean,* taking the first *ho ti* as the neuter of *hostis* and *ean* as equivalent to *an,* as frequently happens in Koine.[218] It will then mean "we quieten our hearts (in respect to all) that they accuse us of." The second *hoti*-clause is then taken in the ordinary causal sense.

The undeniable difficulty of the first interpretation is the repetition of the *hoti,* for which there is no other example in the Johannine literature. On the contrary, the author does not feel it necessary to repeat the *hoti* in similar cases where he uses *hoti ean* (3:2; 5:14).[219] We therefore follow the second interpretation, taking *ho ti ean (an)* as a generalizing relative clause with a conditional character.

Does this form of the text yield a satisfactory meaning? Our spiritual situation would then be as follows: we recognize from love in deed that the divine nature we believe ourselves to possess is no illusion. Even though our conscience is repeatedly troubled by its accusations,[220] we can and will quieten it in the presence of God.[221] When we go beyond what our hearts tell us, we are encouraged to do so by the assurance that God is greater than our hearts and "knows everything."[222]

---

215. Holtzmann, Windisch, BAGD 639, s.v. *peithein* 1, d; cf. Bultmann, *Theology* 2:88 n. *.
216. A 33 218 436 642 808 h q Vg bo arm Aug.
217. See 2 Macc. 4:45; Matt. 28:14; Xenophon, *Hell.* 1.7.7. *Anab.* 3.1.26; *Mart. Pol.* 10.2; BAGD 639, s.v. 1, d. See also the meaning "to corrupt" (ibid.).
218. BDF §107 (further examples in appendix); Radermacher, *Grammatik,* 203f.—So the majority of exegetes (except Camerlynck; Büchsel); the double accusative after *peithein* is classical (cf. Chaine).
219. Büchsel raises objections against the second interpretation, although there are no grammatical reasons against it. He thinks it destroys the parallelism between the two hypothetical clauses in v. 20 and v. 21. But there is no antithesis here (cf. the explanation in the text), unless everything after the second *hoti* is taken *in sensu malo* (see further below).
220. *Hēmōn* is, as its position shows, dependent on *kataginōskē*.
221. *Emprosthen,* which in Koine increasingly replaces *pro* (Mayser, *Grammatik,* II, 2:539), originally had a strict local sense, "in front of," but, like *enōpion,* and similar to the Hebrew *lipnê,* acquired a metaphorical sense, "in the eyes of" (BDF §214.6). On the theological implication of the phrase "in the eyes of Yahweh," see F. Nötscher, *Das Angesicht Gottes schauen,* 98ff. If the preferred meaning of *emprosthen* describes standing before the judge, it is not always so; cf. Matt. 11:26; 18:14; Acts 10:4; 1 Thess. 1:3; 3:9; *T. Iss.* 3:2. The nonforensic sense is required in 1 John 3:19 (cf. BAGD 257, s.v. 2, b). The *present* sentence of condemnation by the heart is silenced by a glance at the God of grace, who is greater. The future *peisomen* is determined by the conditional nature of the sentence.
222. This *ginōskei* (instead of *oiden*), which is probably the counterpart of *kataginōskei* linguistically, has an entirely different resonance: God understands, grasps, is acquainted with, all things, he is the One who knows the heart; cf. BAGD 161, s.v. 6.

That "God is greater than our hearts" is one of the major theological statements in 1 John, the good news of the God of grace and love (cf. 3:1; 4:9f., 16). Every attempt to understand this statement, asserting as it does the terrifying greatness and judicial strictness of God,[223] introduces an uncharacteristic trend into the epistle, concerned as it is to heighten the Christian's consciousness of salvation (2:25; 3:14; 5:13, 19, 20). For the epistle seeks to overcome our discouragement and fear (2:12-14; 4:18). Its aim is to inspire us with confidence in the victory over the destructive power of evil (2:13f.; 4:4; 5:4). This *"Deus semper maior"* knows everything. This is the same thing Peter said to the risen Lord when his confidence was shattered by his guilt (John 21:17). The word "everything" (*panta*) is selected from the broad perspective of this exalted theological position, and the statement is deliberately framed in general terms. When Christians are condemned by their conscience, they not only recall that God knows their deeds of love; they hurl themselves into the ocean of the infinite understanding and mercy of God. This gives these reflections a certain finality and climax, toward which the phrase "before him" right at the beginning of the passage was tending.

Only so can we understand the surprising leap the author takes to the opposite conditional clause in v. 21. This clause is not antithetical to the phrase "if our hearts condemn us" in v. 20, for the ensuing clauses introduce a mainly positive statement about our relationship with God. The new address calls attention to a brief pause in the flow of the thought. Since the heart, when it condemns us, is quietened when we look to God, there is nothing threatening in itself even in that case. Rather, the author takes for granted that our hearts do not accuse us. The thought is expressed not very skillfully in a conditional clause with *ean,* which serves as a bridge to what follows. A certain awkwardness remains, but it does not warrant our seeing here a seam between two different sources.[224]

This verse does not exactly support the Lutheran fideistic interpretation, which clings despite our continuing sinfulness to the grace and forgiveness of God. Rather, it expresses only the deep conviction of all truly religious people that God's wisdom and love are always greater than the human heart when it threatens to break down in fear and trembling. We cannot see whether we have really sinned or whether we only have an exaggerated feeling of guilt. If we put such questions to the text, they only cloud the core of the matter: genuine, practical Christian love is free from all such needs. When we are in fellowship with God, we are assured that he "knows everything."[225]

---

223. This explanation is maintained by Augustine (*PL* 35:2019-21), Bede (*PL* 93:104), and Oecumenius (*PG* 119:657). Its full force was acquired only with Calvin. More recently it has again been put forward by G. Wohlenberg, *Neue kirchliche Zeitschrift* 13 (1902) 632-35. For the controversy, esp. with Calvin, see Büchsel ad loc., on the history of interpretation Wohlenberg, 640-45.

224. The relevant observations by Bultmann ("Analyse," 150f.) have been dealt with by H. W. Beyer in a review, *TLZ* 54 (1929) 611f.; the homiletical parenesis (v. 21) allegedly fails to penetrate the profundity of the *Vorlage.* This solution is upheld even more decidedly by H. Preisker in the appendix to Windisch's commentary, pp. 167, 169. In John 3:19f. we have, he says, "an eschatological word of revelation which speaks about the overcoming of the fear of a guilty conscience before God and his pronouncement of judgment." With reference to his appeal to *emprosthen,* see p. 202 n. 7.— These attempts, which fail to reconstruct any clear text from the *Vorlage,* remain as problematic as the whole redaction hypothesis.

225. On 3:10-20, see also C. Spicq, "La justification du charitable 1 Jo 3, 19-21," *RB* 40 (1959) 915-27 (quotes a comparable Qumran text: 1QH 4:29-37).

3. The Admonition Concluded (1 John 3:21-24)

[21]Beloved, if our hearts do not condemn us, we have boldness before God; [22]and we receive from him whatever we ask, because we obey his commandments and do what pleases him.

[23]And this is the commandment, that we should believe in the name of his Son Jesus Christ and love one another, just as he commanded us.

[24]All who obey his commandments abide in him, and he abides in them. And by this we know that he abides in us, by the Spirit he has given us.

a) THOSE WHO KEEP THE COMMANDMENTS WILL RECEIVE
   AN ANSWER TO THEIR PRAYERS (3:21-22)

3:21 This verse is only loosely connected with the observation just concluded. The question of our hearts condemning us has now been dealt with. "If our hearts do not condemn us" refers to all "those in which there has been no condemnation, and those in which assurance has been gained in spite of the condemnation of the heart" (Brooke).[226]

"We have boldness before God." Boldness presumes a friendly relationship,[227] which allows us to speak freely. We should not emphasize the privilege too strongly. Rather, the author is referring to the inner stance of those who pray to God. They have hope that their prayers will be accepted. Boldness and the certainty of being heard belong closely together here as in 5:14.[228]

3:22 In the farewell discourses of GJohn Jesus assures his disciples repeatedly that God will hear their prayers (John 14:13f.; 15:7; 16:23f., 26). Although these promises are in full harmony with the assurance Jesus gives in the Synoptic Gospels (Matt. 7:7ff.; 18:19; Mark 11:24 par.), 1 John 3:22 should be associated particularly with the dominical saying in John 16:26f. There Jesus tells his disciples that the Father himself loves them and opens his ear to them directly after Jesus has returned to his Father. In this promise we see "what human existence really is when elevated in Christ" (Peterson). For the author of 1 John this promise of the Johannine Christ has become a present reality (note the present tense). The Christians' expectation that their prayers will be heard bears its own stamp, as will be seen when other texts are compared. It depends upon fellowship with Christ and with God. It is not surprising that the idea of prayer being heard is also found among the Mandeans.[229] They had a rich life of worship and prayer. A certain similarity between their piety and that of the Johannine community

---

226. The shorter text without *hēmōn* is the most probable as a quick glance at what precedes will show. *Hēmōn* stands (a) behind *kardia* in ℵ C ℓ Vg sy Clem, but not in BAΨ 33 323 1739 al. Orig. Aug., (b) behind *kataginōskē* in ℵAℓ pl. Vg sy, but not in BC 441 Orig. Aug.

227. See E. Peterson, Festschrift R. Seeberg (Leipzig, 1929) 1:293; according to H. Preisker, the term derives from the original eschatological wording presumed to lie behind vv. 19–20 (appendix to Windisch's commentary, p. 167).

228. Peterson offers examples of *parrhēsia* in prayer from oriental literature and regards the Latin translations, *fiducia* and *confidentia,* as inadequate (in Festschrift R. Seeberg, 296).

229. See *MandLit* 66; 140; *Ginza* 260.6f.; 268.1ff.; 389.27ff.; 396.22ff.

is unmistakable. Yet the function of the heavenly "emissary" who supports the prayer of the faithful is different.[230]

The *hoti*-clause, which explains why God hears our prayers — viz., because we keep his commandments — can hardly be meant to suggest the condition on which their being heard depends.[231] Rather, the entire verse, like John 16:26, is tuned in to the reciprocal love between God and the believers. Out of the love the Father shows to those who believe in Jesus and love their brothers and sisters (cf. v. 23), whatever they ask for in their prayers is granted. The Father loves them because they keep his commandments and, like Jesus in John 8:29, do what is pleasing to him. This is stated as a fact — an example of the untrammeled Christian self-consciousness which was already expressed in 2:13f. and in 3:14. It is obviously in contrast to the perverse attitude of the gnostics that the orthodox Christians at least make a serious attempt to be morally faithful. But in the next verses we get another admonition, for the indicative in v. 22 implies an imperative. This verse clearly serves as a transition, leading into the final admonition. The pleonastic turn of phrase "obey his commandments" and "do what pleases him"[232] betrays a desire to emphasize once more the essential theme of the admonitory section.

b) GOD'S COMMANDMENT CAN BE SUMMED UP AS FAITH IN CHRIST AND MUTUAL LOVE (3:23)

3:23 As far as the wording goes, this verse links up with the phrase "we obey his commandment" (v. 22). The author now tells us that God's ("his") commandment can be summarized as believing in Christ and showing love for the brothers and sisters. Clearly, he intends to summarize the whole admonitory section (2:18–3:20). The basic demand is true faith in Christ. Here, for the first time in this epistle, we meet the concept "faith," which is so central in GJohn. It has, however, already been implicit in the confessional statements of 2:22f. In John faith consists largely in acknowledging Jesus as the One sent from God, the Messiah and Son of God. This is usually indicated by *eis* with the accusative

---

230. See *Ginza* 389.29f.: "Whoever prays my prayer in the light of the Tibil, that prayer I pray from the place of light." At first sight, this looks like an echo of John 14:13 but in gnostic fashion it is the result of the purification of the soul, its assimilation to the prototype of the gnostic, that is, precisely to that (historically incomprehensible) "emissary of light." There is no personal relationship either between the believer and this emissary or between the believer and the "primal life." Cf. fragments 2–10 of Book 16 of the *Right Ginza,* which are to a high degree instructive for the gnostic mentality (Lidzbarski, *Ginza,* 386). Similarly *Odes Sol.* 14.

231. *Contra* Windisch, who relegates 1 John to the level of a legalistic piety, a level that the hymnist of Christian love has left behind him despite all his talk about keeping the commandments.

232. "To do that which is well pleasing unto God" (in the New Testament usually *euarestos*) is a Jewish and Christian motive for behavior. In particular sacrificial offerings should be well pleasing to God, an idea taken over correspondingly into the New Testament; see Rom. 12:1; Phil. 4:10; Heb. 13:16. But human beings, their behavior, and their works, ought to be similarly well pleasing to God; cf. Rom. 8:8; 12:1; 14:18; 2 Cor. 5:9; etc.; Heb. 13:21. In this connection *enōpion autou* (in place of the dative) is probablly derived from spoken Jewish Greek (BDF §4 n. 5). Nevertheless, the preposition had been used in Koine for a long time; see A. Wikenhauser, *BZ* 8 (1910) 263–70; Moulton-Milligan, 220 s.v.

or by a *hoti*-clause ("believe in . . ." or "believe that . . .").[233] In GJohn faith comes about through personal trust and adherence to Jesus. But already there the heart of the matter is an unlimited appreciation of the claim of Jesus indicated by the great "I am" sayings, combined with a readiness to accept all his precepts and to make every effort to obey them. For the epistle, which is concerned not with the beginning and growth of faith but with fortifying the believers against the heretical teachers in an attitude they have definitively assumed, this tendency of Johannine faith is even more marked. More so than in GJohn emphasis is placed on confessional statements. These all have the same christological content. As in GJohn it is the person of Jesus that challenges people to the decision of faith. "The decisive factor is the object of faith, not its subject" (Büchsel).

This relation of faith to Jesus Christ is expressed in 1 John 3:23 by the phrase "in the name. . . ." The word "name" in the Old Testament, as in the Orient generally, stands for the person. What this person means is expressed in the phrase that follows, "his Son." That is also the content of the confession in 2:22b; 4:15; 5:5 (cf. 1:7; 3:8; 4:9f.; 5:9ff., 13, 20). So it is in John 1:34, 49; 3:18; 10:36; 11:4, 27; 20:31. Striking in that passage is the use of the dative, which otherwise in GJohn appears only in connection with the witnesses or testimonies that give rise to faith in Jesus (*pisteuein eis,* "believe in"), or to which Jesus appeals in the face of unbelief.[234] Here it can only mean the same thing as "in the name" (*eis to onoma*) in John 1:12; 2:23; 3:18; 1 John 5:13, that is, faith in Jesus Christ who is the Son of God in an ontological sense.[235] The phrase is synonymous with the Hebrew *he'ĕmîn bĕ* and *lĕ*, a mixed construction with the dative which can easily be observed outside of John.[236] The dative of witness is again found in 1 John 5:10b (cf. also 4:1).

People have often been offended by faith being called a "commandment." After all, it is the basic attitude of Christians, a response to the divine call. It would be more accurate to call faith "a receptive attitude."[237] True, it is not a human achievement, making up for the old works of the law. In John 6:29 Jesus attempts to make clear to his hearers what was expected of the Jews, something completely

---

233. With *eis:* John 2:11; 3:16, 18, 36; 4:39; etc. (a total of 36 occurrences); with *hoti:* 6:69; 8:24; 11:27; etc. (in all, 13 occurrences). On this and on what follows, see J. Huby, "De la connaissance de foi dans s. Jean," *RechScR* 31 (1931) 385–42; P.-H. Menoud, "La foi dans l'Évangile de Jean," *Cahiers bibliques de Foi et de Vie* (1936) 27–43; my dissertation, "Der Glaube im vierten Evangelium" (abridged; Breslau, 1937); Wikenhauser, *Johannes,* 242–47; M. Bonningues, *La foi de Saint Jean* (Paris, 1955); A. Decourtray, "La conception johannique de la foi," *NRT* 91 (1959) 561–76; R. Bultmann, *TDNT* 6:671; F.-M. Willocx, "La notion de foi dans la quatrième évangile" (diss., Louvain, 1962).

234. See esp. 5:38, 46, 47; 10:37f.; 14:11 (a total of 18 occurrences)—a linguistic usage occurring throughout the New Testament.

235. This is particularly clear in John 3:18b. That person ipso facto incurs judgment through not believing "in the name of the only Son of God." The distinction Brooke tries to draw between the dative (=being convinced of the truth of an assertion) and *eis* with the accusative (=surrender to a person) is untenable.

236. See Acts 5:14; 16:34; 18:8. On the Hebrew usage, see L. Köhler and W. Baumgartner, *Lexicon in Veteris Testamenti libros* (Leiden, 1953) 61; further BDF §187.6; Moulton-Thumb, 102f.; H. Bietenhard, *TDNT* 5:271; R. Bultmann, *TDNT* 6:203 nn. 221, 224.

237. Schlatter, *Der Glaube im NT* (4th ed.; Stuttgart, 1927) 218.—On this and on what follows, see my dissertation, pp. 43ff.

different from "works." But as the sole decisive prerequisite for the attainment of salvation, faith in Jesus becomes a demand that confronts the human will, and it is dependent on their overall ethical behavior (cf. John 3:18–21). It is a lively and complete faith, involving obedience to the Son of God (cf. John 3:36) and impelling one to moral fidelity.

The second requirement, which is just as important as the first, is mutual love. Such love is, however, secondary to faith in Christ and a necessary consequence thereof. For Jesus, with whom the believers throw in their lot, and whose words they must endeavor faithfully to obey (cf. John 12:47), gave this commandment. This is expressly stated in the little clause beginning with *kathōs* ("just as"). The subject of the clause, given the obvious allusion to John 13:34; 15:12, 17, can only be Jesus himself, who has just been mentioned. The phrase "just as" does not introduce a comparison, but has a causal sense ("insofar as . . .").[238]

c) THE FRUIT OF OBEDIENCE IS TRUE FELLOWSHIP WITH GOD (3:24)

3:24 Here the author recapitulates and summarizes his argument, reverting to his main theme of fellowship with God. Once again, he takes up the key phrase "obey the commandments" (cf. v. 22b), promising that Christians who do this will "abide in him" (i.e., God). This already familiar assurance (cf. 2:5f.) is expanded further—in defiance of grammatical usage—by the words "and he abides in them." This creates a "reciprocal unifying formula," a stylistic device characteristic of Johannine "God-mysticism" (see Excursus 4).

It is easy for the author to proceed in 3:24 to say "and he abides in them." This is possible because of what has been said about our being children of God or being born of God (3:1ff.). There is a Johannine realism about this. Something of the divine nature (3:9, his "seed"; 3:15, "eternal life") has entered into the children of God. Now we are reminded that we have received the Spirit—which means very much the same thing.

But the author gives this thought a surprising twist. Because we have the Spirit we know we have fellowship with God. Why does the author put it the other way around like this? The easiest explanation is that the author is passing on to a new theme which places the question of discerning the "spirits" in the forefront (4:1ff.).

How did God[239] give the Spirit to the genuine believers as the proof of his love and the seal of theirs? We are never told—any more than we are in 4:13, an almost word-for-word parallel. If we were right in our interpretation of the anointing in 2:20, 27 as a reference to the Spirit, the believers were already being reminded there that they have the Spirit and that they are supposed to follow his instruction. The active role ascribed to the Spirit presupposes the converse truth, viz., that all Christians can have an experience of the Spirit. Such internal revelations

---

238. See BDF §453.2; BAGD 391, s.v. 3; Bultmann, *John,* 382 n. 2 (who, however, expands this usage beyond what is justified).

239. *Edōken* is to be related to God, since there is no reason, as there is in v. 23, to take Christ as the subject; *hou* is attraction of the relative pronoun (BDF §294).

of the Spirit, rather than external charismatic manifestations[240] (which were hardly a universal phenomenon at that time) seems to be the focus of 3:24. Yet this experience of the Spirit, contrary to 2:27, goes beyond instruction in the faith and includes fervent love, peace, and joy—the fruits of salvation which the Spirit imparts, assuring the believers of their fellowship with God (cf. Bonsirven).

EXCURSUS 9

On the Concept of the Spirit in 1 John

I. There are two passages that speak explicitly of the Spirit as a possession of the believers—3:24 and 4:13). Each time it appears as a hallmark of fellowship with God. There is nothing here about manifestations of the Spirit, for it is an experience open to all. There is nothing about the charismata, as in 1 Corinthians 12 and 14. There are three reasons for this: (1) The epistle never mentions such phenomena. (2) The possession of the Spirit is regarded as a general, regular endowment of all who believe in Christ. (3) The epistle rejects any special experiences of God, particularly of the visionary kind (4:8, 20). The Spirit is probably received in a sacramental rite (John 3:5f.). Originally, it is true (Acts 2:38; 8:15f; 10:45; 19:6), visible effects were associated with this eschatological gift of God. But in time the emphasis shifted to the inner experience of salvation (Rom. 5:5; 1 Cor. 6:11). For Johannine thought the soteriological functions of the Spirit are in the forefront.

The similarity between the two passages 3:24 and 4:13 suggests that we have here something in the nature of a catechetical formula. Already in 1 Thess. 4:8 Paul exhorts his readers to holiness and tells them that "(God) gives his Holy Spirit to you" (with an allusion to Ezek. 36:27; 37:14). This Spirit produces many fruits of salvation (cf. Gal. 5:22). In Eph. 1:17 the Spirit is called a "spirit of wisdom and revelation," and in 2 Tim. 1:7 "a spirit of power and of love and of self-discipline." In both places it is God who "gave" the Spirit. The same verb is used in Rom. 5:5 with the Holy Spirit as the object, in a way that suggests that we have here a phrase previously coined. There can be no doubt that this turn of speech was familar from the Old Testament (cf. Ezek. 36:26f.; 37:6, 14 LXX) and late Judaism (1QH 12:12; 13:19; 14:11; 17:17). But in early Christianity it is apparently applied concretely to the conferral of the Spirit in baptism. One should also note the unique formulation in 1 John 4:13, that God has given us "of (*ek*) his Spirit." Virtually synonymous is the saying that refers back to initiation in Heb. 6:4, that the Christians "have shared in the Holy Spirit" (cf. also the Pauline metaphor of the "first installment" of the Spirit which God has given to us, 2 Cor. 1:22; 5:5; Eph. 1:14). We can easily understand how at the end of a section referring repeatedly to baptism (3:1, 9f.) the author of 1 John deliberately takes up an idea and expression that was common to early Christianity and had its *Sitz im Leben* in the baptismal catechesis. This does not exclude the fact that he intends to speak in the next section about "testing the spirits."

---

240. With Bonsirven against Chaine.

II. The main function of the Holy Spirit in GJohn is a revelatory one, leading to divine truth. He is the "Spirit of truth" (John 14:17; 15:26; 16:13; 1 John 4:6). He is himself the truth (1 John 5:6). As the Spirit of truth he assists those who bear testimony for Jesus: "The Spirit is the one that testifies" (1 John 5:6). This probably refers to the support he gives to the Christian proclamation in the world (John 15:26). His function in revealing, confirming (14:26), and completing (16:13) the revelation vis-à-vis the disciples becomes one of testimony in the face of the unbelieving world opposed to God. The Spirit also plays an important role in the controversy between the true believers and the heretics, the enemies of the faith and of God. That is what 1 John has mainly in view. From this perspective the Johannine reflections on the Holy Spirit represent a significant development.

1. The metaphor of anointing in 2:20, 27 probably refers to the Spirit. (a) The expressions "you have" (2:20) and "you received" (2:27) are consistent with the idea of receiving the Spirit as described in John 14:16f. God "gives" (*dōsei*) him; the believers receive (*labein*) him. (b) The "Spirit of Truth" abides in them; cf. John 14:17 with 1 John 2:27a. (c) The Spirit practices the function of teaching (*didaskein*); cf. John 14:26 with 1 John 2:27a–b. (d) The anointing sees to it that the Christians abide in Christ (2:27c), just as the Paraclete in the farewell discourses seeks to bind them in closer fellowship with Jesus; cf. John 14:26; 16:14. For the word of God or the gospel, these terms about the anointing, taken as a whole, would be too strong, especially in view of their personal character.

2. This Spirit of truth is the Spirit of God personified. It is in the true confession of faith in Christ that the operation of the Spirit of God is recognized in human beings (1 John 4:2). This Spirit of God has a counterpart in the spirit of the antichrist (4:3b); the Spirit of truth is the opposite of the spirit of error (4:6d). All of this is consistent with Jewish and early Christian thought. It is true that other traits come out more strongly in ancient demonology. Evil spirits dwell in human beings, sometimes causing diseases and other abnormalities (unclean spirits). Again, satanic teaching and seduction are often attributed to evil spirits; cf. Acts 16:16, "spirit of divination"; Rom. 11:8, "sluggish spirit." They are generally opposed to God: 1 Cor. 2:12, "the spirit of the world"; Eph. 2:2, "the spirit that is now at work among those who are disobedient"; 2 Tim. 1:7, "spirit of cowardice"; Rev. 16:13f., "from the mouth of the dragon, the beast and the false prophet come three foul spirits like frogs. . . . These are demonic spirits, performing signs." Especially close to the spirit of error are the "deceitful spirits" in 1 Tim. 4:1 and the spirits of falsehood often mentioned in *Testaments of the Twelve Patriarchs* (*T. Rub.* 2:1; 3:2, 7; *T. Sim.* 3:1; 6:6; *T. Levi* 3:3; etc.). Religious and ethical admonitory writing traces vices back to evil spirits.

The strong dualistic contrast between the Spirit of God and the spirit opposed to him is also found in the *Damascus Rule* and other documents recently discovered from the Dead Sea. According to CD 2:12, God "made known His Holy Spirit to them (those saved at the end) by the hand of His anointed one, and He proclaimed the truth to them." On the other hand, we hear of the "spirits of Belial," who gain control over human beings (12:2). The most striking point, however, is the strong contrast between the divine Spirit and the spirit opposed to God. This is found in the *Community Rule* of Qumran (3:13–4:26). Here two spirits are fighting for the control of the human race, "the spirits of truth and falsehood"; two realms confront each other, one ruled by the Prince of Light, the other by the Angel of Darkness. The latter is the cause of all the transgression of the children of righteousness. "All his allotted spirits seek the overthrow of the sons of light. But the God of Israel and his Angel of Truth will succour all the sons of light" (3:24f.). Then follows a description of the deeds, virtues, and rewards of those who obey the counsels of the Spirit or spirits of light. These are contrasted with the behaviors, vices, and punishments of those who walk in the darkness according to the spirit of falsehood (4:2-14). Only at the end, at the appointed time, will God destroy the evil spirit and distribute his Spirit of truth among the righteous (4:20f.). The unique description of these two classes of spirits[241] with the appeal for a decision, casts some light on 1 John 4:1-6, though it does not explain the pneumatology in its entirety. Here the conviction prevails that the believers, who are born of God, have already received the Spirit (see Excursus 8.2).

As for the testing or distinguishing of the spirits, Paul also proposes a criterion in 1 Cor. 12:3. This is to test whether the striking or unusual utterances of pneumatics are to be traced to the Spirit of God or the spirit of the devil (cf. also the charisma of discernment of spirits in 1 Cor. 12:10, also 1 Thess. 5:20f.). 1 John 4:1ff. does not constitute a parallel to these pneumatic phenomena. The only parallel is the instruction about testing the spirits for their divine or diabolical origin. Such a test is made necessary not by pneumatic disturbances but by the spread of false doctrine and the arrogance of those who are propagating it.

3. In 1 John 4:1 the spirits are not in themselves superhuman powers. Rather, the human spirit is meant, insofar as it is inspired either by God or the devil (cf. vv. 2 and 3, "from God" and "not from God," respectively). In "the spirits" (v. 1) "every spirit" in vv. 2 and 3 is included. By the way they confess Christ the preachers show by what spirit they are led, by the Spirit of God or by the spirit of the antichrist. Apparently the author, like the Jewish writers mentioned above, imagines that the human spirit is in close association with the superhuman spirit. Instructive in this connection is a passage in Hermas (*Mandates* 11), which also deals with false prophets:

(2) These doubtful-minded ones then come to him (a false prophet) as a soothsayer, and enquire of him what shall befall them. And he, the false prophet, having no power of a divine Spirit in himself, speaketh with them according to their enquiries. . . . (3) . . . but he speaketh also some true words; for the devil filleth him with his own spirit, if so be he shall be able to break down some of the righteous. (4) So many therefore as are strong in the faith of the Lord, clothed with the truth, cleave not to such spirits, but hold aloof from them.

4. This passage also shows that the false prophet was a familiar notion in the ancient church. But the term was applied in various ways, like prophecy as a whole.

---

241. See B. Otzen, *Stud. theol.* 7 (1953) 135-44; F. Nötscher, "Geist und Geister in den Texten von Qumran," in *Mélanges bibliques rédigés en l'honneur de A. Robert* (Paris, 1957) 305-15; E. Schweizer, *TDNT* 6:389ff.; Huppenbauer, *Der Mensch zwischen zwei Welten,* 30-34.

The basic idea is "speaking in the Spirit."[242] This was often understood in an ecstatic sense. The ecstatic element, however, is not inherent in prophecy, as is shown by the example of the great Old Testament prophets.[243] The decisive factor was that the prophet received his call and message from God and proclaimed the words that God had given him. If we stay with the New Testament, false prophets are usually people who claim illegitimately to be prophets or messengers of God like those known from the Old Testament (Matt. 7:15; Luke 6:26; cf. Jer. 23:13ff.; 28; 29:21ff.; Mic. 3:5ff.; Zech. 13:2ff.). A special role is played by the false prophets in the period of the eschatological woes (Mark 13:22=Matt. 24:11, 24) together with false Christs. Finally the false prophet becomes a particular eschatological figure in Rev. 16:13; 19:20; 20:10. Alongside this the general use of the word continues. The Jewish messianic pretenders in New Testament times also hoped to be accepted as prophets.[244] But nowhere in the New Testament do the charismatic prophets, who were so highly esteemed in the early community,[245] have false prophets[246] as their counterparts. Therefore it should not be assumed that there were genuine prophets among the readers of 1 John. Probably false prophets here are not much more than false teachers, as in 2 Pet. 2:1. In *Did.* 11.5-6 false itinerant apostles were called false prophets, and in the *Apocalypse of Peter* it is said of them that "they will teach ways and divers decrees of perdition."[247] Similar opinions are found in CD 1:14f. ("the scoffer . . . shed over Israel the waters of lies"); 8:13; 20:15 and in the Dead Sea Scrolls.[248] The heretical teachers of 1 John 4:1 may claim to be filled by the Spirit and to be prophets. But we cannot assume that they delivered their teachings in ecstasy. We learn with certainty only from later gnosticism that the prophetic elements of vision, ecstasy, and prediction were flourishing and were deliberately cultivated. In fact, there was a special rite for the consecration of prophets.[249] Faced by this movement, the official church became increasingly suspicious of the so-called prophets (see *Did.* 11; *Herm. Man.* 11). Eventually the outburst of prophetic ecstasy in Montanism put an end to the whole prophetic movement. However, this later development tells us nothing about the prophetic or ecstatic element in the early forms of gnosticism that we find in 1 John.

242. Cf. *Did.* 11.7f.

243. See Mic. 3:8: "I am filled with power, with the spirit of the Lord, and with justice and might, to declare to Jacob his transgression, and to Israel his sin." Further Jer. 1:7-10; 15:15-21; 20:7-9; Ezek. 3:17f.; Hos. 12:11; Amos 3:8; etc.

244. Theudas (Josephus, *Antiquities* 20.97f.); the Egyptian (*Ant.* 20.169ff.; *Jewish War* 2.261ff.); another in the time of Festus (*Ant.* 20.188).

245. 1 Cor. 12:28; 14:29; Eph. 2:20; 3:5; 4:11; further Acts 11:27; 13:1.

246. Only the Jewish false prophet Bar-Jesus on the island of Cyprus is mentioned in Acts 13:6. On the false prophets, see G. Friedrich, *TDNT* 6:830.

247. Akhmin-Fragment 1.1; see Lietzmann, *Kleine Texte* 3:8.

248. 1QpHab 2:1f.; 5:11 ("the Liar"); 10:9 ("the Spouter of lies who led many astray"); 1QH 2:31 ("thou hast saved me from the zeal of lying interpreters"); 4:9f. ("they [are] teachers of lies and seers of falsehood"); 4:20 ("thou wilt destroy in Judgment all men of lies, and there shall be no more seers of error").

249. Through the gnostic Marcus; see Irenaeus, *Adv. Haer.* 1.7.3; for the rest, see H. Weinel in Hennecke, *Neutestamentliche Apokryphen,* 294f.

III. In 1 John the word "spirit" has further associations, in addition to truth and revelation. It is also related to life, the divine life. The Spirit represents the principle of life: "It is the Spirit that gives life" (John 6:63). This becomes particularly clear in John 3:5, where baptism is called a birth from water and the Spirit. The Spirit is the creative, life-giving element. In 1 John we hear only of people being "born of God." But in 3:9, under the influence of this metaphor, the expression "God's seed" is used. In view of this allusion to John 3, this "burgeoning seed of divine life" must be substantially identical with the Spirit of God. Later gnostic texts use the term "spiritual embryo" to signify the pneumatic matrix of the elect.[250] For the author of 1 John the power of this divine seed abiding in human beings is displayed in their preservation from sin. He does not derive this pneumatic nature of those born of God from a mythical reception of divine seed. Those born of God are not like the gnostic pneumatics, pneumatic by nature. Rather, they acquire this status through the sacrament, received in faith.

On the other hand, it would be wrong to weaken the significance of the life of the Spirit (sacramentally received) to a mere "begetting."[251] Baptism and Eucharist represent not only the incarnation and the death of Jesus on the cross (cf. on 5:6ff) but really impart divine life, making possible a sinless life-style (cf. on 3:1 and 9). When John 17:3 says that eternal life consists in knowing the one true God and him whom God sent, Jesus Christ, this is not knowledge in the Greek sense, but knowledge as in 1 John 1:3. It is the fellowship resulting from possession of the divine life, fellowship with the Father and his Son Jesus Christ. The real, sacramental impartation of the Spirit is everywhere presumed (as also in John 7:39; note the verb "to receive"). This endowment with the Spirit, of those who believe in Jesus Christ, works itself out in various ways. But basically it means reception into the divine realm of life. This life is derived therefrom as empowerment for a holy life-style in God's light. It is equally an inner illumination, enabling people to abide in the truth and to separate themselves from all falsehood.

Thus the doctrine of the Spirit in 1 John is to a great extent in agreement with GJohn. The various functions of the Spirit are brought out, depending on what needs to be said in the particular context. Because of the battle against the heretical teachers, the predominant emphasis in the epistle is on the Spirit's activity. As the Spirit of truth, his role is to instruct and confirm the believers in the faith.[252]

---

250. See the above passages; see further for the innermost pneumatic being of the gnostics, the fragments from the Baruch-Book of the gnostic Justin in Hippolytus, *Ref.* 5.26.8f. and the information about the Naassenes (*Ref.* 5.8.28f.).

251. *Contra* E. Schweizer, "Das johanneische Zeugnis vom Herrenmahl," *EvT* 12 (1952–53) 341–63 (p. 361: "The meaning of the Lord's supper consists in this, that the reality of the incarnation right through to the death on the cross is being assured against all docetic spiritualization and to attest to it in an even more crass and decisive way . . "); idem, *TDNT* 6:439–42. Here Schweizer says even more forcibly: "For Jn. the function of baptism and the Lord's Supper is to bear witness to the Incarnation" (p. 439) and emphasizes that "ζωή is ascribed to the Word alone" (p. 441).

252. See also T. Preiss, *Das innere Zeugnis des heiligen Geistes* (Zollikon-Zurich, 1947); J. Michl, "Der Geist als Garant des rechten Glaubens," in Festschrift M. Meinertz, 142–51 (he interprets the inner instruction given by the Spirit as *sensus fidelium*); Feine, *Theologie des NT,* 353–56.

PART THREE

The Separation of Those Who Belong to God from the "World," in the True Faith in Christ and in Love (1 John 4:1–5:12)

The new range of thought that begins at 4:1 incorporates all that has been previously expressed and develops the argument further in a particular way. At the end of Part Two stood the divine command, requiring true faith in Christ and mutual love (3:23). These two commandments are now the subject of a protracted discussion. There is a sharp clarion call to combat the heretical teachers, leading to an elucidation of the hallmarks of Christian existence. The theme of love is taken up for the third time (cf. 2:7ff.; 3:11ff.) from this specific perspective, in a depth hitherto unplumbed, and reaching back to the nature and saving work of God (4:7–21). Faith in Christ is summed up in a series of creedal formulas (4:2f., 15; 5:5f.) and is contrasted with the heretical teaching and displayed in its victorious power (4:4; 5:4f.). With all the care lavished on the theme of love, more weight is placed on faith. At this point the debate begins anew (4:1–6), and it is in this section rather than in the parenetic ones that the expositions reach their climax. Then with 5:13 the author begins his concluding remarks. This is similar to John 20:31, except that there the conclusion has undergone considerable expansion. Chapter 5 however should not be separated completely from the previous chapter and treated as a separate section (Büchsel), for the connections, both external and internal, are too strong. Thus we get the structure: A–B–A.

The author expands what he has said already with two more chapters. Apparently this is due to the dangers threatening his readers from the heretical teachers. The defense against them, at first adumbrated (1:5–2:17), then followed (2:18ff.) by an explicit attack on them, suggesting now that the danger had already been dealt with, gives way to a series of new discussions (4:2; 5:6), taking up points in the confession of faith. These show how much the author was impressed by the danger posed by all these false prophets (4:2). The main task now is to warn the Christian community of this danger. They must be on their guard and keep their new spiritual weapons ready to hand (the distinguishing of the spirits). They need to be immunized from within against the destructive poison. How are they to do this? All the author can suggest is what he has already hammered in so hard: the true Christian confession and faithful obedience to God's commandments, especially the command of mutual love. That for him is the infallible expression of the divine nature and a practical proof of genuine Christianity. Thus, egged on by his opponents, driven by a serious concern for the community, he strives to express his thoughts with all the clarity and profundity at his command.

It is not surprising that in doing so the author repeats himself! It is also understandable that while dealing with the theme of love he takes another look at the hallmark of faith (4:11-16). His recapitulations (4:6c, 16b, 19, 21; 5:10c, 11) and the variations in perspective (fellowship with God, 4:12, 13, 15, 16b; eternal life, 5:11, 12; "being from God," 4:1-6; and "being born of God," 4:7; 5:1-4) appear everywhere. So there is no reason to apply the literary scalpel.

The section 4:1-6 cannot be viewed merely as an interruption in the theme of love (Chaine, etc.), for that theme had already been brought to a conclusion in 3:23f. The section 4:7ff., however, builds on 4:1-6. Only because he had dealt with "being from God" previously (4:7) can the author go on to say that love comes from God. Then he can develop the nature of love from its divine origin. On the contrary, 4:1-6 must be regarded as the key for what follows. The author wanted to effect a clear distinction and separation of the true Christians from the false prophets, so he focuses first on love, in order to return later to a discussion of faith.

Thus we get the following structure:

First Section. Distinguishing between the spirits by means of the right confession of Christ and detachment from the "world" (4:1-6).
1. Distinguishing between the spirits is necessary in view of the false prophets, but is also made possible by the confession of Christ (vv. 1-3).
2. In fact the Christians are utterly different from the false prophets in their inner being (vv. 4-6).

Second Section. Love as the hallmark of those born of God, its nature and fulfillment in mutual love (4:7-5:4).
1. Love comes essentially from God, who first loved us (vv. 7-10).
2. The love of those who belong to God is a response to his love and places us in intimate fellowship with God (vv. 11-16).
    Digression: True love of God is known only by those of orthodox faith (vv. 14-16a).
3. Perfect love knows no fear (vv. 17-18).
4. The love of God manifests itself in love for our fellow Christians (4:19-5:2). Renewed call to love (v. 19).

---

1. Cf. 4:3 with 2:18; 4:4 with 2:14; 4:9, 10, 14 with 2:2 and 3:16; 4:11 with 3:11, 16b; 4:12 with 3:24a; 4:13 with 3:24b; 4:15 and 5:1, 5 with 2:22; 4:17 with 2:28 and 3:19f.; 5:3 with 2:5; 5:12 with 2:23, 25.

a) Love for a God we have not seen is not possible without love for a brother or sister we can see (v. 20).
b) Next to the love of God himself mutual love is a positive commandment of God (v. 21).
c) Love of the parent involves love of the child (5:1-2).
5. It is not difficult for those who are born of God to love him (5:3-4).

Third Section. True faith in Christ is the power that conquers the "world" (5:5-12).
1. Only the true and full christological confession grants victory (vv. 5-6).
2. This faith is based on the testimony of three witnesses (vv. 7-8).
3. God himself gave testimony to his Son, and the salvation of all depends on the acceptance or rejection of this God-given testimony (vv. 9-12).

FIRST SECTION

DISTINGUISHING BETWEEN THE SPIRITS BY MEANS OF THE RIGHT CONFESSION OF CHRIST AND DETACHMENT FROM THE "WORLD" (1 JOHN 4:1-6)

4:1Beloved, do not believe every spirit, but test the spirits to see whether they are from God; for many false prophets have gone out into the world. ²By this you know the Spirit of God: every spirit that confesses that Jesus Christ has come in the flesh is from God, ³and every spirit that does not confess Jesus is not from God. And this is the spirit of the antichrist, of which you have heard that it is coming; and now it is already in the world.

⁴Little children, you are from God, and have conquered them; for the one who is in you is greater than the one who is in the world. ⁵They are from the world; therefore what they say is from the world, and the world listens to them. ⁶We are from God. Whoever knows God listens to us, and whoever is not from God does not listen to us. From this we know the spirit of truth and the spirit of error.

1. Distinguishing between the Spirits Is Necessary in View of the False Prophets, But Is Also Made Possible by the Confession of Christ (1 John 4:1-3)

4:1 The renewed warning against the heretical teachers which begins here arises from the concern that the believers are not sensitive enough to resist their seductive talk. This may come as a surprise after what the author has said in 2:20f., 27. However, with all his assurances to his readers that they know the truth and have the inner guidance of the Holy Spirit, the author had already disclosed in 2:18-27 (in his meticulous discussion about the antichrist and especially in the imperatives of v. 24 and v. 27c) that he thinks the danger is far from over. The threat confronting the believers causes him to return once again to the opponents. This time he lifts his visor and shows his face even more than he did before. That the problem is the same is clear from the fact that once again he connects the opponents' machinations with the antichrist (v.3). Once again we have a debate about the christological (4:2, 15) and moral (4:8, 20) heresy, reminding us of theses that are already familiar (christological, 2:22f.; and moral, 2:9, 11; 3:14ff.).

The heretical teachers are now called "false prophets," probably because a prophet is one who speaks in the Spirit of God, and these seducers falsely claim to be filled with the Spirit (v. 1a–b).

It is questionable whether the author is also thinking here of the false prophets who were expected to appear in the great tribulation before the parousia (Mark 13:22 par.), for the latter perform signs and wonders in order to deceive.[2] If indeed that is what he had in mind, he would have recast these heretical teachers and made them into eschatological figures like the antichrist. But this assumption is not necessary. The term "false prophet" can have various connotations, corresponding to the wide uses of the term "prophet."[3] For further discussion, see Excursus 9.

Again, as in 2:18, the author emphasizes how many deceivers there are. This is what makes them so dangerous, especially in view of their self-assurance and convincing eloquence. The phrase "they went out into the world" has nothing to do with the coming of demons into the world (cf. Luke 11:26; Rom. 5:12) nor with the appearance of prophets (cf. John 6:14; 11:24). Nor does it refer to the influx of Jewish false teachers into Asia Minor[4] nor to missionaries going forth from "the churches and in the name of those churches."[5] It merely characterizes their unrestrained appearance in public all over the world. The Christians who are being addressed may come upon them anywhere. Their going out into the world refers to their worldwide activity, similar to that of the evil riders in the book of Revelation (6:2, 4) or Satan (20:8).

The admonition, "test the spirits" (cf. 1 Thess. 5:21), as well as the means used to distinguish the spirits, mainly watching out for the way they confess Jesus (1 Cor. 12:3), have a noticeable echo in the moral rules Paul sets up in his communities for extraordinary charismatic manifestations of the Spirit. It has therefore been suggested that similar things were going on among the readers of 1 John.[6] But this is to overlook the important differences. The Corinthian pneumatics had to face not heretical teachers but pagans inspired by demons (1 Cor. 12:2), while in Thessalonica the apostle seems to be thinking only of testing the various (Christian) charismata to see whether they are useful to the community ("hold fast what is good"). On the other hand, 1 John 4:1 in no way suggests

---

2. Cf. also the apocalyptic figure of the "false prophet," the assistant of the antichirst, in Rev. 16:13; 19:20; 20:10, who likewise supports his satanic propaganda with deceptive miracles.

3. See A. von Harnack, *Mission and Expansion* 1:331–33; 352–54; A. Fridrichsen, *The Problem of Miracle in Primitive Christianity* (Minneapolis, 1972) 147ff.; E. Fascher, Προφήτης: *Eine sprach- und religionsgeschichtliche Untersuchung* (Giessen, 1927) (who believes that the New Testament contains two intersecting trajectories, one coming from the Old Testament and one from Hellenistic syncretism [p. 166]; on false prophets in early Christianity, see pp. 182–90); Dodd, 103–6 (who, however, draws too close a connection between these false prophets and the early Christian charismatic prophets); H. Bacht, "Wahres und falsches Prophetentum," *Bib* 32 (1951) 237–62; G. Friedrich, *TDNT* 6:860f.

4. So Belser, ad loc.—On the other hand, cf. *eis ton kosmon.*

5. So Dodd, 98 and 148.

6. Cf. Chaine, Dodd.

enthusiastic forms of speaking in the Spirit. What these heretics are saying was directed by Satan (v. 4) The orthodox believers could hardly have indulged in extraordinary forms of speech. The spirits in v. 1 are not demonic powers (like, e.g., the "deceitful spirits" in 1 Tim. 4:1), but human spirits inspired either by God or by Satan (v. 3).[7] This is shown by the distinction drawn between the spirits that confess Christ (v. 2) and those that deny him (v. 3).

The sober admonition combined with this, "do not believe every spirit," serves as a warning against blindly attributing things to the Spirit. "Believe" is used with the dative as in John 4:21. It does not have the specific meaning of christological faith which it usually has in John.[8]

4:2 With "by this"[9] the author points to the distinguishing marks of the christological confession. It is the Spirit of God that enables orthodox Christians to hold the confession and conversely it is the Spirit that is validated by that confession. Corresponding to this is the statement at the end of v. 3 that any denial of the confession is due to the "spirit of the antichrist." Just as in vv. 2–3, the Spirit of God and the spirit of the antichrist are powers working against each other, prompting their human underlings in this world to contrary proclamations of faith.

The christological confession that divides the spirits from one another has become a matter of controversy. This is because it is so brief that it is hard to fathom its meaning.[10] In its linguistic form it has to be observed that the verb *homologein* takes a double accusative, an object and a predicate![11] True, the creedal formula contains a didactic statement which requires precise definition.

The question is whether the word "Christ" can be a predicate accusative here. If it is, the formula would be similar to what we have in 2:22 and 5:1, "to confess Jesus as the Christ who came in the flesh." There would be nothing strange about the absence of the article before *Christon* (cf. John 9:22; Rom. 10:9). But this possibility is unacceptable for two reasons: (1) The combination "Jesus Christ" is a fixed expression, especially in this epistle, and is used as a kind of formula (cf. 1:3; 2:1; 3:23; 5:6a, 20c; John 17:3 and later the Ignatian epistles). (2) With the sentence structure *en sarki elēlythota* (NRSV "has come in the flesh"), a participle with a prepositional phrase, the article could hardly be omitted, even when there is no article before *Christon* itself![12]

This makes it impossible to understand the formula in any way other than "to confess Jesus Christ as having come in the flesh."

---

7. Best illustrated in *Herm. Mand.* 11.1–6; see Excursus 9.

8. See above on 3:23.

9. Since it concerns a sign of recognition with permanent validity, it is best taken as an indicative. This is how it is understood in the other readings: *ginōsketai* (Ψ ⅎ Vg syP Cyr. Did. Aug.) and *ginōskomen* (ℵ* al. Bo arm); but they must be regarded as secondary.

10. See Introduction, pp. 18–23.

11. See BDF §157.2; 416.3; Moulton 3:162. The reading of B lat, *elēlythenai,* is certainly an interpretation. Polycarp, who supports this reading also gives a free rendition of the passage, as the context shows.

12. See BDF §272; Radermacher, *Grammatik,* 116f.

But what is the meaning of this formula? The most obvious possibility is that it is directed against docetism. The true corporeality of the incarnate One is emphasized by the crass term "flesh" (cf. John 1:14). On the other hand, it is not likely that *sarx* (flesh) is directed against the idea that Christ's body was a mere phantom (cf. Luke 24:39, "flesh and bones"). The *sarx* in which the Logos is veiled has a soteriological import in GJohn. It enables the One who became human to take upon himself an atoning sacrificial death in order to give life to the world (6:51). But the very sending of the Son of God to redeem sinners is a concern running all through 1 John (2:2; 3:5, 8; 4:10, 14). It seems that this is the reason for the all-embracing importance given to the incarnation, not any anti-docetic tendency. In fact, it serves the same purpose as the other formulas, "Jesus is the Christ" (2:22; 5:1) and "Jesus is the Son of God" (4:15; 5:5). The heretical teachers did not need Jesus Christ as the Redeemer from sins and the Mediator of life. They believed they were able to reach the Father and attain salvation by another way. But the author proclaims nothing other than this all through the epistle: the divine life can only be attained through the incarnate Son of God (1:1-3), only by faith in this divine Bearer of life (5:12f., 20). This point of view is strengthened in the brief Second Epistle of John with its teaching about deceivers and antichrists, who are no doubt identical with those of 1 John and are confuted with almost the same incarnation formula (v. 7). This unmasks the opponents of the true faith over a basic tenet of the Christian message.

Is the formula "Jesus Christ has come in the flesh" specifically an incarnation formula? Nowhere else in the Johannine Epistles does the name "Jesus Christ" refer to the pre-existent One, while the perfect *elēlythota* (has come) lays no particular stress on the historical event or the moment of time when the incarnation occurred. Jesus Christ is the incarnate One who has now returned to his Father (2:1; 5:20c). In view of this the fact of his coming in the flesh becomes known, a fact that continues to be important (perfect tense). But "in the flesh" appears to recapitulate John 1:14, where the incarnation is made the basis for Christian salvation. The perspective of believers making the confession is not that of the evangelist, who is giving a historical overview of the saving event (John 1:14). For believers, Jesus Christ is the living Son of God enthroned at the right hand of the Father (1 John 2:1). It is from this that the saving events mentioned in the confession, events that happened at a particular moment in history, are derived. As soon as the author wants to accentuate the historical aspect, he can add "who came . . ." (aorist, 1 John 5:6). But when he wants to bring out the temporal aspect, he can also say "come (lit., "coming") in the flesh" (2 John 7). It is only too clear that these formulas are on their way to becoming fixed articles of faith. The church needed them more and more as battle cries against the heretics and as liturgical acclamations (cf. 1 Tim. 3:16, "revealed in the flesh").

4:3 In the antithesis the denial of the creedal formula is introduced in an abbreviated way. The early attested reading, "that destroys (*lyei*) Jesus" is, in contrast to the simple negation "that does not confess," so strange that it must surely be regarded as original![13]

---

13. See especially Zahn, *Introduction* 3:365; Westcott, 163ff.; Brooke, ad loc.; Büchsel, Excursus, p. 63, and other modern exegetes.— It is rejected by Bonsirven, 214 n. 1; Lagrange, *Critique textuelle,* 566; Windisch (though Preisker in the appendix disagrees with him); Nauck, *Tradition und Charakter,* 77.

A scholia of the Athos MS 1739 (see Introduction, p. 42) confirms this reading for Irenaeus, Origen, and Clement of Alexandria; additionally Tertullian (*Adv. Marc.* 5.16; *De jejun.* 1), Socrates (*Hist. eccl.* 7.32) and other Latin fathers (Luc Aug Prisc Ticon Fulg) as well as the Old Latin manuscripts (except g) and Vg. It is to be preferred for the following reasons: (1) It can be traced back in textual evidence to the mid-second century and is confirmed not only by the Latin tradition but also by all ancient Greek witnesses. (2) It is more plausible grammatically because of the unusual *mē* ("not") with the indicative "does . . . confess."[14] (3) Internal considerations support it because: (a) *lyein* has a pregnant meaning; *mē homologei* by comparison is colorless, especially in conjunction with *ton Iēsoun;* (b) The continuation in 4:3b, an equally pointed phrase, is meaningful only if it follows this word. To "destroy Jesus" is exactly the role of the antichrist (von Harnack). The disappearance of *lyein* in the later Greek manuscripts can be explained, but not the converse. After *homologein* the negation was inserted mechanically, since it is in accordance with regular Johannine usage.

The various additions to "Jesus" show the embarrassment caused by the concise expression later, and should therefore be regarded as secondary[15]. *Lyei* must not, however, be taken in the pregnant sense of "dissolve." The charge of such a loosening of the bond between the human Jesus and the heavenly Christ might have been directed against the reading "Jesus Christ," whereas the simple "Jesus" designates the historical person whom everybody knew (cf. 2:22; 4:15; 5:1, 5). Rather, *lyei* means (as in 3:8; cf. John 2:19; 5:18; Acts 2:24; 2 Pet. 3:10, 11, 12) "to destroy." The false teachers destroy faith in Jesus as the Son of God made man, whom God sent to save the world. In fact they do away with him as the indispensable Mediator of salvation[16]. This brings out more concisely what every spirit that comes "from God" confesses. We have need of Jesus Christ who came in the flesh for our salvation. Any spirit like this, that contradicts God's revelation and his imparting of life in the historical Jesus, offensive as that may be, is not "from God."

This leads the author to the statement (closely linked to what precedes by the conjunction *kai,* "and") that this spirit is the spirit of antichrist. For the clear reference to "the Spirit of God" (v. 2a) makes it likely that the following definite article (*to*) should be amplified by *pneuma* ("spirit"). The formulation with *estin* ("is") has the same meaning as "by this you know" in v. 2a. Whoever speaks like that against Jesus has the spirit of the antichrist (2:18; 2 John 7)![17] However, the antichrist is not envisioned as a concrete personality. For the relative clause ("of which") does not go with "antichrist" but with "the (spirit)." The curious turn of speech thus created, viz, that "the spirit (of antichrist) is coming," is explained from the community's expectation ("you have heard") of the coming of the antichrist (2:18). But to the author, as we have already seen from 2:18 and elsewhere, this means that the antichrist "comes" in the heretical teachers. In other words,

14. See A. Rahlfs, *TLZ* 40 (1915) 525.

15. ℵ, *kyrion;* ℵ al., *Christon;* ℵ p ℵ pl. sy arm additionally + *en sarki elēlythota.*

16. See BAGD 483, s.v. 4: "annul (the true teaching about) Jesus (by spurning it), "still more forcibly Büchsel, *TDNT* 4:336: "It does not mean 'to dissolve the unity of the person of Jesus from the supernatural λόγος.' The question does not arise in 1 Jn or Jn."

17. Cf. the free rendering in Polycarp 7.1: *pas gar hos an mē homologē Iēsoun Christon en sarki elēlythenai, antichristos estin.*

it is the last hour. The conviction that the spirit of the antichrist is already at work is expressly stated once again. The little phrase "and now" is no longer dependent on the *hoti* ("that") because the author uses the word "now" to give his own interpretation. This interpretation is different from the traditional one ("you have heard"). This represents an original development of the early Christian concept of the antichrist, for which that figure was an individual personality ("the lawless one," 2 Thess. 2:3). But this development does not compromise the essential meaning, since the demonic power that inspired the antichrist represents the decisive factor in both the individual and collective interpretations![18]

2. In Fact the Christians Are Utterly Different from the Prophets in Their Innermost Being (1 John 4:4-6)

4:4 The proven antithesis between the heretics, tainted as they are by the spirit of antichrist, and the believers, who are inspired by the Spirit of God, is broadened out into a basic consideration of the ontological difference between the two groups. At the same time the author attempts to strengthen the faithful believers further so that they need not capitulate before these dangerous opponents. Thus he assures his "little children" that their origin lies in God. They share God's nature and are filled with his power. This phrase, *einai ek,* "to be from," is in accordance with Johannine style. It means to belong to a certain realm ("earth—heaven," John 3:31; "below—above," 8:23), group or category ("my sheep," 10:26), to a "sphere of being ("the truth," 18:37; 1 John 2:21; 3:19). It is in this comprehensive sense that it is used here, where the author is concerned to point out the sharp antithesis between "us" (v. 4) and "them" (v. 5); cf. "from God—from the world" (vv. 4–5); "the One who is in you—the one who is in the world" (v. 4c); "Spirit of truth—spirit of error" (v. 6). The contrast between the faithful Christian believers and those who deny Christ defines being ("is") and behavior ("speak" and "hear"). But these are not dualistic principles any more than it is a matter of *predestinatio ad infidelitatem.* People's characters are judged by their practical behavior, speaking, and hearing, but not vice versa. They are not predestined to faith or unbelief. As in the ethical sphere (3:10), John's dualism remains a practical one, even when he is talking of faith. It skirts around the difficult problem of predestination without getting enmeshed in it. Compare also Introduction, pp. 28f. and 30f., also Excursus 12 at the end.

It is also clear from what he says about the victory over the opponents that practical aims lie close to the author's heart. With deliberate emphasis (note the perfect tense) he seeks to pacify and to encourage his readers by assuring them that they have gained the upper hand over their opponents (cf. 2:13–14). Still more clearly than he had done before, he points to the reason for their victory and the source of their power. He is also moved (v. 14) to assure them that they are strong and that God's word abides in them. But here he gives a clear reason for their victory: "He who is in you" is greater than "he who is of the world."

---

18. Ambroggi: the author is thinking of an evil power of error and seduction, assuming a concrete form in various individuals and in the corrupt teaching.

Precisely because of the close connection between these two references there can be no doubt that the second phrase refers to the evil one, Satan himself. This is theologically important. First, it affirms that the spirit of the antichrist (v. 3) comes from the ruler of this world, who is at enmity with God (cf. John 12:31; 14:30; 16:11). Thus it is no accident that in the phrase required by the parallel, "he who is in them" is omitted. The author does not dare to credit Satan with direct influence, or with the same kind of real indwelling as God has, despite his conviction about the awful power Satan wields in this world (5:19). Together with 2:13f.; 5:4f., 18c this word is one of the finest testimonies to the sense of power and confidence in victory which Johannine Christianity enjoyed. It is an attitude that cannot be explained merely from the surviving idealism of youth or the rhetorical impetus of the original leaders. Nor was it born in the fires of battle. Rather, it comes from the depth of theological conviction.

A similar view is found in the Dead Sea Scrolls. There, too, Satan is the great adversary of God, though he is called by various names. The Angel of Darkness is under his dominion. The "sons of darkness" and all the spirits that are on his side persecute the "sons of light." But God directs everything according to his own plan and helps the sons of light (1QS 3:20ff.). In the world there is a heated battle going on between the two groups. In the *War Rule* of the sons of light and the sons of darkness, which describes this conflict, we have a kind of military text book, setting up the order of battle. There is no doubt that God and his people will be victorious in the end.

4:5 The false prophets are shown that they are "of this world," rather as the Johannine Jesus accuses the unbelieving Jews of being, from "below," "of this world" (John 8:23). Thus the author places his opponents in sharp contrast to the faithful Christians ("you," v. 4) and tries to explain their behavior from their nature. Since they do not belong in spirit to the community, the latter have already excluded them from their midst (2:19). Now they are spreading abroad their heresy all over the world ("they say"). They are doing this in the spirit of conformity with the world, perhaps not in the outward form of their preaching, but certainly in what they are actually saying. The testimony of God is missing from their words (cf. 5:10f.). The world welcomes their message gladly because they are saying just what the world wants to hear. Lurking behind this statement is the admission that the false teachers are having considerable success in the world. The epistle shows how the early church is coming to terms with the outward success of their opponents — rather like the way they came to terms with the riddle of Jesus' rejection by attributing it to the Jewish leaders (cf. John 8:23, 47; 10:26; 14:17; 15:18ff.; 18:37). The cosmos concept is again applied in typical Johannine fashion as it was in 3:13 (see ad loc.).

4:6 This problem of the opponents' success was certainly the main concern of the true Christian preachers. Perhaps this is the reason for the switch to the first person plural. Yet the author can hardly be thinking exclusively and directly of the special circle of witnesses who were called to proclaim the faith (cf. 1:1-3).[19] At most the witnesses are introduced as agents and representatives of the whole

---

19. On the change from the first to the second person plural, cf. 2:19f., 24f., 28; 3:13f.; 5:31f., 20f.

church (cf. Dodd). The contrast between those who are "from God" and those who are "not from God" is meant in a fundamental sense (cf. 2:4f., 23; 3:10; 5:10, 12, 19). The separation between them is a matter of concern for the community (or communities — see 2:19). Compared with v. 5 we may get the impression that this is an excuse for the feeble answer which the Christian missionaries have given to the successful propaganda of the false prophets. Yet the denial in v. 6c and the ending of v. 6d show that the author is primarily concerned to expose the ungodly nature of the false prophets and their followers. He wants to stop his readers from hankering after them. Belonging to God is now referred to as "knowing" him, an expression which the gnostics were using as a slogan in their own interests (2:4). Earlier the author had deprived them of this same weapon when he was discussing moral issues (2:3–6). Then he assured his readers that it is they who really had knowledge (2:13–14). This time, in dealing with the question of faith, he insists similarly that those who truly know God listen to the Christians. It is curious that here the knowledge of God is represented not as the goal but as the origin of the religious pilgrimage. It means the same thing as "belonging to the truth" (John 18:37) and possessing the "Spirit of truth" (cf. v. 6d). The final sentence, v. 6d, does not take up or recapitulate the rules for distinguishing the spirits as in vv. 2–3, for the phrase "from this" can hardly refer back that far. Rather, it means that we can see from their behavior who it is who hears the message of Christ, and which spirit has laid hold of them. "The spirit" is not the human spirit influenced by truth or error, like "every spirit" in vv. 2b and 3a. Rather, as the article also shows, it is the driving power, like "the Spirit of God" in v. 2a and the "spirit of the antichrist" in v. 3b. The term "Spirit of truth" reminds us of the Paraclete sayings in the farewell discourses (John 14:17; 15:26; 16:13). As in v. 3, the phrase "the Spirit of truth" avoids personalizing the opposing power but marks the influence opposed to God as of satanic origin (cf. v. 4).

Planē generally means "going astray, error." It does not usually suggest actively or maliciously leading others astray,[20] though it can have that meaning (cf. Eph. 4:14; Diog. 12.3). Especially instructive are the *Testaments of the Twelve Patriarchs,* in which the doctrine of the spirits or spirit of deception (or of Beliar) occupies a prominent position.[21] *T. Jude* 20:1 speaks of "two spirits" fighting to possess humankind, the "Spirit of truth" and "spirit of deceit" (cf. 14:8). The "Lord of deceit" can blind people to the truth (19:4; cf. *T. Sim.* 2:7); "demons of deceit" may enmesh them in sin (*T. Jud.* 23:1). Only after the coming of the Messiah in the time of salvation would there no longer be a "deceiving demon of Belial" (*T. Jud.* 25:3; cf. *T. Sim.* 6:6; *T. Levi* 3:3). *T. Rub.* 2:1 knows of "seven spirits of deceit" which are enumerated in 3:3–6. *T. Dan* 5:5 teaches that "demons of evil" are responsible for the time of apostasy and disaster (*v.l.* "of deceit"). Repeatedly "truth" and "deceit" (*planē*) are antithetically opposed to each other; cf. *T. Rub.* 3:3–6 with 7f.; *T. Jud.* 14:1; 20:1; *T. Ash.* 6:1 with 2. In all of these texts *planē* is more than "error." It

---

20. See BAGD 666, s.v. — Bauer denies this active aspect additionally for 2 Thess. 2:11 and Diog. 12.3 (*planē tou opheōs*); for a contrary view, see Brooke and Büchsel, as well as H. Braun, *TDNT* 6:238f., 244, 251f.

21. Cf. R. Eppel, *Le piétisme juif dans les Testaments des Douze Patriarches* (Paris, 1930) 83ff.; Noack, *Satanas und Soteria,* 44ff.; B. Otzen, *Stud. theol.* 7 (1953) 135–44; H. Braun, *TDNT* 6:239f.; 240.

means Satan and his spirits, who tempt people to evil, blasphemy, and apostasy. Just as the Dead Sea Scrolls use the terms "lie" (*kzb*) and "error" (*t'wt*), evidently as synonyms, so too there seems to be no real difference between the Johannine use of *pseudos* ("falsehood") and *planē* ("deception"). For this concept see Excursus 9.[22]

SECOND SECTION

LOVE AS THE HALLMARK OF THOSE BORN OF GOD
(1 JOHN 4:7–5:4)

Like the right confession of faith, so too for the author love is the hallmark of those who are born of God. In love their divine nature shines through. This is because God is love by his very nature. In the same way the author understands the love of those who are born of God to be, generally speaking, the hallmark of their nature, though without at first distinguishing between God's love and mutual love. He only treats mutual love thematically at the end of the section (vv. 20f.). (In v. 11 it is not yet the theme). That is where the practical realization of love comes to the fore. In order to recognize the nature of love, which, he says, originates in God, the author examines the way God himself has shown his love *in action*. It became so to speak visible and tangible when God sent his Son for the salvation of the world (vv. 10, 14). This once-for-all divine act of love is the archetype and model for Christian love. Such a genuine, active love, which comes from God and bears the stamp of his divinity, assures the Christian of abundant blessings. It alone unites us completely and lastingly with God (vv. 12–16). It gives hope for ultimate salvation in the last judgment (v. 17) and casts away all fear (v. 18).

Looked at in this light, this new diatribe on love (the longest in the epistle) is far from being an unnecessary repetition of the two preceding ones (2:7–11; 3:11–18 or 24). This is true even though it picks up ideas that are already familiar to the reader. It sets up a reliable hallmark in the defense against the false prophets and their clever disguises. It also gives the moral admonition a profound basis, more so than 3:11ff. This is because it leads to ultimate ontological connections.

The fact that the theological exposition is followed immediately by parenesis — actually the parenesis runs all the way through — does not require the hypothesis of a *Vorlage* that has been exploited for homiletical purposes.[23] It is better explained from the author's idiosyncrasies. Consistent with his sober moral attitude, he casts the entire segment in the form of an admonition. This is shown by the opening words "let us love one another" (4:7). He likes to embellish profound theological argument with words of admonition. This is typical of his style (v. 11, "we ought"; v. 16b, immanence formulas; v. 19, "we love"; v. 21, "the commandment").

---

22. On the doctrine of the two spirits in 1QS, see P. Wernberg-Møller, "A Reconsideration of the Two Spirits in the Rule of the Community," *RevQum* 3 (1961–62) 413–41; Charlesworth, *NTS* 15 (1968–69) 389–419; von der Osten-Sacken, *Gott und Belial.*

23. See Bultmann, "Analyse," 152f.; Windisch prior to 4:7. Preisker assumes for 4:17 an additional eschatological *Vorlage* (169ff.).

Separation from the "World"

1. Love Comes Essentially from God, Who First Loved Us
(1 John 4:7–10)

> [7]Beloved, let us love one another, because love is from God; everyone who loves is born of God and knows God. [8]Whoever does not love does not know God, for God is love. [9]God's love was revealed among us in this way: God sent his only Son into the world so that we might live through him. [10]In this is love, not that we loved God but that he loved us and sent his Son to be the atoning sacrifice for our sins.

4:7 The initial challenge "Beloved, let us love one another" is not meant to open up a discussion of the special theme of mutual love. For the heart of what the author is about to deal with comes out only in the ensuing *hoti*-clause. This places love (*hē agapē*) in the center, though in quite general terms. The author is concerned to differentiate between the Christians and the false prophets, in order to establish that the real Christian is one who loves, while everyone who belongs to the world hates (3:13; cf. John 15:18f.; 17:14). Love is itself the very nature of God ("from God") and of God alone. The world may be able to love its own (*philein*), John 15:19. But what it really desires is lies and murder (cf. John 8:44; 1 John 3:12, 15).

Once this question and the all-embracing theme of love are recognized, the general statement made in v. 7c, "everyone who loves," will stand firm. The reading of Codex A, which adds *ton theon* (God) as an object, as well as tacitly assuming the addition of *tous adelphous* (the brothers), following v. 7a,[24] is an unacceptable narrowing of the meaning.

Everyone who loves, insofar as they actually do so, is born of God. Of course this does not mean that to be born of God consists of love but, as elsewhere in 1 John,[25] that being born of God can be recognized by love.

Next to being born of God comes our knowing him. Love is the criterion of such knowledge, as v. 8 shows. The idea itself, confined only to mutual love or fulfilling the commandments, is already familiar from 2:3ff. If "being born of God" refers rather to the believers' origin, "to know God" means most emphatically to have lasting fellowship with him. Only those who prove themselves by loving—by this very love—share the divine nature and have fellowship with God. The author deliberately adopts these terms, for they define the common religious aspirations both of Christianity and of other religions. This is in order to emphasize the requirement of love and at the same time crush the opponents.[26]

4:8 The author takes us still further into the depths of the divine nature by means of the antithesis that follows. Here he is not only denying—in a polemic against the gnostics—to those who do not love any knowledge of God;[27] but

---

24. So Chaine, who regards 4:7ff. as the immediate continuation of 3:24.

25. 1 John 2:29; 5:1; for the turn of phrase, cf. the clauses with *estin* in 2:22a, b; 3:10b (cf. a); 4:2b (cf. a), 3a (cf. b).

26. On 4:7, see also M. de Jonge, "'Geliefden, laten wij elkander liefhebben, want de liefde is uit God' (I John 4:7)," *NedTTijdschr* 22 (1968) 352–67; J. Coppens, *ETL* 45 (1969) 125–27.

27. The aorist *ouk egnō* (A 33 al. read *ou ginōskei*, in assimilation to v. 7) expresses the fact that

in probing the ground he coins the definitive statement, repeated in v. 16, that God is love. This, along with John 4:24 and 1 John 1:5, is one of the great sayings about the nature of God (see Excursus 10). Here it is stated with reference to the cosmos alienated and hostile to him (cf. 4:4–6). Humanity must decide between a world of unbelief and hatred and the world of faith, obedience, and love. There are no other implications to this word. It is not an analysis of the difference between the God of the Old Testament, the stern lawgiver and tyrant, and the God of the New Testament. 1 John speaks freely and consistently about keeping God's commandments.[28] The author prefers to think rather of the difference between the children of God and the children of the devil (3:9f.). This leads him to the idea of distinguishing what is genuinely Christian. But he does not go about this like a modern devotee of phenomenology or psychology of religion. Rather, he deduces the nature of the children of God from the nature of their Father. In turn, the intrinsically hidden nature of God is disclosed in the self-revelation of God through his saving acts. Of that more in the next verse.

4:9 The love of God has been "revealed," that is, become open to experience through God's sending of his only Son into the world. This expression for God's self-revelation is deliberately chosen because the author has in mind the personal revelation of the Son of God (cf. 1:2; 3:5, 8), in which the love of God — as also the life of God — manifested itself, as it were. The hidden nature of God has only now become recognizable in its fullness. This was not just the revelation of a single divine attribute, but the whole of God as the One who loves. He has always been so,[29] but this has become open to experience "among us"[30] only in the coming of his Son. Here the Son is called *monogenēs,* a term equivalent to the Hebrew *yēḥîd,* the only beloved. This is, in view of God's deed of love, a particularly meaningful attribute. In John — unlike *agapētos* (beloved) in Mark 1:11 par.; 9:7 par.; Matt. 12:18 — it points further to the unique origin of the Son of God (cf. John 1:14, 18), which alone could bring revelation and life from God to humanity.[31] Thus this attribute also prepares for the following *hina*-clause: the only begotten One, who received the divine life in its fullness from the Father (John

such a person has not yet attained to the knowledge of God; it is not a gnomic aorist, a rarity in the New Testament (BDF §333.1).

28. 2:3, 4, 7; 3:22, 23; 4:21; 5:2, 3.

29. See Bonsirven, 28: "until the Incarnation this characteristic of God remained hidden and unknown: but the Incarnation has in a striking way (*éclatant*) made it visible and since then it has been in the forefront."

30. The *en* with *phanerousthai* is hardly to be approximated to *poiein ti en tini* ("in our case") as BDF § 220.1 maintain. Insofar as the *en* with words of appearing does not indicate the object in which something becomes visible (2 Cor. 4:10f.; John 9:3), it has lost much of its force and is equivalent to a dative of the personal object; cf. Rom. 1:19a; Phil. 1:13; 2 Cor. 5:11b; 11:6; Gal. 1:16. Yet even the local meaning may still have some influence; cf. 1 Cor. 11:19b; 2 Cor. 4:3. That is also to be presumed for 1 John 4:9, given its affinity to John 1:14 (*eskēnōsen en hēmin*). Cf. further the usage in *Acts Thom.* 20; *Ep Abgari* 1 (Oepke, *TDNT* 2:539f.).

31. The term is found only at John 1:14, 18; 3:16, 18; 1 John 4:9. For the Old Testament background, cf. Judg. 11:34; Tobit 3:15; 8:17. For the rest, see Bauer on John 1:14 (HNT VI³, 26); Büchsel, *TDNT* 4:737ff. A. Šurjansky, *De mysterio Verbi incarnati ad mentem B. Joh. Ap.* I (Rome, 1941) 103–28. The metaphysical interpretation is rejected by Howard, *Christianity According to St. John,* 69f.; Staerk, *Soter* 1:106, 2:70; Bultmann, *Theology* 2:40f.

5:26), passes it on to those who believe in him. The sending or coming of the Son into the world from the Father[32] is just as much one of the dominant sayings of GJohn as the purpose accorded to it: "that we might live through him." The Pauline perspective on Jesus' death and resurrection and of our dying and rising in him, which he speaks of so often, has given way to the sayings about "life." The imparting of eternal life to humanity by the divine bearer of life, the incarnate Son of God—that is now the joy-giving message.

4:10 The author meditates further on the nature of love. He is profoundly impressed by the unique and supreme deed of God's love as he has just described it. This in turn leads him to recognize that such a perfect revelation of love and the reality of such love exist only as a result of the act of God. It is this act that forms the center of the Christian revelation. Love could not become an existential power effective in the world through human agency, but only through God himself. But in this verse the author cannot indulge in polemic against human arrogance because what he is reproaching his opponents with is a complete lack of love. But the Christians (whom the author has in mind when he uses "we"), as is suggested elsewhere in this letter, have no need of this kind of reprimand. The antithesis "not that . . . but that" only serves to emphasize the importance of what God has done. The true power of love has entered the world solely through God's initiative. The human race stood in *need* of God's merciful love but was quite incapable of producing it. We are reminded of this in the latter part of the sentence which takes up the idea of sending[33] (v. 9) and points to the fact that the Son of God was sent to atone for sins. The same point was already made in 2:2 and—more briefly—with the formula *hyper hēmōn* ("for us") in 3:16 (cf. also 3:8). Any false understanding of the possessive pronoun "our" is ruled out by the expanded commentary in 2:2. The climax of love is that God in his mercy overcame the gulf between himself and a world in need of salvation, a world alienated by sin. The word *houtōs* ("so much") in v. 11 ties in with this.

There is no parallel to these statements outside of Christianity.[34] They contain genuine Christian insights, which the author has plumbed to their very depth. In them the essence of Christianity is recognized as a religion of love—not, however, in the sense that love is the apex and centerpiece of Christian *teaching* but in the much more important sense that the human race only knows what love is since the sending of God's Son. Only in him have they experienced a love bestowed on them to the uttermost.

---

32. See the Excursus in Westcott, 124–28; Staerk, *Soter* 2:87ff.

33. The variation between the perfect and aorist forms in *apostellein* (ℵ reads *apestalken* in v. 10 as well as v. 9) is therefore of no importance; both tenses are consistent with Johannine style, like *edōkas* and *dedōkas* in John 17:6ff., cf. BDF §38; Radermacher, *Grammatik,* 150, 154; Mayser, *Grammatik,* II, 1:140. *Per contra, ēgapēkamen* (so B 1739 pc *contra* ℵ and many manuscripts of the ḥ-type, which have *ēgapēsamen*) certainly denotes the enduring character of love, whereas *ēgapēsen* denotes the once-for-all act of God's love.

34. See Excursus 10.4.

Excursus 10

Love as the Nature of God

The profound discussion about divine love, culminating in the twice-repeated statement "God is love" (1 John 4:8, 16), needs to be evaluated within the framework of Johannine theology. It must also be compared with what the rest of early Christianity and the surrounding world of religion has to say about the subject.

1. The Assertion within the Framework of Johannine Theology

a) The affirmation "God is love" acquires its full meaning only when placed alongside of two other affirmations: "God is Spirit" (John 4:24) and "God is light" (1 John 1:5). We must also bear in mind the dualistic character of Johannine thought. By means of these statements this early Christian theologian aims at expressing the uniqueness of God and his distinction from the world and all its godlessness. His aim is to lay bare something of the glorious nature of God which is shared by those who are born of him — in contrast to those who belong to the world, a world that has turned its back on him. It is no accident that the affirmation "God is Spirit" is found in GJohn and the two other affirmations in the epistle; it is due rather to the subject matter. In GJohn Jesus brings the revelation of hidden mysteries (cf. 1:18; 3:12, 32; 5:37; 6:46). One of those mysteries is the divine nature, the knowledge of which Jesus denies to the unbelieving Jews (7:28; 8:19, 55) but reveals to the Samaritan woman who was ready to believe (4:23f.). The epistle is directed against gnostics, who, while they are receptive to exalted revelations, overlook the moral nature of God. God must be shown to them in his spotless holiness (1:5) and love which urges to action (4:8, 16). Thus these definitive statements about God are not the result of philosophical reflection.They are not intended to be definitions, but are drawn from divine revelation. They throw a clear light upon Christian reflection about God.

b) The author recognizes that God is love in the depths of his being through the divine activity and especially in the sending of the Son into the world and the realm of death in order to give life to humankind (4:9). Only in this way is the love of God revealed among men and women. Only through and in the Son is it possible truly to know the Father (cf. John 8:19; 14:9f.). Only in the giving of the Son as an atoning sacrifice for sin is the transcendent love of the Father for the human race revealed (1 John 4:10). But through his Son, God has enabled us to become his children in a true, existential sense. Thus he has bestowed upon us his fatherly love (cf. 1 John 3:1). This merciful love of God appears so dramatically, so exclusively, that it becomes the sole characteristic of the divine action. "God's love is no longer parallel to his wrath or parallel to his righteousness . . . he *is* love. All his activity is the activity of love" (Dodd). Love therefore becomes the hallmark of God's children. But they love and are enabled to love only by the power of God, only because God first loved them and grafted into them a capacity for love. "This love is a vital movement, a form of existence, an actualization of God in the world."[35]

---

35. Stauffer, *TDNT* 1:52f.; see also Huby, *Mystiques,* 145ff.; Feine, *Theologie,* 348f.

c) The love of those born of God also involves an imparting of the divine nature. It is turning things upside down to infer that the love of God in John is narrowed down to a restricted circle of those who belong to him (from eternity).[36] The idea of predestination is found in other passages in John, namely, in connection with the enigma of unbelief,[37] but has no place in this discussion. The author takes those who are born of God as an empirically existing group. He does not worry about their election or calling, but recognizes them simply by their love. God remains in fellowship with them (4:16) not because they are related to him by nature (the gnostic belief that certain people were pneumatic by nature is rejected by the author), but because and insofar as they have received the divine nature by being born of God (sacramentally) and persist in that state through their love.

d) The universality of the divine movement of love is also preserved in Johannine theology. For God's love is directed in the first instance to the cosmos, the world of humanity in need of redemption (John 3:16; 1 John 4:9f., 14). To enjoy the fruit of this love is a possibility for all who believe in Jesus, the true and only Son of God. Because the eleven who remained with Jesus in the Upper Room love the One whom God sent and believe in his divine origin despite his lowly appearance, the Father loves them (John 16:27). At the time the epistle was written, the author and the Christians associated with him are the believers (the "we"), who accepted this divine revelation of love and thus experienced it as a love which takes away the sins of the world and brings salvation (1 John 4:9f.). But this salvation is in principle open to all (cf. 2:2; 4:14). Just as the love of God is a matter of grace, prevenient and totally unmerited (4:10), so it requires human acceptance through faith in Christ.

2. The Assertion Compared with Other Early Christian Teaching

a) John is expressing an idea that was common in Christianity, but expressing it more forcefully. God in an utterly "unmotivated" way is gracious love, condescending to save the sinner. That is the heart of the good news Jesus brought (Matt. 5:3ff.; Mark 2:17 par.; Matt. 18:23ff.; Luke 15; 18:10ff.).[38] Early Christianity sees this loving attitude of God fulfilled in the giving of his Son to death for our sin and guilt. He did not spare his own Son (Rom. 8:32) and in Christ Jesus has drawn us inseparably into his love (Rom. 8:39). This is why he is a God of love and peace (1 Cor. 13:11). His love is an act of free will proceeding directly from himself for the salvation of the lost (Eph. 2:4). It is directed to those who because of their sin were his enemies (Rom. 5:8). The full breadth of this

---

36. *Contra* H. Preisker, *Die urchristliche Botschaft von der Liebe Gottes im Lichte der vergleichenden Religionsgeschichte* (Giessen, 1930) 47, 58f.; C. R. Bowen, "Love in the Fourth Gospel," *JR* 13 (1933) 39–49.

37. John 6:37, 39, 65; 10:26ff.; (12:37ff.); 17:2, 6, 7, 9, 24; cf. my diss., "Der Glaube im vierten Evangelium," 36ff.

38. This "uncaused" nature in the divine *agapē* has been worked out forcefully by A. Nygren, *Agape and Eros* (Philadelphia, 1953) 75ff. Yet it is hard to understand why Nygren thinks that this idea is "weakened" in John.

dominant thought can be grasped only when we take note of the various synonyms for the love of God, such as "mercy," "righteousness," "reconciliation."[39]

b) There is also the idea that the love of God has been imparted in a certain way to the baptized. It thus becomes an active power within them. The rudiments of this notion can already be traced in Paul. For "God's love has been poured into our heart by the Holy Spirit which has been given to us" (Rom. 5:5). In Paul's dynamic doctrine of the Spirit this divine love imparted to us is more of an agent than a quality. But there can be no doubt from other passages, like Rom. 8:14f.; Gal. 4:6, that the Holy Spirit is thought of not only as the mediator of love toward God but as himself the Spirit of divine love. Through him and with him God's own love enters into us, permeating us, working in us, and assuring us that our salvation will be consummated in the future. John expressed all this in slightly different terms, but put it even more strongly: it is a hallmark of the child of God. But John was not inventing something entirely new.

c) Thus the great achievement of Johannine theology remains within the parameters of early Christianity. It is no more than a pregnant formulation of the fact that the God of the new covenant is by nature a merciful God, the all-giving, self-imparting God of love. Inasmuch as this love is revealed in Christ, this leads to further implications of a slightly different kind. For example, the author of 1 John sees already in the incarnation, in the sending of the Son of God into the world, the manifestation of God's love (1 John 4:9). Christ is the "only-begotten" Son of God, embodying the divine life and proclaiming it to his own. Further, 1 John grasps the connection between God's love for us and our status as his children more firmly than Paul does (3:1) and allows the divine love more emphatically to become a reality in the lives of men and women and a motive for their behavior.

3. The Assertion Compared with the Picture of God in the Old Testament and Late Judaism

a) There is no exact parallel to the pregnant formula of 1 John 4:8, 16 in the Old Testament or late Judaism. In content, however, the saying about the divine nature, apart from its genuine Christian elements, has the closest affinity to the early Jewish concept of God. In the Old Testament God acts in history, and though from a New Testament perspective the sterner elements in the Old Testament picture of God may seem more prominent, nevertheless Yahweh is beyond all doubt a God of election, mercy, and forgiving love. His love for Israel springs from the unfathomable depth of divine choice and acquires a passionate, jealous

39. See R. Schütz, *Die Vorgeschichte der johanneischen Formel* ὁ θεὸς ἀγάπη ἐστίν (Göttingen diss.; Kiel, 1917) 11ff.—On the New Testament idea of God's love, see W. Lütgert, *Die Liebe im NT* (Leipzig, 1905); J. Moffatt, *Love in the NT* (London, 1929); W. Harrelson, "The Idea of Agape in the NT," *JR* 31 (1951) 169–82; V. Warnach, *Agape: Die Liebe als Grundmotif der neutestamentlichen Theologie* (Düsseldorf, 1951); idem, "Liebe," *BibeltheolW* (Graz, 1959) 502–42 (with bibliography); C. Spicq, *Agape dans le NT: Analyse des textes* (3 vols.; Paris, 1958–59).—On John specifically, see A. Šuštar, *De Caritate apud Joa. Ap.* (Rome, 1951); C. Oggioni, "La dottrina della carita nel IV Vangelo e nella prima lettera di Giovanni," *Scrinium Theologicum* I (1953) 221–93; L. Moraldi, *Dio e Amore* (Rome, 1954); J. Chmiel, *Lumière et charité,* 174–212.

power.[40] In the history of the covenant relationship and the experience of Israel's faithlessness, Yahweh's mercy and forgiveness are revealed again and again. He yearns exclusively for Israel's salvation.[41] The Septuagint nearly always translates the Hebrew verb *'āhab* with *agapan*,[42] the very word for love which was hardly ever used for human love in Greek.[43] Despite its stern and uncompromising quality, late Judaism still speaks in glowing terms of God's love for Israel.[44]

b) There is one idea, though, that takes a back seat in Judaism. This is the universality of God's love. That love is directed first and foremost toward the elect people of the covenant, the people who received the Torah as an expression of his preference. The pagan world may, according to the prevailing view, join Israel at the end and share God's love. The other view was that the Gentiles would be justified by their own fulfillment of the commandments.[45] But there was no question of any real equality. For paganism by and large their idolatry was the great barrier that cut them off from God. Israel's advantages are never forgotten. Only after legalism had been overcome in the New Testament was God's universal will for salvation revealed along with his love for sinners. Then God's love came to be realized in all its greatness and incomprehensibility. God's decision is here directed, fundamentally and from the outset, toward the deliverance of all fallen humanity (1 John 4:14, 16). Conversely, individuals exclude themselves from this general salvation insofar as they refuse to believe in the "Savior of the world."

c) To put it in human terms, when God's love is seen as universal in its scope, its character also changes. In the Old Testament the root *'āhab* always has "compassionate overtones of complete engagement."[46] Hosea is the first to apply the metaphor of marriage to the covenant relationship between Yahweh and Israel. But he does not so much portray the passion of love (cf. 2:16ff.) as he shows the horror of Israel's faithlessness (1:2ff.; 2:4ff.). Tenderness is also echoed in the same prophet's description of Yahweh's fatherly care for Israel, his "son" (Hosea 11). Such tender love can turn into boiling rage, then give way to heartfelt mercy. There is no sign of such impulsiveness in the New Testament. Here God is altogether the merciful Father. He knows the frailty and sinfulness of his children,

---

40. See Eichrodt, *Theology* 1:250ff.; Quell, *TDNT* 1:31ff.; J. Ziegler, *Die Liebe Gottes bei den Propheten* (ATAbh 11, 3; Münster, 1930) 19ff.

41. Isa. 54:7f.; 63:7ff.; Jer. 3:12ff.; 31:3ff.; Mic. 7:18ff.

42. Stauffer, *TDNT* 1:39ff.

43. Ibid., 1:36f.; E. Peterson held that the substantive *agapē* was neither created nor used outside Christian-Jewish circles (*BZ* 20 [1932] 378-82); cf., however, C. C. Tarelli, "Agape," *JTS* 51 (1950) 64-67; A. Ceresa-Gastaleo, "'ΑΓΑΠΗ' nei documenti anteriori al NT," *Egyptus* 31 (1951-52) 269-306; idem, "ΑΓΑΠΗ nei documenti estrani all'influsso biblico," *Riv. di Filologia e di Instruzione class.* 31 (1953) 343-56. On the linguistic history, see further Spicq, *Agape: Prolegomines à une étude de théologie néotestamentaire* (Louvain-Leiden, 1955).

44. See Schütz, *Vorgeschichte*, 32-39; Moore, *Judaism* 1:398f.; Bousset-Gressmann, *Religion des Judentums,* 384ff.; Billerbeck, *Kommentar* 3:778; Bonsirven, *Judaïsme* 1:192ff.; esp. well considered in its judgment is E. Sjöberg, *Gott und die Sünder im palästinischen Judentum* (Stuttgart, 1939).

45. Ziegler, *Liebe Gottes,* 104ff.; Volz, *Eschatologie,* 358f.; Moore, *Judaism* 2:385f.; Sjöberg, *Gott und die Sünder,* 86ff., 210ff. (Rabbinic Judaism allows more room for God's mercy than does apocalyptic).

46. Eichrodt, *Theology* 1:250.

yet accepts them with mercy, as Jesus himself shows in the great parable of the prodigal son (Luke 15:11–32). 1 John is speaking of the same God of love who came to meet us and first loved us. This idea of love has a twofold root in the Old Testament. One is its close affinity with God's love for his own people, especially in time of tribulation. The other springs to the lips of the prophet and the one who prays: God of goodness and mercy (*hesed* and *rahămîm*).[47]

4. The Assertions Compared to Syncretistic Texts

a) We look in vain for similar views about the love of God and about his saving acts and mercy in syncretistic thought. In Gnosticism divine love is first and foremost the election of the pneumatics who by nature are related to God. It proves itself when they are led upward to the realm of light. That is why the Mandean texts have so much to say about the "Elect." Only to them is Manda d'Haije sent to guide them upward. "It [viz., the great light] encompassed me about with love, which my friends were to share also. It spoke to me tenderly, in words I was to pass on to my friends. I was to speak to my friends and redeem them from that which passes away" (*Ginza* 333.31ff.). In the *Hermetic Tractate* 1, Poimandres rejects the view that all have *nous*. Only the holy one, the good, the pure, the merciful and pious are approached by *nous*. Its arrival brings them succor, and at once they know all things, "and by their love they cause the Father to be gracious."[48] People here are apparently divided from the outset into two categories, and from those who do not comprehend (*anoētois*), the wicked, evil, covetous, greedy, murderous, ungodly (i.e., those who are imprisoned in the realm of darkness) *nous* remains distant. They are delivered over to the demon of punishment, who prepares them for even greater godlessness and hurls them into even worse perdition (1.23). Not one word about the all-merciful love of God! God only loves his own.[49]

b) The reciprocal love between God and the gnostics who are related to him is described in some texts in affective terms. This is particularly the case in the *Odes of Solomon*. The pictures of marital, paternal, and maternal love are used in similar ways,[50] and often coalesce with one another. But all this is only an expression of their intoxication with "gnosis," to which they have attained and which is the great path to salvation (see Excursus 3). The "Father" is the source of revelation (*Odes Sol.* 7:7). He was merciful in that he allowed himself to be

---

47. See p. 211 n. 38 and Hos. 2:21; Pss. 25:6; 40:12; 51:3; 69:14, 17; 86:5; 90:13f.; 145:7ff. In addition, see Ziegler, *Liebe Gottes,* 28ff., 39ff.; Eichrodt, *Theology* 1:237f.; Bonsirven, ad loc. (p. 223) and *Judaïsme* 1:192f.

48. *Ton patera hilaskontai agapētikōs* (*CHerm* 1.22).

49. See further *CHerm* 4.3f.; 9.5; Ps.-Asclep. 7f. In this passage we do not always find exactly the same ideas about the election of the pneumatic human beings, here called "spiritual by nature," *ousiōdēs*. The strongest expression of this is in 9.5: "not every person is lacking in knowledge, but one is material, the other spiritual. The former of these is involved in evil; he has the seed of knowledge of the demons. The others are involved with the good (by nature); they are saved by God." Scott, it is true, reegards the text as corrupt (cf. 2.214f.), not without justification, given the context; but he proceeds too drastically. The traditional text is equally untenable; see Nock-Festugière, ad loc.

50. (a) bridal relationship (3:3–5, 7; 7:1f.; 8:13, 22; 38:11; 42:8f.); (b) paternal relationship (7:7ff.; 9:5; 14:1; 31:4; 41:1–3, 10); (c) maternal relationship (8:16; 14:2; 19:2ff.; 35:5; 40:1).

known (7:12ff.). Why does a maternal image replace that of the Father? Because milk is a favorite metaphor for love in gnosis.[51] Bridal love depicts the intimate relationship and mystical inclination of the gnostic to the divine realm. It shows the profound understanding and the fervemt urge for union between the gnostics and the deity. The gnostics lose sight of all else. They are alone with God, raised up to the heights of knowledge, united in bliss. One can understand the attraction of this sort of mystical piety in that day and age, as well as the danger it posed for a religion which teaches real salvation coming from God. The verses from the *Odes of Solomon,* which from a superficial point of view sound like 1 John 4 (though couched in the first person singular), are in their true content quite different:

> For I should not have known how to love the Lord,
> if he had not continuously loved me.
> Who is able to distinguish love,
> except him who is loved?
> I love the Beloved and I myself love him,
> and where his rest is, there also am I. (3:3–5)

c) In this type of ecstatic piety the love of God, which is expressed in self-disclosure, is transposed entirely into the present. Gnostics do not look back to God's great act of love in the past, nor do they envision it reaching a final climax in the future. True, after their physical death and release from the material world they will ascend to the glorious realm of light. But though celebrated unceasingly, this ascent is in part no more than a mythological expression of their present union with God, and in part a cry of the soul's yearning. For the soul is unable to realize permanently the brief moment of ecstasy it enjoys in union with the divine, so it hopes for a true fulfillment after death. God's act of love as revealed to the Christians has a genuine climax in time, viz., the sending of the Son of God. That occurred at a particular moment in history (1 John 4:9; cf. Gal. 4:4), and the individual experience of being born of God on becoming a Christian (1 John 3:1), and the perfection of that present status in the eschatological future, the parousia (1 John 3:2; cf. 4:17). Actually, however, the revelation of God's love on a cosmic, universal scale has already reached its climax in the sending of his Son. But the individual's experience of love progresses from today to the eschatological tomorrow.

5. The Assertions Compared with Those of Contemporary Philosophy

Still further removed from the Johannine claim that God is love are the expressions of contemporary philosophy, however attractive they may sound to the popular ear.

a) As early as Plato and Aristotle[52] God is called "Father of mortals and gods,"

---

51. Some of the metaphorical language is strange; see especially *Odes Sol.* 19, where perhaps the gnostic idea of a sacrament in milk is present; cf. Dieterich, *Mithrasliturgie,* 170f.; H. Schlier, *TDNT* 1:646f.

52. Plato, *Tim.* 28c, 41a, 42e; Aristotle, *Polit.* I, 12; he follows the wording of Homer, clarifying it in philosophical terms (Homer, *Iliad* 4.235; 5.33; etc.); cf. Lohmeyer, *Das Vaterunser,* 22f.; G. Schrenk, *TDNT* 5:951f.

and although the same thing is repeated in popular Stoicism,[53] the root of this expression lies for the most part in his attributes as Creator of the universe.[54] The world view may be preoccupied with the problem of pain, but on the whole it remains optimistic. We can see this in the honest attempt to produce a genuine theodicy, which tries to bring home to men and women the goodness and friendliness of the divine Ruler of the world. The world is under the control of reason, and this includes humanity, which consists of reasonable beings able to acknowledge their kinship (*syngeneia*) with God.[55] The cross, the supreme proof of God's love for Christians, looks there like mere folly.

b) The logical consequence of this basic conviction is that God's love for the world and humanity is shown primarily in his providential care.[56] This idea, which was (incorrectly) thought to be close to many sayings of Jesus about his heavenly Father (Matt. 5:45–47; 6:25ff.), is not found anywhere in John. Conversely, we look in vain among the philosophers for the Christian idea of God's love, where the sending of his Son becomes the supreme revelation. Those citizens of the world do not think in historical or soteriological terms. Those who at most sin against their better self and can gain salvation by reflecting on their dignity and freedom as human beings have no need of God's saving mercy and love.

c) God's help, his friendly assistance, is something even the philosophers can feel as a merciful condescension and power from above. But for the deepst human need, for their sense of being lost, for their endemic feelings of guilt, the God of the philosophers is no help whatever. "However much they [the Greek gods] would like to help, it is not written in their faces that they are infinite love, such as makes them ready to to give themselves to men and women and redeem them from all of their distress."[57] The heart of the Johannine message of a loving God who is beyond all doubt the all-merciful, saving love, drawing everyone to himself, is the opposite of the philosophical teaching. It is truly an unprecedented, joyous message.[58]

* * *

53. Epictetus, *Diss.* 1.3.1; 6.40; 9.7; 19.12; 3.24.16; Seneca, *De benef.* 2.29.4f.; *Ep.* 107.11; *De prov.* 1.5.

54. See Plato, *Leg.* 2.678c; Epictetus, *Diss.* 1.9.7: *To de ton theon poiētēn echein kai ton patera kai kēdemona ouketi exairēsetai lypon kai phobōn;* cf. 4.11.3.

55. See Excursus 2. On Plutarch, see Nilsson, *Geschichte der griechischen Religion* 2:385ff.

56. See especially Seneca, *De prov.* 1.1f.; Epictetus, *Diss.* 1.12.1–6. "For the Stoics this belief in the rule of providence becomes one of their favorite ideas" (Preisker, *Urchristliche Botschaft,* 12); cf. also H. Preisker, *Neutestamentliche Zeitgeschichte* (Berlin, 1937) 57–60; Pohlenz, *Stoa* 1:338f.

57. W. F. Otto, *Die Götter Griechenlands* (3rd ed.; Frankfurt, 1947) 242.

58. Nygren places the Platonic idea of Eros in opposition to Christian Agape, as well as its continuation in neo-Platonism (in connection with the mystery religions) (*Agape,* passim). Eros, Nygren maintains, is an upward-moving and in the last analysis egocentric love, whereas Agape is a downward-moving, selfless love. This is overly schematized, though it contains some truth.

2. The Love of Those Who Belong to God Is a Response to His Love and Places Us in Intimate Fellowship with God (1 John 4:11–16)

¹¹Beloved, since God loved us so much, we also ought to love one another. ¹²No one has ever seen God; if we love one another, God lives in us, and his love is perfected in us.

¹³By this we know that we abide in him and he in us, because he has given us of his Spirit. ¹⁴And we have seen and do testify that the Father has sent his Son as the Savior of the world. ¹⁵God abides in those who confess that Jesus is the Son of God, and they abide in God. ¹⁶So we have known and believe the love that God has for us. God is love, and those who abide in love abide in God, and God abides in them.

The author has been discussing the nature of love as God-like behavior. Now, in the section that follows, he draws his conclusions for the benefit of his readers. This is in accordance with his usual practice of deducing the practical implications of his argument—cf. 2:1–2 as against 1:8–10; 2:24 as against 22f.; 3:16f. as against v. 16a. There is thus no reason to suggest that we have here a parenetical commentary on a *Vorlage*, especially since vv. 9–10 can hardly belong to that source.[59] Taken as a whole, this section does not stay consistently with the theme. Verses 14–16a once more place right faith in relation to love, and so form a digression.

4:11 The last thought expressed in v. 10, viz., that the greatness of God's love became visible in the giving of his Son in his atoning death, provides the motivation ("since . . . we also") for Christian love. Here God becomes the pattern of love, like Christ in 3:16b. The way it is expressed ("we . . . ought") also reminds us of that same passage. The practical interest in parenesis is shown in the way the principle of love is immediately applied to the practice of mutual love as its recognizable fruit. In so doing the author returns to the admonition of v. 7a.

4:12 This kind of love, and this kind alone, preserves fellowship between God and humankind. That is the thought that serves as a link to the following verse. As a result, the motif of responsive love (v. 11) joins up with the other motif, that of fellowship with God. The latter provides the basic theme for the whole letter. Verse 12 does not directly anticipate the thought of v. 20, for it lays no stress on the object of love.[60] Rather, love is contrasted with outward show. It is not by such pretense but by love that we are able to remain in fellowship with God. In contradiction to the gnostics, the author still more plainly confutes their claim to a direct knowledge of God (cf. vv. 7d and 8a) and (ecstatic?) visions.

---

59. See Bultmann, "Analyse," 152. The few sentences in the section which Bultmann attributes to his *Vorlage* (vv. 7b–8, 12, 16b) must have been worked into the final document by the author with great ingenuity.

60. The placing of *theon* at the beginning and *allēlous* at the end could be irritating, as though the emphasis rested on *theon*. Yet John 1:18 similarly had *theon* at this place ("as far as God is concerned, this is the case . . "). The emphasis lies on the verbs *tetheatai* and *agapōmen*.

The same polemic against visionary (John 1:18; 5:37; 6:46) or ecstatic (John 3:13) experiences of union with God seems to occur already in GJohn. This polemic is not—in the epistle at any rate—directed against Judaism. It is not attacking apocalyptic speculation about ascensions into heaven.[61] Rather, it is directed against the gnostics, for whom the (ecstatic) ascension of the soul represents a model of divine knowledge or vision.[62] Such gnostic pretensions, represented by the false prophets, are what the author is combating (4:1). God cannot be reached by ecstasy or pretense, involving the elimination of the lower senses.[63] It remains only in those who realize God's commandment of love. Fellowship with God is a pure gift (cf. 3:1) and must be kept pure by moral fidelity. That is why in 4:12 God is the subject: he abides in us—whereas elsewhere the author prefers to say that we abide in God (3:24a; 4:13, 15, 16). The continuation, "his love . . ." concludes the argument: those who actively engage in passing on to others the love they have received put their fellowship with God into practice. In them the divine nature is perfected. The controverted genitive *autou* ("his") must therefore be taken as a subjective genitive, suggesting that we were the recipients of divine love.[64] Nor is it an objective genitive, for that would suggest that our love for him is perfected.[65] On the other hand, taken in a qualitative sense, meaning "the divine love, which is proper to God alone" (cf. 3:17), these words reinforce the main thesis of the section, which is that love comes from God and that everyone who loves is born of him (v. 7). "Perfected" here is not, any more than in 2:5 (see ad loc.) an eschatological term. Rather, it designates reality in its fullness (cf. 4:17 and 18, "perfect love").

4:13 It seems strange that along with the hallmark of love the other point is mentioned, namely, the possession of the Spirit. Perhaps it would be best to take it as a gloss, suggested by the phrase "abide in God."[66] If it is to fit the context, we shall have to assume that the role of the Spirit is to strengthen Christians' awareness that they love God and their brothers and sisters. This, however, would weaken the parenetic emphasis in the words "we ought to love" (v. 12). The almost

---

61. Cf. the ascension of Enoch (*1 Enoch* 71 and *2 Enoch* 1ff.), of Levi (*T. Levi* 2–5), of Baruch (*Apoc. Bar.*), of Esdras (*Apoc. Ezra* 1), etc.; further the assumption of the four rabbis in *Hag.* 14b (Goldschmidt 4:283). See further Bousset-Gressmann, *Religion des Judentums,* 356, 399; Volz, *Eschatologie,* 418; Nötscher, *Das Angesicht Gottes schauen,* 170ff.; Scholem, *Die jüdische Mystik,* 56f. Official rabbinic teaching held strongly to the invisibility of God to those who dwell on earth; see Billerbeck, *Kommentar* 1:362f.; Bonsirven, *Judaïsme* 1:160.

62. Cf. *Mithras Liturgy* 6.9ff. (also Dieterich, *Mithrasliturgie,* 61ff.); *Poimandres* 24–26; Apuleius, *Metam.* 11.23. Cf. Lietzmann on 2 Cor. 12:4 (HNT IX⁴, 153f.); A. Oepke, *TDNT* 2:450ff.; J. Dey, Παλιγγενεσία (NTAbh 17, 5; Münster, 1937) 104ff.; W. Michaelis, *TDNT* 5:323f.; Nilsson, *Geschichte der Griechischen Religion* 2:568; further, Excursus 2 above, p. 67ff.).

63. Cf. *CHerm* 10.5f.: *katargia pasōn tōn aisthēseōn;* 13.7: *katargēson tou sōmatos tas aisthēseis.*

64. Brooke; Schütz, *Vorgeschichte,* 4–6; Bonsirven; Chaine; cf. also Büchsel. However, God's love for us found its supreme climax already in vv. 9–10. How could the perfection of his love (*teteleiōmenē*) now be dependent on our response of love?

65. Belser, Camerlynck, Wendt, Vrede, Windisch, Hauck, Ambroggi, Chaine, Dodd. Our love for God does not suit the context.

66. See Loisy, Windisch.

identical wording of 4:13 and 3:24b[67] suggests a stereotyped formula which presumably comes from the church catechism. "God has given us of his Spirit" was a catechetical phrase, while "we know that we abide in God" is the author's own teaching. He was undoubtedly convinced that everyone who was born in God can possess his Spirit and experience it internally (cf. on 3:24). This agrees with Paul, who is equally aware of the inner testimony of the Spirit, which assures us that we are God's children and inspires deep experiences of prayer in the Spirit (Rom. 8:16, 26f.). The author of 1 John must have felt the same confidence that God will hear our prayers (3:21f.; 5:14), that all our fears will be overcome (4:18), and that the victory of faith will be ours (5:4). In all this he will have felt the breath of the Spirit. But only here does he speak of our partaking of God's Spirit (*ek tou pneumatos*), and that in the context of fellowship with God. This is borne out in v. 15. Love (v. 12), faith (v. 15), and possession of the Spirit (v. 13) are all testimonies and signs of that fellowship with God. We can see in these well-crafted statements and their carefully planned associations the experienced teacher who is attempting to bring home to his readers definite ideas of his own.

4:14 The next two verses are even more clearly a digression. Only in v. 16a does the author return to his theme, the theme of love. In the middle of his discussion about love and the way it is modeled on God's great act of love, he suddenly remembers that faith in Jesus, God's emissary, and in his redemptive death is the presupposition for developing the idea of God's work of love. This is the reason why he again mentions that he and his fellow preachers ("we"; cf. 1:1–4) are witnesses to the faith. Since the phrase "we have seen" must have an object of some sort, that object must be seen formally in the *hoti*-clause. This, however, reproduces the content of the testimony ("do testify"). The phrase therefore must be an abbreviated form of the testimony. "We have seen" summarizes what was said in 1:1. These witnesses have seen the Son, and in the Son they have seen the Father (cf. John 14:9). Through faith in the Son they have acknowledged God's great act of love. To this faith they now give their testimony.

This testimony is formulated in such a way that God's saving act stands out. Since their acknowledgment of it depends on their faith in the Son, it says — contrary to John 3:16 — "the Father." Here, as in 1 John 3:1, the thought that God is a *loving* Father must be implied. The Son is called the "Savior of the world." This really says the same thing as John 3:17. But the substantive "Savior" had a special nuance at that time. For there were saviors both human and divine.[68]

---

67. Differences: in 4:13 *ek tou pneumatos* is dependent on *didonai* and is therefore to be taken as a partitive genitive (cf. BDF §169.2), while in 3:24b it is dependent on *ginōskein*. Further, in 4:13 we have *dedōken* (for this A 33 al. have *edōken*); in 3:24, however, we have *edōken* — a considerable difference. The reciprocal formula for abiding in God in 4:13 occurs already in 3:24a and consequently it is taken up again in 3:24b with the simple formula.

68. Cf. the material in P. Wendland, *ZNW* 5 (1904) 335ff.; F. J. Dölger, *Ichthys* 1:406ff.; Deissmann, *Light from the Ancient East,* 368f.; Bousset, *Kyrios Christos* (Eng. trans.), 310ff.; Dibelius-Conzelmann, excursus on 2 Tim. 1:10 (HNT XIII³; pp. 74ff.); H. Haerens, "Σωτήρ et σωτερία," *Studia Hellenistica* 5 (Louvain, 1948) 57–68. On the connection with ideas of the Son of man in late Jewish apocalyptic, see Staerk, *Soter* 1:72ff.; 2:69f.; F. Büchsel, *Johannes und der hellenistische Synkretismus,* 44–46. The biblical-Jewish components are emphasized more strongly by O. Cullmann, *The Christology*

The only other Johannine passage apart from 1 John 4:14 where Jesus is called Savior is in John 4:42, the Samaritan chapter with its theme of universalism. It also occurs in the Pastorals and 2 Peter,[69] where the uniqueness of the Christian Redeemer is being emphasized. But in 1 John 4:14 the emphasis lies on the *fact* of the world's redemption. This is because the gnostics thought they had no need of salvation by the blood of Jesus (cf. on 1:7c; 2:2; 4:2; 5:6). It is hard to say whether the author, in using the title "Savior of the world," wanted to introduce another, possibly polemical, accent.

The precise wording, "Savior of the world," is confined in the New Testament to John 4:42; 1 John 4:14. It is found several times in inscriptions, where it is used for the emperor Hadrian (117-138 C.E.).[70] Similar titles including the word "Savior" figure elsewhere in the imperial cultus. This is probably the background of the usage in John.[71] At the same time it is remarkable that the title "Savior" occurs nowhere in the polemic of the Johannine Apocalypse against the imperial cultus. If these Johannine references are meant to echo those lofty predicates in the imperial cultus, then at most it is in the way Christ is portrayed as the Savior of the world in a unique religious sense.

Another thread leads to the healing deities, especially Asclepius, who was highly honored in the second century C.E. in Asia Minor and was actually called "savior."[72] But it is doubtful whether the Johannine writings point to the beginnings of the controversy between Christianity and the Asclepius cult, or with pagan healing deities in general.[73] There is no clear connection with the healing miracles. Rather, in both passages the concern is with the universal salvation achieved by Christ. For the same reason there is no question of any competition with the mystery deities, who are also called life-giving saviors. Any contact with the gnostic saviors is at most confined to the fact that the Christian Savior is the source of life—though in a quite different way. All we know for certain is that the title was not adopted independently of the general spiritual and religious environment. This is because of the need to open up an understanding of the unique Christian message of salvation.

4:15 Thus faith in Jesus is the presupposition for belief in God's love for us. This leads the author to raise a point we would have expected him to bring up in 4:1-6. But faith and love as conditions and hallmarks of our fellowship with God simply cannot be separated from each other. The confession "Jesus is the Son of God," harks back to v. 14 ("the [NRSV "his"] Son"), showing how the title Son of God has both christological and soteriological implications. In Jesus we perceive one who is the Son of the Father in an ontological sense (vv. 10,

of the New Testament (Philadelphia, 1963) 239ff.; the main roots are to be found in the Old Testament designations for God which were transferred to Jesus. But in their Greek form (LXX) they acquired a particular resonance in the Hellenistic Gentile environment.

69. Of Jesus Christ, 2 Tim. 1:10; Titus 1:4; 2:13; 3:6 (see H. Windisch, "Zur Christologie der Past," *ZNW* 34 [1935] 213-38, esp. 228); 2 Pet. 1:1, 11; 2:20; 3:2, 18 (see K. H. Schelkle on these passages).

70. See W. Weber, *Untersuchungen zur Geschichte des Kaisers Hadrianus* (Leipzig, 1907) 225f., 229.

71. Cf. Bousset, *Kyrios Christos* (Eng. trans.) 243; Deissmann, *Light,* 369; Bauer, *Johannes* on 4:42; Dibelius-Conzelmann, HNT XIII³, 77.

72. See F. J. Dölger ("ὁ σωτήρ," *AntChrist* 6 [1950] 241-75), who draws his evidence particularly from Aelius Aristides (129-189 C.E.).

73. So especially K. H. Rengstorf, *Die Anfänge der Auseinandersetzung zwischen Christusglaube und Asklepiosfrömmigkeit* (Münster, 1953) esp. 13f.

14). For the only-begotten One was sent into the world to enable men and women to participate in the divine life (cf. v. 9). In a formal sense this confession is repeated in 5:5. But it is also related to the christological confession in 2:22 (cf. v. 23); 5:1.

4:16 In this context the sending of the Son of God is viewed as the great act of God's love. The point is confirmed in v. 16a, which deliberately harks back to v. 11 and possibly to vv. 9–10. By "some" the author means — unlike v. 14 — Christians in general, including both his readers and himself. This is obvious when he says "for us" at the end of the sentence. The Christian believers, unlike the heretics, who exclude themselves from this salvation by denying the divine Sonship of Jesus, have the knowledge that enables them to realize the love of God. Such knowledge (*ginōskein*) is not a matter of logic or theory, but a believing perception, a becoming aware, an apprehending and being apprehended. It is this first verb that governs the object "the love" (cf. John 8:32, 43, 55; 10:14, 15, 27; 14:7, 17 etc.). The phrase *pepisteukamen* (NRSV "we believe") with this kind of accusative of the object is unusual.[74] It is added only because the creedal confession (v. 15, "confess") was mentioned earlier. Hence nothing can be gathered from the order of the two verbs (the reverse of John 6:69). The Greek perfect is significant. It shows that the knowledge of God's love is an abiding and unshakable conviction. There is no doubt of God's love for the Christians. By continuing his works of love,[75] God conveys to them the full effects of Christ's atoning death and makes them his children (cf. 3:1).

At this point the author has returned to the theme of love. So now he summarizes his argument: our love as a response to the love of God guarantees our abiding fellowship with him. Here the author again picks up the ontological statement of v. 8: God is love in his very nature. After the repeated statements about the sending of the Son of God (vv. 9, 10, 14), the meaning of this is crystal clear. God is a loving God who gives his most precious possession to save the human race. In this giving and self-giving mercy and will to save, lies true love. That is God's very nature. Those "who abide in love," that is, who persevere in the attitude God has appointed for them, "abide in God and God abides in them." This happens to the extent that they can as human beings shed abroad the radiance of the divine love. To abide in love is synonymous with the statement that the love of God is perfected in us (v. 12c). By returning to the complete reciprocal formula about our fellowship with God (3:24; 4:13, 15) the author shows that he is wrapping up his argument. Verse 16 represents a climax of the Johannine contemplation of God. It may well be the quintessential expression of the Johannine message, ethical demand, and promise for humankind. This glorious word must not be detached from its context and from the meaning of the entire section.

---

74. Only with the neuter in a general sense in John 11:26; 1 Cor. 13:7; cf. the table of linguistic uses in Moulton 1:68 n. 2.

75. *Agapēn echei en hēmin* here is modeled after *poiein ti en tini,* "to do something to someone" (BDF §206.3); *echein* here expresses that which belongs. Alternatively, *en* is used interchangeably with *eis* (BDF §218; Mayser, *Grammatik*, II, 2:372). In any case it is not to be taken in a literal, local sense, as though God's love were manifested inside of us, e.g., through our possession of *zōē* or of *pneuma* (contra Büchsel, Chaine, Ambroggi).

Nor must it be desecrated or turned into mere sentimentality. It proclaims the Christian Godhead who has revealed his love in Christ. It calls Christians to retain that love and activate it, following the supreme example of Christ. It promises them abiding fellowship with this God of love, a God in whose love their love has its source, its power, and its reward.

3. Perfect Love Knows No Fear (1 John 4:17–18)

[17]Love has been perfected among us in this: that we may have boldness on the day of judgment, because as he is, so are we in this world. [18]There is no fear in love, but perfect love casts out fear; for fear has to do with punishment, and whoever fears has not reached perfection in love.

4:17 The theme of love, which was posed basically in vv. 7–10, and was continued from the perspective of fellowship with God in vv. 11–16, is now developed further. The author argues that we are still in an incomplete state of salvation, still under the threat of future judgment. In this situation love demonstrates its true glory and power by removing from us the justified fear of the heavenly judge and giving us confidence in our salvation. The phrase "love has been perfected among us" does not focus on the demonstration of God's love toward us. That has already been described in 4:9–10. Again, *teleiousthai*, "to be perfected," refers not so much to the degree as to the interior nature of perfection.[76] *Meth' hēmōn*, "with us," may be based on the Hebrew *'ittānû*.[77] The subject of the statement is love as a divine attribute expressing itself to perfection in giving us confidence in the future. The main argument against referring it to the love of God is the sequel in v. 18, which looks for the perfection of love in human behavior. The adjective "perfect" in that verse takes up the verb "has been perfected" in v. 17. Again, the restriction of love toward God or toward the brothers and sisters, or the interpretation of it as the bond of love between God and humankind (= fellowship with God, Büchsel) does not do justice to the context. Rather, it should be clear that since love is able to maintain our present fellowship with God, it also has the capacity to keep alive our hope for the future. The phrase "in this" points to the *hoti*-clause ("because . . .").[78]

The prospect of judgment day—a term taken from ancient Jewish and Synoptic eschatology[79]—confirms (as we have already learned from 2:18ff.) that the

---

76. Cf. on 2:5.

77. Cf. Acts 2:28, quoting Ps. 16:11; the original local sense of *'ēt* sometimes gives way to a metaphorical one. Cf. Jer. 10:5; 23:28; BDF §227.1. The reference made by many exegetes to *meta* = Hebrew *'im* with verbs of action assumes that it is related to the loving action of God toward us, a meaning we have rejected in the text above.

78. Contra Ambroggi, who connects *en toutō* to what goes before (but to what specifically?) and takes *hina* in a consecutive sense.—Such epexegetical *hina*-clauses are possible (in place of the classical infinitive) insofar as they are dealing with consequences not yet realized (when they are realized *hoti* is generally used, cf. 3:16; 5:14), e.g., John 15:3; 17:3; 1 John 3:1; 5:3; 3 John 4.—See BDF §394; Radermacher, *Grammatik*, 190–92.

79. See *I Enoch* 10:4ff.; 16:1; 18:11ff.; 22:4, 11; 4 Ezra 7:113; *Jub.* 5:6ff.; 24:28, 30; *Pss. Sol.* 15:13;

author is faithful to the eschatology of the early church.[80] There is no contra-diction here with John 3:19 (cf. 12:31; 16:8) — passages that describe judgment as a present reality. John 5:24 and 12:48 point to the bridge leading from present to future judgment. Along with judgment we meet other familiar eschatological terminology (cf. 2:28f.). "Boldness" is to be taken here as in 2:28 as the eschato-logical attitude toward the day of judgment, that is, confidence when standing face to face with the Judge (cf. on 2:28 — "assurance of salvation" only in this sense, not in the sense of predestination).[81] "Judgment" refers here to two possibilities, acquittal or condemnation, as in Synoptic usage. It does not refer to the sentence of death, as in John 5:24, 29 (cf. 3:17f.; 12:47f.). Those who belong to God and those who belong to the world look with similar anticipation to the judgment day — the former with confidence, the latter with fear.

The *hoti*-clause states the reason for this. It is because there has been a resurgence of eschatology and ideas associated therewith. Unfortunately this is introduced as a motif which, in the context of the theme of love, is more disturb-ing than helpful.[82] Unless this short clause is excised as a gloss — the pregnant diction does not support this — one must assume that Christ is being envisioned as king (1 John 2:28) and judge (John 5:22) at the parousia and that Christians, who are anxious to follow his example to the best of their ability (cf. 2:29; 3:3, 7), overcome their fear of being "put to shame" and of being rejected by him" (cf. 2:28). It is instructive to note that the heavenly Christ has retained the characteristics of the earthly. He is[83] still, even in the moral sense, what he was on earth, a pattern for those in union with him, with those who are still "in the world."[84] This last addition, inserted as an afterthought, emphasizes that the Christlike manner shows itself in a particularly praiseworthy light. This is true even though in a profound sense it is a gift of God. It shows itself in the midst of a world that is at enmity with God and comports itself in such a different manner.

---

etc.; Matt. 10:15; 11:22, 24; 12:36. The theology of the early church adheres firmly to this (Jude 6; 2 Pet. 2:9; 3:7). Phrases similar in content occur all through the New Testament.

80. Bultmann regards *en tē hēmerą tēs kriseōs* as an interpolation ("Redaktion").

81. The momentary *parrhēsia* in answer to prayer (3:21f.; 5:14) is something different from this; see on 3:21. — Preisker finds here another fragment of his eschatological *Vorlage,* 169.

82. Bultmann's attempt in "Redaktion" to establish the credibility of an original text that was quite different (see Introduction, pp. 16f.) is totally devoid of any positive foundation.

83. To *ekeinos* (= Christ; see on 2:6) *estin* no amplification is necessary (*contra* Windisch); rather, he is put forward as a model and *kathōs* is to be taken in a pregnant sense. The reading of MS 2138 *kathōs ēn en tō kosmō amōmos kai katharos* catches the sense correctly, but misses the theological nuance in *estin.* The present tense should not mislead us into thinking of a similarity with the heavenly Christ (*contra* Chaine).

84. This goes only with *hēmeis esmen; esometha* (ℵ 2138) should be taken as a cohortative (BDF §369.3; Radermacher, *Grammatik,* 216). Otherwise the preceding *estin* would be superfluous. R. Bultmann sticks to this proposal for the text "that we may have confidence in this world": "Because as that one is in the love of the father, so are we in love" (*Johannine Epistles,* 73). In this view the traditional text is not in order. We can agree to that. However, there are other *kathōs*-clauses to be compared, in which Christ appears as a pattern — 2:6 and especially 3:3, 7, where likewise the pres-ent appears, "as he is pure" or "righteous." W. Thüsing interprets thus: "Just as Jesus Christ is our pattern in love, so we, too, are patterns, through him and his anointing, although we, unlike him, are still in this world" (p. 155).

In contrast to this joyous confidence stands the specter of fear. The author now enlarges on this topic, following his usual antithetical style. Specifically he deals with the fear of judgment and the condemnation it threatens to bring in its train. He first speaks of it in general terms. Note that "fear" has no article. This is because it is placed in relation to "love." The author is entitled to follow this procedure all the more because the fear of condemnation is the highest form of fear (Matt. 10:28). Should fear or love play the leading role in religion?[85] That is not the question here. Rather, it is whether fear is still an aspect of love. Now of course the author's central message is fellowship with God (1:3). He defends a view of God in which his luminous being (1:5), his plenitude of life (cf. 1:2; 5:11), and his loving nature (4:7ff.) are developed in sharp contrast to a world darkened by sin, subject to death, and ruled by hatred. Given this situation, the author tries to lead his readers to the clear and total commitment as befits the children of God. This commitment shows itself in perfect love. Fear can only be a disturbing and restricting factor. Of course, there is a legitimate place for the fear of death, whether for the unbelieving world or even for those members of the community who at any time may become its victims. But the author never threatens them with the fear of punishment or eternal damnation. The only danger is that they may be cut off from Christ and God. That would be the most dreadful form of judgment because it would exclude them from the realm of God (cf. John 3:18, 36; 5:24; 8:24; 15:6; 1 John 3:14). It is noticeable that GJohn uses the terms *phobeisthai and phobos* predominantly of *human* fear.[86] The fear of the Jews is typical of this world. God and the world are opposites in their nature. That is the background here. It is not just a psychological way of looking at it. The statement "there is no fear in love," is a general one. The author knows that his readers have not yet attained to perfect love. To that extent it is also an admonition for them.

4:18 We should therefore do all we can to banish fear.[87] But that is not because love has a higher value in religion than fear. The author is not thinking in terms of religious psychology.[88] Rather, fear is the product of the observation that Christians have in fact not yet realized all the potential of their fellowship with God. There is still much of the unredeemed state about them. They show too little joy over being children of God (3:1), too little confidence in the power that comes from God (2:13f.; 4:4; 5:4). Fear is alien to the children of God and must be

---

85. This problem, like the relation between fear and love as the motive of moral behavior, was a topic of lively discussion among the rabbis; see Moore, *Judaism* 2:98ff.; Bonsirven, *Judaïsme* 2:45–47; Büchsel, Excursus, pp. 75–78; R. Sander, *Furcht und Liebe im palästinischen Judentum* BWANT 4.16; Stuttgart, 1935) esp. 125ff.; Sjöberg, *Gott und die Sünder,* passim.

86. Above all, fear of the *Ioudaioi,* John 9:22; 7:13; 19:38; 20:19; otherwise only at 19:8, in an Old Testament citation at 12:15, and in a passage influenced by the Synoptic tradition, 6:19f (cf. Mark 6:50).

87. *Exō ballein,* more forceful than *ekballein,* also occurs at John 15:6; Matt. 5:13 as a metaphor for expulsion or absolute separation from the community; also *ekballein exō* (Matt. 21:39; John 6:37; 9:34; 12:31). Rabbinic parallels are given in Schlatter, *Sprache,* 150f.

88. As in O. Pfister, *Das Christentum und die Angst* (Zurich, 1944), 18f. ("Words which sound like a formula in neurological theory").

dispelled. But this does not mean the gnostic's liberation from the material world and its trammels. Nor is it a rationalistic desire for psychic health. Rather, they should put away every impediment that hinders them from the perfect response of love and from the fellowship God has given them.

The reason for this is that fear still keeps judgment in view. "Punishment" (*kolasis*) is a juridical term for eschatological judgment.[89] Fear is not a punishment in itself, but a kind of mesmerized contemplation of the prospect of future judgment. Verse 18c is hardly a continuation of the *hoti*-clause, but more likely an antithesis to v. 18a. Perfect love tends to reject every impulse of fear. Those who fear obviously fail to show perfect love. The words *teteleiōtai en* corresponds to *teleia agapē* ("perfect love") and places the emphasis on this attribute. When the Christians attain this state of love, an outgrowth of unbroken fellowship with God, they will have overcome all fear and will have achieved perfect confidence.

4. The Love of God Manifests Itself in Love for Our Fellow Christians (1 John 4:19–5:2)

[19]We love because he first loved us. [20]Those who say, "I love God," and hate their brothers or sisters, are liars; for those who do not love a brother or sister whom they have seen, cannot love God whom they have not seen. [21]The commandment we have from him is this: those who love God must love their brothers and sisters also.

5:1 Everyone who believes that Jesus is the Christ has been born of God, and everyone who loves the parent loves the child. [2]By this we know that we love the children of God, when we love God and obey his commandments.

4:19 Only now, at the end of this Johannine Song of Songs, does the author draw from what he has said in general terms certain practical implications for mutual love. Because of its parenetic application, the verb *agapōmen* has to be interpreted as a cohortative ("let us love"; *contra* NRSV "we love"). Since vv. 19–21 form a unity, the author already has the subject of mutual (human) love in mind, and not as the addition "God" (NRSV marg.) or "him" as some manuscripts would suggest,[90] love toward God. Yet v. 19 is only a transition and is still couched in general terms. It takes up what was said in v. 10. The prevenient love of God[91] obliges us to reciprocate with love. The author is feeling his way toward the theme of mutual love. This is shown by his move from the one motif to three further motifs, all of which are intended to provide a foundation for mutual love. In conjunction for these three motifs, v. 19 provides further evidence (cf. 3:16–18) of the moral and practical style of the author. For him the only honest activity and the only response to God's act of love is genuine love on the part of humankind.

89. Cf. Matt. 25:46; *T. Rub.* 5:5; *T. Levi* 4:1; *T. Benj.* 7:5 (*v.l.*); *T. Gad* 7:5; *1 Clem.* 11.1; *2 Clem.* 6.7; *Mart. Pol.* 2.3 (*v.l.*); *Herm. Sim.* 9.18.1; *Diog.* 9.2; etc.

90. *Ton theon* ℵ 33 81 206 al. Vg^cl sy bo arm; *auton* k; a reading without the additions B A 323 614 1739 al.

91. *Prōtos* has a comparative meaning (=*proteros*); cf. John 1:15, 30; BDF §62; Radermacher, *Grammatik*, 71f.

a) Love for a God We Have Not Seen Is Not Possible without Love for a Brother or Sister Whom We Can See (4:20)

4:20 The argument is clear: only those who love the brother or sister they can see are able to love God whom they cannot see. But this conviction does not, as in Philo (*Decal.* 120), stem from general religious considerations, but from the specific thought of v. 12. The way to fellowship with God is not through a visionary experience but only through active love. Now this basic proposition is exploited for the theme of mutual love. While that theme was certainly implied in vv. 11f., the love of God is here made to rest emphatically on the love of brother and sister.

The wording of the verse ("Those who say . . ."; cf. 1:6, 8, 10; 2:4, 6, 9) shows that the author has returned to his polemic against the gnostics. They claim to *love* God as well as to *know* him (2:3f.; 3:6; 4:6). This time he calls them liars for making this claim. He unmasks them with all their specious words, with which they pretend to fellowship with God but fail in showing mutual love. In effective contrast to their supposed love of God, and with emphatic acerbity, he refers to their attitude toward the brothers and sisters (as he had done earlier in 2:9, 11; 3:15) as "hatred." Hatred is something that exists only in this world (3:13) and in those who come from the evil one (3:12, 15). For John's ethical dualism it is quite inconceivable that hatred and love should go together. You might pretend with fine words to love God and get away with it. But everyone can see whether you really love your brother or sister or not. Your relationship to God would lack any proof. Clearly, the author is thinking of the hatred of the gnostics and their secret enmity toward the true believers (3:13).

This is an *a fortiori* argument (*a minore ad maius*), a tactic favored by Jesus himself (Mark 2:9ff.) and in the rabbinic schools.[92] Whoever is incapable of loving those they do see (perfect, denoting a lasting relationship) can on no account love God, whom they cannot see.

b) Mutual Love Is a Positive Commandment of God, Next to Love of God Himself (4:21)

4:21 Along with the reasoned argument comes the positive command of God.[93] This shows that mutual love is unconditional. In the Gospels the indissoluble bond between loving God and loving the neighbor is called "the great commandment" (Matt. 22:37–40 par.). But since v. 21 operates precisely with this inner bond, the author must be referring to this tradition, and not to John 13:34, as he did in 2:7f. He has brought the Synoptic report into conformity with John's new commandment. Love of neighbor becomes love of brother and sister. The

---

92. See H. L. Strack, *Einleitung in Talmud und Midrasch* (6th ed.; Munich, 1930) 97; Billerbeck, *Kommentar* 3:223–26.

93. The application of *autou* to Jesus is to be rejected because (1) he is not mentioned in the context; (2) in similar cases he is introduced with *ekeinos* (2:6 and often); and (3) the *entolē* in Matt. 22:39 is *God's* commandment, which Jesus proclaims only in this form.

latter is seen as a concrete application of the former to the life of the Johannine community. In the Greek text v. 21 begins with the conjunction *kai* ("and"; omitted from NRSV). This forms a close connection with v. 20. At the same time this verse serves as a valuable early Christian commentary on the double command-ment of love as preached by Jesus. The author, speaking only for the commu-nity (note the "*we* have"), is convinced he has understood Jesus correctly in pro-claiming mutual love as a necessary requirement and an unquestionable seal of love for God.

c) LOVE OF THE PARENT INVOLVES LOVE OF THE CHILD (5:1-2)

5:1 Yet a third argument, independent in its own way, is brought to bear as a motivation for mutual love. Only in this way, and not under the rubric of faith,[94] do the two following verses fit into the flow of the argument. Although v. 1a looks like a parallel to 4:7, the continuation in v. 1b shows that the author has finished with the theme of love. Verse 1a is preparatory to v. 1b. The believer (i.e., as in 4:7, the one who loves) is introduced because the author is clearly addressing his readers. In v. 1b he links up with the key phrase "born of God" rather than with "who believes." (Faith would in any case not be a new criterion, since it has already been mentioned in 4:2; what the author still has to say about faith comes later in v. 5 or 4b.)

The creedal formula, which is worded as a positive counterpart to 2:22a, is a brief summary intended to express what is essential in the Christian faith (see Introduction, pp. 18f.). Its brevity shows that there is no concern here for precise definition (that occurs only in 5:6), but rather to pave the way for the phrase "has been born of God."

Following this utterance about the Christian believers, the author makes a general statement about a common experience. The connecting thought — "the parent loves the child" — is omitted, and the author goes on at once to say what he is really concerned about: "Everyone who loves the parent loves the child." Thus he argues from the relationship between fathers and sons to make the point that the lack of love for one's siblings is unusual and unnatural. The present indicative shows what happens as a rule.

5:2 From this general statement the author leads his readers to what they can draw from it for their own status as children of God ("we know"). According to B. Weiss and Dodd, "by this" (*en toutǭ*), as in 2:5; 3:10, 19, looks back to the previous sentence: "From this principle (cf. "From this" [*ek toutou*], 4:6b) we know . . . ." If this prepositional phrase points to the *hoti*-clause,[95] it would result

---

94. So in structure, Häring, Brooke, Windisch, Büchsel, Chaine, et al.

95. So the majority of recent commentators. The fact that *ean* occurs with a similar construction (John 13:35; 1 John 2:3) is not in itself a decisive indication, since *ean* and *hotan* can be used inter-changeably (Abel, *Grammaire*, §68d; BDF §382.4); but it is required because of the association of meaning. *Hotan* then retains its distinctive sense ("every time that . . ."), to denote what occurs as a general rule; cf. Mark 14:7; Luke 11:34; 12:54; John 8:44; 16:21a; 1 Cor. 14:26; 2 Cor. 12:10; 13:9.— BAGD 588, s.v. 1a.

in the strange idea of Baumgarten that "we ought to have in the love of God, which is hidden and beyond our control, the hallmark of the mutual love, which is generally held in high esteem for being open to experience."[96] In that case too the keeping of the commandments would be the criterion of mutual love. That is now firmly established after all the other things that have been said about it (2:7ff.; cf. v. 3f.; 3:10b, 11, 23; 4:21), but especially in connection with the love of brother or sister. The expression "the children of God" instead of "brothers and sisters" confirms the view that v. 2 is merely an application of the rule in v. 1b, though of course with the order reversed. "We always love the children of God when we really love God—who gives birth to them and to ourselves."[97]

With the addition "and obey (*poiōmen,* "do") his commandments," the author gets us onto a familiar track (cf. 4:21). Love for the parent insofar as it is genuine, leads, according to an inherent law, to the love of the other children. In addition, we have in this case the parent's express command. Genuine love of the children is not just a piece of sentimentality, nor is it due to the ties of blood, that is, to natural inclination. Rather, in the relation between parent and child it takes the form of obedience.

5. It Is Not Difficult for Those Who Are Born of God to Love Him (1 John 5:3-4)

³For the love of God is this, that we obey his commahdments. And his commandments are not burdensome, ⁴for whatever is born of God conquers the world. And this is the victory that conquers the world, our faith.

5:3 This essential nature of God's love is now explained (*gar,* "for")—abandoning the analogy which dominated tbe previous verses—once more (cf. 2:5) as the keeping of his commandments. Jesus imposed the same duty on his disciples. They too must love him in no other way than by keeping his commandments (John 14:15, 21a). Emotional love, especially the affection between friends (11:3, 36, *philein,* the verb for the affection of friends; cf. 20:2; 21:15-17, as well as *agapān* the word for Christian love, 13:23; 19:26; 21:7, 30) may not be foreign to him. But in this basic demand for love the author constantly emphasizes the moral element. It also has an anti-gnostic tendency, as was made clear earlier in 2:3-5.

---

96. Baumgarten, who finds here the high point of the writer's ingenious style.—Büchsel tries to get over the difficulty by assuming that v. 2 is directed against the gnostics, who also claimed to love the children of God, that is, people like themselves. Quite apart from the uncertainty of this suggestion we are still left with the tension this causes with *entolas autou poiōmen.* That fraternal love and keeping of the commandments should be played off with one another would be curious, even if the term in question is taken in an "indefinite, general sense."

97. R. Kittler, "Erweis der Bruderliebe an der Bruderliebe?' *Kerygma und Dogma* 16 (1970) 223-28: the statement is answering a hidden objection—How can we know whether a suspected brother to whom we show love is a child of God or a child of the devil? Answer: Through our acting out of love for God!

Next comes a further development and a transition. In his controversy with his opponents, the author seeks to show them that those who are born of God are triumphant in the hard battle against the world. They have a power that comes from God, and that power helps them in their struggle to assert themselves (cf. 4:4-6). Added to this he wants to strengthen his readers and encourage them in their religious and moral endeavor (cf. 2:12-14; 5:13-15, 18-20). Faced with the demand of mutual love (4:19-5:2), they might well have a sense of inadequacy and weakness (cf. 3:20). So he comforts them and assures them that God's commandments are not difficult. There is more in this than the rabbinic teaching about light and heavy commandments (cf. Matt. 23:23).[98] The author in concerned that the commandments should be fulfilled. On that point he can set their minds at rest.

5:4 The commandments are not an intolerable burden for Christians. This is because those who are born of God[99] have overcome the world. The theme of love for God and love for brother and sister yields to a much more basic discussion. The lines are drawn between those who are born of God on the one hand and the world on the other. So far as the moral struggle to keep the commandments is concerned, the assumption is that the world is a threat to our love for God and to moral purity (cf. 2:15-17). The world tempts people into sin and seduces them through the desires that are in the world (2:16). But those who are born of God are able to resist this pressure ("Do not love," 2:15). They refuse to get enmeshed in the world and in the power of sin which dwells in them. Thus they overcome the world. The author is therefore not returning to the Jewish doctrine that people can fulfill the commandments by their own efforts and so merit a reward.[100] As he sees it, the victory is due to God.

The statement in v. 4a is only partly addressed to the theme of moral struggle. However much the gnostics would like to separate religion and morality, these two things are intimately connected for those who believe in Christ. For them there is only one battle against all the enemies of God. For them the cosmos is constituted by immorality and disbelief, and behind them both stands God's great enemy, the evil one. So this reference to victory over the world immediately leads back again to the subject of faith (cf. 4:1-6). Now comes a glorious saying, one with wide implications. This is the only passage in the Johannine writings where the noun *hē pistis* occurs. It is our faith that has conquered the world. Victory over the world has become a reality through faith. In similar cases the author nearly always uses the perfect tense (2:13, 14; 4:4). But if the aorist *nikēsasa* is not exactly equivalent to the perfect,[101] or if it denotes indefinite time, with

---

98. See Billerbeck, *Kommentar* 1:901ff.; Bonsirven, *Judaïsme* 2:73ff.

99. Neuter for masculine; see on 1:1.

100. To be sure, "the whole of Jewish piety in the late Hellenistic period is permeated with a serious mistrust in human capacity" (Bousset-Gressmann, *Religion des Judentums,* 388); but that makes repentance all the more important (ibid., 389f.). Jewish works-piety, attested by both Jesus (Matthew 23) and Paul (Romans 2), was never really overcome. Cf. Bonsirven, *Judaïsme* 2:79f.

101. See Abel, *Grammaire,* §55, 1, 1′ (p. 258); Mayser, *Grammatik,* II, 1:168f. However, the confusion of tenses was mainly characteristic of *narrative* style (see above).

the same meaning as the present tense,[102] it must be explained as suggesting a climax as opposed to *nika* ("conquers") in v. 4a. Those who are born of God not only have the constant strength in themselves to conquer the world; they have actually won the victory already in their faith. If that is the meaning, the thought is intimately connected with the victory that Christ won once for all in salvation history (Rev. 3:21; 5:5, aorist). This victory is repeated in the lives of the Christians (cf. Rev. 12:11). Less likely it refers to the victory of faith which the readers have won over the antichrists (2:18ff.). For in the author's view this battle is not yet over, however much he emphasizes the superiority of the true Christians (4:4 — "have conquered," perfect tense). But in Christ the decisive engagement has already been fought out. Faith is a proof that the Christians have been victorious in their own battle, with Christ as their ally (aorist). In any case, the author is speaking here as the representative and mouthpiece of the Christian community. That community is certain of its victory in the hard struggle with the demonic powers of the world at enmity with God, thanks to the power of Christ. This language of battle and victory comes to full flowering in the book of Revelation.[103]

THIRD SECTION

TRUE FAITH IN CHRIST AS THE POWER THAT CONQUERS THE "WORLD" (1 JOHN 5:5-12)

[5]Who is it that conquers the world but the one who believes that Jesus is the Son of God?

[6]This is the one who came by water and blood, Jesus Christ, not with the water only but with the water and the blood. And the Spirit is the one that testifies, for the Spirit is the truth. [7]There are three that testify: [8]the Spirit and the water and the blood, and these three agree. [9]If we receive human testimony, the testimony of God is greater; for this is the testimony of God that he has testified to his Son. [10]Those

---

102. In itself, the aorist participle need not have a temporal emphasis (Moulton 1:221). According to Abel, *Grammaire,* §73, d, n. (p. 322), the temporal sense remains even with substantival participles (when used instead of a relative clause).

103. *Nikan* occurs in GJohn once, in 1 John six times, in Revelation seventeen times (in the rest of the New Testament only four times). For the content, cf. especially the "victory sayings" (2:7, 11, 17, 26; 3:5, 12, 21), in praise of the victorious Messiah (5:5; 17:14) and the triumphal hymn of the martyrs (12:10-12). See O. Bauernfeind, *TDNT* 4:945.—The Qumran community is filled with the same spirit of conflict and of confidence in victory, with a strong eschatological tension. The clearest evidence for this is in the *War Scroll* (1QM), though its date and meaning are disputed. It is noteworthy that in the *War Scroll* the power to fight and the victory are ascribed exclusively to God. That comes out particularly in the part about the trumpets (e.g., 1QM 3:5: "The mighty Deeds of God shall crush the enemy . . ."; 3:8: "The mighty Hand of God in War": 3:9: "God has smitten all the Sons of Darkness . . .") and the standards (4:6: "Truth of God," "Justice of God," "Glory of God," "Judgment of God"; 4:13: "Salvation of God," "Victory of God . . ."). Later in the Songs of Praise and Victory (in cols. 10-18) we find the same thing expressed. "Truly, the battle is Thine and the power from Thee! It is not ours. Our strength and the power of our hands accomplish no mighty deeds except by Thy power . . ." (1QM 11:5f.). On the other hand it should not be forgotten that the whole unique portrayal represents an eschatological picture; it is about an event that has not yet taken place but is still awaited. The Johannine writings, by contrast, look back at the victory Christ has already won over the world, a victory that continues in his church (John 16:33; 1 John 5:4).

who believe in the Son of God have the testimony in their hearts. Those who do not believe in God have made him a liar by not believing in the testimony that God has given concerning his Son. [11]And this is the testimony: God gave us eternal life, and this life is in his Son. [12]Whoever has the Son has life; whoever does not have the Son of God does not have life.

After the long disquisition about love the author returns once more to speak of faith. This time he goes into it in greater depth, as he does with love. It was mentioned only briefly at the beginning of Part Three, which was occasioned principally by concern for the false prophets, in order to lay down a criterion in the battle of the spirits (4:2). True, in discussing love he pointed to faith as the basis for a right understanding of God's revelation and requirement of love (4:15f.). This time, however, he is seeking to make clear how certain the victory is which the children of God will win over the world (5:5). So he returns once again to the basis of faith. In doing so he develops more clearly than he did before the contrast between the true confession of Christ and the beliefs of the heretical teachers (5:6). Then he goes on to place the community's faith on a firm foundation, viz., on the testimony of witnesses (5:7-8). He refers to the testimony of God himself and evaluates its power to enforce moral obligation (v. 9). Finally, he demonstrates what it means to accept this testimony of God. It means believing it or refusing to believe, that is, rejecting the true faith. On this decision for faith or unbelief depends the salvation (the possession of eternal life) of every individual (5:10-12). It is this section especially which brings forward a viewpoint that can be understood only with the help of GJohn. This section, with its antitheses and its uncompromising demand for faith in the sense of the church's confession, once again produces a powerful argument against the heretical teachers and a fervent appeal to the readers to abide in the truth. Moreover, it draws a bottom line in the controversy with the false prophets. It does this by assuring the Christian believers that they are in possession of salvation ($z\bar{o}\bar{e}$, "life"), while those who deny the Son are excluded therefrom (v. 12)![104]

1. Only the True and Full Christian Confession Grants Victory (1 John 5:5-6)

5:5 Following v. 4 victory is now conceded to those with true faith in Christ. This statement is reminiscent of the assurances of victory in the seven letters of the Apocalypse (Rev. 2:7, 11, 17, 26; 3:5, 12, 21). The paradox of Christ's victory over Satan and the world (John 12:31; 14:30; 16:33) is continued in those who confess their faith in him. In contrast to the victory sayings in the Apocalypse, however, 1 John 5:5 lays no stress on the promise to the victors, but rather on the way they may arrive at this victory, namely, through the true faith. The author wants to encourage them not to martyrdom, not to withstand tribulation coming from the outside, but to resist the heretical teaching. So everything depends on the purity of the faith and on the clarity of their christological confession.

---

104. On 1 John 5:5-11, see Beutler, *Martyria*, 276-81.

The latter is framed in the same terms as in 4:15, "Jesus is the Son of God." This does not mean Son of God in the later metaphysical sense — for example, in the form it took in the Arian controversy, although it is presupposed (5:20). In 1 John the title "Son" is akin to the title "Christ" (cf. 2:23 with 22; 5:5 with 1). All attention is focused on his coming to save the world (cf. 4:15 with 14; 5:5 with 6), not on the metaphysical nature of the Son. Johannine Christology never denies its subordination to soteriology. It is oriented toward salvation history and is thus of a functional type. Johannine thought is dominated not by the divine nature of Christ *per se,* but by his revelatory and saving work in the incarnate Logos, in other words, its meaning for us. On the other hand, this Christology is not to be understood in purely functional terms. It actually presupposes the metaphysical Sonship, and bases its eschatological revelation thereon (cf. John 1:18; 3:31f.) and its work in imparting life (cf. John 5:26; 6:57; 1 John 5:20). Because Jesus is the true Son of God, that is, is of truly divine nature and has appeared as such in the world of death, he is eternal life for us (5:20). But eternal life is not possible without the purification of sins. That is why the Son of God takes upon himself the death of the cross to atone for our sins (4:10, 14). It is precisely this soteriological significance of the Son that the heretical teachers apparently denied. So Jesus must be acknowledged and appreciated, not only in his christological dignity but also in his soteriological significance. The formula "Jesus is the Son of God "must therefore not be isolated from the other christological sayings, such as 4:2f., 14f., and above all not from 5:6. All it does is to form an indispensable basis for those other sayings.

5:6 In open opposition to the heretical teachers (v. 6b), the christological creed is now defined in specific terms. Since Christ and Christ alone is the decisive factor in the confession, the author highlights it by using the demonstrative, followed by the full name: "Jesus Christ." This clearly excludes all other persons or objects of faith. It is to Jesus Christ that the significant formula "came by water and blood" applies. The aorist "came" forces us to envision certain salvation events which took place with Jesus' once-for-all coming into the world. But the preposition *dia* ("by") does not exclude a reference to the sacraments.[105] The context connects these terms with the coming of Christ and its unique significance. All that happened between God and the Redeemer defines the faith and assures us of victory (cf. "has conquered" [NRSV "conquers"], v. 4). In view of the importance GJohn attributes to baptism and to Christ's atoning death, there can be no doubt that this passage focuses on these events, especially on the death of Jesus as a soteriological event with cosmic dimensions. In him is fulfilled and completed what the incarnation ("was revealed," 1:2) basically implies — the inbreaking of divine life into this cosmos under the thrall of death. In his baptism the Messiah is "revealed" (John 1:31) to the people of Israel as the One who

---

105. The preposition *dia* can also indicate an attendant circumstance (Kühner-Gerth 1:482f.; BDF §223.3; Mayser, *Grammatik,* II, 2:354ff.); but after the verb of motion, *elthein,* the original local association ("came by water and blood"(still retains its force; see BAGD 179, s.v. I, 1; A. Klöpper, "1 John 5, 6–12," *ZWT* 43 (1900) 378–400, esp. 382–84. B. Weiss takes what follows in a similar local sense; see also Häring ad loc.

possesses the Spirit in full measure (the Spirit "remained" on him, John 1:32; the Spirit is given to him "without measure," 3:34b). But it is in his atoning death that the redemption is really fulfilled. The blood of the Lamb of God (John 1:29) is offered "for the life of the world" (John 6:51). The Good Shepherd gives his life "for the sheep" (John 10:15). Only so are the sheep enabled to possess the true, divine life (10:10). Only the cross, or, in the profound Johannine perspective, the wound in Jesus' side from which the water and blood flow (John 19:34), becomes for others the source of life. This is what makes the manifestation of the divine life in the cosmos (incarnation) into a fruitful effusion for the cosmos.

At this point the author inserts some more specific points. Jesus Christ came "not with the water only"—as the gnostics admit—but "with the . . . blood." Apparently the heretics attached a certain importance to Jesus' baptism. This comes out often in the teaching of Cerinthus. Jesus was born like any other human being, but after his baptism he became holier and wiser through the Supreme Power (*authentia*). The Christ descended upon Jesus in the form of a dove, but left him again before the passion![106] However similar the treatment of Christ's baptism and death may be, there is nothing to suggest that the pneumatic Christ, who was incapable of suffering, left him then. There is no idea of a *Christus spiritalis* here. "Jesus Christ" (v. 6a) is, as usual (1:3; 2:1; 3:23; 4:2; 5:20b), the full title for the Redeemer. Perhaps the heretics saw in Jesus' baptism the source of his Spirit because they wanted to claim for their own baptism a similar meaning (cf. John 1:33, "who baptizes with the Holy Spirit"; and 3:5). With pneumatics like this in view, the whole passage would emphasize Jesus' historical deed of salvation, assigning to him not merely the role of the first "pneumatic" but above and beyond that the role of the sole and indispensable Redeemer.

The change of preposition in v. 6a (from "by" to "with") might be intended to draw attention[107] to the fact that water not only refers to an event in the life of Jesus but also suggests a further salvific element. However, the sacramental meaning, without which vv. 7f. would be unintelligible, should not be read into v. 6b![108] For in this context "blood" can only refer to the Eucharist. Water and blood are contrasted with one another and especially highlighted. Yet docetists of Ignatius's letter to the Smyrnaeans (7.1) absent themselves from the Eucharist. Here the reference is more likely to their refusal to have anything to do with the blood of Jesus as the means of salvation (1:7)![109] Verse 6b is tied in closely with

---

106. Irenaeus, *Adv. Haer.* 1.26.1 (=Hippolytus, *Ref.* 7.33).

107. *En,* here clearly instrumental, to indicate the attendant circumstances (BDF §298.4; Oepke, *TDNT* 2:538 notes esp. Heb. 9:25), can designate a circumstance accompanying Jesus' own coming (v. 6a) or one that is significant for others as a result of Jesus' coming.

108. Since Tertullian (*De bapt.* 16), the majority of the fathers as well as modern exegetes. E. Günther thinks that *di' hydatos kai haimatos* is actually a sacramental formula (Μαρτύς [Hamburg, 1941] 137 n. 2). True, modern exegetes often emphasize that in v. 6 the author has in view the historical events of Jesus' baptism and his death (see esp. Brooke), but then, with their eyes on v. 7f., they call further attention to the double meaning in the phrase "water and blood." Regardless of this, see for the development of thought especially P. W. Keppler, "Geist, Wasser und Blut: Zur Erklärung von 1 Joh 5, 6–13," *TQ* 68 (1886) 3–25. Equally correct is H. Braun, "Literar-Analyse," 291.

109. The attempt by A. Greiff ("Die drei Zeugen in 1 Joh 5, 7f." in *TQ* 114 [1933] 465–80) to explain the passage in positive terms in the light of the baptismal liturgy, and esp. v. 6b as a polemic against Eucharists celebrated with water only, is to be adjudged unsuccessful.

6a, for the same verb ("came") covers both 6a and 6b. So in both parts of the verse we have a historical reference. The change of preposition may be due merely to stylistic variation. Verse 6 alludes to the conflict with the gnostics, who deny Jesus' messianic significance, his role as Mediator, and especially the necessity of his death, with its significance for cosmic redemption (2:2; 4:14). The whole verse refers to him who "has come," and not to the future liturgy and sacramental life of the church, a life in which the saving acts of Christ are continued through the mediation of the Holy Spirit and made efficacious. Hence there is nothing in v. 6c either about a "sacrament of the Spirit."

If we take note of the context and its reference to faith, we shall leave the Spirit in v. 6c strictly to its function of witness. The little clause leads to the next verses, which are intended to strengthen the basis of faith after referring to its content. Testimony is borne to Jesus Christ. He is the One who is confessed in vv. 5f. He is the Son of God and Redeemer in the fullest sense. But why is the Holy Spirit introduced at this point as the One who bears testimony? The death of Jesus—on which all the emphasis rests—does not speak for itself, at least not before the world. Jesus is more likely to be a scandal and a stone of stumbling (cf. John 14:1, 29). But the meaning of this "departure" is disclosed by the Spirit whom Jesus sent after his return to his Father (John 16:7). The Spirit-Paraclete will bear testimony to Jesus (John 15:26), convincing an unbelieving and hostile world of Jesus' righteousness (16:10; NRSV "judgment") and thus making visible Jesus' victory over the ruler of this world (14:30; 16:33). The Spirit is able to perform this function of witness because he is[110] "the truth," that is, because he has (divine) truth at his disposal and communicates it faithfully. In this sense the Paraclete is repeatedly called the Spirit of truth in the farewell discourses (John 14:17; 15:26; 16:13; cf. 1 John 4:6). The Spirit is "the great commentator, who by his testimony interprets events with reference to the Messiah, events which by their very nature point to the Messiah" (P. W. Keppler).

From all this it emerges, first, that v. 6c is added as a new thought, confirming v. 6b. The Spirit there witnesses to Jesus, that he is come (not only in water but also) in blood as the Son of God and Redeemer. The Spirit is regarded here as the sole witness (kai = "and," not "also"). It emerges, second, that it is not the witness of the Spirit at Jesus' baptism that is intended here,[111] but the witness of the Spirit in the church and through the church, as in John 15:26; 16:10.[112]

Understood in this way, v. 6a-c presents a consistent christological confession.[113]

---

110. Vg reads Christus, thus making the *hoti* clause the content of the Spirit's testimony. But the notion that Christ is the truth does not fit the context and is certainly no more than a reminiscence of John 14:6.—*Contra* A. von Harnack, *Beiträge zur Einleitung in das NT* VII, 69ff., and T. W. Manson, *JTS* 48 (1947) 27 n. 3, with Lagrange, *Critique textuelle,* 566.

111. Otherwise one would expect *ēn* instead of *estin*. The one who gave testimony at the baptism was John the Baptist; cf. John 1:19, 32, 34; 5:33f. There can be no reference here to a testimony given by the Spirit at Jesus' death—though that is precisely what 1 John 5:6 is talking about.

112. Against the view of T. Preiss that the Spirit is an additional internal witness alongside the two external witnesses (*Das innere Zeugnis,* 37).

113. G. Richter interprets the passage as referring to the incarnation ("Blut und Wasser aus der durchbohrten Seite Jesu [Joh 19, 34b]," *MTZ* 21 [1970] 1–21, esp. 1–13). It is supposedly directed against the docetic view that, when Christ came down from heaven, he did not enter the world in the same way as human beings do. He is not composed of "water and blood," like the normal human

The following verses, with their triadic form and their implications for sacramental symbolism, have an aftereffect on v. 6. Traces of this are left in the manuscript tradition too![114]

2. This Faith Is Based on the Testimony of the Three Witnesses (1 John 5:7–8)

5:7f. The witness of the Spirit provided the author with the key word which controls the ensuing argument. In it he shows how close he is to GJohn, where a great deal of space is given to the theme of witness (*martyrein* and *martyria*).[115] The reason for this is that Johannine faith is always grounded on witnesses or testimonies. Just as faith is not a cerebral insight or total comprehension, so too it is not blind trust involving a sacrifice of the intellect. Since the Johannine Jesus in the last analysis demands the acknowledgment of his person ("whoever believes in me"), he supplies at the same time witnesses to support his credibility. This is based further on the Jewish concept of testimony. Their jurisprudence was preeminently the procedure of hearing witnesses![116] At least two witnesses were required, and their testimony had to agree, even in minor cases (cf. Deut. 17:6; 19:15; John 8:17). Only then was it *alēthēs* (=reliable, trustworthy). Following these juridical views, says the author, there are three witnesses to support the Christian confession of faith: the Spirit (first and foremost), the water, and the blood. Their testimony is in agreement (*eis to hen* = [converge] into one). Despite the close connection through the *hoti* at the beginning of v. 7 (NRSV omits),[117] the shift of thought is clear. Earlier water and blood were historical factors that played a major role in the coming of Christ, with the Spirit added as a witness.

---

body. Rather he was formed of water only, without blood (p. 10). The parallels adduced by Richter from the history of religions (especially from the Mandean literature) are noteworthy. But it leaves unexplained the continuation in v. 6c: "and the Spirit is the one that testifies." F. C. Burkitt's explanation that the living human being consists of the three elements of water, blood, and spirit is regarded by Richter himself as "not entirely appropriate" (p. 14). "Spirit" can only mean the Holy Spirit. His function of bearing testimony is directed to the whole advent of Christ in history. As a consequence, "having come" is not to be limited to the incarnation (cf. 1 John 4:2; 2 John 7), at least not in the understanding of the author of 1 John.

114. (a) In v. 6a A pm. sy[h] (von Soden, Vogels, Merk) already have the triad *hydatos kai haimatos kai pneumatos* as opposed to the simple *hydatos kai haimatos* B 1 38 69 209 1175 ℵ q Vg sy[p] Tert. (Tischendorf, Westcott-Hort, B. Weiss, von Harnack, Lagrange [*Critique textuelle*, 565]). (b) The reading *hydatos kai pneumatos* in 43 pc. is evidently a reminiscence of John 3:5. (c) A combination of both these readings is found in P 81 88 915 al. arm: *hydatos kai pneumatos kai haimatos*.

115. *Martyrein* occurs in GJohn 33 times, in 1 John 6 times, in 3 John 4 times, a total of 43 occurrences; *martyria* occurs in GJohn 14 times, 1 John 6 times, 3 John once, a total of 21 times. H. Strathmann emphasizes particularly that the testimony in John is a witness to the nature and significance of Jesus Christ. Its purpose is to produce faith (*TDNT* 4:499ff.). See also H. von Campenhausen, *Die Idee des Martyriums in der alten Kirche* (Göttingen, 1936) 37ff.; E. Günther, Μαρτύς, 135ff.; N. Brox, *Zeuge und Märtyrer* (Munich, 1961) 70–92.

116. See *Sanh.* 5.1–2 (Danby, 388) (the seven "investigations" and the "proofs" for trivial details, carried to the utmost limits).

117. With *hoti* the subordination is often very loose; see BDF §456.1; BAGD 589, s.v. 3, b.

Now vv. 7f. suddenly introduce these witnesses with a masculine gender, despite the fact that all three nouns in the Greek are neuter![118] In connection with the Spirit, water and blood are now considered not as events but as elements, and they are regarded as witnesses. "The terms water and blood are changed without explanation" (H. Strathmann).

Here we are presented with a symbolic figure of speech reminiscent of John 19:34. It is highly probable that the evangelist saw in the flowing of water and blood from the side of the sacrificial lamb at Passover (cf. vv. 36f.) a hint of something deeper. The sacrificial death of Jesus is the source of the saving power of the divine life which the believers share. The elements water and blood particularly recall the two sacraments baptism and Eucharist, to each of which an important section of GJohn is dedicated (chaps. 3 and 6). The Spirit, however, is the leading principle from which these two sacraments derive their supernatural power (cf. 3:6; 6:63). Hence these three major entities, metaphorically speaking, may be considered as three witnesses who agree. That is to say, they act together at the time of Jesus' historical coming and continue to do so for later generations. At the same time the connection is not lost with the major event of salvation, the coming of the Son of God by water and blood. This seems to be indicated by the double meaning and double reference which the author gives to the terms water and blood. They recall the historical context of v. 6 on the one hand and, on the other, the salvific sacraments of baptism and Eucharist, which prolong their effect beyond that time. Since both elements, water and blood, are now given a suprahistorical function of testimony, which is also available to future generations of the faithful, this sacramental interpretation seems appropriate![119] Yet it remains doubtful whether in looking back the author still has the baptism of Jesus in mind or is focusing exclusively on the blood and water that flowed from the side of Jesus. In the light of John 19:34 it may be assumed that here, too, there has been a shift of perspective, in view of the polemic in v. 6. In that verse emphasis is placed on the saving event of the death of Jesus. This brings to the author's mind the scene at the cross. That scene has for him a profoundly symbolic significance. So he immediately pounces on water and blood as witnesses which along with the Spirit continue to proclaim the saving message and to undergird it. Whoever is convinced of the close affinity between GJohn and 1 John cannot regard the curious emphasis on "blood and water" in both John 19:34 and 1 John 5:8 as a mere coincidence. The difference of order may be due to the fact that v. 6 is still echoing in the author's mind, as distinct from the historical scene in John 19:34 from the sequence of baptism and Eucharist in the Christian life. If this is the true explanation of the context and wording, it reveals the author's profound theological insight. The saving act of God, which follows, as a matter of principle and with universal significance, the sending and death of his Son, continues in the life of the church. For by word and sacrament the

---

118. It would be possible to take v. 7 as the statement of a general rule: "Where three are present there are enough important witnesses." In that case the rule is assumed to be known and immediately applicable.

119. Otherwise Brox, *Zeuge*, 87f. (only historical facts are fixed, their application must always be carried out anew).

church extends the divine life to individual believers in subsequent generations. The action of the Spirit in the church becomes a powerful witness, placing the saving significance of Jesus and especially his redemptive death in its true perspective![20]

The sacramental interpretation of vv. 7f. becomes all the more probable when we visualize the way in which the sacraments, and the Eucharist in particular, represent the death of Jesus on the cross. The author is continuing his polemic against the gnostic heretics. In his letter to the church at Smyrna, Ignatius of Antioch expressly provides evidence of this: "They abstain from Eucharist and prayer, because they allow not that the Eucharist is the flesh of our Saviour Jesus Christ, which flesh suffered for our sins."[121] Considering how closely related the heretical teaching combated by the martyr-bishop of Antioch is to the moral and christological "lie" which is presumed in 1 (and 2) John (see Introduction, pp. 20ff.), the shift between v. 6 and vv. 7f. becomes intelligible. The heretical teachers not only deny the saving significance of the death of Christ. They go further than that and deny the need to receive the Holy Eucharist, which represents the redemptive death and by which the redemptive power of the flesh and blood of Jesus is transmitted. Further, Ignatius speaks frequently in this context of the blood of Christ (*Smyrn.* 1.1; 6.1; 12.2), emphasizing, like the author of 1 John, Christ's actuality in the flesh (*Smyrn.* 1.3; 3.1f.). Ignatius reproaches the heretical teachers for denying Christ as "bearer of flesh" and speaks evidently again in view of the Eucharist, of his flesh and blood (12.2). That there is a connection here with the Johannine teaching about the Eucharist can hardly be doubted.

W. Nauck develops the sacramental interpretation even further in a lengthy excursus. He argues that the "Spirit" represents a sacramental rite, the rites of anointing or chrismation. The sequence of the three witnesses, he suggests, reflects the three sacramental acts in Christian initiation as the author knew it, viz., anointing, water baptism, and the eucharistic meal![122] Despite the considerable amount of evidence he offers for comparison (it is undeniable that the Syrian church had a peculiar custom of an anointing prior to baptism) this reading of the evidence is not convincing. Such a rite cannot be proved for New Testament times, and the Johannine writings in other respects are in complete agreement with general early Christianity in their views of baptism. As a symbolic term used

120. On the so-called Johannine comma, which is added here in Vg^{cl}, in a few Old Latin manuscripts, and in many later Western ones, see Introduction, pp. 43ff. Here let us merely note that the insertion of a triad of heavenly witnesses alongside the earthly ones is also suspect on exegetical grounds. The church needs witnesses for its faith who can provide tangible evidence.

121. It is to the merit of E. Schweizer in his essay on the Johannine evidence for the Lord's Supper (*EvT* 12 [1952–53] 341–83) that he refers to the passage (p. 347). That this implies that the Lord's Supper is a representation of Jesus' death on the cross is also rightly seen. But against Schweizer we must, in view of John 6:53–58, question whether this exhausts the meaning of the Supper for John. The Eucharist mediates the divine life in a real and sacramental way, not only through faith but also through the eating and drinking of the eucharistic elements (cf. John 6:55).

122. Nauck, *Tradition und Charakter,* 147–82; see my critique in *BZ* 4 (1960) 297. Nauck's thesis on this passage is followed by I. de la Potterie ("L'onction du chrétien par la foi," in *La vie selon l'Esprit* [Paris, 1965] 107–67, esp. 153). He describes the prebaptismal anointing in the Syrian rite (pp. 150–71), and thinks that it goes back in the last analysis to the earliest church. At that time the Spirit played a part in the genesis of faith and was understood as "anointing" (p. 154).

alongside of water and blood, it would be reasonable to expect "oil of anointing" to be used. Even if the term Spirit was retained simply because of v. 6c, we cannot overlook the fact that "the Spirit," as opposed to "in water," referring to Jesus' baptism, and "in blood," referring to his death, has a new meaning of its own—why then not equally in vv. 7f.? The Spirit acquires in the context of vv. 6–8 a key position. Just as he witnessed those saving deeds of Jesus as the Spirit of truth and interprets their meaning, so he makes them effective in the proclamation and in the sacraments. Similarly, in John 15:26 the Spirit is the witness to Jesus before and in company with the disciples inasmuch as he actually gives his testimony through them.

3. God Himself Gave Testimony to His Son, And the Salvation of All Depends on the Acceptance or Rejection of This God-Given Testimony (1 John 5:9–12)

Governed by the idea of testimony, the author develops a fresh train of thought, enabling him to condemn even more strongly the heretics' rejection of the true testimony to Christ. He places human and divine testimonies in contrast, assuring his readers that God himself has given the same testimony as that which is confessed by the Christian community, namely, that Jesus is the Son of God. Nobody can ignore this divine testimony. It can only be accepted in faith or rejected in unbelief. This is what determines the individual's salvation. Moreover, it is obvious how close this line of thought is to GJohn: the Gospel story is essential to the understanding of what is said here.

5:9 The witness of human beings[123] is accepted provided it is credible. All the more then does the testimony of God demand our attention ("is greater").[124] The conditional clause refers to an actuality (*ei* with the indicative): "We receive" is to be taken literally. We accept the testimony and act accordingly. Thus it makes sense when the author emphasizes in v. 9b that God bore witness to his Son. We are therefore obliged to accept it. This means that we must keep the reading *hoti memartyrēken* ("he has borne testimony"). This is the only reading that satisfies the rules of textual criticism.[125] The awkward but emphatic expression with *hautē* is consistent with Johannine diction.[126] "For that (pointing forward to what follows)[127] is the witness of God. He has given (permanently valid) testimony concerning his Son." Its position at the end places special emphasis on "his Son" (see Brooke). God's testimony has the same content as the community's confession in v. 5. According to the three witnesses in vv. 7f., God himself is named

---

123. The articles are general; there is no reference to any specific testimony.
124. In John 5:36 *meizōn* denotes a higher degree of credibility, while in 1 John 5:9 it denotes the stronger binding force of God's testimony. But the passages are related.
125. *Ēn* is read by P Ψ 104 pm. ℵ. The ancient uncials and most of the versions have *hoti*. The reading *ēn* is advocated by Büchsel.
126. See John 3:19; 1 John 1:5; 4:10; 5:4, 11, 14; with *hina:* John 6:29; 17:3; 1 John 3:11, 23; 5:3.
127. B. Weiss takes it as a backward reference; he goes on to interpret the *hoti*-clause in a causal sense. This, however, is not convincing; cf. Brooke, ad loc.

as the witness to the divine Sonship of Jesus. God confers upon this confession supreme authority and absolute validity. To reject it is therefore a serious evil, and to oppose it a futile project. God's will and power stand behind faith in Christ and assure its victory.

When and where did God give testimony to his Son? No answer is given to this question here. Only the fact is repeatedly stated (vv. 9 and 10). In v. 11 we have no description or definition of God's testimony either (see ad loc.). This is not surprising when we look at GJohn. There, in a context similar to 1 John 5:7ff., Jesus himself points to the testimony of his person, to the witness of his Father. But how this testimony is given we are not told any more precisely. Another related passage is one where Jesus contrasts the human witness of John the Baptist (v. 34) with greater witnesses, the work's that the Father had given Jesus to do (v. 36), the witness of the Father himself (v. 37), and the witness of scripture (v. 39). However we choose to interpret v. 37, the main point is that God himself bears witness to Jesus (vv. 31f.). Not merely the manner but the fact of God's testimony is what counts. The witness of God, dating from the time of Jesus' activity on earth, but retaining its validity still, is what the author must have in mind. This is proved by the perfect tense of the verb *memartyrēken*. The three witnesses in vv. 7f., like the Spirit in v. 6c, are introduced in the present tense. Since these terms refer to what is going on at the present moment in the sacraments, they can hardly be connected with the testimony of God in vv. 9ff. This is because all of God's testimonies (including v. 11) are referred to in the past tense. At most one might consider the possibility that the author is thinking of the blood and water that flowed from the side of Jesus as a divine sign. Yet apart from the mysterious sound of the phrase "water and blood" in v. 8, there is nothing to correspond to it in the text. We must therefore distinguish between the divine testimony in vv. 9ff. and that of the three witnesses, behind which the divine authority also stands. We must content ourselves with the fact that the author is only referring to the existence of that testimony.

The more recent commentaries ignore v. 10a and develop the idea of an internal witness, constituted by the possession of life (v. 11). The inward experience of the Son of God, it is suggested, provides a motive and support for the believers' faith. But this interpretation is untenable. In the Johannine writings *martyrein* and *martyria* always refer to external testimony, as they do in the preceding vv. 6c and 7f. Apart from that, between vv. 10a and 11, from which this view is derived, there is v. 10b, which again refers back to the witness of God. Finally, it is hard to see how the divine life, which in John is always thought of as an objective, invisible gift of salvation, not open to direct experience needing a criterion of its own, could become a "testimony" for faith. See further Excursus 11.

5:10 In the closing verses the author shows the consequences of accepting or rejecting the testimony of God. Verses 10a and b form a genuine antithesis, both in what they say and the way they say it. The meaning of "has the witness in himself"[128] is similar to that in Rev. 6:9; 12:17; 19:10 (cf. 20:4). Those Christians

---

128. The reading *heautō* occurs in ℵ Ψ 104 323 1739 al. Vg. However, instead of the reflexive pronoun the simple personal pronoun may be used, especially after prepositions; see BDF §283.2,

or martyrs "have" the witness of Jesus (cf. 1:2); that is to say, they hold it fast and bear it in their hearts. In exactly the same way 1 John 5:10a tells us that the believers have accepted the witness of God internally and are now bearing it within their hearts. The witness can also be taken into their hearts, as a permanent possession, one that is always valid (cf. *memartyrēken*, v. 9) and allowed there to live (cf. John 8:37c). This is just what the believers do. In this way it corresponds to the obligation to receive it, an obligation which the witness of God requires (v. 9).[129] The testimony of God in v. 10a is not an interior voice, which speaks from inside, but it is certainly interiorized, made the possession of the believers. It is the testimony God has given concerning his Son.

In contrast to this the fault of the unbelievers is that they have made God a "liar" insofar as his witness is concerned (*pisteuein* with the dative).[130] They have made this judgment permanent through their unbelief (perfect tense). The same verdict goes for those who advanced the false thesis: "We have not sinned" (1:10, see ibid.). This contradiction of God is so awesome, so catastrophic, for those who deny him, because they reject the witness God has given to his Son. With the rejection of the only Son of God the unbelievers pronounce their own death sentence (cf. John 3:18). If *pisteuein* is constructed here with *eis* ("believe *in*"), which otherwise gives direction and content to faith, it shows again that the content of God's witness is the Sonship of Jesus (v. 5). The phrase is equivalent in meaning to 3:23b and 5:13c. The entire verse with its sharp antithesis calls for a decision, exactly like John 13:18.

5:11 The last two verses express even more clearly the consequences for the individual resulting from the acceptance or rejection of God's testimony, consequences which the attentive reader will have noticed already in v. 10. Verse 11 contains no definition, any more than John 3:19; 17:3; 1 John 4:10 (for the idea of inner witness, cf. v. 10). Nor does the author specify the content of the testimony (*contra* Belser). The phrase *hautē estin* etc., which always has to be defined more precisely from the context, serves here to clarify the importance of the divine testimony for humankind (cf. *hēmin* in the subordinate clause). By confirming Jesus as his Son, God establishes not only a solemn declaration of the hidden dignity of Jesus but also a binding proclamation of the Mediator of salvation whom he has provided for us. With the gift of his Son he has granted us eternal life (cf. 1:2). The verse unfolds this thought, however, not in a genetic way but in systematic terms. The key word is enunciated first: "God gave us *eternal life*."[131] Then there is added (still dependent on the *hoti*): "and this life is in his

---

3; Radermacher, *Grammatik*, 73. The meaning is the same.—The reading *autǭ* (Westcott-Hort) is untenable linguistically in view of its history; see BDF §64.1.

129. *Lambanein tēn martyrian* and *pisteuein* are generally synonymous; cf. John 3:11 with 12; 3:32f. with 36 (5:34 is a different case); at the same time *pisteuein* in 1 John 5:10 is faith at the peak of its development, having already attained to an interior, living fellowship with God.

130. Cf. John 2:22; 5:24, 46, 47; 10:37f.; 14:11; 1 John 4:1. The only certain exception occurs in 1 John 3:23 (see ad loc.).—The reading *tǭ huiǭ* in A 81 323 1739 al. Vg sy^hmg does not suit the context, which speaks only of the witness of God, not of Jesus' self-testimony.

131. The word order should be noted; the accusative is obviously placed in front for the sake of emphasis (cf. 3:1; John 3:16b). *Hēmin ho theos* is to be read at the end with ℵ A k pm. (with

Son" (=is given to us and in his Son insofar as we believe in him).[132] Since the divine testimony is always related to the Son (vv. 9c, 10c), this last statement is still part of the *martyria*. Indeed, it only now makes v. 11b comprehensible. God has given us everlasting life by sending his Son to mediate that life and by bearing witness to him (note how vv. 9, 10, and 11 all end with "his Son").

5:12 The repeated emphasis on the Son of God gives rise to the pregnant antithesis of v. 12. In order to underscore with emphasis the decisive position of the Son for the confession (v. 5) and salvation (v. 11), the author now transfers a formula that originally described their firm and complete fellowship with God (see on 2:23) to the relation of the believers with the Son. This is another example of the way in which the author takes up certain turns of speech that were current in his religious environment and fills them immediately with his own distinctive spirit.[133] Of course he believes that fellowship with God is attainable only through fellowship with Christ. But because of the complete unity of Father and Son, fellowship with God is experienced therein to a perfect degree (cf. esp. John 14:6–10). Therefore in his view the possession of God which people long for so much is realized through the possession of Christ. However, since in v. 11 the possession of salvation and the goal of salvation are eternal life, already acquired in the present, the author seeks to assure his readers by persuading them that whoever has the Son has life. At the same time this formula reminds us of the preeminent soteriological formula in GJohn: "Whoever believes in him has eternal life" (3:15, 16, 36, etc.; 20:31)![134]

The positive statement is followed by its antithesis, as in John 3:18, 36; 12:46f.; and, in reverse order, 1 John 2:23. Here, however, it acquires greater emphasis as a word of warning and a call to do battle against those who deny Christ (vv. 5f.). But for the Christian this striking verse is necessarily an echo and a confirmation of the fact that their faith is victorious over the unbelieving world (vv. 4f.).

Tischendorf, von Soden, Vogels, and Merk), since the dative of the object usually follows the verb *didonai* immediately.

132. This *en* is not the *en* of Paul's Christ mysticism (the corresponding term *en pneumati* is lacking in John), though it is hardly the *en* of fellowship in John, since for that idea the reciprocal formulas are characteristic (see Oepke, *TDNT* 2:543). It is more relevant to compare such turns of phrase as John 3:15 (*en autǭ* is to be taken with *echę̄*); 16:33; (negative) 14:30; 1 John 4:10.

133. H. Hanse regards the phrase "to have Christ" as analogous ('*Gott haben,*' 107; idem, *TDNT* 2:823f.).

134. Thus we have three parallel formulas with the first two combined in 1 John 5:12:

John 3:36	1 John 2:23	1 John 5:12
ὁ πιστεύων εἰς τὸν υἱὸν	ὁ ὁμολογῶν τὸν υἱὸν	ὁ ἔχων τὸν υἱὸν
ἔχει ζωὴν αἰώνιον	καὶ τὸν πατέρα ἔχει	ἔχει τὴν ζωήν

EXCURSUS 11

The Testimony of God and Faith

1. The close relation between faith and testimony mirrors the place faith occupied in the early church around the turn of the first century. Apparently there had been some evaluation of the validity and binding power of the various testimonies serving as the foundation of the faith. Faith is based on the word and work of Christ and, in the last analysis, on his very person. Yet his figure and voice are no longer present. All the more urgent was the need to elevate past history to a transcendent level. Only so could the past, which would otherwise disappear into oblivion, be retrieved. This ultimate need could be met with relative ease by fixing in written form the history of the past. Probably this was the motive for shaping the distinctive Johannine tradition in permanent form. Thus, alongside the Synoptic Gospels, which were already in circulation, there arose the Gospel of John. But there was also the much more difficult problem of faith: How could the life and death of Christ, embedded as they were in history, be an object of faith for later generations? That problem, too, left its mark on the Johannine writings. At first the Gospel narratives relied on the reports of trustworthy witnesses (cf. John 19:35; 21:24; 1 John 1:1-3). But it had to be made clear that the proclamations of these witnesses were based not merely on their subjective convictions but on objective declarations by God himself. Thus the question of divine testimony arose.

In GJohn Jesus names several witnesses for his claim to be God's final emissary, the only Son of God. They are: John the Baptist (5:33), his [Jesus'] own works (5:36; 10:25; cf. 10:37f.; 14:11), the Holy Scriptures (5:39), his own teaching (7:17), his words (10:38; 14:11; cf. 12:48). The central question is always the reliability of the testimonies. It is, for instance, difficult in the case of Jesus' own words. Intrinsically they can serve as a proof, while Jesus in person is a fully qualified witness (cf. 8:14). But to convince the outside world it is advisable to call on other witnesses, witnesses that may be seen as disinterested and impartial (5:31f.). Such witnesses can carry more weight. Again, with his consciousness of mission (cf. 3:31a), Jesus accepts no human testimony (5:34). In his own discourses the Johannine Jesus appeals to the testimony of the Father himself (John 5:37; 8:18). Further, he points with great decisiveness to the future testimony of the Paraclete. That, too, is a divine witness, since the Paraclete is the Spirit of truth who comes from the Father (15:26). Part of the same train of thought is the constant emphasis in 1 John 5 on the divine testimony. To alleviate doubts and to penetrate more deeply, the relationship of this divine witness to that of the Father himself and to the witness of the Spirit must be clarified.

2. Anyone who points to 1 John 5:10a and 11 for an internal witness, suggesting that those who have it have the divine life within them, may want to identify the divine testimony with the internal witness of the Spirit. Such is the opinion of A. Klöpper in reference to v. 10.[135] The believers have the testimony in

---

135. A. Klöpper, *ZWT* 43 (1900) 396.

their hearts. They have the Spirit of God, who by definition bears witness to the messiahship of Jesus (v. 6), abiding in their hearts. In v. 11 only one accessory effect of this testimony of the Spirit is emphasized. "The blessed consequences for the believer, which are already operative in the present, when the testimony is appropriated, can only serve to reenforce the original assertion of truth."[136] Similarly, T. Häring associates the testimony of God with that of the Spirit,[137] and more recently T. Preiss has developed this view further.[138]

This construction is open to serious objection on exegetical grounds. On the one hand, in 1 John 5:10 and 11 the author is no longer speaking about the Spirit. On the other hand, the word *pneuma* in v. 6 is closely tied to the historical context suggested by the phrase "who came by water and blood." The Spirit does not give direct testimony of this as an inner reality working in the soul. Similarly, in the only passage in GJohn where the Spirit of truth is invoked as a witness (15:26), it is clearly speaking of the role of the Spirit as an external witness to the world. In 1 John 3:24 and 4:13 the Christians' possession of the Spirit is claimed in an entirely different fashion, namely, as a hallmark of their fellowship with God. The teaching (rather than witness), the internal anointing that the Christians have received according to 2:27, certainly refers to the truth of faith as opposed to the heretical teaching. But it does not give access to the material content of faith, only to its formal truth character (cf. "you know," vv. 20f.). The spiritual anointing gives the believers the power to distinguish between truth and error. Inasmuch as it deals with faith in Jesus Christ as the Son of God who appeared in history, the author never returns to the subject of the inner voice of the Spirit but rather to the external witness of the preachers (1:2; 4:14). In 5:9f. *memartyrēken* at the end of both verses looks back on something historical. It does this despite the enduring validity and efficacy of the divine testimony (note the perfect tense).

3. Is this divine testimony itself an interior, direct testimony? This question arises quite apart from the fact of what is meant by the testimony of the Spirit. Bonsirven thinks it is.[139] He claims that it is identical with the "inner testimony of the Father, about which Jesus speaks in addressing the Jews, and which he distinguishes from the testimony of the works that the Father accomplishes through him, as well as from the testimony of scripture." Bonsirven appeals to John 5:37 (cf. 6:45f.). But is this really the meaning of John 5:37? Is it really an *inner* witness of the Father? Is it not rather an *external* one—although it cannot be clarified with certainty in that context?[140] Can the giving of witness by the Father in 5:37 be equated with his inner teaching of human beings in 6:45?

---

136. Ibid., 398.
137. Ad loc. (p. 70).
138. Preiss, *Das innere Zeugnis;* He does not, however, discuss 1 John 5:9f. any further (see p. 39).
139. Bonsirven, *Jean,* 263f.
140. Most modern exegetes equate it with the witness of scripture. The perfect *memartyrḗmen* supports this; though in v. 47 Moses is specified as the witness standing behind scripture. Otherwise in GJohn God's testimony is never anchored to scripture in any special way. Perhaps v. 37 merely emphasizes the fact that God has borne witness, so as to strengthen the statement in v. 32. It is a unitary testimony of God, able to make itself known both in scripture and in the words and works of Jesus. The initial *kai* should therefore be translated "in point of fact"; cf. the *kai* in 1:14.

Bonsirven judges rightly in 1 John 5:10f. that eternal life itself, which believers bear in their hearts, cannot be regarded as a motive for credibility. That would involve a vicious circle. According to Bonsirven, v. 11 describes the essential content of God's interior witness. It does so in two intimately connected statements. God gave us eternal life, and he gave us that life in his Son. Bonsirven would reckon this witness of the Father as one of those heavenly things referred to in John 3:12. It is distinct from the three witnesses mentioned in v. 8. For the latter belong to the order of created reality, to the earthly things.[141] Thus in Bonsirven's exegesis the interior witness (vv. 9–11) follows upon the external testimony (vv. 7f.) of the three witnesses. Unfortunately Bonsirven's interpretation, quite apart from his exegesis of John 5:37, together with 6:45, suffers from the low estimate he gives to the Spirit as a witness in v. 8. Is it not the Spirit that provides the decisive factor in the triad of witnesses in v. 8? Note that the Spirit is mentioned first! Does this mean that the testimony of the Spirit is contrasted with the testimony of God?

4. A satisfactory conclusion can be reached only when we make the following exegetical decisions:

a) The testimony of God in vv. 9–12 is to be distinguished from that of the three witnesses in vv. 7f. The transition from v. 8 to v. 9 is one of external association, brought about by the theme of testimony. The testimony of the three witnesses is meant to place the Christian faith on a firm foundation. The testimony of God, which is much more important than any human testimony, is meant to alert us to the obligation of faith and the sinfulness of unbelief.

b) The testimony of God is a historical fact whose effects are prolonged into the present. This is pointed up by the perfect tense, "has testified." In respect of its content it is determined exclusively by its repeated mention of the divine Sonship of Jesus (vv. 9 and 10). If we accept the more difficult and probably original reading *hoti* in v. 9 (second occurrence), it becomes clear that it is the fact of Jesus' divine Sonship that is being emphasized. The testimony of God is directed to the fact that Jesus is his Son. But we are not told precisely when this happened. To answer that question we have to refer to the events and especially to the words of Jesus in GJohn.

c) The testimony of God in vv. 9–12 is uniform. This can be seen from the way it is spoken of in v. 10b, which is the same as in v. 9. As a result, vv. 10a and 11 do not introduce some special inner testimony. Such testimony from God, internally audible, and rooted in Christian life and Spirit, cannot be traced anywhere in the Johannine writings.

d) Verse 10 does not define the content of the divine testimony any more closely. This has already been done in v. 9, where it says: "this is the testimony of God that he has testified to his Son." Rather, v. 10 draws attention to the meaning of faith and unbelief. This is expressed by the pointed antithesis: those who believe–those who do not believe. But it is equally obvious from the two subordinate clauses. The believers do something important, something that is conducive to salvation. They appropriate the testimony of God internally and they bear it in their hearts. The unbelievers perpetrate something that is shameful

---

141. Bonsirven, *Jean,* 262.

and not conducive to salvation: at the moment of denial they declare God to be a liar. Now we expect the author to continue by telling us what there is about faith that is conducive to salvation and what in unbelief is not.

e) Verse 11 continues the thought of v. 10. It does not give any information about where the testimony of God is available. The believers have perceived the meaning of God's testimony, and precisely by their faith they have fulfilled it for themselves. By bearing testimony to Jesus as his Son, God shows him to be the Giver of life. In v. 11 this is worked out as a matter of fundamental principle. Then in v. 12 it is applied concretely to the believers and the unbelievers (cf. v. 10). Those who accept the Son of God and enter into fellowship with him thereby attain to life. Those who refuse to throw in their lot with the Son of God remain excluded from the divine realm of life.

5. While holding closely to the compact argument of vv. 9–12 it is useful to compare it with the argument of vv. 7f., which likewise stands on its own feet, These two little sections, each of which in its own way deals with the idea of testimony, have something in common. They do not merely remind us of a testimony given in the past. The testimony in each case continues to be effective down to the present time. In vv. 7f. we are told that the testimony of the divine Spirit which is echoed in the proclamation, the testimony to the mighty acts of salvation in the life and death of Jesus, and the testimony of the redeeming water and blood of Jesus continue to be efficacious in the sacraments. In vv. 9ff. the testimony is given once and for all by God himself for the Son. The believers appropriate it so that it becomes a continuing reality for them, again through faith and the sacraments. The thought here is profoundly Christian and existential. It attempts to solve the problem of history and faith. At first sight the terminology and imagery in these verses may seem strange. But behind it all there is a profound reflection on the issues of Christian faith. We have here arguments and reasonings for *believers,* especially for those who are privileged "not to see and yet to believe" (John 20:29) in the face of an unbelieving world.

THE CONCLUSION OF THE EPISTLE (1 JOHN 5:13–21)

[13]I write these things to you who believe in the name of the Son of God, so that you may know that you have eternal life.

[14]And this is the boldness we have in him, that if we ask anything according to his will, he hears us. [15]And if we know that he hears us in whatever we ask, we know that we have obtained the requests made of him. [16]If you see your brother or sister committing what is not a mortal sin, you will ask, and God will give life to such a one—to those whose sin is not mortal. There is sin that is mortal; I do not say that you should pray about that. [17]All wrongdoing is sin, but there is sin that is not mortal.

[18]We know that those who are born of God do not sin, but the one who was born of God protects them, and the evil one does not touch them. [19]We know that we are God's children, and that the whole world lies under the power of the evil one. [20]And we know that the Son of God has come and has given us understanding so that we may know him who is true; and we are in him who is true, in his Son Jesus

Christ. He is the true God and eternal life. [21]Little Children, keep yourselves from idols.

The author is now coming to the end of his letter. This can be seen not only from v. 13, which is very similar to John 20:31, but from the general drift of this last section. He aims at strengthening the healthy self-assurance of the believers, giving them joy over their possession of salvation and renewing their hope for its completion. Note how the phrase "we know" occurs no fewer than six times. Here is a positive reflection on their good fortune. They possess the gift of fellowship with God. They have the divine strength which they derive from that fellowship. All this serves as the strongest bulwark against all destructive influences from without (cf. 2:21, 27). It is the surest support for Christian endeavor in this world (cf. 2:12–17). No attempt is made to minimize the seriousness of the situation. On the contrary, sin is real (vv. 16f.). The power of the evil one, the personal enemy of God (vv. 18f.), is unmasked in all its gravity. After the renewed confirmation of the Christian faith in 5:5–12, the superior counterpart of Satan, the only true Son of God, Jesus Christ, appears his full significance for the existential struggle of Christians in this world (v. 20). The consciousness of superiority, the assurance of victory, all of which are constantly featured throughout the epistle (2:12–14; 3:20; 4:4–6; 5:4) reach their climax here, with a realism free of illusion.

Understood in this way, the last section is to be taken as a unit![142] True, the author still touches on certain specific themes. Some of them have not been dealt with hitherto. They include intercession for the errant brothers and sisters (v. 16); mortal sin and sin that is not mortal (vv. 16b–17). This unsystematic procedure can be explained from the author's peculiar way of thinking. He moves from one idea to another by means of association. That is the key to the structure of this section. There is no connecting link consisting of key words as we find in so many groups of saying in the Gospels. Nor is there any systematic procedure such as we follow when developing an argument. Using the phrase "we know" as a basis, the author proceeds like a musician, introducing a series of musical phrases. Thus one phase of the figure develops after another. There are seven phases in all, though that is probably accidental. There has been no indication thus far that the author uses the number seven as a deliberate stylistic device (*contra* Lohmeyer).

The structure of thought becomes clear from the following list of contents:

1. The aim of the epistle is to assure the Christians of salvation ("that you may know," v. 13).

2. Assurance of salvation is strengthened through constant answer to prayer (vv. 14–15).

3. The power of prayer is shown in intercession for erring brothers or sisters (v. 16a).

Digression: there is mortal sin and sin that is not mortal (vv. 16b–17).

---

142. On Bultmann's hypothesis that 1 John originally ended at 5:13 and that 5:14–21 is to be assigned to an ecclesiastical redaction ("Redaktion," 189ff.), see Introduction, pp. 15f.

4. Those who are born of God overcome sin and are protected from the evil one, that is, Satan (v. 18).

5. Unlike the Christian community, the world is under the sway of the evil one (v. 19).

6. The Christian community has been delivered from the power of the evil one by the Son of God. It lives in fellowship with God through him (v. 20).

7. Therefore the readers must avoid endangering their fellowship with God through idolatry (v. 21).

5:13 This verse harks back to vv. 5–12. That can be seen from the emphasis given to the possession of life (cf. v. 12) and to faith in the Son of God (vv. 10–12). But it leads on to the next verses. The author explains that his readers are conscious of their salvation ("you may know"). They are aware that their salvation is eternal (*aiōnion*).[143] Here the author brings up a concern that has motivated him all along (cf. 1:3; 2:12–14; 3:1, 14; 4:13). The divine life given to the Christian believers must become life with God and with the brothers and sisters. It is a life that requires constant vigilance. It grows out of a happy sense of possession. This supreme treasure must be defended at all costs. In a typically Johannine manner the word order (cf. John 1:12) emphasizes faith again as the basic attitude and condition of the believers. It is faith in the name or person of the Son of God, the perfect bearer of the divine nature (cf. John 1:12; 2:23; 3:18; 1 John 3:23).

5:14 The present awareness of salvation is expressed in boldness and confidence (*parrhēsia*) in prayer. It is expected that prayer will be answered (see 3:21f.). The addition of the phrase "according to his will" suggests that the author has reflected on the promises of the Johannine Jesus. These promises have actually been fulfilled in the life of the early Christian community. By returning again and again to this pragmatic side of Christian fellowship with God, the author shows what a strong impression this confidence in the answering of prayer has made on the minds of the believers. The Son of God had promised as much on the eve of his departure. Often the answer to prayer had been miraculous (cf. Acts 4:23ff.; 12:5ff.). In this the community was confirmed in its belief that it was indeed the eschatological people of God. But sometimes there may have been experiences that contradicted this, especially in private prayer. People were not always conscious of being the people of God. They often lapsed back into purely private prayer (cf. James 5:16f.). They came to expect that the dominical promise would be fulfilled not only in the missionary activity of the church (cf. John 14:12; 15:16), not only in the supernatural fruits of those united with Christ (cf. John 15:7), but also in the private or purely earthly realm. This might have been encouraged by the general way in which the promise was worded (John 16:23f., 26). Thus the question about the object of petitionary prayer becomes important. In 1 John 5:14ff. the author apparently reminds his readers that their prayers should be "according to his will." At the same time he assures them that such prayers will be fulfilled (v. 15, "we know," repeated twice).

143. See above on 1:2.

5:15 The faith of the Johannine community is mature. It leads to fellowship with God as a present reality. That is why such faith likes to speak of "having," possessing. It is also shown in the answers granted to prayer. The confidence of being heard by God is equivalent to "knowing." For the conditional clause ("if we know") sums up the main point of the previous verse. It is not really laying down a condition. *Ean* with the indicative is here used to draw a consequence (=since now).[144] From this certainty that our prayers will be heard without limit ("whatever," *ho ean*)[145] there follows, however, another certainty (again, "we know"), that we have what we have prayed for ("we have obtained"). As surely as the believers in Christ "have" God (2:23), "have" eternal life (5:12), just as surely they "have" everything they asked for. For God grants them a share in it all. The assumption is that it is all connected with fellowship with God (cf. "according to his will," v. 14), about spiritual, heavenly realities. The statement would be senseless if it applied to earthly, tangible realities and if that is what we ask for at the time of prayer. All this is demanded by the theme that governs the author's thought, the theme of fellowship with God. The faithful owe this fellowship with Christ to the far-reaching, gracious generosity of God. They can appeal to that in their prayers (cf. petitionary prayer in the name of Jesus, John 14:13; 15:16; 16:23, 26). In Christ union with the Father includes unrestricted sharing of possessions (John 17:10). We cannot fail to notice how certain the Johannine Christ is of being heard by his Father (John 11:41f.). This provides the supreme example of the power of prayer. Christians share in this power to the same degree or distance that their own fellowship with God approximates to the intimacy of the Father and the Son or fails to do so. At any rate, these texts of 1 John can be explained only in the light of Christ's sayings in GJohn. But they also recall Synoptic texts (Matt. 7:7; 18:19; 21:22; Mark 11:24; Luke 11:5–8). The hearing of prayer, which the Synoptic Jesus assures his followers of on the basis of a charismatic faith excluding all doubt is to be distinguished from 1 John 5:15. Prayer of this type is equally certain of being immediately heard ("believe that you have received it"). But the fulfillment still lies in the future ("it will be yours").

5:16 The petitions of Christians united with God are now channeled into an urgent and concrete concern. It is prayer for the erring brothers and sisters (note the concise repetition of "will ask" without "for them"). The petition of the righteous is equally familiar in the Old Testament and in late Jewish piety.[146] But there is a certain difference. In late Jewish piety this kind of intercession is regarded as efficacious mainly when it is offered by the saints, e.g., the patriarchs.[147]

---

144. *Ean* instead of *ei* is a "vulgarism" (BDF §372.1a); the meaning is like that in John 7:23; 10:35; 13:14, 17, 32; 1 John 4:11 (*ei* with indicative) and 1 John 2:29 (*ean* with subjunctive).

145. *Ho ean*=classical *ho(ti)an* (BDF §107). It takes up the *ean ti* of the preceding verse (stylistic variation or stronger generalization like the classical generalizing relative).

146. See Eichrodt, *Theology* 2/3:448f.; Volz, *Eschatologie,* 272, 290; Johansson, "Parakletoi," 3ff., 65ff., 138ff., 161ff. The clearest place in late Judaism is undoubtedly 4 Ezra 7:102–15 (intercession is possible on earth but has ceased to be so on judgment day; a list of examples is given). Johansson points out that the devout have a duty to pray for one another.

147. For Abraham the best example occurs on Gen. 18:27ff.; cf. 20:7. For Jacob, see especially the *Testaments of the Twelve Patriarchs,* mainly *T. Rub.* 1:7; *T. Jud.* 19:2; *T. Benj.* 3:6; 10:1; *T. Gad* 5:9; for Enoch: *2 Enoch* 64:4; for the rabbinic passages, see especially Johansson, "Parakletoi," 161ff.

Moses,[148] certain of the prophets,[149] and in later days the martyrs[150] in particular. In the Christian community all the believers, in virtue of their union with God through Christ, have an opportunity of saving their erring brothers or sisters. The subject of the verb "will give" is probably God (cf. 5:11).[151] To say that a human being could impart eternal life would seem foreign to Johannine thought, strictly theocentric as it is. Even the Son only imparts the life he has received (5:26) from the Father (John 10:28; 17:2). But the believers possess (*echei*, "has") eternal life but they do not impart it. The absence of the article with *zōēn* ("life") shows that divine life is not given per se or imparted anew. That would create a tension with the phrase "what is not a mortal sin." Rather, its power is rekindled and enhanced in range. The shift from singular to plural ("to those who sin") is abrupt. Such delayed emphasis by means of a participle is found in John 1:12; 1 John 5:13. The participle, when placed in a later position, acquires an importance of its own, in this case with a restrictive sense. But that applies only to those who "commit a sin that is not mortal."[152] What is that sin? The author never makes this clear. The Old Testament already recognizes a difference between lesser (unpremeditated) and greater (deliberate) sins (see Lev. 4:2ff.; 5:1ff.; Num. 15:22ff., in contrast to Num. 15:30f.). Mortal sin originally meant a sin incurring the penalty of physical death (see Num. 18:22; Isa. 22:14). The community must remove from its midst high-handed sinners who "affront the Lord" (Num. 15:30f.). The term is still retained in later times.[153] The expression (*pros* with the accusative) does not call for the actual death penalty but only for the passing of sentence on the deed as being worthy of death. Compare also the phrase "this illness does not lead to (*pros*) death" (John 11:4); "ripe for (*pros*) harvesting" (John 4:35). Death is here to be understood as the opposite of life in the Johannine sense (cf. 3:14; John 5:24). It means spiritual, eternal death (cf. John 8:51). Sin that is not mortal is accordingly an error that does not by its intrinsic nature lead necessarily to eternal death. Yet it can have a serious effect on our union with God. It is therefore not synonymous with the later concept of ordinary, everyday sin (Augustine) or venial sin. Otherwise the admonition to intercede for brothers

148. He is the great intercessor; see Exod. 32:11–14, 31f.; 34:8f.; Num. 14:13–19. For later times, see *As. Mos.* 11:17; 12:6. Among the Samaritans his intercession is effective and will be even at the last day (Volz, *Eschatologie*, 195). See further Johansson, "Parakletoi," 161ff.

149. See already the intercession of Amos (Amos 7:1–6); for Isaiah, 2 Kings 19:4; for Jeremiah, 2 Macc. 15:14; Jer. 37:3; 42:2. For Elijah, see Volz, *Eschatologie*, 195–97.

150. 2 Macc. 7:37f.; 4 Macc. 6:38f.; 17:21f.; *Mek.* on Exod. 22:22.—See Billerbeck, *Kommentar* 2:274ff.; Bousset-Gressmann, *Religion des Judentums*, 189f.; H. W. Surkau, *Martyrien*, 41, 59 and n. 7; Johansson, "Parakletoi," 71ff.

151. *Contra* Brooke, Büchsel, Chaine, Ambroggi.—James 5:15, 20 are parallel in thought though not in wording.

152. In *hamartanonta hamartian* we have an internal accusative ("accusative of content")—a mode of expression that is good Greek; see BDF §153; Radermacher, *Grammatik*, 120.

153. *T. Iss.* 7:1 *v.l.* (β A S¹) *hamartian eis thanaton; Jub.* 21:22; 26:34; 33:13, 18. In *Jubilees* we still have the idea that God himself inflicts death. For the rabbinic *ăwôn mîtā'* see Billerbeck, *Kommentar* 3:779.—On "lesser sins," which do not deserve death, see further *T. Gad* 4:6. The distinction between lighter, not deliberate sins and serious sins committed deliberately with malice aforethought; see also 1QS 8:22–9:2.

and sisters would not be necessary. The idea is that of dying away or becoming powerless (Rev. 3:1). It needs a decisive reversal or thoroughgoing renewal.

Mortal sin is an act God is bound to punish with exclusion from the divine realm of life. It is like the way he punished people with physical death in ancient times. Mortal sin must not be equated with the sin against the Holy Spirit (Mark 3:29) or more generally with the so-called unforgivable sin, where the sinner is beyond repentance (cf. Heb 6:4–8; 10:26–31; *Herm. Sim.* 6.2–3), though many scholars have made that equation.[154] The idea of mortal sin implies nothing about the possibility or impossibility of repentance. The author deliberately makes an exception of mortal sin when he urges his readers to pray for other people ("I do not say that you should pray about that" — note this is not an actual prohibition). A similar consideration may lie behind this as in Heb. 6:4ff., though not necessarily so.[155] But there is a tradition in the Old Testament and in Judaism that distinguishes between unpremeditated sins and those committed in defiance of God and in anger. This distinction is found at Qumran (1QS 8:22–9:2) and in the Epistle to the Hebrews (see 10:26, "if we willfully persist in sin"). If that tradition is accepted as the true background of this verse, the distinction between mortal sin and sin that is not mortal will refer not to two different classes of sinners, but to two kinds of sinners, "conscious sinners" and "remorseful, penitent sinners."[156] However, it might be asked whether the author should not have expressed his point differently and more clearly. This is particularly so since the term he uses, mortal sin, has, in contrast to the usage in the Old Testament and Judaism, already acquired a metaphorical sense, denoting sin that excludes from the supernatural life of fellowship with God. The formulation seems to be pointing to two types of sin rather than to two kinds of sinners. This is true even though there may be an inner connection between the type and sincerity of the deed and the subjective attitude of the perpetrator.

It is equally difficult to explain why the author expressly excludes those who are guilty of mortal sin from our intercession. The suggestion that it is no good praying for those unfortunate people who are hardened in their opposition to God is not necessarily uppermost in the author's mind.[157] A comparison with the situation at Qumran is worth considering. That community was in the habit of handing over deliberate sinners without mercy to the wrath of God (cf. 1QS 10:19ff.). That would make the author of 1 John as concerned as Qumran was with the purity of the community.[158] He would be issuing instructions with the

---

154. For a contrary view, see J. Herkenrath, "Sünde zum Tode," in *Aus Theologie und Philosophie* (Festschrift F. Tillmann) 134f.

155. B. Poschmann connects this passage too onesidedly with Heb. 6:4ff. (*Poenitentia secunda,* 63–81; p. 78: "the same thought as in Heb. 6:4ff."); similarly Charue.

156. So Nauck, *Tradition und Charakter,* 144f.

157. When R. Seeberg supposes that sinners of this kind should not be allowed to confess their sins before the church, he has no support from any comparable New Testament text ("Die Sünden und die Sündenvergebung," in *Das Erbe Martin Luthers* [Festschrift L. Ihmels] 29).—Equally the opinion of O. Bauernfeind ("Die Fürbitte angesichts der 'Sünde zum Tode,'" in *Festgabe V. Schultze,* 51) that intercession for sinners of this kind should be left to the pure impulse of the Spirit has insufficient support.

158. Nauck, *Tradition und Charakter,* 145f.

same wrathful zeal as they did. Now the requirement at Qumran was "that they may love all that He has chosen and hate all the He has rejected" (1QS 1:3f.). Is the Christian author really as harsh and unforgiving as that? In the rest of the New Testament we are frequently told that when heinous sinners are delivered over to divine punishment, this is for the purpose of disciplining them in this life so as to save them in the eternal judgment (cf. 1 Cor. 5:5; 1 Tim. 1:20; also 1 Cor. 11:30; Rev. 2:22f.). In the restrictive formulation "I do not say that you should pray about that (i.e., mortal sin),"[159] all that is being said is that the author would leave the judgment in such cases entirely to God![160]

Thus we can no longer state with certainty what the author really thinks about mortal sin in concrete terms. All speculation is pointless, whether it is apostasy, murder, or idolatry (so Windisch), or the sins that characterize the Way of Death in *Didache* 1-5 (so R. Seeberg), or contempt for God's commandment (so Poschmann). The author presumes that his readers will know what he is talking about, either from the teaching they have already been given or from their own intelligence. Is he thinking of the heresy to which they have succumbed? After all, that is what he has been talking about all through the epistle. Such a suggestion is not as certain as recent commentators seem to think (Bonsirven, Chaine, Charue, etc.). Although John 16:9 designates unbelief simply as "the" sin *par excellence,* nevertheless the general theme of mortal sin (without the article) cannot bear this restrictive meaning. The author draws the line of demarcation firmly enough against those who have fallen from grace. There can no longer be any fellowship with them (cf. 2:19; 4:4f.; 5:12)![161]

5:17   The point of this verse depends on whether we read (with most commentators) "not" before "a mortal sin" or omit it (von Harnack, Büchsel). On purely textual grounds the "not" is firmly established![162] However, on internal grounds it might perhaps be admitted because the crescendo would lead us to expect the mention of "sin not mortal" to come before "mortal sin."[163] Yet the order as we have it provides an intelligible development of thought. The author first depreciates praying for those who have committed mortal sin (v. 16c). Then with utmost gravity he goes on to condemn sin (v. 17a), yet[164] returns to his request for intercessory prayer in v. 17b. All wrongdoing is sin. He does not want to belittle

---

159. *Peri ekeinēs* goes with *legō,* not with *erōtēsē.* One prays for sinners, not for the sin.—The addition of *tis* after *hina* in some manuscripts is superfluous.

160. On 5:16f., see also P. Trudinger, "Concerning Sins, mortal and otherwise: A Note on 1 John 5, 16–17," *Bib* 52 (1972) 541f. (*Erōtan* means here "to ask"; further questioning about "sin not mortal" the author prefers to leave aside).—However, in John 14:16; 16:26; 17:9, 15, 29; 19:31, 38, *erōtan* means "to request," and a change of object is not obvious.

161. Herkenrath makes the cautious observation that the reference is to the sort of behavior that "denies a complete living fellowship with God, Christ, and one's fellow believer" ("Sünde zum Tode," 135f.).

162. The *ou* is lacking only in 33 623 1852 q Vg sy[h] sa arm Tert. For a critique of Harnack's preference for this reading, see Lagrange, *Critique textuelle,* 566.

163. The attempt to place v. 17b before 16c (*estin hamartia pros thanaton*) or 16a (so Windisch), is to be rejected as unfounded.

164. The *kai* has an adversative sense ("and yet"); BDF §442.1.

failure to keep the commandments,[165] for that shows that they do not know God (2:3ff.). They have no fellowship with him (3:24) or love for him (5:3). But not every sin is equally heinous. There are also sins of infirmity, and to confess them is a duty (cf. 1:8f.). Moreover, forgiveness is to be expected in view of God's mercy (1:9) and the intercession of Christ, the divine Mediator (2:1). These hard-to-avoid peccadilloes—their denial becomes a heresy—are "sins that are not mortal."

5:18   The next three verses are notable for the impressive way in which they each begin, with "we know." There is no confession here, only joyful assurance over the Christian state of salvation (cf. v. 13).[166] The author knows that he is at one with his readers, and with all Christian believers, in separation from sin, from Satan, and from a world that has succumbed to Satan's sway. He is also at one with them in fellowship with Christ and with God. Verse 18 broaches the theme of Christ and sin, formulating it apparently in contrast to his earlier claim that those who are born of God are immune from sin. That claim is meant in a general and fundamental sense. It does not imply that they are literally incapable of sin, perhaps because of their possession of a higher nature. That was precisely the gnostic heresy. It only means that in fact they do not sin. In view of the heretical claims (cf. 1:8, 10), the deliberately pointed saying enhances the tension with vv. 16f., but it is the same tension as in 2:1. If the author must speak of sin in the Christian life, he would rather emphasize with all the force at his command that sin ought really to be overcome and that the Christians really do have the power to overcome it (cf. 3:9). Those who are born of God have become different persons. They have supernatural grace, called in the Johannine writings: "being born 'from above,' or 'from God'" (John 1:12f.; 3:3, 5f.; 1 John 2:29; 3:1, 9; 5:1). They bear in their hearts the principle of a new life conveyed by the divine Spirit (John 3:6f.; 1 John 3:9b). Thus they overcome sin, though certainly not without strenuous effort on their own part (1 John 2:29; 3:7; 4:7; see further Excursus 12).

The categorical claim that those who are born of God do not sin is confirmed by the positive turn in v. 8b, a verse that cannot be translated exactly with certainty. Text criticism requires that we read *heauton* rather than *auton*,[167] and *hē gennēsis* instead of *ho gennētheis*,[168] the alternative reading being in each case a simplification, The text we are left with (Nestle) is particularly striking because of the aorist *ho gennētheis* alongside of *pās ho gegennēmenos*. If it refers not to Christ (see below) but to the Christian who is born of God, this clause might

---

165. *Adikia* must be understood as a concrete act because of *pasa*, not as a general attitude= *anomian* (*1 Clem.* 35.5 [*v.l. ponērian*]); 60.1.

166. That this *oidamen* reminds us of "a certain eschatological knowledge of a secret kind" (Preisker, 168, 170), is unproved. This is because *eidenai* in 1 John is not related exclusively to eschatological knowledge (as Preisker himself notes). Moreover, the distinction he draws between *oidamen* and *oidate*, looking back to 5:15, is equally groundless.

167. *Heauton* is read by ℵ ℓ pl. Or. Epiph. (B. Weiss, von Soden, Merk, Vogels); *auton:* B A* 244 1852 2138 q Vg bo Jerome. The first reading must be regarded as secondary.

168. *hēgennēsis tou theou* 2138 (1852) q; *generatio Dei* Vg; *nativitas Dei* Chromatius of Aquil. (*PL* 20:359). For this, see von Harnack in *SB* (Berlin, 1915) 534–42 (and for a contrary view Lagrange, *Critique textuelle*, 566, and most scholars).

be understood as follows: "Those who are born of God (instead of NRSV "The one who was born of God") (also) hold fast to (NRSV "protects") him."[169] This translation explains the repetition of the aorist participle as the subject (cf. "were born," John 1:13, following the preferred reading; also the aorist in 3:3-5). But there is a difficulty: *tērein ton theon* (literally, "to keep God") is a peculiar expression. Yet this phrase might be modeled on "to have God" (1 John 2:23; 2 John 9; cf. 1 John 5:12). In that case it would mean holding fast to fellowship with God. For "to keep" (*tērein*) in this sense, cf. Rev. 3:3; further Eph. 4:3; 2 Tim. 4:7; Rev. 16:15. Against this meaning (followed in the first edition of this commentary), another reading is to be preferred. This has been suggested by K. Beyer in his study of New Testament grammar.[170] It is a semitism associated with a conditional participle. The subject of the verb "keep" is God, and *auton* (NRSV "them") takes up the previous "those who are born of God." Consequently it must be translated: "Those who are born of God, them he [God] protects, so that the evil one cannot harm them." The feasibility of this construction is confirmed only by John 17:2 (*pan ho . . . autois*), perhaps also (as Beyer thinks) by 7:38 or (as several explain it) 1:3. In 1 John 5:18 it makes excellent sense (if we accept the harsh expression, which would be intolerable to Greek ears): God himself protects those who are born of him, keeping them in fellowship with him. In fact, fellowship with God is the dominant theme in these three striking verses, 18-20. Verse 19 contrasts fellowship with God which both the author and recipients of the letter enjoy, as a fact and a status (*einai ek theou*, "to be from God," v. 19; NRSV "are God's children") with the world succumbed to Satan's sway, while v. 20 describes it as a distinctively Christian experience of salvation. This is made possible through Christ, the only Son of God, and realized in him.

With this explanation we have decided against other suggestions for which there are some pros and cons: (1) The interpretation of *auton=heauton*, "those who are born of God keep themselves (sinless)." Apart from the uncertainty on text-critical grounds, a comparison with several other passages (2 Cor. 11:9; 1 Tim. 5:22; Jas. 1:27; Jude 21) shows that in similar cases the predicative amplification is added, for example, "keep themselves *pure*." (2) The acceptance of the reading *hē gennēsis autou*. It is true that this avoids the doubling of the subject, and also follows smoothly on "God's seed" (3:9) as far as the subject matter is concerned. But it is too uncertain, given the overwhelming evidence of the Greek manuscripts. Also it may have originated from the difficulty of the original text. (3) The exegesis of *ho gennētheis*, which has become popular in recent times, with reference to Christ.[171] In favor of this interpretation is (a) that it avoids the tension between *pas ho gegennēmenos* and *ho gennētheis*; (b) the uniform interpretation of the personal pronoun *auton* in v. 18b and *autou* in v. 18c with reference to the Christian believer; (c) the antithesis between "the one who was born of God" (Christ) and the "evil one" (v. 18c); (d) the comparison with John 17:12 and Rev. 3:10. After the positive

---

169. See BAGD 815, s.v. 3; Herkenrath, "Sünde zum Tode," 127. The interpretation of *ho gennētheis* remains uncertain. Bultmann and de Jonge (ad loc.) are more inclined to refer the expression to Christ.

170. K. Beyer, *Semitische Syntax im Neuen Testament* I/1 (Göttingen, 1962) 216f.

171. Wohlenberg, *NKZ* 13 (1902) 233–40; Loisy, Bonsirven, Charue, Büchsel, Ambroggi; Nauck, *Tradition und Charakter*, 139; cf. also Westcott, Brooke, Chaine, ad loc.

explanation (see above) it would seem that the first reason does not hold up. The antithesis between Christ and the evil one would be interrupted by v. 19. Only the place of v. 19c in the structure of the argument remains questionable (see below). The decisive argument against interpreting it as a reference to Christ is the fact that nowhere is he thus designated. He can therefore hardly be referred to in this way here (why not "the Son of God" as in v. 20?).[172]

Because the Christians, being sustained as they are by God and preserved from sin, remain in constant fellowship with him, "the evil one does not touch them." This metaphor refers originally to outward (physical) harm (Job 2:5; Ps. 105:15; Zech. 2:8; *T. Jude* 3:10) and presupposes that the person doing the harm has power over the victim (Job 2:5, where the subject is God). Transferred to Satan, this metaphor means that Satan seeks to bring people under his sway. But he has no power over those who are born of God. For they have a firm union with God, and Satan cannot even take the first step toward subduing (cf. 1 Esdras 4:28 LXX). Where God is, Satan is bound to flee. The same conviction is expressed in the *Testaments of the Twelve Patriarchs* in many places and in divers ways![173] Thus v. 18c does not extend what v. 18a said about sinlessness to cover freedom from temptation. Rather, it illuminates the power of the Christians' union with God (vv. 18a–b) through the powerlessness of the adversary.

EXCURSUS 12

Christians and Sin

The topic of Christians and sin comes to the fore at three places in the epistle: 1:6–2:2; 3:4–10; 5:16–18. Its importance arises from the fact that the statements about the sinlessness of God's children (in 3:9 enhanced to the point of saying that they are unable to sin) as well as the contrary statements about the sinfulness of every human being, Christians included, lack nothing in clarity and precision. That even believing and loving Christians still sin is clear from other passages, such as 3:20. Here there is a discussion of the real possibility that our heart may condemn us. Then again 4:17f. is directed against fear of judgment. The warning against loving the world (2:15); the admonition to abide in Christ and avoid being put to shame at his parousia (2:28); the appeal to be pure and clean (3:3); the rather *sotto voce* encouragement to keep God's not too burdensome commandments (5:3)—all these stand in contrast to the comforting assurance that young and old in the community are powerful in combat with the evil one (2:13f.), that the readers truly love the brothers and sisters (3:14), that they accomplish what is pleasing to God (3:22).

---

172. The reference to John 1:13 holds good only if one assumes the weakly attested reading *egennēthē* or *natus est*. Harnack, *SB* (Berlin, 1915) 537: the aorist would in that case be more appropriate for the believers, the perfect for Christ.—*Gennēthenta* (*ek tou patros*) in the creeds is assured only in the fourth century; see Denziger ##9, 10, 13, 54, 86.

173. See *T. Rub.* 4:11; *T. Sim.* 5:3; *T. Iss.* 7:7; *T. Dan* 4:7; 5:1, 11; *T. Ash.* 1:8; *T. Jos.* 7:4; *T. Benj.* 3:3, 4; 6:1.—Rabbinic parallels are given in Schlatter, *Sprache,* 151.

The problem in 1:6–2:2 is relatively simple. Here the author is combating the gnostic heresy. He is forced to fight on two fronts. On the one hand, he has to confront the moral indifference of the gnostics. He has to emphasize the importance of living in the light, for that is an essential sign of true fellowship with God. It means doing the truth. On the other hand, in the face of their pneumatic conceit he does not and cannot admit that any person, even a Christian, has left the realm of sin behind![174] Yet in the other two principal passages this explicit debate with the opponents is lacking. Even though the controversy with them has not completely disappeared, the discussion becomes much more one of basic principle. The differences between 3:6ff. and 1:6ff. are as follows: (a) The concern is not to confront the heretical claims head-on. Rather, it is to deal up front with positive statements about the being and behavior of those who are born of God. (b) 3:6ff. sets out who the true believers are, not conditionally as in 1:7, but categorically. (c) The reason for this is not derived from their behavior ("we walk," 1:7), but rather from the being and supernatural endowments of the children of God, of all (*pas*) of them without exception. (d) The argument reaches its climax when the author speaks of their inability to sin (3:9b). Only as an afterthought does he draw the consequence (v. 10) that those who do not practice righteousness are not from God.

Our exegesis of 3:6ff. and 5:16ff. was already intended as the positive answer to the problem. But it may help to clarify and enrich that exegesis if we define our position over against other views and thus give it greater precision. In these texts sinlessness or unsinfulness is ascribed to those who are born of God. Here the problem comes to a head. Is the effect of being born of God such as to confer a moral or even physical status, making it impossible to sin?

1. *Attempts have been made to weaken the sense by interpreting these texts in purely ethical terms.*[175] This, however, will not do. The evidence will not support it. For it changes the categorical claim "they do not sin" into a moral admonition, "they may not sin." Even if the entire section 3:4–10 is basically parenetic in intention, the crucial verses, 9–10, are intended to provide a criterion to distinguish between the children of God and the children of the devil. Those who take this line argue that since the sinlessness of God's children is asserted as a fact, we have here not an admonition against sin but an explanation of why they are sinless. In vv. 5f. this intention on the part of the author is still hidden. Verse 6b might serve as a simple admonition, like 2:28. But the antithetical turn of speech surfaces in the tendency to set up a criterion. In the warning against the seducers in v. 7, and the charge in v. 8 that the sinner is diabolical in nature, the way is prepared for a clear distinction between the children of God and the children of the devil. This intention becomes crystal clear in the following two verses. Here we have two *hoti*-clauses leading to a climax (vv. 9a and 9b). These

---

174. Cf. in addition to ad loc., A. Kirchgässner, *Erlösung und Sünde im NT* (Freiburg im Breisgau, 1950) 270–77; Herkenrath, "Sünde zum Tode," 120f.

175. See C. Clemen, *Die christliche Lehre von der Sünde* (Göttingen, 1897) 121f.; Belser, ad loc. (p. 77); Chaine, who seeks to explain the harshness of the expression from a stylistic peculiarity (i.e., exaggeration).

clauses leave no doubt how the author intends the sinlessness of the Christians is to be understood. It is not the goal of their Christian status but the basic sign of what makes them different and distinct from the children of the devil.

2. *Repeated attempts have been made to ascribe to the author a number of different conceptions of sin.*[176]

a) In earlier days the attempt was made to distinguish between the general inclination to sin, that is, concupiscence, and actual sins. "The fact that he has been begotten of God excludes the possibility of his committing sin as an expression of his true character, though actual sins may, and do, occur" (Brooke). Dodd opts for a distinction between habitual and actual sins, depending on the use of different tenses (present and aorist).[177] We have already rejected this interpretation for 1:8 (see ad loc.). In 3:9f. the basic use of the present tense embraces both the ability to sin (v. 10) and actual sin (v. 9, "do not sin").

b) Nowadays most scholars reject the identification with such specific sins as sexual immorality (Belser, ad loc.).

c) The suggestion that the sins of which those who are born of God are incapable include "a state of damnation" (Poschmann), consisting of a deliberate renunciation of Christ and a refusal to acknowledge his commandments (the stance of the gnostic heretics) has more to be said for it![178] At the same time, v. 9a is a categorical statement about not sinning, though with general implications (v. 9b continues in the same vein). It does not just condemn a perverted attitude growing out of a contempt of the law. Also, one can hardly appeal to the distinction the author himself draws between mortal and non-mortal sin (5:16f.)[179] This interpretation of the special expression is highly dubious (see ad loc.). Nor is it permissible to combine 5:16f. with 5:18 in this way. The specific theme of intercession for the erring brother or sister, which provides the context for that distinction, is concluded with v. 17. However, v. 18 belongs with vv. 19 and 20 ("we know"). Here the basic situation of the Christians in the world is described (v. 19), then their situation in salvation history (v. 20). From the concrete experience of life in the Christian community (v. 16) the author turns again in v. 18 to fundamental considerations, to the ideal existence in this world of those who are born of God. Here there is no place for sin, be it heavy or light. The author expresses himself in equally basic terms in 3:9f.

---

176. On the history of interpretation, see A. Zahn, "De notione peccati, quam Johannes in prima epistula docet, commentatio" (diss., Halle, 1872) 30–43.

177. *Johannine Epistles,* 78f.; though he himself goes on to recognize (p. 79f.) the weak basis for this thesis. The same solution is advocated by M. Zerwick in *Graecitas bibl.,* #186.

178. P. Galtier ("Le chrétien impeccable," in *Mélanges de sciences religieuses* 4 [1947] 137–54) interprets the sin Christians are incapable of, following 3:4 (*anomia*) as "a sin committed on principle and out of contempt for the law" (p. 150) (quoted by M.-É.Boismard, *RB* 56 [1949] 379 n. 1). On the question of a Johannine predestinationism, compare my commentary on GJohn, vol. 2, Excursus 11 (pp. 259–74; further H.-M. Schenke, "Determination und Ethik im ersten Johannesbrief," *ZTK* 60 (1963) 203–15.

179. So Poschmann, *Poenitentia secunda,* 71ff.; in the Protestant camp, see A. Zahn, "De notione peccati," 55ff.; also Nauck (see above on 5:16).

d) With this the ground has been cut from under another interpretation. This is that, according to 3:9f., Christians are immune from capital sins but not from venial ones![180] No conclusions about this question are drawn in this passage. Nor can it be cited as an argument against the Council of Trent.

3. *The best way to interpret these texts is to accept the tension between those passages which claim that those who are born of God do not and cannot sin and those which recognize that there is sin in the Christian life.* There is no easy solution to this tension.

a) We must reject the view that this tension is simply incapable of solution![181] Even though the statements are contradictory they must somehow fit together in the author's mind![182]

b) The solution that "the statements about the sinlessness of God's children are (in the last analysis), an expression of faith in God's faithfulness and protection" (cf. 5:18, Büchsel) is equally unsatisfactory. This interpretation dissolves being born of God into a purely personal relationship between God and his children. It merely shifts the problem of the general tension between God's saving activity and human cooperation. If one accepts the view that baptism is the foundation of being born of God (see Excursus 8), this will mean that God's children are granted new powers and abilities to overcome sin. On no account must this be regarded as magical. Rather, the Spirit of God given to Christians does not exempt them from moral endeavor on their own part. It does, however, provide a reality that is more than merely "God's faithfulness and protection."

c) W. Nauck has made a valuable contribution by bringing the Qumran texts into the discussion. First, he points to the dynamic aspect that they give to the situation of the faithful in this world. It is one of conflict arising from temptation to sin. "Insofar as they stand under the power of God, they do righteousness. But insofar as they are in the world and live in the flesh, they succumb again and again to the onslaught of the power of sin, and have to maintain their existence ever anew in the struggle against it."[183] Nauck thinks he can find additional agreement between the Qumran texts and 1 John. Like the latter, they have in view only premeditated sins, not sins of infirmity. Such sins seriously imperil the relation of the devout to God (on this see above on 5:16). Through his Spirit God comes to the help of the infirmities of the flesh. Finally, complete salvation can be expected only in the eschatological future![184] Nauck does not overlook the fundamental difference between Qumran and 1 John. Christians see "the eschatological hope realized in the final conquest of sin through the saving act

---

180. Bonsirven, 174ff.

181. H. Windisch, *Taufe und Sünde im ältesten Christentum bis auf Origenes* (Tübingen, 1908) 266ff.; idem, commentary, 121f. and (assuming redactional reworking) 136; Jülicher-Fascher, *Einleitung,* 228; see also Bultmann's "dialectical" understanding in *Theology* 1:276, 332, and "Redaktion," 193f.

182. The attempt to derive the tension between the texts from the differences of theology between a *Vorlage* and an editor (Bultmann, "Analyse," 148f.) is problematic and unsatisfactory. See also M. Goguel *The Primitive Church* (New York, 1964) 471 n. 4; H. Braun, "Literar-Analyse," 276f.; E. Käsemann, "Ketzer und Zeuge," 306–8.

183. Nauck, *Tradition und Charakter,* 104f.

184. Ibid., 117–22.

of Jesus Christ, the eschatological Mediator of salvation."[185] But Nauck does not appear to recognize sufficiently the reality implied by the possession of the Spirit, which is so strongly emphasized by John. This Spirit of God (imparted sacramentally) makes sin impossible in a different way from the Qumran texts. This is because it is already (as in Paul) an eschatological gift of God. The Qumran texts highlight the situation of conflict in the world. The Christians experience this in a similar way. But the Qumran texts have no adequate understanding of the state of salvation, whereas the Christians know by their faith that they have already been placed in that state. This unfortunately gives rise to the problem of "Christians and sin." For only the double situation, salvation already achieved, on the one hand, and continuing conflict, on the other, provides the basis for these series of statements held in tension. One attributes to the Christians righteousness and sinlessness. The other just as strenuously asserts the need for moral endeavor.

d) It make sense therefore if we explain the tension between the indicative and the imperative from the situation Christians find themselves in in this world. It is an eschatological situation similar to what we find in Paul![186] This would give order to the Johannine texts within a larger framework which is characteristic of early Christianity as a whole. In order to grasp the point more clearly—and avoiding at all costs interpreting John through Paul—let us examine more closely the relevant passages of Johannine theology in their context.

4. *Positive Elucidation from the Spirit of Johannine Theology*

a) The salvation attained by those who are born of God is fundamentally eschatological in character. The clearest indication of this is the central concept of Johannine theology, viz., eternal life. In the Synoptic Gospels eternal life is still something expected in the future (Matt. 7:14; 18:8f.; 19:16f. etc). In John it becomes for the most part a present possession of the faithful (John 3:15f., 36; 5:24, 40; 6:40, etc.; 1 John 3:14f.; 5:11f., 13, 16, 20), though without forgetting its original eschatological character. The author of 1 John is aware that being children of God in this world marks only the beginning of salvation (3:1f.). The promise of eternal life is not superfluous (2:25). Moreover, even the Christians are very concerned to overcome their fear of the day of judgment (4:17f.). This tension between expectation and fulfillment necessitates equally in Johannine theology the moral imperative. It is in fact very forcibly expressed—though in different terms from Paul.

As far as the remission of sin and freedom from it are concerned, these are the basis for all of early Christianity, if not for salvation in its entirety, at least for the basic state of salvation and the foundation for all else. For the Old Testament (Ezek. 11:19f.; 26:25ff.; Jer. 32:39ff.) and late Judaism (*1 Enoch* 5:8f.; *Jub.* 5:12) purity from sin is already one of the blessings of eschatological salvation. With his idea that those who are born of God are free from sin, the author of

---

185. Ibid., 116f. See also A. Merx, "Y a-t-il une prédestination à Qumran?" *RevQum* 6 (1967) 163–82; S. T. Kimbrough, Jr., "The Ethic of the Qumran Community," *RevQum* 8 (1969) 483–98.
186. G. Maier, *Mensch und freier Wille: Nach den jüdischen Religionsparteien zwischen Ben Sira und Paulus* (Tübingen, 1971).

1 John is in the mainstream of this Jewish and early Christian tradition. Rather like the concept of eternal life, the eschatological statements have a certain present validity. True, the author may have adopted some of his terminology from gnostic symbolism (e.g., God's seed) in order to draw out the difference between gnostic and Christian ideas of perfection. There are certain Stoic sayings about the perfection of the wise man, but these lie quite outside the Johannine world of thought![187]

b) The chief method used in Johannine theology to reconcile the palpable tension between salvation and the requirements of morality without eliminating that tension is the use of the verb *menein*, "to abide." The blessings of salvation and the already realized status of being children of God are by their very nature permanent realities; compare 1 John 2:14, 27; 3:9, 24b; 4:13; 2 John 2. The transition from death to life (cf. John 5:24) is basically final (1 John 3:14, note the perfect tense). Alongside of these indicatives we have imperatives. Partly these imperatives serve as a direct challenge to abide in God or Christ (2:24a, 27c, 28; 3:6; 2 John 9). Partly they take the form of religious and moral admonitions, obedience to which is the precondition for continuing to abide in God (2:6, 10, 24b; 3:15, 17, 24a; 4:12, 15, 16). This use of the verb "to abide" brings out the tension between the permanence of salvation already attained and the insecurity and danger salvation has to face in a world dominated by evil. For until the death of the body—or the parousia—Christians are existentially incapable of escaping this tension. The result is that the children of God are, on the one hand, held under the divine protection and are free from sin and eternal death, while, on the other hand, when viewed from the human conditions which limit their state of salvation, they can still fall into sin, and because of their infirmities actually do so. Of course this can still happen in different degrees. Moreover, in the light of the distinctions drawn in 5:16f., we may assume that the author does expect minor lapses to occur. At the same time he considers serious crimes, which make our fellowship with God impossible (3:17; 4:20), to be exceptional. He seems to regard complete apostasy from Christ and God as a sign that such renegades had never really been called as children of God (cf. the verdict on the antichrists in 2:19).

c) This brings us to a difficult aspect of the matter, perhaps one we can hardly hope to clarify. Being born of God—an idea that seems to point back to the sacramental act of baptism—becomes a general affirmation about "being from God" (cf. 3:10 with 9). Sometimes this seems to imply the idea of predestination, especially in 4:4-6, though also in 2:19 (on 5:19 see commentary). This would mean that those who belong to God would be from the very beginning receptive to the Christian revelation. They are called to be children of God who only need to realize their status (cf. also John 11:52). Such people belong to the divine realm of light and life. By their very nature they are separated by an abyss from this world of sin and death. By the life-giving powers conferred by the sacrament of baptism they are enabled successfully to withstand the power of evil (4:4).

---

187. *Contra* Windisch, Excursus, p. 122.—The Stoics reckon with the power of their own virtue, Christians with the strength that God gives them. Philo stands somewhere in between with his doctrine of the Logos preventing sin while dwelling in the soul (*Fuga* 117). But Philo is skeptical with regard to the sinlessness of the wise; cf. *Virt.* 177; *Fuga* 157f.

The author obviously expects that they will never lose their divine nature by falling from faith in Christ or by heinous moral transgression (cf. 5:19 with 18). Yet he nowhere exposes these connections clearly. Instead he contents himself with a few obvious considerations about human behavior. These offer a criterion for distinguishing between the children of God and the children of the devil![188]

d) Thus we get a picture of the children of God that in a unique way combines sacramental efficacy with the need for moral tests. If one strand of this threefold web is removed, the bold claim of 3:9 becomes either unintelligible or downright heretical. Only the divine reality of God's seed guarantees the power to resist sin. If the baptized renege in such a drastic manner as to succumb to the realm of sin, it is clear they are not children of God but children of the devil. But in that case it is their own fault. Nowhere is it said that people are predestined eternally to be children of the devil. Predestination to be children of God remains an unfathomable mystery. To which side do people belong? To God's or to the devil's? The author tells us again and again that the third characteristic of God's children is that they are subject to a religious and moral test. It would be out of line to try and disentangle the various strands in this conception of what it means to be God's children. Christians are challenged, each and all, to believe with all their heart that they are definitively called to be God's children, that they are able to fulfill the moral demands of their calling, and that they have been given the grace to do so through the powers conferred on them. They are convinced that it is not difficult to keep the commandments because all who have been born of God can overcome the power of evil, that is the "world" (5:3f.).

* * *

5:19 The second important statement, v. 19, provides the application of v. 18. The Christians are "from God," that is to say, they are born of God (v. 18a) and abide in him (v.18b). For "to be of God" shows the effect of being born of him and the permanent constitution of nature which is maintained in moral endeavor (cf. 3:10 with 9; 4:7a with 7b). This is true even if in other passages (2:19; 4:4–6) the idea of predestination may be in the background. As v. 19a takes up the first half of v. 18, so v. 19b joins on to the second half of that verse (18c). The evil one, who cannot get those who are born of God into his power, holds sway over a mighty empire—the whole world.

The order of the sentences leaves little doubt that *en tō ponērō* is masculine and personal![189] Even though *keisthai en* usually means "to be in a particular state,"[190] the article

---

188. For the rejection of a false determinism which has been attributed to John especially by A. Hilgenfeld and H. J. Holtzmann, see Feine, *Theologie,* 351–53; Bultmann, *Theology* 2:21ff.; A. Augustinovic, *Critica "determinismi" joannei* (Jerusalem, 1947); Herkenrath, "Sünde zum Tode," 122–24.

189. Cf. *Mart. Isa,* 2:4: "The Prince of Wickedness, who rules over this World, is Belial"; see further the rabbinic discussion about Job 9:24 in *b. B.Bat.* 16a. The learned scholars translate the passage thus: "the earth is given over into the hands of the evil one" and identify the evil one (*rāšāʿ*) with Satan (see Billerbeck, *Kommentar* 3:779). See further above on 2:13.

190. Cf. 2 Macc. 3:11; 4:31, 34; 3 Macc. 5:26. Profane examples are given in BAGD 427, s.v. 2, d.—If it were translated "to lie in the evil one" the article would certainly be lacking. To think of lying down in a lifeless kind of way (Büchsel, Charue) is not natural.

here suggests a more pregnant meaning (for the context cf. Luke 4:6). So the meaning is "to be under the thrall of the evil one" or "to be subject to him."[191]

The "world" is not simply the inhabited earth, but a qualitative entity. It is the world of humanity, whom the Son of God came to redeem (2:2; cf. 4:14). But because of its unbelief it refused Christ and so fell even more under the spell of Satan — a gloomy, pessimistic assessment (cf. John 1:11; 3:19; 12:37ff.), but one that may be explained in part from the sad experience of the churches in Asia Minor. For they were faced with the overwhelming power of unbelief and hatred, of heresy and the worship of idols. There is a similar assessment of the world as the realm of Satan's power in the Qumran texts (cf. Excursus 6, at the end). There, too, God has left the world in Satan's power until the end of this aeon. Yet according to 1QS 3:21ff., the Angel of Darkness is allowed to lead the sons of righteousness astray. All their sins and misdemeanors are subjected to the power of his dominion until the divinely appointed end. Such was the mysterious plan of God. The same holds good for their grief and suffering — only they already have the divine assistance to help them. The Christian community knows that through Christ it is able to be in fellowship with God. It possesses divine power and is completely immune from Satan's hosts. The community does not need to draw an external boundary between itself and this world. It has no need to erect internal barriers by means of purity regulations, rites, and discipline. Rather, it lives in this world, faithfully following the example of Christ (4:17) through the power of God (4:4; 5:18). The Qumraners, that Jewish sect, expected the end of the "final evil time" with passionate yearning. By contrast, the Christian community knows that life and love have already been revealed. With all the similarity in their dualistic outlook, there remain differences that cannot be ignored.

5:20 Only in v. 20 does the Son of God appear on the stage as Satan's counterpart. Here the contrast reaches its climax, the contrast between the divine community and the world dominated by Satan. Here, too, the joyous certainty of the Christians (the third "we know") reaches a crescendo. Despite his usual dislike of connecting particles, the author has inserted a *de* at this point (NRSV "and").[192] Even if the rest of the world is totally under Satan's thrall, the Christian community knows that it is saved by Christ, the Son of God. This takes place in two stages. First there is the historic deed of the Mediator. Then comes our present living union with him. The Son of God — that is now an unquestionable fact — has come, and this coming has remained a tangible reality (*hēkei*, "has come"). The verb, which is used in the rest of the New Testament mainly for the parousia (apart from the quotation in Heb. 10:7, 9), occurs only in John 8:42. There it applies to the first coming of Christ into this world. The decisive theophany has already taken place. For contemporary ears this verb was a sonorous religious

---

191. This meaning is already possible in classical Greek literature; cf. Sophocles, *Oed. Col.* 247f.: *en ymmi gar hōs theǭ keimetha tlamones;* Polybius 6.15.6. Cf. Norden, *Agnostos Theos,* 23 n. 1; Liddell and Scott 934, s.v. V, 3; BAGD 427.

192. At least according to the principal manuscripts B ℵ al.; it is missing from PL al.; A pm. Vg sy read *kai oidamen.*

term.[193] John 8:42 is sufficient testimony for that, for there *hēkō* comes immediately after *exēlthon,* leaving a lasting impression (NRSV "I came from God and now I am here").

This Son of God, who appeared once ("was revealed," 1:2) has given the Christians the capacity (*dianoia*)[194] to know "him who is true" (=God). Christian thinking, superimposed on a Jewish foundation in a world influenced by gnosticism, has here coined an extraodinary expression. For "he who is true" (*ho alēthinos*) is a designation for God in Judaism, serving as a barrier against false, unreal gods.[195] To know means more than just to find the only true God. As elsewhere in 1 John, this knowledge of God must be understood in a highly realistic sense (cf. 2:3f., 13f.; 3:1c; 4:6, 7f.); by knowing him people enter into fellowship with God.

This ontological unity with God is expressed even more clearly in an independent clause (no longer controlled by *hina,* "that").[196] We have not only acquired the capacity to know God; we are in fact in living communion with him. At the same time this verse is intended to highlight the fact that this being in God became a reality for us in his Son Jesus Christ. The brachylogy—presumably intentional—places the full name, Jesus Christ, at the end (cf. John 17:3; 1 John 1:3; 3:23; 5:6a, 13). This turn of phrase may simply, from a formal point of view, stand in apposition, but it actually means: "inasmuch as we are in his Son, Jesus Christ."[197] He is not only the Mediator of revelation (v. 20b; cf. John 1:18). He is also the dispenser of life (1:2; 5:11f.), the constant Mediator of fellowship with God (1:3c; John 1:16f.; 4:10f., 23; 17:21f.). This brings the original Christian element, the christological principle of Johannine theology, into the clearest possible focus. Whatever Christians possess by way of divine gifts, such as truth, grace, life, and the Spirit, they owe it all to the Son of God who appeared on earth. For he is the "only-begotten Son of God." In him the fullness of divine being came to this earth and disclosed himself to all who believe in him (John 1:14; 3:35). From his fullness we have all received (John 1:16).

Therefore there is no longer any doubt (*contra* Dodd) that the following *houtos* (NRSV "he"), like the *houtos* closest to it (cf. 5:6 with 5), refers to Jesus Christ![198]

---

193. See BAGD 344, s.v. 1, d, α; J. Schneider, *TDNT* 2:928.

194. Διανοια=knowledge and capacity for knowledge (Liddell and Scott I, 405), frequently in the *Testaments of the Twelve Patriarchs.* There is a noticeable difference between this word and *exousia* (1 John 1:12), the latter denoting plenitude of power (to attain a new status). The idea in 1 John 5:20 remains more strongly Jewish.

195. Isa. 65:16; 3 Macc. 6:18; Josephus, *Antiquities* 8.13.6; Philo, *Leg. ad Gaium* 366; cf. also John 17:3; 1 Thess. 1:9. The other readings are clearly (unnecessary) attempts to get rid of the absolute *ton alēthinon: to alēthinon* (ℵ* q sa); *ton alēthinon theon* (A K 33 323 1739 pm. Vg bo arm Did. Bas Aug.).—For a different view, see G. D. Kilpatrick, *JTS* n.s. 12 (1961) 272.

196. Despite the better external attestation of *ginōskomen* (ħ against ҟ) the indicative after *hina* must be regarded as a corruption; see BDF §369.6. Consequently *kai esmen* begins a new clause; cf. 3:1.

197. Von Harnack (*SB* [Berlin, 1915] 538f. n. 1) would like to add after *Christou* an *ontes,* which in his view was omitted as a result of scribal negligence, because of the following *houtos.* This conjecture is correct so far as the sense goes, but improbable in form. It destroys the effective conclusion.—On the question of text criticism, see further Lagrange, *Critique textuelle,* 566.

198. Cf. already the illuminating observations of Rothe, ad loc., (203ff. n.), further the Catholic exegetes—*contra* Harnack, Holtzmann-Bauer, Brooke, Windisch (with hesitation), Dodd.—Bultmann,

If we connect it with *alēthinǭ*—which is possible linguistically (cf. 2 John 7)—
it is difficult to avoid a tautology. We would in that case have to look for the
sequence of thought in the statement that this "true" One (God) is eternal life.
But such a claim is usually made for Christ rather than for God (cf. 1:2; John
11:25; 14:6). But in point of fact this strained exegesis is not necessary at all. In
the framework of Johannine theology, the predicate God can be used for Jesus
(John 1:1; cf. 1:18 *v.l.;* 20:28). Admittedly it acquires in 1 John 5:20 an extraordinary, pregnant sense. For here the full identity of Jesus with God is recognized
without reserve (note the article with *theos,* God). This seems to occur intentionally at the end of the letter, at the climax of the triumphant expression of
faith. It is hardly an accident that it is precisely at the beginning (1:1, 18) and
at the end (20:28) of GJohn that the light of Jesus' divinity shines forth most
fully. The climactic christological confession becomes visible here in all its clarity.
Jesus Christ is the true God, not a distant God who is out of reach, but in human
form, to be grasped by faith. That is why he is eternal life. The absence of the
article before *zōē* (life) points to the fact that this word is added as a genuine
predicate to explain the logic of the statement: Jesus Christ is eternal life for
us who believe (cf. 5:11f.). The entire v. 20 forms a compact unit, a brief compendium of Johannine Christology, worthy to stand alongside of 1:2. Fellowship
with God has become for us a permanent reality through and in Jesus Christ.

5:21 Thus there is no reason to understand the *houtos*-clause in the last verse
as an emphatic assertion of Christian monotheism vis-à-vis idolatry (*contra*
Windisch). The final warning against idolatry of course sounds strange, introduced here as it is for the first time. Nowhere until now has this topic been raised
before. Idols are in themselves pagan images or deities![199] Perhaps the meaning
is that in contrast to him who is true they are referred to disparagingly as devoid
of substance and being (thus in the first edition of this commentary). On the
other hand, it cannot be denied that such a warning, addressed to people who
had been believers for a long time and were thoroughly at home in Christian
worship and the Christian life, would be strange. That is so even if their pagan
environment still exercised a magnetic attraction over them. Hence W. Nauck
might be right when he associates idols with sin as a satanic power. "The concluding admonition says nothing else but 'keep yourselves from sin.'"[200] The
linguistic justification for this interpretation is now provided by the Qumran texts,
which use the term *gillûlîm* frequently in a metaphorical sense, already common
in the Old Testament (especially in Ezekiel) meaning real idols, including amulets,
to express the heinousness of sin. For these texts idols are objects that draw the
human heart away from God: "the idols of his heart" (1QS 2:11), "his idols" (2:17).
"Whoever walks in the paths of light, illuminated by the 'spirits of light,' seeks
admirable purity, which detests all unclean idols" (4:5). Especially clear is the

who thinks it more probable on exegetic grounds that it goes with *Iēsous Christos,* ascribes the clause
to an "imitator" ("Redaktion," 195f.).

199. Büchsel, *TDNT* 2:377.
200. Nauck, *Tradition und Charakter,* 137.

connection between "idol" and "sin" in 1QH 4:15, "they walk in stubbornness of heart and seek Thee among idols," compared with lines 18f.: "but Thou, O God, wilt reply to them, chastising them in their might, because of their idols and because of the multitude of their sins." Again, in CD 20:9f. we read: "They have taken idols to their heart and walk in the stubbornness of their hearts." Though perhaps in concrete terms the thought is about impure things, yet the metaphorical sense is obvious. We had no proof of this until now.[201] With this explanation the final verse fits nicely into the context. After reassuring his readers of their fellowship with God through Jesus Christ (v. 20), the author adds another brief, forceful admonition. They must beware of the sin of "idolatry" which will separate them from God and drive them back into the realm of Satan (v. 19) — indeed a most moving conclusion to the letter and its admonitions.

---

201. The passage quoted by Nauck (*Tradition und Charakter,* 137) from the *Testaments of the Twelve Patriarchs* (*T. Rub.* 4:5f., does not, strictly speaking, belong here. The first part must be translated "Little children, observe all (*phylaxate panta*) that I have commanded you" (not "keep yourselves from all . . ."), and the second part is a warning against sins of licentiousness, which separate from God and lead to idolatry. The interpretation of "idols" in reference to sin, developed by W. Nauck and adopted by me in the second edition, has met with criticism. See H. Braun, *Qumran und das Neue Testament I* (Tübingen, 1966) 304f.; R. Bultmann, *Johannine Epistles,* 90 (he interprets the "sin that is mortal" and "idolatry" as a reference to apostasy from the true faith).

THE SECOND
AND THIRD EPISTLES
OF JOHN

INTRODUCTION

1. Epistolary Character

Earlier it was assumed that the two short Johannine epistles were put into this form artificially only so as to lend them a personal imprint.[1] That view, however, loses force in view of the constant rediscovery of private letters from antiquity written on sheets of papyrus. This provides a broader basis for comparison. Among all the letters of the New Testament 2 and 3 John (along with Philemon) have a breath of originality and freshness about them. Their length (2 John: 1,126 letters; 3 John: 1,105) reveals that each filled a single sheet of papyrus of the same size.[2] The design of both epistles, their style, including certain phrases common in Hellenistic letter writing (see also on 3 John 2), the concise treatment of concrete questions, the mention of specific individuals (3 John 1, 9, 12; cf. 15) — all this guarantees that they were designed as letters from the outset. However, 2 John is a brief letter addressed to a community,[3] a precious relic of what was probably a lively correspondence, whereas 3 John is a private letter (cf. the address), though it also discusses important issues affecting the life of the community. It is addressed to an active member of that community.

2. The Author

The two letters achieve their full importance from the personality of the author. Who is this "elder" (for the term itself, see the commentary)? For that is what

---

1. So even Dibelius, *RGG²* 3:348.

2. This may have been the same size as the one evidenced by Deissmann (*Light from the Ancient East,* 167ff.) containing two letters of an Egyptian in the second half of the second century C.E. (1,124 letters) or as a letter of the third century C.E. given in M. David and B. A. van Groningen, *A Papyrological Primer* (2nd ed.; Leiden, 1946) 152f.

3. R. Bultmann advocates the view that 2 John is a fictitious letter, whose author used both 1 John and 3 John. The messenger who delivered it was supposed to present the writing to all the churches to whom it was of concern (*Johannine Epistles,* 1, 107f.). For a contrary view, see R. W. Funk, "The Form and Structure of II and III John," *JBL* 86 (1967) 423–30; J. B. Polhill, "An Analysis of II and III John," *Review and Expositor* 67 (1970) 461–71; Kümmel, *Introduction,* 448, 450.

the author calls himself. The authorship of John the son of Zebedee, that is, his identification with the elder, appears to be no longer tenable today. If even GJohn, in its present form does not derive directly from him,[4] it is improbable that the three epistles were written by him. Moreover, if in 1 John 1:4 a group of witnesses is speaking who were not direct eyewitnesses of the earthly career of Jesus, but appeal to their association with men of the first generation, then the elder of 2 and 3 John must belong to those presbyters who, according to Papias, Irenaeus, and Clement of Alexandria preserved the apostolic tradition. In any case, he was a man who in a preeminent sense was able to call himself *"the* presbyter"* (=the elder). It is hardly possible to identify him more precisely. To focus better on him let us use several different approaches.

a) A Closer Definition of *ho presbyteros*

α We must reject the hypothesis that there was originally a name attached to it that was later cut out, also the other suggestion that the anonymous author "placed the mysterious superscription 'the presbyter'—one that could be deciphered only in one particular way" at the head of both letters, so as to create the fiction "that it was the one great witness of Asia Minor that was writing, one who in a special sense is 'the presbyter.'"[5] Since we are dealing with a genuine letter, not a fictitious one (cf. the epistolary character), which in each case arises from a concrete situation (see the exegesis), the author must have been known to his readers. Since too he introduces himself merely by calling himself "the elder," this cannot be understood in any way other than as a title of honor. By this title he discloses himself unambiguously to his readers (cf. on 2 John 1).

β Historical-critical method requires us to ask whether the same pregnant formulation is to be found in any other writing, without mention of any specific name. As a matter of fact, this is just the case in the early Papias fragment quoted by Eusebius (*H.E.* 3.39.15 regarding the Gospel of Mark). In the preface to his work Papias calls this presbyter by name: "the presbyter John" (Eusebius, *H.E.* 3.39.4).

γ The fragment continues to discuss whether this elder is identical with John the apostle, the son of Zebedee. Reputable scholars still believe that this is the correct interpretation of the Papias passage as given in Eusebius (*H.E.* 3.39.3–4).[6] Other scholars, Roman Catholics as well as Protestants, even today opt for that understanding of the famous text which Eusebius, the first tradent of the text, deduced for himself: contemporary with the apostle John or after him there was another John who was called the Presbyter to distinguish him from the apostle

---

4. See the Introduction to GJohn I; see also *BZ* n.s. 14 (1970) 1–23.

5. E. Hirsch, *Studien zum vierten Evangelium* (Tübingen, 1936) 178.—For a critique of Hirsch's fiction theory, see Haenchen, *TRu* 26 (1960) 281f.

6. Poggel, 27ff.; T. Zahn, *Forschungen zur Geschichte des neutestamentlichen Kanons und der altkirchlichen Literatur* VI, 1: *Apostel und Apostelschüler in der Provinz Asien* (Leipzig, 1900) 112–52; Feine-Behm, *Einleitung,* 107ff.; Meinertz, *Einleitung,* 218f. and the scholars mentioned on p. 219 n. 2; Michaelis, *Einleitung,* 93ff.; H. P. V. Nunn, *The Authorship of the Fourth Gospel* (1952) 52–70.

of the Lord and was held in high esteem.[7] Here recent scholarship tends to follow the second opinion, which seems to commend itself more easily to an unprejudiced interpretation of the Papias quotation. For a more detailed discussion, see the Introduction to the commentary on John.

δ There is no other evidence for John the Presbyter apart from the Papias fragment. The assumption that there was another John distinct from the apostle in Eusebius (see above) and Jerome (*Vir. ill.* 18) rests on their exegesis of the Papias quotation in connection with information given by Dionysius of Alexandria. He says that there were two graves in Ephesus, both graves of "John."[8] Jerome takes up the hypothesis as an argument against those who wanted to assign 2 and 3 John to a different author from that of GJohn and 1 John. Dionysius of Alexandria himself, who postulates a different author for the Apocalypse, knows nothing, however, of a John the Presbyter. He obviously considers John the apostle to be the author of the two shorter Johannine epistles.[9] In any case, the Papias fragment is strong enough to prove that there did exist a John the Presbyter alongside of John the apostle.

ε But the question arises whether the anonymous presbyter of 2 and 3 John should be identified with Papias's John the Presbyter. The extant Papias quotations do not help us to answer this question, for the two shorter Johannine epistles are nowhere mentioned. It is worth noting that Papias also speaks in the place already mentioned of the presbyters (in the plural) from whom he either learned directly or whose teaching he learned from others (Eusebius, *H.E.* 3.39.3, 4). Some of these presbyters, he seems to have thought, were bearers of the apostolic tradition, as is also shown by the linguistic usage in Irenaeus, and mainly disciples of the apostles![10] Since these people held high authority, it is possible that Papias's presbyter John was hiding himself behind the self-designation of the author of 2 and 3 John. This makes it impossible to decide the question of authorship from the title of elder or presbyter.

b) Internal Comparison with 1 John and GJohn

α There can hardly be any doubt that 2 and 3 John were written by the same author. Though the letter mentioned in 3 John 9 cannot be our 2 John (see ad loc.), yet the designation of the sender of both letters as the elder carries such great weight that only very strong arguments against it would be sufficient to prove that they were different authors. Added to that, the almost identical length

---

7. Among the Catholics, see M.-J. Lagrange, *Jean,* xxixff.; P. Vannutelli, "De presbytero Ioanne apud Papiam," *Scuola cattolica* 58 (1930) 366–74; 59 (1931) 219–32; Chaine, 236f.; G. Bardy, *DBSup* 6:843–47; Wikenhauser, *Einleitung,* 206f.; F.-M. Braun, *Jean le Théologien,* 357–64.

8. In Eusebius, *H.E.* 7.25.16.

9. Ibid., 7.25.11.

10. As F.-M. Braun, *Jean le Théologien,* 361 observes: "Since Dom Chapman presented his observations on the meaning of *presbyteros* in the Apostolic Fathers and notably in St. Irenaeus (*John the Presbyter* [Oxford, 1911] 13–19), any confusion between the Apostles and Elders is scarcely tolerable." See further G. Bornkamm, *TDNT* 6:676–78.

of both letters plus certain stylistic peculiarities,[11] especially in the conclusion, point in the same direction. The deviations can be explained from the different concerns which moved the author to write 2 John as a general letter and 3 John as a private one.

β The subject matter of 2 John has many affinities with 1 John, especially in vv. 4–9. Love (and its practical expression in love for the brothers and sisters) and faith (i.e., orthodox Christology) form the main themes. Heretical teaching is refuted as an innovation (against the emphasis on what was heard "from the beginning") with a confessional formula that is almost identical with 1 John 4:2. The expression "to have God" (2 John 9) serves as another strong link between the two letters. The concrete situation in 2 John rules out any suggestion of mere plagiarism.

γ Stronger objections have been raised against certain allegedly un-Johannine expression in the two short letters.[12] These are supposed to make it impossible to ascribe these works to the author of GJohn. It is true that the concept of "full reward" and the phrase "Be on your guard" have a Synoptic ring to them. Yet anyone seeing how the sayings about judgment in 1 John 2:28; 4:17 do not contradict GJohn (cf. John 5:22, 24, 29f.) cannot raise any objection here. Turns of speech such as "that we become co-workers" (3 John 8) and "does good" (3 John 11) do not prove much since they are very close to typically Johannine expressions. "To see God" (3 John 11) is similar to 1 John 3:6; cf. John 6:40; 12:45; 14:17 (*contra* Jülicher-Eascher). 3 John 12b draws a strong line of connection with John 19:35; 21:24. Of course the two letters cannot be used to substantiate the identity of the presbyter with the author of GJohn.

δ The outlook and phraseology in all three Johannine letters are similar in certain instances ("to be of," "to abide in," etc.).[13] One must therefore postulate the same author at least for all three letters. True, Jerome contemplated the possibility that 2 and 3 John came from a different hand, but there are no firm grounds for this. It is not surprising that the author of 1 John, who introduces himself to his readers in 1:1–3 as a well-known personality, only needs to refer to himself briefly as "the elder" in the two short letters.

c) Internal Objections against the Apostle John as the Author

Apart from the question of the presbyter, internal grounds have been advanced for ruling out the apostle John as the author of 2 and 3 John. No apostle could have been challenged by a local church leader like Diotrephes in 3 John 9 or take such liberties as he does with the elder. References to the experiences of Paul have been put forward in answer to this, but they are not very convincing. For

---

11. See B. Bresky, *Das Verhältnis des 2 Joh zum 3 Joh* (Münster, 1906) 31f.

12. E. Schwartz, *Über den Tod der Söhne Zebedaei* (Göttingen, 1904) 47f., 52f.; Jülicher-Fascher, *Einleitung*, 236f.; Hirsch, *Studien zum vierten Evangelium*, 177ff.

13. Cf. Poggel, 111ff.; Brooke, lxxivff.; Chaine, 233ff.; Dodd, *Johannine Epistles*, lxff.

Paul had to fight to be recognized as an apostle, whereas that was not the case with John the son of Zebedee. True, "does not receive us" (NRSV "does not acknowledge our authority") does not necessarily mean a complete rejection. In questions of organization there might well have arisen a stubborn desire for independence vis-à-vis an apostle. The elder's reaction gives the impression of self-assurance. He is convinced that his personal appearance will lead to a drastic change in the situation (v. 10). Even Harnack, in his study of the development of church polity attested in 3 John, does not find anything strange about the picture as compared with Paul's relation to his churches![14]

Nor again is the special circle of friends the elder gathered around him an argument against his position as an apostle. Paul also had a circle of friends in his churches who were particularly devoted to him, fellow workers and disciples. If Gaius does not possess the same authority, that is because he was not a missionary assistant or an official representative of the elder. It is clear that according to the Johannine letters the local churches and their leaders were becoming more independent than is the case in the Pastoral Epistles. According to 3 John the elder exercises more of a patriarchal than a juridical supervision over the local churches. His authority was moral rather than institutional. This might have been possible for a disciple of the Lord outside the college of apostles or for a disciple of the apostles. Yet it is by no means impossible that an apostle is hiding himself behind the title of elder.

d) E. Käsemann's Hypothesis

A very different theory about the author of the Johannine epistles has been advanced by E. Käsemann![15] He reverses the situation by declaring that it was not the presbyter but Diotrephes who was the representative of legitimate ecclesiastical authority. The presbyter was supposedly under admonition for holding gnostic views and had been expelled by the orthodox authorities. In his turn, he is fighting back, opposing another gnostic tendency, this time that of docetism. This would also explain his anonymity, though he does retain the title of presbyter as a designation of the office he had previously held. He had the impertinence to construct a gospel about Christ slanted in a gnostic direction. Diotrephes viewed him as a heretic and drew the consequences. Thus the presbyter in 2 John is forced back on the defensive.

This bold hypothesis, which seems to make the remarks in 3 John 9–10 plausible in a surprising way, breaks down mainly in the light of the Johannine writings as a whole: (1) It can hardly be established that the presbyter's views were heretical or represent an attack on early Catholicism. Indeed that would implicate the Johannine epistles as a whole. In the light of 1 John 2:27 (see the commentary), it can hardly be claimed that the presbyter "has attributed the anointing of the Spirit to every Christian believer, whereas early Catholicism ties the Spirit to office

---

14. On the third Johannine epistle, see *TU* 15, 3 (1897) 17. Cf. also R. Schnackenburg, "Der Streit zwischen dem Verfasser vom 3 Joh und Diotrephes und seine verfassungsgeschichtliche Bedeutung," *MTZ* 4 (1953) 18–26.

15. Käsemann, "Ketzer und Zeuge: Zum johanneischen Verfasserproblem," *ZTK* 48 (1951) 292–311.

and tradition."[16] Tradition and the operation of the Spirit in the individual believer are not necessarily opposed to each other in early catholicism. It cannot be proved that "Bishop" Diotrephes would have taken offense at this notion. (2) There is no justification for shifting the opposition between the presbyter and Diotrephes from the sphere of practical discipline to that of dogmatics. There is no evidence for this in the text. (3) Käsemann's explanation of the author's anonymity is improbable. A presbyter who had been excommunicated might conceivably continue to use that title when addressing friends as in 3 John. But it would have been impossible for him to do so in a letter to the whole community, like 2 John. (4) 2 John cannot be excluded from the discussion. This letter is hardly addressed to a circle of private persons. It is close in style and form to 3 John, which maintains an attitude that is markedly authoritative and conservative (see v. 9). This makes it impossible to see in the presbyter anything other than a genuine and acknowledged authority.

e) E. Haenchen's Theory

Finally E. Haenchen has addressed himself to the whole complex of problems![17] His judgments, which are critical though well thought out, led him to the following view with regard to authorship: "He is a church leader who pleads in 3 John for a mission to the Gentiles. This brings him into conflict with the leader Diotrephes, while in 2 John he is suggesting to a neighboring community that they should reject certain itinerant gnostic preachers" (cf. the "apostles" in Rev. 2:2). In this basic interpretation of the two letters Haenchen is in close agreement with the present commentary, except that he takes a different view of the author and his authority. From Käsemann's hypothesis, which Haenchen in general rejects, he takes up the suggestion that the presbyter held a definite office, but he does not regard him as a simple presbyter among others. Rather, he thinks he held the position "of a president over a presbytery, which was practically the same position as that which was held by Diotrephes" (p. 290). At the same time Haenchen combines with this the well-known concept of presbyter from Papias, Irenaeus, and Clement of Alexandria, according to which the functionaries thus designated were "guardians and transmitters of the apostolic tradition" (p. 291). This is because Haenchen rightly sees that an ordinary official could hardly have introduced himself simply by name. Against this there are further implications of greater importance. If the author of the two letters writes self-consciously, using this title by itself, he must have set more store on it and must have used it in a special sense. The problem of the two short letters must not be separated from that of the longer one. The latter is evidently written as an admonition, addressed to a wider circle of churches, or at least (should it have been addressed only to a single church) with great authority, exceeding that of the leader of a local church. Of course it is possible that the author himself was the leader of a local church. But when he writes to the "elect lady" (2 John) and to Gaius (3 John), he does so not as a local leader but as the "presbyter," that is, as the bearer of apostolic tradition, in which capacity they all knew him.

16. Ibid., 308.
17. Haenchen, *TRu* 26 (1960) 267–91.

Introduction

Was John the apostle, the son of Zebedee, the author of all three Johannine epistles? Given the complications of the Johannine question, one is driven to the conclusion that it is impossible to answer that question with any certainty. At least he was an outstanding personality from the Johannine circle, perhaps an apostolic disciple, who represents the Johannine tradition and upholds it.

3. The Origins of the Letters

Aside from the question of authorship, the two short letters offer few criteria for a more precise view of their circumstances of origin. 2 John must be close in date to 1 John because of the battle against heresy. The features of this heresy are similar to those of the better-known heresy in 1 John (v. 7), as are the prescriptions against heretical teachers (v. 10). There is no reason to place it later in the second century; its church organization shows signs of the early stages of the development of monarchical episcopacy. The two letters presuppose at least two local churches, over which the elder keeps a watchful eye and where he has a voice. Probably there were more, though the "lady" of 2 John was hardly the church in which Gaius was a member. This reminds us of the seven letters of the Apocalypse. The elder exercises a far-reaching influence, probably extending over a large territory. After all is said and done, the most likely area in question is somewhere in Asia Minor.[18] The epistles of Ignatius show that the monarchical episcopate came to be accepted in that area very rapidly.

It is not necessary to suppose that there was a great distance in time between 2 and 3 John, so long as we do not assume that the recipients in both cases represented the same community.[19] All three of the Johannine epistles may come from the same time slot, though it must be remembered that 1 John is directed to a wider circle of churches, 2 John to a single local church, and 3 John to a private individual.

4. 2 and 3 John in the History of the Canon[20]

Origen does not include the two short epistles among the generally accepted writings;[21] neither does Eusebius.[22] The fact is, however, that their testimony is "not all that impressive" (Meinertz).

---

18. The attempt of J. Chapman (*JTS* 5 [1904] 357ff., 517ff.) to interpret the "lady" of 2 John as Rome is misplaced; cf. Bresky, *Verhältnis,* 55–63.—A more precise definition of the recipients (Findlay, 31: Pergamum) may be absolutely impossible.

19. The arguments Bresky employs to establish this hypothesis are not convincing (above all, 3 John 11b is not directed against heresy, but is a Johannine mode of speech). Further, H. H. Wendt is particularly to be mentioned: in a series of articles (*ZNW* 21 [1922] 140ff.; 23 [1924] 18ff.; *Johannesbriefe,* 3ff.) he seeks to prove that all three epistles are addressed to the same single community (in the order 2-3-1 John). The attempt to see *egrapsa* (3 John 9 and 1 John 2:14) as a reference to 2 John is, however, untenable (see commentary).

20. On this topic, see Poggel, 51–108; Bresky, *Verhältnis,* 47–55.

21. *In Joa.* 5.3, in Eusebius, *H.E.* 6.25.10.

22. *H.E.* 3.25.3.

a) The echoes of 2 and 3 John in the Apostolic Fathers hardly help us to decide whether they knew the two letters or not. That is true for Polycarp (7.1; cf. 2 John 7, as well as 1 John 4:2f.), for a turn of speech in the Papias fragment quoted by Eusebius (*H.E.* 3.39.3; cf. 3 John 12 as well as John 14:6); and for an instruction of Ignatius of Antioch (*Smyrn.* 4.1) against the heretical teachers, which overlap in content with 2 John 10f. The same applies to Tertullian, *De carne Christi* 24, as to Polycarp.

b) Clear evidence for the use of the two letters is available only from the time of Clement of Alexandria. According to Eusebius (*H.E.* 6.14.1), Papias wrote a commentary on them but in the *Adumbrationes* there are only elucidations of 1 and 2 John.[23] Irenaeus quotes 2 John 11[24] and 2 John 7f.[25] For the Latin African church a bishop at the Synod of Carthage in 256 C.E. quotes 2 John 10f.[26] Dionysius of Alexandria, like Origen, knows all three of the Johannine epistles.[27]

c) It is a debated question whether the Latin church knew only two of the Johannine epistles, our 1 and 2 John. This need not be the case for Clement of Alexandria (see above); the citation formula was often inaccurate.[28] Though Tertullian and Irenaeus never mention 3 John, this may be due simply to the minimal theological content of this letter, or it may be just an accident. But the reference in the Muratorian Fragment is puzzling. This list, compiled in poor Latin from the second century, says in line 68f. "superscriptio Johannis duas (duae) in catholica habentur." Here we should probably read *superscripti* for *superscriptio* (so Lietzmann et al.), hardly *superscriptae* (Zahn). Does this fragment know only two Johannine epistles?[29] Or, after quoting 1 John in lines 26ff., is it referring to two additional Johannine epistles?[30] Should *Johannis* be corrected to *Petri?*[31] A plausible solution has been offered recently by P. Katz.[32] He thinks that *catholica* means not the "catholic church" (*ecclesia* would not be omitted), but "the catholic letter" [*sic*], viz., 1 John. "In," however, is a corruption for "sin," which is a transliteration of the Greek *syn*. The sense of the reconstructed text, according to Katz, is "*dyo syn catholicē = dyo syn catholica*": "of the aforementioned John two in addition to the 'Catholic' are held." Though this explanation must remain hypothetical, there can be no doubt that it is essentially correct.

d) By the fourth century all of the Johannine epistles are known everywhere except in the Syrian church, though their canonical status is still in dispute

23. See also Bresky, *Verhältnis,* 48; further, J. Ruwet, *Bib* 29 (1948) 95ff.
24. *Adv. Haer.* 1.9.3.
25. *Adv. Haer.* 3.17.8.
26. See Zahn, *Geschichte des ntl. Kanons* 1:216f.
27. Eusebius, *H.E.* 7.25.11.
28. *Strom.* 2.15.66 *en tē meizoni epistolē;* cf. also Poggel, 78ff.; Meinertz, *Einleitung,* 284.
29. So T. W. Manson, *JTS* 48 (1947) 33. He assumes that the Latin version of 3 John had a different translator from 1 and 2 John.
30. Zahn, *Geschichte* 1:219f.; Poggel, 68ff.; Bresky, *Verhältnis,* 52; Meinertz, *Einleitung,* 284.
31. So Lagrange, *Histoire du canon,* 74.
32. Katz, "The Johannine Epistles in the Muratorian Canon," *JTS* n.s. 8 (1957) 273f.

Introduction

(Eusebius). This small collection of Johannine epistles (parallel to the Paulines?) is vouched for among others by Athanasius (39th Paschal Letter), Cyril of Jerusalem (*Cat.* 4.36), the Council of Laodicea (ca. 260), the Mommsen Catalogue (ca. 360 in North Africa), the Sahidic and Bohairic versions. Those who express doubts about their canonicity include Amphilochius of Iconium (d. ca. 400 C.E.)[33] and Jerome (d. 420 C.E.).[34]

e) While the Old Syrian translation totally ignores the Catholic Epistles, the Peshitta contains only James, 1 Peter, and 1 John. Whether Ephraim Syrus quoted 2 and 3 John is doubtful.[35] Only the Philoxeniana (beginning of the sixth century) includes these letters, though the Nestorians never accepted them.

There were various reasons why the Johannine epistles, short as they were, did not have an easy acceptance into the general canon: first, there was their brevity and their minor theological importance. Then there was doubt over their apostolic origin (the problem of the presbyter). Their eventual acceptance was probably due to the growing conviction that they too were genuine writings of the apostle John, and therefore form with 1 John a little corpus of Johannine epistles.

---

33. See Zahn, *Geschichte* 2:219, lines 63f.
34. *Vir. ill.* 9 (*PL* 23:623, 625), and 18 (*PL* 23:637); see above, p. 268.
35. W. Bauer, *Der Apostolos der Syrer* (Giessen, 1903) 40ff.; Lagrange, *Histoire du canon,* 129.

EXEGESIS OF 2 JOHN

This letter addressed to a local church (see Introduction) was occasioned by a concrete pastoral situation and accordingly exhibits a clear and unified structure. After the prescript (vv. 1–3), which is already completely tailored to the author's concern (with "the truth" as the leading motif), the first part (vv. 4–6) contains an admonition to a genuine Christian life-style. The author considers this to be the fulfillment of the love commandment. Inner solidarity and mutual bonds are in his view the surest guarantee for the strength of the Christian community in the face of the dangers it is exposed to from the heretical teachers. It is the defense against these teachers that provides the real reason for this letter. In the second part these heretics are branded for the denial of true faith in Christ. They are the antichrist personified (vv. 7–9). But for this the author would have hardly bothered to write so shortly before his visit to the community. There is an actual concrete reason that comes out in the third part of the letter, which contains practical advice (vv. 10f.). The author is afraid that even before his arrival some of these heretical teachers might turn up in the community and receive at least a formal welcome. Once that happened, the heretics would have a chance to poison the minds of the believers. That is why he urges them to refuse hospitality to the heretics from the very outset. Even a superficial association with them would mean participating in their nefarious works. Having once expressed his real concern, he interrupts what he is writing to tell them about his intention to visit them (v. 12) and ends with greetings from the sister community where he is at the present time (v. 13).

The structure of the letter is entirely consistent with its purpose. The author does not burst in immediately with his news, yet he leaves nothing to be desired as far as clarity is concerned. He writes with authority and yet with a father's warmth. His thought revolves — as in 1 John — around two themes: mutual love and true Christian faith.

Despite the brevity of the document, its structure reveals the writer's character and shows that he is the same author as the one who wrote 1 John. The two writings share the same characteristics. First, the love commandment is brought to the fore, and only then does the writer turn to the christological heresy. This is true despite the fact that — especially in 2 John — his practical concern is focused on the heresy. The author does not notice that in doing so he makes it easier for critics in time to come to point out the tension between the demand for love in vv. 4–6 and the harsh and unyielding admonition regarding the heretical teachers in vv. 10f. There is no sign of any particular concern about the inner unity of the community. This short letter does not give the impression that the elder is using the opportunity to introduce a variety of admonitions. His constant desire is to encourage mutual love. This is only the first step in defending his readers against the threat of the moment. The structure brings out the individuality of the author, while the affinity between 1 and 2 John is equally evident from other considerations, such as language, thought, and the heresy under attack (see Introduction).

THE PRESCRIPT (2 JOHN 1–3)

[1]The elder to the elect lady and her children, whom I love in the truth, and not only I but also all who know the truth, [2]because of the truth that abides in us and will be with us forever:
[3]Grace, mercy, and peace will be with us from God the Father and from Jesus Christ, the Father's Son, in truth and love.

1 The prescript of this document, a genuine letter (see Introduction) betrays Johannine characteristics. This is true despite its similarities with the usual Christian style of letter writing. There are specific expressions such as "to love" or "love" (v. 3), and "truth" (three times). The Pauline epistles already exhibit features that distinguish them from early Hellenistic letters, where the sender (*superscriptio*), addressee (*adscriptio*), and good wishes for the recipient's well-being (*salutatio*) are featured. In Pauline prescripts there is a considerable expansion and reshaping of these elements in a Christian direction.[36] The author of 2 John follows this precedent while at the same time impressing them with his own style as contrasted with Paul. While the *intitulatio* in Paul emphasizes his own apostolic office, the Johannine author gives himself the honorific title of "the elder" (*ho presbyteros*).

Unlike the plural, the singular can hardly be used as an official title. This is because for the institution of elders it is their collegiate character that is important.[37] The

---

36. See O. Roller, *Das Formular der paulinischen Briefe*, 57ff. and nn. 263ff. (pp. 445ff.).

37. It is certainly no accident that *ho presbyteros* never occurs anywhere for an individual member of the presbyterium; only in 1 Pet. 5:1 do we find *ho sympresbyteros*. In addition the *presbyterion* is more of a patriarchal institution than a body of officials. As distinct from the presbyterate, the episcopate clearly developed into an office of leadership; cf. 1 Tim. 3:2; Titus 1:7. Moreover, committees of presbyters were very different in origen (Judaism, Hellenism), function (political entities, clubs, religious institutions), composition (honorific, and partly on ground of seniority). See A. Deissmann, *Bible Studies*, 153ff.; *Neue Bibelstudien* (Marburg, 1897) 60ff.; M. L. Strack, *ZNW* 4 (1903) 213–34; H. Hauschildt, *ZNW* 4 (1903) 235–42; M. Dibelius-H. Conzelmann, Excursus on 1 Tim. 5:17 (HNT XIII [3rd ed., 1955] 60f.); A. Wikenhauser, *Die Kirche als der mystische Leib Christi*, 82f.; G. Bornkamm, *TDNT* 6:653f.

comparative is no longer regarded as having comparative force,[38] as is the case with other frequently used adjectives. The article introduces the writer as a well-known and unmistakable personage who does not need to mention his name. If we take "the elder" as an epithet denoting authority and honor, it does not necessarily imply seniority, although it is likely that the author was an elderly person, judging from his paternal style.[39] Had he wanted to introduce himself as a church official, he would hardlly have omitted his name; otherwise he would have been mistaken for one of his colleagues.[40] But there is no reason to suppose that the name was (deliberately?) omitted quite early on in the manuscripts.[41] Such a possibility is even less likely in view of the fact that 1 John also uses similar substantival adjectives, pointing to a well-known personage in a pregnant manner.[42] See the Introduction for resulting questions regarding authorship.

The "lady" who is being addressed is not an individual named Eclecta or Kyria as has been suggested. The former suggestion is ruled out by the final greeting,[43] which adds "the children of your elect sister" (v. 13). The believers liked to refer to themselves as the "elect" or "chosen."[44] In 1 Pet. 5:13 the community giving the greeting is called "your sister the church in Babylon, chosen together with you." Ignatius of Antioch bestows upon the church at Tralles the honorific title, "the elect and worthy of God" (*Trall. inscriptio*). In the second instance one would expect the name to be placed first, as it is in the epistolary inscriptions of 1 and 2 Timothy, Titus, Philemon, and 3 John, with the article before the attributive "elect" as in Rom. 16:13; etc.[45] The community is likened to a mother with all her children (cf. v. 4). This is proof for the distinctive value that the early church bestowed on each community. It did this without removing the local church from the church of God as a whole.[46] "Lady" is also found as an honorific designation for a political community (*curia patris*), and it seems that the church took over this usage from the profane sphere.[47] Originally the apostolic preacher himself

38. See BDF §244.2; Radermacher, *Grammatik,* 69f.; Moulton 3:30; Mayser, *Grammatik,* I, 1:49ff.

39. In non-Christian bodies of presbyters *presbyteros* was not always a designation of age, but often one of honor; see Hauschildt, *ZNW* 4 (1903) 239. The advanced age of the *presbyteros* in 2 and 3 John is emphasized too strongly by Wendt, *Johannesbriefe,* 7f.

40. On E. Käsemann's hypothesis, see Introduction, pp. 271f.

41. So E. Schwartz, *Über den Tod der Söhne Zebedaei,* 52f.; E. Meyer, *Ursprung und Anfänge* 3:638; for a contrary view, see, e.g., Jülicher-Fascher, *Einleitung,* 237.

42. Cf. *ho hagios* (1 John 2:20); *ho alēthinos* (5:20); *ho ponēros* (2:13, 14; 5:18); *ho ap' archēs* (2:13, 14).—BDF §263.

43. Already Clement of Alexandria, *Adumb.* (GCS 3:215); in more recent times Estius, Cornelius a Lapide, Poggel, and esp. R. Harris (*Exp* 6, 3 [1901] 194–203).

44. Rom. 16:13; 2 Tim. 2:10; 1 Pet. 1:1; Rev. 17:14; *1 Clem.* 6.1; *Herm. Vis.* 2.4.2; *eklektoi theou* (Rom. 8:33; Col. 3:12; Titus 1:1; *1 Clem.* 1.1; 2.4; 46.3; etc.; *2 Clem.* 14.5; *Herm. Vis.* 1.3.4; etc.— According to Harnack (*Mission and Expansion* 2:403), the designation "the Elect" became (later) almost a technical term.

45. See BDF §270.

46. Cf. the designation of the local congregation as *hē ekklēsia tou theou* in the prescripts of 1 and 2 Thessalonians, 1 and 2 Corinthians, Galatians; and on this point, see Wikenhauser, *Die Kirche,* 5f.; K. L. Schmidt, *TDNT* 3:506; R. Schnackenburg, "Episkopos und Hirtenamt," in *Festschrift Cardinal Faulhaber* (Regensburg, 1949) 84ff.

47. See the inscription in St. George's Church at Gerasa, printed in F. J. Dölger, *Antike und Christentum* 5 (1936) 214f. (ca. 115–116 C.E.). For its use in connection with the church, see Tertullian, *Ad mart.* 1: *domina mater ecclesia;* Dölger shows that this relates to the local church of Carthage (p. 216).

begets "children in the Lord."[48] But now we are in a period when a considerable proportion of converts came from the missionary activity of the community itself. The faithful are also referred to as children of a community in Hermas (*Vis.* 3.9.1, 9). The metaphor is found already in Jewish writings, which refer to the city of Jerusalem and her "children."[49] In Rev. 2:26 the followers of heretical teachers are metaphorically referred to as "children" of the whore. This does not mean that the elder himself made converts in the community; their children would also be his children (cf. 3 John 4).

These children, that is, the faithful of the community, are loved by the author "in truth," that is to say, in integrity and sincerity. In this context the turn of phrase without the article does not mean "based on the common possession of truth" or "in the divine nature of truth." Rather, it retains the Old Testament associations of "truth."[50] It has become almost like a formula, synonymous with *alēthōs,* "truly" (cf. John 17:19 — John 1:47; 7:26; 8:31; 17:8) or *ep' alētheias,* "truly" (Mark 12:32; Luke 4:25; 20:21; 22:59; Acts 4:27; 10:34).[51] If we read this into the phrase (as most commentators do), then the express reason given in v. 2 becomes superfluous. "Truth" is one of the favorite words of John. It can have many different nuances, depending on the context.[52]

This becomes immediately obvious in v. 1b, with its assurance that mutual love is something that the whole community can share, all "who know the truth." For here truth means the divine revelation that brought Jesus, the light of the world. Jesus "speaks" the truth, not in formal terms as contrasted with lying but in substance. He proclaims what he has heard from God (John 8:40; cf. 45; 3:11, 32; 7:16; 8:26), in all its fullness (3:34). The "Spirit of truth" will continue this work of "guiding (you) into all truth" (16:13). The Christian believers, to whom God has given the Spirit (1 John 3:24; 4:13; cf. 2:20f., 27), have reached full and abiding knowledge (*egnōkotes,* perfect) of the divine revelation. This profound knowledge of the divine truth, effected by Jesus, who embodied it in his person (John 14:6), and which the unbelieving world cannot receive (John 8:43, 45; 14:17) is the goal of faith (John 6:69; 8:31f.; 1 John 4:16a).

2 We should understand knowledge of the truth (acceptance of the revelation) in terms of Johannine thought. According to this it is only those of peculiar sensitivity who hear the voice of Jesus (John 8:47; 10:27; 18:37). If that is the case, it is not a great step to the distinctively Johannine concept of truth (see on 1 John

48. Cf. 1 Cor. 4:14, 17; 2 Cor. 6:13; Gal. 4:19; Phlm. 10; 1 and 2 Tim. 2:2; Titus 1:4; cf. 1 Thess. 2:11; 3 John 4.

49. Isaiah 54; Bar. 4:9–5:9; on this, Gibbins, *Exp* 6, 6 (1902) 228ff., esp. 232.

50. Cf. 1 Sam. 12:24; Ps. 145:18; Mark 12:14 par.; 1 Cor. 5:8; 2 Cor. 7:14; Eph. 5:9; 6:14; Phil. 1:18; 1 John 3:18; 3 John 1: Pol. *Phil.* 4.2. On this see Bultmann, *TDNT* 1:243; further Dodd, *The Bible and the Greeks,* 68f.

51. On the formulalike phrases, see Bultmann, *TDNT* 1:243; Mayser, *Grammatik,* II, 2:35ff.

52. See R. Bergmeier, "Zum Verfasserproblem des II. und III. Johannesbriefes," *ZNW* 57 (1966) 93–100. He investigates the concept of *alētheia* and is of the opinion that it denotes orthodox (ecclesiastical) doctrine. From this he concludes that 2 and 3 John were by the same author as 1 John. Against this, see R. Schnackenburg, "Zum Begriff der Wahrheit in den beiden kleinen Johannesbriefen," *BZ* n.s. 11 (1967) 153–58. Similarly, R. Bultmann asserts that *alētheia* and *didachē* are not identical.

1:8). This step we now take (cf. 1 John 2:21a, b, and c) in v. 2. The bond of love ties together the author, his readers, and all faithful believers "because of the truth that abides in us." Truth here means the divine reality that is always with us (cf. 1 John 1:8; 2:4), just like "life" (cf. 1 John 3:15) and the Spirit of truth itself (John 14:17b). With the Spirit-filled word God's very being has flowed into us. God's word and God's life are intimately bound together. That is why John likes to use double phrases, like "grace and truth" (1:14, 17), "Spirit and truth" (4:23f.), "the truth and the life" (14:6). In this encompassing sense we get "truth" in v. 2, as the continuation in v. 2b especially shows. Insofar as "truth" means revealed truth, expressed in doctrine and confession, it is the duty of the believers "to abide in it" (cf. v. 9). But insofar as it fills people with the divine wisdom and life, it may be said to "abide in us." The continuation of v. 2b is—similar to 1 John 3:1—formed as an independent clause. Like everything belonging to the divine realm, truth abides "forever" (cf. the same saying about the Paraclete in John 14:16; also 6:51; 8:35; 11:26; 1 John 2:17).[53] The preposition *meta,* "with," makes "truth" look almost personified. Yet this statement—again in view of 1 John 4:17a—must not be pressed too far (Büchsel); the change to *en,* "in," is just for the sake of variation (cf. John 14:16f.).

3 Under the stimulus of what he has just written, the author continues by repeating "will be with us,"[54] and proceeds to pronounce an opening greeting, the *salutatio.* We should not fail to notice how this happens, following the words of blessing in v. 3, "Grace, mercy, and peace." This is not just a wish but a deliberate and confident affirmation.[55] The whole verse is a beautiful example of the way Christians freely expand the conventional epistolary greeting, normally a brief and stereotyped beginning to a letter. Instead of the profane greeting *chairein* ("greetings"), the author wishes them *charis* ("grace"), as Paul invariably does. This custom seems to have become common among Christians from very early days. Instead of the usual twofold Pauline formula "grace and peace," this author uses a threefold one, "grace, mercy, and peace" (cf. 1 and 2 Timothy). Perhaps this is like *2 Apoc. Bar.* 78:2, a combination with the Jewish greeting "grace and peace" (Gal. 6:16; Jude 2, Polycarp *Inscriptio*).[56]

---

53. *Eis ton aiōna,* in GJohn twelve times, is purely Johannine; it has a Semitic root. Cf., however, the Hellenistic inscriptions given in E. Peterson, Εἷς θεός (Göttingen, 1926) 168ff. On *menein,* see J. Heise, *Bleiben: Menein in den Johanneischen Schriften* (Tübingen, 1967) 164–70 (for authorship he advocates a hypothesis similar to that of Bultmann: the author wanted to correct the third letter in the name of the presbyter as well as Johannine theology in its entirety in the sense of the official church).

54. The reading *meth' hymōn* (048 K pm. Vg sy^h bo arm) is the result of reflection and assimilation to greetings in the second person.—*estai meth' hēmōn* (om. A al.).

55. That the future tense was felt to express a wish, as most exegetes assume, is not all that certain. The future as a substitute for the imperative is the "legal language of the OT" (BDF §362), or a peremptory command that does not expect to be contradicted (Moulton, 278). A wish is expressed by the optative or by *ophelon* with future indicative (BDF §384; Moulton, 309 and 317f.); in vulgar usage the subjunctive is also found (Radermacher, *Grammatik,* 166; BDF §364.3). We may compare the *negative* form with ou mē and the future indicative, as well as a wish (BDF §365; Moulton, 300f.).

56. See L. Brun, *Segen und Fluch im Urchristentum* (Oslo, 1932) 38.

In substance the blessing is a powerful expression of the grace of Christian salvation. This is reinforced by "from God the Father." All good things come from God (cf. Jas. 1:17). Whereas *charis* as used in the New Testament often includes the blessings of salvation,[57] *eleos* ("mercy") is more the gracious attitude of God who grants salvation beyond our deserts (cf. Eph. 2:4; Titus 3:5; 1 Pet. 1:3). The same combination of grace with mercy occurs in Wis. 3:9; 4:15. In Christian circles "peace" has a stronger resonance than the Jewish *shalom,* for peace is, in Christian understanding, the messianic salvation (Isa. 52:7). By the addition of "from Jesus Christ" the distinctive Johannine nuance becomes audible. Peace, which Jesus Christ brought from God, is something the world does not know (John 14:27; 16:33). For "Jesus Christ" the author uses not the Pauline "our Lord" but the Johannine "the Father's Son." This implies that the Son of God was sent into the world to be the Bearer and Mediator of the divine blessings of salvation.

The addition of *en alētheia kai agapē* ("in truth and love") is superfluous, for this twofold phrase can hardly be applied to God's act of blessing.[58] Probably it is intended to bring out the effect the divine blessing has upon the believers.[59] The phrase serves as a bridge. The author still has the words about truth (vv. 1f.) ringing in his ears, so he adds "love" because he wants to mention it next (vv. 4–6). He does not intend to change the train of his thought (*contra* Chaine and Ambroggi).

FIRST SECTION

THE TEST OF GENUINE CHRISTIAN LIFE IS FIDELITY TO GOD'S COMMANDMENTS (2 JOHN 4–6)

[4]I was overjoyed to find some of your children walking in the truth, just as we have been commanded by the Father. [5]But now, dear lady, I ask you, not as though I were writing you a new commandment, but one we have had from the beginning, let us love one another. [6]And this is love, that we walk according to his commandments; this is the commandment just as you have heard it from the beginning—you must walk in it [love].

4 The regular *captatio benevolentiae* (cf. 3 John 3) is not an expression of thanks to God as it is in Paul, but is formulated in personal terms. The author has had the pleasure[60] of meeting some of the members of the

---

57. Cf. John 1:16 and esp. Paul in Rom. 5:15, 17, 20; 1 Cor. 1:4; 2 Cor. 4:15; 6:1; 8:1; 9:8; Eph. 4:7, 29; also J. Wobbe, *Der Charis-Gedanke bei Paulus* (NTAbh 13, 2; Münster, 1932) 40ff.; P. Rousselot, "La grâce d'après S. Jean et d'après S. Paul," *RechScR* 18 (1928) 87–108; Bultmann, *John,* 74 n. 1 and 78 n. 1; Dodd, *The Bible and the Greeks,* 61ff.

58. Büchsel takes the phrase with *tou huiou tou patros,* referring to John 1:14 and 17. That would not only be awkward, but would also be a singular assertion about the relation of sonship.

59. The vague *en* is undoubtedly to be taken instrumentally; cf. BDF §219.4.

60. The aorist *echarēn* is probably ingressive.

community,[61] who are really leading Christian lives. That is shown in their behavior (cf. 1 John 1:6, 7; 2:6, 11), which transfers God's commandments into deeds. "In truth"—contrary to v. 1 and 3 John 1—here denotes the genuine Christian way of life corresponding to the true nature of God's children.[62] It was easy for the author to adopt the image of "walking in the way" in combination with "truth," for it is already suggested in the Septuagint by 3 Kingdoms 2:4; 4 Kingdoms 20:3, which speak of "going" or "walking" in the way. But of course the author does not mean it quite in the Old Testament sense of "fidelity." In the Qumran writings, which use the term *alētheia* or *'mt* extensively, we meet similar turns of phrase.[63] The following clause introduced by *kathōs* then explains how it is that this life-style of the members of the community can be characterized as "walking in the truth." It is because they hold faithfully to the instructions of the Father. Genuine Christians receive instructions for their way of life from their Father, like Jesus himself (cf. John 10:18; 12:49; 14:31; 15:10). It is not, however, meant as inner promptings but as commandments coming from outside (*entolēn* used generically). The aorist *elabomen*, "we have received" (NRSV "we have been commanded"), and the comparison with v. 6 ("according to his commandments"). The content of God's commandment is to be taken as all-embracing, perhaps in the sense of 1 John 3:23. The whole verse testifies that those believers comply with what is demanded in 1 John 1:7; 2:3ff. as well as 2:24, 27.

5 An equally exemplary Christian life cannot be realized by everyone in the community (cf. v. 4, "some of your children"). In a well-crafted continuation (*kai nyn* as in 1 John 2:28 = "now therefore"; NRSV "but now") he admonishes the entire community, addressed once again as "Lady," "let us love one another" (the *hina*-clause depends on *erōtō*, "I ask"). Verses 5f. are typically Johannine, both in style and thought. Outwardly the author joins the sentences by single identical words;[64] inwardly the sentences circle around a single thought, namely, the love commandment. He uses similar words to 1 John 2:7 as he describes it as something they have had "from the beginning," that is, ever since they first had the gospel preached to them (for the imperfect, cf. 1 John 2:7). He includes himself here because he too has received it from Christ. The original tradition serves as an edge against the craze for novelty on the part of the heretical teachers

---

61. *Heurēka* can have a concrete meaning, stating that the author has met such members of the community, perhaps on a visit (cf. v. 12), or conversely when visited by one of them (cf. 3 John 3). In that case the restrictive phrase (*ek tōn teknōn sou*) can mean only that the author knows that part of the community is exemplary. But the construction with a connecting participle, as well as the perfect, expressing a concrete experience, makes a metaphorical sense more plausible: I have found them to be such; see BDF §416.2; BAGD 325, 1, c and 2. In that case there is an implied rebuke of other members of the community, those of whom he does not have such a high opinion.
62. Cf. BAGD 36, s.v. 2, b.—In the first edition, based on the construction without an article, suggesting a formulalike expression, we express the opinion that *en alētheiạ* was equivalent to "in reality" (=*alēthōs*).
63. Cf. 1QS 5:25; 7:18 (to be unfaithful to the truth); 8:5 (to stand firm in the truth); 1QSb 3:24 (strengthen in truth [. . . and in righteousness observe all his laws]; 1QH 16:7 (in truth and with the whole heart). In all these passages *b'mt* occurs.
64. Cf. *entolēn* (v. 4 and v. 5); *agapōmen* (v. 5)–*agapē* (v. 6a); *tas entolas* (v. 6a)–*hē entolē* (v. 6b).

(v. 9). Probably the challenge to love is deliberately couched in terms that the members of the community will discern, not only the admonition to fraternal behavior among themselves but also the warm-hearted contact with the elder. It is possible that he has here to deal with difficulties in the community as he has to in 3 John.

6 This verse ties in externally with the previous words (*ad vocem agapōmen*, "we love"). It can hardly mean either the love of God specifically (as in 1 John 5:3)[65] or the love of brother or sister, as seems to be required by "let us love one another."[66] The author speaks in both basic and general terms — as in 1 John 4:7ff. — about the nature of love. For him it is neither a matter of empty assurances (1 John 3:18) nor yet a gnostic infatuation with knowledge (1 John 2:3ff.; 4:7f.), but is demonstrated in action. The phrase "to walk according to God's commandments" serves to make this point. The author combines the two concepts closely, allowing the one to explain the other. True "walking" consists in obedience to the commandments ("according to his commandments"; cf. v. 4). The commandment, however, can only be fulfilled only by "walking" ("you must walk in it"). Thus it becomes intelligible from v. 6b that the second "this" in v. 6 points to the *hina*-clause (introduced by a dash in NRSV). But this does not so much indicate the content of the commandment. Rather, it puts emphasis on "you must walk" (note the position of the verb at the end in the Greek). In that case "in it" can be understood indefinitely, with v. 6b as a playful reversal of v. 6a, relating to the word "love."[67] Whether the *hina* before *kathōs* is original or not[68] is of no consequence for this accentuation. In any case, the author wants love to be demonstrated by concrete behavior. That is the point here. The phrases "walking in the truth, just as we have been commanded by the Father" (v. 4), and "that we walk according to his commandments" (v. 6b) express this idea in different ways.

SECOND SECTION

THE RECIPIENTS MUST GUARD THEMSELVES AGAINST THE VIEWS OF THE HERETICAL TEACHERS (2 JOHN 7-9)

[7]Many deceivers have gone out into the world, those who do not confess that Jesus Christ has come in the flesh; any such person is the deceiver and the antichrist! [8]Be on your guard, so that you do not lose what we have worked for, but may receive

---

65. So Camerlynck, Vrede, Bonsirven, Chaine.
66. So Brooke, Windisch, Büchsel (who connects it with vv. 11f.; that can hardly be right).
67. So also Calmes, Camerlynck, Belser, Vrede, Bonsirven, Chaine, Dodd, et al.; Brooke, Büchsel, Ambroggi take it with *entolē;* cf. Windisch. Regarding the style, cf. John 13:34, where the second *hina*-clause takes up the first one, and, because of the *kathōs*-clause, modifies it with *kai hymeis;* similarly 17:21.
68. *Hina* is read before *kathōs* in ℵ A K Ψ 33 69 81 323 1739 al. Vg sa bo arm, most of which except ℵ A Ψ go on to leave out the second *hina;* a single placement of the *hina* at the second position is attested by B L pm. sy.

a full reward. ⁹Everyone who does not abide in the teaching of Christ, but goes beyond it, does not have God; whoever abides in the teaching has both the Father and the Son.

7 With the explanatory *hoti* ("for" — omitted by NRSV) the author indicates that he had already had the heretical teachers in view. Now he mentions them explicitly, branding as such those who deny the christological confession of the orthodox community. He first refers to them in general terms as "deceivers."⁶⁹ He says of them as he had said of the false prophets in 1 John 4:1 — that they "have gone out into the world" (see on 1 John 4:1).⁷⁰ There are many of them (*polloi*), and they are spreading a lively propaganda all over the place (*exēlthon*). The hallmark of true faith is defined by a confessional formula, almost identical with that in 1 John 4:2 (see ad loc.).

The only noticeable difference is the present participle, contrasted with the perfect participle in 1 John 4:2. There is no question of its referring to the parousia, for in early Christian usage that is generally referred to as a coming not "in the flesh" but "in glory."⁷¹ Christ's fleshly form is then glorified through the Spirit (cf. John 6:63a) and could not be emphasized as though it were characteristic of him. The formula, which in style is identical to 1 John 4:2, emphasizes (like the perfect participle in 1 John 4:2; see ad loc.) the supratemporal significance of the incarnation. Ignatius of Antioch similarly, in his attack on the heretical teachers in his letter to the Smyrnaeans, underscores in quite general terms the fleshly state of Jesus. This applies not only to the moment of his crucifixion (1.2) but also to the period after the resurrection (3.1; cf. 3.2f.). His concern is that Jesus should become known as *sarkophoros* (bearer of the flesh, 5.2). It seems that the formula in 2 John 7 has the same meaning. The present participle is perhaps influenced also by the phraseology in GJohn about Jesus as the one who comes (*erchomenos*) occurring in a variety of contexts.⁷² But it may simply be a "didactic formula" (Windisch).

The shift to the singular may suggest that *houtos* (NRSV "such a person") is the predicate. In that case it defines who is the deceiver and antichrist. But if the latter nouns form the predicate, the article shows⁷³ that the reference is to one or two eschatological figures. The antichrist is expected to precede the parousia of Christ as in 1 John 2:18; 4:3 (see above), but the elder visualizes him as having come already in the people who deny Christ. The deceiver may well be the same figure in a different guise. He would then be first called the deceiver

---

69. *Planos* is primarily an adjective (1 Tim. 4:1) but is also used as a substantive in the New Testament in Matt. 27:63 (cf. *T. Levi* 16:3, probably an addition from the Christian era); 2 Cor. 6:8; further Vett. Val. 2.16. See H. Braun, *TDNT* 6:233.

70. The reading *eisēlthon* (P ⅙ 33 al.) is perhaps influenced by the following *eis* or by passages like John 6:14; 9:39; 11:27; 12:46; 16:28; 18:37.

71. See 1 Cor. 15:43; Phil. 3:21; Col. 3:4; 1 Tim. 3:16; Titus 2:13; Heb. 2:9; 1 Pet. 4:13. — One should not appeal to *Barn.* 6.9 since as already in 6.7 we are dealing with the prophetic foresight of Jesus, who from the Christian perspective has already come.

72. John 1:15, 27; 3:31; 6:14; 11:27; cf. also 1:9 (also 12:46). If these passages are in part connected with the messianic expectation of a particular "Coming One" (note the article) as further attested in the Synoptics (Matt. 11:3; cf. Mark 11:9 par.), nevertheless 3:31 especially echoes the distinctive Johannine understanding of the "coming" of Jesus. Like the "coming from above" in John 3:31, the "coming in the flesh" of 2 John 7 is a permanently valid fact (both occurrences are in the present tense). Cf. further Staerk, *Soter* 2:89f.; J. Schneider, *TDNT* 2:671ff., 674.

73. BDF §273.

because the heretics have already been referred to as "many deceivers" at the beginning of the verse. This is then clarified as the "antichrist." The latter explanation is the more probable. There seems to be no reason to envision two distinct eschatological figures. The activity of the second beast (from the earth) in Rev. 13:11ff. would in itself suit the deceiver here (cf. "deceiver" in v. 14), although it does not deceive by false doctrine, but by miraculous signs wrought by magic. The antichrists in 1 John 2:18ff. are also described as "deceivers" ("those who would deceive you," v. 26). It is probable that the only certain tradition the author knows about the eschatological times is the one about the antichrist (2:18; 4:3). This figure he proceeds to identify with the heretical teachers of his time.[74] These words now recover their eschatological significance.

8 "Be on your guard" is here an eschatological admonition.[75] The promise of a full reward (at the end) is reminiscent of Jewish thinking and somewhat surprising. For v. 9, again in a genuine Johannine way, is focused on our present fellowship with God. This motivation may be due to the eschatological perspective. The metaphor in v. 8 is taken from strenuous physical labor. The readers should not lose what they have worked so hard for (cf. the phrase "will by no means lose the reward," Mark 9:41 = Matt. 10:42). In John 6:27–29 "to work" is used metaphorically for the will to believe. That 2 John 8 involves the use of a metaphor is shown by the second half of the verse, where the statement is reversed and put positively. "To receive a full reward" is a phrase that occurs frequently in Judaism.[76] It is already found in Ruth 2:12. No doubt what is really meant is fellowship with the Son and the Father (cf. v. 9b) the grace and bliss that come from possessing salvation. The full reward then is the eternal life promised to the believers (cf. 1 John 2:25; also John 6:27).

The textual tradition leaves us in doubt as to whether the individual verbs are in the first or second person plural. In favor of *apolesēte* and *apolabēte* is the weight of the textual evidence.[77] Against this, *ērgasametha* is read by B* ℵ al. sy^hmg sa^codd. Intrinsically the latter represents the more difficult reading, but for the suspicion that would imply that the author was presenting himself as the missionary who founded the community (cf. the same image in Paul, 1 Cor. 3:8, 14; 15:10; Gal. 4:11; Phil. 2:16). On grounds of textual criticism *eirgasasthe* deserves preference despite B*.[78]

---

74. Chaine: "As in John 2:18, 19, St. John spiritualizes the current idea of the eschatological adversary and shows how this terrifying event is realized in contemporary facts." In general, Ambroggi conceives of the antichrist as a "collective opposition to Christ."

75. In a formal sense with a reflexive pronoun = Mark 13:9; though cf. Mark 13:5 par.; in content the meaning is reminiscent of Rev. 3:1.

76. See targums on Ruth 2:12; Eccl. 1:3; 2:10, 11; 5:18, "where rewards are always referred to in a set formula." (Büchsel, ad loc.). R. Harris assumes that there is a direct allusion to Ruth 2:12, *Exp* 6, 3 (1901) 194ff.

77. *Apolesōmen* and *apolabōmen* only ℵ 69 al.

78. This reading is attested by ℵ A Vg sy Ir. Luc. Isid. Dam. It is preferred by Tischendorf, von Soden, Vogels, Merk, and esp. by Harnack (*SB* [Berlin, 1923] 97); among more recent commentators, by Windisch, Büchsel, Bonsirven, Dodd. The reading is rejected by Westcott-Hort, B. Weiss, (E. Nestle), Lagrange (*Critique textuelle,* 538), and among the commentators by Brooke, Chaine, Charue, Ambroggi.

9 The believers hold on to what "they have heard from the beginning" (vv. 5f.). Unlike them, the heretics progress further (*proagōn*, "going beyond").[79] They are not satisfied with "the teaching of Christ," but aspire to higher insights[80] in a manner typical of gnostic behavior. How their gnosis goes beyond the teaching of Christ we are not told. It is not clear whether "of Christ" is an objective or subjective genitive. This is because apostolic or internal teaching has as its content Christ and the meaning of his salvation.[81] But there is an explanation that is more profound theologically and closer to Johannine thought. This is that it is the teaching given by Christ himself (subjective genitive).[82] Jesus speaks of his "teaching" in GJohn (7:16). He is asked by the high priest "about his teaching" (18:19). "Of Christ" instead of "of Jesus" or "of Jesus Christ" is in that case the language of faith.

Whoever does not remain within the parameters of this teaching "does not have God"—the equivalent of fellowship with God, an idea we have already encountered in 1 John 2:23 (cf. 5:12; see ad loc.). Altogether the passage 1 John 2:22f. is closely related to the present one. The antithetical style, repeating the negative statement in positive terms, the emphasis created by *houtos* (picking up "whoever"; see NRSV), the absolute language, "the Father" and "the Son," the precedence of the Father over the Son (cf. also 1 John 1:3) where the opposite order would have been expected—all these similarities are found in both passages. The replacing of "to have God" in v. 9a with "has the Father and the Son" in v. 9b arises once more from the basic Johannine conviction that fellowship with God is attainable through the Son (1 John 2:23; 5:12). At the same time we have the further result that the heresy is not merely the focus of the special statement in v. 7, but permeates the whole letter. It is of crucial importance, as we know from 1 John.

THIRD SECTION

PRACTICAL INSTRUCTIONS: THE RECIPIENTS ARE TO REFUSE HOSPITALITY TO THE HERETICS (2 JOHN 10–11)

[10]Do not receive into the house or welcome anyone who comes to you and does not bring this teaching; [11]for to welcome is to participate in the evil deeds of such a person.

---

79. The picture given by the multivalent word *proagein* is given a precise nuance by the closely related phrase *mē menōn en* (related to our term "progress").—The reading *parabainōn* (ᵏ pl. sy, Vogels) is either a weakening ("to go astray," "wander from the path") or a correction in the interests of ecclesiastical authority ("to transgress"—the correct doctrine of Christ imposed like a command).

80. Well put by Zorell (*Novi Testamenti Lexicon graecum* [2nd ed.; Paris, 1931] 1119f., s.v. 2a): omnis, qui ultra (limites verae doctrinae christianae ad nescio quam ficticiam sublimiorum perfectionem) procedit.

81. Windisch thinks it refers to a fixed "canon of true faith," and compares with Eph. 4:31. Similarly Rengstorf (*TDNT* 2:164) takes *Christou* as an objective genitive, though he understands *didachē* differently: "the traditional and familiar way of speaking of Christ," which is certainly incorrect.

82. So most of the recent commentaries. In addition the subjective genitive is much more frequent.

Exegesis

10 Because the salvation of his readers is in danger (v. 8), the elder now delivers a series of concrete instructions that were probably the reason for writing the letter. He is afraid the itinerant heretical teachers may turn up and receive an unsuspecting welcome. By "anyone who comes" he therefore means not just ordinary travelers but, as the continuation of the letter shows, people who champion the "lie" (cf. 2 Cor. 11:4). Ignatius of Antioch has similar reports of itinerant preachers and calls them bad names (Ignatius, *Eph.* 7.1; 8.1; 9.1; *Smyrn.* 4.1; 5.1; 7.2). He too issues sharp warnings to his flock, similar to those in 2 John (cf. also Jude 23). Later the precautions multiply concerning such itinerant brethren. Everywhere the ancient church insists on strict avoidance of heretical teachers.[83] The refusal of hospitality is frequently urged upon the churches. This is especially striking in view of the high regard for hospitality in the early church.[84] But the enemies of the faith are more insidious than personal opponents. That is why the need for forgiveness (Matt. 5:23–25) and love of the enemy (Matt. 5:44–48) must not be played off against it. Faced by a refusal to accept the good news of the kingdom of God, Jesus ordered his disciples to break off fellowship (Matt. 10:14; Luke 10:10f.). How much more is this true when the church is faced by people who seek to destroy it! Just as Paul calls down destruction upon those who destroy God's temple, that is, the Christian church (1 Cor. 3:17); just as the author of Jude brings all his guns to bear against the heretical teachers of his time, so too does the elder show his combative side, which springs from his responsibility for his churches.

11 The readers should not even greet the heretics. In Jewish eyes a greeting is something more than a mere formality. The greeting of peace is equivalent to a blessing (cf. Matt. 10:13 = Luke 10:6).[85] The Greek greeting (*chairein*) is by comparison colorless. That is why the author feels obliged to give his Greek readers a reason for the prohibition. People enter into fellowship with those they greet. They associate themselves[86] with their evil deeds. They share responsibility for their aberrations (cf. 1 Tim. 5:22). For Christians to greet their enemies would seem not only to be consenting to their previous malefactions, but also to be sanctioning their future misdeeds. These "evil deeds"[87] include not only immoral acts in general (John 3:19) but specifically the spreading of lies directed against

---

83. See *Did.* 11 and 12; Irenaeus, *Adv. Haer.* 3.3.4; Tertullian, *De praescr. haer.* 7.37 (the heretics have no rights in the church). The excommunication of the Essenes and associated groups such as the community of the new covenant at Damascus and the Qumran community are products of a different spirit; the idea of purity, pride in one's election, esotericism, and only in part the desire for protection against degeneration.
84. See Rom. 12:13; 1 Tim. 5:10; Heb. 13:1f.; 1 Pet. 4:9; 3 John 5–8; *1 Clem.* 1.2; 10.7; 11.1; 12.1; *Herm. Man.* 8.10; *Herm. Sim.* 8.10.3; 9.27.2; Aristides, *Apol.* 15; Tertullian, *Ad uxores* 2.4; Cyprian, *Ep.*7; *Const. Apost.* 3.3.—Findlay, 11–20; G. Stählin, *TDNT* 5:22ff.; H. Rusche, *Gastfreundschaft in der Verkündigung des NT und ihr Verhältnis zur Mission* (Münster, 1958).
85. See L. Brun, *Segen und Fluch*, 109.
86. *Koinōnein* is constructed with a genitive and a dative of the object. In the New Testament the dative is used in connection with spiritual entities (Rom. 15:27), with the sufferings of Christ (1 Pet. 4:13), and the sins of one's youth (1 Tim. 5:22); see further Plato, *Leg.* 801 E (*euchais*); Epictetus, *Diss.* 4.6.30 (*ergō*); *Gnom. stob.* C 36 (*kakiq* and *douleiq*); *POxy.* 1223.19 (*peristasei*). Seesemann, *Begriff* κοινωνία, 8f.
87. Note the emphasis created by placing the attribute after the noun.

Christ. In John 8:41 Jesus reproaches his unbelieving adversaries for doing their "father's," that is, the devil's, desires. This radical view, which sees everything in black and white, is retained in 1 John 3:8, 10. The elder makes no clear-cut decision between moral and religious conduct. He is quite certain that their deeds are evil. There is every excuse for this judgment, for we know from 1 John that heresy combined both christological and moral "lies." This prohibition of greeting is a consequence and practical application of that basic separation from sin arising from the community's sense of faith. It must not, however, be detached from its historical context and applied indiscriminately to entirely different situations. There is no mention in this verse of excommunication as such (*contra* Ambroggi).

THE CONCLUSION OF THE EPISTLE

INTENTION TO VISIT AND FINAL GREETINGS
(2 JOHN 12–13)

[12]Although I have much to write to you, I would rather not use paper and ink; instead I hope to come to you, and talk with you face to face, so that our joy may be complete.
[13]The children of your elect sister send you their greetings.

12 After presenting his main concern, the author breaks off. Although he still has much to write about,[88] he has to forgo it because he plans to visit the community.[89] He is all the more keen to do so (*eboulēthēn* is another epistolary aorist; see on 1 John 2:14, 21), because speaking face to face[90] is preferable to writing with pen and ink.[91] This need mean no more than a preference for verbal communication to an exchange of letters. But there may be more to it than this. He may have certain unpleasant matters to bring up, perhaps involving personal relations between the writer and individual members of the community. This surmise is all the more plausible if the challenge to mutual love in v. 5 acts as a bond between the elder and his readers. The added sentence, "so that our[92] joy may be complete,"[93] corresponds literally to 1 John 1:4, "our" (*hēmōn*) being

---

88. There are a few uncertain points in the text: *echō* (ℵ* A* 81 323 431 915 1739) in place of *echōn* must be an error of ear or eye on the part of the copyist; *grapsai* (A 93 436) is an assimilation to the aorist *eboulēthēn*.
89. *Genesthai,* for which P ℵ pm. sa arm read *elthein,* has the meaning "to come," for which there is abundant attestation; see BAGD 159, 4, c.
90. The phrase derives from the Old Testament: Num. 12:8; Jer. 39:4; though cf. ZP 1.39 *to stoma pros to stoma.*
91. *Chartēs* for paper (papyrus leaves; see, however, 2 Tim. 4:13, where a different word is used) only here in the New Testament. Elsewhere it occurs frequently; see Liddell and Scott 1980, s.v. *Eboulēthēn* has no infinitive of its own (Büchsel: *gnōrizein*), but again *graphein* has to be understood (cf. 3 John 13).
92. In place of *hēmōn* (ℵ ℵ sy arm) *hymōn* is read by AB 33 81 323 1739 al. Vg bo. *Hēmōn* is not necessarily an assimilation to 1 John 1:4 (*contra* Brooke); *hymōn* was probably introduced under the influence of *hymin* and *hymas.*
93. *Peplērōmenē* here means the height of joy; see BAGD 671, s.v. 3.

the plural of authorship as in 3 John 9b (see ad loc.). The author is only referring to himself.

13 The usual concluding greeting then follows. The author returns after *hymin* ("to you") in v. 12 (and earlier) to his original metaphor of the "lady" and her "children" and continues to speak of the children and their "sister," that is, the faithful members of the church where he is residing. This community also, like the recipients, is accorded the title of honor, "chosen" (see on v.1).[94] A few late manuscripts add *meth' hymōn* ("with you") on the analogy of the Pauline writings (cf. also Rev. 22:21): *hē charis meta sou* ("grace be with you [sing.]") or *meth' hymōn* (𝕜 pm sy) ("with you [plur.]"), *amēn.*

---

94. The reading *ekklēsias* (307 321 fu) is evidence for interpreting it as a reference to the church; 465 + *tēs en ephesō* introduces the tradition that the elder was a resident of Ephesus.

EXEGESIS OF 3 JOHN

3 John is a Christian letter written to a single individual, one Gaius, otherwise unknown. It has all the charm of an occasional writing and shows how a Christian person in authority speaks to a friendly member of the laity. Added to this, it gives us a brief glimpse into the everyday life of an early Christian community. This charm of a unique, nondidactic missive is counterbalanced by certain difficulties and disadvantages. We can no longer reconstruct the precise situation or fully understand much of what the author is getting at.

Just as in a regular private letter, the author discusses in succession a series of problems that are giving him some concern. There are three of these. First, he has a request for hospitable reception and care of itinerant missionaries, whose arrival in the community is expected shortly (vv. 2–8). Then there is information for the recipient about a letter sent by the elder to the community and about the behavior of Diotrephes (vv. 9f.). Lastly, there is a commendation of a certain Demetrius (vv. 11f.). The letter closes, like 2 John, with the hope that the author will soon be able to visit the recipient, and with greetings (vv. 13–15).

Since the letter is addressed to a believer whose faith ("truth," v. 3) and love (v. 6) have been proved, admonitions to mutual love and the rebuttal of heretical teachers retreat into the background. The main interest of 3 John for us lies not in its theology but in what it tells us about the history of church polity. The author allows us a glimpse of the ongoing life of the church, the many things that are going on there and the way the Spirit is at work, as well as the inadequacies and tensions current among human beings. It is closely related in language and theology to 1 and 2 John and offers a welcome supplement to the other two Johannine letters, in which it is more the theologian and father of the community who speaks.

THE PRESCRIPT

(3 John 1)

[1]The elder to the beloved Gaius, whom I love in truth.

1 The prescript is shorter than that of any other letter in the New Testament. This brings it closer to a lot of extant private letters from Greco-Roman times than any other Christian letter that has survived.[95] This prescript (to be distinguished from the address, which was placed on the outside of the letter)[96] mentions only the sender and the recipient. Curiously enough, there is no opening greeting (*salutatio*)[97] at the beginning, though there is a wish for peace at the end of the letter (v. 15). The elder is no other than the writer of 2 John. This self-appellation in such a friendly and fatherly letter (v. 15) heightens the certainty that the author is some outstanding person. He deserves this epithet in a special, exclusive way (see 2 John 1). Gaius was a very common name. We know other Christians of that name in the New Testament: There was a Gaius at Corinth (1 Cor. 1:14), who was probably identical with Paul's host mentioned in Rom. 16:23. There is also another Gaius from Macedonia, one of Paul's travel companions mentioned in Acts 19:29. Finally there is a Gaius from Derbe in Acts 20:4. The recipient of 3 John was apparently the center of a circle of friends (cf. v. 15), an exemplary believer and a confidant, though not a church official.[98] The sender calls him his "beloved," which is how Paul and the Christian community at large addressed one another among themselves.[99] The author also adds, as in 2 John 1, "whom I love in truth." "In truth" underscores as in 2 John 1 the genuine and sincere nature of his love. He does not merely love Gaius for his loyalty to the faith (v. 3, "to the truth") but also for his active fraternal behavior (v. 6, "your love"). It is possible that Gaius owed his faith to the elder (v. 4, "my children"). This, however, is uncertain since the elder appears to regard all of the faithful to whom he feels an obligation as his children (1 John 2:1 *teknia mou*—though this is not so strong as *ta ema tekna;* see on v. 4).

FIRST SECTION

PRAISE FOR GAIUS AND A REQUEST THAT HE SHOULD SUPPORT ITINERANT PREACHERS WHEN THEY ARRIVE (2 JOHN 2-8)

[2]Beloved, I pray that all may go well with you and that you may be in good health, just as it is well with your soul. [3]I was overjoyed when some of the friends arrived and testified to your faithfulness to the truth, namely how you walk in the truth. [4]I have no greater joy than this, to hear that my children are walking in the truth.

95. See Roller, *Das Formular der paulinischen Briefe,* 61 and n. 263 (pp. 445–47).

96. See Deissmann, *Light from the Ancient East,* 148f. n. 5; Roller, *Das Formular,* 59 and n. 204 (pp. 392–94).

97. In private letters that happened "very rarely" and "only accidentally" (Roller, *Das Formular,* 61; cf. n. 265). Was it lost in copying perhaps because all it said was *chairein?*

98. *Const. Apost.* 7.46 would have us believe that the recipient was (later?) bishop of Pergamum. J. Chapman thinks that 3 John was addressed to Thessalonica (*JTS* 5 [1904] 357); V. Bartlet opts for Thyatira (*JTS* 6 [1905] 204ff.). Both suggestions have too little to commend them.

99. Rom. 16:5, 8, 9, 12; Eph. 6:21; Col. 1:7; 4:7, 9, 14; 2 Tim. 1:2; Phlm. 1.—Acts 15:25; Rom. 1:7; 1 Cor. 4:14; 10:14; etc.; Jas. 1:16; 1 Pet. 2:11; 4:12; 2 Pet. 3:1, 8, 14, 15, 17.

⁵Beloved, you do faithfully whatever you do for the friends, even though they are strangers to you; they have testified to your love before the church. You will do well to send them on in a manner worthy of God; ⁷for they began their journey for the sake of Christ, accepting no support from non-believers. ⁸Therefore we ought to support such people, so that we may become co-workers with the truth.

2   The good wishes usual in ancient letters for the welfare and health of the recipients are employed here by this Christian author. He hopes that things will go well with Gaius in every way (*peri pantōn* is to be taken with *euodousthai*);[100] as he says emphatically. After the general *euodousthai* ("go well");[101] the elder particularly wishes him good health. Probably he does so out of politeness, not because Gaius was ill. Very similar formulas are found in many private letters written on papyrus.[102] The following *kathōs*-clause draws attention to the inner well-being of the recipient. The elder wishes for Gaius the spiritual well-being that he also wishes for him physically. This should not be taken in the Greek sense of a dichotomy between body and soul, an idea that is hardly known in the New Testament.[103] There is no contrast between body and soul here.[104] Rather, Gaius is being addressed in his entire *persona* though from different angles. As the sequel shows, the term *psychē* points to his religious and moral behavior, his efforts to attain salvation. The most likely parallel in the New Testament is the phrase "salvation of the *psychē*" or similar phrases, again not intended in the sense of the salvation of the soul as distinct from the body, but for the salvation of the whole person in the totality of his or her being.[105] The word to Gaius may be compared with what is said to the recipients of 1 Peter: "You have purified your souls (*tas psychas hymōn*) by your obedience to the truth, so that you have genuine mutual love" (1:22).

3   Thus the elder can provide a reason for addressing Gaius in this way.[106] He has heard a good testimony about the way Gaius is living the Christian life

---

100. BDF §229.2 think that it has the same meaning as the usual *pro pantōn* (=primarily), as in the papyrus letters (see below, n. 102), though they are unable to give any more examples.

101. The word generally has the sense even in the Septuagine (Josh. 1:8; Judg. 18:5; 1 Chron. 13:2; 2 Chron. 7:11; 13:12; etc.; see esp. Tobit 4:6 (*hoi poiountes alētheian euodōthēsontai*); in the New Testament, see 1 Cor. 16:2; Rom. 16:10; according to BAGD 323, s.v., it is also found in papyri; see Moulton-Milligan, 263, s.f.

102. *Pro de pantōn hygiainein se euchomai* (*POxy.* 292.11 [a. 25 p.]; *BGU* 2.423; *PFay.* 117.27; *BGU* 3.846 [*dia pantōn* . . .]). *POxy.* 119.5: a refractory son threatens his father: *oute hygienō se* (=*hygiainō* from *hygiainō*), "nor do I wish you good health" (Deissmann, *Light from the Ancient East*, 176). See also Deissmann, *Bible Studies;* also *Light from the Ancient East*, 179 n. 25; Moulton-Milligan, 647.—*Euchomai* thus means "to wish" not "to pray" (if that is the meaning *pros ton theon* is added, 2 Cor. 13:7); "to pray" is otherwise expressed by *proseuchomai*.

103. See J. Schmid, *LTK* 1:604–15; for Paul, see also Bultmann, *Theology* 1:203–5; W. D. Stacey, *The Pauline View of Man* (London, 1956) 121–27.

104. Philo (*Heres* 285) on the other hand formulates it from a Greek understanding: . . . *euodē de ta sōmatos pros hygieian te kai ischyn, euodē de ta psychēs pros apolausin aretōn.*

105. Cf. Heb. 10:39; Jas. 1:21; 5:20; 1 Pet. 1:9; though already in Mark 8:35, 36, 37 and par.; Matt. 10:28; Luke 21:19. Cf. BAGD 893, s.v. 1, c.

106. *Gar* is missing from ℵ 5 33 218 al., Vg sa bo arm eth; but on text-critical grounds it may be regarded as assured.

Exegesis

and it has given him great pleasure (the same phrase as in 2 John 4). The brothers and sisters in the faith, who praised Gaius so highly after visiting him, had come to where the elder was and reported to him how Gaius had offered them hospitality (v. 6) although they were strangers (v. 5). So the *alētheia* ("faithfulness") of Gaius they attested to must mean not only his orthodoxy, his knowledge of the revelation (2 John 1), but also his perseverence in love by "walking in the truth, just as we have been commanded by the Father" (2 John 4). *Alētheia* is here the human, outward, and visible sign of that *alētheia* which belongs to the divine nature and fulfills the very being of those who are born of God (cf. 1 John 1:8; 2:4; 2 John 2). The *kathōs*-clause, joined to *sou tē alētheia* (NRSV "your faithfulness to the truth") brings the witness of these brothers and sisters still more to the fore; they show how[107] Gaius "walks in the truth" (see on 2 John 4). In other words, they gave a lively description of how Gaius was helping the brothers and sisters out of a spirit of faith. The *sy* ("you") in the *kathōs*-clause need not be emphasized or have a polemical nuance, but like the *egō* ("I") in v. 1 may be a peculiarity of style.[108] Of course a polemical tone may be there too (cf. vv. 9f.).

4 The author had apparently had other painful experiences in his communities. So he underscores his joy over Gaius by assuring him of his paternal feelings. He was overjoyed[109] to hear such good reports about his children. Referring affectionately to his protégés as his children, the elder is not necessarily suggesting that, like Paul, he had converted them by his preaching (1 Cor. 4:15; Phlm. 10). This is not probable for one who uses this metaphor for being born of God, which was a supernatural process. He calls them his children (*teknia*, 1 John 2:1, 12, 28; 3:7, 18; 4:4; 5:21; *tekna*, 2 John 1, 4) because of his special patriarchal position. The possessive pronoun strengthens his close relationship to them.[110] Along with *ta ema* (instead of *mou*) this verse exhibits still further peculiarities of style (*meizoteran, toutōn . . . hina*).[111]

5 Following his words of praise for his "children," the elder starts with a new address ("Beloved"). Then comes an admonition. They must continue to be active

---

107. On this use of *kathōs* to introduce indirect speech, see BAGD 391, s.v. 5 (referring further to Acts 15:14). *Kathōs* is said to stand for the otherwise usual *hōs* or *pōs* (BDF §396).

108. We need not conclude that it is an Aramaism, since it occurs equally in Greek; cf. Moulton, 136f.; Mayser, *Grammatik*, II, 1:62f.

109. The reading *charin* (instead of *charan*) in B 1891 2143 2298 Vg bo perhaps betrays theological reflection on the grace of the preaching ministry, or it is modeled on Pauline sense and language (Rom. 1:5; 1 Cor. 3:10; Phil. 1:7; etc.) *Charan* in 3 John 4 clearly follows upon *echarēn* in v. 3 and is certainly original (*contra* Chaine and Lagrange, *Critique textuelle*, 565.

110. Thumb, *TLZ* (1903) 421; Moulton (59) see in the use of *emos*, which had otherwise become rare, a peculiarity of dialect in the Koine of Asia Minor. Its position before the article could lead to a certain emphasis (BDF §285.1), which, however, would be sufficiently explained by the fatherly joy; but there is no need for this assumption; see Mayser, *Grammatik*, II, 2:67f. There is no suggestion of any *opposition* to other preachers.

111. *Meizoteros* is a double comparative, a vulgar neologism in Koine; see BDF §61.2.—The *hina*-clause is, as often in John, epexegetic (instead of *tou*+infinitive); cf. esp. John 15:13; BDF §394; Radermacher, *Grammatik*, 190, 192.

in support of the itinerant missionaries on their way through.[112] The urgency of supporting Gaius is pinpointed by the disapproval of Diotrephes (v. 10) who, it seems, is trying to bar his community from all external influences, depriving them of all vital contact with their sister churches from an egotistic desire to lord it over them. In opposition to such unwholesome endeavors the elder introduces his younger friend to the wider world of the universal church. The Christian spirit of mutual love and missionary zeal bursts the constricting fetters of ecclesiastical parochialism. It is possible that Diotrephes was making trouble for Gaius on account of his hospitality toward the missionaries (v. 10, "he refuses to welcome the friends"). In view of this the elder assures Gaius that he is acting faithfully (*piston poieis,* "you do faithfully").[113] He is sustaining all of the brothers and sisters in Christ, especially the guests from out of town. Gaius must be supported in this fraternal behavior. The kind of help he was giving (*ergazesthai*)[114] is made clear by the next verse. He has received them (as guests, and then) supplied them with everything they needed for their journey (*propempsas,* "to send them on") in a generous spirit, "worthy of God" (*axiōs tou theou*). This verse is a fine example of early Christian hospitality.[115]

6   These itinerant preachers whom Gaius had helped reported gratefully "before the church," presumably their own home church. The term *ekklēsia,* which is found only here in the Johannine writings (except in the Apocalypse) and in vv. 9f., refers to the local community (as is usually the case in Paul). The phrase *enōpion ekklēsias* means "before (the assembled) congregation."[116] That need not necessarily be the church in which the elder resides. It could be that he has just heard of it. The purpose for mentioning the laudatory report is to encourage Gaius to further efforts on behalf of the missionaries ("you do well to send them on"). This fresh look at the further travel plans of the missionaries (the Greek is actually future, "you will do well," contra to NRSV) begins only in the relative clause, v. 6b, while previously (v. 5, "you do well," present tense) it was the general conduct of Gaius that was being praised.[117] When the impending visit of the itinerant missionaries takes place on their way through, Gaius is urged to behave

---

112. On itinerant missionaries, see Harnack, *Mission and Expansion,* 319ff.; Goguel, *The Primitive Church,* 136f.

113. *Piston poiein ti*=to act in a loyal way (BAGD 662, s.v. 1, b); *piston* is placed first predicatively to give emphasis. Gaius has shown himself to be *pistos,* that is, reliable, obedient to the instructions he has received; cf. the *doulos agathos kai pistos* in the parables of Jesus (Matt. 24:45; 25:21, 23; Luke 12:42), as well as the way Paul speaks of his fellow workers (1 Cor. 4:17; Eph. 6:21; Col. 1:7; 4:7, 9). Gaius has shown himself to be a true disciple of the elder (cf. v. 4) and a co-worker with the "truth" (v. 8).

114. *Ergazesthai* does not denote the work of an office bearer in the church or a semiministerial activity like *kopian* in 1 Thess. 5:12; 1 Cor. 16:16; 1 Tim. 5:17 (*contra* Windisch); rather, it denotes voluntary acts of charity performed for other people, as in Matt. 26:10; Gal. 6:10; Col. 3:23.

115. Cf. on 2 John 10.

116. The absence of the article, which causes Brooke to plead for "assembly," does not speak unconditionally for a special use of *ekklēsia;* cf. *en mesō ekklēsias hymnēsō se* (Heb. 2:12, quoting Ps. 22:23). The article is often dropped after prepositions (Mayser, *Grammatik,* II, 2:35ff.; BDF §255). The local association of *enōpion* is in favor of "congregation."

117. *Piston poieis* in v. 5 is therefore not to be taken as a future (Büchsel), but suggests the rule for behavior generally; cf. *opheilomen* (v. 8), with *oun* drawing the consequence.

in a manner "worthy of God."[118] For they are engaged in the service of God's word. Their behavior must be different from that of the itinerant Cynic philosophers, with their bedraggled appearance, and from the rapacious mendicant priests of Dea Syria![119]

7   They went forth "for the sake of the name" (NRSV marg.), that is, for the sake of Christ or for his honor. The phrase is too vague to refer to God![120] Moreover, "the name" seems to have become a generally accepted designation for Christ![121] Paul similarly regards it as his obligation through the grace of his apostolate to bring about obedience to the faith among the Gentiles "for the sake of his name" (Rom. 1:5). It was for no other purpose, certainly not for their personal esteem or selfish gain ("accepting no support") that the missionaries mentioned here went out to proclaim the faith. Christ's charge to his disciples (John 20:21) was taken up by the second generation, who delivered the gospel message far and wide with conspicuous zeal. The picture we get here is of itinerant messengers like those of the *Didache* (11.3–5). Insofar as they prove their legitimacy as genuine envoys of the church, they must be welcomed "like the Lord" (*Did.* 11.4; cf. Matt. 10:40=Luke 10:16; John 13:20).

Yet unlike the *Didache,* 3 John does not seem to know anything of *false* itinerant preachers, profiting financially from their high office. On the contrary, these missionaries have high ideals. They refuse to accept support from nonbelievers. As a result they are in danger of being reduced to penury. The principle that Christian brothers and sisters must supply their needs had been followed since the earliest days of the Christian mission and goes back to the instruction of Jesus himself (Matt. 10:10=Luke 10:7; 1 Cor. 9:14; 1 Tim. 5:18). The nonbelievers, whose help they refuse, are not newly converted Christians but the general public who listen to their preaching, from whom they refuse to accept any money, unlike pagan preachers (see on v. 6). But they may also be following the example of Paul (1 Cor. 9:15-18; cf. 4:11f.), who refused to receive alms from his recent converts.

8   The early Christians ("we"), many of whom had by that time been Christians since their earliest days,[122] are under obligation to support the missionaries,

---

118. *Propempein* here does not mean merely "to escort" as in Acts 20:38; 21:5; Rom. 15:24; but "to equip for a journey," as in Acts 15:3; 1 Cor. 16:6, 11; 2 Cor. 1:16; Titus 3:16.

119. See the inscription from Kefr-Hauar in Syria, in which a slave of the Syrian goddess boasts that "each journey brought in 70 bags," goods he had begged for (Deissmann, *Light from the Ancient East,* 109) and the picture Lucian describes (*Lucius* 35ff.; *Metam.* 8.24ff.) of the efforts made by the devotees of Dea Syria (collections taken up from the spectators after ecstatic dances). Their reputation was just what would be expected; cf. Harnack, *Mission and Expansion* 2:140.

120. The reference to the use of *haššēm* for Yahweh (Büchsel) would be out of place at this time in a letter to a Gentile Christian.

121. Cf. Acts 5:41 with 4:17f.; 5:28, 40; 8:14; 9:10; etc.; 1 Pet. 4:14, 16; further Ignatius, *Eph.* 3.1; 7.1; *Phld.* 10.1; *Barn.* 16.8; the use probably follows dominical sayings such as Matt. 10:22, 40ff.; 18:5; 19:29; 24:5, 9 par.; John 15:21; see Billerbeck, *Kommentar* 3:779; Bietenhard, *TDNT* 5:272f.

122. Cf. the conversion of whole families in John 4:53; Acts 10:48; 16:15, 33; 1 Cor. 1:16; 2 Tim. 1:16; 4:19.

mainly by meeting their material needs, that is, almsgiving![123] This explains a good deal about the early Christian understanding of missionary obligation. Support "worthy of God" and supplies for the journey are the way those who cannot literally follow Jesus' missionary command make their contribution. In this way they become "co-workers with the truth." The dative (*tȩ̄ alētheia̧*) probably indicates their personal commitment, not the reason for their cooperation![124] The "truth" is thus in a way personified![125] It is hardly a power working independently for the missionary cause (cf. Büchsel), but only working in partnership with the missionaries themselves. It is a vital, effective power in their hearts (cf. John 17:17f.; 1 John 4:6; 2 John 2). The phrase "so that we may become" probably does not indicate a totally new relationship, but suggests rather that we must prove ourselves as co-workers with the truth![126]

SECOND SECTION

THE BEHAVIOR OF DIOTREPHES (3 JOHN 9–10)

[9]I have written something to the church; but Diotrephes, who likes to put himself first, does not acknowledge our authority. [10]So if I come, I will call attention to what he is doing in spreading false charges against us. And not content with those charges, he refuses to welcome the friends, and even prevents those who want to do so and expels them from the church.

9 The second concern that moves the author follows closely on his words of praise for Gaius. The author spends so many words on this because there are opposing powers at work, trying to frustrate the elder's attempts to further the mission. The letter he mentions here must have been concerned with the welcome and assistance given to the itinerant missionaries. So it cannot be identified with 2 John![127] It must be one of the lost letters. Later copyists tried to argue from the little particle *an* (giving the meaning "I would have written") that it refers to a letter that was never written![128] Although the elder mentions that letter here,

---

123. In profane literature *hypolambanein* often means "to welcome as a guest" (so too BAGD 845, s.v. 2), but it can also have the general sense of "to support"; cf. Moulton-Milligan 658, s.v.; Passow, *Handwörterbuch* II, 2:2137, s.v. 1, b. This general meaning is preferable here after *mēden lambanontes*. The continuation of the journey (*propempsas*) was already envisioned in v. 6.

124. So too BAGD 788, s.v.; the dative of the person is usual (Passow, *Handwörterbuch* II, 2:1715, s.v.; Liddell and Scott 1711, s.v. Cf. the parallel in content (quoted by Windisch) in *Ps. Clem. Hom.* 17.19 (*tȩ̄ alētheia̧ synergēsai*). On "cooperation in view of . . ." (*eis*), cf. Col. 4:11.

125. Cf. Papias in Eusebius *H.E.* 3.39.4, according to whom the commandments originate *ap' autēs tēs alētheias*.

126. Cf. John 15:8 and W. Bauer, *Johannes*, ad loc. Of the passages quoted there a few perhaps should be dropped (e.g., John 20:27; 1 Cor. 14:20), since *ginesthai* can also be used in place of *einai;* but there are still enough passages left to confirm this nuance.

127. *Contra* Bresky, Zahn, Calmes, Loisy, Wendt, Dibelius (*RGG* 3:348), Jülicher-Fascher (*Einleitung,* 235), Meinertz (*Einleitung,* 282), et al.; with Brooke, Büchsel, Bonsirven, Chaine, Charue, Dodd, Feine-Behm (*Einleitung,* 264f.), Michaelis (*Einleitung,* 305), et al.

128. Instead of *ti* the reading *an* occurs in ℵ³ 33 81 181 307 431 436 al. Vg sy. The anxiety was not about the loss of the letter but about the authority of the elder. On the textual criticism, see Lagrange, *Critique textuelle,* 566f. (*contra* Harnack).

it does not follow that Gaius was somewhere else at that time (Büchsel). Nor is it certain that Diotrephes had suppressed the letter from the community. The author points to what he had written previously in order to focus more sharply on the stubborn and uncooperative Diotrephes.

This Diotrephes — the name was not unusual[129] — is marked by a desire to lord it over other people, combined with a lack of moral authority. This is described by the word *philoprōteuein*. The expression — found thus far only in 3 John 9 — is probably synonymous with the adjective *philoprōtos* = "loving the first place."[130] This need not imply that he was claiming a new office. Rather, all suggestions, whether it means aspiring to an office or misusing the same, striving for pre-eminence or autocratic rule, ambition, vanity or conceit, are open to question. The actual position of Diotrephes can perhaps be gathered from the information given in v. 10![131] He refuses to accept the authority of the elder (*ouk epidechetai*).[132] On what grounds we are unfortunately not informed, but it may refer to the dispatching of the itinerant missionaries. The switch to the first person plural (*hēmas*) may be due to the author's style; it is hardly an authorial plural![133] The plural occurs again with *phlyarōn* ("spreading false charges") in v. 10 and *martyrein* ("every one has testified") in v. 12. Thus he is obviously referring to himself.

10   In a visit planned shortly (*eutheōs*, "soon," v. 14) the elder will "call attention"[134] to the deeds of Diotrephes. This does not sound like a disciplinary action — the juridical terminology of a later period would be out of place here. But it does sound like a serious public rebuke. There are four charges which the elder levels against this all-too-independent leader of the community. First, Diotrephes maligns him using bad language and bringing baseless charges against him![135] This is more than just name-calling or gossip. It has to do with their different standpoint in ecclesiastical and especially missionary questions. The connection with what follows ("not content with these charges") makes it likely that Diotrephes took a different line over missionary policy, directed as it was by the

---

129. See the excursus in Windisch, ad loc.—Findlay argues from the rarity and the etymology of the name that D. belonged to the aristocracy—a farfetched notion (p. 41).

130. See Liddell and Scott II, 1939; Moulton-Milligan, 671; BAGD 860f.

131. The position that Diotrephes occupied in the church remains in question, and opinions vary. See the views collected together by E. Haenchen (*TRu* 26 [1960] 267–81). Following him, E. Käsemann has modified his view; see *Exegetische Versuche und Besinnungen II* (Göttingen, 1964) 133f. n. 1. See further R. Bultmann, *Johannine Epistles*, 101 n. 8.

132. This is the only example of this meaning in the New Testament, though cf. 1 Macc. 10:46; Sir. 51:46; Polybius 6.24, 7; *PPar.* 63.161 (BAGD 292, s.v. 2.—The reference in Polybius is to be corrected).—E. Käsemann interprets it in accordance with his hypothesis (see Introduction), *epidechesthai* = to enter a closed society ("Ketzer und Zeuge," 294).

133. Mayser speaks of a "generalizing" plural, appearing in official and, more rarely, in private correspondence, when the writer includes other people like himself (*Grammatik*, II, 1:40f.). However, in everyday language the singular and plural alternate without any obvious psychological reason. According to Moulton (137f.) "I" and "we" alternate in these documents (papyri) without reason.

134. *Hypomimnēskō* in the same sense, that is, in the parenesis given by a church officer, as also in 2 Tim. 2:14; *1 Clem.* 62.3.

135. This is the only occurrence of *phlyarein* in the New Testament, though it is sufficiently attested in Koine; see BAGD 862, s.v.; Moulton-Milligan 673, s.v.; Liddell and Scott 1945, s.v.

elder from headquarters. So he was trying his best to counteract this wider influence. Along with this he may have been making further accusations of a personal kind ("false charges") against the elder. Perhaps he was protesting the way Diotrephes was hampering the community. Paul had to put up with similar disputes over his authority, though the slogans that were being used in his case were different (cf. 2 Cor. 3:1; 4:11f.; 10:7ff.; 12:19ff.; Phil. 1:17; 3:2ff.). The main difference was that with Diotrephes his egotism was being concealed under the cloak of ecclesiastical superiority![136]

Above and beyond this personal squabble over the elder's authority, Diotrephes has been guilty of a second misdemeanor: he has refused to show hospitality to the missionaries. His shortsighted struggle against the influence of the wider church has driven him to refuse lodging to the missionaries on their way through![137] That would have been a special duty incumbent upon him in view of his position. This means therefore that he was sinning against the basic commandment of Christian faith, against mutual love (cf. 1 John 2:9f.; 3:11ff., 23; 4:11f., 19ff.; 2 John 5).

Closely connected with this ("not . . . and even")[138] is the third charge the elder brings against Diotrephes. He compounds his faults by misusing his position and preventing members of the community from showing hospitality to the missionaries when they were ready to do so![139] But there are difficulties. Gaius is clearly one of those who were ready to welcome the missionaries and was trying to stop Diotrephes from carrying out his wishes (vv. 5f.). However, he was not—as the sequel makes clear—excluded from the community. Such an interpretation would be avoided if *kōlyei* ("prevents") and *ekballei* ("expels") were taken as conative presents![140] But this solution does not commend itself because the last three complaints against Diotrephes are closely tied together by *oute-kai-kai* ("neither-and-and"). Also the first of them, viz., that he refused to welcome the missionaries, is an actual fact. However, the context shows that the attempt to "refuse" the church members remained an unsuccessful attempt. The community set limits against this individual and his ambitions. The faithful saw no reason to give him unqualified obedience because of his official position—despite the threat of excommunication. Evidently he had no jurisdiction in this matter.

We come now to the fourth and last complaint against Diotrephes. He is trying to expel his opponents from the community. The Greek expression used (*ekballei*) does not seem to be a technical term. It is not equivalent to excommunication

---

136. In his study of 3 John, von Harnack tries to explain the tension between the elder and Diotrephes as due to the opposition between the old order of the Spirit with its missionary zeal and the institutionalization of the church with its structured ministry. *Per contra,* Streeter attributes it to the differences between the "Archbishop" in Ephesus and his local suffragan (*Primitive Church,* 88f.). On this matter, see R. Schnackenburg, "Der Streit zwischen dem Verfasser von 3 Joh und Diotrephes und seine verfassungsgeschichtliche Bedeutung," *MTZ* 4 (1953) 18–26.

137. *Epidechesthai* thus has a different meaning from that in v. 9; the same shift of meaning occurs in 1 Macc. 10:1 (cf., on the other hand, 46); 12:8, 43, etc.

138. As in John 4:11; cf. BDF §445.3.

139. *Epidechomenous* is read by C 323 1739 Vg[cl] sy sa arm obviously because of *epidechesthai.*

140. So in the first edition with Westcott, Findlay (42 n. 1); *per contra* Dodd ad loc.—Poggel (163) prefers to take *adelphous* as the object of *ekballei;* that is too harsh linguistically and farfetched.

from synagogue or church.[141] There is no need to think of any such formal act. Diotrephes may merely have turned up at the gathering of the community and tried to get together a majority against the refractory members and railroad a ban against them. If however we take *ekballei* as a statement of fact (see above) and compare it with Luke 6:22 ("exclude you, revile you, and profane you") it would necessarily be a judicial act, even if not quite the same thing as the later ecclesiastical excommunication.[142] But in effect the attempt was unsuccessful, for the author does not tell us that Gaius was actually excommunicated. Rather, he still seems to belong to the same community after it has all blown over.

After all this, it is difficult to get a picture of Diotrephes' official position. Possibly he was a monarchical bishop who was disregarding the admonition of 1 Pet. 5:3 (Chaine; cf. Charue). He may also have been one of a circle of elders who, on the strength of his character, his "successful demagoguery," had risen above his colleagues.[143] But we get a stronger impression that he was the sole leader of the community. Otherwise why would the elder not have resorted to the collective body? Yet his position could not have been one of sole rule. The community seems to continue to have a say, just like those ancient authorities, as represented by the elder. We are in a period of transition; the monarchical episcopate, as we know it from the letters of Ignatius, is in the process of being established.

THIRD SECTION

COMMENDATION OF DEMETRIUS (3 JOHN 11-12)

[11]Beloved, do not imitate what is evil but imitate what is good. Whoever does good is from God; whoever does evil has not seen God. [12]Everyone has testified favorably about Demetrius, and so has the truth itself. We also testify for him, and you know that our witness is true.

11   The letter writer is motivated by yet another, pleasant request, and he leads into it with a new salutation and a general observation. In admonishing his readers not to imitate what is evil, he still has Diotrephes in mind, just as in turning to the positive side he is already thinking of Demetrius, whom he wishes to

---

141. Similarly, John 9:34f. should not be taken as an official sentence of excommunication from the synagogue (cf. 9:22); it is a spontaneous action of rejection of a healed man and implies in the first instance banishment from the temple (cf. Lagrange, ad loc.; *contra* Tillmann, Bauer, Bultmann, et al.). No formal decision is involved. Similarly, the man who was formerly blind is not guilty of the "crime" mentioned in 9:22 (the crime of confessing Jesus as the Messiah). At the same time the expression may have been in the evangelist's mind a deliberately vague one with an ambiguous meaning; see BAGD 237, s.v. 1; Hauck, *TDNT* 1:528, n. 6. Against the history-of-religions background, John 9:34f. ("they drove him out") certainly means exclusion from the synagogue (see the commentary on GJohn, 2:252). Exclusion from the building denotes at the same time being driven out of the Jewish religious fellowship.

142. *Contra* the first edition; on this point, see esp. W. Doskocil, *Der Bann in der Urkirche* (Munich, 1958) 42f., 100f.

143. See Dodd, ad loc.; Michaelis, *Einleitung*, 303.

commend. He uses the neuter because he does not wish to identify Diotrephes directly as an evil person, only to characterize his type of behavior. But he warns them seriously against such un-Christian conduct; it destroys fellowship with God. Verse 11b (in chiastic arrangement) mentions the evildoer after the one who behaves well and once again stresses the warning. What is said about the two types is substantially the same. "To be from God"=to share God's nature and being (cf. 1 John 3:10; 4:4, 6; 5:19; John 8:47) and "to have seen God"=to know God, to be in union with him (cf. 1 John 3:6; John 14:9) are simply different terms for the leading Johannine theme of fellowship with God (see Excursus 2). Doing good is not based on the direct vision of God (something John has previously rejected; see John 1:18; 5:37; 6:46; 1 John 4:12), *contra* Windisch. Nor could v. 11 refer to the heretical teachers. Basically, this verse, like 1 John 3:10, contrasts the children of God with the children of the devil, though not with the same acerbity. In any case it provides strong support for regarding 1 and 3 John as the work of the same author.

12   Now the author expresses openly his positive request by beginning right away with the name of his protégé, thus bringing him to the fore — still in implicit contrast with Diotrephes. Who this Demetrius was — it was a common Hellenistic name[144] — and what role he played at that particular moment are completely unknown to us. He is not the same as the Ephesian goldsmith mentioned in Acts 19:24, Paul's opponent, who by this time was probably long dead. We may perhaps surmise that he was one of the itinerant preachers whose arrival had just been announced (vv. 6–8). Perhaps he was one of their leaders. He might also have been the bearer of the letter (cf. the commendation of Silvanus in 1 Pet. 5:12), who acted as a commissary for the elder. The commendation is threefold: (1) "Everyone" gives him a good testimony. This refers to his general reputation as a Christian in the local churches; cf. the testimony given to Gaius in vv. 3 and 6. (2) This testimony is confirmed "by the truth itself." This is perhaps a general turn of speech![145] It hardly justifies deeper reflections about the specifically Johannine personification of *alētheia*.[146] This acquires personality as a divine being and reality at most in the concept of "Spirit of truth" (cf. John 14:17; 15:26; 16:13; 1 John 4:6; 5:6). However, it is not to be supposed (see Ambroggi) that the Spirit has borne testimony to Demetrius in some special way (cf. Acts 13:2). Like v. 3, it only provides additional confirmation. (3) This general testimony of the church, supplemented by the personal testimony of the elder, has intrinsic significance of its own. For this recommendation is of special importance for Gaius ("and you know . . ."). The elder has a unique authority which makes his witness trustworthy (*alēthēs*). His exalted position is recognized by Gaius and his friends. Demetrius is probably also one of this circle of friends who share

144. See Moulton-Milligan 144, s.v.; Dittenberger, *Syll²*, index.

145. A certain personification of "truth" is also found in Demosthenes, *C. Neaer.* 15 (quoted in Windisch and Büchsel, ad loc.); *PPar.* 46: *parakolouthēsanta se tē alētheiạ* cf. Mayser, *Grammatik*, II, 2:31, 3f.); Polybius 1.21.3; 84.6. Thus it is possible in non-Christian literature.

146. Windisch thinks it refers to Christ (John 14:6); cf. further Belser, Dodd, ad loc. Bonsirven and Chaine, among others, are critical.

the elder's confidence. This verse also suggests how the Christian community in a time of consolidation and expansion knows how to protect itself from alien influences — the positive side of the admonition given in 2 John 10f. Such letters of commendation are known to us from other literature![147]

THE EPISTOLARY CONCLUSION (3 JOHN 13-15)

[13]I have much to write to you, but I would rather not write with pen and ink; [14]instead I hope to see you soon, and we will talk together face to face.
[15]Peace to you. The friends send you their greetings. Greet the friends there, each by name.

13   The conclusion of this letter is very similar to that of 2 John. It confirms what was already suggested by the opening salutation, viz., that the sender of 2 and 3 John was the same person. Moreover, the author assures his recipient that he has much more to write to him![148] But he does not wish to do this — *ou thelōn* — is more decisive than *ouk eboulēthēn* in 2 John (NRSV translates both "I would rather not") — with pen and ink. The writer does not pull his punches when judging other people. He is not hiding anything. "With pen and ink" is almost a conventional formula![149]

14   The elder announces his intended visit to the local community (cf. v. 10) in the near future ("soon"). He plans then to speak "face to face" with Gaius — the same phrase as he used in 2 John 12. The word "soon" (*eutheōs*) justifies our thinking that the elder's departure is more imminent than it was when he wrote 2 John, for he does not use the word *eutheōs* there. But whether it is the same journey or not we do not know. Does it mean he is planning a round trip, or even a tour of inspection? Even if it is the latter, he hardly intends to exercise juridical authority (see on v. 10).

15   Before his final greetings the author inserts a wish for their peace, though without any Christian amplification or rewording (cf. Gal. 6:16; Eph. 6:23; 2 Thess. 3:16). So it is quite brief and terse (cf. 1 Pet. 5:14). This is consistent with the distinctly private character of the letter. The peace greeting betrays the born Semite (cf. on 2 John 3). He has, however, adopted the Hellenistic epistolary style, including formulalike expressions (see on v. 2). The Christians preferred to use the same greeting the risen Christ gave to his disciples (John 20:19, 21, 26) to the conventional *errōso* ("farewell"). Also, the final greetings are kept short, with no mention of the names of the persons being greeted. The elder and his readers constituted a circle of friends in both churches. These friends may have regarded

---

147. Cf. e.g., Lietzmann, *Griechische Papyri* (Kleine Texte 14⁴) #13, line 16 (*POxy.* 6.930); #15, line 16 (*PGrenf.* 2.73).
148. The imperfect *eichon* denotes (as in classical Greek) obligation or possibility (BDF §358), and the aorist infinitive *grapsai* is accordingly quite natural (as in Matt. 23:23; 26:9; 1 Cor. 5:10; etc.).
149. See Windisch, ad loc.

the elder as their "master." That is why he passes on to them the greetings of the friends who are with him[150] and asks Gaius to greet the friends in his church individually. *Kat' onoma* ("by name") in this sense is found elsewhere, mainly in letters.[151] The elder's circle of friends can hardly have formed a "party" in the two local communities (*contra* Büchsel). There is nothing striking about this special greeting to his friends. After all, this is a highly personal letter.

---

150. The reading *adelphoi* (A 33 69 81* 436 1827 sy[hmg]) is secondary and obliterates the special coloring of this confidential letter.

151. Cf. the letter of the Egyptian Sempronius to his mother (second half of the second century) in Deissmann, *Light from the Ancient East,* 161, lines 14f.; *POxy.* 2.123; *PTebt.* 2.299 (quoted in Brooke); *POxy.* 6.930, line 26 (Lietzmann, Kleine Texte 14, p. 14); Arist 247; Ignatius, *Smyrn.* 13.2.

BIBLIOGRAPHY

TEXTS (SOURCES AND TRANSLATIONS)

BIBLE

Biblia Hebraica Stuttgartensia. Edited by K. Elliger and W. Rudolph. Stuttgart, 1967–77.

Septuaginta. Edited by A. Rahlfs. 2 vols. Stuttgart, 1935.

The Greek New Testament. Edited by K. Aland et al. 3rd ed. New York, 1975. UBS Greek NT. On this see B. M. Metzger, *A Textual Commentary on the Greek New Testament* (New York, 1991).

Novum Testamentum Domini nostri Iesu Christi latine secundum editionem S. Hieronymi. Edited by J. Wordsworth and H. J. White (1–3 John, ed. A. W. Adams).

Novum Testamentum graece. Edited by E. Nestle and K. Aland. 26th ed. Stuttgart, 1979.

Novum Testamentum graece et latine. Edited by A. Merk. 8th ed. Rome, 1958.

Novum Testamentum graece et latine. Edited by H. J. Vogels. 4th ed. Freiburg im Breisgau, 1955.

Vetus Latina. Edited by Beuron Abbey. Vol. 26/1, *Epistulae Catholicae,* edited by W. Thiele. Freiburg im Breisgau,1965–.

Vetus Testamentum Graecum. 9 vols. to date. Göttingen, 1931–.

JUDAISM

Aristeas to Philocrates (Letter of Aristeas). Edited and translated by M. Hadas. New York, 1951.

Avigad, N., and Y. Yadin. *A Genesis Apocryphon.* Jerusalem, 1956.

The Babylonian Talmud. Eng. trans. edited by J. Neusner. New Haven, 1988.

Bardtke, H. *Die Handschriftenfunde am Toten Meer.* 2nd ed. Berlin, 1953.

———. *Die Handschriften am Toten Meer: Die Sekte von Qumran.* Berlin, 1958.

Barthélemy, D., and J. T. Milik. *Qumran Cave I.* Discoveries in the Judaean Desert 1. Oxford, 1955.

Burrows, M., ed. *The Dead Sea Scrolls of St. Mark's Monastery.* New Haven, 1950–51.

Charles, R. H., ed. *The Apocrypha and Pseudepigrapha of the Old Testament in English.* 2 vols. Oxford, 1913.

Charlesworth, J. H., ed. *The Old Testament Pseudepigrapha.* 2 vols. Garden City, NY, 1983.

The Greek Versions of the Testaments of the Twelve Patriarchs. Edited by R. H. Charles. Oxford, 1908.

Joseph et Aséneth. Edited by M. Philonenko. Leiden, 1968.

Bibliography

Josephus. Translated by H. St. J. Thackeray. Loeb Classical Library. London, 1961.

Kautzsch, E., ed. *Die Apokryphen und Pseudepigraphen des Alten Testaments.* 2 vols. Tübingen, 1906. Reprinted, 1921.

Le Livre de la Prière d'Aséneth. Edited by P. Batiffol. Studia patristica 1–2. Paris, 1889–90.

Le Livre des Secrets d'Hénoch. Texte slave et trad. franc. par A. Vaillant. Paris, 1952.

Maier, J. *Die Texte vom Toten Meer.* 2 vols. Munich/Basel, 1960.

The Mishnah: A New Translation. Translated by J. Neusner. New Haven, 1988.

Philo of Alexandria. Translated by F. H. Colson and G. Whitaker. Loeb Classical Library. 10 vols. London, 1929–62.

Rabbinische Texte. Edited by G. Kittel and K. H. Rengstorf. Stuttgart, 1952–.

Riessler, P. *Altjüdisches Schrifttum ausserhalb der Bibel.* Augsburg, 1928.

Sukenik, E. L., ed. *The Dead Sea Scrolls of the Hebrew University.* Jerusalem, 1955.

The Tosephta. Translated by J. Neusner. New York, 1977.

Vermes, G., ed. and trans. *The Dead Sea Scrolls in English.* Penguin Books. Baltimore, 1975, etc.

The Zadokite Documents. Edited by C. Rabin. 2nd ed. Oxford, 1958.

EARLY CHRISTIANITY

Acta Apostolorum apocrypha. Edited by R. E. Lipsius and M.Bonnet. 2 vols. Leipzig, 1891, 1903. Reprint Darmstadt, 1959.

Corpus Christianorum. Turnhout/Paris, 1953–. (=CC)

Corpus scriptorum ecclesiasticorum latinorum. Vienna. (=CSEL)

Eusebius. *The Ecclesiastical History.* Loeb Classical Library. New York, 1926–32. (=H.E.)

Funk, F. X., and K. Bihlmeyer. *Die Apostolischen Väter I.* Tübingen, 1924.

Goodspeed, E. J. *Die ältesten Apologeten.* Göttingen, 1914.

Griechische christliche Schriftsteller. Edited by the Prussian Academy of Sciences. Berlin (=GCS)

Hennecke, E., and W. Schneemelcher. *New Testament Apocrypha.* Eng. trans. edited by R. McL. Wilson. 2 vols. Philadelphia, 1963.

Ignace d'Antioche. *Polycarpe de Smyrne, Lettres. Martyre de Polycarpe.* Greek texts with French translation by P. T. Camelot. Sources chrétiennes. 2nd ed. Paris, 1951.

S. Irenaei Libri quinque adversus Haereses. Edited by W. W. Harvey. 2 vols. Cambridge, 1857.

Lightfoot, J. B. *Die Apostolic Fathers. Greek and English.* London, 1912.

Migne, J. P. *Patrologia graeca.* (=PG)

———. *Patrologia latina.* (=PL)

GNOSTICISM AND HELLENISM

Charlesworth, J. H., ed. *The Odes of Solomon.* Oxford, 1973.

Drower, E. S. *The Canonical Prayerbook of the Mandaeans.* Leiden, 1959.

Lidzbarski, M., ed. *Ginza, der Schatz oder das Grosse Buch der Mandäer.* Göttingen/Leipzig, 1925.

——. *Das Johannesbuch der Mandäer.* Giessen, 1915.

——. *Mandäische Liturgien.* Berlin, 1920. Reprinted Berlin/Hildesheim, 1962.

Nock, A. D., and A. J. Festugière, eds. *Corpus Hermeticum.* 4 vols. Paris, 1945–54.

Robinson, James M. *The Nag Hammadi Library in English.* Rev. ed. San Francisco, 1988.

Scott, W., ed. *Hermetica.* 4 vols. Oxford, 1924–26.

Turchi, N. *Fontes historiae mysteriorum.* Rome, 1930.

LITERATURE

GENERAL AIDS

Abel, F. M. *Grammaire du Grec biblique.* Paris, 1927.

Bauer, W. *A Greek-English Lexicon of the New Testament and Other Early Christian Literature.* Translated and edited by W. F. Arndt, F. W. Gingrich, and F. W. Danker. 2nd ed. Chicago, 1979.

Blass, F., and A. Debrunner. *A Greek Grammar of the New Testament and Other Early Christian Literature.* Translated and edited by R. W. Funk. Chicago, 1961.

Feine, P., and J. Behm. *Einleitung in das Neue Testament.* 9th ed. Heidelberg, 1950.

Gesenius, W., and F. Buhl. *Hebräisches und Aramäisches Handwörterbuch über das Alte Testament.* 17th ed. Leipzig, 1921.

Hatch, E., and H. A. Redpath. *A Concordance to the Septuagint.* 2 vols. Oxford, 1897. Reprint Graz, 1954.

Jülicher, A., and E. Fascher. *Einleitung in das Neue Testament.* 7th ed. Tübingen, 1931.

Köhler, L., and W. Baumgartner. *Lexicon in Veteris Testamenti libros.* Leiden, 1953.

Kümmel, W. G. *Introduction to the New Testament.* Rev. ed. Nashville, 1975. Pp. 434–52.

Liddell, H. G., and R. Scott. *A Greek-English Lexicon.* Revised by H. S. Jones. Oxford, 1940.

Mayser, E. *Grammatik der griechischen Papyri aus der Ptolomäerzeit.* 2 vols. Berlin/Leipzig, 1906–34.

Meinertz, M. *Einleitung in das Neue Testament.* 5th ed. Paderborn, 1950.

Michaelis, W. *Einleitung in das Neue Testament.* 3rd ed. Bern, 1961.

Moulton, J. H., and G. Milligan. *The Vocabulary of the Greek New Testament.* Revised by H. K. Moulton. London, 1978.

Moulton, W. F., and A. S. Geden. *A Concordance to the Greek Testament.* 3rd ed. Edinburgh, 1926. Reprint 1950 etc.

Passow, F. *Handwörterbuch der griechischen Sprache.* 4 vols. 5th ed. Leipzig, 1841–57.

Bibliography

Preisigke, F. *Wörterbuch der griechischen Papyrusurkunden.* 3 vols. Berlin, 1925–31.

Radermacher, L. *Neutestamentliche Grammatik.* Lietzmann I. 2nd ed. Tübingen, 1925.

Robert, A., and A. Feuillet, eds. *Introduction à la Bible. II, Nouveau Testament.* Tournai, 1959.

Robertson, A. T. *A Grammar of the Greek New Testament in the Light of Historical Research.* New York, 1919.

Theological Dictionary of the New Testament. Edited by G. Kittel and G. Friedrich. Translated by G. W. Bromiley. Grand Rapids, 1964–1976.

Trench, R. C. *Synonyms of the New Testament.* New York, 1871.

Wikenhauser, A. *New Testament Introduction.* New York, 1958. Pp. 520–33.

Zerwick, M. *Graecitas biblica exemplis illustratur.* 2nd ed. Rome, 1949.

Zorell, F. *Novi Testamenti Lexicon graecum.* 2nd ed. Paris, 1931.

Zorell, F., and L. Semkowski. *Lexicon Hebraicum et Aramaicum Veteris Testamenti.* Rome, 1940–.

COMMENTARIES

Ancient

Augustine. *In ep. S. Ioannis ad Parthos. PL* 35:1977–2062.

Venerable Bede. In *PL* 93:85–124.

Cassiodorus. *Complexiones. PL* 70:1369–76.

Catenae graecorum Patrum in NT VIII. Edited by J. A. Cramer. Oxford, 1844. Pp. 105–52. On the catenae, which yield little for the Johannine Epistles, see also K. Staab, "Die griechischen Katenenkommentare," *Bb* 5 (1924) 296–353; and R. Devreesse in *DBSup* 1:1224–28.

Clement of Alexandria. *Adumbrationes* (1 and 2 John). Edited by O. Stählin. GCS 3:206–25.

Didymus. Fragmenta. In *PG* 39:1775–1812. A better edition is F. Zoepfl, *Didymi Alexandrini in Epistolas canonicas brevis enerratio.* NTS 4, 1. Münster, 1914. Pp. 37–88 (questions the authenticity).

Ps.-Oecumenius. In *PG* 119:617–704.

Theophylact. In *PG* 126:9–84.

Medieval

There were many commentaries on the Johannine Epistles in the Middle Ages, more than were hitherto known, as can now be seen from the great collection by F. Stegmüller, *Repertorium biblicum medii aevi,* 7 vols. (Madrid, 1950–62). Among them we should mention the following:

Augustinus Triumphus de Ancona (Augustinian hermit; d. 1328). Ep. Can., unpublished. See Stegmüller 2:1531–33.

Dionysius the Carthusian (d. 1471). Commentary on the whole of Holy Scripture. *Opera omnia.* 42 vols. Montreuil/Tournay, 1896–. Johannine Epistles: vol. 14 (1901) 3–64.

Bibliography

Ericus Olaf (Prof. in Uppsala; d. 1486). Brief gloss on 1-3 John, unpublished. See Stegmüller 5:8365-67.

Hilary (identity uncertain; 5th cent.?). See Stegmüller 3:3528-30.

Hugo a S. Caro (Dominican; d. 1264). His commentary on the Catholic Epistles is preserved in two versions. See Stegmüller 3:3761-66.

James of Lausanne (Dominican; d. 1322). Commentary on 1-3 John, unpublished. See Stegmüller 4:6721-23.

John Hus (d. 1415). Ep. Can. See Stegmüller 3:4574-76. Ed. Monumenta Johannis Hus II (1558).

John Wyclif (1384). Ep. Can., unpublished. See Stegmüller 3:5114-16.

Lambert von Geldern (Prof. in Vienna; d. 1419). Commentary on 1-3 John, unpublished. See Stegmüller 3:5361-63.

Martin of Leon (priest and Augustinian canon of St. Isadore in Leon; d. 1221). Wrote a major commentary on James, 1 Peter, 1 John. In *PL* 209.

Nicholas of Lyra (Franciscan; d. 1349). *Postillae perpetuae in Vetus Testamentum.* 1st ed. Rome 1471-72. Repeatedly published later, generally with the ordinary and interlinear gloss, further with the additions by Paul of Burgos and the "Repliken" of Matthias Doering. Final ed. Antwerp, 1634.

Nikolaus Gorran (Dominican; d. ca. 1295). Commentary on James, Peter, John. Printed under the name of St. Thomas Aquinas. Paris, 1543. Rome, 1570 (vol. 17). Paris, 1876 (vol. 31). See Stegmüller 4:5806-8.

Petrus de Tarantasia (Dominican, later Pope Innocent V; d. 1276). Ep. Can., unpublished. See M. H. Laurent, *Le bienheureux Innocent V (Pierre de Tarantaise) et son temps* (Studi et testi 129; Rome, 1947); Stegmüller 4:6910-12.

Petrus Johannes Olivi (Franciscan; d. 1298). Commentary on 1-3 John, unpublished. See Stegmüller 4:6721-23.

Smuczben (probably Dominican; 15th cent.?). Commentary on James and 1 John, unpublished. See Stegmüller 5:7696-97.

Langton, Stephen (Archbishop of Canterbury; d. 1226). Commentary, unpublished. See G. Lacombe and B. Smalley, *Studies on the Commentaries of Stephen Langton* (Archives d'hist., doctr. et litt. du moyen Âge 5 (1930) 1-266; Stegmüller 5:7924-26, 7931-33.

Werner Rolevinck (Carthusian; d. 1502). Major Commentary on 1-3 John, unpublished. See Stegmüller 5:8365-67.

Anonymous

Basel A X, 40. See Stegmüller 6:8651 (1 John).

Firenze, Laurenziana, Conv. Soppr. 465. See Stegmüller 6:9268-70.

Lüneburg, Ratsbibl., theol. Fol. 60. See Stegmüller 6:9730 (1 John).

Paris, nat. lat., 14798. See Stegmüller 7:10525-27.

Paris, nat. lat., 15247. See Stegmüller 7:10552-55.

Paris, nat. lat., 17289. See Stegmüller 7:10667-69.

Paris, Mazarine 179. See Stegmüller 7:10781 (1 John).

Paris, Ste Geneviève 1207. See Stegmüller 7:10841-43.

Prague, University, 405. See Stegmüller 7:10895-97.

Bibliography

Troyes 1861. See Stegmüller 7:11357–59.
Vatican, vat. lat. 996. See Stegmüller 7:11461–63.

Modern Times

Catholic

Commentaries from the sixteenth to eighteenth centuries:

Cajetan (d. 1534). Notae in ep. II Pet., I-III Ioa., Iud. Rome 1532 etc.
Calmet, A. (d. 1757). Comm. littéraire VIII. Paris, 1726.
Cornelius a Lapide (d. 1637). Commentary. Milan, 1870.
Estius, W. (d. 1613.). Commentary, final ed., 2 vols. Paris, 1892.
Justiniani, B. (d. 1637). In omnes Ep. Cath. explanatio. Lyons, 1621.
Salmeron, A. (d. 1585). Disputationes in ep. canonicas. Op. omnia XVI. Cologne, 1640.

Recent commentaries:

Belser, J. E. Die Briefe des hl. Johannes. Freiburg im Breisgau, 1906.
Bisping, A. Erklärung der kath. Briefe. Münster, 1871.
Bonsirven, J. Épîtres de S. Jean. Verbum salutis 9. New ed. Paris, 1954.
Braun, F.-M. Les Épîtres de S. Jean traduites. Bible de Jerusalem. 2nd ed. Paris, 1960.
Calmes, T. Épîtres Catholiques. Paris, 1907.
Camerlynck, A. Comm. in Epistolas Catholicas. Bruges, 1909.
Chaine, J. Les Épîtres Catholiques. Études bibliques. Paris, 1939.
Charue, A. Les Épîtres de S. Jean. La Sainte Bible 13. Paris, 1938.
de Ambroggi, P. Le Epistole Cattoliche. La Sacra Bibbia, ed. S. Garofalo. 2nd ed. Turin/Rome, 1949.
Lauck, W. Das Evangelium und die Briefe des hl. Johannes. Freiburg im Breisgau, 1941.
Mayer, G. K. Comm. über die Briefe des Apostels Johannes. Vienna, 1851.
Michl, J. Die Katholischen Briefe. RegNT 8. Regensburg, 1953. 2nd ed. 1968.
Poggel, J. Der 2. und 3. Brief des Apostels Johannes. Paderborn, 1896.
Thüsing, W. Die Johannesbriefe. Geistliche Schriftlesung. Düsseldorf, 1970.
Vawter, B. "The Johannine Epistles." In The Jerome Biblical Commentary, edited by R. E. Brown, et al., 2:404-13. Englewood Cliffs, NJ, 1968.
Vrede, W. Die Briefe des hl. Johannes. Bonner NT 9. 4th ed. Bonn, 1932.

Protestant

Alexander, N. The Epistles of John. Torch Bible. London/New York, 1962.
Asmussen, H. Wahrheit und Liebe: Eine Einführung in die Johannesbriefe. 3rd ed. Hamburg, 1957.
Baumgarten, O. Johannesbriefe. Gött. NT 4. 3rd ed. Göttingen, 1918.
Brooke, A. E. The Johannine Epistles. ICC. Edinburgh, 1912. Reprint 1957.
Bruce, F. F. The Epistles of John. London, 1971.
Büchsel, F. Die Johannesbriefe. Theol. Handkomm. 17. Leipzig, 1933.

Bibliography

Bultmann, R. *The Johannine Epistles.* Hermeneia. Philadelphia, 1973.

de Jonge, M. *De brieven van Johannes.* Nijkerk, 1968.

Dodd, C. H. *The Johannine Epistles.* Moffatt. 2nd ed. London, 1947.

Findlay, G. G. *Fellowship in the Life Eternal.* London, 1909.

Gaugler, E. *Die Johannesbriefe.* Zurich, 1964.

Gore, C. *The Epistles of St. John.* London, 1920.

Häring, T. *Die Johannesbriefe.* Stuttgart, 1927.

Hauck, F. *Die Kirchenbriefe.* NTD 20. 5th ed. Göttingen, 1949.

Haupt, E. *Der erste Brief des Johannes: Ein Beitrag zur biblischen Theologie.* Colberg, 1870.

Holtzmann, H. J., and W. Bauer. *Johannesbriefe.* HCNT 4, 2. 3rd ed. Tübingen, 1908.

Horn, F. *Der erste Brief des Johannes.* Munich, 1931.

Houlden, J. L. *A Commentary on the Johannine Epistles.* Harper NT. San Francisco, 1973.

Kohler, M. *Le coeur et le mains: Comm. de la première ép. de Jean.* Neuchâtel, 1962.

Law, R. *The Tests of Life.* London, 1909.

Loisy, A. *Le quatrième Évangile: Les Épîtres dites de Jean.* Paris, 1921.

Ross, A. *The Epistles of James and John.* NIC. Grand Rapids, 1954.

Rothe, R. *Der 1 Joh.* Wittenberg, 1878.

Schneider, J. *Die Briefe des Jakobus, Petrus, Judas und Johannes.* NTD 10. Göttingen, 1961.

Stott, J. R. W. *The Epistles of John.* Tyndale NT. Grand Rapids, 1965.

Weiss, B. *Johannesbriefe.* Meyer 14. 6th ed. Göttingen, 1899.

Wendt, H. H. *Die Johannesbriefe.* Stuttgart, 1927.

Westcott, B. F. *The Johannine Epistles.* 5th ed. London, 1908.

Williams, R. R. *The Letters of John and James.* Cambridge, 1965.

Windisch, H. *Die Katholischen Briefe.* Lietzmann XV. 3rd ed. Tübingen, 1951.

STUDIES ON THE JOHANNINE EPISTLES

Alfaro, J. "Cognitio Dei et Christi in 1 Joh." *VD* 39 (1961) 82–91.

Ayuso, T. "Nuevo estudio sobre el 'Comma Ioanneum.'" *Bib* 28 (1947) 83–112, 216–38; 29 (1948) 52–76.

Bardy, G. "Cérinthe." *RB* 30 (1921) 344–73.

Bartlet, V. "The Historical Setting of the Second and Third Epistles of St. John." *JTS* 6 (1905) 204–16.

Bauernfeind, O. "Die Fürbitte angesichts der Sünde zum Tode." In *Von der Antike zum Christentum.* Festschrift V. Schultze, 43–54. Stuttgart, 1931.

Belser, J. E. "Erläuterungen zu 1 Joh." *TQ* 95 (1913) 514–31.

———. "Zur Textkritik der Schriften des Johannes." *TQ* 98 (1916) 145–84.

Bludau, A. "Die 'Epistula ad Parthos.'" *ThGl* 11 (1919) 223–36.

———. "Die ersten Gegner der Johannesschriften." *BS* 22, 1–2. Freiburg im Breisgau, 1925.

Boismard, M.-É. "La connaisance de Dieu dans l'Alliance Nouvelle d'après la première lettre de S. Jean." *RB* 56 (1949) 365–91.

———. "Je ferai avec vous une alliance nouvelle." *LumVi* 8 (1953) 94–109.

Bott, J. C. "De notione lucis in scriptis S. Ioa." *VD* 19 (1939) 91ff., 117–22.

Braun, F.-M. "L'Eau et l'Esprit." *RevThom* 49 (1949) 5–30.

Braun, H. "Literar-Analyse und theologische Schichtung im 1 Joh." *ZTK* 48 (1951) 262–92.

Bresky, B. *Das Verhältnis des 2 Joh zum 3 Joh.* Münster, 1906.

Büchsel, F. *Der Begriff der Wahrheit in dem Evangelium und den Briefen des Johannes.* BFCT 15, 3. Gütersloh, 1911.

———. "Zu den Johannesbriefen." *ZNW* 28 (1929) 235–41.

Bultmann, R. "Analyse des 1 Joh." In *Festgabe für A. Jülicher,* 138–58.

———. "Johannesbriefe." In *RGG* 3 (1959) 836–39.

———. "Die kirchliche Redaktion des 1 Joh." In *In memoriam E. Lohmeyer,* 189–201. Stuttgart, 1951.

Chapman, J. "The Historical Setting of the Second and Third Epistles of St. John." *JTS* 5 (1904) 357–68, 517–37.

———. *John the Presbyter.* Oxford, 1911.

Chmiel, J. *Lumière et charité d'après la 1. épître de s. Jean.* Rome, 1971.

Clemen, C. "Beiträge zum geschichtlichen Verständnis der Johannesbriefe." *ZNW* 6 (1905) 271–81.

Conzelmann, H. "Was von Anfang war." In *NT Studien für R. Bultmann,* 194–201. BZNW. Berlin, 1954.

de Ambroggi, P. "La teologia delle epistole de S. Giovanni." *Sc* 76 (1946) 35–42.

de Keulenaer, J. "De 1 Joh. 2, 15–17." *Collat. Mechlin* 6 (1931) 189–90.

———. "De interpretatione 1 John 1, 5–10." *Collat. Mechlin* 28 (1939) 279–82.

———. "De interpretatione prologi 1 John 1, 1–4." *Collat. Mechlin* 6 (1931) 167–73.

del Alamo, M. "Los tres testificantes de la 1 Ep. de Juan." *Cult. bibl.* 4 (1947) 11–14.

de la Potterie, I. "L'impeccabilité du chrétien d'après 1 Joh 3,6–9." In *L'Évangile de Jean,* 161–77. Rech. bib. 3. Louvain, 1958.

———. "L'onction du chrétien par la foi." *Bib* 40 (1959) 12–69, esp. 30–47.

———. "'Le péché, c'est l'iniquité' (1 John 3,4)." *NRT* 78 (1956) 785–97.

Denney, J. "He that Came by Water and Blood (1 John 5.6)." *Exp* 7, 5 (1907) 416–28.

Dodd, C. H. "The First Epistle of John and the Fourth Gospel." *BJRL* 21 (1937) 129–56.

Dolger, F. J. "Domina Mater Ecclesia und die 'Herrin' im 2 Joh." *AntChrist* 5 (1936) 211–17.

Eichholz, G. "Der 1 John als Trostbrief und die Einheit der Schrift." *EvT* 5 (1938) 75–83.

———. "Erwählung und Eschatologie im 1 Joh." *EvT* 5 (1938) 1–28.

———. "Glaube und Liebe im 1 Joh." *EvT* 4 (1937) 411–37.

Feuillet, A. "Les épîtres johanniques." In *Introduction à la Bible,* 2:685–708.

Filson, F. V. "First John: Purpose and Message." *Int* 23 (1969) 259–76.

Findlay, G. G. "The Preface of the First Epistle of John." *Exp* 4, 7 (1893) 97–108.

———. "Studies in the First Epistle of John." *Exp* (1903–1905).

Galtier, P. "Le chrétien impeccable (1 Joh 3, 6 9)." *Mel. de science rel.* 4 (1947) 137–54.

Gibbins, H. J. "The Second Epistle of St. John." *Exp* 6, 6 (1902) 228–36.

———. "The Problem of the Second Epistle of St. John." *Exp* 6, 12 (1905) 412–24.

Greiff, A. "Die drei Zeugen in 1 John 5, 7f." *TQ* 114 (1933) 465–80.

Guy, H. A. "I John 1.1–3." *ExpT* 62 (1951) 285.

Haenchen, E. "Neuere Literatur zu den Johannesbriefen." *TRu* 26 (1960) 1–43, 267–91.

Häring, T. "Gedankengang und Grundgedanke des 1 Joh." In *Theologische Abhandlungen für C. von Weizsäcker,* 171–200. Freiburg im Breisgau, 1892.

Harnack, A. von. *Über den 3 Joh.* TU 14, 3. Leipzig, 1897.

———. "Das 'Wir' in den Joh. Schriften." In *SB,* 96–113. Berlin, 1923.

———. "Zur Textkritik und Christologie der Schriften des Johannes." In *SB* 534–73. Berlin, 1915.

Harris, R. "The Problem of the Address in the Second Epistle of St. John." *Exp* 6, 3 (1901) 194–203.

Henle, F. A. *Der Evangelist Johannes und die Antichristen seiner Zeit.* Munich, 1884.

Héring, J. "Y a-t-il des Aramaïsmes dans la Première Épître Johannique?" *RHPR* 36 (1956) 113–21.

Herkenrath, J. "Sünde zum Tode (1 Joh 5,16)." In *Aus Theologie und Philosophie.* Festschrift F. Tillmann, 119–38. Düsseldorf, 1950.

Howard, W. F. "The Common Authorship of the Johannine Gospel and Epistles." *JTS* 48 (1947) 12–25.

James, A. G. "Jesus Our Advocate (1 John 2.1f.)." *ExpT* 39 (1929) 473–75.

Joüon, P. Ἀλαζονεία τοῦ βίου." *RechScR* 28 (1938) 479–81.

———. "Le verbe ἀναγγέλλω dans Saint Jean." *RechScR* 28 (1938) 234–35.

Käsemann, E. "Ketzer und Zeuge: Zum joh. Verfasserproblem." *ZTK* 48 (1951) 292–311.

Katz, P. "The Johannine Epistles in the Muratorian Canon." *JTS* n.s. 8 (1958) 273f.

Keppler, P. W. "Geist, Wasser und Blut: Zur Erklärung von 1 Joh 5, 6–13." *TQ* 68 (1886) 3–25.

Kilpatrick, G. D. "Two Johannine Idioms in the Johannine Epistles." *JTS* n.s. 12 (1961) 272–73.

Klein, G. "'Das wahre Licht scheint schon': Beobachtungen zur Zeit- und Geschichtserfahrung einer urchristlichen Schule." *ZTK* 68 (1971) 261–326.

Klöpper, A. "1 Joh 5,6–12." *ZWT* 43 (1900) 378–401.

———. "Zur Lehre von der Sünde in 1 Joh." *ZWT* 43 (1900) 585–602.

Künstle, K. *Das Comma Ioanneum auf seine Herkunft untersucht.* Freiburg im Breisgau, 1905.

Leconte, R. "Jean, Épîtres de saint." In *DBSup* 4:797–815.

Le Fort, P. *Les structures de l'Église militante selon s. Jean.* Geneva, Switzerland, 1970.

Lee, G. M. "I John 1.1–3." *ExpT* 62 (1951) 125.

Lemonnyer, A. "Comma Johannique." In *DBSup* 2:67–73 (with further bibliography).

Lohmeyer, E. "Über Aufbau und Gliederung von 1 Joh." *ZNW* 27 (1928) 225–63.

Manson, T. W. "Entry into Membership of the Early Church." *JTS* 48 (1947) 25–33 (on 1 John 5:7f.).

Marty, J. "Contribution à l'étude des problèmes Johanniques: Les petites épîtres II et III Jean." *RHR* 91 (1925) 300–311.

Michl, J. "Der Geist als Garant des rechten Glaubens." In *Vom Wort des Lebens*. Festschrift W. Meinertz, 142–51. Münster, 1951.

Nagl, E. "Die Gliederung des 1 Joh." *BZ* 16 (1922) 77–92.

Nauck, W. *Die Tradition und der Charakter des ersten Johannesbriefes*. WUNT 3. Tübingen, 1953.

Noack, B. "On 1 John 2. 12–14." *NTS* 6 (1959–60) 236–41.

O'Neill, J. C. *The Puzzle of 1 John* London, 1966. (He offers new hypotheses on the structure, the origin, and the recipients; see the relevant sections in the Introduction.)

Pecorara, G. "De verbo 'manere' apud Ioa." *DivThom* 40 (1937) 159–71.

Phythian-Adams, W. J. "The New Creation in St. John." *CQR* 144 (1947) 52–75.

Piper, O. A. "1 John and the Didache of the Primitive Church." *JBL* 66 (1947) 437–51.

Poggel, H. *Der 2. und 3. Brief des Apostels Johannes*. Paderborn, 1896.

Review and Expositor 67,4 (1970) (with various contributors).

Riggenbach, E. *Das Comma Johanneum*. BFCT 31, 4. Gütersloh, 1938.

Rivera, A. *La redención en las epistolas y en el Apocalypsis de S. Juan*. Rome, 1939.

Robinson, J. A. T. "The Designation and Purpose of the Johannine Epistles." *NTS* 7 (1960–61) 58–65.

Rougé, P. "Dieu le Père et l'oeuvre de notre salut d'après l'Évangile et la première Épître de S. Jean." Diss., Carcasonne, 1938.

Salom, A. P. "Some Aspects of the Grammatical Style of 1 John." *JBL* 74 (1955) 96–102.

Schnackenburg, R. "Johannesbriefe." In *LTK* 5:1099f.

———. "Der Streit zwischen dem Verfasser von 3 Joh und Diotrephes und seine verfassungsgeschichtliche Bedeutung." *MTZ* 4 (1953) 18–26.

Schütz, E. *Die Vorgeschichte der joh Formel* ὁ θεὸς ἀγάπη ἐστίν. Göttingen diss. Kiel, 1917.

Schwarz, E. "Johannes und Kerinthus." *ZNW* 15 (1914) 210–19.

Schweizer, E. "Der Kirchenbegriff im Evangelium und den Briefen des Johannes." In *Studia Evangelica*, 363–81. TU 73. Berlin, 1959.

Schwertschlager, R. *Der 1 Joh in seinem Grundgedanken und Aufbau*. Diss., Gregorian. Coburg, 1935.

Seeberg, R. "Die Sünder und die Sündenvergebung nach dem 1. Brief des Johannes." In *Das Erbe Martin Luthers*. Festschrift L. Ihmels, 19–31. Leipzig, 1928.

Shutt, R. J. H. "I John IV.12a," *ExpT* 65 (1953–54) 29f.

Bibliography

Simpson, J. G. "The Message of the Epistles: The Letters of the Presbyter." *ExpT* 45 (1933) 486–90.

Škrinjar, A. "Maior est Deus corde nostro." *VD* 20 (1940) 340–50.

———. Various essays in *VD* 41 (1963)–47 (1969) (chiefly on the theology of 1 John).

Smit Sibinga, J. "I Johannes tegen de achtergrond van der teksten van Qumran." *Vox theologica* 29 (1958–59) 11–14.

———. "A Study in 1 John." In *Studies in John.* Festschrift J. N. Sevenster, 194–208. Leiden, 1970.

Soltau, W. "Die Verwandtschaft zwischen Ev Joh und dem 1 Joh," *StudKrit* 89 (1916) 220–33.

Suitbertus, S. J. C. "Die Vollkommenheitslehre des 1 Joh." *Bib* 39 (1958) 319–33, 449–70.

Šurjanski, A. J. *De mysterio Verbi incarnati ad mentem B. Ioannis Apostoli* (Rome, 1941).

Synge, F. C. "1 John 3.2." *JTS* 3 (1952) 79.

Thiele, W. "Beobachtungen zum Comma Johanneum (1 Joh 5, 7f.)." *ZNW* 50 (1959) 61–73.

———. *Wortschatzuntersuchungen zu den altlateinischen Texten der Johannesbriefe.* Freiburg im Breisgau, 1958.

Thornton-Dewsberry, J. P. "1 John 1.9" *ExpT* 45 (1933) 183f. On this, see L. M. Rogers, *ExpT* 45 (1933) 527.

Tomoi, K. "The Plan of the First Epistle of John." *ExpT* 52 (1940–41) 117–19.

Trépanier, B. "Contribution à une recherche de l'idée de témoin dans les écrits johanniques." *Rev. de l'Université d'Ottawa* 15 (1945) 5–63.

von Dobschütz, E. "Johanneische Studien I." *ZNW* 8 (1907) 1–8.

Wendt, H. H. "Der 'Anfang' am Beginn des 1 Joh." *ZNW* 21 (1922) 38–42.

———. "Die Beziehung unseres 1 Joh auf den 2 Joh." *ZNW* 21 (1922) 140–46.

———. "Zum 1 Joh." *ZNW* 22 (1923) 57–79.

———. "Zum 2 and 3 Joh." *ZNW* 23 (1924) 18–27.

Westcott, B. F., and F. J. A. Hort. "The Divisions of the First Epistle of St. John." *Exp* 7, 3 (1907) 481–93.

Wilson, W. G. "An Examination of the Linguistic Evidence Adduced against the Unity of Authorship of the First Epistle of John and the Fourth Gospel." *JTS* 49 (1948) 147–56.

Wohlenberg, G., "Glossen zu 1 Joh." *NKZ 13 (1902) 233*–40 (on 5:18), 632–45 (on 3:18–22).

Wurm, A., *Die Irrlehrer im 1 Joh.* BS 8, 1. Freiburg im Breisgau, 1903.

Zahn, A. "De notione peccati, quam Johannes in prima epistola docet, commentatio." Diss., Halle, 1872.

Zerwick, M. "Veritatem facere." *VD* 18 (1938) 338–41.

WORKS FREQUENTLY CITED IN ABBREVIATIONS

Abramowski, R. "Der Christus der Salomooden." *ZNW* 35 (1936) 44–69.

Barrett, C. K. *The Gospel According to St. John.* London, 1955.

Barth, M. *Der Augenzeuge*. Zurich, 1946.

Bauer, W. *Das Johannesevangelium*. Lietzmann 5. 3rd ed. Tübingen, 1933.

Billerbeck, P. *Kommentar zum NT aus Talmud und Midrasch*. 4 vols. Munich, 1922–28.

Bonsirven, J. *Le judaïsme palestinien au temps de Jésus-Christ*. 2 vols. Paris, 1934–1935.

Botterweck, G. J. *"Gott erkennen" im Sprachgebrauch des AT* BBB 2. Bonn, 1951.

Bousset, W. *Die Hauptprobleme der Gnosis*. FRLANT 10. Göttingen, 1907.

——. *Kyrios Christos*. Nashville, 1971.

Bousset, W., and H. Gressmann. *Die Religion des Judentums im späthellenistischen Zeitalter*. Lietzmann 21. 3rd ed. Tübingen, 1926.

Braun, F.-M. *Jean le Théologien et son évangile dans l'église ancienne*. Etudes bibliques. Paris, 1959.

Brox, N. *Zeuge und Märtyrer: Untersuchungen zur frühchristlichen Zeugnis-Terminologie*. SANT 5. Munich, 1961.

Büchsel, F. *Johannes und der hellenistische Synkretismus*. BFCT 2, 16. Gütersloh, 1928.

Bultmann, R. *The Gospel of John*. Oxford, 1971.

——. *Theology of the New Testament*. 2 vols. New York, 1951, 1955.

Burrows, M. *The Dead Sea Scrolls of St. Mark's Monastery*. New Haven, 1950.

——. *More Light on the Dead Sea Scrolls*. New York, 1958.

Colpe, C. *Die religionsgeschichtliche Schule: Darstellung und Kritik ihres Bildes vom gnostischen Erlösermythus*. FRLANT n.s. 60. Göttingen, 1961.

Cross, F. M., Jr. *The Ancient Library of Qumran and Modern Biblical Studies*. London, 1958.

Deissmann, A. *Light from the Ancient East*. New York, 1927.

Dieterich, A. *Eine Mithrasliturgie*. 3rd ed. Leipzig/Berlin, 1923.

Dodd, C. H. *The Bible and the Greeks*. London, 1935.

——. *The Interpretation of the Fourth Gospel*. Cambridge, 1953.

Dupont, J. *Essais sur la Christologie de S. Jean*. Bruges, 1951.

Eichrodt, W. *Theology of the Old Testament*. 2 vols. Philadelphia, 1961, 1967.

Feine, P., and K. Aland. *Theologie des NT*. 5th ed. Berlin, 1949–51.

Goguel, M. *The Birth of Christianity*. London, 1953.

——. *The Primitive Church*. New York, 1964.

Grant, R. M. *Gnosticism and Early Christianity*. New York, 1959.

Hanse, H. *'Gott haben' in der Antike und im frühen Christentum*. RVV 27. Berlin, 1939.

Harnack, A. von. *The Mission and Expansion of Christianity in the First Three Centuries*. 2 vols. 2nd ed. New York/London, 1908.

Heinisch, P. *Theologie des AT*. Bonn, 1940.

Huby, J. *Mystiques paulinienne et johannique*. Paris, 1946.

Johansson, N. "Parakletoi: Vorstellungen von Fürsprechern für die Menschen vor Gott in der alttestamentlichen Religion, im Spätjudentum und Urchristentum." Diss., Lund, 1940.

Jonas, H. *Gnosis und spätantiker Geist I: Die mythologische Gnosis*. FRLANT n.s. 33. Göttingen, 1934.

——. *Gnosis und spätantiker Geist II/1: Von der Mythologie zur mystischen Philosophie.* FRLANT n.s. 45. Göttingen, 1954.

Jones, M. *The New Testament in the Twentieth Century.* London, 1924.

Lagrange, M.-J. *Critique textuelle II: La critique rationelle.* Paris, 1935.

——. *Évangile selon S. Jean.* 4th ed. Paris, 1927.

——. *Histoire ancienne du Canon du NT.* Paris, 1933.

L'Évangile de Jean: Études et Problèmes. Recherches bibliques 3. Louvain, 1958.

Lütgert, W. *Amt und Geist im Kampf.* BFCT 15, 4–5. Gütersloh, 1911.

——. *Die joh. Christologie.* 2nd ed. Gütersloh, 1916.

Maurer, C. *Ignatius von Antiochien und das Joh.-Ev.* ATANT 18. Zurich, 1949.

Meinertz, M. *Theologie des NT.* 2 vols. Bonn, 1950.

Menoud, P.-H. "Les études johanniques de Bultmann à Barrett." In *L'Évangile de Jean,* 11–40. Recherches bibliques 3. Louvain, 1958.

——. *L'Évangile de Jean d'après les recherches récentes.* 2nd ed. Neuchâtel/Paris, 1947.

Meyer, E. *Ursprung und Anfänge des Christentums III.* 3rd ed. Stuttgart/Berlin, 1923.

Moore, G. F. *Judaism in the First Centuries of the Christian Era, the Age of the Tannaim.* 3 vols. Cambridge, 1927–1930.

Mussner, F. ZΩH: *Die Anschauung vom 'Leben' im 4. Ev. unter Berücksichtigung der Johannesbriefe.* Munich, 1952.

Nilsson, M. P. *A History of Greek Religion.* Oxford, 1949.

Norden, E. *Agnostos Theos: Untersuchungen zur Formengeschichte religiöser Rede.* Leipzig/Berlin, 1913.

Nötscher, F. *Gotteswege und Menschenwege in der Bibel und in Qumran.* BBB 15. Bonn, 1958.

——. *Zur theologischen Terminologie der Qumran-Texte.* BBB 10. Bonn, 1956.

Omodeo, A. *La mistica Giovannea.* Bari, 1930.

Percy, E. *Untersuchungen über den Ursprung der joh. Theologie.* Lund, 1939.

Pétrement, S. *Le dualisme chez Platon, les Gnostiques et les Manichéens.* Paris, 1947.

Poschmann, B. *Paenitentia secunda.* Bonn, 1940.

Pribnow, H. *Die johanneische Anschauung vom 'Leben.'* Greifswald, 1934.

Prümm, K. *Der christliche Glaube und die altheidnische Welt.* 2 vols. Leipzig, 1935.

Quispel, G. *Gnosis als Weltreligion.* Zurich, 1951.

Reitzenstein, R. *Die hellenistischen Mysterienreligionen.* 3rd ed. Leipzig, 1927.

——. *Das iranische Erlösungsmysterien.* Bonn, 1921.

——. *Poimandres.* Leipzig, 1904.

Riddle, D. W. "The Later Books of the New Testament: A Point of View and a Prospect." *JR* 13 (1933) 50–71.

Rigaux, B. *L'Antéchrist.* Gembloux/Paris, 1932.

Roller, O. *Das Formular der paulinischen Briefe.* BWANT 4.6. Stuttgart, 1933.

Ruckstuhl, E. *Die literarische Einheit des Johannesevangeliums.* Freiburg, Switzerland, 1951.

Rudolph, K. *Die Mandäer. I, Prolegomena: Das Mandäerproblem. II, Der Kult.* FRLANT n.s. 74, 75. Göttingen, 1960–1961.

Schlatter, A. *Der Evangelist Johannes.* 2nd ed. Stuttgart, 1948.

———. *Sprache und Heimat des vierten Evangelisten.* BFCT 4, 4. Gütersloh, 1902.

Schoeps, H. J. *Aus frühchristlicher Zeit: Religionsgeschichtliche Untersuchungen.* Tübingen, 1950.

———. *Theologie und Geschichte des Judenchristentums.* Tübingen, 1949.

Scholem, G. *Die jüdische Mystik in ihren Hauptströmungen.* Zurich, 1957.

Schubert, K. *Die Gemeinde vom Toten Meer: Ihre Entstehung und ihre Lehren* Munich/Basel, 1958.

Schulz, S. *Komposition und Herkunft der johanneischen Reden.* BWANT 5 series 1. Stuttgart, 1960.

Seesemann, H. *Der Begriff* κοινωνία *im NT.* BZNW 14. Giessen, 1933.

Sjöberg, E. *Gott und die Sünde im palästinischen Judentum.* Stuttgart, 1938.

Spicq, C. *Agapè dans le Nouveau Testament: Analyse des textes III.* Études bibliques. Paris, 1959.

Staerk, W. *Die Erlösererwartung in den östlichen Religionen (Soter II).* Stuttgart/Berlin, 1938.

———. *Soter: Die biblische Erlösungserwartung als religionsgeschichtliches Problem. I, Der bibl. Christus.* BFCT 2, 31. Gütersloh, 1933.

Stauffer, E. *NT Theology.* New York, 1956.

Streeter, B. H. *The Primitive Church.* London, 1929.

Twisselmann, W. *Die Gotteskindschaft der Christen nach dem NT.* Diss., Gütersloh, 1940.

Völker, W. *Fortschritt und Vollendung bei Philo von Alexandrien.* TU 2, 1. Leipzig, 1938.

Volz, P. *Die Eschatologie der jüdischen Gemeinde im neutestamentlichen Zeitalter.* 2nd ed. Tübingen, 1934.

Wikenhauser, A. *Die Kirche als der mystische Leib Christi nach dem Apostel Paulus.* 2nd ed. Münster, 1940.

———. *Das Evangelium nach Johannes.* RegNT 4. 3rd ed. Regensburg, 1957.

Wilson, R. McL. *The Gnostic Problem.* London, 1958.

Zahn, T. *Geschichte des neutestamentlichen Kanons.* 2 vols. Erlangen/Leipzig, 1888, 1890.

INDEX OF SUBJECTS

INDEX OF GREEK WORDS

Index of Greek Words